solutions@syngre

MW01140784

With over 1,500,000 copies of our MCSE, MCSD, CompTIA, and Cisco study guides in print, we have come to know many of you personally. By listening, we've learned what you like and dislike about typical computer books. The most requested item has been for a web-based service that keeps you current on the topic of the book and related technologies. In response, we have created solutions@syngress.com, a service that includes the following features:

- A one-year warranty against content obsolescence that occurs as the result of vendor product upgrades. We will provide regular web updates for affected chapters.

- Monthly mailings that respond to customer FAQs and provide detailed explanations of the most difficult topics, written by content experts exclusively for solutions@syngress.com.

- Regularly updated links to sites that our editors have determined offer valuable additional information on key topics.

- Access to "Ask the Author"™ customer query forms that allow readers to post questions to be addressed by our authors and editors.

Once you've purchased this book, browse to www.syngress.com/solutions.

To register, you will need to have the book handy to verify your purchase.

Thank you for giving us the opportunity to serve you.

SYNGRESS®

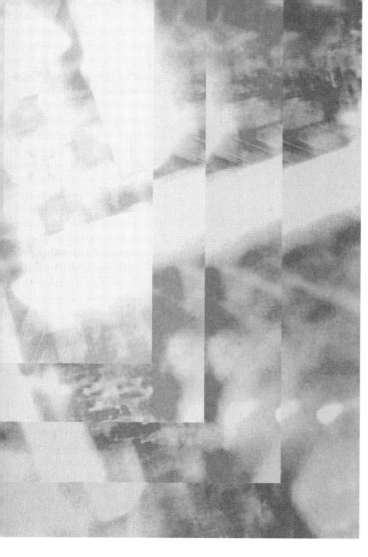

MISSION CRITICAL!
WINDOWS 2000
SERVER ADMINISTRATION

SYNGRESS®

KEY	SERIAL NUMBER
001	9TATW2ADSE
002	NF4TRA7TC4
003	CDE3C28FV7
004	DC5C8NVT4N
005	Z745QQE2BR
006	PF62RT652H
007	DTP252ZX44
008	NT3F743RTG
009	6532M977LS
010	SMWR8P554N

PUBLISHED BY
Syngress Publishing, Inc.
800 Hingham Street
Rockland, MA 02370

Mission Critical Windows 2000 Server Administration

Printed in the United States of America

1 2 3 4 5 6 7 8 9 0

ISBN: 1-928994-16-4

Copy edit by: Beth Roberts
Technical edit by: D. Lynn White
Index by: Robert Saigh
Co-Publisher: Richard Kristof

Proofreading by: Fred Lanigan
Page Layout and Art by: Reuben Kantor
and Shannon Tozier

Distributed by Publishers Group West

Acknowledgments

We would like to acknowledge the following people for their kindness and support in making this book possible.

Richard Kristof, Duncan Anderson, Jennifer Gould, Robert Woodruff, Kevin Murray, Dale Leatherwood, Rhonda Harmon, and Robert Sanregret of Global Knowledge, for their generous access to the IT industry's best courses, instructors and training facilities.

Ralph Troupe and the team at Callisma for their invaluable insight into the challenges of designing, deploying and supporting world-class enterprise networks.

Karen Cross, Kim Wylie, Harry Kirchner, John Hays, Bill Richter, Kevin Votel, Brittin Clark, Sarah Schaffer, Ellen Lafferty and Sarah MacLachlan of Publishers Group West for sharing their incredible marketing experience and expertise.

Mary Ging, Caroline Hird, and Simon Beale of Harcourt International for making certain that our vision remains worldwide in scope.

Annabel Dent, Anneka Baeten, Clare MacKenzie, and Laurie Giles of Harcourt Australia for all their help.

David Buckland, Wendi Wong, David Loh, Marie Chieng, Lucy Chong, Leslie Lim, Audrey Gan, and Joseph Chan of Transquest Publishers for the enthusiasm with which they receive our books.

Kwon Sung June at Acorn Publishing for his support.

Ethan Atkin at Cranbury International for his help in expanding the Syngress program.

Special thanks to the professionals at Osborne with whom we are proud to publish the best-selling Global Knowledge Certification Press series.

From Global Knowledge

At Global Knowledge we strive to support the multiplicity of learning styles required by our students to achieve success as technical professionals. As the world's largest IT training company, Global Knowledge is uniquely positioned to offer these books. The expertise gained each year from providing instructor-led training to hundreds of thousands of students worldwide has been captured in book form to enhance your learning experience. We hope that the quality of these books demonstrates our commitment to your lifelong learning success. Whether you choose to learn through the written word, computer based training, Web delivery, or instructor-led training, Global Knowledge is committed to providing you with the very best in each of these categories. For those of you who know Global Knowledge, or those of you who have just found us for the first time, our goal is to be your lifelong competency partner.

Thank your for the opportunity to serve you. We look forward to serving your needs again in the future.

Warmest regards,

Duncan Anderson
President and Chief Executive Officer, Global Knowledge

About the Author

Robin Walshaw (B.Sc Computer Science, MCSE, DPPM) is an independent consultant who delivers strategic Windows 2000 solutions to large corporations around the globe. Born in England, Robin spent the majority of his earlier years in Scotland and South Africa. One of the first MCSEs in Africa, he enjoys being at the forefront of new developments in network and operating system architecture.

With a flair for developing strategic IT solutions for diverse clients, he has worked in the world of computers in eight countries, and has traveled to over thirty countries in the last ten years. A veteran of numerous global projects, Robin has honed his skills across of a wide variety of platforms and technologies.

Though an industrious computer professional by day, by 'night' Robin is an experienced mountain guide. Robin is a keen sportsman and has managed to balance work with a passion for climbing the world's highest mountains, culminating in an attempt on the North Ridge of Mount Everest.

Residing with his wife, Natalie, in London and South Africa, Robin can be contacted via email at rwalshaw@hotmail.com. Displaying Herculean resolve, Natalie simultaneously manages to keep Robin's feet on the ground and a smile on his face. Some men just have all the luck.

Contributors

Melissa Craft (CCNA, MCSE, Network+, CNE-3, CNE-4, CNE-5, CNE-GW, MCNE, Citrix) is a Director of e-Business Offering Development for MicroAge. MicroAge is a global systems integrator headquartered in Tempe, Arizona. MicroAge provides IT design, project management and support for distributed computing systems. Melissa develops enterprise-wide technology solutions and methodologies for client organizations. These technology solutions touch every part of a system's lifecycle—from network design, testing and implementation to operational management and strategic planning. Melissa holds a bachelor's degree from the University of Michigan and is a member of the IEEE, the Society of Women Engineers and American MENSA, Ltd. Melissa currently resides in Phoenix, Arizona with her family, Dan, Justine and Taylor, and her two dogs, Marmaduke and Pooka.

Debra Littlejohn Shinder (MCSE, MCP+I, MCT) is an Instructor in the AATP program at Eastfield College, Dallas County Community College District, where she has taught since 1992. She is Webmaster for the cities of Seagoville and Sunnyvale, Texas, as well as the family Web site at www.shinder.net. She and her husband, Dr. Thomas W. Shinder, provide consulting and technical support services to Dallas area organizations. She is also the proud mom of a daughter, Kristen, who is currently serving in the U.S. Navy in Italy, and a son, Kris, who is a high school chess champion. Deb has been a writer for most her life, and has published numerous articles in both technical and non-technical fields. She can be contacted at deb@shinder.net.

Thomas W. Shinder, M.D. (MCSE, MCP+I, MCT) is a Technology Trainer and Consultant in the Dallas-Ft. Worth metroplex. Dr. Shinder has consulted with major firms, including Xerox, Lucent Technologies, and FINA Oil, assisting in the development and implementation of IP-based communications strategies. Dr. Shinder attended medical school at the University of Illinois in Chicago, and trained in neurology at the Oregon Health Sciences Center in Portland, Oregon. His fascination with interneuronal communication ultimately melded with his interest in internetworking and led him to focus on systems engineering. Tom works passionately with his beloved wife, Deb Shinder, to design elegant and cost-efficient solutions for small- and medium-sized businesses based on Windows NT/2000 platforms.

Technical Editor

D. Lynn White (MCPS, MCSE, MCT, MCP+I) is President of Independent Network Consultants, Inc. Lynn has more than 14 years experience in networking and programming. She has been a system manager in the mainframe environment as well as a software developer for a process control company. She is a technical author, editor, trainer, and consultant in networking and computer-related technologies. Lynn has been delivering mainframe, Microsoft-official curriculum and other networking coursed in and outside the United States for more than 12 years.

Contents

Chapter 4: Implementing Domains, Trees and Forests 103

Chapter 8: Managing Settings, Software, and User Data with IntelliMirror   263

Introduction

Just a few short years ago, no one could have foreseen the huge impact that the personal computer would have on the working lives of so many people. Idling on the desk of millions of office workers around the world is a tireless instrument that extends and facilitates our ability to deliver work. Today, the personal computer and the operating systems that run it are as ubiquitous as the car, with which it shares several powerful characteristics.

The modern car comes with a surfeit of features—sleek lines, aggressive low-cut features, and a powerful engine—all intended to tempt the buyer. But, it is the road that the car travels along that makes it truly productive. Without the road, the modern car would be sleek, beautiful, and useless. Windows 2000 Professional and most other modern personal operating systems are armed with the same sleek lines, powerful engines, and aggressive features as the modern car. To guide operating systems such as Windows 2000 Professional down the road of increased productivity, flexibility, and reliability, a robust and mission-critical server operating system infrastructure is required—an operating system infrastructure like Windows 2000 Server.

A significant portion of the design objectives for the Windows 2000 development team was to ensure that Windows 2000 Server was the most efficient, scalable, and reliable Microsoft operating system for the enterprise. Complex decision-making issues that arose during the design of Windows 2000 Server were handled with ruthless efficiency. If a choice arose between compatibility and stability, it was ruled as no competition—stability won every time. That has left us with an operating system that has gone through one of the most rigorous testing cycles in operating system history. Compound this with the involvement of some of the best minds in the computing business, and you have a network operating system that can only be described as a winner.

What does Windows 2000 Server signify to information technology professionals? It means an exciting opportunity to learn new skills, provide better services, and enhance productivity (and to use cool-sounding words like ADSI and Kerberos). Windows 2000 Server ushers in a bevy of features that leverage best-of-breed technology sets. This is not technology for technology's sake, but a technical architecture geared toward providing an infrastructure based on delivery.

Even on first appearances, it is obvious that Windows 2000 Server is a vastly complex operating system. With functionality literally bursting from the seams, it creates the dual opportunity for success and failure. The correctly prepared professional who understands the nature and complexities of Windows 2000 Server can provide an outstanding infrastructure based on its reliable, extensible, and flexible feature set. Those unprepared for managing and working with a product as far-reaching and complex as Windows 2000 Server should prepare for a good deal of confusion and reactive problem solving.

Windows 2000 Server is the next-generation operating system from Microsoft that not only replaces, but also revolutionizes the network operating system product space that Windows NT 4 Server occupied. With adequate preparation, appreciable benefits can be realized by all information technology professionals, from the Dilbert-style network manager, to the technical developer who sits in a lotus position chanting C++ mantras. But, more importantly, your clients—the users—will be able to reap the rewards that go hand in hand with Windows 2000 Server.

Mission-Critical Windows—A Contradiction in Terms?

Rightly or wrongly, Microsoft has been soundly chastised on more than one occasion for supplying server-based operating systems that fail ungracefully under pressure. Mention *Windows* and *Mission Critical* in the same sentence, and most people are likely to choke on their coffee. In the last 10 years, mainframes and several flavors of UNIX have been the first choice for providing mission-critical services, and for very good reasons. The message chanted by hardware and software vendors alike was, "Don't use Microsoft for anything that just *can't* go down"—a statement that most times I would have agreed with. Windows 2000 Server has changed all of that.

The Windows 2000 product group represents the largest and most technically advanced body of work undertaken by the most successful software company in the world. It is considered by many to be the single most important milestone in the evolutionary development of the Windows family. By providing a computing platform that offers stability, high productivity, and compatibility, Microsoft is extending its software presence even further into the server space.

The deluge of complaints that Microsoft has received (not to mention the battering suffered at the hands of the press) regarding its server-based operating systems has ensured that the Windows 2000 core services are built around a reliable and scalable architecture. Don't get me wrong, blue screens of death are not a thing of the past, nor have required reboots been relegated to the dust pile of Windows anachronisms. What has changed is the refocus on stability and on user requirements.

I am not alone in wanting 99.999% uptime, scalable directory services, and a secure computing platform. Windows NT went some way to addressing all of those concerns, but not nearly far enough. Mission critical means different things to different organizations—to supermarkets, point-of-sale systems are mission critical; to e-businesses, Web farms are mission critical. The common thread that runs through these disparate businesses is the requirement to provide a stable, supporting infrastructure that technologically enables mission-critical business services—a requirement to which Windows 2000 Server provides an almost unbeatable solution. That's the good news. The bad news is that you need more than a superficial level of understanding of your network operating system, you need to get your hands dirty with the real technical nuts and bolts.

This book is aimed at ensuring that your hands never look the same again!

Who Should Read This Book?

If you work with Windows 2000 Server, or are planning to, then this book will be of use to you. It is not meant to be light bedtime reading, but an exploration of the more technical issues of Windows 2000 Server. I recommend that you gain some familiarity with Windows 2000 Server concepts before reading this book (though it is not entirely necessary, since most chapters have introductory material), and that you understand general networking and operating system concepts. Don't let that scare you though—you don't need a degree in Quantum Physics, or need to own a personalized pocket protector to derive value from this book. What you do need is a will to get involved with the most exciting development in operating systems in the new millennium.

Windows 2000 Server is not a lightweight operating system. As users have become more demanding, there has been an associated increase in the complexity of the supporting technical infrastructure. But even among scary-sounding Windows 2000 Server acronyms like FSMO, SDOU, and LDAP, you will find concepts such as ease of use, security, and decreased support overhead. These are certainly concepts that most people can identify with, and if you do, then you *want* to understand the contents of this book.

How This Book Is Organized

When I was initially putting together the outline for this book, I realized that it would be impossible to cover all the technology sets in as great a detail as I would have liked—not unless I was prepared to have a book published that no one was physically able to pick up! As a result, certain features of Windows 2000 Server have received greater coverage than others. Core Windows 2000 Server features like Active Directory, IntelliMirror, network services, and security rightfully receive the lion's share of the coverage.

For relative newcomers to Windows 2000 Server, I recommend that you read the chapters in the order presented in the book. Not all chapters are freestanding, and certain chapters should be grouped together around the core Windows 2000 Server features I have mentioned. For those of you looking for particular technical information, or those who need no introduction to Windows 2000 Server, feel free to page through and use this book as a technical reference. Hopefully, within no time your copy of *Mission-Critical*

Windows 2000 Server will take on the appearance of a truly useful book—in other words dog-eared and discolored, with a fair amount of pencil work in the margins!

Acknowledgments

There are a number of people I must thank; some of them provided invaluable help in writing this book, while others taught me many of the things worth knowing in life. Thanks go to Sonia Barrett, for teaching me to laugh, to smile, and to appreciate real music. To Ray Walshaw, for gifting me with confidence and teaching me the courage of my convictions. Martin Walshaw—big brothers just don't come any better. Costas Kellas, for starting me down the road. The lads from the valley—Uruman Gwuafi, Alex Harris, David Ker, Sean Disney—thanks for teaching me that no mountain is too high—literally. Andrew Williams and Syngress, for being all the things a good publisher should be. D. Lynn White, for a great job of technical editing this back breaker.

My last and most important acknowledgment goes to the person who brings the light into my life. Natalie—thank you for helping me climb mountains, write books, sleep late, and most of all for being my wife—this book is yours as much as mine. Just you know why.

Chapter 1

Introduction to Windows 2000 Server

Solutions in this chapter:

- What's New in Windows 2000 Server?

- What's Not New in Windows 2000 Server?

- Windows 2000 Challenges

Introduction

Significant changes in the way that computers are used in the workplace have heralded an increased focus on issues such as security, manageability, scalability, and reliability. The use of information technology has ushered in an era characterized by high availability, high productivity, and increased support levels. Unfortunately, the burden of responsibility rests squarely on the shoulders of the IT professional to ensure that the infrastructure meets the requirements of the modern demanding user.

It is no great secret, or surprise, that legacy technologies are beginning to creak under the strain of ever-increasing user requirements, stability initiatives, and management drives to lower the cost of ownership. A new technology set was needed to provide services that existing operating systems could not. Microsoft itself was guilty of a lack of technical delivery with glaring omissions in the Windows NT 4 technical strategy that included the lack of a perceived stable mission-critical server platform and the absence of a cohesive infrastructure to manage configuration changes.

With a vision of providing an operating system for the future, Microsoft began development on its most ambitious project to date: Windows 2000. The aims of the design team, though simple in theory, proved to be much more difficult to achieve in reality. They had to provide scalable answers to the deficiencies in Windows NT 4, and satisfy design objectives that included:

- Increasing reliability, availability, and scalability
- Reducing costs through simplified management
- Providing a powerful and robust Internet and application server

Much has been said about the complexity and size of this new brainchild. The modern-day software malady of ever-increasing size and complexity has certainly directly affected Windows 2000 Server, but not necessarily in the manner that many people perceive.

There is no doubting that Windows 2000 Server is a mammoth exercise in coding complexity. Can a software project so large and intricate escape its unwieldy foundation to provide a truly stable computing platform? I can cite a classic modern example in defense of Windows 2000: its older sibling, Windows NT 4. Comparatively speaking, Windows NT 4 included a veritable minefield of code and feature changes over the ground-breaking Windows 3.x. The new operating system was to support memory protection, preemptive multitasking, and a limited directory service in a time when DOS and Windows 3.1 ruled the roost. Is the difference between Windows 2000 and Windows NT so substantial that we cannot draw confidence from the benefits gained during the migration from the veritable Windows 3.1 to the (then) cutting-edge 32-bit Windows NT platform?

Whether you plan to deploy it or are already using it, a lasting first impression of Windows 2000 Server is the vast array of integrated functionality. Casual inspection reveals a hauntingly familiar interface—is it just Windows NT 4 with a slick version of the Windows 98 GUI? Actually, nothing could be further from the truth. By probing a little deeper it soon becomes apparent that Windows 2000 Server combines an evolutionary upgrade path with a revolutionary feature set.

This chapter touches on the powerful features of Windows 2000 Server, and its effect on the organization and Administrators. Windows 2000 Server presents a radical change from its predecessor, and knowledge of its myriad of features is required to leverage its true power.

What's New in Windows 2000 Server?

When confronted by the sea of features and changes that accompany Windows 2000 Server, it is easy to understand the need to address some of the new features in detail, while touching on others in no more than a cursory fashion. Microsoft supplies a "feature highlight" that includes almost 80 major features—enough to make the eyes water!

Microsoft, to its credit, has learned that it is not possible to satisfy the diverse set of server requirements with a "one package fits all" strategy. To allow Windows 2000 Server to scale from the small business right into the multinational corporate server farm, it has been divided into a family of server operating systems (Table 1.1).

Each of the various flavors supports the much-touted Active Directory, which is probably the most critical element of the Windows 2000 Server family. Active Directory simplifies management, extends interoperability with applications and devices, and improves security.

The entry-level and most commonly used edition is Windows 2000 Server Standard Edition. The nomenclature for Windows 2000 Advanced Server hearkens back to the early days of Windows NT, when the name Advanced Server made its debut. Aside from its nostalgic name, Advanced Server maps most closely to Windows NT Server Enterprise Edition. It contains all the features and benefits of Windows 2000 Standard Edition, but includes support for larger deployments. The inclusion of support for network load balancing, clustering, and a more scalable memory and CPU architecture makes Advanced Server an excellent candidate for large SQL Server databases, for high-end Web servers, and for meeting the demands of high-end, critical file and application services.

Windows 2000 DataCenter is Microsoft's top-of-the-line model. In addition to having all the features of the Standard Edition and Advanced Server, DataCenter supports more processors and larger amounts of memory. Windows 2000 DataCenter Server is ideal for extremely large-scale

Table 1.1 Windows 2000 Server Family

	Description	Features
Windows 2000 Server	Designed to be a powerful multipurpose server. Ideal for workgroup and departmental servers.	■ During upgrade four-way SMP support. Fresh install supports two-way SMP. ■ Supports 4GB of memory. ■ Active Directory. ■ Kerberos security. ■ Enhanced Internet and Web services.
Windows 2000 Advanced Server	Designed for intensive enterprise applications. Provides further availability and scalability enhancements.	■ All Windows 2000 Server features. ■ Up to eight-way SMP support. ■ Supports up to 8GB of memory. ■ 32-node network load balancing. ■ Two-node clustering.
Windows 2000 DataCenter	Designed for massive enterprise solutions providing maximum levels of scalability and availability.	■ All Windows 2000 Advanced Server features. ■ Up to 32-way SMP support. ■ Supports up to 64GB of memory. ■ Four-node clustering.

deployments with the most demanding needs, such as high-end clustering, data warehousing, and Internet Service Providers (ISPs).

As usual, Microsoft has published a minimum hardware specification for the Windows 2000 Server family (Table 1.2)—and also, as usual, you can totally disregard them. I would be sorely taxed to think of anything as mind-numbingly boring as watching Windows 2000 Server run on a Pentium 133MHz. So this said, the recommendations should be read care-

Table 1.2 Minimum Hardware Requirements for Windows 2000

Microsoft published minimum requirements for Windows 2000 Server and Windows 2000 Advanced Server
■ 133MHz or higher Pentium-compatible CPU
■ 256MB RAM (128MB minimum supported)
■ 2GB hard disk with a minimum of 1GB free hard disk space

fully, and then thrown away. Hardware specifications are very much dependant on the type and volume of usage, but to provide a decent level of performance for the base operating system (but without leaving too much room for applications), I would recommend at a minimum a Pentium II 500MHz, 256MB of RAM, and a 100MB network interface card (NIC). The same rule that applies to luck also applies to RAM in the context of Windows 2000 Server: There is no such thing as too much of it!

The Key to Unlocking Your Network: Active Directory

The success or failure of a Windows 2000-enabled network will, in the majority of cases, hinge on the implementation of Microsoft's directory service, Active Directory. It is a fundamental change that affects the Windows operating system and Windows networking from top to bottom, and provides a structure for other applications to integrate more tightly into your Windows network than ever before.

"What exactly is a directory service?" you ask. A directory is a place to store interesting (and sometimes not-so-interesting) information (Figure 1.1). A directory service includes *both* the entire directory and the method of storing it on the network so that it is available to any client or server.

Figure 1.1 Directory service structure.

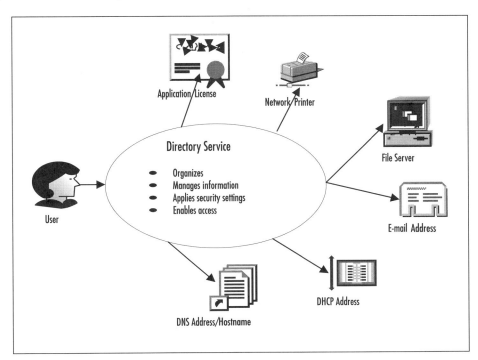

The type of information that is stored in a directory falls into three basic categories:

Resources Resources are the items attached to the network and made available to users. A resource can be a server's hard drive, an IP address, an application, a fax modem, a scanner, a printer, or any "thing" that can be used by a client workstation.

Services A service is a function on the network that makes resources shareable. Most services are simply network applications. These two categories are typically related. For most services, there is an analogous resource, and for most resources, there is an analogous service. Sometimes, however, a resource or a service stands alone.

Accounts The final category in a directory is an account. An account is usually a logon ID and associated password used for access to the network. It is used to grant the right to use a service or a resource.

Now that we know what a directory service is, we now need to find out how the Active Directory fits into the picture. Active Directory offers a nearly ideal set of directory characteristics so that a single directory and logon is available to all users. It also allows administration to be centralized or distributed according to requirements. The directory and its inherent security can be extended and scaled from small to large enterprises. Simply put, the Active Directory allows your users to find the resources they need on the network, while simultaneously facilitating administration, flexibility, and scalability.

Why Should I Use the Active Directory?

At first, it can be difficult to see the need for a directory service when, on first inspection, your current infrastructure suffices. This is abetted by the fact that many IT professionals live by the tried and tested maxim "if it ain't broke, don't fix it." Active Directory should only be implemented if it meets well-defined business requirements, and if it satisfies carefully thought-out technical considerations. Once it is implemented, though, you will wonder how you ever lived without it. Some of the advantages of Active Directory include:

Inherent scalability Active Directory has been designed to provide reliable services that scale from the small office to the multinational corporation. Multiple indexes of the directory provide swift information retrieval even in large distributed environments.

Enhanced security Active Directory integrates with a number of security mechanisms. It includes support for Kerberos, Secure Sockets Layer (SSL), smart cards, and X.509 certificates.

Standards based In a move away from proprietary architecture, Active Directory supports LDAP access, and uses TCP/IP with DNS as a namespace. This also implies that Active Directory can be easily integrated into an Internet or intranet environment.

Extensibility Active Directory provides a host of built-in functionality, including an inherent extensibility supplied through a definable schema and the Active Directory Services Interface (ADSI). Active Directory also provides tools for synchronizing with other directory services and managing identity information stored in multiple directory services.

Ease of administration Active Directory acts as publishing service for resources, allowing for centralized administration. The hierarchical directory structure simplifies administrative tasks and allows for the delegation of authority.

Inherent flexibility and scalability provides almost limitless applications for Active Directory, whether it is as the backbone of your distributed security environment or as a framework for client management and support. With the adoption of Active Directory by software vendors, the benefits of the Windows 2000 directory services will not only be available to the supporting infrastructure, but to applications themselves.

Change and Configuration Management

A great deal of attention has been focused on the cost of owning computing platforms; in particular, client workstations. Microsoft has aggressively addressed this issue by providing a series of technologies for Windows 2000 that support change and configuration management (Figure 1.2). The term *change and configuration management* encompasses all of the corrective, configurative, and preventative tasks that an Administrator must perform to keep his user base productive, including the deployment of software to the desktop. As is typical in the computing world, fancy multibarreled words can be boiled down to very basic principles: Change and configuration management is quite simply desktop and user management and configuration.

Figure 1.2 Change and configuration management in Windows 2000.

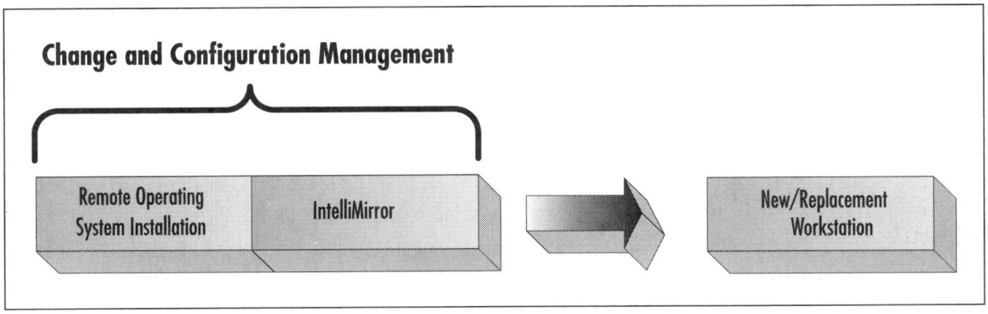

After consulting customers and the IT sector, Microsoft realized that its change and configuration management feature set needed to meet at least the following requirements:

- The ability to store user data centrally.
- Support of a personalized computing environment; data and applications should follow the users as they roam around the network.
- The ability to work on or offline.
- Reduction of administrative overhead by providing the ability to centrally configure clients by policy, including software deployment by policy.
- Self-healing desktops that reduce support call incidents.
- The ability to add/replace desktops without prestaging.

A number of factors have contributed to the increased costs associated with managing and owning a network and its infrastructure; more demanding users, increasingly complex products, and a growing user base are just a few of them. Windows 2000 certainly does not break the mold when it comes to developing complex products, but it does provide an infrastructure to lower the cost of owning a Windows-based infrastructure.

Change and configuration management centers are the continuing requirement for Administrators to manage the change and configuration issues that arise during the support of their user base. Two main concepts that support the new change and configuration management techniques are IntelliMirror and remote operating system installation. IntelliMirror is a set of tools and technologies that increase availability, reduce support costs, and allow the users' software, settings, and data to follow them. Three pillars support the IntelliMirror technology:

User data management Users can have access to their data whether they are online or offline. This feature leverages the Active Directory, Group Policy, folder redirection, disk quotas, and file synchronization—technologies that increase data availability. In Microsoft parlance: *"My data and documents follow me."*

User settings management Allows preferences to follow the user. The user's personalized settings such as desktop arrangements and software and operating system settings follow the user. This feature includes the Active Directory, Group Policy, roaming profiles, and particular shell enhancements—technologies that increase computer availability. In Microsoft parlance: *"My preferences follow me."*

Software installation and maintenance Ensures that users have access to their required software. Software can be advertised to install on demand, or be installed by default. This feature includes the Active Directory, Group Policy, self-repairing software, and application deployment—technologies that increase application availability. In Microsoft parlance: *"My software follows me."*

NOTE

A word of caution, do not tell friends or family that your software, data, and preferences are following you. They could take it upon themselves to retire you to a room with soft padded walls.

The second concept, remote operating system installation, allows Administrators to build a functional, standardized workstation remotely. Providing a solid and flexible infrastructure for operating system deployment is imperative for a successful operating system installation strategy.

A brief summary of some of the technologies used with IntelliMirror include (Figure 1.3):

Active Directory A scalable directory service that stores information about the network that can be accessed by users and Administrators alike. It can act as both an information source and a centralized administrative tool.

Group Policy A technology that enables Administrators to precisely define the configuration of the users' computing environment. It can satisfy such diverse requirements as setting security settings to application deployment. Group Policy can control both user- and machine-based configuration settings.

Offline Files and Folders A technology that allows users to access defined files and folders while offline. Entire mapped drives can even be accessed while offline. The Synchronization Manager can be used to synchronize offline resources.

Folder Redirection The ability to point a folder, such as My Documents, to another (network) location.

Distributed File System (DFS) This service can build a single namespace consisting of multiple shares on different servers. DFS provides the ability to load share and increase data availability.

Roaming User Profiles A centrally stored user profile that follows the user around the network.

Windows Installer A standardized, scalable installation service that is customizable, consistent, and provides diagnosis and self-repair functionality.

Disk Quotas A technology that enables Administrators to monitor and limit disk space usage on a per-volume per-user basis.

Figure 1.3 IntelliMirror and associated technologies.

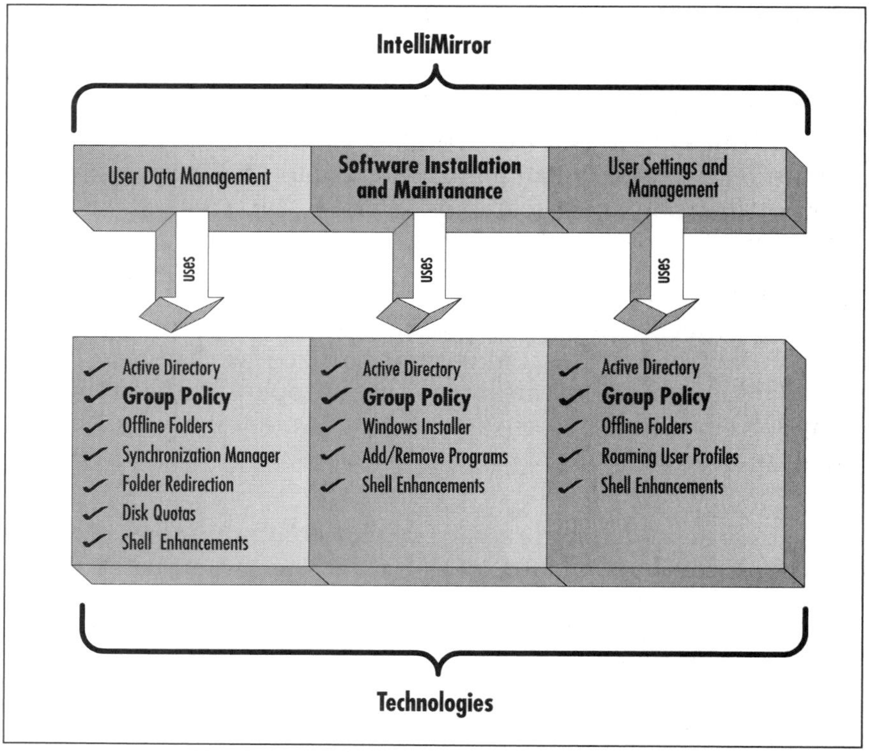

Group Policies

At times, it seems that as soon as your back is turned, more clients attach themselves to the network. The growing hunger of businesses to technologically enable their workforce is creating a mounting headache for the Administrator of today's networks. Maintaining and enforcing a standardized configuration while allowing the users freedom to work unhindered is a juggling act that sometimes requires the Administrator to have too many balls in the air at once. The only way to ensure that the configuration of possibly thousands of workstations is maintained in a consistent manner is by allowing the network to enforce the rules for software deployment and other change and configuration issues. Policy-based management is one answer to Windows 2000 change and configuration management challenges.

Group policies can be used throughout Windows 2000 to define user and computer configuration settings such as scripts, software policies, security settings, application deployment, user settings, and document options. Using group policies, these settings can be controlled centrally and applied across the business. Group Policy leverages the Active Directory and supports the IntelliMirror technology to control the scope and granularity of changes in configuration. By providing a well-managed desktop environment through group policies, Windows 2000 eases the resolution and elimination of change and configuration management issues.

The ability to control and manage the network in a scalable environment ensures that small, medium, and large businesses have the tools to lower the cost of owning PCs and supporting users. The vast array of configurable settings ensure that there is a wealth of usage scenarios for Group Policy, with just a few of those possible being:

- Install the accounting package on all computers in Finance.

- Run acclogon.cmd when users in the Accounts department log on.

- Do not save settings on exit for all consultants.

- Disable the RunAs service for the whole organization except Administrators.

- Launch this Web page at user logon.

Windows 2000 Security

Windows 2000 Server serves up a great number of security enhancements compared to what was available in previous incarnations of the operating system. These enhancements include Public Key Infrastructure capabilities, the Kerberos v5 authentication protocol, smart card support, the Encrypted File System (EFS), and IPSec. These new additions to security are necessary to protect data as more organizations come to the realization that their information technology infrastructure is business critical. It can be very hard to quantify the benefits of an enhanced security infrastructure—that is, until it's too late. Legacy security infrastructure and exploitable vulnerabilities have the potential to leave the doors in your network invitingly ajar, allowing havoc to be wreaked on mission-critical systems.

In today's ever-changing global environment, the more security that can be provided by a network operating system, the better off the organizations that use it will be. Security for Microsoft's network operating system has undergone major surgery with the arrival of Windows 2000 Server. What has emerged from the operating theatre is a product family that includes extensible, standards-based, mission-critical security. Some of the new features include:

- Multiple methods of authenticating internal and external users

- Protection of data stored on disk drives using encryption

- Protection of data transmitted across the network using encryption

- Per-property access control for objects
- Smart card support for securing user credentials securely
- Transitive trust relationships between domains
- Public Key Infrastructure (PKI)

Why the Change?

The change in security in Windows 2000 Server is necessary as more organizations use the operating system for mission-critical applications. The more widely an operating system is used in industry, the more likely it is to become a target. The weaknesses of Windows NT came under constant attack as it gained popularity. One group, L0pht Heavy Industries, harshly highlighted the frailties of Windows NT's password encryption for the LAN Manager hash. Due to the fact that the LAN Manager hash was always sent (by default) when a user logged in, L0pht produced a tool to crack the password. Microsoft made provisions for fixing the problem in a Service Pack release, but in Windows 2000 Server, it has replaced the default authentication with Kerberos v5 for an all-Windows 2000 domain controller based network—a system where passwords are never transmitted along the network.

Alarming figures based on intrusion detection statistics indicate that the majority of security violations occur *internal* to the corporate network. Accordingly, emphasis has moved from protecting against "black hat" external hackers to securing the corporate network as a whole.

Differences in Windows 2000 Server Security

One of the enhancements to the security in Windows 2000 Server is the support for two authentication protocols, Kerberos v5 and NTLM (NT LAN Manager). Kerberos v5 is the default authentication method for Windows 2000 domains, and NTLM is provided for backward compatibility with Windows NT 4.0 and earlier operating systems. Transitive trust relationships—a feature of Kerberos v5—are established and maintained automatically. Transitive trusts rely on Kerberos v5, so they are applicable only to Windows 2000 Server-only domains.

Another security enhancement is the addition of the Encrypted File System (EFS). EFS allows users to encrypt and decrypt files on their system on the fly. This provides an even higher degree of protection for files than was previously available using NTFS (NT File System) only.

The inclusion of IPSec (IP Security) in Windows 2000 Server enhances security by protecting the integrity and confidentiality of data as it travels over the network. It's easy to see why IPSec is important; today's networks consist of not only intranets, but also branch offices, remote access for travelers, and, of course (fade in scary music), the Internet.

Each object in the Active Directory can have its permissions controlled with a high level of granularity. This per-property level of permissioning is available at all levels of the Active Directory. Smart cards are supported in Windows 2000 Server to provide an additional layer of protection for client authentication, as well as providing secure e-mail. The extra protection is derived from adversaries needing not only the smart card, but also the Personal Identification Number (PIN) of the user to activate the card—a feature called two-factor authentication. Windows 2000 Server depends heavily on Public Key Infrastructure (PKI). PKI consists of several components: public keys, private keys, certificates, and certificate authorities (CAs).

Windows 2000 Network Services

The cliché that the world is getting smaller is used and derided on a daily basis, but that does not detract from the fact that it has become a truism. Communications, both data- and voice-based, have reduced the world to a global village. One of the factors that have hastened the arrival of the global village is the drive to well-connected networks. Operating systems such as Windows 2000 Server provide a number of advanced network services that facilitate reliable and scalable communication and connectivity. A few of the network services Windows 2000 offers include:

Certificate Services Several of the services available in the Windows NT 4.0 Option Pack are now included in Windows 2000 Server, including Certificate Services. Certificates are used most commonly to implement Secure Socket Layer communications on Web servers for the transmission of private information—your credit card number, for example. Certificate Services can also be used to make e-mail secure, provide digital signatures, and set up certification authorities that issue and revoke certificates.

DHCP Dynamic Host Control Protocol (DHCP) is certainly not new, but now interfaces with DNS and Active Directory. This feature illustrates an important point: Active Directory integration is pervasive throughout Windows 2000, and you'll find it in the most unlikely places!

DNS Domain Name Services (DNS) have been included with Windows 2000 as the default namespace provider. Additional benefits include the adoption of Dynamic Domain Name Service (DDNS), allowing clients to update details in DNS automatically.

Internet Authentication Service Internet Authentication Service (IAS) brings the ability to manage the authentication, accounting, authorization, and auditing of dial-up or virtual private network (VPN) clients. IAS uses the Remote Authentication Dial-In User Service (RADIUS). Setting up a VPN will allow you to provide secure network connections to users over the Internet, and IAS is a service used to manage these types of connections.

Internet Connection Sharing Many homes and small offices have a need for sharing an Internet connection, and there are a number of third-party products on the market that have filled this need. Windows 2000 can now share an Internet connection with a small network with a service that provides network address translation (NAT), addressing, and name resolution for other computers on the network.

Internet Information Services 5.0 The newest version of Microsoft's Web services is much like IIS 4.0, but has a truckload of new features. These include support for Web Distributed Authoring and Versioning (WebDAV), Web Folders, integrated FrontPage Server Extensions, support for some of the latest Internet standards, FTP Restart, Browser Capabilities Component, Self-Tuning ASP, encoded ASP scripts, process throttling, and the list goes on.

Network Address Translation Network Address Translation (NAT) is a feature that is used on many routers to connect networks using private IP address ranges to the Internet. NAT, as its name implies, translates addresses on IP packets so that devices on the Internet return all packets to the computer or router running NAT. The NAT device then forwards the data to the client that initiated the communication. This service also provides a layer of security, because a device on the Internet can only initiate communications with a host that has a routable IP address. Computers communicating behind a NAT device are much safer from outside attack than systems that have Internet routable IP addresses.

Quality of Service Windows Quality of Service (QoS) allows you to tune how applications are allotted bandwidth. With the increased use of audio and video over networks, it is necessary to ensure that enough bandwidth is available for these applications to deliver acceptable performance. QoS-based hardware and protocols, such as ATM, will enable multipurpose networks to meet the needs of voice and video applications in addition to the traditional uses of networks.

Routing and Remote Access Routing and Remote Access, affectionately known as RRAS, was introduced for Windows NT 4.0 as an add-on. Remember that cool Steelhead code name? Just like all those Option Pack features, RRAS is now a service bundled with the OS. You can use RRAS to terminate dial-up or VPN clients, and provide IP, IPX, and AppleTalk routing. Windows 2000 can function as a remote access server, a VPN server, a gateway, or a router with the capabilities of RRAS.

Virtual Private Networking Deploying a virtual private network (VPN) enables users to access your network via the Internet with a secure, encrypted connection. Organizations can use L2TP and IPSec to create VPNs and reduce or eliminate the need to maintain dial-in services for remote users, who will simply use a national or global ISP.

Managing and Supporting Windows 2000 Server

Another key goal of Windows 2000 Server's design was to simplify system management, ultimately lowering organizations' overall computing costs, also referred to as the total cost of ownership (TCO). Reducing the TCO for a Windows 2000 environment is partially fulfilled by IntelliMirror, but the total solution has been achieved by integrating this with a set of powerful services, including:

- Integrated directory services
- Comprehensive management solutions
- Comprehensive file, print, and Web services

Integrated Directory Services

As discussed earlier, the Active Directory stores information about the various resources on a network, much as a telephone directory stores information about people and businesses with telephones. Active Directory takes this concept a bit further; it not only stores directory information, but also provides the services that make this information available and useful. This is a major design feature of Windows 2000, which seeks to simplify and improve management while reducing the total cost of ownership. Active Directory contributes to Microsoft's design goals by providing these advantages:

- Simplified management
- Strengthened security
- Extended interoperability

Active Directory provides a single repository for managing users, groups, and network resources, eliminating redundant tasks by providing a single-point of management. An Administrator can easily deploy applications, find network resources, and even delegate administrative tasks and privileges easily and quickly. In addition to centralizing management, Active Directory improves security because of its tight integration with various security features, including a number of authentication mechanisms and Internet-secure protocols. Finally, Active Directory serves as a key integration point for application and system integration through such standard interfaces as the Microsoft Management Console (MMC). Windows 2000 Server improves management and lowers overall costs through its directory service by providing a focal point for securing network resources, reducing the number of places where Administrators need to manage information, and making it possible to integrate with other systems.

Comprehensive Management Solutions

Windows 2000 Server includes a broad range of solutions designed to assist Administrators. Using the management infrastructure and the many tools provided, Administrators can provide a broad range of services both quickly and reliably; they can better manage the network, while increasing server availability through improvements in:

- Management infrastructure
- Change and configuration management
- Storage management

The management infrastructure of Windows 2000 Server includes the presentation services, which incorporates the Microsoft Management Console (MMC). The MMC acts as a standard host for management applets, providing a consistent and customizable user interface. Windows 2000 management infrastructure also includes scripting services, which provide Administrators with the flexibility to automate processes using well-documented scripting languages. Gone are the days of incomprehensible batch files that seem to have been written in ancient Phoenician by a bleary-eyed technocrat referred to as "He Who Must be Obeyed."

Several new developments have heralded an increased ability to manage and support Windows-based infrastructure. Increased manageability translates into a more effective and customizable means of managing, upgrading, and installing operating systems and applications.

The technologies and tools detailed next are an essential part of Microsoft's Windows 2000 strategy, though it is important to note that the advantages of these tools can be realized prior to Windows 2000 deployment and can pave the way to a well-controlled deployment process.

Windows Scripting Host (WSH) The limitations of batch files are well documented, and the need for a replacement mechanism to automate tasks has been long overdue. WSH is a language-independent scripting host that natively supports VBScript and JScript (and the ability to leverage Internet Explorer). Scripting is a powerful way to efficiently automate tasks, both for the Administrator and the power user. Run from either the desktop or from the command prompt, it uses an ActiveX scripting architecture. Additional languages, such as Perl, TCL, and Python, can be incorporated through the use of third-party scripting engines. VBScript and JScript are easy-to-use scripting languages that can "get inside" Windows-based operating systems using Windows Management Instrumentation (WMI) and Active Directory Services Interface (ADSI).

Windows Management Instrumentation (WMI) To provide a comprehensive management platform, Microsoft has developed a means of instrumenting software and hardware components. WMI's kernel-level technology allows it to monitor, view, and manipulate components. WMI publishes information, configures device settings, and supplies event notification from device drivers.

Active Directory Services Interface (ADSI) In businesses today, there are usually a number of disparate directories—repositories of information—such as network operating systems and e-mail systems, each with its own method to access the information it contains. ADSI provides a well-defined, open set of interfaces for managing these directories. ADSI can be used with equal ease to add a user to the Active Directory, to the Windows NT Directory Service, and to the Novell Directory Service. ADSI can be considered the ODBC (Open Database Connectivity) of directory services.

Microsoft Installer (MSI) In order to address the shortcomings of the installation processes during deployment in Microsoft-based environments, MSI was developed to provide a more robust installation method. It provides the ability to manage shared resources effectively, enforce installation rules, reduce DLL conflicts, rollback installations, ease customization, and offer a self-repair facility.

Also part of the management infrastructure are the directory service, security services, and group policy services, which are tightly integrated with the Active Directory. Terminal services, which Microsoft has kindly included free with Windows 2000 Server, can be used to administer a Windows 2000 Server (or desktop computer) remotely. It also provides an excellent platform for sites that have decided not to embrace fat client technology, but have determined that thin is in.

Windows 2000 supplies added management solutions by incorporating change and configuration tools such as IntelliMirror, which is designed to lower the total cost of ownership and uses caching and centralized synchronization to mirror network users' desktop settings as well as applications and data.

IntelliMirror can also be used in conjunction with the storage management features included in Windows 2000, such as the Hierarchical Storage Management System. This combination, along with data archiving services and the improved backup and recovery utility, makes protecting users and the organizations data easier and more manageable.

Comprehensive File, Print, and Web Services

In addition to the support for disk quotas and volume management, Windows 2000 Server also seeks to improve management and lower costs by providing a broad set of file, print, and Web services with:

- Improved file system
- Faster printing
- Integrated Web services

The file system that Windows 2000 Server is built upon is a new version of the NT File System (NTFS), which provides added flexibility. It introduces new concepts such as reparse points, which allow file systems to be enhanced by additional installable file system filter drivers. Microsoft provides its own reparse points that support remote storage and volume mount points.

Organizations are now able to migrate data to less-expensive forms of media through the use of Remote Storage Service (RSS), yet the migrated data is still available to users because of pointers, which remain in the original location. The Windows 2000 file system also increases file system and data availability through features such as Dynamic Volume Management and the distributed file system (DFS). Both of these reduce downtime, which provides a definite added cost benefit to organizations.

Windows 2000 Server also supports the new UniDrive5 driver standard, which makes printing faster while improving its quality. In addition, the management of printers is simplified because of both Plug and Play support and support for the Internet Printing Protocol (IPP). IPP is an application-level protocol that can be used for distributed printing on the Internet, and it allows the management of printers through Uniform Resource Locators (URLs).

Finally, Windows 2000 Server is packaged with an updated version of Internet Information Services (IIS). IIS 5.0 makes it easy to share and publish information and documents across a company intranet or on the Internet. IIS is tightly integrated with Active Directory and the Windows 2000 security features, and it supports Active Server Pages (ASPs), Windows Media Services, CPU throttling, and HTTP compression.

Reliability and Availability

Windows 2000 Server provides an improved framework for reliable and available solutions with:

- Improved system architecture
- Support for various RAID levels
- Distributed File System (DFS)
- Clustering technology
- Disk defragmentation
- Plug and Play

Windows 2000 supports the various levels of RAID that Administrators may require; it includes support for disk mirroring (RAID level 1), disk duplexing (RAID level 1), and disk striping with parity (RAID level 5).

Another feature, the Distributed File System (DFS), improves fault tolerance by providing increased data availability and load balancing when it is integrated with Active Directory. DFS makes finding and managing information much easier by implementing a single namespace for miscellaneous file system resources, which allows shares to be maintained redundantly among multiple servers. Clustering is only available with Windows 2000 Advanced Server, providing failover capability to high-availability server farms.

A comprehensive part of the design of Windows 2000 was ensuring that the operating system suffered less system crashes and required fewer reboots. This entailed some aggressive coding to ensure that the operating system experienced fewer memory leaks. Additionally, many configuration changes—such as binding a new protocol—no longer require reboots. Server reboots may not yet be a thing of the past, but the number of times you will have to reboot your Windows 2000 Server has been dramatically reduced. More than 90 percent of the situations that once required a reboot have been eliminated.

Disaster and System Recovery

Some disenchanted readers may respond to this topic with the observation that if Windows 2000 Server provides such stupendous availability and reliability, you shouldn't even need disaster and system recovery tools. Now, I suppose the Microsoft line on that would be that they, unfortunately <sigh>, cannot guarantee the reliability of other operating systems and infrastructure that may interact and possibly "affect" Windows 2000 Server, and this is the reason why they provide the aforementioned tools <grin>.

Windows 2000 Server does provide the following methods for disaster and system recovery:

- Backup and UPS support
- Recovery Console
- Safe Mode Boot
- System File Protection

Windows 2000 includes an enhanced and powerful backup utility, and support for uninterruptible power supplies through a UPS service, which sends alerts in the event of a power failure. In addition, the service is capable of safely shutting down the system before the battery power in the power supply is depleted.

Another useful utility allows access to the NTFS file system for authorized users in case the server becomes inaccessible. Using the Windows 2000 CD-ROM or a version installed on the local drive, you can access this utility, called the Recovery Console. Before Windows 2000, many Administrators would resort to installing a parallel copy of Windows NT into a different directory in order to gain access to the file system. The other option was to install NT on a FAT partition so access could be gained to the file system through the use of a Windows 98 boot disk. Fortunately, the Windows 2000 Recovery Console provides an alternate way to safely and efficiently gain access to the file system and operating system services.

Windows 2000 Server incorporates great features from operating systems such as Windows 98, by allowing a computer to be started in Safe mode. Often a computer will not start because of a corrupt or misconfigured driver. In the past, Administrators often relied upon the "Last known good configuration" menu selection; however, this did not always work. With the ability to boot into Safe mode, the system can be started with the minimal number of drivers loaded, which allows you to make modifications or remove the faulty driver.

Windows 2000 also avoids file version mismatches, through the System File Protection (SFP) system. SFP monitors protected files and keeps a cache of original system files in case it becomes necessary to restore one of them. SFP tracks the proper file versions and stores this information in catalogs with a *.cat* extension. The system performs a check of these catalog files, and if any of the files are missing or corrupted, SFP will pull the good file from its cache, or ask the original media to restore the file.

Reliable Storage

Windows 2000 also increases reliability by providing enhancements to the storage system such as:

- Remote Storage
- Server Dynamic volumes
- Disk quotas

Remote Storage Server (RSS) works with the Hierarchical Storage Management (HSM) system, which allows different types of media to be part of the file system. RSS can automatically monitor the amount of space available on a local disk and is capable of moving data if free disk space drops below a specified level to secondary storage devices. Reparse points exist on the primary storage so that the migrated files can easily be retrieved from secondary storage.

Windows 2000 also increases reliability by the use of dynamic volumes. Dynamic volumes function much like partitions; however, volumes are not limited to only four, as partitions are. In addition, an Administrator can create, extend, and mirror volumes without rebooting the system.

Finally, Windows 2000 increases storage reliability by providing disk quotas, a much-desired feature found in other network operating systems. By using quotas, an Administrator has control over the amount of data that is allowed on NTFS volumes by users. Windows 2000 provides quota management at the volume level and does not support quotas on directories; therefore, you will need to acquire a third-party utility if you need to limit directories.

What's Not New in Windows 2000 Server?

So far, we've spent our time covering what's new. How about what isn't new? How much of your Windows NT knowledge will be useful for working with Windows 2000 Server? Quite a lot, actually. A good understanding of Windows NT is a great foundation for working with Windows 2000.

Core Architecture

Fortunately, the foundation of the operating system has remained intact. All of the things you learned about the Windows NT core architecture are still good to know—how it handles memory, interfaces with hardware, runs programs, etc. Despite the many changes that have been made, it is essentially the same operating system at its lowest layer. A good understanding and working knowledge of Windows NT will be a great foundation for working with Windows 2000.

Although the exact steps to configure many things have changed, you will find yourself swimming in well-known waters once you get started. For instance, the Windows NT Network Neighborhood icon on the desktop is named My Network Places in Windows 2000, and the familiar right-click and select Properties brings up the new Network and Dial-up Connections window. To install and configure clients, protocols, and services, you must view the properties of one of the connections. To install a new network adapter, however, you must use the Add/Remove Hardware Wizard in the Control Panel. Some things have been shuffled around a bit; you may spend a little time figuring out how to complete some operations the first time, but once you find out exactly where to do it, you'll have no problems if you are comfortable doing the same things in Windows NT.

Application Support

Since the core architecture has remained intact, Windows 2000 will still run most applications that run on Windows NT 4.0, including 16-bit programs. However, the more tightly an application was integrated with the Windows NT operating system, the more likely it is to have problems running on Windows 2000. You will certainly want to test every application thoroughly before upgrading any production computers.

Check with the software publisher for information regarding Windows 2000 compatibility first, so you won't spend time rediscovering problems they've already uncovered, or be unaware of an issue they have discovered that your testing missed.

User Interface

The graphical user interface (GUI) that you've come to know and love in Windows NT 4.0 is, for the most part intact, but many enhancements have been made. If you are familiar with the changes made by Active Desktop, you will find many of the same things in the Windows 2000 interface. Some of the improvements are merely aesthetic, such as the shadow behind the mouse cursor when running in high color or better video modes. You can also get more use out of your right mouse button, so be sure to try right-clicking for options where you tried with no success in Windows NT 4.0. One really great GUI enhancement is the drop-down list that appears when you are typing paths in Run or Open commands. As you begin typing a path, Windows 2000 moves ahead and displays folders and files that might complete or partially complete what you are typing. It even works when you are typing Universal Naming Convention (UNC) names! This is a great feature for those of you who shun the mouse to gain the speed of typing. Now you don't have to remember the path exactly—you'll be getting some help.

Client Support

Windows 2000 will still offer file and print services for Windows, Windows NT, and Macintosh clients. An Active Directory client is available on the Windows 2000 Server CD for Windows 95 and 98. This will allow Windows computers to take advantage of Active Directory services when possible, and will allow developers to write Active Directory-enabled applications for Windows 9x PCs.

Windows 2000 Challenges

In an effort to portray a realistic view, warts and all, of Windows 2000 Server, it is important to discuss all facets of the operating system. An entire book could be filled with the multitude of benefits to be gained from Windows 2000 Server—this is not that book. Windows 2000 Server is unarguably a fantastic leap forward for server-based operating systems, but at the same time, there are challenges to be faced:

Plug and Play A common complaint is the lack of comprehensive Plug and Play support. When Plug and Play is not adequately supported, some of the device's more advanced features may not function, and in some instances the device itself will not function at all. This should not be as much of a problem when using server platforms, which usually have a relatively static hardware profile and are subject to stringent change control procedures. All the same, it is important to consult the Hardware Compatibility List (HCL) whenever implementing hardware for Windows 2000.

BIOS versions Particular BIOS revisions may be required to take advantage of certain Windows 2000 features. Older BIOS versions may even cause stability issues.

Device driver compatibility This is related to the Plug and Play issue described earlier. Many Administrators have found they can "fool" Windows 2000 into using older drivers by combining Windows 9x and Windows NT .inf files. I recommend heartily that you wait for the vendor-released driver—Would you want mission-critical servers to be based on homegrown driver sets? Driver compatibility is building up a head of steam for Windows 2000, and it should not be long before they are almost on a par with personal operating systems such as Windows 9x and Windows Millennium.

Application compatibility   Many applications that are compatible with Windows NT will function under Windows 2000. Remember that during the design phase, Microsoft engineers made the conscious decision to forsake compatibility for stability if so required. This means it is important to verify compatibility by running the application through a rigorous test cycle and checking whether the application complies with the Windows 2000 Application Specification. If the application sports the *Made for Windows 2000* logo, you can be sure it is compatible.

Hardware requirements   Much like Windows NT, it was generally considered during initial release that Windows 2000 was very resource intensive. And just like Windows NT, by the time Windows 2000 achieved real market penetration, such requirements were passé. "Canny planning," some would call it.

Service Release levels   Windows NT has undergone extensive trial by fire and is now a stable, well-patched operating system. Windows 2000 has not undergone the trials and tribulations of many years of operational service.

Directory architecture   Existing architectures may need to be remodeled to take advantage of Windows 2000 Server, and in particular, Active Directory. One of the biggest challenges lies in the integration or redesign of existing directory services to take advantage of Active Directory. In networks that consist mainly of NetWare or UNIX, Active Directory may be difficult to implement, since Windows 2000 and Active Directory cannot be uncoupled. Other hurdles could include DNS requirements, existing domain design, and current business models.

Cost of deployment   Deploying Windows 2000, and in particular, Active Directory, can generate a significant cost implication. Microsoft's spin on this is that the organization must be willing to absorb a significant initial outlay to reap the long-term rewards.

Client management   Windows 2000 provides little management for non-Windows clients. Group policies are Windows-centric.

Skills base   It will take some time before Windows 2000 has the same diverse pool of technical know-how as its more mature rivals. Due to the fundamental changes ushered in by a directory service, expensive specialist skills may be required.

Competition   Some of the competition has stolen a march on Windows 2000 by offering an intriguing combination of services coupled with a mature product set. In particular, Novell's NDS has long been considered to have a best-in-class enterprise directory service space and has been widely available for some time.

Summary

Operating systems have progressed remarkably in terms of capability and complexity in recent years. Unfortunately, productivity gained by using technologically advanced operating systems has been offset by the high cost of owning, maintaining, and deploying them. Windows 2000 Server provides an answer to many of the escalating server operating system issues.

Windows 2000 design goals included:

- Increasing reliability, availability, and scalability
- Reducing costs through simplified management
- Providing a powerful and robust Internet and application server

The Windows 2000 Server family of products has been demarcated according to required scalability and availability. The standard edition, Windows 2000 Server, is designed to be a powerful multipurpose server. Windows 2000 Advanced Server provides all the benefits of the standard edition, along with increased scalability and availability. Windows 2000 DataCenter is targeted at those businesses whose requirements extend into the highest levels of availability, scalability, and capacity.

A plethora of features are bundled with Windows 2000 Server, with the most important feature undoubtedly being Active Directory. A directory consists of interesting information about the organization that can be used by Administrators, applications, services, or users. The responsibility for storing directory information and the service for accessing this information within Windows 2000 can be defined as the Active Directory.

The use of Active Directory is encouraged because it provides a number of considerable benefits. These include inherent scalability, advanced security, extensibility, ease of administration, and the facility to use standards-based services and protocols that integrate with the Internet.

Microsoft has developed a cohesive strategy for addressing change and configuration management issues. IntelliMirror and Remote Operating System installation are technology sets designed to address change and configuration management. Features of IntelliMirror include software installation and maintenance, user data management, and user settings management.

Group policies enable the Administrator to define the state of the users' computing environment, and uses the network to enforce that definition according to the required scope.

Security within organizations is of paramount importance, and Windows 2000 Server attempts to address security issues with a range of scalable security services. These services include Kerberos, Public Key Infrastructure (PKI), IPSec, Encrypted File System (EFS), and smart card support.

Windows 2000 network services provide the basis for a well-connected and manageable network environment. Services such as Dynamic Host Control Protocol (DHCP) and Domain Name System (DNS) are not only supported, but also integrated into Active Directory. Windows 2000 also provides other features such as Quality of Service (QoS), Internet Information Services v5 (IIS), Routing and Remote Access Services (RRAS), and virtual private networking (VPN).

Though providing a rich feature set is a requirement in modern server-based operating systems, it is also equally important to maintain a suitable cost of ownership. Microsoft has answered the questions surrounding management by providing technologies such as the Microsoft Management Console (MMC), Windows Scripting Host (WSH), Microsoft Installer (MSI), and Windows Management Instrumentation (WMI).

Supported by the improved file system, faster printing services, and integrated Web services, Windows 2000 Server is the ideal Internet and file and print platform.

FAQs

Q: What is Microsoft Windows 2000 Server?

A: Windows 2000 Server is the successor to Windows NT 4.0 Server. It provides networking, application, communications, and Web services with increased reliability, scalability, and manageability.

Q: How does Windows 2000 Server differ from the others in the 2000 Server family?

A: Within the Windows 2000 Server family, there are three different versions: Windows 2000 Server, Windows 2000 Advanced Server, and Windows 2000 DataCenter Server. Windows 2000 Server is the primary product aimed at small to medium deployments. Windows 2000 Advanced Server (formerly known as Windows NT Server 4.0, Enterprise Edition) is much more powerful than Windows 2000 Server. Advanced Server is more scalable, and can support memory up to 8GB. Windows 2000 DataCenter server is the high-end version of Windows 2000, and it supports up to 32-way symmetric multiprocessing (SMP) and 64GB of memory. This edition is geared to very large deployments.

Q: Why does Windows 2000 use Kerberos?

A: Previous authentication infrastructures for Microsoft products had very well-known weaknesses. Kerberos provides a scalable, fast, and secure authentication protocol that never transmits sensitive data (such as passwords) along the network.

Chapter 2

Active Directory— The Heart of Windows 2000 Server

Solutions in this chapter:

- Mission-Critical Active Directory Concepts
- Developing a Naming Strategy
- Designing Active Directory Domains

Introduction

Network and operating system vendors would have you think that directory services are a startling new advance ushered in by the Information Age, but in fact, directory services have been available as tools for organizing, locating, and managing information for many years. Network directories are similar in concept to the telephone book Yellow Pages. The Yellow Pages are a listing of businesses and phone numbers that are indexed by the type of business and then alphabetized. Anyone can look up a business by type and name in order to get the correct phone number. On the network, a user could use a directory service to find all printing services, and then browse the listing of the one that is most appropriate.

The directory service is a concept that organizes all the pieces of a network together (and for someone like me, that in itself is a minor miracle). It is available to each server that participates in the directory, and to each client that wants to access a server. Domain Name System (DNS) is one type of directory well known to Administrators. The DNS directory lists computers by their hostnames and associates them with their respective IP addresses. When a user needs to access a computer on the network and uses its hostname, the client computer contacts the DNS server to request an IP address.

Microsoft has answered the directory service challenge by creating the Active Directory as a standards-based system, accessible via the Active Directory Services Interface (ADSI) API and standard protocols such as LDAP (Lightweight Directory Access Protocol).

As mentioned earlier, Windows 2000 is packed with new and improved features, with the Active Directory itself offering:

- The ability to promote and demote domain controllers (DCs) as they act as domain controller peers within the directory structure
- Granular, policy-based administration easing management concerns
- Decentralized administration using an organizational unit (OU) and domain hierarchy
- Improved security

Active Directory can be seen as a unifying engine and information source that integrates with many network and application functions. The Active Directory, which is at the heart of the fundamental changes in Windows 2000, abounds with functionality and features. Unfortunately, when software positively bristles with features, it usually means that it is a bit prickly to learn. Several important concepts and issues that form the backbone of the architecture and structure of Active Directory will be discussed in detail in the coming chapters.

Mission-Critical Active Directory Concepts

No single book can purport to explain all of the features of Windows 2000 Server, and this book certainly does not buck that trend. That said, there are several fundamental concepts and technologies that need to be understood before you will be able to leverage the full power of Windows 2000 and the Active Directory. In this section, you will find a brief description of the terms and concepts that are critical to understanding and using Active Directory. However, one critical concept that I have not covered is *perseverance*—clothe yourself in it and the Active Directory will become a welcome friend, shrug it aside and you may regret it!

As this book is aimed at the network-literate reader, some explanations and definitions in the Mission Critical Concepts section are meant to act as reminders only.

For IT Professionals

Directory Enabled Networks

The Distributed Management Task Force (DMTF), whose Web site is www.dmtf.org, is currently developing a standard for Directory Enabled Networks (DEN). Even though many network operating systems support directory services of various types, most are vendor specific. This means that one server might be able to access a directory, but another will not, simply because it is running a different vendor's network operating system. The result might be multiple directory services running on a single network, which poses problems for users who are faced with multiple logons (again) and for Administrators who must manage multiple directory structures.

Once vendors create DEN-compliant directories, multiple network operating systems will be able to participate in a single directory service. Don't worry! DEN compliance is a goal for Microsoft Active Directory services once the standard has been finalized. In fact, Microsoft and Cisco were the pioneers of the DEN initiative.

A directory service such as the standard being developed for DEN will go beyond the simple organization of addresses and hostnames that DNS provides. Instead, the directory service will organize all the services and resources participating in a network.

Where Active Directory Fits in the Overall Windows 2000 Architecture

Microsoft has attempted to integrate Active Directory into all aspects of Windows 2000, be it management, resource location, or application integration. It is a fundamental change that affects the Windows operating system from top to bottom.

Each time a Windows 2000 Server (any version) is installed with a new install, by default it becomes a member server. Upgrades are handled differently if a Windows NT primary domain controller (PDC) or backup domain controller (BDC) is being upgraded to Windows 2000. Member servers use an identical security architecture to the Windows 2000 Professional client workstations, which has a flat-file local database. The flat-file database allows for local users and groups, as well as shared files and printers, in a server-centric model. Only when a member server or client workstation joins an Active Directory domain can it participate in the Active Directory. This does not remove the local database, and a user can still log on locally to the server using it.

When a Windows 2000 Server joins an Active Directory domain, it can communicate with any DC for Active Directory Service (ADS) security information. Domains are configured as top-level containers in a tree structure. Each domain is configured into a hierarchical structure using organizational units (OUs). Domains sharing a contiguous namespace are organized into domain trees. There can be multiple domains in ADS, and multiple domains with different namespaces that participate in a single ADS are considered a forest of multiple domain trees.

Active Directory Concepts

The contents of the Active Directory are stored in a database, the structural organization of which is called the *schema*. The schema defines the types of objects that can exist in the directory. When updates are made, they are most effectively distributed via a transaction-oriented database update protocol, since only updates need to be changed throughout and not the entire database.

Any changes made to the directory can be made to any directory server, which then propagates that change to the remaining directory servers. This method, called *multi-master replication*, provides fault tolerance and distributed administration and directories. However, the multi-master method does require a way to handle conflicting changes in the directory.

What's in a Name?

In the ever-growing world of information technology, one of the most vexing problems is how to track and address the resources in your network. Active

Directory provides a scalable hierarchical structure for finding and organizing resources, helping you manage your network entities. As you can guess, understanding how these resources are named, addressed, and structured is fundamental to understanding Active Directory itself.

Namespace

A *namespace* is any dataset in which standardized names can be looked up and resolved. This broad definition includes all directory services, from DNS to ADS. In ADS, the name of any object (whether it is a user account, resource, or service) is resolved to that object itself. Once a user or even an application resolves the name to the object, the user or application can browse the object's property values, if permitted to do so. If that user or application has security access, it can even manipulate the values of those objects. The ADS namespace is directly related to DNS. Each domain is granted a DNS domain name.

Name

Each object has a name that represents it in the ADS tree. The name for a server would be its DNS name, such as server.company.com, while the name for a user account would be the simple logon name.

Container

A *container* is an object in the directory that simply contains other objects. Containers are similar to folders in a file system. Container objects can contain other containers in the same way that a file system folder can contain other folders. A container does not represent any user, service, or resource, but it does have its own attributes and values.

X.500

X.500 is a directory service standard ratified by the International Telecommunications Union (ITU-T) in 1988 and modified in 1993 and 1997. It was intended to provide a means to develop an easy-to-use electronic directory of people that would be available to all Internet users. The X.500 directory specifies a common root of a hierarchical tree. Contrary to its name, the root of the tree is at the top level, and all other containers are below it. The X.500 standard includes several types of containers with a specific naming convention for them. In this naming convention, each portion of a name is specified by the abbreviation of the object type or container it represents. A user has a CN= before the username to represent its "Common Name," a C= precedes a country, and an organization is heralded by an O=. When compared to IP domain names—for example, host.subdomain.domain—the X.500 version of CN=host/C=US/O=Org appears excessively complicated.

Each X.500 local directory is considered a Directory System Agent (DSA). The DSA can represent either a single or multiple organizations.

Each DSA connects to the others through a Directory Information Tree (DIT), which is a hierarchical naming scheme that provides the naming context for objects within the directory. Although ADS is derived from the X.500 model, ADS does not implement all of the X.500 protocols because of the excess overhead involved or the lack of their general usage.

Distinguished Name

Each ADS object possesses a *distinguished name* (DN). The DN identifies the object by its name, and includes the trace of all of the containers above it with their respective names, until the top of the tree (a hierarchy of containers) is reached. Each DN is unique within a forest (multiple trees), even if multiple objects have the same name in different domains. For example, Benjamin Johnson with the name BJOHNS can exist in the Panther domain, while Beverly Johnston with the name BJOHNS can exist in the Cheetah domain (Figure 2.1). They may appear to have identical names, but in the Active Directory, their DNs are different because they include the domain name as part of the DN:

/O=MicroAge/DC=Cheetah/CN=Users/CN=BJOHNS

/O=MicroAge/DC=Panther/CN=Users/CN=BJOHNS

Relative Distinguished Name

The *relative distinguished name* (RDN) of any object is the part of the DN that represents the object. In the example (Figure 2.1) for Beverly Johnston in the Cheetah domain, her DN is /O=MicroAge/DC=Cheetah/CN=Users/ CN=BJOHNS, and her RDN is CN=BJOHNS. The RDN is typically the simple name of the object.

User Principle Name

The *user principle name* (UPN) is a naming format that uses a domain name as part of the username. It is a new concept for usernames. Since DNS is provided in ADS as the locator service, incorporating the domain name as part of the username means that user objects are easily located and authenticated. This can facilitate the logon process for users who roam from site to site. Additionally, the UPN format—user@subdomain.domain.com— can be identical to the e-mail address for that user, making it easier for that user to remember.

GUID

A *Globally Unique Identifier* (GUID) is a 128-bit identifier that is used to identify an object within Active Directory. The GUID is assigned once an object is created, and will remain the same even if an object is moved or renamed. This allows services to find an object even if its name or attributes are modified.

Figure 2.1 Tracing DNs through the Active Directory tree.

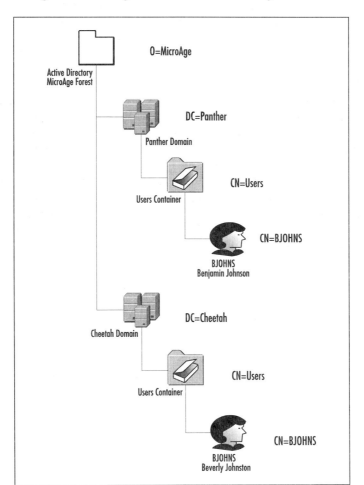

NAMING SUMMARY

The Active Directory is based on the X.500 model. The objects within the directory are resolved within the namespace. Each object has a name and is held within a container. Every ADS object possesses a Distinguished Name (DN). The Relative Distinguished Name (RDN) is the part of the Distinguished Name that represents the object, while the User Principle Name is a format that uses the domain name as part of the username. A Globally Unique Identifier is a number used to identify any object regardless of location or name.

Naming Contexts and Partitions

A naming context is also known as a *partition* because it is the part of the Active Directory database that is replicated to other domain controllers. There are three types of naming contexts:

- Schema
- Configuration
- Subtree

The schema is the description of the types of objects and properties that are available throughout the ADS database. The schema must be identical on all DCs so that objects and their properties can be recognized from any point in the internetwork. The configuration of the Active Directory is principally the method of replication and any ADS database descriptor information. The method of replication must be known throughout the internetwork, so that DCs know where to send updates within domains, and when to send updates outside of the domains. The ADS database configuration includes information about the shape of the Active Directory itself, such as which domains are connected to which other domains through what bridgehead servers. Finally, subtree information is a contiguous set of database objects. Subtrees are typically separated at the domain level. This information must be replicated in order for authentication and access control to function properly.

The Architecture of Active Directory

Architecture implies structure and building of something. So how do you construct an Active Directory? The answer to that question is, *any way that will fit your organization.* You see, the way that Microsoft developed the Active Directory provides a flexible model that can incorporate any type of physical internetwork and any type of logical organization. The network impacts the Active Directory Service design in four ways:

- Data model
- Schema
- Security
- Administration

Data Model

The data model for Active Directory is derived from X.500; however, it is not identical to X.500. When X.500 was first implemented, it was discovered to have some significant overhead issues in its use of OSI protocols encapsulated in TCP/IP. Later, LDAP was developed to access an X.500 directory and avoid the overhead, which is why its name begins with the word *lightweight*. Active Directory uses a similar data model and the

LDAP protocol to gain the best of the X.500 directory standard and avoid the worst.

The ADS data model provides for a hierarchical directory that uses objects to represent services, resources, and users. It further enables attributes to describe the objects. This hierarchy, however, can be created for any type of enterprise, and can be developed to encompass both a physical structure and a logical organization of the users and groups within the enterprise.

Schema

The *schema* defines what types of objects can be stored in a specific Active Directory. For example, an extremely simple schema might define three object classes as a server, an OU, and a user. Each of these object classes would have attributes such as the server IP address, the OU name, and the user e-mail address. When an actual server, OU, and user object are created, those attributes are given values. The value for the server IP address attribute might be 10.10.10.5, the value for the OU name attribute might be HQ, and the value for the user e-mail address attribute might be user@mail.corp.com. This is summarized in Table 2.1.

Table 2.1 Schema Objects, Attributes, and Values

Object Class	Object	Attribute	Value
Server	Server.domain.com	IP address	10.10.10.5
Organizational unit	CN=HQ	Name	HQ
User	USER	E-mail address	user@mail.corp.com

The Active Directory schema can be extended to include additional objects. For example, a backup program that is written to take advantage of the Active Directory could add an object class for the backup service and add an attribute to the server object class to enable it as a backup service provider or a backup service requester. The schema must be updated across all the DCs that contain a replica of the Active Directory in order for those objects and properties to be recognized and administered from any point in the internetwork.

The ADS schema is stored within the directory itself. This reduces the overhead involved with users or applications that run queries on the Active Directory. It also allows the schema to be extended dynamically, with immediate access to the new object classes and attributes. The ability to perform schema extensions is protected by Access Control Lists (ACLs) so that only authorized users can extend the schema.

TIP

When an application that extends the schema is installed on the network, the application will require the name and password of a user who has the capability of extending the schema. Otherwise, the installation will fail.

Security Model

When a Windows 2000 Server joins a domain or becomes a DC, it automatically begins participating in the Active Directory. The Active Directory uses the Kerberos security model. The ADS uses Kerberos version 5.0, an authentication protocol that was developed by MIT and is published by the IETF in RFCs 1510 and 1964. Using Kerberos, the ADS can verify the identity of any user, service, or resource on a network that without this verification would otherwise be unprotected from public use. Kerberos does not rely on the NOS to authenticate, and does not trust specific IP addresses, which are both common security methods in use today. Instead, Kerberos uses credentials to verify identities.

Once an identity is authorized to access the directory, the security within ADS takes over. In the Active Directory itself, ACLs are defined by the Administrator to allow any user, resource, or service to access any other user, resource, or service. The ACLs are flexible enough to enable access to use a service or resource, or even to change the values of their attributes.

Administration Model

The Active Directory allows an Administrator to delegate authority to segments of a domain. In the legacy domain model for Windows NT, the Administrator delegation level was set for an entire domain, regardless of the groups and organizations that participated in the domain. Now, with the ability to segment a domain into a hierarchical tree structure using nested organizational units (a type of container), the administration model can be set to whichever level best suits the enterprise. The result is that an Administrator is granted an appropriate area of control.

Putting the Pieces Together

Once we understand how objects are addressed within the Active Directory, we progress into the logical organization and structure of the Active Directory. The ADS logical architecture consists of three main organizing concepts:

- **Forest**   A set of namespaces representing multiple domain trees.
- **Domain tree**   A set of domains that are hierarchically named to participate in a single namespace.
- **Organizational unit**   A container within a single domain that organizes the domains users, resources, and services.

A forest is global, which means that it can include any or all users, resources, domains, and physical LAN and WAN connections on the internetwork. The domain tree is based on the DNS domain name. The OU is a logical container that can organize the resources, services, and users within a domain in a nested hierarchical tree structure.

Global Catalog

The *global catalog* (GC) is a listing of the objects within the Active Directory. It contains enough information to locate a replica of the ADS partition, which contains the object without the querying user or application needing to know the location of that object within the ADS hierarchy. The user or application will need to know one or more attributes of the desired object to perform the query.

Objects and Organizational Units

Objects are the items that are organized in the Active Directory. The objects can be anything that the schema allows, such as users, groups, printers, servers, and so on. The objects are stored in organizational units (OUs), which then become an administrative tool for grouping objects in a hierarchical system similar to a folder on a hard drive. The interesting concept about OUs is that they are themselves a type of object. A user can be granted access rights to an OU for administration purposes, while another user would not have administrative access to that OU, even though that other user has administrative rights elsewhere within the same domain.

Tree

A *tree* is a hierarchical organization of containers and objects. The tree is similar to the entire file system on a computer's hard drive. The tree has multiple branches created with nested containers. Nested containers are similar to folders in the file system. The ends of each branch are objects that represent users, services, and resources. These objects are analogous to the files inside containers.

Domains

The *domain* is a group of Windows 2000 computers that participate in the same security subtree. The Active Directory consists of one or more domains. Each domain can span both LAN and WAN links, depending on the network design and subsequent domain implementation. Multiple domains can exist on the same LAN. When there are multiple domains using different namespaces in the Active Directory, it is considered to be a forest of domain trees. This forest must enclose domains that share a common schema and configuration, though the domains do not necessarily share the same contiguous namespace. They produce a GC of users, services, and resources.

The domain hierarchy follows a rigorous definition where a child domain has only one parent domain, and two children with the same parent have the same name.

Domain Trees

The *domain tree* is a group of contiguous domains that share a common schema and configuration, and are united by trust relationships to create a single namespace. ADS can contain one or more trees, which can be depicted via their trust relationships or via their namespace.

Viewing Trust Relationships

Trust relationships are the connecting points in a domain tree. To illustrate this relationship, picture a logical structure of each domain with arrows showing the explicit trust relationships between domains, and any implicit trust relationships that result from them. ADS uses the Kerberos security protocol to establish trust relationships between domains. The Kerberos trusts are transitive and hierarchical.

NOTE

Transitive trusts are new to Windows 2000. The legacy Windows NT trust relationships were nontransitive. In the legacy Windows NT domain architecture, for example, the Tabby domain can trust the Calico domain, and the Calico domain can trust the Persian domain, *but* the Tabby domain does not automatically trust the Persian domain. However, in the Windows 2000 architecture, trust relationships are transitive. In this architecture, and using the Tabby -> Calico->Persian trust relationships, there is a new *transitive trust relationship* in which the Tabby domain trusts the Persian domain.

Forests

As mentioned earlier, a forest is a set of domain trees that share a common schema, configuration, and GC. However, a forest has one more requirement: It has two or more namespaces among the participating domain trees.

The forest uses the name of its root domain. It exists as a set of domain trees that trust each other via transitive and hierarchical trust relationships using the default Kerberos security trust model that is implemented by ADS. Figure 2.2 depicts a forest.

Figure 2.2 Multiple namespaces in a forest.

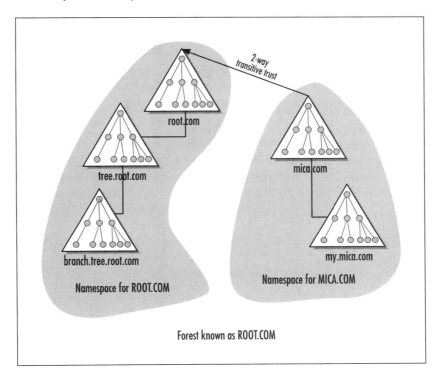

Sites

Think of a *site* as a geographically-based location for servers. The official definition for a site is one or more IP subnets that share a fast and reliable connection. It is recommended that a site consist of links with greater than 512 Kbps of available bandwidth. Available bandwidth is the amount of bandwidth that is not being used by other network traffic. If a link exists for a T1 line of 1.44 Mbps, it would appear that it has more than enough bandwidth to meet this recommendation. However, if that T1 line was saturated with network traffic, it would not be sufficient.

The site definition is vague enough to allow a site to encompass high-speed WAN links; however, a site is best configured as one that only contains LAN connections that are less likely to become saturated with network traffic. IP subnets of a single IP network typically are designed to share LAN connectivity.

The servers that are in a single site are automatically configured for replication to each other. If those servers are only connected with high-speed reliable links, then the replication traffic can take advantage of the physical network.

Authentication traffic also takes advantage of site configuration. When a user logs on to the Active Directory, the workstation will try to locate servers in the same site as the user first, and then try other servers in other sites. The local site is determined by the IP subnet in which the workstation exists. It looks up a server that is in a site that contains that IP subnet in order to log on. Taking advantage of a physically close server, and a fast connection, makes the user perceive a higher performance from the network.

Multi-Master Replication

Multi-master replication occurs when each DC is a peer to all other DCs in a single domain. A change made to any replica of the Active Directory database on any DC is automatically updated on all the others. Changes are replicated within the domain, but changes can be replicated to other domains through what is best described as bridgehead servers. A bridgehead server is one in the network that is designated to send and receive replication traffic from other domain sites so that there is a management method to the traffic direction on the network. Using bridgehead servers enables the network designer to direct how replication traffic traverses the internetwork.

Active Directory can use two transports for this replication traffic:

- **SMTP**   Asynchronous replication via the Collaborative Data Objects (CDOv2) interface to Simple Mail Transfer Protocol (SMTP).
- **RPC**   Synchronous replication via Remote Procedure Calls (RPCs) over Transport Control Protocol/Internet Protocol (TCP/IP).

Keep in mind when designing your bridgehead servers that RPC communication is appropriate for most LAN and WAN connections between sites. However, SMTP communication is most effective for low-speed WAN connections, such as remote access connections over modems, between sites.

Developing a Naming Strategy

Understanding trees and forests does not imply that we are out of the woods yet! Planning the Active Directory naming strategy is the launch point for deploying Windows 2000. This may seem a tedious task, but it is critical to the performance and usability of your network. In order to determine the naming strategy, you will need to gather information about the enterprise. This information includes the existing Domain Name System (DNS) configuration, the existing NT Domain configuration, and the current naming conventions used on the network. Before deploying Windows 2000, the project team should fully understand the components of the Active Directory namespace plan. The namespace plan incorporates the naming strategy for DNS, since it is so tightly integrated in the Active Directory. It also describes the domains and their structure for all of the Windows 2000 domains, and the standards that the team will adhere to when creating objects and published resources in the Active Directory tree. Do not make the mistake of discounting the importance of a solid namespace design. The namespace plan impacts all sorts of network mechanisms, including:

- Administrative efficiency
- Change management
- Network usability
- Bandwidth overhead issues
- Network availability and fault tolerance

Active Directory's Integration with DNS

DNS is a general-purpose data query service for the TCP/IP protocol suite. The data typically queried is hostnames (a.k.a. the name of the computer), and the responses are typically the hosts' IP addresses. DNS requires name servers that maintain the information about the domain tree structure. These servers will maintain a subset of the domain information and are considered an authority for that subset of the tree. That subset of the domain, consisting only of the authoritative information, can be organized into zones, which are then automatically distributed to redundant DNS name servers. Clients use an application called a *resolver* to query their DNS server. DNS servers also have an application called a resolver that extracts data from the DNS database in order to respond to a client request. When the resolver cannot extract data from that particular name server, it can pursue the query through referrals to other name servers via a recursive process to resolve the names for which they are not authoritative.

Active Directory Services (ADS) are so tightly integrated with DNS that it is amazing that Microsoft did not name it Active DNS instead! DNS is required on the network for Active Directory to be installed and to function. This is a major change for those who are migrating from non-TCP/IP networks. There are two significant DNS implications when employing ADS:

- In order for clients to log on to Active Directory, DNS is required to locate the DCs. The Net Logon service requires a DNS server that supports the Service Locator Resource Records (SRV RRs), because SRV RRs both register and identify the DCs in the DNS namespace.
- The Active Directory can stow DNS zone information and replicate it throughout the enterprise. The requirement of being able to contact a compatible DNS server by Active Directory DCs is absolute. When a Windows 2000 Server is promoted to a DC, it must have a DNS server available to it. If no DNS server is discovered on the network, the DNS service is installed by default on the new DC.

For IT Professionals

About SRV RRs

SRV (service locator) RRs are used to locate Active Directory domain controllers (DCs). This type of RR enables multiple servers that provide the same type of service to be located with a single DNS query. Under Active Directory, the SRV RR is the means by which clients locate DCs using LDAP (Lightweight Directory Access Protocol) via TCP port 389.

SRV RR fields consist of *service.protocol.name ttl class SRV preference weight port target*:

- **Service**   A name for the service. RFC1700 defines the names used for well-known services. Otherwise, the Administrator can specify his own name.
- **Protocol**   The transport protocol used. RFC 1700 defines the available protocols, but usually this is TCP or UDP.
- **Name**   The DNS domain name.
- **TTL**   Time to Live. This field can be left blank.
- **Class**   One of four classes. IN is the most common and represents the Internet. This field can be left blank.
- **Priority**   The number between 0 and 65,535 representing whether the target host should be contacted first. The lowest number has priority over others.
- **Weight**   The number between 1 and 65,535 used to load balance when two or more target hosts have the same priority. Usually set to 0 when load balancing is not used.
- **Port**   The transport protocol port represented by a number between 0 and 65,535. Well-known services use ports that are listed in RFC 1700.
- **Target**   The host's DNS domain name that is providing the service.

An example of an SRV RR that will look for a service from one of two different servers is:

```
ldap.tcp.name SRV 0 0 389 dns1.root.com
SRV 1 0 389 dns2.branch.root.com
```

DNS is required by Active Directory, but can also interact with WINS, the Windows Internet Naming System. WINS provides NetBIOS computer name mappings to IP addresses. DNS can provide name resolution for any names that it learns from WINS.

After Active Directory is installed, there are two ways to store and replicate DNS zones.

- Standard text-based file storage for the zone
- Active Directory integrated storage for the zone

Text files that store zones have a .DNS extension and are stored in the %SystemRoot%\System32\DNS directory on each Windows 2000 server acting as a DNS server. The first part of the name is the name of the zone; for example, the ARABLE zone will be stored in the ARABLE.DNS file. An important point to remember is that the local zone file is deleted once a zone is upgraded to an integrated Active Directory zone.

How DNS Zones Function

Primary DNS name servers maintain local files for the zone. Any changes to the zone must be made to the primary name server. Secondary DNS name servers obtain their information from any server that has authority for the zone in a zone transfer. A master name server is one that a secondary name server contacts in order to initiate the zone transfer.

Zones are part of the DNS namespace for which a specific server, or redundant servers, is responsible. The zone represents a single database of records containing information about a specific part of the domain namespace. A DNS name server can then be a primary name server for one zone, as well as a secondary name server for another zone. The zone does not need to hold all the subdomain information beneath the root domain of the zone. Zones are aware of the subdomains for which they are not authoritative through the use of name server (NS) records for the subdomain authoritative DNS servers.

How Active Directory Uses DNS

Windows 2000 DCs register SRVs so that Administrators can use several servers for a single domain and move services among the DCs. Every DC that has a registered SRV RR also registers an A RR, so that its individual host address can be found. For example, when looking for the address http://www.mycorp.com, the lookup is for http.tcp.www.mycorp.com. The www, in this case, refers to a service that is shared by multiple individual servers. The query retrieves a Web document from any of the available servers.

The main impact that SRV records have on the internetwork is that the DNS servers must support them, and preferably would support dynamic updates as well. SRV records are described in RFC 2052, and dynamic updates are discussed in RFC 2136. These requirements limit the versions of DNS that can be used. The following are supported:

- Microsoft's Windows 2000 DNS, which supports SRV records and dynamic updates for DNS (of course!)
- UNIX BIND version 4.9.7, which supports SRV records
- UNIX BIND version 8.1.2, which also supports Dynamic DNS updates

DNS has its own Microsoft Management Console (MMC) snap-in utility. All management for DNS can be executed from this utility. If you are tied to the command line, Microsoft also provides a command-line tool for DNS called DNSCMD.

When DNS is integrated into the Active Directory, the DNS zone benefits from multi-master replication (Figure 2.3). An update is received for a zone by any DC. The DC writes the update to the Active Directory, which is then replicated to all other DCs. Any DNS server that queries the Active Directory anywhere in the internetwork will receive the updated information. When you use the Microsoft Windows 2000 DNS integrated with Active Directory, there is no need to implement any other type of replication for DNS other than that already configured for Active Directory.

Dynamic updates are helpful for reducing the administration needed for DNS. However, a primary DNS server can be the single point of failure when it becomes unavailable. Since the primary server holds the only DNS database that can be updated, a dynamic update will fail when that server is down.

There is always the chance for conflicts when multi-master replication exists. When Microsoft's DNS is integrated with Active Directory, name-change conflicts are handled on a first-come, first-served basis. If two DNS servers create the same name or make changes to an RR, the first one to write it to the Active Directory wins.

Dynamic updates allow computers to register themselves in the DNS system. Windows 2000 and its DNS service all support this, as well as the Windows 2000 DHCP service. The Windows 2000 DHCP service will remove any records that it registered upon the DHCP lease's expiration. In order to use the benefits of dynamic updates, the DNS server must support RFC 2136.

Active Directory has an additional benefit for keeping the DNS records up to date. Active Directory timestamps each RR, and RRs are refreshed periodically. When an RR does not refresh for a number of intervals, it is considered stale and is then scavenged from the database. In order to enable the aging and scavenging of Active Directory-enabled DNS:

- RRs must be timestamped.
- Zones must have a refresh interval and a no-refresh interval set.
- Scavenging must be enabled for each zone and name server.
- The name server must have a scavenging period established.

Figure 2.3 Multi-master replication for DNS.

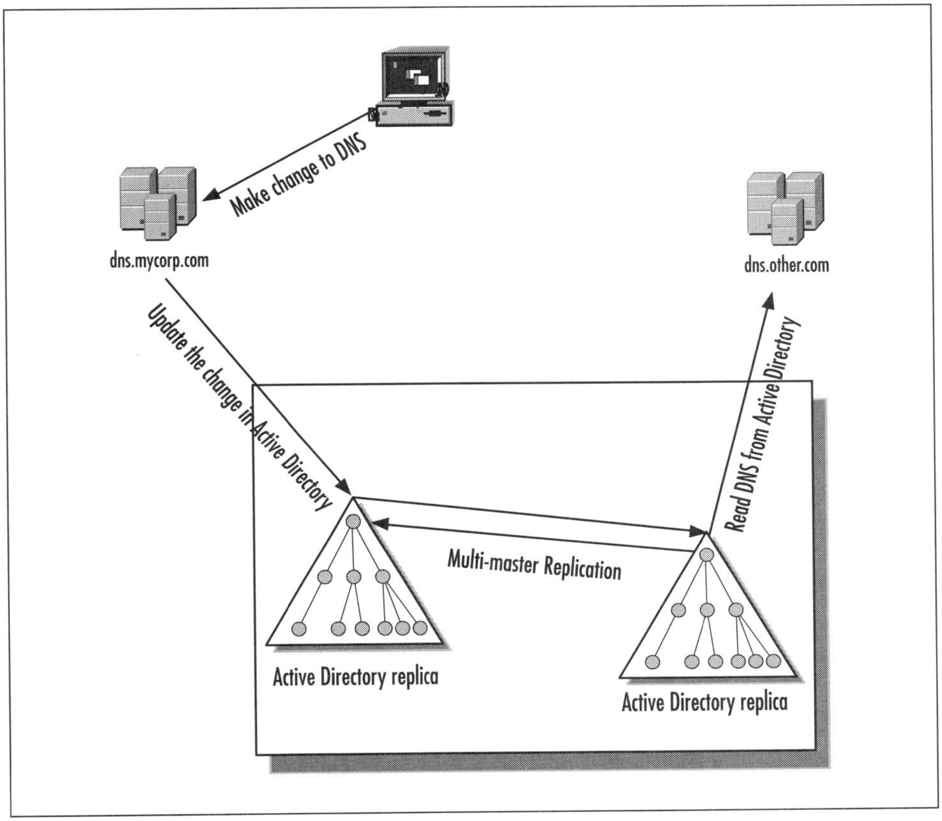

Planning Active Directory and DNS

There are four areas to document for an Active Directory and DNS name-space design. These will encompass both a logical organization of your network, including joint ventures, business units, and workgroups, and the physical network, including the geographic distribution of the users and the network topology. The four areas include:

- Forest plan
- Domain and DNS strategy
- Organizational units (OUs)
- Site topology

Forest Plan

The forest plan document for most enterprises will be a short document because of the nature of forests. A forest is a collection of multiple domain

For IT Professionals

Designing Active Directory on a Network Connected to the Internet

When you select your Active Directory domain names and you are planning to be connected to the Internet, you can do one of the following:

- Select a brand new, unique DNS name (or names) that you must register with InterNIC.

- Use an existing DNS namespace that has already been registered with InterNIC and is running on the Internet providing Web services.

- Use a subdomain of an existing DNS namespace that has already been registered with InterNIC, but is NOT running on the Internet providing Web services.

- Use a local DNS name that is completely outside the Internet.

You can have a separate DNS zone for a new DNS namespace, for a subdomain of an Internet-used DNS namespace, or for a local DNS namespace. However, you will have the most problems when you use an existing DNS namespace and share it with Internet Web servers.

Sharing a DNS namespace with Internet Web servers provides a way for unintended persons to access your network simply by having the names of your Windows 2000 servers available in the DNS server that services the Internet. A person can run nslookup and check out the entries against your DNS server. The way to get around this is to establish two DNS servers with primary zone authority for the same namespace. Place one of the DNS servers inside your firewall and include all the Active Directory servers in that zone, as well as the Internet servers required for users to access the Internet. Place the second DNS server outside the firewall and make certain to exclude all the Active Directory servers. While this setup is confusing and requires extra management, it does provide a way to use the same namespace and maintain a measure of security.

trees with multiple namespaces that trust each other, and share a common configuration, schema, and global catalog (GC). The trust relationships within a forest are transitive, and configured automatically. A forest is a logical formation that does not significantly impact, nor is impacted by, the network's topology. The structure within a forest is transparent to users. The GC shields them from domains and OUs. A forest should encompass most of the computers in any enterprise network, if not all of them. The forest plan should document the namespaces and trust relationships expected between domains. A pictorial representation of a forest was shown in Figure 2.2.

There are causes for having two or three forests, however. Since a forest will share:

- **Common schema**   Collection of objects and attributes allowed in the Active Directory database.
- **Common configuration**   Globally available configuration for replication and interdomain activity.
- **Common GC**   Actual user accounts and published resources in the tree.

the production network will benefit by being separated from any domains and forests that are connected to the Internet. This also applies to lab networks, since testing a different configuration or adding to the schema should be kept outside the production network until deployment. A separate lab forest or Internet forest keeps test users and public user accounts out of the GC.

The final reason that a network may implement more than one forest is for administrative separation. This is a common situation in companies that interconnect for joint ventures, or for those that have subsidiaries. The forest is the absolute separation of administrative authority. Two forests allow Administrators to have the authority over the configuration, the schema, the GC, and security, completely separated from another Administrator's sphere of control.

When a domain is initially created, it must join a forest. That domain cannot be moved between forests; it is a permanent member of the original forest. Furthermore, a forest cannot be split or merged (yet), but there is a tool for importing and exporting Active Directory objects, LDIFDE.EXE, which is found in the WINNT\SYSTEM32 directory. LDIFDE stands for LDAP Directory Import File Directory Export, and uses the LDAP protocol to access the forest's GC, and export the objects into a text file that can be imported into another forest.

TIP

When you implement more than one forest, your users will need to learn about their namespace if they will be accessing resources outside of their own GC. They will be forced to query each domain directly for all resources that exist outside their forest.

Domain and DNS Strategy

Domains are the top-level division within a forest. The domain should be treated as a logical division and as a physical division. The reason for this is that there is significantly more traffic within the confines of a domain than there is between domains. New domains should be added only when the replication, query, and authentication traffic will overwhelm the available bandwidth of a slow network link and it is not feasible to upgrade the link.

The domain is an administrative division, offering a boundary for security policies. All objects within a domain are granted identical security policies, which can be accessed through the Security Settings Microsoft Management Console (MMC) utility found in the Administrative Tools menu. These include:

- Password policy
- Account lockout policy
- Kerberos ticket policies

Since the domain is the division for policies, it is also the division for authentication. In this case, a user authenticates for logon and access to resources to any of the DCs that belong to the user's domain. The user cannot authenticate to any other domain even if it is in the same namespace or forest.

Root Domain

The first domain that that is installed within the forest is the *root domain*. This domain will be the first domain created in the forest, and since it contains the management information for the schema of the entire forest, it should contain servers that are distributed to all physical sites (if feasibly possible). The Domain Admins group of the forest root domain is, by default, the schema administrator group for the entire forest. In view of this requirement, there are two ways to design the root domain:

- As a standard domain that contains user accounts and published resources
- As an empty domain that has no purpose other than to publish the schema and make it available to all other domains

The advantages of dedicating a root domain as in the second option is that there are no Domain Administrator conflicts and the domain never becomes obsolete. The first option has the advantage, especially when there is only a single domain, of being able to distribute more than just the schema to multiple sites.

About Domains

The main recommendation for planning domains and DNS is simply to delegate a separate DNS zone for each Active Directory domain. You should ensure that there are at least two DNS servers running on DCs, or available to those same DCs, in the Active Directory domain.

When planning domains, there are a few rules to consider that may impact the decisions you make for your network:

- A domain's name cannot be changed.
- Two domains cannot be merged.
- A single domain cannot be split into two.

You can, however, still use the import/export tool called LDIFDE.EXE to move objects outside both the domain and the forest. To move objects within the forest, but to a different domain tree, use the MOVETREE tool from the Windows 2000 Resource Kit.

DNS Servers

Active Directory requires DNS servers to be available at all times. While it is convenient to use Active Directory DCs to provide the DNS services, this may not always be feasible. In order to ensure that DNS is always available for Active Directory, the recommendation is to provide, at a minimum, one primary and one secondary name server per domain. This will enable:

- Load balancing between the name servers
- Faster access, especially when placing the secondary name server across a WAN link
- Redundancy, in case of failure of one of the name servers

If possible, it is recommended that there is at least one DC running the DNS service in each site. This will enable much faster access and ensure that DCs are not cut off from DNS if a WAN link goes down. These servers can be secondary servers for the zone, rather than primary.

The minimum hardware requirements for a Windows 2000 DC running the DNS service on an Intel processor server are 100 bytes of RAM per RR on top of the RAM required for the server operating system, and at least a Pentium II 500MHz processor.

Organizational Units (OUs)

OUs are the container objects that exist within domains. They are a logical arrangement of objects, that can be nested, and have no impact on the network traffic. Two items will impact the OU design:

- Group Policy
- Administration

For Managers

Naming Conventions for the IT Manager

Naming conventions for user accounts are sometimes the keys to the internetwork for hackers. Many organizations use a standard of the first letter of the first name and the first five to seven letters of the last name as a standard for usernames. Hackers find it effortless to discover a user's name. The only other piece of information is the user's password, which is sometimes written on a Post-It note and pasted on the PC itself, or sometimes given by an unsuspecting user to a call from "IT Support" (a.k.a. the hacker).

The other thing that organizations typically do is to leave the default administrator name for the network. In Windows 2000, this is a domain administrator named "Administrator." Again, hackers have half the key to the network when an organization leaves this account with its original name intact.

Finally, organizations that are on the Internet already have a widely published domain name for their Internet presence. Many of them use that same name, or a subdomain of it, for their private, internal network. Again, there is no guessing involved in locating servers on the private network for a hacker.

So what does an IT Manager do to secure the network through naming conventions?

- Do not use the user's name, or permutations of it, as the user's logon ID unless you add numbers or other data to the logon ID to disguise it.

- Do not be tempted to use a United States social security number for a user's ID. A social security number not only places a user's personal information at risk, but companies with international sites will have users who do not have social security numbers.

- Rename the Administrator account. Remember, however, some applications are written to look for the "Administrator" account in order to be installed, although most allow you to input a different name.

- Create Administrator accounts with randomly generated names using both upper and lowercase letters and numbers. Who is to know that the Administrator's name is X3460GzwGm?

- Always remember to enforce a strict password policy, especially if the organization is connected in any way to the Internet.

- Register a new domain name with InterNIC for your internal network that is completely different from the one used on the Internet. This will provide you with flexible naming options.

Aside from DNS naming conventions, there are other interoperability issues with names for most internetworks because of legacy systems. The following rules will help evade many trials and tribulations when connecting to legacy systems:

- Always create unique names for users, computers, printers, and other resources.

- Avoid the following characters when creating user or computer names, since many computers will translate these as encoding characters or will not understand them:

    !@#$%^&*()_?<>'";:[]{}\|/.,

- Keep object names for logon IDs to eight characters or less. Many legacy systems stop after eight characters.

- Keep object names for computers to eight characters or less. Many legacy systems stop after eight characters.

- Do not depend on the letter case (upper and lower) to create unique names. Many computers translate both Frank and fRANK to equate to FRANK, so they would no longer be unique.

- Do not depend on a distinguished name to create unique names. Legacy systems may not understand context-sensitive names, and will translate /CN=M1craft3/CN=USERS/DC=Panther/DC=MicroAge/DC=com to simply be M1craft3. Therefore, if there is another M1craft3 in the Active Directory, but in a different tree location or domain, the name will not be unique.

In both of these cases, the OU is the boundary. Different group policies can be applied to different OUs. Different Administrators can be granted administrative access to different OUs, without concern for conflicts over administrative control.

How you create the OU hierarchy can reflect the company org chart, or some other tree structure that seems sensible. The Microsoft utilities do not require users to navigate the hierarchy of OUs, although some tools do expose them, so there is no true need to create OUs that serve no purpose other than the reflection of an org chart. Instead, focus on the purpose that the OU will serve, whether to provide group policy, administrative area, or to group a set of users logically together.

OUs are the most flexible container objects in the Active Directory. Unlike forests and domains, OUs can be created, moved, added, or deleted whenever needed. These changes have no impact on the network. Objects within OUs can also be easily moved, created, added, and deleted. When these changes are made, the major considerations are simply about how the group policy and administration issues will change.

Group policies will affect the time that it takes for a user to log on; the more group policies there are, the longer it takes. If an Administrator applies multiple group policies to a single OU, the user's logon time will suffer. If the user is located three nested groups down, and the Administrator has applied a single group policy at one of the levels, that user will log on faster than the user with multiple group policies applied to a single OU. Group policies are the reason for logon times being increased. The problem, however, with OU design is that when there are multiple nested OUs, Administrators are more likely to apply group policies to each OU in the hierarchy than apply multiple group policies to a single OU. When planning the OU structure, make sure to state where group policies will be applied, and whether multiple group policies will be acceptable.

Site Topology

The *site topology* is a representation of the physical network. It consists of sites that are connected by site links. (Note that this is very similar to Exchange Server's directory in which sites are connected by site connectors.) The site is a physical division of the network. When users authenticate to the network, their authentication traffic will be directed to a DC within their own site. Additionally, sites will maintain more query and replication traffic within them.

Sites, as well as their Active Directory names, should represent the physical network, and should have a DC within each. The site should consist of networks that are connected by fast and reliable links. They can be

LAN or extremely high-speed WAN links. A site should not span a medium- or low-speed WAN link (e.g., less than 10 Mbps).

Unlike domains, sites are easily added, moved, changed, or deleted. This is one of the methods that make Active Directory scalable with the internetwork's growth. In order to manage sites, you can use the Active Directory Sites and Services MMC utility. This can be located by clicking Start | Programs | Administrative Tools | Active Directory Sites and Services.

Naming Conventions

The key to a solid namespace design is simplification. The simpler the namespace design, the easier it is to manage and add to later on.

The namespace should fit the ideal network for the enterprise, even if the ideal network is not what exists currently. After designing the ideal network's namespace, make adjustments only for the anomalous network devices. Eventually, the network will adjust toward the ideal by taking this approach.

Finally, the namespace design should be enabled for change management. Most enterprises are not static entities. People are promoted to new positions, move to different departments, start new business units in another city or country, leave the company, and so on. The PCs that they use either move with them, or change hands and are reconfigured. New PCs, servers, and printers are added to the network, and old ones are retired. All organizations experience these changes to some degree. If the Active Directory namespace does not support changes, it will not be a success. Instead, it should support changes so that it is easy to move objects around the tree. One way to enable the Active Directory for change management is to standardize unique names throughout the tree. This simple standard will ensure that no conflicts from moves, adds, or changes will ensue.

Defining DNS Names

The rules regarding DNS names are simple:

- Each host in the DNS database is allowed to have a name of up to 63 characters in length, and many allow names up to 255 characters.
- All hosts must have unique names. For example, a host named george.microage.com and a host named george.eng.microage.com are each considered unique.
- All subdomains must have unique names within their parent domain.

For IT Professionals

Naming Convention Rules

Microsoft's DNS service that comes with Windows 2000 is more forgiving when it comes to naming conventions than the DNS applications from other vendors. Even if you are using Microsoft's version of DNS, you may, at some point in time, connect to a network that uses a different vendor's DNS. When that happens, the naming conventions that you are using will need to be compatible with both DNS versions. Otherwise, you will encounter a few problems.

Standard DNS naming rules, which are understood by all DNS versions, are as follows:

- Use a registered DNS name. You can register DNS names with InterNIC.

- Use the standard character set of A through Z, a through z, and 0 through 9 and the dash (-) character. Note that the Windows 2000 DNS will support both the underscore (_) and Unicode characters.

- When in doubt, verify your naming strategy with RFC 1123, which is available on the Internet at http://freesoft.org/CIE/RFC/1123/index.htm.

DNS names for each domain should be defined when creating the domain plan. Each domain should be assigned a name that follows the format of root.com. Domains that will share the same namespace as the forest root domain will have a subdomain name format of parent.root.com. Any domains beneath them in the domain tree hierarchy will have the sub-subdomain name format of child.parent.root.com. Further subdomains are allowed, but not recommended because of the complexity added to the internetwork. Trust relationships will follow the tree structure.

Each DNS root domain namespace should be registered with InterNIC. This will avoid conflicts if there is another one being used on a connected network or the Internet.

The DNS name for a domain in the Windows 2000 is defined when the first DC for that domain is installed with Active Directory.

Defining DNS Zones

All DNS zones and RRs are managed in the DNS Management Console. To add a zone, follow these steps:

1. Click Start.
2. Select Programs.
3. Select Administrative Tools.
4. Choose DNS. The DNS Microsoft Management Console utility will start.
5. Select either Forward Lookup Zones or Reverse Lookup Zones below the server that will be managing the zone, depending on which type of zone you are adding.
6. Click the Action menu.
7. Select Create a New Zone. The Add New Zone Wizard will begin.
8. Select the zone type.
9. Assign a name and complete the wizard. The new zone will appear in the DNS utility.

Adding an RR also occurs in the DNS Microsoft Management Console utility.

Naming Conventions for Active Directory

Active Directory is an open directory service in that it supports a wide range of protocols, objects, and application programming interfaces (APIs). These are the mechanisms that define the availability of the Active Directory to various types of clients.

As a result of Active Directory's support for diverse protocols, Active Directory supports many different name formats:

- Internet e-mail addresses, as described in RFC 822— name@mycorp.com
- Uniform Resource Locators (URLs) for HyperText Transfer Protocol (HTTP)—http://www.mycorp.com
- Lightweight Directory Access Protocol (LDAP) names—LDAP:// myserver.mycorp.com/CN=myname,OU=Users,O=Mycorp,C=US
- Universal Naming Convention (UNC) names—\\myserver.com\ myvolume\file.ext

Such diversity in naming format support enables companies to select nearly any names that are appropriate for their company. The major influence on a naming convention will be the connectivity to external systems on the internetwork. Windows 2000 Active Directory is more forgiving than other systems for names in that it supports a wider variety of characters and character sets, and even lengthier names.

Migrating an Existing Exchange Server Design

The Active Directory inherited many of its characteristics from Exchange Server's directory system. Additionally, the design premises are nearly identical. If an organization already has a well-tuned Exchange Server directory with basically the same scope of sites, users, computers, and servers, then it can mirror the design of the Active Directory and expect good results.

Migrating an Existing Novell Directory Services Design

Many organizations have invested a significant amount of time and effort in a Novell Directory Services design. This design is generally a geographical division at the top of the tree and an organizational division lower down. If the Novell Directory Services design follows this scheme *and* it has the same scope, it is easy to translate it into an Active Directory design. Instead of each top-level OU, replace it with an appropriate domain. Then retain the hierarchy of OUs that exist within that top level and place them within the domain.

You will find a handy wizard for migrating Novell Directory Services information into the Active Directory in the Administrative Tools menu.

Virtual Containers

The Active Directory can incorporate information from other directory services through a *virtual container*. The other directory service must be LDAP compliant for this to work. The Active Directory implements a virtual container in what amounts to a pointer to the foreign directory service. The foreign directory server's DNS name is contained as part of the virtual container's properties. When a client performs a query on the virtual container, DNS locates the foreign directory and passes an LDAP query to it. The response to that query is returned to Active Directory, which then presents it to the client.

Designing Active Directory Domains

The previous sections barraged you with an alarming number of new terms and concepts, but in fact by now you should be able to discuss the importance of trees and forests so naturally that people mistake you for a Green Peace activist. The strategy for constructing domains involves leveraging these concepts to provide a comprehensive and detailed design statement.

The enterprise's business requirements will guide the Active Directory domain design. The design will depend not only on business requirements, but also on the network that already exists and the way that the enterprise is organized. Rules regarding network design are never hard and fast; some network designs simply result in more optimal performance than others.

However, performance is not necessarily the top business driver for an organization. Each company, organization, or government office is different and has its own requirements for technology. Windows 2000 Server with Active Directory Services is flexible enough to meet most business requirement sets, but its implementation will vary widely.

Providing a detailed domain design involves generating the following:

- Forest plan
- Domain/DNS strategy
- Organizational unit (OU) structure
- Site topology

It also implies that you should be in possession of a great deal of supporting information about the enterprise. This information will reflect both the network's physical structure and the enterprise's logical organization. The following list represents the types of documents that are recommended to discover the network's physical structure. Note that the documentation of your network may be structured differently, and will not map directly to this list.

- Topology maps detailing the WAN links of the internetwork
- Topology maps detailing the LANs that make up the internetwork
- Lists of servers, including current NOS version, service pack updates, and services that are provided to the network (file, print, RAS, SQL, e-mail, etc.)
- Hardware specification of relevant computing infrastructure
- Lists of printers and their locations
- DNS structure
- Lists of other network resources and their locations
- Traffic flow and network baseline performance
- Inventory of the client workstations

Aside from the physical structure of the network, you will also need information on the logical organization of the enterprise. This information is typically documented in:

- Org charts
- Lists of users and their locations
- Lists of groups and their purpose
- Workflow between groups
- Information regarding future growth plans

TIP

Microsoft provides a number of tools to help with the migration to Windows 2000. One of them, the Active Directory Sizer tool, can be very useful during the design stages. This tool can provide information on:

- CPUs per machine and type of CPU.
- Disks needed for Active Directory storage.
- Amount of memory required.
- Domain Database size.
- Domain controllers per site.
- Global catalog servers per domain per site.

Forest Plan

The first thing to do is review what a forest is, what belongs in a forest plan, and the rules surrounding forests. Remember that a forest is a group of multiple DNS namespaces (and multiple domains) that shares a common configuration, schema, and global catalog (GC). A forest plan typically contains the number of forests, the reasons they were selected, the names of the root forest domain, and an optional pictorial representation. Rules surrounding forests are few:

- A forest cannot be merged with any other forest.
- A forest cannot be split.
- The root domain of the forest is the name the forest takes on.
- A forest is a logical grouping, and has little impact on network bandwidth.

Domain Plan Including DNS Strategy

You should begin your domain planning session with the same step as in the forest planning, with a review of domains, DNS, and the rules surrounding them.

A domain is the top-level division within a forest. There is significantly more traffic within the confines of a domain than there is between domains. The traffic between domains is mainly replication of schema, configuration, and GC data. The traffic within a domain includes query, authentication, and further replication of the domain objects in the Active Directory. Sites centralize this traffic somewhat by formalizing the paths for replication traffic. There is a preference to send query and authentication traffic to domain controllers (DCs) within the same site as the user making the request. New domains should be added only when the total of the replication, query, and authentication traffic will overwhelm the available bandwidth of a slow network link and it is not feasible to upgrade the link. With the capability of domains and sites to be able to cross each other's boundaries, determining the traffic needs becomes somewhat of an art. The following traffic guidelines are not absolute, but look for minimum bandwidth of:

- 512 Kbps available bandwidth within a site, whether or not it spans multiple domains.
- 256 Kbps available bandwidth within a domain that spans multiple sites, where no sites span it and other domains.
- 56 to 128 Kbps available bandwidth where a domain and site share a boundary—larger for those GCs with more than half a million objects.
- If using a single domain model, these issues do not apply.

Aside from traffic issues, a domain should be added when the domain-level security policy for passwords and account lockouts must be different for two separate sets of users. Other reasons for implementing separate domains include wanting to decentralize administration, and support of geographical boundaries.

DNS provides mapping between IP addresses and hostnames. It can also map to further information such as service resource records (SRV RRs). DNS is used by the Active Directory as a locator service for logon, for locating DCs, and GC servers.

Rules surrounding domains and DNS are as follows:

- A domain's name cannot be changed if it is a root domain, or easily changed otherwise. Note that the domain's globally unique identifier cannot be changed, but display names for nonroot domains can be renamed in the Active Directory.
- Two domains cannot be merged.
- A single domain cannot be split into two.
- DNS must support SRV RRs.
- DNS must be available for DCs at all times.
- At a minimum, there should be one DC and one DNS server in each site.
- A DC is allowed to also be the DNS server running Microsoft's DNS service.
- One recommendation is to have a single root domain hold the schema, and lower-level domains contain the resources and users in the tree.

- Domains are an administrative and security boundary, so plan domains accordingly.
- DNS names should be registered with InterNIC. InterNIC does not require subdomains to be registered, simply the parent domain level.

Organizational Unit Strategy

OUs are container units that can be nested into a tree structure, or hierarchy, within a domain. OUs can contain user accounts, resource objects, and other OUs. OUs reside within a single domain. The OU strategy is an initial hierarchy within each domain. OUs are flexible enough to be changed as needed, so this strategy may change over time, or at any time, to better meet the changing needs of the enterprise. The rules regarding OUs are as follows:

- OUs can be created, moved, added, or deleted whenever needed.
- OU changes have no impact on the network traffic.
- Objects within OUs can also be easily moved, created, added, and deleted.
- OUs are containers for implementation of group policy.
- OUs are containers for delegation of administration.

Organizational Unit Structure

OUs are containers within a domain that can nest within each other to develop a hierarchy. They are not used for user account policy, but are used for group policy and for the delegation of administrative authority. An Active Directory user does not always have to navigate the OU hierarchy to locate services and information, so the optimal structure for OUs should reflect the boundaries needed for applying group policy or for delegating authority. It is a good rule of thumb to keep the OU names short enough to remember.

OU Objects in the Active Directory

OUs are container objects within the Active Directory. They contain other objects, but they also have attributes and values applicable to them. Policies can be applied to OUs, and those policies can be inherited by sub-OUs. This facilitates administration of group policy.

Group Policy and OUs

Group policy settings are applied to users and computers in order to manage the desktop configuration. A specific policy is applied to a site, domain, and/or an OU as needed. The group policy can be filtered to control access. Group policies will affect users' logon time when they are in a

For IT Professionals

Designs

There is more than one right way to design a network. Optimal designs take into account the business requirements, current network environment, and potential growth of a company. The designs for forests, domains, OUs, and sites could be completely different for two companies and still be considered "correct" or "good." This reflects the flexibility of Active Directory more than it does the benefits of a good design.

In many cases, network design and selection is based on the business requirements for the company and its existing environment. Here are some design tips:

- Do not be afraid to create a design that seems aberrant from standard models, if it supports business requirements.

- Try to keep your designs as simple as possible.

- Pay strict attention to the design of items that cannot change or be moved, merged, or split, such as forests and domains.

- Play with a couple of design scenarios before you select a final design. Make sure it supports each of your business objectives, and you can justify that design above the others.

- Make sure that whatever design you specify, you will have enough servers to support its creation.

- Always register your DNS names with InterNIC.

- Wear caffeine-tolerant clothing during your design process—you will probably spend long hours on this part of the job. <grin>

nested OU that has multiple group policies. Longer names for OUs will also affect processing at logon time.

Delegating Administration

The Legacy NT delegation of administration did not offer much in the way of flexibility.

- Administrators were forced to use built-in local groups on the servers for administrative authority.

- They had to adjust predefined rights, if they were not sufficient or too lax.

- Their administrative design typically resulted in oodles of Domain Administrators so that everyone could access what they needed to.

- They created resource domains just to delegate administration, which then resulted in too many domains and complex trust relationships.

Delegating administration is more powerful and flexible in Windows 2000 than it was in earlier versions of NT. Using the flexibility of the Active Directory, delegation of administrative responsibility can be applied at the OU level. The Administrator can assign administrative rights for each object's attributes and whether that control can be inherited. The result is that the appropriate Administrators are granted the appropriate control of their assigned users and published resources. If an Administrator delegates "Full Control" to another user, then that user is able to delegate administrative authority to others. Otherwise, the delegation of administration is completed by selecting the authority level over each object class and the ability to modify specific attributes. The process is fairly simple:

1. Create a group.

2. Grant the group specific access.

3. Populate the group with users.

Site Topology

For the final design component, we should consider Active Directory sites. A site is a collection of IP subnets that are connected by fast, reliable links. Sites are typically LANs, and do not contain WAN links except where the WAN link is very fast and reliable. The site is used to create physical divisions of the network. It directs authentication and query traffic for users within a site to a DC within a site. Replication traffic is similarly controlled. The following design rules apply to sites:

- The site topology should reflect the network's topology.

- Each site should have a dedicated DC.

- No site should span a slow or unreliable network connection, especially WAN connections.

- Sites do not need to be created for clients that connect via remote access.

- Sites are easily added, moved, changed, and deleted.

Summary

DNS (Domain Name System) is tightly integrated with Windows 2000 Active Directory Services. Active Directory uses DNS for its locator service for the NetLogon service. The DNS must support SRV resource records (RRs), and preferably will support dynamic updates as well. This integration runs in both directions. Not only does Active Directory use DNS as its locator service, but the Active Directory can manage and maintain the DNS information within itself as well.

When Active Directory manages the DNS information, there are many benefits:

- Multi-master replication
- Scavenging of stale RRs
- Support for dynamic updates

Because of DNS integration, the entire Active Directory planning is involved in the DNS namespace design. There are four planning areas:

- Forest
- Domain
- Organizational unit (OU)
- Sites

Naming conventions should be defined for the user accounts and published resources within the Active Directory. The naming conventions should support the Active Directory and any legacy systems to which users or computers may connect. Legacy systems tend to have stricter naming requirements than the Active Directory.

The DNS domain name is applied to a domain at the installation of the first domain controller (DC) in that domain. If using the Microsoft DNS service, DNS can be managed through the Microsoft Management Console DNS utility found in the Administrative Tools menu. The Active Directory also uses DNS to locate and connect to foreign directory services, and treat them as virtual containers.

Designing an Active Directory structure consists of four design objectives:

- The forest plan
- The domains and DNS strategy
- The organizational unit (OU) strategy
- The site topology

All designs should be based on the business requirements of the enterprise. When a design is based on a business requirement, it will better serve that enterprise—even though another design may be more optimal for a different company with the same size and locations, but different business objectives.

Although the forest plan is a simple document detailing the number, root domain, and purpose for each forest, it is the first set of decisions that must be made toward the final Active Directory implementation. This plan must be made wisely, because the forests cannot be merged, split, renamed, or otherwise redesigned after they are implemented.

The most critical decisions that will be made are those that affect the Active Directory domains and DNS strategy. DNS is compulsory for Active Directory to function. The DNS names used should be registered with InterNIC, if new ones are required for the DNS strategy. Domains are both a physical and logical structure for Active Directory. Each domain has its own DNS name. The design for the domains should be treated with as much assiduousness as the forest plan, because domains have the same permanent features: They cannot be merged, split, or renamed, after they are first created.

Since an OU is a logical grouping container in the Active Directory and has no real impact on the network traffic, it can reflect the organization or another functional plan. OUs can be used for applying group policy and for delegating administration. OUs can be renamed, moved, created, and deleted at any time.

Sites are a representation of the physical network. Sites are considered to be a group of IP subnets that share fast and reliable network connections. The site should not span any slow or unreliable WAN links. Each physical campus or building can be considered a site, or when using extremely fast WAN links, a group of geographically distant but well-connected areas can become a single site.

Using OUs for delegating administration is a great tool for Administrators that prevents all the legacy Windows NT issues of creating groups of Administrators and multiple domains and trusts. An OU can be created arbitrarily, and specific rights can be assigned to a user or group for administration; this is both flexible and effective. This capability can enable Administrators to provide password reset rights only to a group, which means that they can reset a password and not change any other information in the Active Directory. Windows 2000 Server provides a wizard to delegate control, which simplifies this activity. The Delegate Control Wizard is accessed by right-clicking an OU in the Active Directory Users and Computers MMC, then selecting Delegate Control from the pop-up menu.

FAQs

Q: I have a test network and a production network. I want to make sure that users do not see my test lab users when they query the global catalog (GC). Should I put my lab servers in the same forest as the production servers?

A: Not if you want them to have a different GC. Since a forest shares the same schema, configuration, and GC, the test network should not be part of the same forest as the production network. If testing a new application that extends the schema, using a different forest will prevent extra objects and attributes from being added to the production schema. The configuration can be changed for the test forest without impacting the production network by using separate forests. Finally, a separate test forest will prevent test users from showing up in the GC.

Q: Our company uses a DNS server that does not support SRV resource records (RRs). Can we use it when we implement Active Directory?

A: No. The Active Directory relies on SRV RRs in order to locate domain controllers (DCs). All DNS servers for the namespaces that the Active Directory encompasses must also support the SRV RRs.

Q: Our group has created a forest plan that consists of three forests. We only have a single registered DNS name. We would like to use the same DNS namespace for each of the forests. Can we do this?

A: No. Each forest must have its own dedicated DNS namespaces. A namespace cannot cross forests.

Q: We are planning to create two forests on the internetwork. We will use one forest as a testing area and the other for production. We plan to develop the domains and their DCs on the test forest, and then move them to the production forest later on. Is this a viable plan?

A: No. Although the use of a separate test forest and a production forest is recommended, domains do not have the ability to be moved from one forest to another. In this case, domains cannot be moved from the test forest to the production forest.

Q: There are two office buildings in our organization and we have a fractional T1 line running between them at 256 Kbps. We have a legacy Windows NT domain that covers both sites. Can we keep this same domain design?

A: Yes. The domain design is flexible enough to span WAN links, but it is preferable not to. This should not prevent an existing legacy NT domain structure from being upgraded into the Active Directory in its existing configuration. It is recommended to create two separate sites with their own DCs—one site to represent each building—in the Active Directory. This will help manage the traffic crossing the WAN.

Q: Two people in our OU planning group want to recreate the org chart for the OU structure. The rest of the group wants to create a structure that reflects the administration of the network. We intend to delegate administration through the OUs. Which is the right way?

A: That depends. If the administration of the network is in a one-to-one correspondence with the org chart groups, or even if there is one administration group to several org chart groups, then the org chart method will be effective for both. If there are two groups of Administrators who are each supposed to manage a part of an org chart group, then they will end up stepping on each others toes by sharing the OU administrative rights. In this case, the OUs should reflect the administration groups, or a combination of the two.

Chapter 3

Migrating to Windows 2000 Server

Solutions in this chapter:

- Introduction
- Server Migration Strategies
- Upgrading with the Windows 2000 Setup Wizard
- Installing Active Directory Services
- Interim Mixed Domains
- Migrating Components
- Delegating Administrative Authority
- Insert into the Replication Topology
- Migrating from Novell Directory Services
- Upgrade Clients to Windows 2000 Profressional

Introduction

It is often the case that upgrading a server, which everyone is used to using, causes more problems than installing an entirely new server from the ground up. Additionally, it is common knowledge that an upgrade requires significant preparation prior to the migration itself. Unfortunately, common knowledge does not always translate into common practice.

Migrations typically take place over a weekend and during evenings so as not to interrupt users during business hours. Contingency planning during these activities is of prime importance. To paraphrase the airlines, "in the unlikely event of a failure," you must be ready. New installs do not face several of the issues that plague upgrades, although it is usually preferred that they take place during evenings and weekends to avoid business interruptions.

A whole slew of preparatory work is required in order to migrate any operating system successfully. This can be compounded significantly by migrating to a new directory service. Typical migration projects consist of the following basic phases:

1. **Vision**. The migration team is assembled, and the members of the team determine the business requirements and vision for the Active Directory and Windows 2000. Too often, technology drives migrations rather than the business fundamentals. How do the business requirements and Windows 2000 relate to your existing security, administrative model, directory service, and network infrastructure?

2. **Plan**. The technical requirements for the Active Directory and Windows 2000 are defined and the tasks to complete them are determined. Resources for the project are gathered and team members are assigned tasks and given dates and milestones.

3. **Develop**. A lab or test system is created where the migration team can test the proposed technical configuration and ensure that it meets the business requirements defined by the Windows 2000 vision phase; the team may develop an automated installation process and a quality assurance process, and will deploy to a pilot group of users to ensure success.

4. **Deploy**. Windows 2000 and Active Directory are installed across the production network, clients are granted access to the Active Directory, the system is assured to be stable through quality assurance, and the systems are turned over to the operations support staff.

Don't be surprised if your migration project encompasses more planning and development issues than are described here. Each enterprise has its own business requirements and usually a unique internetwork with its own technical requirements. The project must take into account these factors when planning things such as the Active Directory security strategy and the Domain Name System (DNS) requirements.

TIP

Before beginning your migration, make sure to have your Active Directory sites, forest, domain, and organizational unit (OU) structure documented, as well as your DNS strategy and your security strategy. For more information on these subjects, review Chapters 2, 4, and 8.

Server Migration Strategies

To determine the strategy for migrating servers, the first task to complete is to examine the existing domain structure and network environment. In addition, standard Active Directory planning tasks, which are discussed in Chapter 2, "Active Directory—The Heart of Windows 2000 Server," should be undertaken.

- Develop a DNS namespace and domain plan.
- Create a forest plan.
- Devise the OU hierarchy.
- Create the site topology plan.

The planning tasks will involve documentation of the existing network. Most organizations have some documentation already existing for their networks. This documentation should be gathered, and if not current, updated to represent the present network. The documentation will validate the design plans and must include the information listed in Table 3.1.

TIP

A number of extremely useful tools can be downloaded from the Microsoft Web site to help in migration and migration planning. What's more, they are free! A must for any migration toolkit includes:

- **Windows 2000 Readiness Analyzer** When run provides details on known hardware and software incompatibilities on your system. This tool is the standalone equivalent of the analyzer incorporated into the Windows 2000 setup program. The standalone version can be run in logon scripts and used with SMS. It can be found at www.microsoft.com/ windows2000/ downloads/deployment/readiness.

- **Active Directory Sizer Tool** Provides estimates on Active Directory hardware requirements based on information passed to the tool. It can be found at www.microsoft.com/Windows2000/downloads/deployment/sizer.
- **Active Directory Migration Tool** Allows you to trial run migrations and is suitable for most small and medium-size corporations. A variety of wizards such as the User Migration Wizard and Computer Migration Wizard make the task of migrating to Windows 2000 less onerous. It can be found at www.microsoft.com/ windows2000/downloads/deployment/admt.

Table 3.1 Analysis Requirements

Documented Item	Purpose	Example Usage
Network server hardware	To determine compatibility, and if not compatible, an upgrade strategy.	Refer to the Microsoft Hardware Compatibility List at www.microsoft.com/hcl. Check hardware specification.
Applications running on the servers	To determine compatibility, and if not compatible, an upgrade or replacement strategy.	Refer to application vendor's site or Microsoft Application Compatibility List at www.microsoft.com/windows/server/deploy/compatible/default.asp.
Network infrastructure	To determine the bandwidth available to new network traffic, assist in the domain and site designs; if not sufficient, to determine an upgrade strategy, to assist with protocol requirements.	Large DNS zone transfers, replication traffic.
Server locations and functions	To determine which servers are best as domain controllers (DCs) and DNS servers, to determine site locations.	Dedicated file or Web servers, PDCs or BDCs. Review functions and needs by users.
Security policies	To assist in the design of domains and group policies, to determine which security components to include in the Active Directory.	Account policies in User Manager for Domains. Review functions and needs for network.

Once the network documentation has been gathered and the design completed, the migration strategy must be planned. Although there are many methods of doing this, the plan that follows is a solid approach. First, look at the forest plan. If there is a single forest, then selecting a forest is easy. If there are multiple forests, the optimal selection is to migrate the forest that is least likely to have an impact on production if the migration fails for any reason.

For example, The Honey Bee Corporation has three namespaces: honeybeeswax.com, honeybee.com, and workerbee.com. The workerbee.com namespace is dedicated to a lab network, and the other two namespaces are on the production network. The Honey Bee Corporation decided to have two forests, one for the lab network and the other for the production network. For their migration strategy, then, the forest least likely to cause problems when it is migrated is the lab network forest, of which the root is the workerbee.com DNS namespace. Figure 3.1 illustrates the Honey Bee Corporation forest plan including subdomains.

There are two options for migrating each domain when migrating a legacy Windows NT domain structure: domain upgrade and domain restructuring. A domain upgrade is simply migrating each domain to a Windows 2000 domain. This method begins with the upgrade of the primary domain controller (PDC), followed by the backup domain controllers

Figure 3.1 Honey Bee forest plan.

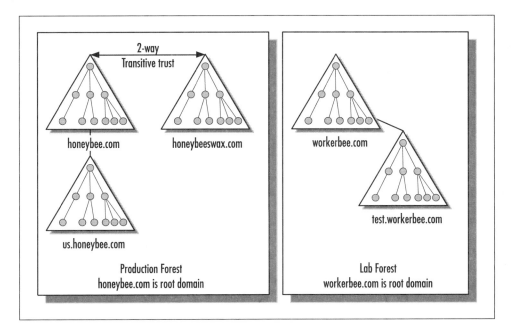

(BDCs), and finally the member servers. A domain restructuring is a complete redesign of the domain structure either prior to or after the upgrade to Windows 2000. Because of the Active Directory capabilities for delegation of administration and site-centric traffic management, many organizations may consolidate their domain structure into a simpler design that still satisfies business requirements.

Deciding whether to upgrade or restructure is a matter of reviewing the optimal plans that the Active Directory can offer. Although a legacy Windows NT domain structure may satisfy many business requirements, simply upgrading it to the Active Directory may not be the optimal Active Directory design. Take a company that has two business units, Payroll and Service, that each have separate administration. A legacy domain structure would be two separate domains, even though the two business units may share the same facilities, as illustrated in Figure 3.2.

If this company simply upgraded the existing domains from Windows NT to Windows 2000 Active Directory domains, the network would experience more traffic than necessary. Network traffic within a domain is higher than that between domains. When the traffic from two separate domains travels across the same links, it is not optimal for the network because there is higher bandwidth utilization. In Figure 3.2, there would be more

Figure 3.2 Legacy domains can cross physical boundaries.

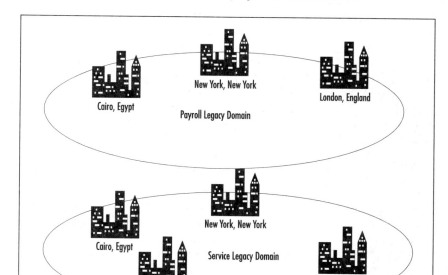

traffic in the links between Cairo, Egypt or New York, New York and every other site because of the two domains having domain controllers (DCs) in those sites.

However, if the company with these two legacy domains restructured into a single larger domain under Active Directory, it would not experience the higher bandwidth utilization. The company could easily create OUs to delegate administration in the restructured domain. It would use sites within the domain to centralize traffic at each of the locations.

An organization can best evaluate whether to upgrade or restructure by starting with a blank page. If there were no domain structure in place, what would be the optimal Active Directory domain for the organization? If that domain structure matches the existing domain structure, an upgrade path is best. Otherwise, the organization should consider a restructuring process.

TIP

If you plan a new domain structure and realize that there are more domains in the Active Directory than there were in the legacy structure, you will want to revisit your plans. The Active Directory can be optimized in a simple structure. The simpler the structure, the easier it is to manage the Active Directory.

The first domain that is created in a forest is the root domain. This means that the first set of DCs that must be installed and/or migrated must belong to the root domain. Take the Honey Bee Corporation, for example. In the lab network, there is a single DNS namespace with the root domain of workerbee.com. As its first task, Honey Bee Corporation simply migrates an existing lab server acting as a PDC over to the workerbee.com domain as a DC. The remaining servers designated for that domain are then migrated, starting with the BDCs and ending with the member servers. After migrating the root domain, Honey Bee Corporation follows the namespace down to the subdomain test.workerbee.com and begins by migrating servers. Honey Bee Corporation does not have another domain in the lab to migrate, so it migrates member servers and then promotes at least one to a DC using the Active Directory Wizard to create the new domain.

The following are high-level overviews of the migration process. If you have vertigo, be careful—we are more than 1000 feet up from the tactical steps of actual deployment.

If there are multiple forests, one must be selected for the first migration. As stated previously, the first forest migrated should be the one with

Figure 3.3 Migration strategy for a single domain.

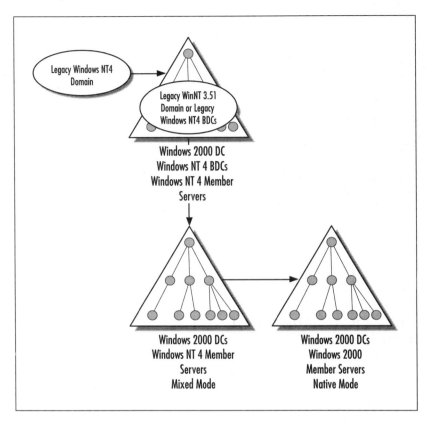

the least impact on the daily production network. Once the forest has been selected, the forest migration strategy is as follows:

1. Migrate the root domain first. If creating a new root domain instead of migrating an existing domain, then create the root domain first. Figure 3.3 illustrates the process of migrating a single domain to Windows 2000.

2. Completely migrate the root domain before starting the next domain. When migrating from an existing Windows NT domain to an Active Directory domain, there will probably be a period of time during which the domain works in mixed mode. A mixed-mode domain has at least one Windows 2000 Server DC and one or more legacy Windows NT BDCs. Transitive trusts are only supported in native mode. A native-mode domain just has Windows 2000 DCs. For this reason, each domain should be migrated in its entirety

before migrating the next domain in the Active Directory forest. A migrated domain will remain in mixed mode even after all the DCs have been upgraded to Windows 2000 until the Network Administrator switches it to native mode.

3. Follow the DNS namespace for each domain thereafter so that each domain tree is migrated completely before migrating the next domain tree. For example, if migrating the root.com first, the second domain to be migrated is trunk.root.com, and the third is leaf.trunk.root.com.

4. When migrating the next domain tree, start at the root of its namespace and work through each domain to the end of the domains. For example, after migrating the root.com domain tree, migrate the nextdomaintree.com and its subdomains trunk.nextdomaintree.com and leaf.trunk.nextdomaintree.com in that order.

Within the forest, each domain should be migrated completely before starting the next. The domain has its own migration strategy.

1. Complete all preparation work of cleaning users, groups, and applications. Perform a full backup of the PDC before migrating.

2. When migrating, begin with the PDC first. Even if you intend to have newly installed Windows 2000 servers installed as DCs, you must migrate the PDC before installing the new Windows 2000 servers. If you attempt to install an Active Directory DC into an existing Windows NT 4.0 domain with an existing PDC, it will fail. An Active Directory DC cannot exist in the same domain with a legacy PDC.

3. Perform a full backup of each BDC before migrating it.

4. After the PDC has been migrated, the BDCs should be migrated next.

5. Perform a full backup of each member server before migrating.

6. After all DCs have been migrated, the member servers should be migrated to Windows 2000.

7. The last step in the domain migration is to perform a quality assurance check to verify the printers, clients, users, and other resources that were migrated.

Domain restructuring is the migration strategy for merging two or more domains into a single Active Directory domain. This may be necessary if the domain and DNS plan collapses domains in favor of using sites to manage the physical network traffic and using OUs for delegating administration. The destination domain is the one in which all the users, computers, and resources will reside when migrated to the Active Directory (Figure 3.4).

Figure 3.4 Domain restructure: collapsing domains into a single Active Directory domain.

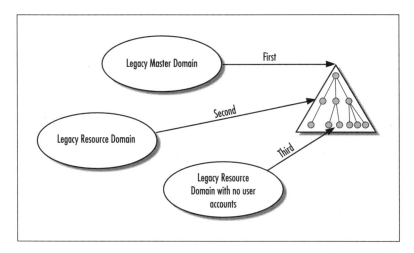

1. Begin by migrating legacy Windows NT domains to the destination domain first, or create a new domain for destination by installing at least two Active Directory DCs. By installing more than one DC, additional copies of the Active Directory exist for fault tolerance.

2. Move user and group accounts into the destination domain from the other domains.

3. Move computers and member servers into the destination domain from the other domains.

4. Back up data on merging DCs from the other domains, and run fresh installation into the Active Directory domain as DCs, or as member servers if they are no longer needed as DCs.

5. Reinstall applications on the newly installed servers.

6. Restore backup data to the newly installed servers.

7. Upgrade member servers into the Active Directory domain as members.

8. Verify resources, users, groups, and computers as a final quality assurance check.

Primary Domain Controllers (PDCs)

Some preparation should be completed prior to migrating a PDC. The first effort is in streamlining the domain. Before starting this, a complete backup should be executed in case some account was deleted that should

For IT Professionals

Cleaning Up the Legacy Domain

Migrations tend to be more of a problem than fresh installations because they pull along all the old problems that were sitting in the legacy domain. The domain upgrade migration takes the entire legacy Windows NT domain Security Accounts Manager (SAM) and translates it to the corresponding Active Directory components. If there is an empty Windows NT global group, it will be migrated. If user accounts still exist for people who have left the organization, they will be migrated. If there is a right to access a resource that may have been granted in error to a local group, it will be migrated.

Not only do these objects cause a security risk, but the additional objects will increase the time it takes to upgrade the SAM to the Active Directory. This is additional time that is completely unnecessary, because after being migrated, cleaning up those objects would still require the same amount of time as before. Cleaning up the legacy domain is a vital step in the migration process!

have been retained. After that, the Network Administrator has the following tasks to complete:

1. Delete old user accounts.
2. Delete the home directories associated with the old user accounts.
3. Remove empty groups.
4. Consolidate groups and simplify the group structure.
5. Remove computer accounts from the domain if they are no longer used.
6. Verify that the domain security policies are correct.
7. Simplify protocols so that only TCP/IP (if possible) is used.
8. Verify and validate the DNS, DHCP, and WINS configurations.
9. Make sure that existing DNS systems support Service Locator Resource Records (SRV) and, preferably support dynamic updates.
10. Update Windows NT and any applications with the latest service packs.

11. Convert the file system to NT File System (NTFS) on all DCs.

12. Verify that the server hardware is compatible with Windows 2000.

13. Make sure that any Windows NT 4.0 clients are upgraded with the latest service pack.

14. Uninstall third-party backup programs and virus detection programs. These applications have been proven to cause failures during Windows 2000 upgrades.

15. Run WINNT32/CHECKUPGRADEONLY from the Windows 2000 setup files to ensure that the server can be upgraded.

Before migrating any servers, a test should be conducted. This pilot migration should verify not only that the migration will work, but that a contingency plan to back out of the Windows 2000 migration will also work. One way to do this is by creating a backout BDC. The tasks involved in creating a backout BDC are as follows:

1. Use legacy Windows NT servers with hardware comparable to that available on the production network.

2. Back up each pilot server.

3. Create a synchronized BDC for the domain.

4. Remove the synchronized BDC from the domain.

5. Execute the migration with the PDC first.

6. Recover the domain with the BDC.

7. Repeat the process, but recover the domain using the backup tape.

Changes Required when Upgrading a Domain Controller

When legacy Windows NT 4.0 DCs are upgraded to Windows 2000, two components on the network must typically be upgraded as well.

- DNS
- NTFS

Active Directory requires DNS in order to function. The DNS server must support SRV because they are used to locate Windows 2000 DCs. Another feature that can facilitate DNS administration is dynamic update protocol. If upgrading an existing Windows NT 4.0 DC that is also a DNS server, these capabilities are automatically upgraded with the new Windows 2000 DNS.

Active Directory DCs must have NTFS in order for Active Directory to be installed. If the server is already running NTFS v4.0, it will be upgraded to NTFS v5.0. If the server is not running NTFS, the file system must be converted to NTFS in order for the Active Directory to be installed.

Backup Domain Controllers (BDCs)

Before upgrading the domain, one recovery method is to prepare a recovery BDC. This BDC is useful if there is a need to roll back changes if something goes wrong. The first thing to do is make sure that the legacy Windows NT domain has a BDC. If it does not, a BDC should be installed.

The BDC should have a copy of each of the services that are running on the PDC. For example, if the PDC is also a DNS server, DNS should be installed and configured on the BDC. Other services that should be copied are DHCP, WINS, and any business-critical messaging, print, and file services. A backup copy of the data used by each of these services should be placed on the BDC. There is no need to start any of these services unless there is a failure.

The BDC should be synchronized with the PDC so that it has the most current security account data in it. This can be done through the Server Manager utility, shown in Figure 3.5. The steps you take to synchronize the entire domain, including the recovery BDC, are to click the Computer menu and then click Synchronize Entire Domain.

Figure 3.5 Synchronizing a legacy domain.

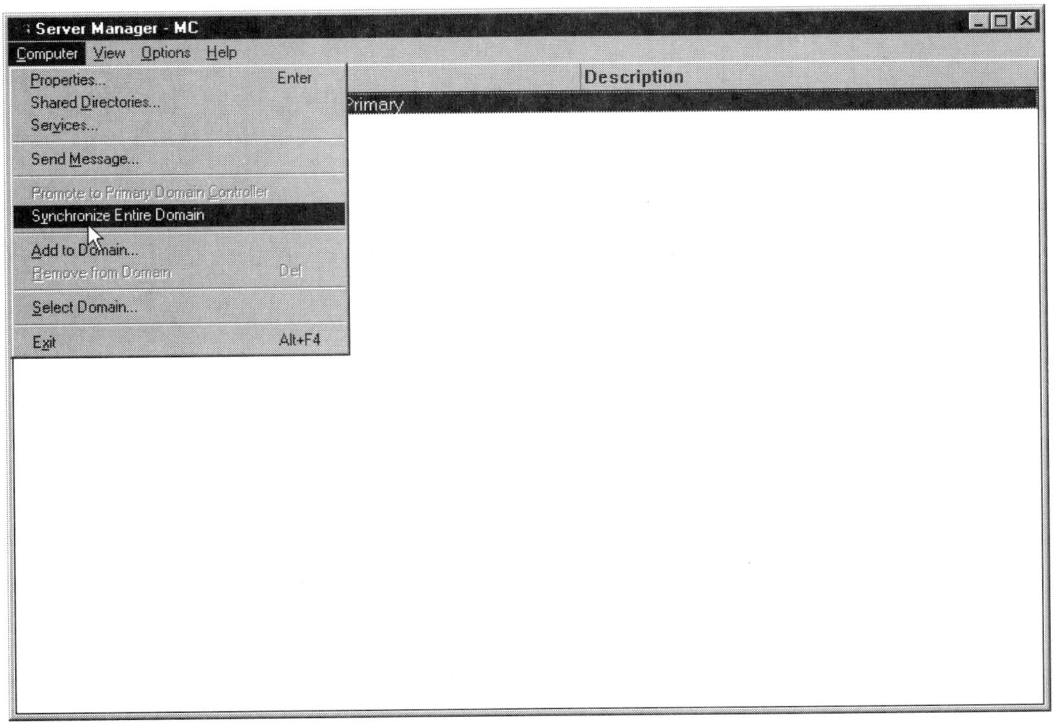

For Managers

About Windows NT 3.51

Migrating computers from one operating system to another can be a dilemma. There are issues with application compatibility and hardware compatibility—especially when the operating systems have great differences. It is more likely for a successful migration from Windows NT 4.0 to Windows 2000 than it is for a migration from Windows NT 3.51 to Windows 2000.

The Windows NT 3.51 operating system is ancient in terms of software age. When it was developed, computers in the workplace tended to be 486s. The Windows 2000 operating system does not support most of the computers that were around when Windows NT 3.51 was developed.

Even if the hardware is compatible, the applications may not work. Applications that were developed to be installed into either Windows NT 3.5x or Windows NT 4.0 tended to create different Registry keys for each operating system at the time of installation. Migrating the more similar Windows NT 4.0 may work, but migrating from Windows NT 3.51 probably will have errors and issues.

To solve these issues, an incremental upgrade strategy may succeed better than a direct upgrade. For instance, the Windows NT 3.51 computers can first be upgraded to Windows NT 4.0. After that is completed, the computers can be upgraded to Windows 2000.

Two known issues regarding using Windows NT 3.51 in a Windows 2000 environment involve authentication and SIDHistory. Authentication problems occur when a user from a Windows 2000 domain attempts to access a resource on a Windows NT 3.51 server in a resource domain. The Windows NT 3.51 domain does not construct tokens including any groups except those from the account domain that the user is logging in from. This is unlike the behavior of both Windows NT 4.0 and Windows 2000, and may result in a denial of access to a resource, or access to a resource that should be denied.

The SIDHistory issue occurs when a user account is moved from one domain to another and receives a new security identifier (SID). The SIDHistory attribute will "remember" the old SID and enable access to the old resources by using it. However, Windows NT 3.51 does not use the SIDHistory attribute and will not use them for access. This, again, may result in either the denial of access to a resource, or access to a resource that should be denied.

After synchronizing, the BDC should be taken offline. An interim step can be taken before taking the BDC offline to ensure that the network is recoverable. This process is to promote the BDC to a PDC and verify that each service will work. If that is successful, then promote the former PDC back to the PDC, which automatically demotes the recovery machine to a BDC. After verifying data integrity, simply shut the recovery BDC down and take it off the network.

Member Servers

Member servers are designated as resources in both the legacy Windows NT domains and the Active Directory domains. A member server does not have a copy of the domain security accounts or active directory. Instead, member servers provide services to users such as file and print services, Web services, databases, messaging, remote access, and so on. What often confuses the Active Directory neophyte is that even though a member server participates in the Active Directory, it still maintains its own local account database.

A user can gain access to the member server either by authenticating through the domain in which the member server is a part, or authenticating to a domain that trusts the member server's domain, or authenticating to the member server's local accounts database.

Promoting Member Servers with DCPROMO

Even though a server was a member server in a legacy Windows NT domain, it can easily be promoted to an Active Directory DC after it is upgraded to Windows 2000 Server. This is a change from legacy Windows NT where DCs had to be specified during installation only. The legacy Windows NT server's role could not be changed afterward. Now, the server can be promoted to a DC and demoted to a member server whenever deemed necessary.

Windows 2000 Server provides a tool with which to promote a member server to a DC: the Active Directory Wizard, or DCPROMO.EXE. As a member server, the Windows 2000 Server uses DNS to contact a DC and check to make sure that requesting users actually have the correct rights to use whatever resource they are requesting. When a member server is promoted to a DC, the server copies the Active Directory locally. As a DC, the server simply uses its local database to ensure that there are appropriate permissions.

Another change that occurs when a member server is promoted to a DC is that it can now make changes to the Active Directory on its locally stored database. The server then participates in the replication topology, which increases the traffic between it and its peer DCs on the network.

Upgrading with the Windows 2000 Setup Wizard

Late amendments to the operating system and known "features" (that is, bugs) are often squirreled away in the Readme.doc on the Windows 2000 Server distribution. Make sure you review it completely before commencing. The final step before upgrading a legacy Windows NT server to Windows 2000 is to run the WINNT32 setup file with the /CHECKUPGRADEONLY switch. This action will be a final verification that the server can be upgraded.

If upgrading directly from the CD-ROM, after inserting it, the dialog box shown in Figure 3.6 will appear. If upgrading from a network share, this prompt does not appear.

The installation wizard begins with the screen shown in Figure 3.7. This dialog lets the installer select between an upgrade of the existing server, or a new installation of Windows 2000 in a different directory. The second option creates a dual-boot machine.

The second wizard screen is a standard license agreement dialog. After selecting the agreement option and clicking NEXT, the third screen appears as shown in Figure 3.8. This screen is significant because it will show any running services or programs that are known to be incompatible with Windows 2000 Server. If any of these services or programs are vital to the production network, the following steps should be taken:

1. Click DETAILS and investigate the compatibility issue.

2. If the answers are not satisfactory that the installation can continue, click CANCEL and bail out of the setup program.

3. Further investigate the compatibility by checking Microsoft's Web site at www.microsoft.com and the vendor's Web site.

4. Create a strategy for removing, replacing, or upgrading the application.

5. Upgrade or replace the application, or uninstall it.

6. Begin setting up Windows 2000 Server again.

Figure 3.6 Upgrading from the CD-ROM.

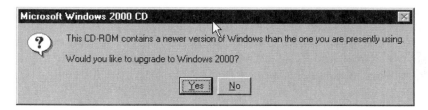

Figure 3.7 Selecting between an upgrade and a new install.

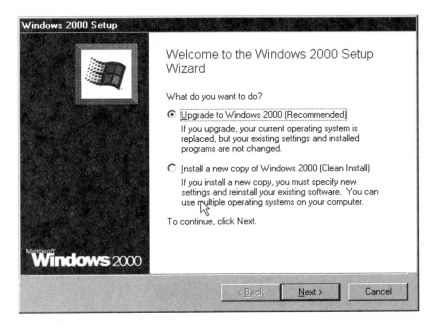

Figure 3.8 System compatibility issues.

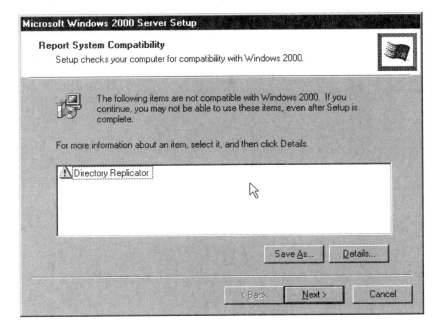

After clicking NEXT in the System Compatibility dialog, the rest of the installation continues without user input. Files are copied. The system reboots automatically and enters the Windows 2000 text-mode setup portion. This completes without user interaction and automatically reboots. The Windows 2000 Server graphical setup completes without need for user input. After a final reboot, the server starts for the first time as a Windows 2000 Server. If the upgraded server was a PDC or BDC on a legacy Windows NT domain, the Active Directory Wizard begins automatically.

Installing Active Directory Services

The Active Directory Wizard installs Active Directory Services. This wizard is available from the Windows 2000 Configure Your Server screen, or can be launched with the DCPROMO.EXE command.

The Active Directory Wizard branches out at each screen to enable you to install the right configuration. Table 3.2 lists the steps you need to take to reach the configuration you desire.

Table 3.2 Active Directory Installation Scenarios

Prior Server Role	Action Taken	Resulting Role	Resulting Domain and Forest	Steps in Active Directory Wizard
Domain controller	Demote server	Member	N/A	1. Click NEXT for first screen. 2. If this server is also a Global Catalog Server (GCS), a warning message will pop up. Click OK to confirm. 3. If this is the last DC in the domain, check the box. Click NEXT. 4. Provide the Administrator name and password that is authorized to remove this DC. Click NEXT. 5. Provide a password for the new local Administrator account. Click NEXT. 6. Click NEXT on the Summary, then click FINISH.

Table 3.2 *continued*

Prior Server Role	Action Taken	Resulting Role	Resulting Domain and Forest	Steps in Active Directory Wizard
Member server	Promote	First domain in controller new domain	Root domain in new forest	1. Click NEXT for first screen. 2. Select "Domain controller in new domain." 3. Select "Create a New Domain tree." 4. Select "Create a New Forest." 5. Either select to configure the DNS client on the server, or install and configure DNS on this server. 6. Give the new domain a DNS name. 7. Give the new domain a NetBIOS name. 8. Select a location for Active Directory files. 9. Select a location for the system volume. 10. Select whether users will access this domain via Windows NT 4 RAS servers. 11. Provide the password to be used for Active Directory restore.
Member server	Promote	Additional domain controller in existing domain	Any domain in any forest	1. Click NEXT for first screen. 2. Select "Additional domain controller in existing domain." 3. If the DNS client is not configured on this server, this will need to be done prior to continuing with Active Directory setup. 4. Select a location for Active Directory files. 5. Select a location for the system volume. 6. Provide a password to restore Active Directory.

Table 3.2 *continued*

Prior Server Role	Action Taken	Resulting Role	Resulting Domain and Forest	Steps in Active Directory Wizard
Member server	Promote	First domain controller in new domain	Subdomain in existing domain tree	1. Click NEXT for first screen. 2. Select "Domain controller in new domain." 3. Select "Create a new child domain in an existing tree." 4. Either select to configure the DNS client, or install and configure DNS on this server. 5. Give the new domain a DNS name. 6. Give the new domain a NetBIOS name. 7. Select a location for Active Directory files. 8. Select a location for the system volume. 9. Select whether this domain will have Windows NT 4 RAS servers. 10. Provide a password to restore Active Directory.
Member server	Promote	First domain controller in new domain	New domain tree in existing forest	1. Click NEXT for first screen. 2. Select "Domain controller in new domain." 3. Select "Create a New Domain tree." 4. Select "Place this new domain tree in an existing forest." 5. Either select to configure the DNS client on this server, or install and configure DNS on this server. 6. Give the new domain a DNS name. 7. Give the new domain a NetBIOS name. 8. Select a location for Active Directory files.

Table 3.2 *continued*

Prior Server Role	Action Taken	Resulting Role	Resulting Domain and Forest	Steps in Active Directory Wizard
				9. Select a location for the system volume. 10. Select whether this domain will have Windows NT 4 RAS servers. 11. Provide a password to restore Active Directory.

TIP

To install the Windows 2000 Server Administrative Tools on a workstation, run the Microsoft Installer package AdminPak.msi in the \i386 directory on the Windows 2000 Server CD-ROM.

Interim Mixed Domains

A mixed-mode domain is one that includes both Windows NT 4.0 BDCs and Windows 2000 DCs. This should not be confused with *native mode*, which is discussed in this section. There are some benefits to having mixed domains:

■ Multi-master replication can occur for the Windows 2000 DC that acts as a PDC.

■ The Network Administrator can retain Windows NT 4 BDCs for as long as needed and still be able to use Windows 2000 Server features.

There are drawbacks to using the mixed-mode domains:

■ The domain size is constrained by Windows NT 4 requirements for a maximum number of 40,000 objects.

■ The Network Administrator cannot implement new Active Directory security groups, such as Universal Groups.

■ Other features for the Active Directory are not completely implemented until the domain is changed to native mode. These features are listed in Table 3.3.

Table 3.3 Active Directory Features and Mode Compatibility

Active Directory Features	Native-Mode Function	Mixed-Mode Function
Kerberos transitive trusts	Available	Available
Kerberos authentication	Available	Available only on Windows 2000 DCs and used by Win2k clients and other Kerberos clients
Organizational units (OUs)	Available	Available, but only can be administered using Windows 2000 tools
Active Directory scalability	Available	Available only when no DCs are running NT4
Active Directory security groups (nested groups)	Available	Not available; can only use legacy Local and Global groups
Multi-master replication	Available	Only available on Windows 2000 DCs
Group Policy	Available	Only available on Windows 2000 Servers
Netlogon Replication	Not available; replaced by the File Replication System (FRS)	Available as a backward compatibility feature for NT 4 BDCs

Mixed Mode

After migrating the PDC and while running in mixed mode, the new Windows 2000 DC will act as a PDC Emulator in the domain. There is only one PDC Emulator in the domain, regardless of the number of Windows 2000 DCs. The PDC Emulator acts as a PDC for nonmigrated BDCs and clients. It will handle password changes for clients and BDCs, act as a Windows NT Master Browser, and provide the replication source for BDCs.

Native Mode

Native-mode domains are those that only have Windows 2000 DCs and have been manually changed to native mode. After upgrading the PDC, the BDCs should be upgraded as soon as possible. This will enable the domain to be switched to native mode, at which point clients and servers alike will

For IT Professionals

Windows 2000 without Active Directory

Though Active Directory is undoubtedly the most important feature of Windows 2000, there are several compelling reasons (other than increased stability) to install Windows 2000 Server in a non-Active Directory environment:

- **File and Print Services** Windows 2000 Server supports features such as disk quotas, Internet printing, hierarchical storage management, and dynamic volume management.
- **Web Services** Windows 2000 Server is bundled with IIS 5.0 and supports XML.
- **Communications** Remote connectivity is robustly supported by virtual private networks (VPNs), Remote Access Dial In User Service (RADIUS), and Remote Access services.
- **Infrastructure** Windows 2000 Server supports remote management and the swiftly developing Public Key Infrastructure (PKI).
- **Applications** It is bundled with Terminal Services and supports expanded availability features.

For IT Professionals

What Happened to NetBIOS?

NetBIOS does not go away in Windows 2000; instead, it is present as a backward-compatibility feature for legacy Windows NT. You may not see the word "NetBIOS," but the "Down-level name" that appears in various dialog boxes and installation screens is the NetBIOS name.

be able to participate in the Active Directory advanced features. Once a domain is in native mode, it cannot be switched back.

For example, in mixed mode, the domain will be limited to a total number of 40,000 objects, whereas in native mode, this number can be at

Figure 3.9 Switching to native mode.

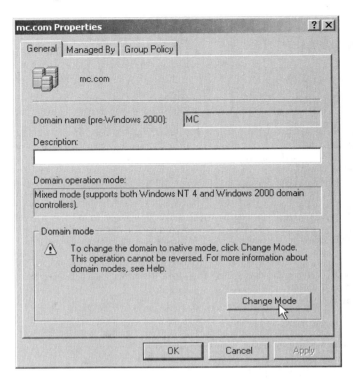

least 1 million. To switch a domain to native mode, start the Active Directory Users and Computers console by clicking Start | Programs | Administrative Tools, and then selecting Active Directory Users and Computers. In the left pane, click on the domain that will be changed to native mode. From the Action menu, choose the Properties option. When the properties dialog appears, on the General tab that is shown in Figure 3.9, click CHANGE MODE.

Migrating Components

When performing a domain upgrade, the domain components, such as users and groups, are migrated automatically. However, restructuring domains into a single Active Directory domain will require components to be migrated. The scenarios listed in Table 3.4 will apply to a domain restructure that requires migration of components.

Table 3.4 Restructuring Scenarios

Restructure	Process
New forest migration	Create a new forest of Windows 2000 servers and migrate components from existing legacy Windows NT domains. Take existing domains offline and remove. The process for a new forest migration is illustrated in Figure 3.10.
Merge domains	Perform domain upgrade of those legacy domains that will participate in the new forest, then migrate components from the remaining legacy Windows NT domains. Take legacy Windows NT domains offline and remove.
Split domains	Create a new domain and migrate components from the legacy NT domain. Delete the components from the legacy NT domain that remain within the Active Directory. Either create a new domain and migrate the remaining components, or perform a domain upgrade.

Using Organizational Units (OUs) to Create a Hierarchical Structure

Even when upgrading a domain, the OUs will need to be established and users moved into the correct container OUs. When restructuring domains, one of the first steps is to create a hierarchical structure for each domain with OUs before migrating the components.

OUs are created in the Active Directory Users and Computers Management Console. They should be planned out prior to being created, and typically provide one of four functions:

- Delegating administration
- Hiding objects
- Applying group policy
- Organizing objects logically

The OUs designated for delegating administration will typically be the top-level OUs in the hierarchy, because that will simplify the administrative structure. Administrators may be separated by geography or by business unit. There may also be levels of administrative authority, such that some Administrators have more control over more objects or properties than

Figure 3.10 Domain migration.

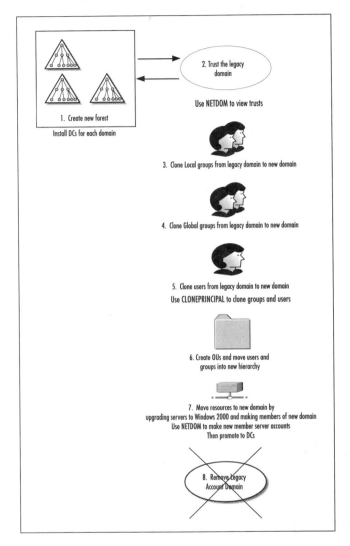

others. When delegating administration, the highest level of administrative authority should be granted at the top, and then lesser authority in OUs further down the tree. Below those top levels, the OUs for hiding objects and applying group policy will further organize objects.

User Accounts

Network Administrators usually want the users migrated along with their rights to network resources. The only way to accomplish this is to make

For IT Professionals

How to Hide Objects

Sometimes Administrators do not want some objects to be seen in the tree, even when users have the authority to view their attributes. One use of OUs is to place one or more objects into OUs and limit the ability of users to see the objects in the entire OU by removing the List Contents for those OUs. To hide objects in this way:

1. Open the Active Directory Users and Computers Management Console.
2. Navigate to the OU where you will place the hidden objects.
3. Right-click on the OU and select Properties.
4. Click on the Security property page.
5. Revoke all permissions by removing them from the Security property page.
6. Click ADVANCED.
7. Uncheck the box for Inherit Permissions from Parent, and click OK to return to the Security property page.
8. Add the groups that need to have rights to this OU on the Security property page with the appropriate rights.
9. Add any objects into the OU that you want hidden from users' view.

sure that when a user is migrated from one domain to another, and that user account belongs to one or more Global groups, the Global groups are moved as well. Some Global groups associate users with network resources via ACLs. In order to maintain users access to those resources, both the users and the group must be migrated at the same time.

The utility used for migrating user accounts is called ClonePrincipal. The name is derived from the fact that it can clone a security principal. Security principals are users and groups. ClonePrincipal uses customizable Visual Basic scripts for migrating objects incrementally to the Active Directory from a legacy Windows NT domain. The migration of Global groups is discussed later in this chapter.

Machine Accounts

Machine accounts are comprised of both Windows for Workgroups and Windows NT computers. Some of those machine accounts can be clients, and others can be servers and DCs.

Each legacy Windows NT computer has its own local SAM. Each SAM contains Local groups. In the legacy system, users became members of domain Global groups, and domain Global groups became members of computer Local groups. Then the Local groups were granted access to resources on the local machine. When migrating machine accounts, all the Local groups should be migrated as well.

Joining a domain can be completed at the member server or client computer. From the Network Properties, there is a button enabling domain membership that can be changed to an Active Directory domain. However, the computer account must be available within the new domain, or the user making the change must have a name and password to an account with the proper administrative rights for joining a domain.

NETDOM is a command-line utility that can manage computer accounts, domains, and trust relationships. The NETDOM utility can perform the following functions:

- Add, remove, and query machine accounts in a domain, even specifying the OUs.
- Join Windows 2000 computers to a domain.
- Establish and manage a domain's trust relationships.

Nested Groups

Windows 2000 has four types of groups: Local, Domain Local, Domain Global, and Universal. A Local group is limited to resources within a single computer, but can have members from any trusted domains. Domain Local groups are limited to resources within a single domain, but can have members from any trusted domains. Domain Global groups are capable of being granted access to any trusted domain, but can have members only from the local domain. Universal groups can be granted access to any trusted domain running in native mode, and can have members of both users and computers from within the local forest.

Nested groups are a method of reducing the numbers of members in an Active Directory group. Group memberships are limited to 5000 or fewer members. The limitation is placed on the group because an update to the group membership requires that the entire group's membership list be replicated.

Nested groups not only help reduce the number of members in a group, but also facilitate administration by enabling a master security group that can have multiple logical groups of users that share work functions.

Table 3.5 Nesting Groups in Native Mode

Container Group	Group Members	Other Members	Member Source
Universal group	Universal groups Global groups	User accounts Computer accounts	Any domain, same forest, or trusted
Global group	Global groups	User accounts	Same domain
Domain Local group	Universal groups Global groups	User accounts	Any domain, same forest, or explicitly trusted
Domain Local group	Domain Local group		Same domain

The ability to nest the groups is available when the domain is in native mode, and nesting configurations are listed in Table 3.5. The reason for this is that legacy NT domains do not support nested groups. For backward compatibility, Local groups can contain Global groups, which then contain user accounts.

Global Groups

Since Global groups are security principals, migrating Global groups can be performed with the ClonePrincipal utility. To ensure that the correct users can access the correct resources through the migration of the Global group, the user accounts must be migrated at the same time.

Another method of moving a Global group is to recreate the group in the Active Directory and then add the correct members to it. The Global group is traditionally a holder of users and less likely to be granted access to resources directly. Instead, it was usually granted rights to resources by being made a member of Local groups that had those rights. So, in order to grant permissions to resources, the Global group must be made a member of other Local groups in the Active Directory that have those rights until the domain is switched out of mixed mode and into native mode. Once the domain is in native mode, the Global group can be changed to a Universal group or become a member of other Global, Universal, or Domain Local groups.

Delegating Administrative Authority

One reason for merging legacy NT domains that were used for ensuring separation of administration is to take advantage of Windows 2000 Active Directory for the delegation of administration. In the Active Directory, responsibility is delegated by the OU, but can be inherited by lower, nested

Figure 3.11 Delegation of administration design.

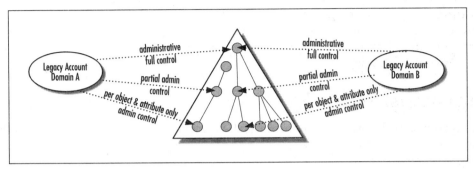

OUs. This directly affects how OUs are designed, since the simplest design would place the highest level of administrative capabilities at the highest level of OUs. The migration strategy is to map out which users should have the highest level of administrative control, which should have partial control, and which may have the object- and attribute-level control. After completing that, delegate authority to those users at the top of the OU hierarchy for the full control, mid-level for partial control, and closest to the users for per-object and attribute control, as illustrated in Figure 3.11.

To start the Delegation of Control Wizard, in the Active Directory Users and Computers Management Console, right-click on an OU and select Delegate Control. As you follow the wizard through the steps needed for delegating control in the Active Directory, you will find that there are predefined roles. A Network Administrator should not limit himself to this predefined set, and should investigate the variety of permissions allowed by selecting the "Do customized delegation" instead of a predefined role. The Network Administrator can use the customized delegation to grant control over certain object types, such as only user accounts or only computer objects.

Insert into the Replication Topology

When there is a single DC in the Active Directory, there is no need to establish replication. Replication only concerns the DC computers in the Active Directory, because they hold the copies of the Active Directory databases. When there is a single DC, there is no other DC to replicate changes to or receive updates from.

The issues arise as soon as the second DC is installed. Now, there is a need to replicate something depending on whether the second DC is in the same site or a different site. Same site, or intrasite replication occurs automatically. Each DC has a function within it called a Knowledge Consistency Checker (KCC). The KCC generates an intrasite topology running over RPC (Remote Procedure Calls) whenever a new DC is installed into a site.

When a DC is installed into a different site, the Network Administrator has the option to let the KCC automatically generate the intersite replication topology, or to manually establish it. When the Network Administrator manually establishes the connections for replication, there is the opportunity to create bridgehead servers that direct the replication traffic over certain network links.

Migrating from Novell Directory Services

Many organizations have invested time and effort in creating a directory services tree (NDS) for Novell NetWare and then educating their users on navigating its specific OUs. The NDS model they used can be migrated to the Active Directory so that users have a familiar navigational structure to use. There is a Directory Services Migration tool used specifically for this process.

1. The Directory Services Migration tool must run on Windows 2000.

2. Network traffic is reduced if the Directory Services Migration tool runs on a DC.

3. The tool can be used for multiple migrations of NDS trees, as well as legacy NetWare server binderies.

4. Each migration is established as an individual project within the tool. A migration can consist of a portion of an NDS tree or the entire tree itself. This enables an incremental migration.

5. Before beginning a migration, the Network Administrator should have complete documentation of the NDS design, administration, and groups. Additionally, the Administrator should have full documentation about the Active Directory design, administration, and groups.

6. The Active Directory should be readied to receive the new resources by having the domains, DCs, OUs, and groups already designed and implemented.

7. Each migration project begins with the selection of the Novell NetWare resources that will be imported offline. The Network Administrator has the option to change some of the resource properties to fit the Active Directory model. Then the offline project can be exported to the Active Directory. Additionally, files can be moved from NetWare servers to the Windows 2000 servers for any NetWare servers that will be taken offline through the tool. The project should end with a quality assurance check to ensure that the migration was successful.

Installing the Directory Service Migration tool is a matter of starting the Windows 2000 Configure Your Server from the Administrative Tools menu, then selecting the Add/Remove Windows Components selection. The Directory Service Migration tool can be found within the Management and

Monitoring Tools Details section of components. Selecting this tool will automatically install Gateway Services for NetWare if it has not already been installed. The new Directory Service Migration tool can be found in the Administrative Tools menu.

After starting the Directory Service Migration tool, a new project must be created. To create a new project, click the Action menu and select New Project. After creating the project, the first item is finding what NetWare resources are available on the network. Creating a new view will start the Discover wizard and do just that. To create the view, right-click on the new project, select New and then View from NetWare. This step allows you to select the source users, groups, and containers that will be used for that project.

The objects are stored in an offline project database. The next step is to make any necessary changes to the objects, whether to conform to a new naming convention, establish new passwords, or move them into different containers.

The project data can be exported into the Active Directory next. This is done by right-clicking an object in the Directory Service Migration tool project, selecting Task from the pop-up menu, and then selecting Configure Object to NTDS. The Configure Objects to NTDS wizard will prompt for the Active Directory destination OU, and after clicking FINISH, the object will be exported. Migrating files is performed by right-clicking NDS volume objects in the project and selecting File Migrate from the pop-up menu.

Upgrade Clients to Windows 2000 Professional

Whether to upgrade a client workstation or not is a concern for many organizations. Some organizations have legacy applications that are not compatible with Windows 2000 Professional, although many will find comparable applications that are Windows 2000 compatible. Some will be faced with extra costs required to upgrade hardware to be compatible with Windows 2000 Professional, although many have planned for this change since the announcement of Windows 2000's release. All organizations will need to plan for user support and training. Even though the usability features of Windows 2000 can make end users more productive in the long run, there is a learning curve at first. These organizations must weigh these concerns against the overall benefits that Windows 2000 Professional can bring them:

- **Enhanced security** Support for smart cards and the Public Key Infrastructure.
- **Enhanced reliability** More reliable than previous versions of Windows NT; fewer reboots when changing configuration of the workstation.

- **Enhanced usability** Proven graphical user interface with improvements geared toward the way people work.
- **Enhanced performance** Snappier performance.
- **Enhanced manageability** Plugs right into the Active Directory and takes advantage of all the Active Directory management features.

Once a decision has been made to upgrade to Windows 2000 Professional at the desktop, there is a secondary decision about whether to upgrade the servers or the clients first. If an organization plans to roll out Windows 2000 Professional by using the Remote Installation Service (RIS) of Windows 2000 Server, the "which first" decision is fairly obvious— Windows 2000 Server first. This decision is in line with long-standing networking best practices when deploying new networks:

1. Establish the network infrastructure first.
2. Security and servers next.
3. Workstations last.

NOTE

RIS is a new feature of Windows 2000 that enables the operating system to remotely install software from a central distribution point. It requires either a BIOS or chip on the network interface card (NIC) that will enable it to be managed remotely. These chips are called PXE ("pixie"), which stands for Pre-boot eXecution Environment. PXE is part of the Wired for Management protocol set. Although these are not the only manufacturers with WfM technology, Phoenix BIOS produces a BIOS that is PXE capable, and 3Com produces NICs that are PXE capable.

Additionally, when installing the Windows 2000 Server first, there is only a single, Active Directory-enabled Windows 2000 Professional image that must be created and maintained. However, when installing the Windows 2000 Professional workstations first, they will probably need to be updated immediately after the Windows 2000 Servers are installed in order to be able to access resources that are migrated to a new area in the new Active Directory. A second image must be created for all new workstations deployed after the Windows 2000 Servers are installed. This translates into additional work and affects the bottom line of a deployment project's budget.

When an organization has Windows 95 or Windows 98 clients, it will need to provide access to the Active Directory in order for the clients to function on the network. An interim solution is found in the DS (Directory

Services) Client. The DS Client enables Windows 95 and Windows 98 computers to work in the Active Directory in the same way as a native Windows 2000 Professional computer would. This includes the ability to:

- Query the Active Directory for users and resources
- Install Active Directory printers
- Use Kerberos authentication

Summary

Migrating to Windows 2000 from legacy Windows NT domains can take the form of one of two types of migrations:

- Domain upgrade
- Domain restructure

The type of migration depends entirely on the plans for the Active Directory for the forests, domains, and Domain Name System (DNS) namespace, organizational units (OUs), and site topology, and how they fit with the existing domain structure. A domain upgrade occurs if the legacy domains will remain intact as Active Directory domains after migration. A domain restructure is when the domains are merged or split into different configurations. The first place to start when migrating is with the forest:

1. Migrate root domain first.
2. Migrate each domain completely before starting the next.
3. Follow the DNS namespace to the next subdomain to migrate each domain tree before starting the next.
4. Completely migrate each domain tree before starting the next forest.

Drilling down further into the migration strategy, the method of migrating each individual domain is next.

1. Complete all preparation work and back up the PDC.
2. Migrate the PDC.
3. Perform a full backup of each BDC before migrating it.
4. Migrate each of the BDCs next.
5. Perform a full backup of each member server before migrating.
6. Migrate each member server next.
7. Verify the working condition of printers, clients, users, and other migrated resources.

When restructuring a domain, there are additional steps that require individual components to be migrated from source legacy domains to the target Active Directory domain(s). For example, the process to merge domains is as follows:

1. Migrate the destination domain or create a new Active Directory destination domain.

2. Move user and group accounts into the destination domain from the other domains.

3. Move computers and member servers into the destination domain from the other domains.

4. Back up data and install DCs from the merging domains into the Active Directory domain.

5. Reinstall applications.

6. Restore backups of data.

7. Upgrade member servers with Windows 2000.

8. Verify resources, users, groups, and computers.

When Windows 2000 Server is installed on a new computer, it will automatically install as a member server. However, when upgrading a PDC or BDC, Windows 2000 Server will automatically begin the process to install the Active Directory by starting the Active Directory Installation Wizard as soon as the Windows 2000 Server installation is complete.

An Active Directory domain has two modes: mixed mode and native mode. When running in mixed mode, the Active Directory will act as a PDC for any legacy Windows NT BDCs. This enables backward compatibility, as well as an incremental upgrade strategy such that each server can be migrated and verified before beginning the next. Native mode is required for using Active Directory features such as nested groups. Native mode cannot be used until all BDCs are upgraded, and the domain cannot be returned to mixed mode after switching.

Two utilities are critical components for moving users, groups, and computers: ClonePrincipal and NETDOM. ClonePrincipal is a customizable scripting program that can copy a security principal (example, user or group) from one domain to another. NETDOM is a command-line utility that can manage domain trusts, machine accounts, and domain memberships.

After components have been migrated, the Administrator may want to delegate control over some of them. Delegation of administration is necessary when merging two legacy Windows NT domains and using the OU structure to separate the administrative duties. The Delegation of Control Wizard is available in the Active Directory Users and Computers Management Console.

Inserting into the replication topology is an automatic function within a site. The Knowledge Consistency Checker (KCC) will generate the replication topology whenever a new domain controller is added. Only domain controllers are involved in the replication topology. New sites require that connection objects are created to establish replication between sites.

Migrating from NDS is a process that many organizations will be required to undergo. This process is simplified by the Directory Services Migration tool. The tool allows the import of objects from NDS into an offline project database that can be remodeled to fit the new Active Directory structure. The objects can be exported incrementally to the Active Directory thereafter.

FAQs

Q: I want to migrate our network by starting with the member servers, then follow with the BDCs, and finally migrate the PDC so that we can have a working copy of the NT domain SAM constantly updated until we are ready to cut over. Can this migration strategy work?

A: No. Active Directory domain controllers cannot exist in the same domain as a Windows NT PDC. The strategy should be changed to start with the PDC and follow with the remaining BDCs and then member servers.

Q: When I tried to upgrade a Windows NT 3.51 member server to Windows 2000, it failed. What should I do?

A: After reverifying that the hardware and applications are compatible, and that the users, groups, and Registry are cleaned up of any unnecessary entries, you should try to upgrade the Windows NT 3.51 server to Windows NT 4.0 first. After a successful upgrade to Windows NT 4.0, try upgrading to Windows 2000 Server.

Q: What types of applications will cause the worst problems with upgrades?

A: The two types of applications that cause the worst problems are virus detection applications and tape backup applications. Not only do these applications have very specific Registry entries that are difficult for the upgrade to process, but their nature is one that prevents the operating system from being changed. Take a virus detection program: It looks for changes to the boot files and has different methods of preventing them from being changed, whereas the upgrade process makes necessary changes to those same critical files. The conflict causes errors and issues. The backup application is necessary for restoration of the server files if there is a problem, so completely removing it is probably not the best tactic. The best thing to do is to uninstall all virus detection programs and turn the backup application service off. If, after upgrading, the backup application does not work, it can be reinstalled over the old one.

Chapter 4

Implementing Domains, Trees and Forests

Solutions in this chapter:

- Introduction
- Implementing a Domain
- Building Trees and Forests

Introduction

In Chapter 2, "Active Directory—The Heart of Windows 2000 Server," you learned that Active Directory is at the heart of Windows 2000 Server. Well, now it's time to get that heart pumping! This chapter provides descriptions and best practices for installing and configuring your domain, along with the process of building trees and forests.

When it is agreed that the domain structure design is in hand, implementation can proceed in accordance with the design strategy. This requires that the installation team has reviewed the design documents and understands them before installing the servers into the domain. Sometimes the installation team and the design team are the same set of people. Other times, they are two different sets of people with different ideas on how the domain should be structured. When design decisions are made for business-specific reasons that are understood by all involved, the two teams can generally come to an agreement on design implementation.

The scope of the design may include the creation of multiple related domains that form a domain tree. Disparate domain trees may then be incorporated into a forest. This chapter discusses how to implement your domain design by using domains, trees and forests.

Implementing a Domain

Often, implementing a domain can be as simple as installing a single domain controller. Beware of giving in to the false impression that the hands-on installation seems a great deal easier than the time and effort spent preparing for it would indicate. Microsoft has made installation even easier for Windows 2000 than it ever was for its predecessor, Windows NT.

There are three basic steps for the Windows 2000 Active Directory domain installation.

1. Running the Windows 2000 Server WINNT/WINNT32 command to install the operating system for the domain controller itself.

2. Configuring DNS (Domain Name System) as a client or as a service on the Windows 2000 Server.

3. Running the Active Directory Installation Wizard.

Active Directory installation and configuration is completed using the Active Directory Installation Wizard after Windows 2000 Server has been installed. DNS is required for the Active Directory, so if it is not detected on the network at the time of the Active Directory installation, the Active Directory Installation Wizard installs the service on the Windows 2000 Server. If DNS is configured as a client, the installer must ensure that the domain's DNS name is registered in the DNS tables before installing the

Active Directory domain. Dynamic updates should be turned on for the DC to register itself. If DNS is configured as a DNS server on the DC, the DNS tables must include the domain name, and dynamic updates must be turned on so that the DNS entries can be created for the Active Directory domain.

After installing a DC, the hierarchical structure within that single domain can be created, populated, and managed. This is performed by creating organizational units (OUs), creating objects within the Active Directory, and establishing a group policy system to enable role-based administration.

Installing the First Domain in Active Directory

The first DC in the Active Directory has the honor of being the DC for the root domain of the first forest. In other words, installing Active Directory on the first DC is the same as installing the root domain. Installation of the DC requires some information gathering. Table 4.1 lists the type of information needed to install the first Windows 2000 DC.

Table 4.1 Information Required for Windows 2000 Installation

Server Information	Example
Domain name	Root.com
Server DNS name	Server.root.com
Server NetBIOS name	Server
Partition and size	C: and 4 GB
File system	NTFS
System directory	\WINNT
Name of license owner	M.Y. Name
Organization of license owner	My Org
Language	English
Keyboard	U.S.
License mode (per seat or per server)	Per seat
Administrator's password	Hx346xqmz3
Time zone	Arizona GMT -7

After logging on to Windows 2000 Server for the first time, you will be confronted by the Windows 2000 Configure Your Server screen. While this wizard may not whisk away all your configuration woes, it does provide a single interface to assist in configuring Windows 2000 Server. Browsing through its contents, you will realize that it is simply a compilation of all the utilities that are useful during the configuration of Windows 2000 Server. All of these items can be accessed through the Control Panel, the Administrative Tools, or through the command-line interface. This console utility was developed to simplify the Administrator's tasks for configuring any new Windows 2000 Server, and can be launched at any stage after installation.

Active Directory Wizard

When Windows 2000 Server is initially installed, the server becomes a member server, unless an upgrade is being performed on a legacy NT primary or backup domain controller (BDC). When an upgrade is performed, the Active Directory Wizard begins automatically. The Active Directory Wizard is also available from the Configure Windows 2000 Server screen under Active Directory. If the file system is not NTFS, it will need to be converted to NTFS before Active Directory will install. To quickly convert the file system, the command CONVERT <drive> /FS:NTFS can be executed from the command prompt. The next time the server boots, the file system will then be converted to NTFS.

To access the Active Directory Wizard, select Active Directory from the navigation bar in the Configure Windows 2000 screen, which takes you to the Active Directory page. This page will not only lead you to the Active Directory Wizard, but also offers links to more information about DCs, domains, and forests. Click on Start the Active Directory Wizard (note that the wizard can be run at any time by executing DCPROMO.EXE).

The first screen of the wizard is a Welcome screen. Click NEXT to continue. The Domain Controller Type page is displayed, requesting you to select whether this will be the first DC in a new domain, or a DC in an existing domain. Assuming this is the first DC in the domain, select the first option. After clicking NEXT, the Create Tree or Child Domain window appears, as shown in Figure 4.1. This allows you to select whether this is the first domain in a tree, or if it is a child domain. Since this is a DC for a root domain, select the "Create a new domain tree" option.

After creating a new domain tree the Create or Join Forest page is displayed, allowing you to create a new forest, or to place this domain tree in an existing forest. The option to select for a forest root domain is to create a new forest. The new domain being created will need a DNS name. Unlike Windows NT, this name is not a NetBIOS name such as MYDOMAIN, but a true DNS name such as mydomain.com. The wizard dialog that appears after prompting for the DNS configuration establishes the DNS name for the domain, as shown in Figure 4.2.

Even though the domain will have a DNS name, it will also have a NetBIOS name for compatibility with legacy domains. The next screen prompts for the NetBIOS name. This does not have the same format as the

Figure 4.1 New domain tree or child domain.

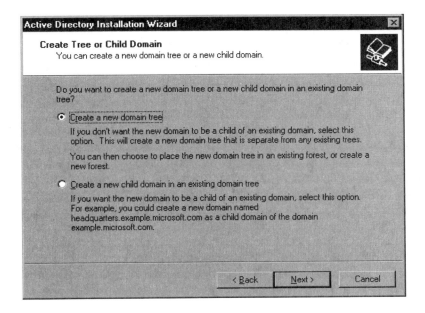

Figure 4.2 New DNS domain name.

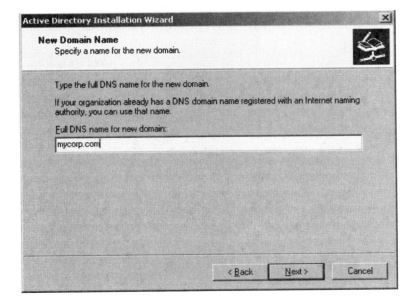

DNS name, nor does it have to have the same name. For example, if the domain's DNS name is mydomain.com, the NetBIOS name could be CAPNKIRK or something else totally unrelated to the DNS name. Even though this is a capability for backward compatibility, using a similar name for both the DNS and NetBIOS names will reduce confusion and make the domain easier for users to use. For example, mydomain.com can be the DNS name, and MYDOMAIN can be the NetBIOS name. Type in the NetBIOS name and click NEXT to access the following wizard screen.

You are then prompted to select the location for the Active Directory database and logging files. Make sure that the location has enough space for growth of the directory. For optimal performance and to enable recovery of the server, these two files should not be in their default locations, but on separate partitions on different physical disks. The default locations for these files are on the system partition within the WINNT directory, as shown in Figure 4.3.

The next wizard dialog allows you to select a folder for the system volume. The system volume is a folder that is replicated to every DC. SYSVOL contains the directory service information that must be replicated. Because of the replication, the SYSVOL directory must be placed on an NTFS 5.0 partition. Information that must be replicated for the Active Directory includes the files necessary to enable logon. Traditionally, this was handled by the NETLOGON share. Logon still is handled by NETLOGON, but now the NETLOGON folder is a subdirectory of SYSVOL, which

Figure 4.3 Default locations for Active Directory database and log files.

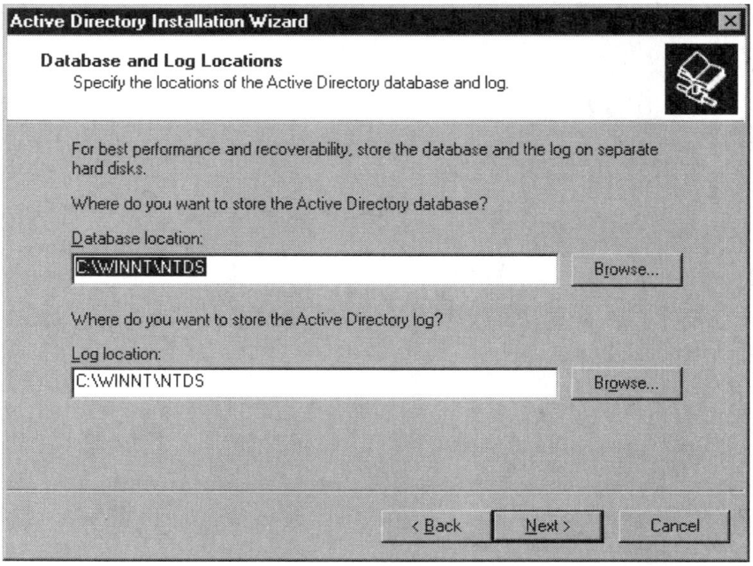

For IT Professionals

Active Directory Recovery Console

Directory Service Restore mode is applicable only to Windows 2000 DCs for restoring the Active Directory service and SYSVOL directory. Restore mode is a command-line console that can be used to:

- Start or stop services
- Format a hard drive
- Copy or view files on the server's NTFS drives
- Repair the system by copying a file from a floppy or other drive
- Reconfigure a service that is preventing the system from starting

If the Recovery console has been installed, it is available from the list of operating systems in the startup of the computer. If it has not been installed, you can run it from the Windows 2000 Setup program on the CD-ROM. This will only function if the server can boot from the CD-ROM.
To install the Recovery console as a startup option for Windows 2000:

1. Start Windows 2000 Server and log on as Administrator.
2. Click Start | Run, and type **CMD** in the box to open a command prompt.
3. Make sure that the Windows 2000 Server CD is in the drive, or that the CD's contents are available on a network share.
4. At the command prompt, change to the drive that contains the I386 directory.
5. From the I386 directory, type **WINNT32 /CMDCONS**.
6. The first dialog will allow you to bail out of the install by clicking No, or continue by clicking YES. Click YES to continue.
7. After files are copied, a final dialog screen appears, stating that the console has been installed. Click OK to close the screen.
8. To run the Recovery console, restart the server and select the Recovery Console option from the list of operating systems in the Boot menu.

means it will be replicated with the Active Directory system information and enable logon. Group policy templates and information are also replicated as a consequence of being placed within SYSVOL. These files are required by all DCs when applying group policy. The default folder is the WINNT\SYSVOL directory. Like the database and log files, ensure that this folder is on a partition with sufficient space for growth.

After clicking NEXT, the Active Directory Wizard will attempt to contact a DNS server for your domain to determine if it supports Dynamic DNS. If a DNS server has not been configured to support the new domain, then the Active Directory wizard will allow you to select whether to install DNS on the current server.

The next window asks whether this is a mixed domain that uses Windows NT 4 RAS (Remote Access Service) servers. The issue is security-related and revolves around the inability, under certain circumstances, of a Windows RAS server to authenticate clients. In order to use Windows NT 4 RAS servers, permissions must be less secure. Select the option that makes sense for your network, and click NEXT.

The following dialog will provide the Administrator password to be used when restoring the Directory Services. This is a different password to the server's local Administrator account, which means that the password can be the same or may be different. Ensure that the password is available in case of a disaster. Click NEXT.

The wizard will display a summary page. Review this page to ensure that the options selected are the ones required for your installation. If the options are not correct, this is the last chance to click BACK to change those options. If they are correct, click NEXT, and . . . wait. The Active Directory Wizard will take a considerable amount of time to install Active Directory Services, and even longer if installing a DC that is not the first in the forest, and must replicate to an existing, populated Active Directory.

Integrating DNS into the Active Directory

Today, the only way to integrate DNS with the Active Directory is to implement the Microsoft Windows 2000 DNS service on a Windows 2000 Server. When DNS is integrated in the Active Directory, there are some immediate benefits:

- It can coexist with other DNS servers.
- It automatically supports DHCP, and no DHCP-integration testing is required.
- It will support multi-master replication of the DNS within the Active Directory.
- It is able to scavenge stale records and keep the DNS database up to date.

If the Windows 2000 Server DNS service is implemented exclusively on the network, it will add the additional capability for using the Unicode extended character set. (Briefly, Unicode is a character set that is based on 16 bits of information. Compared to standard 7- or 8-bit ASCII or 8-bit EBCDIC, which have 128 or 256 characters, the Unicode character set can have up to 65,536 characters. This enables it to encompass most of the world's languages in one set of characters.) Additionally, the Windows 2000 Server DNS supports all the require-ments for Active Directory such as Service resource records (SRV RRs) and dynamic updates.

Configuring DNS

If the network does not have DNS installed or configured on it, it will not have Active Directory installed either, because Active Directory depends on locating a DNS server. To configure DNS before running the Active Directory Wizard:

1. Either select Start | Programs | Administrative Tools | DNS, or from the Windows 2000 Configure Your Server screen, select the Networking option in the left-hand pane. When it expands, select DNS, and finally click the Manage DNS option in the right-hand pane that appears.

2. Select the server that you will be configuring DNS on.

3. Click the Action menu.

4. Choose the Configure the Server option.

5. The Configure DNS Server Wizard appears with a Welcome screen. Click NEXT.

6. If this server will be a root server for DNS, select the first DNS server on the network. If DNS is already installed and configured on the network, select the second option.

7. The Configure DNS Server Wizard will next prompt to create a *forward lookup zone.* If Active Directory is installed, then you will be able to use the "Active Directory-integrated" option. However, if the server is a stand-alone or member server and you attempt to create a forward lookup zone, you will see the Active Directory Integrated option is grayed out. Not to worry, simply select the second option to Create a Standard Primary for now and click NEXT.

8. The Configure DNS Server Wizard will provide a Summary page. If you need to make changes, you can click BACK. If not, click FINISH to close the wizard screen.

Active Directory Integrated Zones

If you install Active Directory after configuring DNS on a server, you can still create Active Directory Integrated zones. To create an Active Directory Integrated zone, do the following:

1. Enter the DNS Management Console by clicking Start | Programs | Administrative Tools | DNS, or from the Windows 2000 Configure Your Server screen, select the Networking option in the left-hand pane. When it expands, select DNS, and finally click the Manage DNS option in the right-hand pane that appears.

2. Click the plus sign (+) next to the server you are adding the zone to and expand it.

3. Select the Forward Lookup Zones folder below the server.

4. Click the Action menu, and click New Zone.

5. The New Zone Wizard will display a Welcome screen. Click NEXT.

6. The Zone Type screen will appear. Select the "Active Directory-integrated" option. (This will be grayed out if Active Directory is not installed.) Click NEXT.

7. Type in the name of the zone, such as myzone.com or myzone.mydomain.com. Click NEXT.

8. The New Zone Wizard will display a Summary page. If the summary is correct, click FINISH. If not, click BACK and change the options.

About Zones

The DNS namespace can be divided up into zones. Each zone stores information about a DNS domain and is the source of information for that domain. A zone can include information about subdomains, or a new zone can be created for the subdomain. When a subdomain is contained in a new zone, the parent domain's zone must still contain a few records, called Name Server (NS) records, to be able to delegate information to that new zone. Zones can be fault tolerant by creating secondary servers for them. Any time a zone is replicated to a secondary server, that replication is considered a zone transfer.

A forward lookup zone is the most common. This type of zone represents a query by a client based on the DNS name of another computer that is stored as an Address (A) RR. The DNS server will respond to a forward lookup with an IP address.

A *reverse lookup zone* is used to find the DNS name of a computer with a certain IP address. It is the same as a forward lookup, but backwards.

The client will submit a query with an IP address, and the DNS server will respond with the hostname of that computer.

Dynamic updates function in a similar fashion to DHCP addresses. The dynamic updates self-register DNS names on a DNS server without requiring an Administrator to set the DNS name and address. This is similar to DHCP, which applies updates to the workstation without requiring an Administrator to set the IP address. In both cases, from the user's perspective, it is a transparent process. In fact, the two work quite well together. When a DNS server supports dynamic updates, clients can register and update their own A RRs with the server. With DHCP, for example, a client can receive an IP address and register it with the A RR on the DNS server. If the client does not renew the DHCP lease and is granted a new IP address the next time it accesses the network, it can update the A RR on the DNS server with its new IP address. This functionality is especially helpful for companies with active intranets published on users' computers. Until dynamic updates are enabled on the network, dynamic addressing via DHCP would make parts of the intranet difficult, if not impossible, to access and manage, because the DNS servers would need to be updated each time a new address was granted to a computer. Dynamic updates must be supported by both the client and the server, if the client needs to register its DNS name. Legacy Windows 9*x* and Windows NT 4 clients do not currently support this functionality. There is a DS Client that can be installed to overcome this problem. To manage the Windows NT 4 Servers that may remain on the network, it is recommended to statically list their DNS names until they are retired, upgraded, or replaced by Windows 2000 Servers.

Windows 2000 clients will attempt to register A RRs dynamically for their IP addresses. This process can be forced by entering the command ipconfig /registerdns from the client. The DHCP service will register the IP address dynamically on the Windows 2000 client.

Scavenging is a new option within the Microsoft Windows 2000 DNS service. It enables the automatic management of RRs. What the scavenging system does is set a timestamp on all RRs. Then the DNS service attempts to refresh the record at a set interval called the "no-refresh interval." If the RR cannot be refreshed, the DNS service will wait a second period of time, called the "refresh interval," and if the record is not refreshed during that second interval, the DNS will then scavenge the record. These intervals can be set within the MS DNS Microsoft Management Console (MMC) for a server by selecting the server, clicking the Action menu, and selecting the "Set Aging/Scavenging for all zones" option. Or, a zone can have its own unique aging and scavenging properties. This is performed by selecting the zone, then clicking the Action menu, and selecting Properties. On the General tab, click Aging to see the screen similar to Figure 4.4.

Figure 4.4 Zone Aging/Scavenging Properties window.

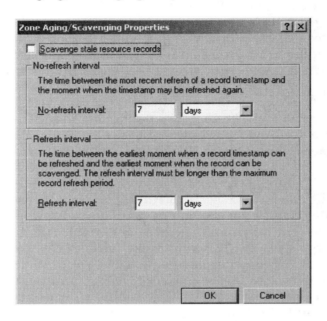

Service Resource Record Registration

SRV RRs are not created the same as a standard A RR. To create an A RR, the Administrator would simply add a new computer to the zone by right-clicking on the zone and selecting New Host. But to create an SRV RR, the Administrator must select Other New Records. This prompts a dialog box that allows the Administrator to select from a list of RR types, as shown in Figure 4.5. The Service Location record is actually an SRV RR. After selecting the Service Location option, a dialog appears for selecting the SRV RR properties.

Creating Organizational Units

The hierarchy within the domain consists of nested OUs. OUs are created in the Active Directory Users and Computers MMC. Creating OUs is a privileged task, so the user who will execute this should be logged on as an Administrator, belong to a group with explicit permissions, or have been granted explicit permissions to do so.

The following procedure is used to create OUs:

1. To invoke the Active Directory Users and Computers MMC, click Start | Programs | Administrative Tools | Active Directory Users and Computers.

2. Click the domain or OU in which you will be placing the new OU.

3. Click the Action menu.

Figure 4.5 SRV RR creation.

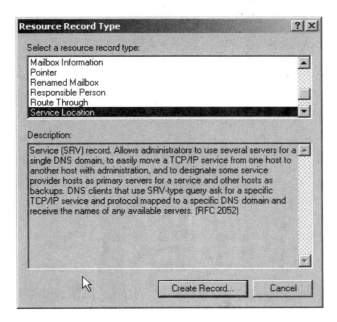

4. Click New.

5. Select Organizational Unit, as depicted in Figure 4.6. Note that you can also right-click the parent object, select New from the pop-up menu and Organizational Unit from there to get the same result.

6. The New object dialog will appear. Make sure that the destination for the OU is correct by checking the "Create in:" statement at the top of the dialog. Type a name in the box for the OU, and click OK.

The OU will appear below its parent object in the left-hand pane of the window. As new OUs are created, the left-hand pane will develop a hierarchical structure as shown in Figure 4.7.

Managing Objects in Active Directory

A significant feature of Active Directory is the ability to provide resources throughout an entire organization via one central repository. In addition, the advanced security permissions make it possible to further delineate permissions based upon user requirements. A Network Administrator will probably spend a lot of time managing objects in the Active Directory. Each time a new person is hired, every time new Windows 2000 Professional PCs are installed, whenever someone is promoted, and whenever someone moves to a different office, a corresponding change must be made to objects in the Active Directory.

Figure 4.6 Creating a new OU.

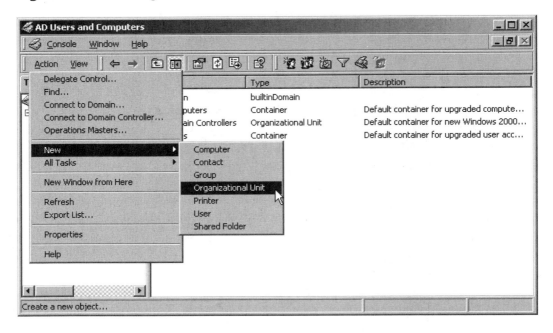

Figure 4.7 Hierarchical OUs.

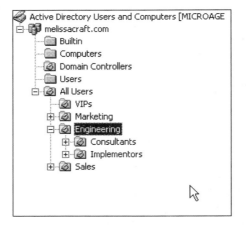

Managing User Accounts

If a person is hired at the company, the Administrator must create a user account in the Active Directory. To create a user account:

1. In the Active Directory Users and Computers console, right-click the OU, select New, and then select the User option.

Figure 4.8 New Object-User dialog.

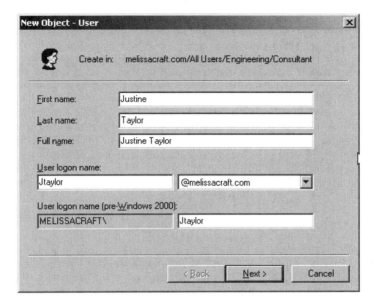

2. The New Object-User dialog, as shown in Figure 4.8, will appear.

3. Complete the user's name and logon id boxes, then click NEXT.

4. Set the password, select the password options in the subsequent dialog box, and click NEXT.

5. Accept the confirmation dialog and the user account will be created and appear in the OU that was originally selected.

The New User Wizard will complete all the necessary information for the user account to be usable on the network. However, to enable the user to access resources and to store relevant information about that user, the New User Wizard is not enough. To make changes to the user's information, right-click the user account object and select Properties from the pop-up menu. The User Account Properties dialog is displayed as in Figure 4.9.

When a user moves to a different department, not only will user account information such as group membership need to be changed, but also it is likely that the user account will need to be moved into a different OU. To move a user account from one OU to another, simply right-click the user account and select Move, then select the destination container from the resulting dialog.

Managing Groups

To create a group in the Active Directory, follow the same process as creating a user or an OU. Right-click on the OU that will contain the group,

Figure 4.9 User Properties.

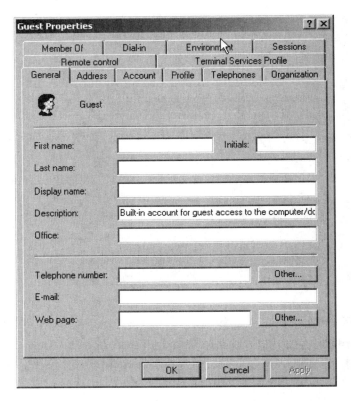

click New, and then click Group. In the New Object-Group dialog box shown in Figure 4.10, type the name of the group, select the Group Scope and the Group Type. The Group Scope establishes where the group can be seen and the types of objects that can be within it. These are listed in Table 4.2. The Group Type "Security" sets whether the group can be used for the assignment of permissions to other network resources, which is why it does not cross over into another domain tree. "Distribution" is a standard group type that is used for nonsecurity-related tasks.

There are two ways to add users to groups. One is from the Group's Properties, and the other is from the User account Properties. To add a user to a group from the Group's Properties, right-click the group and select Properties. Click the Members tab, then click ADD. Use the dialog box to find the user to add to the group, then click ADD.

To add a user to a group from the User account properties, right-click the user and select Add to Group. This can be used for multiple users at a single time.

Figure 4.10 New Group.

Group Scope	Group Type	Where Seen	Content Objects
Domain Local	Security Distribution	Domain	Users Global groups Universal groups
Global	Security Distribution	Domain tree	Users Global groups
Universal	Distribution	Forest	Users Global groups Universal groups

Managing Computers

When a new computer is added to the network, it has a corresponding computer object in the Active Directory. Windows 2000 PCs are capable of adding themselves to the Active Directory domain, as long as the installer

For IT Professionals

How Native Mode Affects Groups

While universal groups are restricted to distribution in mixed-mode domains, this is not the case in a native-mode domain. Universal groups can be security principals in a native-mode domain. The reason for the restrictions in mixed mode is to ensure backward compatibility with Windows NT 4 BDCs, since universal groups have no equivalent within the Windows NT SAM database.

Not only that, but in native mode, both a domain Local group and a Global group can be elevated to Universal group status. Once the configuration has changed, however, the group cannot be changed back—once Universal, always Universal.

Best practices for groups are to avoid using Universal groups as much as possible. The main reason for this is that Universal groups are placed into the GC along with their entire contents. This is necessary in order to publish the group to the entire forest of domains, and the GC is the only database (or index) that connects the forest's multiple domain contents.

has an Administrative password. In many cases, it is preferable to not give out the Administrative name and password for this purpose, but to simply create the computer account prior to its installation. To create the computer account:

1. Right-click on the destination container, and select New.

2. Select Computer from the pop-up menu.

3. Complete the computer name.

4. If the computer is a Windows 3.*x*, Windows 95/98, Windows NT 3.5*x*, or Windows NT 4.0 system, check the box to Allow pre-Windows 2000 computers to use this account.

5. Click NEXT.

6. The second screen allows the Administrator to mark this computer as a managed PC and to set a GUID, Globally Unique Identifier, for it. If it will be managed, complete this information. If not, do not check the box stating that this is a managed PC.

7. Click NEXT to see the summary page.

8. Click FINISH to add the computer to the network.

If the computer is designated as a managed PC, the Administrator can invoke the Computer Management MMC Console from the Active Directory Users and Computers console. To do this, the Administrator simply needs to right-click on the computer object and select Manage from the pop-up menu, as shown in Figure 4.11.

Managing Shares

When publishing a resource, the resource is more than just an object within the Active Directory; it is also a searchable entity. That is, users can execute queries to find published resources, or they can browse around to look for them.

Not only should you determine what is going to be published, but also where in the directory should it be published. If a SalesReports user is in an OU for Sales, then publishing the SalesReports share in the Services OU would not be as helpful as publishing it in the Sales OU. Select meaningful placement of resources, and pay attention to the location from which users may be suddenly browsing. If publishing a file from New York in a container that only holds Florida users, there may be more traffic on the WAN than desired. In these cases, another option is to use File Replication Services (FRS), which is a fault-tolerant form of sharing files automatically configured for each DC through the SYSVOL share.

To set up a published file share:

Figure 4.11 Invoking computer management.

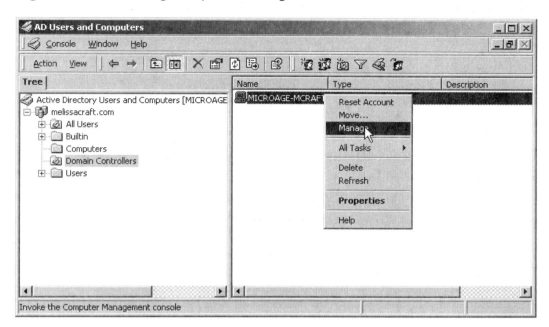

1. In the Active Directory Users and Computers console, right-click the OU, select New, and then select the Shared Folder option.

2. The New Object-Shared Folder dialog will appear.

3. Complete the name of the share and its network path, then click NEXT.

Another feature provided with published resources is keywords. This allows you to specify information found within this share for the purposes of searching.

Managing Printers

Printers are published in the Active Directory through the Add Printer Wizard of a Windows 2000 computer. The default behavior for shared printers is a listing in the Active Directory.

To verify whether a printer is shared in the directory, right-click the printer object and select Properties. Click the Sharing tab. Verify that the box for List in Directory is checked. If a legacy Windows NT printer must be shared in the Active Directory, you can right-click any container, select New, and then Printer from the pop-up menu. Enter the UNC name for the shared printer.

Another method of publishing printers from non-Windows 2000 networks is through the use of the script in Winnt\system32\pubprn.vbs. This Visual Basic script can be executed with the syntax:

```
cscript pubprn.vbs servername "ldap directory services path"
```

For example, executing the command:

```
Cscript pubprn.vbs \\printserver "LDAP://cn=printers,dc=root,dc=com"
```

will publish all the printers located on the server named Printserver into the Active Directory OU named Printers within the domain root.com.

Common Object Management

With ever-changing network environments, objects will move around the Active Directory—following their real counterparts around the network. Objects will be renamed and deleted too. No amount of planning will prevent changes affecting the network on a daily basis.

Moving an object is as simple as right-clicking it and selecting Move from the pop-up menu. This will produce the Move dialog with the Active Directory hierarchy available to be navigated to the destination container.

Renaming an object is just as simple. Right-click the object and select Rename. This does not produce a dialog box, but allows the Administrator to type in the new name of the object directly into the window.

There are two ways of deleting an object. You can click on the object in the right-pane window and then press DELETE on the keyboard, or you can right-click on the object and select Delete. Both of these actions will result in a Delete Confirmation box.

Nesting Groups

Nested groups cannot be used in mixed domains; that is, those domains that include Windows NT 3.5x and Windows NT 4.0 DCs and member servers. They can only run in domains that are in native mode. A nested group is one that is a member of another group. By nesting groups, the child group automatically inherits the permissions of the parent group, plus it can have its own additional permissions. Nesting groups makes it easier to manage them, but only if they are carefully planned.

To create a nested group, start with the parent group.

1. Right-click the parent group.
2. Select Properties from the pop-up menu.
3. Click the Members tab.
4. Click ADD and navigate the hierarchy to the child group.
5. Select the group, and click ADD. The group should appear in the Members window.

Role-Based Administration

Administrative roles are useful for enterprises that have a distributed network management structure with different levels of access required for the Administrators. For example, distributed network management is used by a business that establishes a single group to have access to full administrative rights to a domain, a second group to have the administrative rights to add, delete, and change user accounts, and a third group to reset passwords. Distributed network management is implemented in the Active Directory through created roles for Administrators, or *role-based administration.*

Microsoft Management Console

Microsoft created the Microsoft Management Console (MMC) to aid with the administration of Windows 2000 Servers. It was developed to simplify administration through the use of a consistent interface. Microsoft is expected to continue the development of MMC and extend its capabilities to be usable by third-party software tools.

The interesting thing about the MMC is that it is not a management application itself. Instead, the MMC provides the User Interface (UI) for the administrative application. The snap-in (similar, I suppose, to plug-ins for Web browsers) is the administrative tool. The snap-in will also create menu items, pop-up menus, and drag-and-drop actions that are specific to that administrative tool. Extensions provide even further capability to a snap-in. Windows 2000 Server provides a set of preconfigured MMC consoles, more of which are added when Windows 2000 Server additional components are installed. MMC consoles appear under the Administrative Tools menu when you click Start | Programs | Administrative Tools.

MMC can run in two modes:

- User mode
- Author mode

User mode limits the functionality of the MMC so that its configuration cannot be saved. It also prevents the user from adding or removing snap-ins. Author mode lets the user do everything, including adding and removing snap-ins, creating a new window, viewing all portions of the console tree, and saving the console's configuration.

Administrative Roles

In order to economize, most large enterprises create a tiered structure for administration. A three-tiered structure might resemble Table 4.3.

Obviously, an enterprise would not want their first tier to have the ability to change the way the MMC worked. It is probable that they would not want the second tier to have this ability either. Therefore, they should

Table 4.3 Tiered Support Structure

Tier Level	Support Experience	Example
First tier	Minimal	Help Desk: Reset passwords.
Second tier	Mid-level	Desk-side support: Adds, deletes, changes user accounts and computer accounts, install member servers.
Third tier	Highly experienced	Network Design and Engineering: Manages the site topology, hierarchical structure, and advanced troubleshooting.

ensure that those administrative roles are restricted to user mode for the MMC. The way that this is done is through applying a group policy. For those organizations that wish to restrict some MMC consoles to user mode and allow others to be in author mode, it can be done. Individual snap-ins can be restricted via group policy.

Delegating Administration

Windows 2000 even supplies a Delegation of Control Wizard in the Active Directory Users and Computers Microsoft Management Console (MMC) utility (which can be found in the Administrative Tools folder under Programs in the Start menu). This makes the process even easier to execute. The following steps must be taken to use the Delegation of Control Wizard (Figure 4.12) in order to delegate Full Control to another Administrator for a single OU (the OU is also called a folder in the wizard).

1. Click Start | Programs | Administrative Tools on any DC.

2. Select Active Directory Users and Computers.

3. After the window opens, in the left pane of the window, navigate to the OU to which you will be delegating administrative rights.

4. Right-click on the OU and select Delegate Control from the pop-up menu.

5. The wizard box will start with a Welcome dialog. Click NEXT.

6. The Group or User Selection screen will appear. Click ADD.

7. Select the group to which you will be giving administrative access.

8. The group's name will appear in the window. Verify it is correct, and click NEXT.

Figure 4.12 Customized delegation.

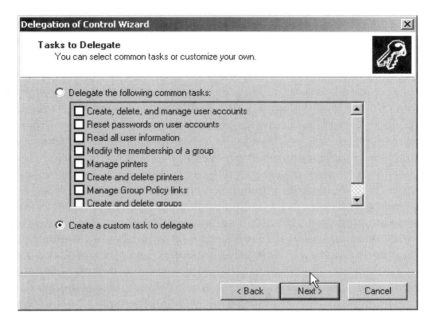

9. In the Active Directory object type window, you can select either the entire folder or a custom list of objects that are in the folder. Select the first option (This folder...), and click NEXT.

10. In the Permissions box, you can select a variety of permissions. To delegate full administrative rights, you will need to select Full Control. Then click Next.

11. The final dialog will show you a summary of the options you have selected. Click Finish to enable delegation. If you click Back, you can change your options. If you click Cancel, no changes will be applied.

After completing this exercise, there is a way to verify that the changes are applied. In the Active Directory Users and Computers window, select the View menu and then the Advanced Features option. You can then right-click the OU for which you delegated control, then select Properties. On the Security page, click Advanced. The Permissions tab will show you the additional permissions created for the group. If you double-click the group, you will see that it has been granted full rights to all of that OU and any OUs within it.

Another way to verify that the group has been correctly granted access is to log on as a user account that is a member of that group. Then start the Active Directory Users and Computers Wizard and try creating a new group.

Controlling Who Can Reset Passwords

One of the most common problems users run into is that they forget their password. Usually this happens the day after they were required to change their password. Only certain Administrators can access that type of user control in legacy environments, so this capability is typically retained by a high-level IT group. In a large organization, it can become a huge headache!

Active Directory can be an aspirin for this particular headache, if an organization has a group such as a Help Desk that is connected to the network. In this case, the Active Directory allows the delegation of only the password resetting right. The Help Desk would have no other rights to the directory and could handle the password resets immediately.

To delegate this specific right, create a group for the Help Desk. Then follow the Delegation of Control process up to the Active Directory Object Type window. Here you would select "Only the following objects in the folder," and from the check box list, select "User Objects." Click NEXT and progress to the Permissions window. Select only the "Reset Password" box in the list. It is a simple matter of finishing the wizard after that.

There are some challenges with delegating administration. For many with experience in other directory services, the most difficult problem with delegating administration for a container is with somehow losing the delegated Administrator's password—whether the Administrator has forgotten it, or left the company, or some other mishap has occurred. For this reason, it is good practice to always have a master administrative account that is granted access to every container, even if it is intended to be completely cut off. The account should be set aside in a secure place for disaster recovery purposes only.

Object-Based Access Control

Access control lists can be used to assign security permissions to objects. This is accomplished by assigning security descriptors to each individual object. This methodology can be used both to control the object itself, and to secure its attributes. It goes one step further by providing additional security features to meet the needs of most organizations. For example, users' descriptions, but not their phone numbers, may be available for modification. You can also set up permissions to be allowed or denied. Some permissions are granted by group memberships to read information. You may choose to deny this to a user group such as external contractors. When a user is granted permission by two different memberships, both sets of permissions are applied in combination. For example, if a user has Read through one group and Write through another, the effective permissions will be Read/Write.

There are two types of object access: standard permissions and special permissions. Standard permissions consist of normal permissions applied such as Read or Write. These provide the normal level of permissions similar to those associated with the NTFS file system. The standard permissions for files include Read, Write, Read & Execute, Modify, and Full Control. Standard permissions for directories include Read, Write, Read & Execute, List Folder Contents, Modify, and Full Control.

Special permissions allow an even finer degree of administration by breaking down the standard permissions one step further. For example, the Read permission might have three special permissions associated with it. To access the special permissions, click ADVANCED on the Security tab of an object. Next, click VIEW/EDIT to specify specific special permissions.

Building Trees and Forests

Each time a DC is installed, it must be installed into a domain. If it is a new domain, it must be installed into an existing tree in an existing forest, form a new tree in an existing forest, or form a new tree in a new forest. The forest is the largest holder of the schema, configuration, and global catalog (GC). It is the ultimate division for an enterprise. Building a forest can be as simple as installing a single domain with a single DNS namespace, or as complex as installing multiple domains with multiple child domains and namespaces among them.

A forest is a collection of domain trees that do not have to form a contiguous DNS namespace. For example, one tree may have the root.com namespace, and another tree may have the corp.com namespace. Each tree can consist of multiple domains, but they must all share the same namespace.

The forest is created with the installation of the root domain's first DC. When installing a new Windows 2000 Server to be a DC, it must be promoted to a DC after the operating system is installed. The Active Directory Wizard is the application used for promoting the server to a DC. During the installation process, you will be prompted as to which forest the new domain should join, or if you are creating a new forest. The command line for the Active Directory Wizard is DCPROMO.EXE.

Forest Characteristics

The forest is a collection of domain trees with multiple namespaces that share a common schema, configuration, and GC. Technically, a forest can exist as a single domain with a single namespace. In essence, the Active Directory forest lets an organization use domain names that are not part of the same DNS namespace to work seamlessly together. For example, a forest could contain a domain tree with the root.com namespace and another domain tree with the tree.com namespace. There can be as many namespaces as needed in a forest.

Common Schema

Each forest shares a common schema. The schema is the list of all the object types, called object classes, that can exist in the Active Directory. The schema lists the objects, as well as the attributes that each object class can have.

Since it is possible to add object classes or attributes to existing object classes, the schema is not necessarily going to be identical between two different forests. However, within the forest, the schema is replicated throughout the forest, and all object classes and attributes will be available at any point in the forest.

Common Configuration

The configuration for a forest is a naming context container object of which every DC in the forest contains a copy. Information that must be applied to the entire forest is stored in the configuration container object. The configuration container is used to generate the replication topology because it contains data about the underlying network infrastructure.

Global Catalog

Each forest has a single GC that contains information about each object within it. The GC is basically an index of the Active Directory database. It has a partial replica of all forest-contained objects. The GC has a larger scope than that of the domain since it will cover the entire forest. A GC server processes all UPN (User Principal Name) logons for a single forest.

Some DCs are also GC servers for the forest. The first DC installed into a forest will become the forest's first GC server. All other DCs must be specifically designated as GC servers.

When a DC processes the logon request and needs to find Universal group memberships, it queries a GC DC. If a GC server is not available when a domain controller tries its query, the logon is rejected completely to guard against security blunders. For example, user Billy is a member of the Universal group NonPayroll, which explicitly denies Billy access to a resource share for Salary.XLS. If the GC was not reachable and he was allowed to log on, then he would potentially have access to Salary.XLS.

Instead, the DC will reject Billy's logon request until a GC server can be reached.

The obvious impact of this tactic is at the design level. The most logical place to put GC servers is one in each site. Because sites are groups of well-connected IP subnets, and because well-connected implies LAN connections, it follows that there would be fewer network failures within a site than between sites. This is not necessarily true for WAN connections. If a site does span a WAN connection, even if it is a high-bandwidth link, the network designer may want to place a GC server on each side of that link.

GC DCs generate more replication traffic than regular DCs because they are replicating the GC as well as the contents of the Active Directory domain. The GC contains a read-only, partial copy of the Active Directory database for every other domain in the forest. DCs already have a read-write, complete copy of their own domain's Active Directory database.

Keep in mind the following GC rules:

- The GC includes only a single forest's set of objects for users to browse. If users need to access objects in another forest, they must know which domain in that other forest to query.

- Query traffic is generated to GC servers, when users browse the "entire network" or use search commands to find network resources.

- The settings in the schema will determine whether an attribute is available within the GC. If it is not, users will not be able to see it.

Contiguous Namespace

Domain trees are a set of domains that have a contiguous namespace. The forest can have multiple domain trees. A continuous namespace is a set of DNS names that have the same root namespace. A forest can have multiple domain trees, but only contains a single root domain. The first domain installed into a forest, regardless of the number of different namespaces, will always be the root of the forest. Each domain tree will have a root DNS namespace, but that does not designate that domain as a root of the forest.

Trust Relationships

Legacy Windows NT domains enabled access to each other's users via trust relationships. These trust relationships were explicitly set between domains. Not only that, but trusts were one-way. That is, domain A trusted domain B in a single trust, but domain B did not trust domain A unless a second trust was established. Not only were trusts one-way, but they were nontransitive. That is, when domain A trusted domain B, and domain B trusted domain C, then domain A did not automatically trust domain C. This system had limitations that the Active Directory fixed.

Transitive Bidirectional Trust

Active Directory trust relationships are different from the legacy NT domain trusts. First of all, within a forest, the trust relationships are created automatically. They are bidirectional and transitive. If a forest contains domain A, domain B, and domain C, then domain A trusts both domain B and domain C, and they both trust domain A and each other, as illustrated in Figure 4.13.

The Active Directory forest contains multiple domain trees that are connected via a transitive, bidirectional Kerberos trust relationship. Child domains always have Kerberos transitive trusts between themselves and their parent domain. A forest always contains entire domain trees. The domain tree cannot be split between multiple forests.

When migrating from a legacy Windows NT domain to an Active Directory domain structure, there will be changes in the way that the domains trust each other. Before migrating Windows NT domains to Active Directory, the Network Administrator should review the existing trust relationships and note any trust relationships that should not exist after migration. By default, domains that are migrated to the Active Directory forest will connect to each other through transitive trusts. Any domains that are not moved into the new forest will require explicit, nontransitive, trust relationships to be created between themselves and any new domains within the forest. However, any upgraded domains will retain their existing trust relationships as nontransitive, one-way trusts.

Because of the way that trust relationships work during migration, a legacy Windows NT domain structure that uses a Master or Multi-Master domain model requires that the Master domains are migrated to Windows 2000 first. Resource domains should be migrated to Windows 2000 after all

Figure 4.13 Transitive trusts in Active Directory forests.

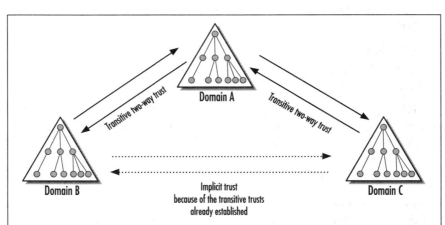

Master domains have been completely migrated. Resource domains are best migrated as child domains of already migrated Master domains.

Trusts that Cross Forests

Within a forest, there is no need for establishing trusts because of the Kerberos transitive two-way trusts. However, sometimes users in one forest need to access resources in another, or during migration, users may need to access resources in a legacy Windows NT domain. For example, the XYC Corporation has two forests that were created for the sole purpose of separating the global catalogs (GCs), schemas, and configurations. One forest is dedicated to a lab environment, and the second forest is dedicated to the production network. When Administrators are working in the lab environment, they still need to access their corporate e-mail and manage the production forest domain. They will be able to perform their job functions if they are able to establish a domain trust relationship.

NOTE

Domain trusts within a forest are transitive, benefiting from Kerberos authentication. If a domain in one forest requires access to resources in another forest, a nontransitive NTLM trust has to be established between domains in the disparate forests. These types of trust relationships can quickly evolve into the same tangled web of trusts experienced with operating systems prior to Windows 2000. This should be taken into consideration during forest planning.

Trust Utilities

There are two tools that are useful for handling trust relationships in Windows 2000:

- NETDOM
- Active Directory Domains and Trusts Management Console

NETDOM is a command-line tool found in the Windows 2000 Resource Kit that can list existing domain trust relationships, establish new trust relationships, and manage machine accounts in a domain. Establishing a trust relationship with NETDOM can be executed with the following command:

```
NETDOM /DOMAIN:RESOURCE MASTER MASTERDOMAIN PASSWORD /TRUST
```

This command will establish a one-way trust in which the domain named RESOURCE trusts the domain named MASTERDOMAIN. It can be

For IT Professionals

NETDOM

Command-line programs such as NETDOM are confusing at first because they do not usually have easily understood help options. However, these programs are a blessing when you need to automate procedures to happen after hours or without user input. There are five major commands: NETDOM BDC, NETDOM MASTER, NETDOM MEMBER, NETDOM QUERY, and NETDOM RESOURCE. Each of these commands has a group of options that affect how they work. In general, the options are:

- **/Domain:domainname**   The command is executed on the PDC or DC of the domain listed.
- **/User:domain\user**   The command uses this user account.
- **/Password:password**   The command uses this password for the user account.
- **/noverbose**   The command does not display much text on the screen.

The syntax of the commands is as follows:

- **NETDOM [/options] BDC [\\BDC] [/Command]**
- **NETDOM [/options] MASTER [masterdomain] [password] [/command]**
- **NETDOM [/options] MEMBER [\\member] [/command]**
- **NETDOM [/options] RESOURCE [resourcedomain] [password] [/command]**

NETDOM QUERY is unique—it has a single option, /noverbose, and all you need to type at the command prompt is NETDOM QUERY \\computername, where computername is the name of the DC that you want to list trust relationships for.

Notice that each of the NETDOM commands other than NETDOM QUERY ends in /command. The available commands for this are as follows:

- **/Add**   Adds a machine account.
- **/Delete**   Deletes the machine account.
- **/Query**   Finds out domain information.
- **/Fullsync**   Starts a full synchronization of the domain.

- **/Partialsync**   Starts a synchronization with the PDC.
- **/Trust**   This is only available with the NETDOM RESOURCE and NETDOM MASTER commands. This command establishes the trust relationship for the domains.
- **/joindomain**   This is only available with the NETDOM MEMBER command. It joins the member to a domain.
- **/joinworkgroup**   This is only available with the NETDOM MEMBER command. It joins the member to a workgroup.

One of the ways to use the NETDOM command is when migrating servers to Windows 2000. For example, GRAY Corp. decides to restructure domains when deploying Windows 2000. Each new Active Directory domain is a new domain name deployed on new servers. The old servers in the legacy domains are to remain on the network until each legacy domain has been completely migrated to a new Active Directory domain. The Network Administrator needs to join each of 5000 Windows NT 4.0 Workstations and Windows 2000 Professional computers to the new Active Directory domains.

The Network Administrator decides to create a login script for each group of migrated clients rather than go to each desktop and run through the domain-joining process, and rather than giving an Administrative password to users and walking them through the process.

The Network Administrator edits the login script in the old domain to add the line: NETDOM /Domain:newdomain /User:newdomain\admin /Password:password /Noverbose MEMBER /JOINDOMAIN

This line will join the computer that the login script is executing for to the domain named NEWDOMAIN. It will use the Admin account in the NEWDOMAIN, but will not display any text on the screen due to the /Noverbose command. Even so, using the Admin account and password in a script is not recommended, since security may be breached simply by a user viewing the login script if it is in a noncompiled format.

Once the computer has joined the new domain, it will have a new login script and it will not attempt to join the domain again.

used across forests, or between legacy Windows NT domains and Windows 2000 domains.

The Active Directory Domains and Trusts management console is the main utility that Network Administrators will use to manage trust relationships and, oddly enough, the UPN suffix for the forest. The default UPN suffix is that of the forest's root domain's DNS name. This is where they would establish a trust between two domains in two separate forests. The steps to take in establishing the trust relationship are as follows:

Figure 4.14 Establishing trusts for domains.

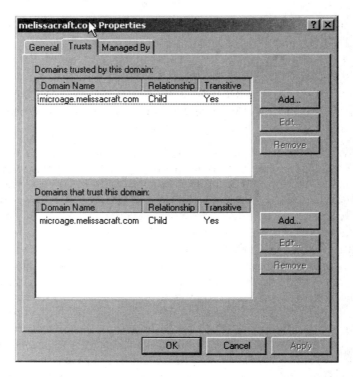

1. Click Start | Programs | Administrative Tools | Active Directory Domains and Trusts.

2. Right-click the domain to which a trust will be added.

3. Select the Properties option from the pop-up menu.

4. Click the Trusts tab. The resulting screen will resemble Figure 4.14.

5. If the domain that you are editing is the resource domain, click ADD under "Domains trusted by this domain." If this domain will be the Master, click ADD under Domains that trust this domain.

6. Select the appropriate domain, and click OK.

7. Repeat this action on the other domain to establish the trust. Both sides of the trust must be established or the trust is invalid.

Planning a Forest Structure

There are some general design principals to keep in mind when planning forests:

- Incorporate areas in the forest plan that will enable growth of the organization.

- Design as simple a structure as possible to reduce administrative overhead.

- Understand the incremental bandwidth overhead that is incurred when implementing multiple forests.

- Keep all domains that are allowed to trust each other within a forest.

- Refer to the existing network configuration and documentation to support decisions about the forest structure.

The primary purpose of the forest plan is to determine how many forests are required for the network. Since each forest can contain multiple domains, a single forest structure is typically sufficient for any enterprise network. Situations requiring multiple forests include those in which there must be separate schemas or GCs, or in which there should be absolute division in administrative authority.

For example, in a corporation that implements Windows 2000 and Active Directory to support the Internet and also implements it for the internal, private enterprise network, it may be necessary to separate the private forest from the Internet forest so that the private GC is not available publicly. Another example is when a company implements a lab network in which various technical scenarios are tested before being implemented on the production network. If changes to the schema need to be tested before being deployed, they must be tested on a separate forest, or else the changes will be made enterprisewide automatically through the multi-master replication of Windows 2000. The advantage to having a separate lab network is that most labs are confined to a single geographical area, and many do not share the same cabling and infrastructure that is used on a production network. When a lab is constructed this way, a separate forest for a lab will not impact traffic on the network to any great degree. A final reason that an organization may decide to have multiple forests is when there is a clear separation of administrative authority. In this case, a company may have two clearly separate business units that use completely separate administrative groups and change management methods. Although administration is best delegated through OUs or even through separate domains, it may become necessary to have separate forests for each of the administrative units.

When multiple forests do exist to separate schemas or GCs, there is an impact to administration. Either a trust relationship must exist between the forests and Administrators granted administrative authority in both forests, or separate Administrator accounts must be created for each Administrator who must manage both forests.

Administrators must also be aware of the impact they may have on the network within any particular forest. This necessitates a close working relationship amongst administrators and the clear communication of large

Figure 4.15 Multiple forests with interdomain trust relationships.

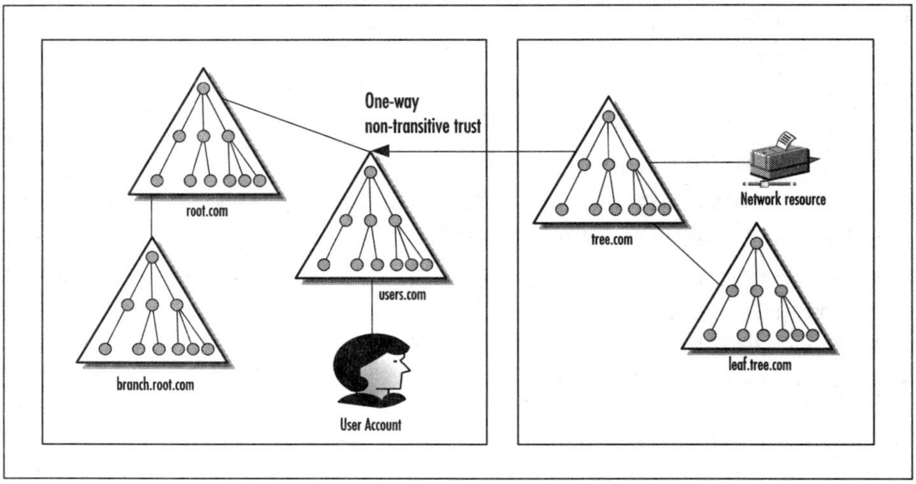

changes planned for the Active Directory. When multiple forests are involved, each one should be easily identifiable. For instance, rapidly performing moves, adds, and changes on objects within the forest creates a large amount of replication of the GC (which contains a partial copy of every forest object) among DCs forestwide. This may prevent users from logging on to the network or being able to access network resources. Additionally, every change to the schema, to the configuration container, and additions or removals of entire domains has a forestwide consequence.

Multiple forests also impact on the way in which users are able to work. If users remain within a single forest, they can browse or query the GC to find resources. The GC makes the forest structure transparent to users. When a user accesses a network resource that exists in a different forest, that resource will not be found in the GC since it is not shared. In this case, the user must be aware of the other domain where the resource exists. In addition, there must be a trust between the domain in which the resource exists and the domain where the user exists. This type of a trust is an explicit, one-way, nontransitive trust. Basically, it is the same type of trust relationship that legacy Windows NT domains relied upon. Because it is a one-way trust, the direction of the trust matters. The rule of thumb is that a domain that contains a resource must trust the domain that contains the user account, as illustrated in Figure 4.15.

Multiple forests will also affect the way in which users log on. A UPN using the format user@domain.com can only be applied to a single forest. If there are multiple forests, one will use the UPN of user@domain-one.com, and the other will use the UPN of user@domain-two.com. UPNs are stored in the GC and must be unique within the enterprise network.

Forests do not share information well outside of themselves. Administrators will have additional work with moves, adds, and changes to objects when there are multiple forests. A user account or other Active Directory object cannot be moved between forests. Instead, the objects must be cloned using a utility such as ClonePrincipal, or migrated with a utility such as LDIFDE.EXE, or manually created. Regardless of which method is used, a copy of the object remains in the original domain until it is manually deleted. Domains cannot be moved between forests, and forests cannot be merged or split. A DNS namespace cannot be split between two forests either. Finally, using multiple forests means that data cannot use the same replication topology. If multiple forests are used, data must be manually replicated and updated between them, thus increasing the administrative overhead for that network.

The Domain Tree Structure

The domain tree is a set of domains that are arranged in a hierarchical structure due to their DNS names. The forest can have multiple domain trees. Each domain in a domain tree is separate from the parent and child domains. A domain tree makes use of a single DNS namespace, enabling multiple domains to exist within it. This reduces the need for registering several DNS namespaces. For example, a company named XYZ can have seven domains in their forest, but only needs to register a single DNS namespace if all the domains are within that namespace, such as xyz.com, one.xyz.com, two.xyz.com, three.xyz.com, four.xyz.com, five.xyz.com, and six.xyz.com, as illustrated in Figure 4.16.

Figure 4.16 Wide and flat domain tree structure.

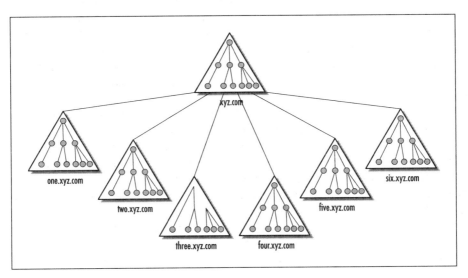

Figure 4.17 Tall domain tree structure.

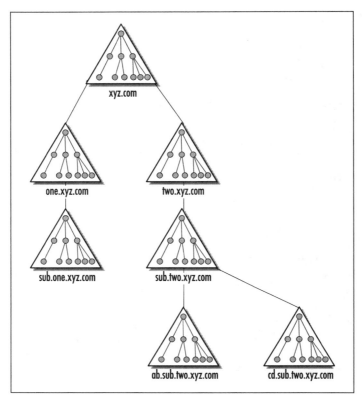

The domain tree can be wide and flat as depicted in Figure 4.16. The domain tree can also be tall, with multiple subdomains, as shown in Figure 4.17. The configuration of a domain tree is entirely up to the network designer, since the Kerberos, two-way, transitive trusts essentially make a domain tree into a group of domains that completely trust each other and trust all other domains within their designated forest.

Each domain in the Active Directory forest defines a partition of the forest's database. The partition is a subset of a larger database that is distributed to multiple DCs. This method of partitioning makes the Active Directory scalable from small to extremely large enterprise networks. In addition, it is beneficial to have redundant replicas of the domain partitions when multiple DCs exist for each domain.

A DC can only contain a copy of the database partition for its own domain. This implies that copies of different domain database partitions cannot be contained on a single Windows 2000 Server. However, the forest configuration and schema are hosted by all DCs throughout the forest.

Adding a Child Domain

Child domains are installed when the first domain controller of the child domain runs DCPROMO. When that child domain is formed, Active Directory creates a two-way transitive Kerberos trust automatically between it and the parent domain. Schema and configuration data for the forest are copied from the parent domain to the new child DC.

The relationship of a parent domain to a child domain is strictly one of the DNS subdomain name and trust relationship. For example, a parent domain in a domain tree would be PARENT.COM. The child domain would be CHILD.PARENT.COM. The trust relationship is bidirectional and transitive. An Administrator in PARENT.COM does not have administrative authority in CHILD.PARENT.COM. Instead, the Administrator in PARENT.COM must be granted administrative authority to CHILD.PARENT.COM. Likewise, group policies set in PARENT.COM are not applicable to CHILD.PARENT.COM.

Another change to the Active Directory occurs with a new child domain—a new replication topology is created. More about replication can be found later in the book.

Sizing the Active Directory Store

Each DC contains a copy of the Active Directory Store for the domain. Some of the DCs are also GC servers. They contain a copy of the GC for the entire forest. Other DCs have a copy of the forest configuration. Determining the size requirements for DCs is somewhat of an art form.

One thing to remember is that the Active Directory store does not automatically shrink in size when its objects are deleted; it typically stays the same size or grows. If space within the store is freed up, it remains available for new objects and properties to fill. Space is freed up when objects are deleted, but not immediately. Deleting an object creates a tombstone, which marks the record for deletion, but does not delete it immediately. The tombstone, which is replicated to the other DCs, has a lifetime value, known as a *tombstone lifetime*, to it. When the object reaches the lifetime value, it is physically deleted from the Active Directory Store.

The ADSIEdit utility is used to view or change the tombstone lifetime value. ADSIEdit is a Resource Kit utility that has access to the inner workings of the Active Directory. It is comparable to the regedit utility that has access to the Windows 2000 Registry. When starting the ADSIEdit utility, it will most likely not be in the area of the Registry that accesses the tombstone lifetime. In order to access the configuration container, right-click on the domain and select Settings as illustrated in Figure 4.18. Then select the Configuration container.

Once the Configuration container is visible in the left pane, navigate through CN=Configuration/CN=Services/CN=Windows NT/CN=Directory Service.

Figure 4.18 Accessing the Configuration container in ADSIEDIT.

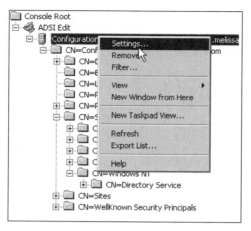

Right-click on Directory Service and select Properties from the pop-up menu. When the Properties dialog appears, under the "Select which properties to view" drop-down list, select tombstoneLifetime. To change the value, type in a number in the Edit Attribute box, and click SET.

Garbage collection is the process used to free up space. It deletes expired tombstones and defragments the Active Directory database. Each DC runs garbage collection independently of the others, and the default 12-hour value can be changed in the ADSIEdit Resource Kit utility in the same place that tombstone values are changed in the Directory Service Properties dialog. To change the garbage collection period, select garbageCollPeriod from the drop-down list and place a number in the Edit Attribute box, which is shown in Figure 4.19. Garbage collection frees up space in the database, but does not reduce the size of the database.

In order to truly reduce the size of the Active Directory store, use NTDSUtil. NTDSUtil.exe is an offline defragmentation utility, which after execution reduces the size of the Active Directory database. Note that the server must be taken offline to use NTDSUtil; consequently, it should be used sparingly.

Security principals such as user objects and groups use approximately 3.5KB of space in the database. Nonsecurity principals, such as an OU object, use about 1KB of space each. When sizing the database, count the number of security principals and multiply by 3.5, count the number of nonsecurity principals, and add the two figures. Divide this sum by 1000 to receive the number of MBs. Add approximately 1000MBs for the base size of the store. Then double the final amount to account for growth. To find what is needed for the entire server hard drive, add in the amount required for Windows 2000 Server, the amount needed for applications, and additional space for growth.

Figure 4.19 Changing the garbage collection interval.

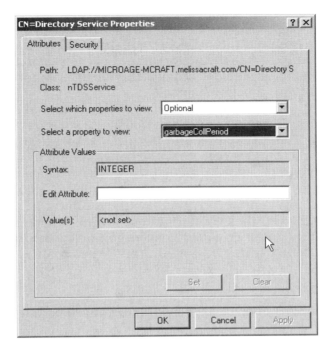

If there are 100,000 security principals and 20,000 nonsecurity princi-pals, the result will be 370,000KB, or 370MB. Added to the 1000MB, the result is 1370MB. Double this for growth and the minimum size reserved for the Active Directory store would be 2.7 GB.

NOTE

The optimal storage system for a Windows 2000 DC is a hardware-based RAID drive using RAID 5. Such a RAID system would be able to recover from a hard drive failure while the server was still running and providing services to the network. Although RAID 5 is recommended for speed and redundancy, it certainly is not a requirement. If using regular hard drives, however, performance on a DC is best if the system, database, and log files for the Active Directory are placed on separate hard drives. When these files are on separate hard drives, they can be written to simultane-ously, thus increasing performance. Not only is this helpful with speed, but this will enable a faster recovery if one of the hard drives happens to fail, since log files will assist in rebuilding the database to a current state.

Managing the Forest

The most obvious place to manage the forest is within the Active Directory Domains and Trusts management console, shown in Figure 4.20. This console, found in the Administrative Tools menu on a Windows 2000 DC, displays all of the domain trees in the forest and can view, change, or create any trust relationships that exist outside the forest. The forest's UPN format is also configured in this console.

There are many other utilities that can manage the forest aside from the Active Directory Domains and Trusts console, such as MOVETREE.EXE. This utility is found in the Windows 2000 Resource Kit utilities and is used to move objects within one domain to another domain, as long as both domains exist in the same forest.

Objects that are domain-specific, such as domain Global groups or Local groups, cannot be moved by the MoveTree utility. If MoveTree executes a move for the OU that contains these groups, then the groups remain behind in a container called LostAndFound in the domain. Some things are not objects within the domain, but are domain-specific data that

Figure 4.20 Domains and Trusts management console.

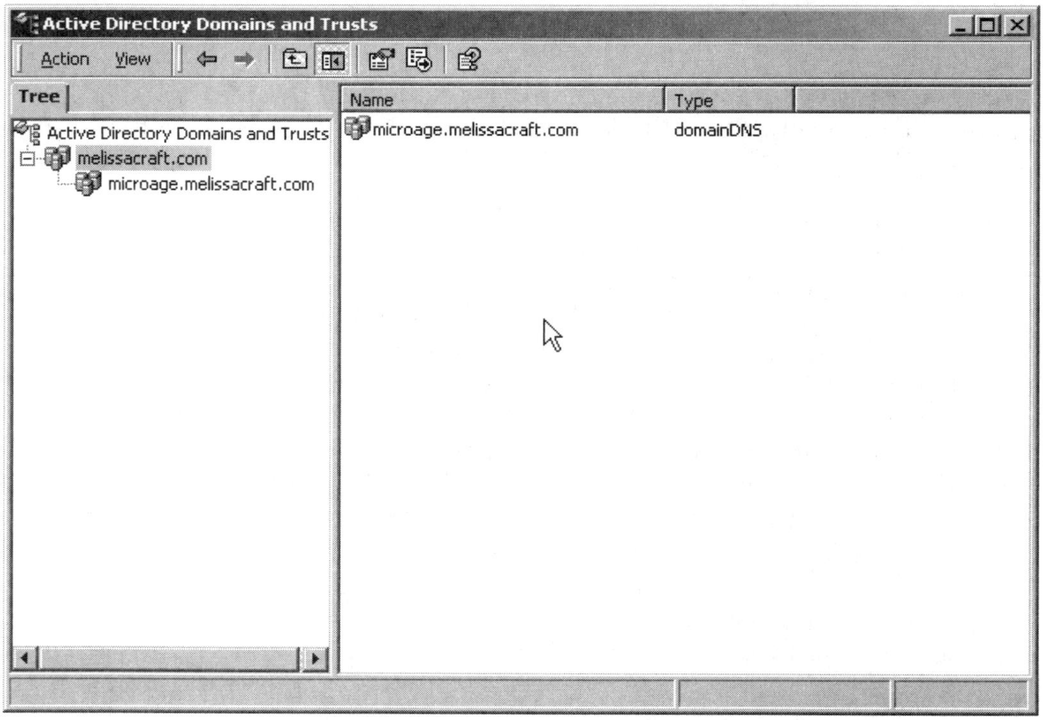

exist within the Active Directory. This includes logon scripts, policies, and profiles. These will not be moved by MoveTree either.

MoveTree is a command-line utility that can execute in batch mode. One of the switches for MoveTree is /check, which runs MoveTree but does not complete the move of the objects. Instead, it verifies that it will work. If MoveTree /check executes without errors, then the same command will be successful in /start mode. For example, if moving a user from one.xyz.com to two.xyz.com, the MoveTree command to check would be:

```
Movetree /check /s server1.one.xyz.com /d server2.two.xyz.com /sdn
cn=user,cn=users,dc=one,dc=xyz,dc=com /ddn
cn=user,cn=users,dc=two,dc=xyz,dc=com
```

If the command does not report any errors, the MoveTree command that can execute the move is:

```
Movetree /start /s server1.one.xyz.com /d server2.two.xyz.com /sdn
cn=user,cn=users,dc=one,dc=xyz,dc=com /ddn
cn=user,cn=users,dc=two,dc=xyz,dc=com
```

Another utility can be used to move objects outside a domain to any domain. The Lightweight Directory Access Protocol (LDAP) is a standard supported by the Active Directory Service. LDAP is an open standard supported by many different directory services, making it an ideal interchange point between two different directories, or even between two different forests.

LDIFDE.EXE is an LDAP Data Interchange Format utility included with Windows 2000. It can export and import objects in the Active Directory using the LDAP protocol. The process to export objects from the current domain using LDIFDE, which can be found in the WINNT\SYSTEM32 directory, is as follows:

1. Log on to a DC in the domain from which you want to export objects, as a user with Administrative authority.

2. Open a command prompt window (Start | Run | cmd).

3. Type **ldifde –f filename.ldf**, and press ENTER.

The screen should look like Figure 4.21.

The resulting file is a plain-text listing of the objects in the Active Directory. It will include records that look like the following user account object:

```
dn: CN=my self,OU=Sales,OU=All Users,DC=melissacraft,DC=com
changetype: add
accountExpires: 9223372036854775807
badPasswordTime: 0
badPwdCount: 0
codePage: 0
cn: my self
countryCode: 0
```

Figure 4.21 LDIFDE.

```
D:\>ldifde -f c:\ldifde.ldf
Connecting to "MICROAGE-MCRAFT.melissacraft.com"
Logging in as current user using SSPI
Exporting directory to file c:\ldifde.ldf
Searching for entries...
Writing out entries.................................................
...............................................................
136 entries exported

The command has completed successfully

D:\>_
```

```
displayName: my self
dSCorePropagationData: 19990816040611.0Z
dSCorePropagationData: 16010101000001.0Z
givenName: my
instanceType: 4
lastLogoff: 0
lastLogon: 0
logonCount: 0
distinguishedName: CN=my self,OU=Sales,OU=All
Users,DC=melissacraft,DC=com
objectCategory:
CN=Person,CN=Schema,CN=Configuration,DC=melissacraft,DC=com
objectClass: user
objectGUID:: SxvF1yYMEkmBBksImyTCqQ==
objectSid:: AQUAAAAAAUVAAAAiqcyPyPz9mP4n7R0dQQAAA==
primaryGroupID: 513
pwdLastSet: 125781260326329120
name: my self
sAMAccountName: myself
sAMAccountType: 805306368
sn: self
userAccountControl: 512
userPrincipalName: myself@melissacraft.com
uSNChanged: 2084
uSNCreated: 2077
whenChanged: 19990803035352.0Z
whenCreated: 19990803035334.0Z
```

The LDIFDE command used to import objects is:

```
Ldifde -i -f ldifde-ldf
```

LDIFDE can be used to perform mass changes across all objects in a particular OU or across an entire domain. The LDIFDE command has extensive capabilities for managing the Active Directory. Since LDIFDE is a command-line tool, it can be executed in batch mode. To find out what options are available, type **LDIFDE /? |more** at the command prompt.

Summary

When the first domain controller (DC) is installed on a network, so too is the first domain in the first forest of the Active Directory. The process of installing Windows 2000 Server will create a member server. The Windows 2000 Server is functional as a member server with a local database of user accounts and groups that can access and use it. However, to use the Active Directory functionality, the member server must join an Active Directory domain or become a DC for an Active Directory domain.

To install the Active Directory service, the installer can invoke the Active Directory Wizard from the Configure Your Server screen that starts when the server starts. The Active Directory Wizard guides the installer through the options for installing the Active Directory. The information required for installing the Active Directory Service includes the DNS information for the computer and its domain. DNS is required by Active Directory. DCs must be configured as DNS clients, or they must provide the DNS service itself.

Configuring DNS as a service is a simple matter of starting the DNS administrative tool, selecting the local computer, and selecting "Configure this server" from the Action menu. If the Active Directory is not installed on the local computer, however, the DNS service cannot create Active Directory-integrated zones. If the Windows 2000 Server is a DC, and is running the DNS service, it can create Active Directory-integrated zones and bring the following benefits to the network:

- It can coexist with other DNS servers.
- It automatically supports DHCP, and no DHCP-integration testing is required.
- It will support multi-master replication of the DNS within the Active Directory.
- It will be able to scavenge stale records and keep the DNS database up to date.

The DNS console application is started by clicking Start | Programs | Administrative Tools | DNS. The first task is to create a DNS zone. The second task is to create the resource records (RRs), both A, or address records, and SRV, or service location records.

The majority of the Active Directory management will occur in the Active Directory Users and Computers console. In this console, the organizational units (OUs) can be created in a hierarchical structure. New users, computers, and groups can be created within the OUs and then moved, renamed, and deleted as needed. Most actions can be executed by right-clicking the object and selecting the appropriate action item, or by manipulating the object's properties.

An Active Directory forest is a collection of multiple domains using multiple DNS namespaces. Each domain within a forest shares a common configuration, schema, and global catalog (GC). The configuration container and schema is replicated to every domain controller (DC) in the forest. The GC is a partial copy of every object in each domain that belongs to the forest.

Domain trees within a forest use a contiguous DNS namespace. A top-level domain in the domain tree would have the DNS name parent.com, and directly below it the child domain would have the DNS name child.parent.com.

Each domain within a forest is connected to others via a two-way transitive trust relationship. This results in each domain trusting every other domain within a forest.

When planning a forest, the main decision is whether or not the network will have multiple forests. Multiple forests are necessary if there is a reason to have:

- Separate schemas
- Separate configuration
- Separate GC
- Completely separated administration

There is some impact in having multiple forests on the network. Additional bandwidth is required for replication of a separate GC and Active Directory databases. Users are affected in how they work across forests. The resource domain must trust the domain that the user belongs to in order for the user to access the resource. If the resource domain is in a different forest, then the Administrator must establish that trust explicitly. Trusts between forests are one-way and nontransitive. A user must know which domain the resource belongs to and be able to query that domain directly.

Creating a domain tree in a forest is simply the process of adding new child domains using subdomains of the same DNS namespace. The tree can be wide and flat, or tall and thin.

When a new DC is added to manage a new domain, its storage space should be adequate to support the objects that will exist in the Active Directory. Storage requirements are larger for DCs that contain a copy of the GC because they will have two databases on them.

Several utilities are used to manage the Active Directory forest.

- NETDOM is used for domain trust management.
- NTDSUtil is used to defragment the Active Directory database while the DC is offline.
- ADSIEdit allows editing of specific internal parameters of the Active Directory.
- Active Directory Domains and Trusts offer a graphical view of all the domains within a forest and enables trust relationship management.
- LDIFDE is used to import and export objects from an Active Directory domain.
- ClonePrincipal is used to clone objects from a domain.
- MOVETREE is used to move objects from one domain within a forest to another domain within the same forest.

FAQs

Q: Our plan is to create a nested set of groups. We want to keep some Windows NT 4.0 domain controllers (DCs) for the first six months after installing the Windows 2000 Servers with Active Directory. Will we be able to use the nested groups right away?

A: No. Active Directory must be running in native mode, as opposed to mixed mode, in order for nested groups to work. That means that the Windows NT 4.0 DCs will need to be migrated before using nested groups.

Q: How do you switch a domain from mixed mode to native mode?

A: Click Start | Programs | Administrative Tools | Active Directory Domains and Trusts. Right-click on the domain and select Properties. The General tab should be the first screen shown. Click CHANGE MODE on the General tab page. Click YES to confirm. Either click APPLY or OK to change the mode.

Q: I am concerned about the extra traffic that multiple forests can have on wide area network (WAN) links. However, I want to have a separate forest for my lab network, which is confined to a single room. Will creating two forests, one that is confined to that room and another that is used for production, cause significant WAN bandwidth consumption?

A: No. In the situation described, the lab forest would not span any WAN links and would have no effect on the bandwidth utilized across the WAN.

Q: I have a group of people in CORAZON.COM who must access a printer in New York that is in the CARTA.COM domain in a different forest. Which domain must trust the other in order for the users to be able to print?

A: CARTA.COM must trust CORAZON.COM. Resource domains must always trust the account domain in order for the users to access the resources.

Q: We want to move the domain Global groups from one domain to another in the same forest. What is the best utility to use, ClonePrincipal or MoveTree?

A: ClonePrincipal can clone security principals, such as users and groups, from one domain into another. MoveTree cannot move domain-specific objects such as domain Global groups.

Chapter 5

Planning and Implementing Active Directory Sites

Solutions in this chapter:

Introduction

The modern world is a global village with millions of computers connected by high-speed backbones weaving a gloriously chaotic web spanning the globe. The focus of our concerns surrounding connectivity has undergone a subtle shift – the concern is no longer *if* you can connect, but *how*.

Most medium or large companies will implement Active Directory in multiple locations, spanning their directory database across disparate geographical locations. The bandwidth available to connect these locations is usually limited, raising issues such as quality of service and link saturation due to network traffic patterns. Active Directory Services brings new traffic to the network in the form of:

- Query traffic
- Authentication traffic
- Replication traffic

Consider a network with multiple offices around the globe. Some offices are close to each other and have fast network links between them with T3 lines and more than 1.5 Mbps of available bandwidth. Other offices are simply connected with slow network links such as ISDN 128 Kbps or Fractional T1 lines at 256 Kbps. There is a concern about the way the added network traffic caused by Active Directory Service may affect the available bandwidth on these connections. Using sites to delineate the divide between high- and low-speed connections can go some way to alleviating this concern.

Active Directory's method of managing network traffic centers on its use of sites. Sites are considered to be regions within the enterprise network that share high-bandwidth connectivity. In essence, they are an assembly of well-connected Internet Protocol (IP) subnets.

The Function of Sites in Active Directory

The founding rationale of sites is that they should be created based on the geography of the network, centralizing the domain controllers to which traffic should be directed. Basically, a site can be considered to be a concentration of well-connected network servers and computers in a single geographic location. For example, if a corporation had a headquarters office in Boston, Massachusetts and a satellite office in London, England, its Network Administrator should create two separate sites: one for Boston and the other for London.

Sites are very flexible and can span domains. This means that several domains, or parts of domains, can exist within a single site. This occurs when a domain design separates each domain by its location. A sample design illustrating this is detailed in Figure 5.1. When a site spans multiple domains, there is an increase in the replication traffic within that site, because multiple domain databases must be replicated in addition to the schema, configuration, and GC for the forest.

Domains can span sites, and there can be several sites within a domain. This design results from domains spanning multiple geographic locations, as illustrated in Figure 5.2.

Sites are specific to a forest, meaning that if there are multiple forests in the same location, a site must be created in each forest for that location. There are few limitations on how a site or domain is designed, and sites can be created, deleted, or changed at any point in time, which may result in a rather confusing arrangement. In fact, a single forest can have sites spanning domains, and domains spanning sites, as shown in Figure 5.3.

Sites are not part of the DNS namespace; they simply set a geographic boundary for managing network traffic. Sites determine the proximity of network computers for those that are sending Active Directory-based data, such as replication, authentication, and query traffic. For instance, clients will be directed to DCs within their designated site when authenticating or querying.

Figure 5.1 Sites span domains.

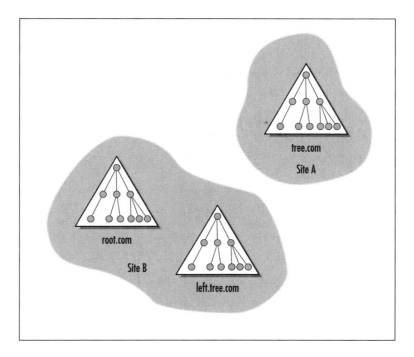

Figure 5.2 Domains spanning sites.

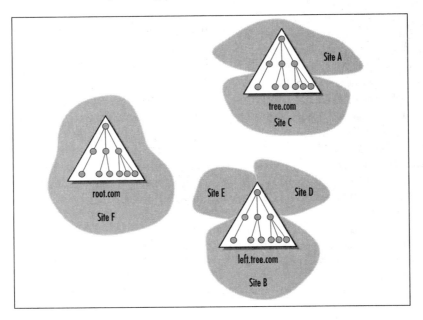

Figure 5.3 Domains and sites spanning each other.

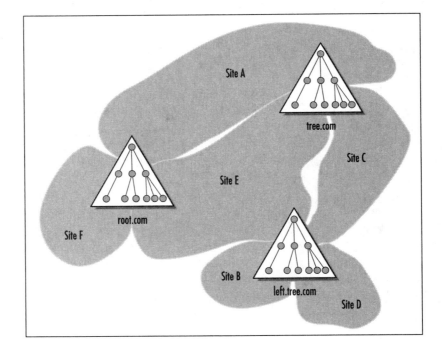

Default-First-Site-Name

Amazingly, or maybe not so amazingly, the first DCs that are installed within the Active Directory are automatically placed within a site called Default-First-Site-Name, as shown in Figure 5.4. This can be viewed in the Active Directory Sites and Services utility found in Administrative Tools.

Figure 5.4 Default-First-Site-Name.

The Default-First-Site-Name name can be changed by opening Active Directory Sites and Services and selecting rename after right-clicking Default-First-Site-Name.

Replicated Active Directory Components

Several components within the Active Directory must be replicated. Some of these are replicated solely within a domain, whereas others are replicated to all parts of a forest.

Domain Partitions

The Active Directory database is partitioned for each domain. The DCs maintain a replica of the partition for their own domain and no other. This replica is identical to all other domain replicas until an Administrator makes a change to the domain. At that point, the change is replicated to all other domain replicas. The domain partitioning enhances performance for the database, since smaller database parts enable faster response to queries and more efficient processing.

Using Figure 5.5 as an example, if a change is made to a user account in tree.com, the replication is only affected in tree.com. Neither leaf.tree.com nor trunk.tree.com are impacted. The sites that are affected with the update replication are site A and site C. Sites B and D are not affected because they do not contain any DCs for tree.com.

Figure 5.5 Domain partitions.

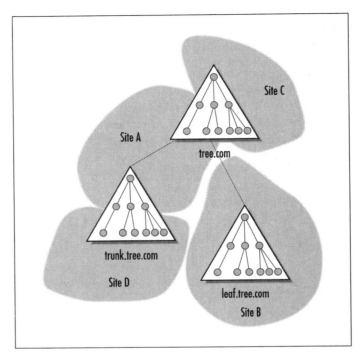

Global Catalog

When there is a single domain within the Active Directory, there is no real need for a GC server since all users have the same context (and User Principle Names (UPNs) are not required), and Universal groups are mostly useful in distributing objects between domains (and so would not be required). The entire Active Directory forest is represented by the GC, which is a database that contains a partial replica of every object in each Active Directory domain within a single forest. The GC provides a single database to search for users or resources.

Any DC can be designated as a GC server. Because the GC server provides logon authentication for UPNs and the source data for queries, there should be at least one per site to retain query traffic within the site boundaries. Additionally, Universal groups publish their entire group memberships within the GC. If there are thousands of users within a Universal group, the GC will increase tremendously. However, if nesting global groups within Universal groups, then the published membership in the GC is greatly reduced even though the membership within the Universal group is the same.

To designate a server as a GC server, use the Active Directory Sites and Services utility. Expand the Sites container by clicking the plus (+) sign to

Figure 5.6 NTDS Settings for a GC server.

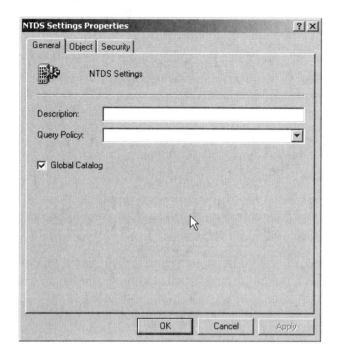

the left of it. Expand the site that contains the server, then expand the Servers folder, and then expand the server itself. Below the server there is an item called NTDS Settings. Right-click NTDS Settings and select Properties from the pop-up menu. In the Properties dialog, check the box for Global Catalog server, as shown in Figure 5.6.

Schema and Configuration Containers

All DCs in an Active Directory hold a copy of the schema and the configuration for their designated forest. Both the Schema and Configuration containers must be replicated to ensure consistency throughout the entire forest.

Modifying the Schema

We know that the Active Directory is a database that uses multi-master replication with a list of objects that it can contain. Whenever a new object is created, it is selected from that list. Each object has its own attributes, such as a user account First Name. This list of objects and all their possible attributes makes up the *schema*.

Active Directory is an extensible system. The originally installed list of objects can grow over time to include others. New applications can be cre-

For IT Professionals

Think Twice Before Modifying the Schema

Modifying the schema is an advanced administrative right for a good reason. There are impacts and potential problems that can raise their ugly little heads whenever a change is made. The issues revolve around:

- Creating invalid objects in the Active Directory
- Replication impacts to the network

No one intends to create invalid objects. Consider the following example, a user account named Joe has an attribute called Spouse that the Administrator added to the schema. The value "Mary" was then placed into the Joe object instance. Later on, it is decided that the Spouse attribute is not required, so the Administrator deletes it from the schema. Joe's object is not like the rest because it has the Mary value in an attribute that does not exist. Active Directory lets Joe's object remain in the forest, but it does not clean up the invalid attribute. Instead, the Administrator must perform a query and delete that attribute manually.

Replication is affected whenever a schema change is made. That change is replicated to every domain controller (DC) in a forest. Latency inherent in the propagation process and exacerbated by replication schedules will cause a temporary inconsistency in the schema between various DCs. Objects that are created during the inconsistency period can be replicated before the schema changes, which results in a failure. Active Directory responds to the failure by initiating a new, explicit schema replication from the DC where the schema was changed.

A level of control can be exerted over who can modify the schema by controlling who belongs to the Schema Admins global group in Active Directory.

ated to take advantage of its existing schema, and they can create new objects or properties of objects to be added to the schema. Network Administrators may want to add attributes to objects to meet their own specific business requirements. Whether an application or an Administrator makes the change, this process is called *extending the schema.* Extending the schema can have a significant impact on your Active Directory configuration, so it is important to understand the consequences of schema changes.

The schema defines classes of objects and their attributes for the Active Directory. An object class is simply the type of object, such as a user account, and all its applicable attributes, such as the user's first and last names. When the Active Directory is populated with objects, the new objects are considered *instances* of the object class.

Each object class contains both Mandatory and Optional attributes. The attributes also have a syntax, which explains what type of data can be contained in an instance of the object class. The postalCode attribute for an instance of a user object can only have a numeric value; therefore, its syntax is string (numeric).

The definitions of the Active Directory objects and attributes are contained in schema objects. A classSchema object defines an Active Directory object, and an attributeSchema object defines an attribute. When a classSchema object lists attributes under mustContain, those attributes are mandatory.

Schema Management Console

The Schema Management console is a Resource Kit utility that enables the Schema Administrators to access and change the schema in the Active Directory using a graphical interface. Not only does it enable the Schema Administrators to edit or create schema object classes and attributes, it also lets them select which object classes and attributes should be available in the GC.

In the Schema Manager, the left pane displays the scope of the schema, and the right pane displays the results. The top container, or node, in the left pane is the root node containing the forest schema, and the two below it are the class node and the attributes node, which contain schema specifiers for classes and attributes, respectively.

Flexible Single Master Operation

Make sure that the Schema Manager console specifies the Operations Master for the schema of your forest. The Operations Master for the schema is a role that is granted to a single DC for making updates to the schema. Only one DC at a time can occupy this role. After the changes are completed, they are replicated to the remaining DCs in the forest. To see the Operations Master role, open the Schema Manager console, right-click on Active Directory Schema Manager root, and select Operations Master from the pop-up menu. Make sure that the box for "The Schema may be modified on this server" is checked. Checking this box sets the value "Schema Update Allowed" to 1 under the Registry key HKLM\System\CurrentControlSet\Services\NTDS\Parameters. This method of enabling any DC to be a single master of the schema is called the Flexible Single Master Operation model, or FSMO (pronounced FIZZ-MO).

TIP

The Schema Manager is not a utility that shows up in any menu, and can only be found in the Resource Kit utilities. First, the Resource Kit must be installed. Then, open the Schema Manager (schmmgmt.exe) and select the Console menu. Click Save As and save the file to the Documents and Settings\<your username>\Start Menu\Programs\Administrative Tools directory. You may rename the file from schmmgmt to Schema Manager at the same time.

There are five FSMO roles in Windows 2000:

Schema Master   Controls schema updates.

Domain Naming Master   Controls all the additions and removals of domains from the Active Directory.

RID Master   Controls the allocation of Relative IDs (RIDs). Relative IDs are allocated as a sequence of numbers to each domain. The RID is concatenated with the domain's SID (Security Identifier) whenever a new object is created, and then assigned to the new object as a unique object SID.

PDC Emulator   In mixed mode, the primary domain controller (PDC) emulator controls backup domain controller (BDC) replication and backward compatibility. In native mode, the PDC emulator controls password updates.

Infrastructure Master   Controls group-to-user references, so that updates of group memberships are propagated throughout the Active Directory.

You can view various FSMO roles whenever you see the Operations Master option in an Active Directory console menu or pop-up menu.

How to Modify the Schema

The schema can be modified through the addition, deletion, or updates to any objects or attributes within it. The schema is the structure of the Active Directory and manages how the content of the Active Directory is presented to users, Administrators, and applications. When changes are made to the schema, the Active Directory validates the changes to make sure that the entire Active Directory database retains integrity.

Class

It is recommended that you create attributes before creating classes, so that new attributes can be designated as Mandatory in the class. A new class can be created without creating any new attributes, however. Before creating a new class of object in the schema, the information listed in Table 5.1 should be determined.

Table 5.1 Object Class Information Needed for New Object

Class Object Dialog Options	LDAP Property Name	Function	Example
Common name	Cn	Name of the class of object. This name must be unique in the schema.	My Object
LDAP Display	LDAPDisplay Name	This name, similar to the common name, is used by programmers and is guaranteed to be unique. It has a format of being multiple words concatenated with capitals separating each word, but the first letter being lowercase.	myObject X.500 Object ID
X.500 OID	object Identifier	This is a unique number where each set of numbers is separated by a period. It is guaranteed to be unique worldwide for standard object classes since it is usually issued by a standards organization, including the ISO, ITU, and ANSI. If creating a new class, the OID (Object ID) can be obtained from these standards groups. It is not recommended that you make up a number for this, since it could conflict with other classes that are added later.	1.1.111. 111111. 1.1.111
Parent Class	Poss Superiors	The class from which the new class will inherit default attributes. If a new object is a subclass of Person, it will inherit all the Person attributes. Person is a subclass of top, and inherits all the top attributes.	ParentClass

Table 5.1 *continued*

Class Object Dialog Options	LDAP Property Name	Function	Example
Class Type	objectClass	The class type is an X.500 class type. There are three from the 1993 X.500 definition:	Abstract Auxiliary Structural
		Abstract Template class for all three types of classes.	
		Auxiliary List of attributes that can be included in Structural and Abstract classes.	
		Structural True object class that will enable new objects to be created within Active Directory.	
		There is one class type from the 1988 X.500 definition: 88. 88 does not have the same structure as the other classes, and is not available within Active Directory.	

Follow these steps to create a new class in the Schema Manager console:

1. Right-click the Classes Node in the Schema Manager.

2. In the pop-up menu, click Create Class…

3. A warning will appear; click CONTINUE to bypass it.

4. In the Create New Schema Class dialog box illustrated in Figure 5.7, complete the information that was listed in Table 5.1, and click NEXT to continue.

5. In the next dialog, you can select the attributes that will be part of this class. For any attributes that an Administrator *must* fill out when creating one of the instances of this object, add them to the Mandatory section by clicking ADD next to the section and selecting the attributes. Add any discretionary attributes to the Optional section by clicking ADD next to the Optional section. You do not need to add any attributes, although some will be added by default.

6. Click FINISH to create the object.

7. Expand the Classes node by clicking the plus sign to its left in the scope pane.

Figure 5.7 Create New Schema Class dialog.

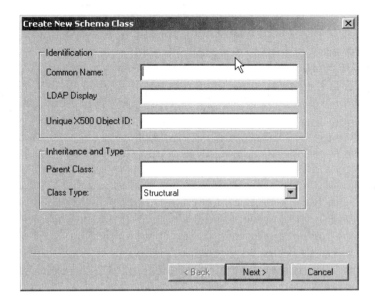

8. Under the Classes node, locate the new object and select it. The Results pane will display all the attributes that were added, along with many that are automatically defaults of that type of class. The attributes that are inherited are displayed with the name of the parent class in the Source Class column.

Once a class has been created, it can be modified by right-clicking the class and selecting Properties. The resulting dialog allows the Administrator to change the selected attributes, the description, the possible superiors, and security. It also lets the Administrator deactivate the object or enable it to be browsed in the Active Directory by checking the boxes for these options on the General tab. Note that some of the properties are grayed out, and therefore cannot be changed. These include the Common Name, the X.500 Object Identifier, and the Class Type.

Inheritance occurs when one object class is designated as a parent to another. This designation enables the attributes of that parent class to flow down to the child class. For example, if making a new class a child of a User class, all the attributes of Users will be available as part of the new class. To change the inheritance of the object or the attributes that it uses by default, select the Relationship tab. Click Add next to Auxiliary classes in order to select a list of attributes that should be included in this class. Then select an Auxiliary class from the list of available schema objects and click Ok. The new attributes will be added to the defaults in the results pane when you are finished.

To add the inheritance from parent classes, click ADD next to the Possible Superiors box, and "Add a class" from the list that appears. After clicking OK for either of these operations, the possible superior's or auxiliary class's X.500 Object Identifier will appear in the window.

To select or deselect attributes for the class, click the Attributes tab. You cannot add or remove any Mandatory attributes, but you are able to add or remove Optional attributes, even if they were added during the object's creation. The process is the same as during the creation of the class.

NOTE

The objects in the original Active Directory schema cannot be deactivated; however, those that are added later can be. Deleting a schema object is not supported by the Active Directory because of the inconsistencies that could result. Deactivation is the next best thing since the object class is unusable, but the instances of the class can still exist, just not be newly created.

The object class can be deactivated by checking the box in the Schema Manager. The object class can be reactivated by unchecking it later.

When a class is deactivated, it cannot be added as an instance afterward. Those existing instances cannot be modified. Queries made by users, or deletions of the Active Directory instances, can still occur as though nothing has happened.

After deactivation, schema updates will only modify the isDefunct attribute of the schema object. The isDefunct attribute is set to true when the object is deactivated. No other modifications will be made except for that isDefunct attribute value.

Attributes

When creating a new object class that includes new attributes, it is recommended that the attributes be created first. Then, the new class can use the new attributes immediately upon creation. The attribute requires the same common name, Lightweight Directory Access Protocol (LDAP) display name, and Unique X.500 Object Identifier that is required by a new class object. Additionally, the new attribute will require the information contained in Table 5.2.

Table 5.2 Required Information for a New Attribute

Dialog Options	Purpose
Syntax	The syntax determines what type of information can be contained. This field is a drop-down list with several options, including Octet string (such as an IP address) and Boolean (true and false values).
Minimum	This is the lower limit on the syntax's value. For example, if using an Integer syntax, the default lower limit is 0, but placing 1 here will eliminate 0 from being used.
Maximum	This is the maximum limit on the syntax's value. If using a String syntax, the maximum limit would be the length of the string. Placing 50 in this field would limit a String syntax attribute to 50 characters.
Multi-Valued	When checking this box, it means that the attribute can have a one-to-many relationship with the resulting properties. For example, a multi-valued item is the Possible Superiors attribute. There can be many superior class objects. However, each Boolean attribute (true/false) can only be single-valued, since an item should not be true and false at the same time.

In order to create a new attribute, you must start with the Schema Manager.

1. Right-click on the Attributes node in the Scope panel.

2. Select New Attribute.

3. Click CONTINUE to bypass the warning.

4. The Create New Attribute dialog box will appear. Type in the Common Name, LDAP Display, and X.500 OID, as well as the information determined for the items in Table 5.2, and click OK.

5. The object will be created and will appear in the Results window in the Attributes node.

6. The attribute can be modified somewhat after it is created. This is done by double-clicking the attribute in the Results pane, or right-clicking it and selecting Properties. Note that the Common Name, X.500 OID, and Syntax are grayed out and cannot be changed. There is a statement about whether the attribute is multi-valued or single-valued, and that cannot be altered either. The remaining items can be updated.

Schema Container

The Schema container holds the entire schema, inclusive of attribute and class definitions. It must be replicated to each DC that is part of the same forest. The Schema container is located in the Configuration container, at cn=Schema, cn=Configuration, dc=mysubdomain, dc=mydomain, dc=com. The Schema Configuration container cannot be viewed with the default Windows 2000 Active Directory tools; however, it can be seen using the following Resource Kit utilities:

- Schema Manager
- ADSI Edit
- LDP

The first time that ADSI Edit is executed, the user must connect to a naming context. This requires right-clicking the ADSI Edit container and selecting "Connect to" from the pop-up menu. The ADSI Edit tool must be pointed to the schema in order to see it. This requires right-clicking the root and selecting Settings, then changing the Naming Context to Schema.

The Cache

When a DC initializes, it reads the schema from the Schema container into memory. This version of the schema sitting in RAM is called the *schema cache*. Whenever changes are made to the schema, they are validated against the schema cache rather than the schema on the hard drive to enhance performance. Whenever replication or changes are made, they are first made to the schema on the DC's hard drive and then are automatically updated in the cache five minutes after the first change was made. The file on the hard drive that initializes the schema when it is first installed is the SCHEMA.INI.file located in %systemroot%\ntds. The Active Directory database is the NTDS.DIT that is located in the %systemroot%\ntds directory by default. NTDS.DIT contains the entire Active Directory, including schema and GC.

The tables in the schema cache are called ATTCACHE and CLASSCACHE, and represent each attribute and class in the schema. There are hash tables of ATTCACHE and CLASSCACHE to enable lookups in the cache. The table sizes are dynamic, based on the number of items (attributes and classes) that exist in the schema. The table sizes increase or decrease based on the schema changes made.

The schema cache is updated every five minutes. This means that changes made to the schema may not appear immediately. To update the schema cache from the hard drive without waiting for the five-minute interval to pass, in the Schema Manager, right-click the Active Directory Schema Manager root node and select Reload the Schema.

Schema Utilities

The Schema Manager is not the only utility that can update the schema, although it is probably the most user-friendly. LDIFDE and CSVDE are two command-line tools that can also update it, as well as ADSI Edit.

LDIFDE and CSVDE are two data format exchange utilities. The first, LDIFDE, uses LDAP Data Interchange Format. The second, CSVDE, uses a Comma Separated Value. Both of these utilities take files that contain data to be added or modified in (LDIFDE can modify, CSVDE can only add) the Active Directory, then import it to the Active Directory. Both of these utilities can also export directory data from the Active Directory.

It is recommended that the Schema Manager be used to update the schema. But for die-hard command-line utility users, the following is an LDIFDE file format representing an addition to the schema. Because CSVDE does not have as many features as LDIFDE, it is recommended that LDIFDE be used for the command-line format tool.

```
dn: CN=myAttribute,CN=schema,CN=configuration,dc=microage,dc=melissacraft,dc=com
changetype: add
objectClass: attributeSchema
ldapDisplayName: myAttribute
adminDisplayName: my-attribute
adminDescription: A new schema attribute
attributeID: 1.2.840.113557.8.8.999
attributeSyntax: 2.5.5.12
omSyntax: 64
isSingleValued: TRUE
systemOnly: FALSE
searchFlags: 0
showInAdvancedViewOnly: FALSE
```

Querying the Active Directory

The schema affects end users in a fundamental way. It provides the basic layout of information about users, computers, and other Active Directory objects. This layout is copied fully within each domain and partially to the forest's GC.

First, an attribute has to be replicated to the GC. This is accomplished in the Schema Manager by double-clicking any attribute and selecting "Replicate this attribute to the Global Catalog."

Display Specifiers

The user interface can be specified for each object within the Active Directory. The user interface information is stored in an Active Directory object called a *display specifier*. The storage of the user interface information (UI) plus the ability to secure who sees which attributes allows the Active Directory to adapt to the needs of both end users and Administrators.

For example, a Network Administrator JUDY may create a display specifier for CUBE NUMBER as an attribute for a user account that only Administrators need to see. The PAYROLL business unit may also want to add display specifiers for SALARY and VACATION HOURS, but would not want JUDY to see the values for those fields. Both JUDY and the PAYROLL unit can add the display specifiers and then apply security to them so that JUDY cannot see SALARY and VACATION HOURS, and PAYROLL cannot see CUBE NUMBER.

Display specifiers are Active Directory objects stored in cn=Display Specifiers, cn=Configuration, dc=mydomain, dc=com. They include property sheets, context menus and icons, and more. Display specifiers are available in the ADSI Edit utility.

Configuring Site Replication Components

Several components must be configured within an Active Directory forest in order to enable replication:

- Site objects
- Connection objects
- Site links
- Site link bridges
- NTDS Settings

Creating Site Objects

A site object represents an Active Directory site. A site is a set of well-connected IP subnets, implying that the subnets are linked together and have substantial bandwidth available to those links.

There are no hard-and-fast rules regarding which links are considered well-connected and which are not, so designating an IP subnet to a particular site can be somewhat of a confusing decision. The characteristics of sites can help make this decision. Microsoft designed sites to reduce bandwidth consumption between sites, yet still enhance performance of the replication topology.

Workstations attempt to contact DCs within their own site for logon. The Knowledge Consistency Checker (KCC) will designate more replication connections between DCs within a site than with DCs in other sites. When replication occurs between different sites, the replication traffic is compressed to reduce the bandwidth consumption. Where replication occurs within a site, the replication traffic is not compressed to increase the speed of processing the replication. Finally, the replication within a site is triggered whenever a priority change is made to the domain database, as well as on a default five-minute interval, and replication between sites occurs based on a preset schedule.

The first DC installed is placed in the Default-First-Site-Name. All other DCs are placed within the same site as the first DC, or into a site designated as the default site for the Active Directory forest. If another site is created that contains an IP subnet to which a new DC's IP address belongs, the new DC will automatically join the other site rather than the default site. After installation, new DCs can be a member of any single site within the Active Directory.

Creating Connection Objects

A connection object represents the flow of replication between DCs within a site. Connection objects are found below the replication target DC, and they point to the replication source DC. In this way, the connection object flows in a single direction. The only way to have replication occur in both directions is to create two connection objects, one for each target DC.

An Administrator can create a connection object, or it can be created by the KCC on the destination DC. The KCC connection objects are created automatically and are sufficient for replication. The only time that an Administrator needs to create connection objects manually is to reduce latency. The KCC will not delete any manually created connection objects, nor will it create a duplicate connection object where a manually created one exists.

Creating Site Links

Without site link objects, DCs in different sites would not be able to communicate. Site link objects guide traffic between sites using a protocol, such as IP or Simple Mail Transfer Protocol (SMTP). Each site link object represents a link of a particular type and all the attached sites to that link, and should have an equal cost. For example, a Frame Relay network may have several sites attached to it, and that Frame Relay network would be represented by a single site link object.

The site link object contains information such as availability for replication, cost of using the link, and how often replication can occur for the link, as shown in Figure 5.8. The site link object offers a way for the Active Directory to understand how to use the connection. Site link objects are used to connect DCs from different sites together.

The properties that influence how a site link object is used are:

- Cost
- Replication frequency
- Schedule of availability

Cost is the logical expense of using a site link object. When a cost number is high, then the logical expense of the messages is high, and that cost of messages is directly translatable into the amount of bandwidth that is available for them. Microsoft designed replication to select a link more frequently for low-cost messages and less frequently for high-cost messages.

Figure 5.8 Site Link Object properties.

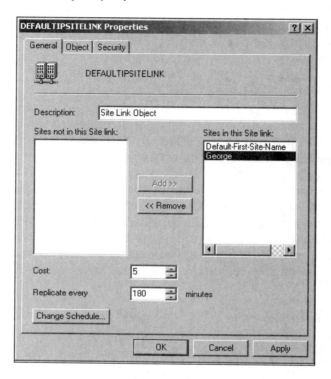

In routing scenarios, cost is traditionally established in inverse proportion to frequency or priority of a link's usage. Since the site link object represents an actual network connection, replication frequency should be increased as the cost decreases in any particular object. When this value is configured, provide a value for the number of minutes, between 15 and 10,080 minutes. When there are redundant site links representing redundant network connections, the Active Directory will select only the site link with the lowest cost.

Less bandwidth = higher cost = less frequent replication

The schedule can intervene in an automatic replication system by simply setting up whether the link can be accessed. The schedule enables the link for certain blocks of time, then disables it during the remaining hours.

Creating Site Link Bridges

A site link bridge object creates a forwarding system, which models multiple segment routing, between site link objects that have sites and protocols in common. A site link bridge cannot exist between site links that have no mutual sites. When a site link bridge is created, the cost of the site links is additive. Be aware that in a fully-routed network it is not required to create site link bridges manually.

Figure 5.9 Joe's Parts, Inc. site link bridge.

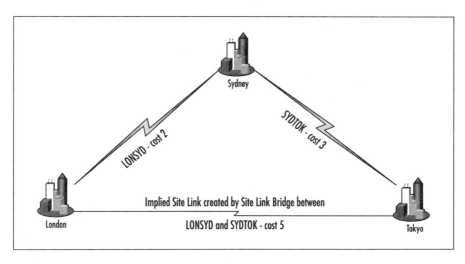

For example, Joe's Parts, Inc., shown in Figure 5.9, has three sites: one in London, one in Sydney, and the third in Tokyo. Joe's Parts' Administrator creates a site link between London and Sydney called LONSYD, and another site link between Sydney and Tokyo called SYDTOK, because those site links represent the WAN links on the network. To ensure that replication will flow through from London to Tokyo, the Administrator must create a site link bridge between LONSYD and SYDTOK. If LONSYD has a cost of 2 and SYDTOK has a cost of 3, then the site link bridge has a cost of 2+3=5.

Replication Protocols

Two protocols are used for replication traffic:

- Remote Procedure Calls (RPCs) over IP
- SMTP

RPCs over IP are used for traffic within a site between DCs over connection objects, and for replication traffic between sites across site links. RPCs are a Session-layer API that executes applications on remote computers, but appears to be executing them locally. RPCs can be executed over other protocol stacks, such as VINES and IPX. However, in the Active Directory, RPCs are only supported when executed over IP. In order to execute an RPC, the underlying network protocols must be in complete working order. If a DC's network interface card (NIC) or DNS configuration is not working correctly, an RPC error may result.

IP seems an obvious choice for a replication traffic protocol, but SMTP is not. SMTP was selected as the protocol to use solely for intersite (between

Figure 5.10 Site links are created within the appropriate Transport container.

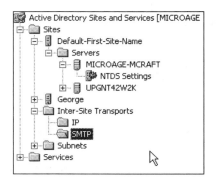

sites) replication. SMTP, in this case, is asynchronous and appropriate for slow or low-bandwidth WAN links. SMTP-based replication is not supported for sites that contain DCs from the same domain; it only can be used to replicate GC, schema, and configuration data. Site links and site link bridges are created below the transports they utilize, as shown in Figure 5.10.

Replication in Active Directory

The function over which sites have the most control is replication. Replication is an essential component to distributed database systems such as the Active Directory. When copies of the database exist in multiple locations, and a change is made in one copy, the other copies must be synchronized with that update. The synchronization of updates is accomplished through replication. The result is that users are able to access the Active Directory at any time, in any site or domain within the forest. Replication in the Active Directory will:

- Select efficient connections and site links
- Use multiple routes through the internetwork to provide fault tolerance
- Minimize the cost of replication by updating only the changed information
- Provide a method of conflict resolution

Replication will occur between any two DCs with the minimum of the Schema and Configuration containers being replicated. Replication between any two GC servers includes the schema, configuration, and GC. Replication between two DCs within the same site consists of the schema, configuration, and domain database. If those two DCs are also GC servers, then the replication traffic will have schema, configuration, domain database, and GC.

Figure 5.11 Setting up a bridgehead server.

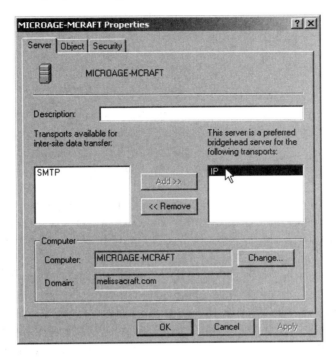

Replication traffic will treat bridgehead servers with preference. A bridgehead server in a site will receive all updates from within the site and exchange those updates with other sites via site links and site link bridges. The bridgehead server will receive replication traffic from other sites and then replicate that to DCs in its own site. To establish a server as a bridgehead server, in the Active Directory Sites and Services management console, right-click the server and select Properties from the pop-up menu. Click on a transport (either IP or SMTP), and then click ADD to make this server a bridgehead server for the selected transport, as shown in Figure 5.11.

Replication Topology

The replication topology is the configuration of connections within a site, and the site links between sites. The intrasite (connections inside a site) configuration is automatically generated by the KCC. The KCC is a service that operates on each DC. It creates the connection objects between DCs that are located within the same site, and executes every 15 minutes to reconfigure the replication topology.

The KCC ensures that replication occurs by reviewing the replication topology and creating additional connection objects to provide redundancy or to overcome a failure in the replication. To do this, the KCC attempts to establish a replication topology that includes a minimum of two connection objects to each DC. Although the KCC automatically generates a replication topology, it can be overwritten by an Administrator creating new connection objects. The replication topology manages how DCs communicate with each other.

The replication topology between sites can be manually created by an Administrator. The use of bridgehead servers and site link bridges can enable an efficient design. Scheduling the intersite replication can further make the replication topology effective.

Each naming context has its own replication topology. This is mainly due to the fact that each context has a separate place to be replicated to.

- The schema and the configuration's naming context applies forest-wide, so they share a single replication topology across all sites and domains.
- Each domain has a separate naming context, and its replication topology applies across all DCs within it, and any sites to which they may belong.

The replication topology is built on top of the sites in a single forest. There is no replication between forests. Within each naming context, a bidirectional ring is created and the spanning tree algorithm is used to prevent routing loops of replication traffic when redundant links exist.

The optimum site topology is one in which domains and sites are in a one-to-one correspondence. For example, if domain A is completely within site A, and domain B is completely within site B, the intersite traffic only consists of GC, schema, and configuration information, and the intrasite traffic is limited to a local domain plus the GC, schema, and configuration traffic.

If a site consists of four DCs that are within the same domain, the replication topology resembles Figure 5.12. Note that in these diagrams, wherever one or more double arrows exist between DCs, two connection objects must exist, one in each direction.

The replication ring for a single site with two domains in it is more complex. This replication topology demonstrates the incremental bandwidth overhead of sites that span multiple domains. The replication topology is depicted in Figure 5.13.

The replication topology becomes more intricate as multiple sites are added. As you have seen in each of the previous figures as well as the following, there is no stated path for the GC namespace. GC replication is somewhat counterintuitive, since the data for the GC will simply follow the same path that the domain namespace follows. Figure 5.13 illustrates a replication topology for two sites that each contain DCs from two separate

Figure 5.12 Replication topology in same site for same domain.

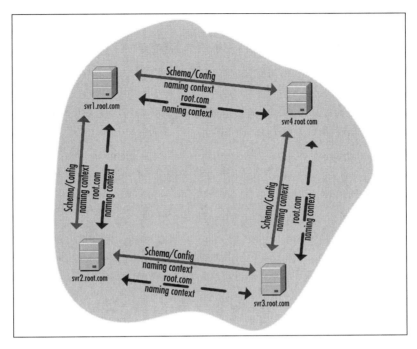

Figure 5.13 Replication topology in single site for two domains.

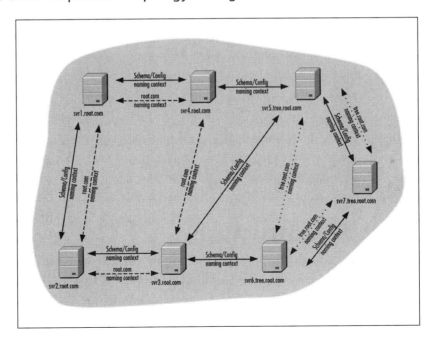

domains. Note that in Figure 5.14, two DCs in each site have been designated as bridgehead servers.

Figure 5.14 Replication topology for two sites with two domains.

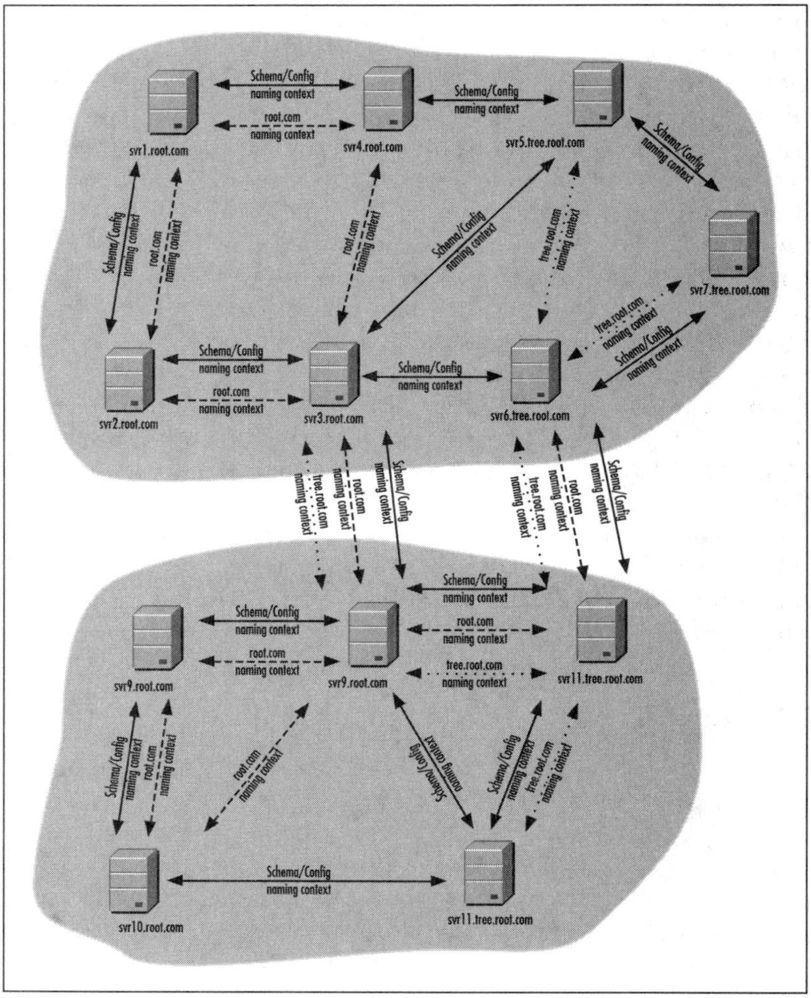

Planning a Site Structure

One of the first planning decisions is whether to establish multiple sites, and if so, how many. Separating the network into sites gains the following:

- Traffic from workstations and servers is localized.
- Replication traffic is optimized between DCs.

- Response performance from DCs is increased, typically resulting in reduced response time.
- Overhead traffic is reduced over WAN links.

All of these items translate into enhanced performance from the perspective of the end user. The reasons to create a new site would be to gain performance and reduce overhead on the network. A site should only be created separately from the default site if it has a DC dedicated to it, since otherwise it would not be involved in the replication topology. A separate site should be created for any office that has enough users to rate a dedicated DC. A site that has more than 30 users probably would benefit from having a DC. A site with less than five users would probably not. These are only suggested guidelines. The actual decision to place a DC and create a new site is one built of business requirements, usage, and performance requirements.

Site links should be created to provide reliability and fault tolerance to the intersite replication topology. A single site link is sufficient to send data between two separate sites. However, multiple redundant site links can make the topology fault tolerant.

When planning the site structure, the main organizing factor is the physical network infrastructure. The infrastructure is typically built to mirror the geography of the organization's places of operation. For example, Grape Drapes has its headquarters in Paris, a manufacturing plant in Florence, and sales offices in New York and London as depicted in Figure 5.15. The infrastructure would most likely have a hub-and-spoke configuration, with links between Paris and all other locations. A single domain could encompass the entire corporation, and separate sites dedicated to

Figure 5.15 Grape Drapes' network infrastructure.

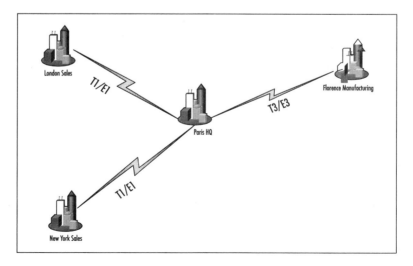

each location would be most effective to centralize traffic. Since the KCC automatically generates each site's internal replication topology, the only thing that must be planned are the site links, site link bridges, and bridge-head servers between the sites.

In the Grape Drapes scenario, there are three WAN links, for which three site links should be created. Remember, a site link represents a network connection and the sites involved in that connection. Each link will require cost and frequency of replication. Florence has the fastest link to Paris with the T3/E3 link, whereas the other two links have much less bandwidth in T1/E1 links; therefore, the Florence cost should be lower and the frequency should be higher. The New York sales office is not available for replication during 10 A.M. to 2 P.M. in order to reduce the cost of the overseas link. The three site links can be created as shown in Table 5.3.

Table 5.3 Site Links for Grape Drapes

Site Links	Cost	Frequency of Replication	Schedule
London–Paris	5	45 minutes	Available all hours
NY–Paris	5	45 minutes	Available 12:00 A.M.–10:00 A.M. and 2:00 P.M.–11:59 P.M.
Florence–Paris	1	20 minutes	Available all hours

This will enable replication to occur between any site and Paris, but does not enable replication traffic to occur between New York and Florence, New York and London, or London and Florence. To enable this type of connection, site link bridges must be created. The site link bridges should use Paris as the site in common. Since the network is not fully routed, site link bridges in Table 5.4 would be created for Grape Drapes.

Table 5.4 Site Link Bridges for Grape Drapes

Site Link Bridge	Site Link 1	Site Link 2	Cost
London–NY	London–Paris	NY–Paris	10
Florence–London	Florence–Paris	London–Paris	6
NY–Florence	NY–Paris	Florence–Paris	6

WARNING

SMTP is asynchronous, and will normally ignore the schedule set on the site link properties. The only time that the SMTP site link schedule should be set is when the underlying network link itself is only live during certain time periods.

Placing Domain Controllers

There should be at least one DC in each site. This will provide an efficient localization of traffic for queries and authentication. Every site should have at least one site link associated with it.

Each site has to be associated with a subnet in order to be functional. Since a site is defined as a collection of well-connected subnets, each subnet associated with the site will automatically place a client workstation, server, or DC that is on that subnet into the site. It is recommended that the sites and their subnets are designed and implemented prior to installing any machines; except, of course, for the first DC in that forest.

When using a firewall, or when a site is connected to other sites only through a low-bandwidth network connection, a bridgehead server should be designated for intersite replication traffic. If using any SMTP-based site links, then a Certificate Authority (CA) service must be installed in the forest. The CA signs the SMTP packets, which enables their acceptance by the receiving DC.

Where to Place Global Catalog Servers

There should be at least one GC server on a DC in each site. The main issue with the GC is how large the forest is: the larger the forest, the larger the GC, and the greater the replication traffic. This replication traffic is simply between GC servers.

When there are fewer GC servers, there is less replication traffic, but there is more traffic for queries and authentication from workstations. When there are more GC servers, there is more traffic for replication, but less for queries and authentication from workstations. Replication traffic can be controlled between sites via the frequency and scheduled availability for the site link, so the most effective placement of GC servers is to ensure at least one server in each site.

Another issue to consider when placing GC servers is that there will need to be an Infrastructure Flexible Single Master Operations (FSMO) server for the forest. This Infrastructure FSMO cannot be run on the same

DC as the GC. Since the Infrastructure FSMO is "flexible" and can be changed from DC to DC as needed, each site that may possibly host the Infrastructure FSMO must also have a separate DC for the GC.

The GC cannot be run on the same DC as the Infrastructure FSMO because the FSMO is responsible for cleaning up stale references from objects in its domain to objects in other domains of the forest. The stale references are those objects that have been moved or renamed. This means that the local data is out of sync with the GC. The only way that the two can synchronize is by the FSMO server verifying the objects' validity against the GC. If the Infrastructure FSMO and GC are housed on the same server, it will never recognize any references as stale, and cleanup will not occur.

Implementing a Site Structure in Active Directory

Implementing sites is accomplished through the Active Directory Sites and Services management console found in Administrative Tools. Since the first DC in the forest automatically created the Default-First-Site-Name site, then the console will display this site.

After that first DC is installed, the entire site structure can be created before installing any other domains and DCs.

The following examples use Bland Blinds as an example organization with the network infrastructure and designed site structure shown in Figure 5.16.

The first item is to rename the Default-First-Site-Name. Since the first DC installed is la1.blandblinds.com, then the site name should change to LA. In the Active Directory Sites and Services console, right-click Default-First-Site-Name and select Rename from the pop-up menu. Then change the name to LA.

The next thing we can do is create the PHX and LON sites. In the Active Directory Sites and Services console, right-click the Sites container and select New Site. Type in the name for PHX, and select a site link—DEFAULTIPSITELINK is fine for now, we will edit the site links later. Then click OK. You should see a dialog similar to the one shown in Figure 5.17. Click OK to bypass it. Repeat this procedure for the LON site.

The next step is to add the correct IP subnets to the site. Even though the Default-First-Site-Name was used as the LA site, it will not have any IP subnets assigned to it. Right-click the Subnets container and select New Subnet. In the LA site, one of the subnets is 10.10.10.0. Although it is not listed here, the subnet mask is 255.255.255.0. In the New Object-Subnet dialog shown in Figure 5.18, type in the address and subnet mask, click on LA in the Site Name box, and click OK.

Figure 5.16 Bland Blinds' network infrastructure.

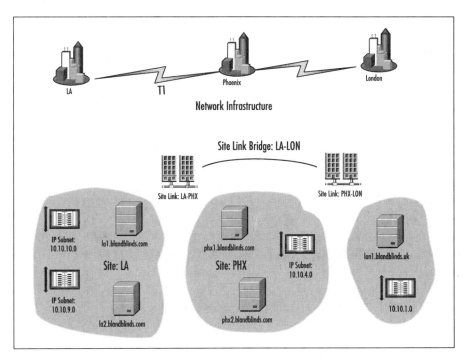

Figure 5.17 Create an Active Directory site.

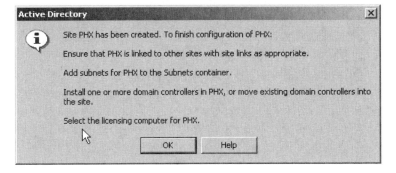

The name will build as you type in the subnet mask; it is merely a different notation for subnetting that is commonly used for Variable Length Subnet Masking (VLSM). The /24 represents the number of bits assigned to the subnet mask. To generate the remaining IP subnet objects, repeat this process and assign the subnets to the appropriate sites. The final IP subnet set for Bland Blinds should resemble those shown in Figure 5.19.

Figure 5.18 Create an IP subnet object.

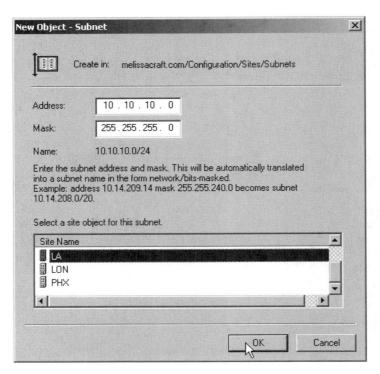

Figure 5.19 Resulting IP subnets for Bland Blinds.

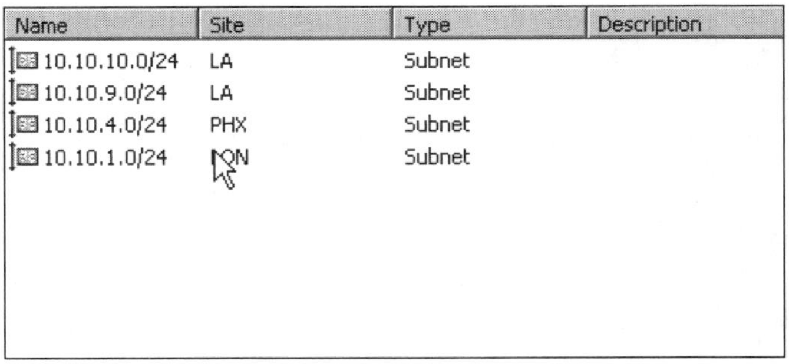

Name	Site	Type	Description
10.10.10.0/24	LA	Subnet	
10.10.9.0/24	LA	Subnet	
10.10.4.0/24	PHX	Subnet	
10.10.1.0/24	LON	Subnet	

After assigning the IP subnets to the sites, the next task is to create the two site links: LA-PHX and PHX-LON. It will be assumed that the links are approximately equal in bandwidth availability, and that they will be IP site links and have a cost of 7 and a replication frequency of 60 minutes. (Please note that these figures were arbitrarily selected for this scenario.)

Figure 5.20 Site link creation.

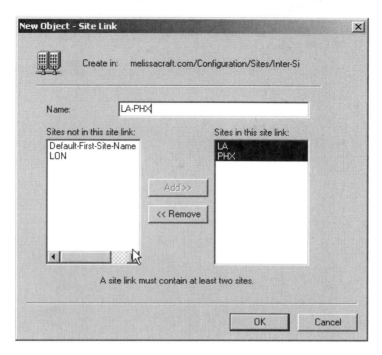

To create a site link, in the Active Directory Sites and Services console, expand the Sites container, then expand the Inter-Site Transports container. Right-click the IP container and select New Site Link. In the dialog box, select the LA site and the PHX site, and click ADD to incorporate them into the site link. At the top of this dialog box, name the site link LA-PHX as shown in Figure 5.20, and then click OK. Repeat this process for the second link.

To change the cost and frequency of each site link, double-click it to display the Properties, as shown in Figure 5.21. Change the Cost from the default value to 7. Then change the value of the frequency from the default value to 60. Click OK to complete the configuration, and repeat for the other site link object.

Now that site link objects are configured, if a site link bridge is needed from LA to London, it can be created. This is a nearly identical process to creating a site link. In the same IP container below the Inter-Site Transports container, right-click the IP container and select New Site Link Bridge. In the resulting dialog, similar to that shown in Figure 5.22, select each of the new site link objects in the left-hand pane and click ADD to move them to the right pane. Give the site link bridge a name, and click OK.

Figure 5.21 Site link configuration.

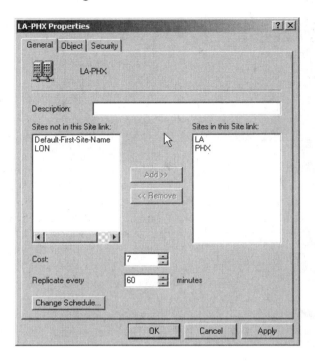

Figure 5.22 Site link bridge creation.

Replication Utilities

Once replication has been configured, how can an Administrator verify that it works? Microsoft provides utilities to monitor and manage the replication for the Active Directory.

Replication Monitor (REPLMON)

The replication monitor is provided with the Windows 2000 Resource Kit utilities to view the replication topologies and monitor the traffic. It is a graphical tool that uses icons to represent server roles, such as a globe to designate a GC server, and their status, such as a red X to indicate a replica that is out of date. The Administrator can select which DCs to monitor by selecting the Edit menu and the Add Site/Server option.

This utility enables the Administrator to specify the naming contexts and sites, then track each naming context's replication traffic for each DC by creating log files. Statistics are placed in the log files for each replication partner and each replication topology (for example, naming context level).

Administrators should use the replication monitor after establishing the site structure to verify that it is working. If testing various site structures, which is entirely possible given the fact that sites are easily moved, changed, or deleted, Administrators can use this tool to validate the best replication topology set for their environment.

Replication monitor also serves as a troubleshooting tool. If there are persistent errors with replication, or if there are bandwidth utilization concerns, the replication monitor can provide the statistics. The replication monitor can be used to recalculate the replication topology by triggering the KCC. Additionally, if a naming context appears to be out of sync on separate DCs, the replication monitor can be used to force a synchronization.

Replication Administrator (REPADMIN)

REPADMIN is a command-line tool used to diagnose replication problems between DCs. This tool can provide the same functions as replication monitor; as a command-line tool, it is less intuitive, although it can produce some very precise results.

DSASTAT

Although not specifically geared toward replication or sites, the DSASTAT command-line tool can help diagnose problems with naming contexts. This tool would be used if there were no obvious source of problems from the replication monitor log files.

DSASTAT compares naming contexts on different DCs. Additional statistics regarding the Active Directory store capacity, at a granular level, can further detect divergence of replicas.

Understanding Time Synchronization in Active Directory

Time synchronization is an important subject in distributed databases. One reason is that most distributed databases use a "last write" date and time-stamp to determine which change should be considered final when there are conflicts.

If, for example, a change is made on a replica in New York at 3:08 P.M., and another change is made on a replica in Los Angeles at 12:09 P.M. (which would be exactly one minute after the New York change given the time zones), the change that would "win" during replication would be the change made in Los Angeles. However, if the DC's time clock had drifted to 12:07 P.M., the New York change would win. A change to a user object that was made in error at one site and then corrected on the other site could be the difference between that user being able to log on the next day or not. This is not the best situation, especially if that user happens to be a vice president of a corporation, which that user always seems to be when these types of glitches occur.

So how does time synchronization work with the Active Directory? The goal of time synchronization is to eliminate the consequence of drifting computer clocks and enable a common time for all participants on the internetwork. Common time does not necessarily refer to correct time, such as the atomic clock can provide. Rather, a common time is simply the same designated date and time that all computers agree upon. Keep in mind the following factors that are looked at by Active Directory when evaluating a conflict in replicated data:

1. The version number of an attribute has changed. If a user's password is changed in two locations (once by the user, once by the Admin), the attribute's version number is incremented by 1 on that DC. The change with the highest version number wins during a conflict. If the version numbers are equal such as when the changes are made within two different sites, then...

2. The change timestamp is evaluated. If the timestamps are equal, then...

3. The Globally Unique IDs (GUIDs) of the originating write Directory Service Agents (DSAs) are evaluated.

Active Directory reaches this goal through the W32TIME service running on Windows 2000 Servers. A simple command, NET START W32TIME, will start the service, which is implemented as SNTP (which is described in RFC 1769 and is available on each Windows 2000 Server or Professional machine). The service designates two types of machines:

- Time servers
- Time clients

The first installed DC acts as a primary SNTP server. Other DCs are also time servers for all time clients. Time servers implement synchronization between sites when Active Directory replication initiates a connection between DCs. If the time server is pointing to another Active Directory-based time server, the time source can be validated, but this cannot happen if pointing to a standard SNTP time server.

Time clients contact the time servers at logon. There is a five-minute difference in time allowed by Kerberos. Time is checked in eight-hour intervals after logon to verify time compliance. If the time client's clock is off, it will adjust its clock to match the time server's clock, log the change into its event log, and cut the interval check to every four hours.

The legacy NET TIME command is still available, but is not the same as the SNTP-compliant W32TIME service. However, NET TIME can use NTP services.

Summary

A site is defined as a set of IP subnets that have a high amount of bandwidth available between them. The purpose of a site is to localize traffic from queries, authentication, and replication. Replication is the process of synchronizing all the copies, or replicas, of the distributed Active Directory database. Queries and authentication traffic is generated at the will of clients. Replication traffic occurs actively and frequently within a site, but can be managed through intervals and scheduled availability between sites. Because of the nature of replication traffic, sites typically define a single geographic location.

When planning a site structure, make sure to place at least one domain controller (DC) and at least one global catalog (GC) server (they can be the same server) in each site. The configuration that will have the least amount of traffic between sites is that where sites and domains are in a one-to-one correspondence. This ensures a minimum of intersite and intrasite traffic, making this an optimum topology.

The Active Directory schema is the underlying layout for the Active Directory database. It is comprised of classes of objects and attributes. The objects that are within the Active Directory are instances of the schema classes. The properties of these objects are the schema attributes.

The schema is replicated in its own container, which is located in the Configuration container, to all domain controllers (DCs) within a forest. Each DC loads the schema into a memory cache. The only group that has access to the schema is the Schema Admins group. There can only be a single DC with the capability to extend the schema, since it uses the Flexible Single Master Operations (FSMO) method. FSMO lets any DC become the Operations Master for the schema, but only one DC at a time.

Additions and modifications to the schema can be made in several utilities:

- Schema Manager console
- ADSI Edit
- LDIFDE
- CSVDE

When a new class or attribute is added, it should have the complete information documented prior to its implementation, since the schema safety and consistency checks will not allow some changes to be made to the attribute or class after its creation. Classes and attributes cannot be deleted, but they can be deactivated. Classes and attributes within the default schema that Active Directory starts with cannot be deactivated. When a new attribute is created, it must be replicated to the global catalog (GC) in order for users to search for objects based on that attribute. This is available as a property of the attribute. Users and Administrators can easily search for objects within the Active Directory Users and Computers console.

The replication topology is the configuration of the physical flow of information between DCs. Each naming context (schema, configuration, and domain) has a separate replication topology. Replication traffic increases when sites span two or more domains. The Knowledge Consistency Checker (KCC) generates the replication topology within a site by creating a bidirectional ring for each naming context. Each direction in the ring is represented by a one-way connection object that can be found below each DC.

The replication topology between sites can be manually created by an Administrator. The Active Directory Sites and Services console is used to create the replication topology. Within it:

- Sites are created and assigned to a transport type, currently IP or SMTP.
- IP subnets are created and assigned to sites.
- Site links are created to connect those sites that have actual network connections between them.
- Site link bridges are created to connect sites by hopping over sites in common when two sites do not have network connections between them.
- Servers can be moved into sites, or if installed after the site has been assigned IP subnets, they will install into the site that contains their IP subnet.

Three utilities can assist in managing replication traffic:

- Replication Monitor—REPLMON
- Replication Administrator—REPADMIN
- DSASTAT

These tools are capable of monitoring traffic on selected DCs, as well as forcing a replication synchronization and other troubleshooting options.

Time synchronization has an impact on replication in that if all Active Directory DCs do not agree on a common time, then updates may be applied out of order, resulting in possible logon failures and other access problems. Time synchronization is handled through the W32Time service, which is an SNTP-compliant time service. There are both time servers and time clients in this service. Time servers synchronize on a common time setting. Time clients check with time servers at logon to validate their time. If a time client is not synchronized, it will update its clock and log the event.

FAQs

Q: I would like to test three different site topologies on a production network. Can I do this, or must I select one and stay with it?

A: Sites are easily created and changed as needed. They were developed that way to incorporate growth and change within an organization. Therefore, any number of site topologies can be tested before selecting the optimal version. This, however, does not apply to a domain structure, since domains cannot be merged, split, or easily deleted.

Q: I made a change to the schema, but the change did not appear on the network right away. Why is that?

A: What you see when you look at the schema is actually the schema cache in RAM of the DC. When changes are made, they are made to the schema located on the hard drive. There is a five-minute interval for the schema cache to be updated by the changes made to the schema on the hard drive. This interval can be bypassed by manually reloading the schema from the Schema Manager console.

Q: How can I change the schema FSMO to the current DC?

A: In the Schema Manager console, right-click the root and select the Operations Master. If the current DC is not listed, click CHANGE and select the current DC. Then, return to the Operations Master dialog and select "The Schema May Be Modified on this Server."

Q: We have three sites: site A is in Phoenix, site B is in Mexico City, and site C is in Vancouver. Both Mexico City and Vancouver have WAN links to Phoenix. Since there is no network connection between Mexico City and Vancouver, how do we enable replication between those two sites?

A: This can be enabled by a site link bridge. A site link bridge is generated by connecting at least two site links that have at least one site in common. It duplicates a multihop routing system for the replication traffic.

Q: We want to limit the number of servers that can send replication traffic between two sites. Can we?

A: Yes. Designate each server that is allowed to transmit replication traffic as a bridgehead server.

Q: We do not want to use the automatically generated intrasite replication topology. Can we delete and create some different connection objects without the KCC reconfiguring them later?

A: Yes. The KCC will not change or delete any connection objects that were manually created by an Administrator. In order to reduce the cost of administration for replication, use the KCC-generated site topology. Whenever a manually generated connection object is created, an Administrator would be required to analyze each change to the site's configuration (such as a new DC) and make appropriate changes to the connection objects.

Q: We would like to use a third-party time service that is SNTP compliant. Is this possible?

A: Yes, an SNTP-compliant time source can be used as the primary time server with the W32Time service.

Q. How can you filter group policy for a group of users that exists in an organizational unit (OU) with other users so only the first group receives the group policy and the rest do not?

A. When you want to apply a group policy object to a group of users that exists within an OU and it is not feasible to move that group into its own OU, you can rely on applying rights to filter the group policy. To filter a group policy for a select group, edit the properties of the group policy object. Click the Security tab, and then remove the Authenticated Users group from the ACL. Add the selected group and make sure to grant the Read and Apply Group Policy permissions. This will provide an effective filter.

Q. Where are my group policy objects? They don't appear as objects within their applied containers?

A. Group policy objects are stored in two places: in the GPT folder below SYSVOL on each replicated DC's hard drive, and within the System\Policies container in the Active Directory. The System container is not available by default in the Active Directory Users and Computers console. To view the System container and the Policies subcontainer, you can select Advanced Features from the View menu of the Active Directory Users and Computers console.

Chapter 6

Advanced Active Directory

Solutions in this chapter:

- **Introduction**
- **Interfacing with Active Directory**
- **Microsoft's Metadirectory**
- **Implementing a Disaster Recovery Plan**
- **Recovering a Failed Domain Controller**
- **Troubleshooting Tips**

Introduction

Active Directory is full of subtle nuances usually only unearthed over time by the adept. As your Active Directory infrastructure matures and your requirements grow, a number of more complex technical issues will cross your path, such as: How do I interface with Active Directory? How do I get other directory services to interface with it? Can I automate Active Directory tasks? How does an LDAP query access Active Directory?

Other issues not so subtle, but equally as important, also need to be considered. Disaster recovery is a critical element of any infrastructure plan and should be an integral part of your design and management processes. Not all advanced Active Directory concepts are technically complex, but it does help to have a level of experience beyond that of an Active Directory neophyte.

Interfacing with Active Directory

It's no secret that there are directory services other than the Active Directory. These directories can be accessed in a number of ways, with some methods based on protocols, while others are based on application programming interfaces (APIs). Using these methods, two or more directory services can be synchronized. Understanding these methods will assist in managing and synchronizing multiple directory services. Methods include:

- Active Directory Services Interface (ADSI)
- Remote Procedure Calls (RPC)
- Windows Sockets (Winsock)
- Distributed Component Object Model (DCOM)
- Exchange Active Directory Connector (ADC)
- Microsoft Directory Service Synchronization for Novell (MSDSS)

ADSI

Active Directory Services Interface (ADSI) is a set of COM programming interfaces aimed at providing a well-documented API that can access and manage multiple directory services (including the Active Directory). It can be used by Network Administrators to automate Active Directory tasks, and by developers to connect their applications to the Active Directory. ADSI has been gaining momentum within the industry, and it has been adopted by vendors to enable connectivity between their directories and ADSI-enabled applications. Broadly speaking, ADSI is to directory services what ODBC is to databases: It provides open interfaces to multiple providers.

Four ADSI objects are capable of extending a directory service schema. They are called schema management ADSI objects.

- **Schema container** Contains the target directory service schema.
- **Class container** Defines object classes for the target directory service.
- **Property object** Defines object attributes for the target directory service.
- **Syntax object** Further defines the syntax used for a property object.

In addition to schema management objects, ADSI has directory objects that represent the directory service components. There are two types of directory objects: container and leaf objects. Container objects include namespaces, country, locality, organization, OU, domain, and computer. Leaf objects include users, groups, aliases, services, print queues, print devices, print jobs, file service, file shares, sessions, and resources.

To manipulate a property value, ADSI uses two commands: GetInfo to read information about a directory service object and refresh cache from the directory, and SetInfo to establish new information for a directory service object to ensure it is written to disk.

Windows 2000 ships with a scripting host, Windows Scripting Host (WSH), which supports Visual Basic Script and JScript out of the box. The combination of WSH and ADSI provides an incredibly powerful tool to "get inside" Active Directory and automate tasks that in previous versions of Microsoft operating systems were almost impossible. Minimalist command-line batch files can be forsaken for the smoother and more flexible advantages of JScript and VBScript. It is now a snap to create Active Directory-enabled scripts that can use both Windows and Internet Explorer.

ADSI uses its own naming convention so that the object can be identified regardless of which namespace it will be ported to. For example, the directory is identified in a string called AdsPath along with the container and object names. A user named Joe in an Active Directory OU named Sales and a domain called XYZ.COM would have an AdsPath of:

```
LDAP://cn=Joe,ou=Sales,dc=XYZ,dc=com
```

If you wanted to use ADSI to log on to Active Directory, you could use a script similar to the following:

```
Dim dsobj As IADsOpenDSObject
Dim dom As IADsDomain
Set dsobj = GetObject("LDAP:")
Set dom = dsobj.OpenDSObject("LDAP://DC=XYZ,DC=COM", "MyUser",
  "password", ADS_SECURE_AUTHENTICATION)
```

Another ADSI script can be used to run a backup of Windows 2000 computers.

```
Set cntnr = GetObject("LDAP://OU=Sales, DC=XYZ, DC=COM")
Cntnr.Filter = Array("computer")
For each comp in cntnr
    Comp.BackupNow()
Next
```

The following sample script could be used to add users to the Active Directory.

```
Set ou = GetObject("LDAP://OU=Sales,DC=XYZ,DC=com")  '—— Bind to target OU  ——
Set usr = ou.Create("user", "CN=Bart Johnson")       '—— Create user object ——

'—— Mandatory Attributes——
usr.Put "samAccountName", "bjohnson"

'—— Optional Attributes, you can optionally skip these——
usr.Put "sn", "Johnson"
usr.Put "givenName", "Bart"
usr.Put "userPrincipalName", "bjohnson@xyz.com"
usr.Put "telephoneNumber", "(555) 123 4567"
usr.Put "title", "Knower of all things"
usr.SetInfo                                          '—— Apply changes     ——

usr.SetPassword "startup password"                   '—— Set password      ——
usr.AccountDisabled = False                          '—— Enable account    ——

usr.SetInfo                                          '—— Apply changes     ——
```

RPC

RPCs are a Session-layer API that makes remote applications appear to be executing locally. The activity of an RPC is completely transparent to the end user. At the Session layer, RPC is able to run over other lower-level protocols such as IPX, Vines, NetBEUI, and TCP/IP. RPCs may use other interprocess communications to access remote systems, including named pipes and Winsock.

An application that uses RPCs can place portions of the application on different computers. This is the definition of true client/server networking, in which a server can execute part of the processing and the client executes the remainder. The components of an RPC-enabled application include the items listed in Table 6.1.

Windows Sockets

Windows Sockets, also known as Winsock, is a standard interface based on the original Berkeley Sockets interface specification. The intention of sockets was to enable multiple applications to be able to access and use the same network connection, consequently sending data across a network from two or more separate applications. Winsock standardized this system further, and can work over the NetWare-compatible (IPX) protocol, as well as TCP/IP.

Table 6.1 RPC Components

Component	Component Full Name	Function
Proc Stub	Remote Procedure Stub	Packages the calls to be sent to a remote server by RPC RT.
RPC RT	RPC Run Time	Manages the communications between local and remote computers.
APP Stub	Application Stub	RPC RT sends RPC requests to APP Stub, which then unwraps the package and sends the call to a remote procedure.
Proc	Remote Procedure	The procedure called by the network.

DCOM

DCOM, or the Distributed Component Object Model, is actually a form of network-aware object linking and embedding. It has grown to be a software development system wherein software objects can be reused and/or replaced. Each object represents multiple sets of functions, with each set being considered an interface. The reason why more than one interface can be supported by a DCOM object is that any change or addition to an interface can only be achieved with the creation of a new interface.

Exchange Server Active Directory Connector

The ability to synchronize accounts between disparate systems can prove to be extremely useful to the underpaid and overworked Administrator—at times, this facility can almost cut workload in half. A symbiotic relationship between Windows NT and Exchange Server enabled mailboxes and Windows NT accounts to be synchronized. However, with an upgrade to Windows 2000, Exchange Server can no longer use the same mechanism to synchronize accounts. Though the mechanism has changed, the same functionality has been carried over to Active Directory, allowing Exchange Server to synchronize using the AD connector.

The technical requirements for deploying the Exchange Server Active Directory connector are:

- For each Active Directory domain, plan to have at least one Active Directory Connector server.
- Exchange Server 5.5 must be installed with Service Pack 2, at a minimum.
- Exchange Server's LDAP port must be changed to a port number that will not conflict with Active Directory.

- If upgrading a Windows NT domain, first complete the upgrade to Windows 2000 before implementing the connector in order to avoid duplicate accounts.
- Whenever possible, place the Active Directory connector server on the same subnet as the Exchange Server bridgehead to Active Directory.

If a single Active Directory domain is connected to a single Exchange site, the requirements are simplified: a single Active Directory connector with two primary connection agreements (each connection agreement is configured from its starting point), one pointing at Exchange from Active Directory, the other pointing at Active Directory from Exchange. Even though the connection agreement is configured from a starting point, it can designate either one-way or two-way traffic. Select two-way if you are unsure which your connection should be.

When two Active Directory domains are connected to a single Exchange site, a decision must be made as to which domain will be the primary connection for Exchange. To avoid confusion over which is the master over the connection, always designate the domain closest to the root of the Active Directory forest to be the primary connection.

When there are multiple sites and multiple domains, there can be any number of complex arrangements for connections. In these situations, planning is essential to ensure that redundant connections do not end up creating multiple duplicate accounts in either Exchange or Active Directory. There should only be one primary connection pointing to each Active Directory domain. Likewise, there should only be one primary connection pointing to each Exchange Server site.

Designated bridgehead servers should be assigned for the connections between Exchange and Active Directory. When designating a bridgehead server for Exchange, select any servers that are solely used as gateways or "connector servers" first. After that, select a server that is well-connected to the network and has available resources for the connection processing overhead. When designating a bridgehead server for Active Directory, select (in order of preference) a global catalog (GC) server first, a DC second, and a member server last. Also select a server that is well-connected to the network and has available processing resources.

To install the Exchange Server Active Directory Connector, look on the Windows 2000 Server CD-ROM for the \valueadd\msft\mgmt\adc directory.

Execute the setup.exe program to begin the Active Directory Connector Installation Wizard. When prompted for the component selection, select both the Microsoft Active Directory Connector Service and Microsoft Active Directory Connector Management components. Specify the install folder for ADC. Finally, designate a service account to manage the connection, and then finish the wizard.

After the installation has completed, there will be a new program in the Administrative Tools menu called Active Directory Connector Management. This is the program used to configure the connector. Open it, right-click the Active Directory Connector Management object, and select Properties from the pop-up menu. The default properties for information originating in Exchange and for information originating in Active Directory will be available in this dialog after creating a new connection agreement. To create a connection agreement, right-click the Active Directory Connector for your server, select New, and then Connection Agreement.

After configuring the connector, you can create new users in Active Directory or new mailboxes in Exchange, or change information to verify that communication is taking place.

Synchronizing with the Novell Directory Service

Microsoft Directory Synchronization Services (MSDSS) is a connector between Novell's Novell Directory Services and Microsoft's Active Directory that enables synchronization from either directory service to the other. MSDSS also connects to legacy Novell NetWare bindery servers, but will only send data to those binderies in one direction. It will not receive updates from a Novell NetWare bindery server.

MSDSS requires that there is at least one Active Directory DC to manage the MSDSS synchronization. It also requires a Windows 2000 (Professional or Server) machine to run both the MSDSS client and the Novell Client32 redirector. This second machine acts as a gateway between the two directory services, taking information in the form of updates from one directory service and passing it on to the other. Because the gateway runs the Novell Client32 redirector, MSDSS is capable of synchronizing passwords between the two directory services while maintaining a secure environment.

Microsoft may have developed the Active Directory, but they did not create it in a vacuum. Microsoft made every effort to ensure that the Active Directory would be representative of Internet standards, and be able to interoperate with third-party applications. It should also be wryly noted that MSDSS, though targeted at providing support for heterogeneous environments, doubles as an excellent NDS to the Active Directory migration tool.

Microsoft's Metadirectory

Many enterprise networks have a common set of business requirements for their networked systems, including:

- Single logon and synchronized passwords across systems to simplify network access from the user's perspective, translating directly into a reduction in support overhead.

- Propagation of human resources information throughout multiple systems during the enrollment of new staff. This provides the dual ability to grant network access and revoke it as required.
- Single global address book containing current information, including e-mail addresses regardless of the messaging system used.

Metadirectories have come to the fore in networked environments due to the proliferation of directory databases. The average enterprise has approximately 10 directories residing in their multiple network operating systems, databases, groupware, PBX telephone systems, and infrastructure operating systems. For example, when a new employee is hired, a company may need to enter that employee's data into an HR database, a security badge database, the PBX voice mail system, an electronic messaging application, Novell Directory Services, a legacy Windows NT domain, the Active Directory, and so forth.

Confusion often mounts over the differences between synchronization services and metadirectories. Synchronization is the process of ensuring that when an Administrator makes a change to one database, that change is synchronized across all other databases. This is like multi-master replication among dissimilar databases. As unlikely as it seems, this is a common system already developed for many messaging systems. It enables global address books from different vendors to be synchronized when a change is made to one of those vendors' directories. This type of synchronization is traditionally implemented through gateway or connector software.

A metadirectory, on the other hand, is a superset of all directories. Primarily, these directories manage identity information, but many of them extend into other resource information, such as data, files, printers, shares, applications, policy rules, and so on. Not all directories have common content, but most have a commonality in the identity of users who are allowed to access this information, as shown in Figure 6.1.

The metadirectory is actually a directory itself, or an index, of all the information that can be synchronized between these various databases. There are two approaches to metadirectory products:

- Identity information index
- Single point of administration

The identity index approach enables centralization of the common identity information from the various databases mapped to each other. In the early development of metadirectories, this approach is most common. The single point of administration approach includes a further extension into the security aspects of the various directories by including the resource information and the rules that apply to how users are granted access to those resources. Regardless of which approach is used, the capability of managing identity from a single point is a major administrative process

Figure 6.1 Identity management with a metadirectory.

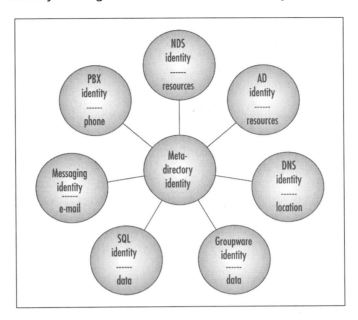

improvement over the problems incurred through managing an average of 10 directories containing information about the same user identity.

The challenge with metadirectories is to establish rules to manage the updates when they can be initiated from any one of the directories. The question at hand is, "which directory owns that particular identity attribute?" For example, is it more sensible to have the messaging database own the e-mail address, or the SQL database? Probably the messaging database should own that piece of information. That means, if an Administrator made a change to the e-mail address on a SQL database, and another Administrator made a change to the messaging database, the change that would win is the messaging database e-mail address. This is achieved by establishing the messaging database as the master of the e-mail address attribute, whereas other databases are slaves to the messaging master.

Microsoft acquired Zoomit Corporation, a company that developed metadirectory technologies, in 1999. This acquisition enables Microsoft to implement a metadirectory that is able to access and interact natively with the Active Directory, and to work with other directory services. Such directories include:

- Messaging address books
- DNS and DHCP databases
- Third-party directory services
- Database directories
- Mainframe and minicomputer account managers

In essence, a metadirectory enables an Administrator to have a single interface into multiple directory services, and manage those directory services using intelligent rules. The metadirectory must be able to integrate with those other directory services in a way that can maintain integrity across directories, and translate between different types of data representing the same value. For example, the e-mail address in one directory might be given two fields: a string representing the user ID, and a string representing the Internet domain. A different directory might keep the e-mail address in a single field as a string value. Phone numbers can include area codes and symbols in one directory, represented by a string value, but they could be seven-digit phone numbers in another directory with no symbols and represented by a number.

The metadirectory must be able to understand these values and map them between directories. This can be done by using a native API for each directory, or by using a common protocol to access each directory (such as the Lightweight Directory Access Protocol, or LDAP) and then manipulating the data to ensure that the data is correct in each directory that the metadirectory touches.

The optimal architecture for a metadirectory is one in which the metadirectory is the central connecting point between all the other directory services (Figure 6.2). If a directory service were connected to others in a serial fashion, it would be less likely that the metadirectory could apply business rules regarding the ownership of values in the data (Figure 6.3).

Figure 6.2 Hub-and-spoke metadirectory.

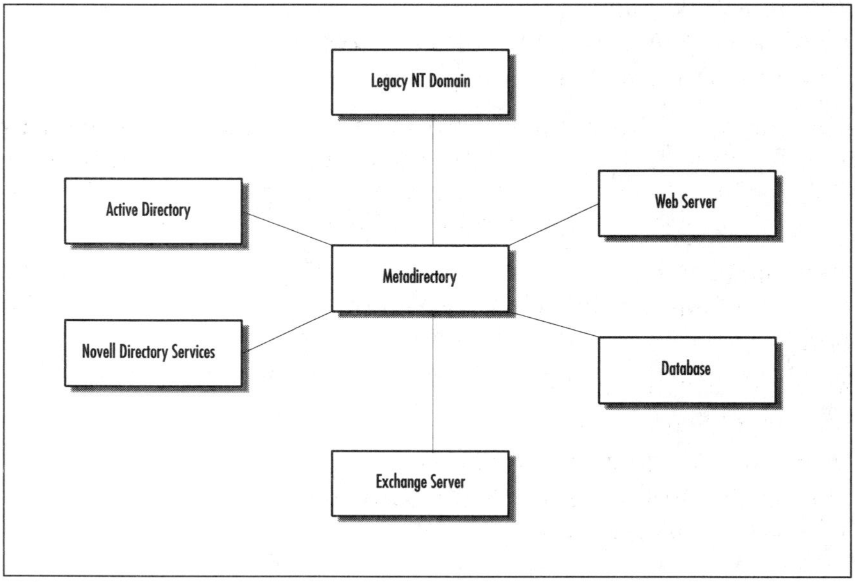

Figure 6.3 Serial directories.

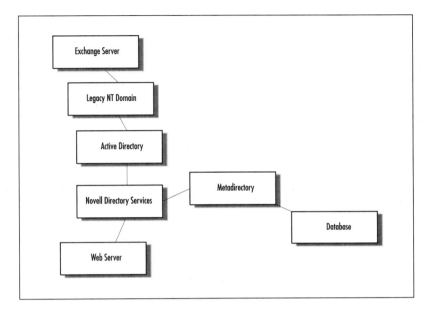

VIA Architecture

VIA is the name of the metadirectory product that Microsoft acquired when they bought Zoomit. It can run as a service or a console on a Windows NT 4 or Windows 2000 Server. To access the VIA metadirectory, a client can be a:

- Web browser
- LDAP client—either LDAP v.2 or LDAP v.3
- Zoomit Compass client

The VIA "metaverse" database connects to multiple directories through management agents that work in a bidirectional flow that can be scheduled by the Administrator. There are management agents currently available for the following directories (future versions may contain more):

- Banyan VINES
- GMHS (BeyondMail and DaVinci)
- Lotus Notes
- Microsoft Exchange Server
- Microsoft Mail
- Microsoft Windows NT domains
- Microsoft Windows 2000 Active Directory
- Netscape Directory Server

- Novell NetWare bindery
- Novell Directory Services
- Novell GroupWise (4.*x* and 5.*x*)
- SQL databases, via ODBC
- X.500 directories, via LDAP, such as ISOCOR, ICL, and Control Data

Additionally, a "report" management agent is available for reporting on the metaverse, and a "generic" management agent is available to use in creating a custom version for a different database.

The metaverse can synchronize directories to the attribute level. In fact, new objects can be created in any directory or the metadirectory, or attributes can be changed, and then those objects and attribute changes will be propagated to the metadirectory (if made from a different directory). From the metadirectory, they will be propagated to the rest of the connected directories.

VIA also supports ownership of data to the attribute level. This further maintains the referential integrity of the data when there are two or more different sources for identity information.

Implementing a Disaster Recovery Plan

Disasters and timeshare salesmen both have the nasty habit of creeping up on you by surprise. Fortunately, the farsighted Administrator can plan to avoid disasters. A pity about the timeshare salesmen.

Disasters can range from the corruption of mission-critical data to the total destruction of a company's sole office building, along with all systems within it. Regardless of the extent of the destruction, the result is an interruption in business that can result in a loss of revenue.

There are a variety of disaster recovery plans that provide some form of protection against a bewildering number of disasters. Generally, these can range from storing backup tapes offsite, to the relocation of critical personnel to a hot standby site that is ready to commence close-to-normal business activities. When developing a disaster recovery plan, you must estimate the likelihood of a disaster and the scope of destruction that a disaster might have. It may be more likely that you will experience a virus spread by e-mail than a hurricane if your office is located in a desert and you are connected to the Internet. But don't dismiss the possibility of natural disasters; Nature has its own way of making itself known.

For example, if your building is located in an area that experiences hurricanes, establish a plan that will mitigate the disastrous effects of a hurricane but that is also realistically in line with the potential revenue loss. If you have a small branch office that generates $30,000 profit per month, the plan should not exceed the revenue-generating potential of the office over a period of time during which the disaster's effects could be reversed.

If the hurricane damage can be repaired within three months, then the disaster recovery plan should not cost more than $90,000 to implement.

However, there are considerations other than loss of revenue that should be taken into account. It is difficult to quantify the impact of a negative public perception due to a loss of service. In the previous example, costs significantly higher than $90,000 may be justified if there is a strong desire to limit negative publicity.

For further information on general disaster recovery techniques and planning best practices, check out these Web sites:

http://admin5.hsc.uth.tmc.edu/ishome/dr/drwhy.html

www.paaet.edu.kw/Info/HomePage/shaheen/security.htm

www.disaster-survival.com/Planning_Overview.html

Modeling Sites with Disaster Recovery in Mind

When planning for Active Directory, it is important to keep disaster recovery in mind. Sites offer an obvious facilitator to recover from disasters if their structure is implemented according to a disaster recovery plan. Let me elaborate: If there is a planned cold standby or hot standby office (cold standby offices are available to begin business after being set up and data and personnel have been transferred to them, and hot standby offices have recent data and available personnel to staff them should an emergency take place), an Active Directory structure can be implemented in that office with an up-to-date copy of all identity information and resource information simply by placing appropriate DNS, DHCP, global catalog (GC) and domain controller (DC) servers for each domain that will use that standby site in addition to a link from the production network to the standby site.

For instance, fobya.com is run by a company that has incorporated a standby site into their disaster recovery plan. The Network Administrator establishes two sites within the fobya.com domain, one for the main office and one for the standby office. The company that sponsors the standby office establishes a T1 line between fobya.com and their data storage warehouse that houses the fobya.com standby servers. A minimum of two servers are located at the standby site: a server that manages DNS and DHCP, and a second server that acts as a DC and GC server. The fobya.com office maintains several servers and ships data backups to the warehouse on a weekly basis. The Administrator then sets replication to occur every 30 minutes because the servers can handle the extra processing and there is no other data traveling across the site link. The configuration is similar to Figure 6.4.

Dealing with a single production office means that a Network Administrator must manage to a single point of failure. But what would happen if fobya.com grows to include multiple domains placed around the globe? Figure 6.5 illustrates the domain configuration for fobya.com after it

Figure 6.4 fobya.com single-domain site model for disaster recovery.

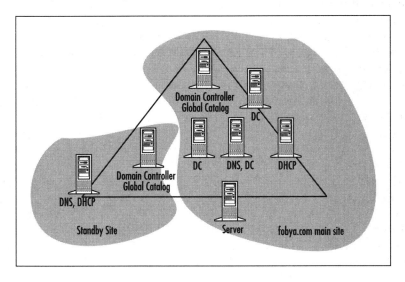

Figure 6.5 fobya.com global site and domain configuration.

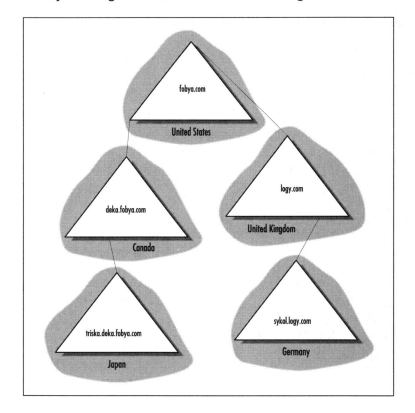

has merged with other companies and become a global entity. In the new fobya.com forest, each domain exists in a separate country.

If the Network Administrator creates a second recovery site for each of the domains, he or she will need to establish two links from that recovery site: one to the domain that will be recovered, and a second link to some other site. The reason for the dual links is that if a site crashes, the standby site will lose its link to the forest unless it has that second link.

Because the sites are in different countries, the likelihood of a disaster wiping out more than one site is extremely small. Using standby sites for each domain may not be feasible or cost effective. Instead, the Network Administrator can configure sites in a way that provides redundancy and backup of the domain by placing a DC from one domain into a site that houses most of another domain. The result would be similar to Figure 6.6.

Figure 6.6 ensures that the destruction of a single location, such as Japan, would not cause a complete loss of all the domain information for the triska.deka.fobya.com domain. There will be an incremental increase in traffic between sites when domains span sites, since more data (from the domain partition) than the GC, schema, and configuration will be traveling across the wire.

Figure 6.6 Modeling multiple domains and sites for disaster recovery.

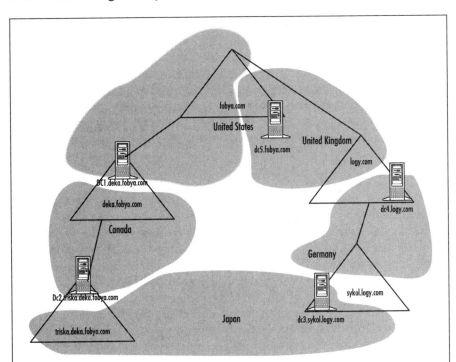

The Active Directory Database File Structure

Each DC contains a set of files that hold its portion of the Active Directory. The file structure is a fault-tolerant transaction-based database, which is based on ESE (Extensible Storage Engine). Transactions occur in a short sequence of actions:

1. The Administrator creates an object, which initiates the transaction.
2. The transaction is written to a log file.
3. The transaction is then committed to a database buffer.
4. The transaction is completed when the database on the disk is written.

Several files are involved in this process. The NTDS.DIT file is the database file that stores all the objects for that DC's partition of the Active Directory. There are also several log files:

- Transaction logs
- Checkpoints
- Reserved logs
- Patch files

Transaction log files can reach 10MB in size. A current transaction log, called edb.log, is used until it reaches the 10MB limit. At that point, the log is saved as a separate file, edb00001.log—where the numerical portion of the filename is incremented as new full log files are saved—and the edb.log is emptied for new transactions.

Circular logging will not create the past transaction log files, such as edb00001.log, edb00002.log, and so on. Instead, it will rewrite over the current transaction log. The circular logging can be turned on to reduce the number of log files on the hard drive. Avoid circular logging as a practice. The default behavior of Windows 2000 Active Directory is to not execute circular logging. However, you can change the default behavior through a Registry key:

`HKLM\CurrentControlSet\Services\NTDS\Parameters\Circular Logging`

Set the circular logging to 0 to turn circular logging off, and to 1 to turn circular logging on.

There is a checkpoint file named edb.chk that is stored in the same directory as NTDS.DIT. This file holds the pointers to the transactions in the transaction logs that have actually been written to the database. The file literally checks the point at which the log file and the database are consistent.

Two reserved log files, res1.log and res2.log, are also placed in the same directory as NTDS.DIT. These files are each 10MB in size and will become log files if there is not enough space on the disk to create a new edb.log file. Any outstanding transactions are copied from memory into the reserved logs, and then the Active Directory will shut down with an "out of disk space" error.

Patch files are used to track transactions written to the Active Directory database during backup. Split transactions are those that are written across multiple database pages. A split transaction can be written to a portion of the Active Directory database that has already been backed up. The backup process is as follows:

1. A patch file with a .pat extension is created for the current database written to disk.

2. Backup begins.

3. Active Directory split transactions are written both to the database and to the patch file.

4. The backup writes the patch file to tape.

5. The patch file is deleted.

Do not delete log files. The Active Directory will automatically run a garbage collection process to delete unused objects, delete unused files, and defragment the database. When files are manually deleted, the Active Directory can become corrupted. Garbage collection will take place on a 12-hour interval basis.

NOTE

Offline database management is performed with the NTDSUtil.exe program. To run the offline database tool, start the server and at the initial boot menu screen press F8. Select the Directory Services Repair Mode option, and then run the ntdsutil.exe tool.

Backup

Windows 2000 has a Backup utility program found in the Programs\Accessories\System Tools menu. This utility is shown in Figure 6.7.

The Backup utility provides the following features:

- Data backup of files, folders, Active Directory, and system information
- Scheduled backups
- Storage of backup data on networked systems and removable media
- Data and Active Directory restoration
- Emergency repair disk creation

To create a backup job, select the files and folders to back up, the location to place the backed-up data on, and options such as data verification or compression of the data. One of the new items in the Backup utility is

Figure 6.7 Backup.

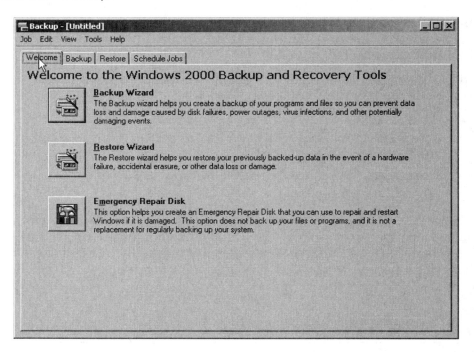

System State data. System State data can potentially refer to (depending on the operating system installed) the server's Registry, component services Class Registration database (storing COM data), startup files, Certificate services data, Active Directory, and SYSVOL. Whenever you create a backup that is intended to be able to repair a server, select the System State in addition to the data that is being backed up. The System State data is selected by checking it off, as shown in Figure 6.8.

The Backup utility does support a scheduled backup. This is a common feature in many backup utilities, where a backup automatically executes after standard business hours and is completed when Administrators return. Scheduling backups to occur after standard business hours reduces the impact to network performance that a backup may cause.

Creating an Emergency Repair Disk

In Windows 2000, the emergency repair disk is included as a backup option, rather than a separate application. Emergency repair disks contain minimal system data, although typically enough to get a downed server to restart. To create an emergency repair disk, select the option in the Backup utility as shown in Figure 6.9. The Backup utility will prompt for a diskette to be placed in the default drive A:.

Figure 6.8 Checking off System State data.

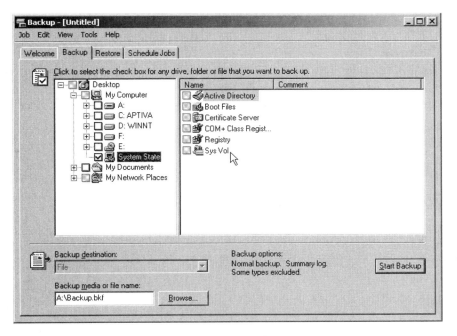

Figure 6.9 Create an Emergency Repair Disk.

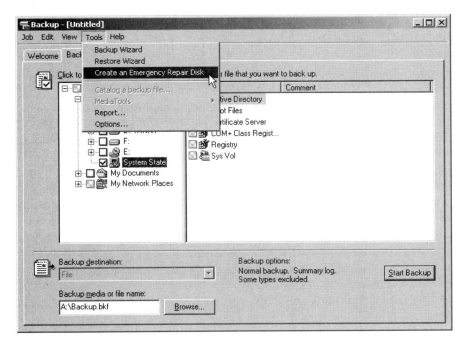

Recovering a Failed Domain Controller

When a DC fails, there is typically more to be restored than just files and folders. There are two issues involved:

- Transactions may not have been committed to the disk, but written to log files for the Active Directory.
- Data in the Active Directory databases on other DCs may have changed since the failure.

This means that the log files must be used to bring the written transactions to a current state. Additionally, when the Active Directory database is brought online, it must be synchronized with the rest of the domain and forest. To ensure that this happens, make certain to restore the System State data. After that is restored, an automatic consistency check occurs on the DC's Active Directory database. The consistency check is then followed by an indexing operation. Finally, replication takes place and the Active Directory is updated with the latest information, and file replication services restore the latest data versions from other DCs.

WARNING

If the DC has a corrupted Active Directory database, you must use the Directory Services Restore Mode startup option before restoring the System State data.

Authoritative Restore of Deleted Objects

Call me a prophet of doom, but it is going to happen at some point. Someone will delete an organizational unit (OU) filled with user accounts or other objects. It will be an accident, of course, but an accident that you will need to fix quickly. The place to start is restoring your last backup. But, there will be a problem...

Unfortunately, when you restore deleted objects from the Active Directory, those objects will be deleted (actually, they are tombstoned) the next time that replication takes place. The reason for this is that the objects have been marked for deletion in another DC's replica of the Active Directory, and replication will then reproduce the accidental deletion. This is normally the behavior you want, except in the case of accidents!

To prevent this you must execute an authoritative restore. This process will enable the objects that are restored to resist deletion when replication occurs. Each object that is restored in this manner will be marked as "authoritative." The authoritative attribute prevails over the tombstone attribute when replication next occurs. To perform this operation:

1. Boot the computer.
2. At the startup screen, press F8 for Advanced startup options.
3. Select Directory Services Restore mode.
4. Restore the System State data of a backup that contains the objects that you want to restore.
5. After restoration has finished, close Backup.
6. Run NTDSUtil.exe.
7. Type **Authoritative restore** at the prompt.
8. Type **Restore subtree** and the distinguished name of the object or OU (for example, restore subtree ou=sales,dc=xyz,dc=com).
9. Exit the NTDSUtil program and restart the computer normally.

Startup Options

There are several options available when Windows 2000 starts. These can assist in returning a failed server to normal operations in different ways. Table 6.2 lists the startup options.

Table 6.2 Startup Modes

Startup Option	Function	Purpose
Debugging Mode	Sends the debug data to another computer through a serial cable.	Only use this when you need to do high-level debugging, or are sending a report to a debugging expert.
Directory Services Restore Mode	Allows restoration of the Active Directory and SYSVOL files.	Use this whenever you need to do offline defragmenting of the NTDS.DIT file using the NTDSUtil.exe utility, or when you need to restore or repair the Active Directory on a DC.
Enable Boot Logging	Creates an ntbtlog.txt file in the systemroot showing all device drivers loaded during startup.	Use this if you want to find out which device drivers are loading. This is helpful if you suspect one of them is causing problems on the server.

Table 6.2 *continued*

Startup Option	Function	Purpose
Enable VGA Mode	Runs Windows 2000 using a standard VGA driver.	Use this if you accidentally selected the wrong display driver and it will no longer load properly. When in this mode, you can change the display driver and then test it by rebooting normally.
Last Known Good Configuration	Starts up Windows 2000 with the last configuration that a full logon was executed on.	Use this if you changed the server's configuration and the server will no longer get to the point of a logon screen. Or, if you have reached the logon screen, but really don't want to save your changes, reboot instead of logging on and select this option.
Safe Mode	Runs Windows 2000 with the most basic drivers, creates a log file.	Use this if the server will not function properly and you suspect a device driver of some type is causing the problem. If it starts properly in Safe Mode, it is most likely a new device driver.
Safe Mode with Command Prompt	Runs Windows 2000 with the most basic drivers at a command prompt rather than the GUI, creates a log file.	Use this if you want to change that device driver by copying over a file from a command prompt. This option is rather handy.
Safe Mode with Networking	Runs Windows 2000 with the most basic drivers, loads networking drivers, creates a log file.	Use this if you need to get the server into a file and print sharing mode and you have been able to get the server into Safe Mode, or if you want to test that the network device driver is not the one that has caused the server to stop functioning—if it has, this option will not work.

The Recovery Console

The Recovery console does not automatically install on a Windows 2000 machine, nor does it have to be installed to be used. It can be executed from the Windows 2000 CD-ROM using the Recovery Console option when given the Repair Options screen. If you want to install the Recovery console, insert the Windows 2000 Server CD, open a command prompt, and execute:

```
<cdrom drive>:\i386\winnt32 /cmdcons
```

When you use the Recovery Console option, you can configure a service to start or stop when the server boots—a handy tool for corrupted services that cause a server to hang before logons can begin. The Recovery console can also be used to copy files to an NTFS partition, which is particularly useful when files on the hard drive have become corrupted. (Previously, this could only be attempted with a third-party tool that could access an NTFS drive from a DOS prompt.) Finally, you can manage files, folders, partitions, and disk drives. It is even possible to delete, recreate, and format partitions. However, changing partitions and formatting them should be a last resort undertaken by those with a strong stomach and a very sick server.

For Experts

There are some tasks and concepts that not every Network Administrator needs to know. For example, I own a car, and when I am feeling brave I attempt to fix the odd problem with it (this is usually followed by me catching the train to work for the next two weeks while a real mechanic rectifies the problem). But, for everyday maintenance I don't need to know how to bore the cylinders or change the engine timing. Network administration can be much the same; you are not required to know every trick in the book—just which book to look in!

For those of you who administer larger networks and are involved with the more tricky Active Directory problems, then perhaps the next section will be of interest.

PDC Emulation and Native Mode

When Active Directory is working in mixed mode, it has a Flexible Single Master of Operations (FSMO)that is set to act as the "PDC Emulator." The PDC Emulator takes on the tasks of a primary domain controller (PDC) to down-level Windows NT backup domain controllers (BDCs). This is an intuitive role for a PDC Emulator to play.

What is interesting is that the PDC Emulator does not go away after the Active Directory is migrated to native mode. Instead, the PDC Emulator remains as a primary checkpoint for password changes. When a password is changed in the Active Directory, the PDC Emulator is the preferred target for the replication traffic. The reason for this is to manage situations where replication of password changes may take several hours to synchronize across an entire Active Directory database.

For example, if a password is changed, it will be replicated as a changed password to the PDC Emulator. Then, if the user attempts to log on at another domain controller (DC) that has not yet received the update to the Active Directory including that user's password, the DC will not immediately reject the logon. Instead, the DC contacts the PDC Emulator and checks with it first to make sure that the password is correct. The PDC Emulator FSMO gets all password changes immediately. This should drive placement of that FSMO in a central location, well connected to the other subnets. A DC can be set to not contact the PDC Emulator if the PDC Emulator role owner is not in the current site. If the AvoidPdcOnWan Registry entry in HKEY_LOCAL_MACHINE\CurrentControlSet\Services\Netlogon\Parameters\ is set to 1, the password change reaches the PDC Emulator nonurgently, through normal replication.

The PDC Emulator in the root domain of the forest provides one other function, regardless of which mode the domain is in: the authoritative time source for the forest. This root domain PDC Emulator is the one that should be set up with an external time source in order for the forest to use an external time provider. The hierarchy of time providers is as follows:

- Client workstations and member servers use the authenticating DC as a time provider.
- DCs in a domain use the PDC Emulator of their own domain as the time provider.
- Each PDC Emulator will use the PDC Emulator of its parent domain, or the forest's root domain if they are the top of a domain tree, as its time provider.
- The root domain's PDC Emulator is the top of the hierarchy and can be used to connect to external time sources.

How Active Directory Prevents Unnecessary Replication

The bidirectional loop created for replication provides multiple paths for DCs to send and receive updated information. This results in both fault tolerance and enhanced performance. A less desirable result could be that multiple instances of the same update are sent to the same DC. Active Directory prevents this through propagation dampening.

In Figure 6.10, there are three servers that are direct replication partners to each other in a bidirectional ring. (They each have connection objects beneath their NTDS Settings for the other two servers.)

When an object in the Active Directory is updated on Server A, it changes the object's Update Sequence Number, or USN. Replication occurs to both Server B and Server C, since they are both direct replication partners. Servers B and C detect that Server A had replicated the change to both, so they do not send the update to each other.

To make this process work, the Active Directory uses two vectors:

Figure 6.10 Server replication ring.

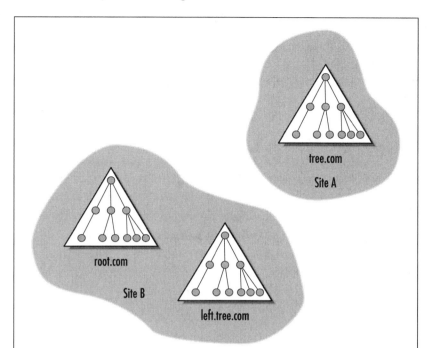

- Up-to-date vector
- High watermark vector

The up-to-date vector is comprised of pairs of server USNs. The high watermark vector is the highest USN stored for each object. Propagation dampening occurs because each DC keeps track of its direct replication partners' high watermarks.

How an LDAP Query Accesses Active Directory

The Lightweight Directory Access Protocol (LDAP) query will start in the domain where the query was generated. In the Active Directory forest using LDAP, each domain knows about the other domains within their own trees, so LDAP gets referred within a single tree. To use an expanded scope including domains with other namespaces in a forest, the global catalog (GC) must be used.

The LDAP referral process for an LDAP query acquires an authoritative answer first. In the following example, the LDAP client is asking for information about an Active Directory object within a sister domain.

1. The LDAP client queries DNS for an LDAP server in the current domain.
2. DNS responds with a DC in the current domain.
3. The LDAP client queries the DC for information about an Active Directory object.
4. The DC refers the client to the parent domain.
5. The LDAP client queries DNS for an LDAP server in the parent domain.
6. DNS responds with a DC in the parent domain.
7. The LDAP client queries the parent DC for information about an Active Directory object.
8. The parent DC refers the client to another of its child domains.
9. The LDAP client queries DNS for an LDAP server in the sister domain.
10. DNS responds with a DC in the sister domain.
11. The LDAP client queries the sister DC for information about an Active Directory object.
12. The sister DC responds to the request.

Renaming Domains

A domain cannot be renamed. However, if you demote and repromote each of the DCs into a new domain, and then either recreate accounts or migrate them to the new domain, and finally join clients to the new domain, you will achieve the same effect. Do not attempt this with a domain that has child domains. If this is the case, you will need to migrate all the child domains first, and then attempt the parent domain.

The only way you can change the computer name on a DC is to demote the DC, rename it, and then repromote it. If there are no other DCs in the domain, all the user accounts will be lost.

Add a Server to Two Different Sites Simultaneously

Using the Active Directory Sites and Services console will allow you to configure a server as a member of a single site. If you want a server to be available in multiple sites, you will need to use a different method—this is by design. Having a server as a member of two or more sites may result in poor network performance, so only use this as a last resort.

Begin by logging on to the server that you want to be a member of more than one site. Make sure to use an Administrator's name and password. Then, click Start and then Run. Type **regedt32**, and click Oκ.

In the Registry Editor, navigate to HKLM\System\CurrentControlSet\Services\NetLogon\Parameters. Select the Edit menu and choose Add Value.

In the resulting dialog box, type the name **SiteCoverage** and select the type of REG_MULTI_SZ, then click OK. After that, enter the names of each site of which the server will be a member, each site name on a new line with the identical spelling and capitalization used. After the last entry, press SHIFT and ENTER to move to the next line, and click OK to finish.

Now the server is a member of more than one site, but it will not show up in the Active Directory Sites and Services console. You can manually create the server objects by right-clicking on each additional site and selecting New, and then selecting Server. Place the NetBIOS name of the server in the space provided, and click OK.

Once the server object has been created, right-click on it and select Properties from the pop-up menu. In the section under Computer, click CHANGE. Select the correct server from the ones available on the network. This capability is useful when a site exists without a DC. It allows a DC in another site to become the preferred logon DC.

Removing Phantom Objects

A phantom object is one that has been removed from the Active Directory, but for some reason still appears as an object within it. This type of error can happen when a command has not completed properly (the server lost power, received an unrecoverable network packet during the change to Active Directory, etc.). This can prove to be troublesome because the Active Directory does not truly reflect the current network configuration. The good news is that this is not a difficult problem to solve.

First, note the full path of the object, such as cn=object,cn=ou,dc=domain,dc=com. Boot the DC into DS Repair Mode. Start NTDSUtil.exe. Type **Files** and press ENTER. Remove the object using its full path. Run a Header check, and then run an Integrity check. After these complete, reboot the server normally and initiate replication.

Sometimes an object is left as a logical placeholder in the Active Directory, even though its physical component has been removed. For example, if a DC is removed from the Active Directory and does not appear in the Active Directory Users and Computers console (or when you run NTDSUtil), it may still appear in the Active Directory Sites and Services console. When this happens, you can safely remove that object by right-clicking on the server object and selecting Delete from the pop-up menu.

Phantom Domains

When an Administrator demotes the last DC for a domain, he or she should select the option for "This server is the last domain controller in the domain." This will remove the metadata for the domain from the Active Directory forest. If the Administrator does not select it, the metadata for that domain must be removed.

1. Log on to the domain naming master FSMO DC as a member of the Enterprise Admins group, and force replication to take place.

2. Open a command prompt, type **Ntdsutil**, and press ENTER.

3. Type **Metadata cleanup**, and press ENTER.

4. Type **Connections**, and press ENTER.

5. Type **Connect to server nameofdomainnamingmasterFSMO**, and press ENTER.

6. Type **Quit**, and press ENTER.

7. Type **Select Operation Target**, and press ENTER.

8. Type **List Domains**, and press ENTER. You will see a list of domains associated with numbers.

9. Type **Select Domain Numberofdomain**, and press ENTER.

10. Type **Quit**, and press ENTER.

11. Type **Remove Selected Domain**, and press ENTER.

12. Type **Quit**, and press ENTER until you have exited the NTDSUTIL.

Transferring FSMO Roles

Moving the RID master, which is a single designated DC in an entire forest that provides the relative ID (RID) portion of the SID to other DCs, entails one of two methods.

1. In the Active Directory Users and Computers console, right-click on the domain and select Connect to Domain Controller from the pop-up menu.

2. Select the DC that will be the new RID Master, and click OK.

3. Right-click on the domain again, and select Operations Masters from the pop-up menu.

4. Select the Rid Pool tab.

5. Click CHANGE at the bottom of the dialog.

6. Click OK.

Or, using NTDSUTIL, the Administrator can do the following to change the RID master:

1. Log on as a member of Enterprise Admins to any DC.

2. Open a command prompt, type **Ntdsutil**, and press ENTER.

3. Type **Roles**, and press ENTER.

4. Type **Connections**, and press ENTER.

5. Type **Connect to server servernameofnewRIDMaster**, and press ENTER.

6. Type **Quit**, and press ENTER.

7. Type **Transfer Rid Master**, and press ENTER.

8. You will be prompted by a dialog to transfer the role. Select YES.

9. Type **Quit**, and press ENTER until you have exited NTDSUTIL.

The PDC Emulator is a computer that acts as the PDC for Windows NT BDCs in a mixed domain. It also handles password changes and has authority for time for its domain. To change the PDC FSMO role:

1. In the Active Directory Users and Computers console, right-click on the domain and select Connect to Domain Controller from the pop-up menu.

2. Select the DC to be the new PDC Emulator, and click OK.

3. Right-click on the domain and select Operations Masters from the pop-up menu.

4. Click the PDC tab.

5. Click CHANGE, and Click OK.

Or, using NTDSUTIL, the Administrator can do the following to change the PDC Emulator:

1. Log on as a member of the Enterprise Admins group on any DC.

2. Open a command prompt, type **Ntdsutil**, and press ENTER.

3. Type **Roles**, and press ENTER.

4. Type **Connections**, and press ENTER.

5. Type **Connect To Server ServernameofnewPDCEmulator**, and press ENTER.

6. Type **Quit**, and press ENTER.

7. Type **Transfer Pdc**, and press ENTER.

8. You will be prompted by a dialog to transfer the role. Select YES.

9. Type **Quit**, and press ENTER until you have exited the NTDSUTIL.

The Infrastructure master is responsible for managing the group-to-user references. This will ensure that users are able to access resources. To change the Infrastructure master, do the following:

1. In the Active Directory Users and Computers console, right-click on the domain and select Connect to Domain Controller from the pop-up menu.

2. Select the DC that will be the new Infrastructure master, and click OK.

3. Right-click on the domain, and select Operations Masters from the pop-up menu.

4. Click the Infrastructure tab.

5. Click CHANGE, and click OK to confirm.

To do this same change with NTDSUTIL, execute the following:

1. Log on as a member of the Enterprise Admins group on any DC.

2. Open a command prompt, type **Ntdsutil**, and press ENTER.

3. Type **Roles**, and press ENTER.

4. Type **Connections**, and press ENTER.

5. Type **Connect To Server ServernameofnewInfrastructureFSMO**, and press ENTER.

6. Type **Quit**, and press ENTER.

7. Type **Transfer infrastructure master**, and press ENTER.

8. You will be prompted to transfer the role. Select YES.

9. Type **Quit**, and press ENTER until you have exited NTDSUTIL.

There is only one domain naming master FSMO per forest. This designated DC ensures that any domain added to the forest has a unique name. To change the server that handles this role, first make sure that the new DC is also a GC server.

1. In the Active Directory Domains and Trusts console, right-click on the Active Directory Domains and Trusts root, and select Connect to Domain Controller from the pop-up menu.

2. Specify the name of the DC that will be the next domain naming master FSMO (remember, it must also be a GC server), and press ENTER.

3. Right-click on the Active Directory Domains and Trusts, and select Operations Masters from the pop-up menu.

4. Click CHANGE.

5. Click OK to confirm.

To execute this same process using NTDSUTIL:

1. Log on to a DC as a member of the Enterprise Admins group.

2. Open a command prompt, type **Ntdsutil**, then press ENTER.

3. Type **Roles**, and press ENTER.

4. Type **Connections**, and press ENTER.

5. Type **Connect to server servernameofnewdomainnamingmasterFSMO**, and press ENTER.

6. Type **Quit**, and press ENTER.

7. Type **Transfer domain naming master**, and press ENTER.

8. A dialog will appear to confirm the role transfer. Choose YES.

9. Type **Quit,** and press ENTER until you have exited the NTDSUTIL.

The schema master is the one DC upon which the schema can be changed. There is only one schema per forest. To change this role, you must use the Active Directory Schema Manager console.

1. Log on to a DC as a member of the Schema Admins group.

2. Start the Active Directory Schema Manager console and right-click on the Active Directory Schema root.

3. Select Change Domain Controller from the pop-up menu.

4. Specify the name of the DC that will be the new schema master, and click OK.

5. Right-click on the Active Directory Schema, and select Operations Master from the pop-up menu.

6. Click CHANGE.

7. Click OK when a dialog confirms the role transfer.

The change of the Schema Master FSMO can be accomplished using NTDSUTIL.

1. Log on to a DC as a member of the Enterprise Admins group.

2. Open a command prompt, type **Ntdsutil**, then press ENTER.

3. Type **Roles**, and press ENTER.

4. Type **Connections**, and press ENTER.

5. Type **Connect To Server ServernameofnewSchemaMasterFSMO**, and press ENTER.

6. Type **Quit**, and press ENTER.

7. Type **Transfer Schema Master**, and press ENTER.

8. Select YES for the dialog regarding the role transfer.

9. Type **Quit**, and press ENTER until you have exited NTDSUTIL.

Troubleshooting Tips

A raft of problems inevitably follows the implementation of any complex system. Good planning and preparation contributes extensively to reducing issues, though even the best plan is open to human error. Your ability to resolve problems quickly and efficiently may be the fulcrum that levers your Active Directory infrastructure into being a productive environment.

Avoiding Errors When Migrating a Domain

Do not try to add a Windows 2000 server as a DC into a Windows NT 4.0 domain that has a Windows NT 4.0 PDC. The Windows 2000 DC will automatically emulate the PDC for that domain and cause conflicts.

Remote Procedure Call (RPC) Errors

A strange but true fact: When you receive an RPC error, you are most likely having problems with DNS. Or worse, there is a hardware problem, or an IP address is not applied to the network interface, or some other lower-layer problem. RPC is the session-level protocol that runs procedures transparently on remote hosts. It can run over multiple lower-layer protocols including TCP/IP. It uses DNS to find remote services. DNS depends on IP addressing, which further depends on the Physical and Data Link layer protocols such as Ethernet or Token Ring, and those lower-layer protocols can only function if the network interface is working and connected to a functional network. So, the order in which to troubleshoot an RPC error is this:

1. Run NetDIAG.
2. Check your DNS server's configuration (DNSCMD on a Windows 2000 DNS Server).
3. Verify that your workstation's network interface has an IP address (you can use WINIPCFG or IPCONFIG on most Windows machines).
4. Check to make sure the network interface card (NIC) is functioning. (If the NIC has lights, are they green? Did you run the vendor diags?)
5. Check the network cable.
6. Check the hub and switches to make sure that they are functioning.

TIP

No self-respecting IT professional involved with Microsoft products would be caught dead without a subscription to *TechNet*, so make sure you keep your subscription up to date! Alternatives to the trusty almanac for all things Microsoft (the *TechNet*), is Microsoft's troubleshooting Web site, the Diagnostic Solution Guide to Windows 2000 and Windows NT, at http://dsg.rte.microsoft.com.

Summary

RPC, DCOM, and Winsock are all part of a developer system for network-aware Windows applications. These work alongside the Active Directory Services Interface to provide a method for both Administrators and developers to manage and extend the Active Directory.

The Active Directory will not stand alone in the network as a directory service. As time goes by, an enterprise may add other applications and systems that integrate with the Active Directory. There may be some directories that cannot be integrated or synchronized directly with the Active Directory. If the network grows with multiple directory services, it may simplify processes to use a metadirectory.

A metadirectory is a database that serves as an index of other directories. This index can propagate data throughout the various directory services. It can synchronize data between them. Microsoft purchased Zoomit Corporation, which produced a metadirectory called VIA. VIA is now a Microsoft metadirectory that can access Active Directory information. In addition to being a standard metadirectory, VIA can apply business rules in order to place ownership of data for certain directories over others.

When designing the Active Directory, a part of the design should take into account the plans for disaster recovery. Because each DC holds several partitions of the Active Database—at a minimum, the schema, configuration, and the domain in which they belong—with some DCs containing a copy of the GC, they can become a point of failure if they are all held within the same physical location. If all the controllers in a single domain were held in a single building, the loss of that building would become the loss of that domain. Sites can be designed by adding an extra site for each standby office, or by maintaining at least one DC in another location.

The Active Directory database consists of several file types:

- The database itself—ntds.dit
- Checkpoint files—edb.chk
- Transaction logs—edb.log
- Patch files—*.pat
- Reserved log files—res1.log, res2.log

The patch files are used during backup. The checkpoint and log files are used to indicate which files have been written to disk and which have not.

The Windows 2000 Backup utility can be used to both back up and restore the Active Directory. The key to this process is to back up the System State data.

If restoring the Active Directory, an authoritative restore created with the NTDSUtil.exe utility can restore deleted objects and ensure that they persist after replication takes place.

FAQs

Q: Is Microsoft's Directory Synchronization Service (MSDSS) for Novell NetWare a metadirectory?

A: No. MSDSS is not a metadirectory, since it does not create a centralized index that connects the Active Directory to others. Instead, it works more closely to a multi-master replication scheme, since no single directory owns any data.

Q: Is there a DSClient for Windows 3.1?

A: No. There is no DSClient for Windows 3.1. There is a single DSClient for both Windows 95 and Windows 98, and a DSClient is expected for Windows NT 4.0.

Q: I have many files named edb000xx.log on my Windows 2000 Server and I would like to delete them to free up space. Can I delete them from Windows Explorer?

A: No. These log files are essential for ensuring that data is able to be restored to a current state. When a backup is performed, log files will be deleted automatically. If the log files are manually deleted, they may cause corruption to the Active Directory.

Q: When browsing the Registry, I noted that a Circular Logging key was set to 0. Should I change it to 1 in order to make sure that circular logging is not used?

A: No. The default behavior of the Active Directory is to have circular logging turned off (corresponding to a Registry key value 0). If circular logging is turned on, then past log files are not created. If these past log files are not created and a disaster does occur, it is probable that some Active Directory data will not be able to be restored.

Chapter 7

Configuring IntelliMirror

Solutions in this chapter:

- **Introduction**
- **What Is IntelliMirror?**
- **Configuring Group Policies**
- **Troubleshooting Group Policies**
- **Security**
- **Object Protection**
- **Summary**

Introduction

It is no secret that network clients are becoming more complex, harder to manage, and further geographically dispersed. Network managers lost in glassy-eyed reverie often regal their younger colleagues with tales of the "wonder years" when men where men and terminals where dumb. Unfortunately, the advent of the more intelligent and flexible client workstation has raised the specter of increased maintenance costs. As client workstations became more intelligent, so the software followed suit with increasing complexity and size. A glaring omission in the Windows technical strategy was the lack of a cohesive infrastructure to manage client configuration changes and administration. With IntelliMirror, Microsoft has provided a number of symbiotic technologies that enable Windows 2000 users to be productive under a variety of circumstances, and allow the Administrator to manage a user's environment from a central location.

Remote administration and maintenance is a key factor in the fight to lower Total Cost of Ownership (TCO). Allowing increased control and manageability over client workstations provides Administrators with an effective method of reducing the time required for configuration and problem resolution. Centralized remote administration can also provide a scalable way to manage desktops, control configuration changes, and deploy software to a burgeoning user base. Microsoft has recognized this as an essential requirement to redress the imbalance in corporate computing ownership, and has provided a tool set and infrastructure that eases the rocky road traveled by Administrators as they attempt to deploy and maintain operating systems and software within the business.

IntelliMirror is a Windows 2000 feature that is enabled by the Active Directory through the use of group policies. When IntelliMirror is implemented, a user's environment, even his personal documents, can intelligently follow him around the network. If there is no other reason to implement Active Directory Services, then do it for the group policies. This is one of the most functional components of the Active Directory for Administrators, making user and computer settings easier to manage.

What Is IntelliMirror?

Quite a bit of confusion surrounds the use of the term *IntelliMirror*. I know of several people who hunted high and low for several unhappy hours searching for the IntelliMirror utility. The manic gleam in their eye when I told them that IntelliMirror is a concept brought into existence by the collaborative use of a number of technologies was enough to make me take a step back—hastily followed by several more.

By using a comprehensive array of supporting technologies, IntelliMirror provides users with the same personalized working environment regardless of which Windows 2000 computer they use. User data is made consistently available, whether online or offline, while being simultaneously maintained on the server. Policy-based user and computer configuration settings ensure a consistent and personalized workspace. In short, IntelliMirror ensures the high availability of personal computer settings, software, and user data by combining centralized administration with distributed client computing. Three major features support the IntelliMirror technology:

User data management   Users can have access to their data whether they are online or offline. This feature includes the Active Directory, Group Policy, folder redirection, disk quotas, and file synchronization—technologies that increase data availability.

In Microsoft parlance: *"My data and documents follow me."*

User settings management   Allows preferences to follow the user. The user's personalized settings such as desktop arrangements and software and operating system settings follow the user. This feature includes the Active Directory, Group Policy, roaming profiles, and particular shell enhancements—technologies that increase computer availability.

In Microsoft parlance: *"My preferences follow me."*

Software installation and maintenance   Ensures that users have access to their required software. Software can be advertised to install on demand, or be installed by default. This feature includes the Active Directory, Group Policy, self-repairing software, and application deployment—technologies that increase application availability.

In Microsoft parlance: *"My software follows me."*

The *"follow me"* model of IntelliMirror ensures the high availability of a user's personalized computing environment, including their data, settings, and software. The design of IntelliMirror is intended to please both the Administrator by offloading some of the work to the supporting infrastructure, and management by lowering the cost of change and configuration management.

The three features of IntelliMirror are scalable from the small business to the global enterprise. With the support of Active Directory and policy-based management, features can be assigned a granularity defined by the Administrator. A brief summary of some of the technologies used with IntelliMirror include:

Group Policy   A technology that enables Administrators to precisely define the configuration of the user's computing environment. It can satisfy such diverse requirements as setting security settings to application deployment. Group Policy can control both user- and machine-based configuration settings.

Offline Files and Folders   A technology that allows users to access defined files and folders while offline. Entire mapped drives can even be accessed while offline. The Synchronization Manager can be used to determine when offline files should be updated.

Folder Redirection   The ability to point a folder, such as My Documents, to another (network) location.

Distributed File System (DFS)   This service can build a single namespace consisting of multiple shares on different servers. DFS provides the ability to load share and increase data availability.

Roaming User Profiles   A centrally-stored user profile that follows the user around the network.

Windows Installer   A standardized, scalable installation service that is customizable, consistent, and provides diagnosis and self-repair functionality.

Disk Quotas   A technology that enables Administrators to monitor and limit disk space usage on a per-volume per-user basis.

IntelliMirror is not an all-or-nothing technology—the Administrator can choose the features that best meet the needs of the organization. By identifying the particular features required, the relevant technology can be implemented without having to configure a host of supporting technologies. Though IntelliMirror uses a variety of technologies, by far the most important is *group policies*.

Configuring Group Policies

When Microsoft released Windows 95 in August 1995, a new feature called system policies was a slick way to manage Windows 95 computers and their users across a network. This functionality was included in Windows NT 4.0 when it was released later. Now, for Windows 2000, system policies have grown up to become group policies in the Active Directory. System policies may still exist on a Windows 2000 system, but since they have been displaced by group policies, it is not recommended that they be used.

Group policies are a constantly evolving administrative system. They can be used for managing computers and the end-users' environments. They can even be a method of deploying software to client workstations and as a configuration management tool. If an organization intends to use group policies in this manner, it is recommended that the Windows 2000 domain controllers (DCs) are established before creating the group policies and installing or upgrading client workstations. In order to use the group policies attached to organizational units (OUs), domains, or sites, the Active Directory must be functional; otherwise, only Local group policies can be used.

Group policies are rules that the Network Administrator sets for users and computers on the network. Rather than a single flat file located in a file-based directory, group policies take advantage of the Active Directory distributed database. The result is a managed user environment and desktop configuration.

Group policies are stored in Group Policy Objects (GPOs). The Group Policy Objects are associated with Active Directory containers. The settings in a Group Policy Object are inherited by child containers. For example, users will receive the group policy settings in all the policies leading from their current OU up to the top-level group policy, as shown in Figure 7.1.

You can launch Group Policy Editor by opening Active Directory Users and Computers. When open, click on the domain or OU desired, then open the Properties for that object. Clicking on the Group Policy tab will show which GPOs are active for that object (Figure 7.2). To open the editor for a particular GPO, select the GPO from the list, then click Edit. This will open the Group Policy Editor (GPE) for that policy.

Multiple Group Policy Objects can be associated with the same container, too. The depth of a user's location in the OU hierarchy does not

Figure 7.1 Group policy objects are inherited.

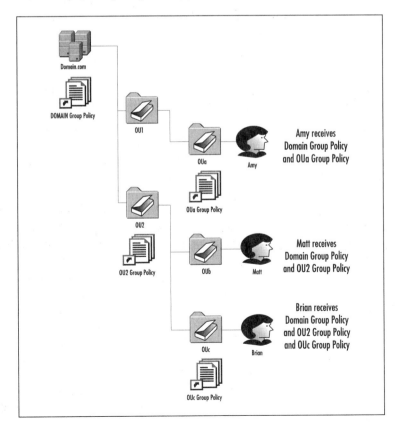

Figure 7.2 Blocking inheritance.

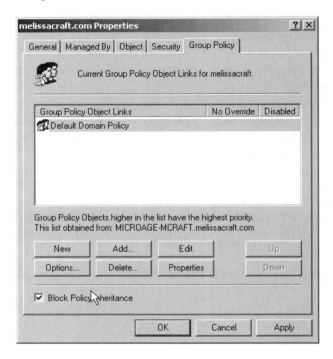

affect the length of time it takes to log on. Instead, it is the number of Group Policy Objects that must be read and applied. If there is a single group policy for each OU, and a user is located five OUs deep, it will take the same amount of time for the user to log on if the user is in a top-level container that has five Group Policy Objects associated with it.

The group policy itself is contained within a Group Policy Object in the Active Directory. The object is created in the Group Policy Editor (discussed later in the chapter), which can be launched in three different ways:

- From the Active Directory Users and Computers console, from the Group Policy tab on container objects
- From the Active Directory Sites and Services console, from the Group Policy tab on container objects
- As a separate management console using MMC and opening gpedit.msc

There are four policy types that can be applied to specific containers:

Local group policy   The Local Group Policy Object exists on each Windows 2000 computer. It contains, by default, only policies regarding security. The policy is located in the %systemroot%\system32\GroupPolicy directory.

Site group policy   Site Group Policy Objects are linked to site objects and can affect any object across the entire forest, since sites can span domains.

Domain group policy   Domain Group Policy Objects are linked to a single domain and affect all user and computer objects within the domain.

Organizational unit group policy   OU Group Policy Objects are linked to a specific OU. The OU group policy will affect all objects within the OU and within any OUs nested below it in the hierarchy.

WARNING

Group policy objects (GPOs) work only for users and computers, not groups. If an organizational unit only contains group accounts, the users will not receive the GPOs linked to that container.

How Group Policies Are Applied

When a computer boots into the Active Directory, it grabs the settings in the computer configuration of its associated GPOs and applies them. When a user logs on, the settings in the User Configuration portion of the group policy are applied to the user's environment. No other Active Directory objects receive group policies. Computer configuration and user configuration are discussed in further detail later in this chapter.

The order of policy application will begin with legacy NT4 system policies, if they exist. If they do not, the order follows the **SDOU** sequence:

1. Local Group Policy Object
2. **S**ite Group Policy Object
3. **D**omain Group Policy Objects
4. **OU** Group Policy Objects from the parent OUs down to the user's or computer's OU location

NOTE

Group policy objects are stand-alone objects that can be associated with multiple sites, domains, and organizational units (SDOUs). GPOs by default affect all the users and computers in a container. Group policies are only inherited from the domain that the computer or user belongs to, and not from higher-level domains. Conversely, group policies are inherited down the organizational unit tree within a domain.

Refresh Interval

Both the user and computer configuration settings include options for refreshing group policies. The interval can be set for 0 to 45 days. Zero essentially establishes a constant dialog from the client computer to a DC every seven seconds to determine whether updates to group policies have been made. The default setting for the refresh intervals is every 90 minutes. To change the refresh intervals for the computer, within the Group Policy Editor, expand the Computer Configuration container, then the Administrative Templates, then System, and finally click Group Policy in the left-hand pane. In the right-hand pane, double-click on the Global Policy Refresh Interval and establish the interval. The navigation is essentially the same for the User Refresh Interval, except that the first container to expand is User Configuration, and the item to double-click is the Global Policy Refresh Interval for Users.

Blocking and Enforcing

Group Policy provides a great deal of flexibility in the manner with which settings are applied using the SDOU scheme, but additional tailoring can be undertaken by using the Enforce and Block Policy Options. Enforcing a group policy prevents other GPOs from overriding a policy. If you enforce the site GPO, then group policies in lower containers (domains and organizational units) would not be able to change the settings set by the site GPO. On the other hand, blocking policy inheritance prevents GPOs in higher-level containers from applying their policies to the blocked container and its children. It should be noted that enforced GPOs always take precedence over blocked containers.

A group policy that can be inherited from a higher level can be blocked so that it does not pass further down the hierarchy. To block a policy:

1. Right-click the site, the domain, or the OU, and select Properties.
2. Click the Group Policy tab.
3. Check the box at the bottom of the dialog that states "Block Policy Inheritance," as illustrated in Figure 7.2.

If there are conflicts between a policy setting in two different GPOs, the last GPO will override the setting applied previously. An Administrator can stop a policy from being blocked or overridden. To enforce a policy:

1. Right-click the site, the domain, or the OU, and select Properties.
2. Click the Group Policy tab.
3. Click Options.
4. Check the box for No Override, as depicted in Figure 7.3.

Figure 7.3 Enforcing a policy.

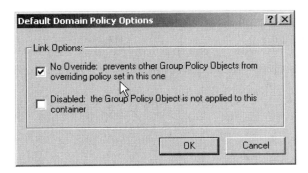

As shown in Figure 7.3, a group policy can also be disabled. An Administrator should exercise this option when retiring a group policy. By disabling the policy, the Administrator can reenable it later, should the need arise.

Group Policy Information Storage

A Group Policy Object is a virtual container that stores information in the Group Policy Container and a Group Policy Template. Group Policy Containers are Active Directory objects that store the GPO properties. Group policy objects store information in the Active Directory and in a Group Policy Template. The Active Directory storage is a Group Policy Container (GPC) that further contains subcontainers for user and computer information. The GPC has the following properties:

- **Version information**   Information that it used to ensure that GPC information is synchronized with GPT information.
- **Status information**   Information that indicates the status of the GPO, enabled or disabled.
- **List of components**   Information about the policies that have been configured in the GPO.

The Group Policy Template is actually an entire folder structure stored in the SYSVOL of the Active Directory DCs. The Group Policy Template top-level folder is \Policies. Below that, each GPO is granted its own subfolder using its GUID (Globally Unique Identifier—a long, indecipherable string of numbers and characters) as the folder name. Below that there is a GPT.INI file and further folders that are created whenever changes are made to the following:

- **Adm**   Additions of Administrative Templates files (.adm files).
- **Apps**   Application deployment files for Windows Installer advertisements (.aas files); appears as a subfolder of both User and Machine.

- **Files**   Contains files to be deployed to the client; appears as a subfolder of both User and Machine.
- **Machine**   Contains the registry.pol file for the computer configuration changes.
- **Scripts**   Contains all scripts for the entire group policy.
- **User**   Contains the registry.pol file for the user configuration changes.

Both the Active Directory and the SYSVOL directory structure participate in multi-master replication. This ensures that the group policies are available anywhere within a global enterprise.

Administrative Templates

The source settings for group policies can originate from an MMC extension, or, as is more commonly used, an Administrative Template. Administrative Templates consist of ASCII text files with the extension .adm. The files include the Registry settings in a format of categories with subcategories. These appear to the user in a Group Policy Editor interface as a hierarchy of settings, some with default settings already selected. Windows 2000 Group Policy can use the .adm files described in Table 7.1, as well as others. It is not recommended that the legacy system policy .adm files be loaded because they can result in persistent Registry settings. Once an .adm file is loaded, it can be found in the SYSVOL directory, ensuring that it will participate in multi-master replication as well as netlogon.

Table 7.1 Administrative Templates

Template	Policy Editor	Installed by Default	Function
System.adm	Group Policy	Default	This is the default Administrative Template and is used for Windows 2000 client workstations.
Inetres.adm	Group Policy	Default	This is an Administrative Template installed by default and is used to set Internet Explorer policies for Windows 2000 client workstations.
Winnt.adm	System Policy	Not default	This is a legacy system policy Administrative Template for Windows NT 4.0 clients.
Windows.adm	System Policy	Not default	This is a legacy system policy Administrative Template for Windows 95 and Windows 98 clients.

Table 7.1 *continued*

Template	Policy Editor	Installed by Default	Function
Common.adm	System Policy	Not default	This is a legacy system policy Administrative Template for the common interface items of Windows NT4, Windows 98, and Windows 95.
Wmp.adm	Group Policy	Not default	This is a template for Windows Media Player.
Conf.adm	Group Policy	Not default	This is a template for NetMeeting.
Shell.adm	Group Policy	Not default	This is a template for additional interface options under the User Configuration options.

An Administrator can create Administrative Templates to include Registry settings that are not default selections. Software developers may include .adm files for their Windows 2000 applications. If an .adm file is included, an Administrator can take advantage of the template to establish settings for the users, and perhaps even deploy the software.

To open an .adm file, start in the Group Policy Editor. Expand the Computer Configuration or User Configuration container and right-click the Administrative Templates container. Select Add/Remove Templates from the pop-up menu, as shown in Figure 7.4. Click ADD, and then select the .adm file that you wish to add from the dialog. If you click REMOVE, you can remove an .adm template. Finally, click CLOSE. New options will appear immediately in the Group Policy Editor.

Registry.pol

While the Administrative Template files are the source for group policy settings, the actual resultant information is saved as registry.pol files. The User settings are saved in the Policies\<Group Policy GUID>\User\Registry.pol file, and the Computer settings are saved in the Policies\<Group Policy GUID>\Machine\registry.pol file.

Group Policy Settings

The Group Policy namespace consists of two components, user and machine configuration. Policies can be created that take advantage of only user settings or only the machine settings. These settings can then be subdivided into five main areas of configuration (Figure 7.5):

Figure 7.4 Adding an Administrative Template.

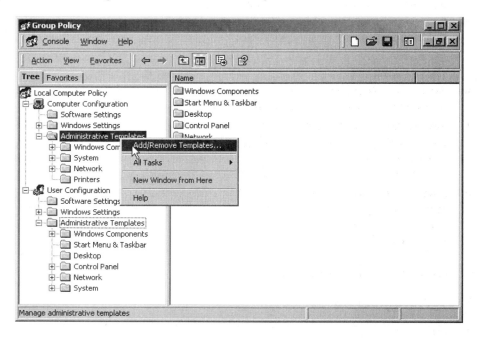

Figure 7.5 Group Policy namespace.

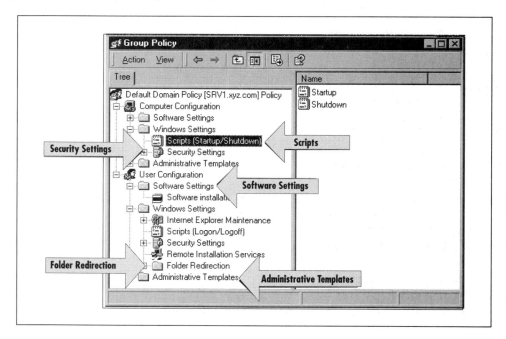

- **Software Settings**   Allows software to be managed centrally, including application deployment and removal.
- **Scripts**   Contains configuration information for scripts such as Startup/Shutdown scripts and Logon/Logoff scripts. These scripts can take advantage of new technologies such as the Windows Scripting Host.
- **Security Settings**   Contains configurable settings relating to security for a particular machine or user.
- **Administrative Templates**   These are Registry-based settings that configure a number of components, from disk quotas to printers to the user's desktop. These settings are written to the Registry each time the Group Policy is applied.
- **Folder Redirection**   Applicable only in the user-based configuration of the policy, folder redirection allows well-known folders such as My Documents to be located centrally instead of on the local machine.

Computer Configuration

The Computer Configuration settings stipulate operating system behavior. All options for the desktop, security settings, and even startup and shutdown scripts can be found in this area. Since the Computer Configuration settings are applied to a computer, regardless of who logs on to it, this policy is best applied to computers that require being locked down to protect local data or applications from being misused.

The Computer Configuration portion of group policies includes a profusion of security settings, as shown in Figure 7.6. This is by design, since these policies are applied to individual computers. An example of a computer that can benefit from computer security policies would be a kiosk computer that is placed out for public use. The kiosk needs to be secured, regardless of the user logged on, since anyone can log on.

User Configuration

The User Configuration settings are similar to the Computer Configuration settings. These are user-specific settings that follow a user around a network wherever that user may log on. Many of these settings are similar in content to the Computer Configuration set, but there are many more settings for the interface in the User Configuration set. This enables the same interface to appear wherever a user may choose to log on, which is desirable especially for roving users.

Scripts exhibit the reasons behind the selection of a setting to be placed under the computer configuration as opposed to the user configuration. Script settings for users are different from those for computers. Whereas computer settings include startup and shutdown scripts, which

Figure 7.6 Computer Configuration and its security settings.

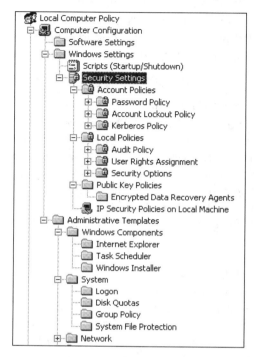

run automatically for a computer regardless of whether anyone has logged on, the user settings include logon and logoff scripts. Logon and logoff scripts occur only when a user accesses the network.

Designing a Group Policy Strategy

Group policies should be taken into consideration when designing an OU structure. The number of group policies affect the user's experience for logging on, and the placement of machines and users in the OU structure will determine how many group policies are required.

For example, FrigidMidgets is a small-sized refrigerator rental service that is located in seven cities with large universities across the United States. There is a sales group, a service group, and a collections group in the FrigidMidgets company. All of sales must have identically configured computer and security settings. If the Network Administrator designs an OU structure that places seven cities at the top, with three nested OUs for Sales, Service, and Collections in *each* of those seven top-layer OUs, then there will be seven identical group policies in each of the Sales containers, along with all the additional traffic to replicate those policies. However, if the Network Administrator designs three top-layer OUs for Sales, Service, and Collections, there will only be one group policy for the Sales OU and a considerably more efficient system.

This example demonstrates the primary rules for designing OUs with group policies in mind:

- Group similarly configured computers in the same OU.
- Group users with similar requirements in the same OU.

Additionally, the fewer settings that a group policy contains, the less time it will take to download and apply that group policy to a computer. Therefore, an Administrator should take care to only establish a group policy setting that is absolutely required. The sequence of events from the time a computer is booted to the time that the final user interface is applied is illustrated in Figure 7.7.

Multi-master replication pledges that information will be synchronized across the entire forest of DCs. However, in any multi-master replication system, there exists the potential for conflicting group policy settings where one setting overrides another. This typically occurs when two different Administrators make contradictory modifications to the same group policy, or make a change to a lower-level group policy setting that overrides a parent group policy setting. To reduce the risk of this happening, organizations should only empower a small number of Administrators to manage group policies.

TIP

User-based configuration settings in the Group Policy Object (GPO) are applied at logon and include software deployed to the user, desktop configuration, security settings, and logon scripts. By default, the CTRL+ALT+DEL screen will not be displayed until the computer settings of the GPOs have been applied, and the user's desktop will not be displayed until the user settings of the GPOs have been applied. This behavior can help with troubleshooting.

The option to apply GPOs synchronously (default) or asynchronously can be configured through the policy, though applying GPOs asynchronous is not recommended.

Group Policy in WAN Environments

Network environments with slow WAN links present other issues for group policy. Because of the excess time that it takes for a logon to complete

Figure 7.7 Sequence of startup events for group policies.

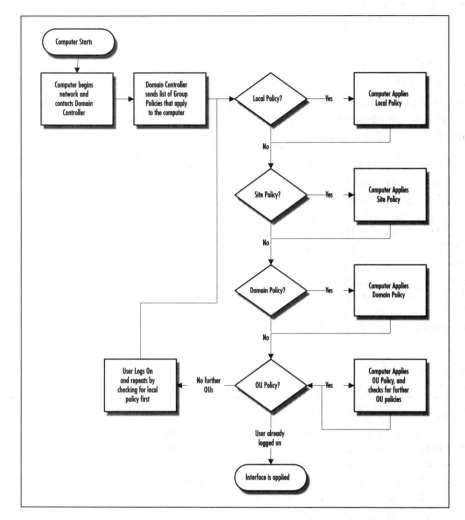

when group policies are present, a slow WAN link or a RAS connection may result in exceptionally poor performance for end users.

Netlogon is capable of detecting a slow link by sending a test ping from the client to the server. If the ping response is slow, netlogon sets a GPO_INFO_FLAG_SLOWLINK value to indicate that the connection is a slow link. A slow link is considered to be 500 Kbps or less. A Network Administrator can change this default value through the Computer Configuration | Administrative Templates | System | Logon | Slow network connection timeout for user profiles policy and the Computer Configuration | Administrative Templates | System | Group Policy | Group Policy slow link detection policy. Various group policy settings may be deactivated for that particular client, but not all group policy settings. When the slow link flag is set, the following are default actions:

- Software policy remains active and cannot be deactivated.
- Application deployments are deactivated.
- File deployments are deactivated.
- Scripts remain active but can be deactivated.
- Registry-based policies remain active and cannot be deactivated.
- Security settings are active but can be deactivated.

WAN environments typically implement sites to manage WAN traffic. A group policy that is linked to a site object will be applied to every machine within that site, even if that site spans multiple domains. The site-linked group policy stays within the domain in which it was created. This means that clients will contact that one domain to apply that group policy. This can cause unnecessary traffic if the domain spans the site. Site-linked group policies should be applied sparingly, and with the traffic implications

For IT Professionals

Using Group Policy to Secure the Management Console

The Active Directory and its schema are dangerous things to enable people to access and use if those users have the ability to make changes to them. Accessing the Active Directory, the schema, and many other system functions in Windows 2000 is executed through a common interface: the Microsoft Management Console (MMC).

Group Policy contains a section for securing the MMC. This section of the group policy, which is located in the User Configuration | Administrative Templates | Windows Components | Microsoft Management Console, allows the Administrator to effectively stop any user from using specific console applications.

Sometimes, however, it is necessary to enable the viewing of a console, but the Administrator may not want the user to *change* anything. In this case, the Administrator will want to turn off the Author mode for that user in the group policy. This particular group policy setting is entitled "Restrict the user from entering Author mode." When this policy is enabled, the user can browse any console that the Administrator has left enabled, but is unable to make any changes within it, thus adding another layer of security to the network.

understood, so that only domains that are held entirely within a site are used as the creators of that site's site-linked group policy.

Implementing Group Policy Strategies

The Network Administrator creates the group policies using a utility called the Group Policy Editor, which is a management console that can be launched separately, or from the Active Directory Users and Computers.

Configuring Group Policy Objects

Group policies can be accessed in three ways, all of which involve using the Microsoft Management Console. The first method uses the stand-alone Group Policy snap-in to launch a Microsoft Management Console with the focus on a particular Group Policy Object. The second method uses the Group Policy snap-in from within the Active Directory Users and Computers snap-in, while the third uses a similar method within the Active Directory Site and Services snap-in.

Using either the Active Directory Users and Computers snap-in or the Active Directory Site and Services snap-in allows Administrators to browse to containers (or sites) that they wish to link GPOs to. Launch the Active Directory Users and Computers snap-in and right-click on the container you wish to associate a group policy with (or to edit an existing Group Policy Object). Click on Properties toward the bottom of the pop-up list. Approximately five tabs will be displayed in the Properties window. Clicking on the far right tab, Group Policy, provides a window displaying any Group Policy Objects associated with this particular container, as shown in Figure 7.8.

Six buttons in the lower portion of the window detail management actions for the Group Policy Objects. If there is more than one GPO associated with a container, then the UP and DOWN buttons are activated, allowing the Administrator to specify the order of priority of the GPOs for that container.

Group Policy Objects are processed from the bottom up as they are displayed on the Group Policy tab, with the topmost GPO overriding settings in the lower GPOs.

The management buttons allow you to:

- Create a new GPO by clicking NEW.
- Associate a GPO already in existence with this container by clicking ADD.
- Edit the currently selected GPO by clicking EDIT.
- Enforce a policy (GPO settings cannot be overridden) or disable a policy by clicking OPTIONS.
- Delete a GPO, or delete its link to the current container by clicking DELETE.

Figure 7.8 New Group Policy Object.

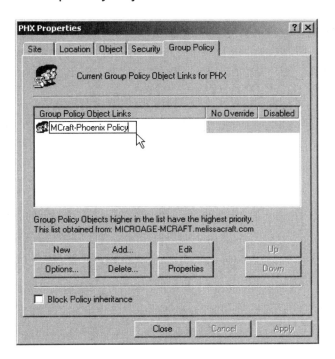

- View summary information, disable computer or user settings, find what containers are associated with this GPO, and set additional filtering security by clicking PROPERTIES.

Double-clicking on the Group Policy Object, or selecting the Group Policy Object and clicking EDIT launches the Group Policy console. The Tree pane in the Group Policy management console contains two main components, Computer Configuration and User Configuration, each with child nodes containing particular configuration policy settings (similar to Figure 7.5).

Link a Group Policy Object to a Container

An Administrator may create a GPO linked to a specific OU, domain, or site, and then wish to deploy the identical GPO elsewhere. Recreating the GPO may take a tremendous amount of time if it is a complex set of policies. The optimum solution would be to link the existing GPO to the other container, which is possible within the Active Directory. To do this, right-click the site, domain, or OU, and select Properties. Click the Group Policy tab. Click ADD. In the resulting dialog box, click the All tab. All of the GPOs for the entire domain will appear. Select the GPO that you want to use, and click OK. The linked group policy will be added to the bottom of the list of

Figure 7.9 Linked containers for a Group Policy Object.

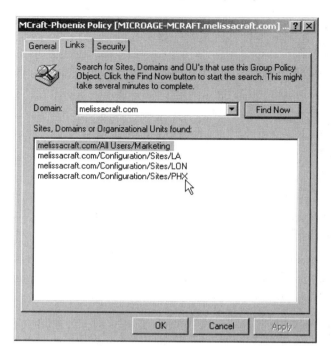

group policies for that container. If you want the group policy to be processed after the others, select the group policy and then click Up. Group policy objects cannot be moved outside of the domain in which they were created; they can only be linked. This will force the users in a linked domain to contact a DC in a different domain to access the group policy, which in turn may cause undesirable network conditions. If not carefully managed, linked GPOs can cause significant network traffic.

Administrators may need to find out which containers a group policy is linked to when they need to troubleshoot the group policy, or when they intend to delete the group policy. The way to go about this is to open the Group Policy Object in the Group Policy Editor and right-click the root container of the group policy. Then select Properties from the pop-up menu.

The Properties dialog for the Group Policy Object will appear. Click the Links tab for the dialog, then click FIND NOW. All of the containers that the group policy is linked to will appear in the dialog, as shown in Figure 7.9.

Keeping Groups from Growing Over Time

One of the challenges with managing a network is to be able to keep administrative groups from growing too large. For example, Joe may leave for a conference out of town. While Joe is away, he may have Susan take over his duties. To grant Susan access, the Administrator adds her account to all of Joe's groups. When Joe returns, no one thinks to remove Susan from the groups. Multiple occurrences like these make groups grow, and too many people end up with more rights than are actually needed.

Group policy has a way to keep groups from growing overly large. By adding groups to the computer configuration group policy, any computer that the group policy applies to will reset permissions according to the group policy, even if changes have been made to that group through the Active Directory Users and Computers console. This does not prevent changes to the groups while the computer is up; instead, it cleans up those changes after the computer reboots. The next time that the computer is booted, it will apply the group policy and remove any extra entries.

To use restricted groups, open a Group Policy Object and navigate to Computer Configuration | Windows Settings | Security Settings | Restricted Groups. Add groups to the Restricted Groups node by right-clicking the Restricted Groups node and selecting New Group. After adding the groups, configure their appropriate user list.

After applying the group policy to a set of computers, only changing the group policy will change the list of users in those groups. It is recommended to use this only with sensitive groups to keep them from growing over time.

Group Policy Objects are not the only features in Windows 2000 that can create restricted groups. The Domain Security Policy console can also establish restricted groups to be applied domainwide.

Delegating Control of Group Policy

As is the case with many tasks associated with the Active Directory, Group Policy management can be delegated. Tasks that can be delegated include:

- Managing Group Policy links
- Creating GPOs
- Editing GPOs

To delegate the management of Group Policy links, right-click on the container for which you wish to delegate authority and select Delegate Control. The Delegation of Control wizard then guides you through the process of determining which users or groups require delegated authority. The next window provides a list of tasks to delegate with an option to Manage Group Policy links (Figure 7.10) toward the bottom of the list. Select this task and proceed to the next screen, which provides a summary of who is receiving the delegated authority. Click FINISH and the users or groups you selected previously now have the authority to manage GPOs linked to the specific container. The user, or group of users, can now add, delete, or reorder GPOs linked to the specified container to which the user has delegated authority.

Figure 7.10 Delegating the management of Group Policy.

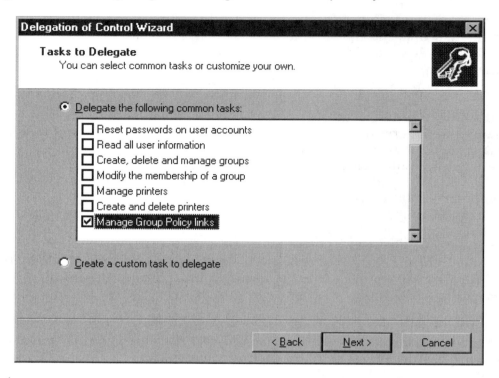

NOTE

Using the Delegation of Control wizard to allow users to manage linked Group Policies does not allow the user to edit or create new Group Policy Objects. Delegating the managed linked Group Policies grants the user read-and-write access to the gPLink and gPOptions properties of the container.

To delegate the creation of GPOs, a user must be added to the Group Policy Creator Owners security group. This security group will allow users to create new GPOs, but edit only the ones created by that particular user or delegated to that user. Another restriction is that members of the Group Policy Creator Owners security group cannot link GPOs to a container.

A user can edit a GPO if the user is granted all permissions on the GPO except Apply Group Policy. Providing the user with the ability to edit a GP does not provide the ability to link the GPO with a container.

Troubleshooting Group Policies

There are three issues with group policies that need troubleshooting:

- The policy does not execute.
- The policy does not execute the way that was expected.
- Logging on takes a really long time.

Policy Does Not Execute

When the policy does not execute, it is usually a problem with an Access Control Entry (ACE) or multiple group policies that conflict with each other, or that part of the policy has been disabled. When the user does not have an ACE directing a Group Policy Object to be applied, then the group policy is skipped completely. To check on the ACEs for a Group Policy Object:

1. Right-click the OU or DC in Active Directory Users and Computers (or right-click the selected Site in the Active Directory Sites and Services console).

2. Select Properties from the pop-up menu.

3. Click the Group Policy tab.

4. Click once on the policy that is not executing to select it.

5. Click PROPERTIES.

6. Click the Security tab.

7. Select the group or the user account from the list in the upper box and review the rights assigned in the lower box.

8. To see a more detailed view, click ADVANCED.

9. Make sure that the user or a group to which the user belongs has the Read right and Apply Group policy right. Also make sure that no group to which the user belongs has been denied rights to either of these rights.

If the user has multiple group policies applied, some may conflict with others, and the result is that the last one that applies usually overrides all previously applied policies. A group policy does not override previously applied group policies if the No Override feature has been checked on one of the upper-level group policies. Upper level can be one of the policies in the list applied to that container, or a group policy that has been applied to a parent container. The best method is to start with the group policy that did not execute correctly, and ensure that it is configured correctly. Then work backward to the top of the tree until all the policies have been reviewed. This would be in the order of OU, parent

OUs, domain, site, and then the Local group policy. To check them, click on the group policy, then click OPTIONS, and make sure that the No Override check box is clear.

Finally, if a policy has been disabled, it will not execute. To see if a group policy has been disabled, select it and then click OPTIONS. Make sure that the Disabled check box is clear. To see if part of the policy has been disabled, select the group policy and then click PROPERTIES. On the General tab, make sure that the check boxes for disabling either the User or the Computer portion of the policy have not been disabled.

Policy Executes in the Wrong Way

A policy may execute in an unexpected manner for a couple of reasons. It could be a legacy NT 4 system policy that was applied accidentally. A good practice to follow is to not use any legacy system policies.

If a group policy is created to install software, and the installation does not occur correctly, it could be that the software transform file is not correct. Transform files are those that custom configure Windows Installer packages. If the transform file is not added to the Modifications tab, the plain vanilla installation of the software will proceed. If the wrong transform file is added to the Modifications tab, then errors may occur or the wrong configuration of software will be a result.

It is possible that the same software application is applied to the same group policy software installation. If so, then the application may install incorrectly. Make sure that an application only appears once within any Group Policy Object, or within a string of nested GPOs.

If you receive a "Failed to open the Group Policy Object" error, then you will need to recheck the network connection and DNS configuration. This error indicates that the policy was not located.

Logging On Takes a Long Time

The primary thing to do when there is an extended logon period is to reduce the number of Group Policy Objects that are applied to a user. This can be done by removing group policies, combining multiple group policies into a single group policy, or by removing the "Apply Group Policy" right from the user's Access Control Entries (ACEs).

The next thing that can be done is to disable parts of GPOs. This is achieved through the Properties dialog box for the group policy. It will avoid processing the settings, even for unconfigured policies.

There may be a GPO that is applied to a site, where the GPO belongs to one domain and the user belongs to another. When this happens, the user must be authenticated back to the DC that "owns" that particular group policy. This excess processing causes a slower logon. Where possible, remove site-linked group policies and apply them to containers instead.

If none of these tactics work, you may need to look at the site topology and whether there are enough DCs available to service logon requests from users.

NOTE

The Windows 2000 Resource Kit includes some essential Group Policy tools, such as:

- **Gpolmig.exe**   During the migration from a Windows NT 4 environment to a Windows 2000 environment, this utility can migrate Windows NT 4 system policies to Windows 2000 Group Policy Objects.
- **Gpotool.exe**   The Group Policy verification tool can check the consistency and replication state of Group Policy Objects.
- **Gpresult.exe**   The Group Policy Result tool details information about the application of group policy to the current machine.

Security

Rights can only be assigned to security principals. Security principals consist of user accounts and security groups. Security groups are either Domain Local groups or Global groups. (Universal groups exist only as distribution groups in mixed mode, but can be made into Security groups in native mode.)

Unlike Novell's directory service (NDS), OUs are not security principals. You cannot assign rights to an OU and expect those rights to be inherited by the users and groups within them. If you are an NDS Administrator and would like this same functionality, you can muddle through with strategic placement and organization of Global groups. The procedure or process Microsoft recommends is to create a Global group within each OU, and name it accordingly. Then include all the users and groups within that OU as members of the Global group. Plus, add the Global groups of the next level down OUs. This nesting system will permit rights to flow down through the tree. Assign rights to these OU Global groups as though assigning them to the OU itself. The only thing that is not achieved with this system is the ability to block inheritance. An example of this system is shown in Figure 7.11.

Groups

Three types of groups are available for the Active Directory: Domain Local, Global, and Universal. Of these types, there are several default groups

Figure 7.11 Nesting Global groups to flow rights down the Active Directory hierarchy.

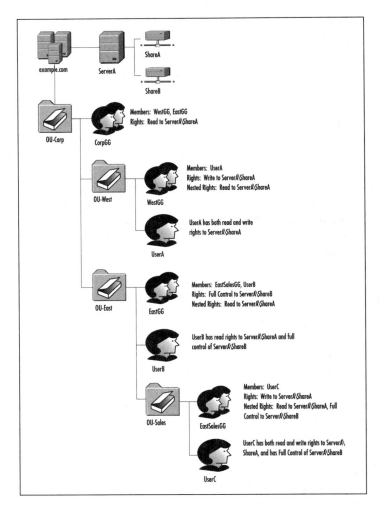

that are provided automatically within the Users container in each domain. Another set of groups is placed in the Builtin container in each domain. Builtin groups are provided for local group usage and backward compatibility.

There are yet other groups available for security reasons that are not provided as Active Directory security principals. These are special groups that define default behavior for users. The reason that they are provided as special groups is so that the Network Administrator can define that default behavior in ACEs for various objects. The special groups are:

Anonymous Logon   This group handles anonymous logons, and is used for Microsoft Message Queuing (MSMQ). When MSMQ clients use RPCs to reach an MSMQ server, the call is considered an anonymous logon.

Authenticated Users   This represents any user who can log on to a machine or to the Active Directory. This group is automatically made a member of the Power Users Local group, so that all users are "Power Users" on Windows 2000 PCs. To reduce those users' rights to be equivalent to standard users' rights, you will need to remove the membership for Power Users and leave the membership to the Users Local group. All Authenticated Users are given the Read and Apply group policy rights to each group policy, so this will need to be removed from a group policy if the Administrator wants to filter the group policy and apply it to only certain security groups. Of course, the Administrator will need to apply explicit rights for those security groups in order for the group policy to become effective.

Everyone   This group includes all current users, including guests and users from other Active Directory domains.

Interactive   This group includes any user who is currently logged on to a specific computer locally and given access to its resources. There can be multiple user accounts in this group when the DC is providing terminal services.

Network   This group is the antithesis of the Interactive group. It includes all users who have been authenticated and granted access to a specific computer's resources over the network.

There are other special groups that are installed with certain services. For example, a Dialup group is created for remote access services, and a Proxy group is created for Internet Information Services. Your Windows 2000 system may have additional special groups depending upon which services have been installed. The service's documentation should explain the purpose of those groups and what security may be required to manage them.

Group Strategy

The group strategy in legacy Windows NT was summarized by the acronym AGLP. This stood for **A**ccounts added to **G**lobal groups that are placed in **L**ocal groups, which are assigned **P**ermissions. The strategy for Windows 2000 is nearly identical. In this strategy, user accounts should be placed within Global groups. Here we depart from the former standard with options—the Global groups can be placed within other Global groups or within Universal groups in whatever nesting strategy is established. Then we pick up with the recommended strategy again, place the Global groups within Domain Local groups, which are assigned Permissions. The resulting acronyms? AGDLP is standard, AGUGDLP is nested.

For more information on groups and users, refer to Chapter 9, "Managing Users and Groups."

Viewing Security Features in Active Directory Users and Computers

When viewing the Active Directory Users and Computers console, it is sometimes necessary to view who has rights to individual objects. To see the permissions for each object, click the View menu and select Advanced Features. You will see an additional two folders: Lost and Found, and System. Lost and Found holds orphaned objects. System holds other Active Directory objects such as Group Policy Objects in its Policies subcontainer.

Not only will you be able to see the additional features, but you will have a Security tab added to the properties of Active Directory objects. The Security tab will lead to the discretionary Access Control List (ACL) for the object. Any users or groups who have rights will be listed. You can add, remove, or edit properties for the object. Note that whenever you add a right, you add it explicitly for that object. If you want to add a right that is propagated to other objects within a container, you must select the Advanced tab and drop down the box that states "This object only" to change it to "This object and child objects."

Domain Security Console

Security for the Active Directory is configured in many places, but domain-wide policies are configured in the Domain Security console shown in Figure 7.12. The Domain Security Policy is located in the Administrative Tools menu.

There are several containers for security policy in the Domain Security console:

- Account Policies
- Local Policies
- Event Log
- Restricted Groups
- System Services
- Registry
- File System
- Public Key Policies
- IP Security Policies on Active Directory

Account Policies

There are three account policies: Password, Account Lockout, and Kerberos. Kerberos policy is new to Windows 2000, while Password and Account Lockout policies are similar to the ones in the legacy Windows NT Server. All are listed in Table 7.2.

Figure 7.12 The Domain Security console.

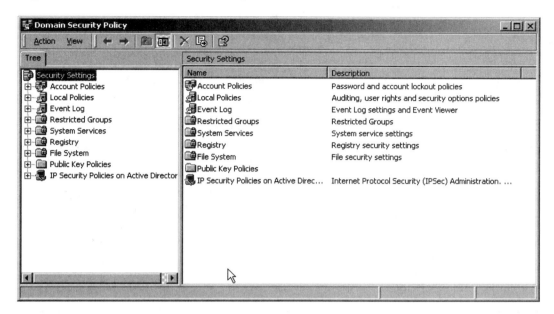

Table 7.2 Account Policies

Policy Type	Policy	Default Setting	Security Feature	Minimum and Maximum Values
Password	Enforce password history.	1 password remembered	Users are prevented from reusing the same password over and over.	0 (do not keep password history) to 24 passwords.
Password	Maximum password age.	42 days	When set to a low number, users are forced to use fresh passwords, making the system more secure.	0 (passwords do not expire) to 999 days.
Password	Minimum password age.	0 days	When set to any number other than 0, users are forced to retain a password for a duration of time, preventing immediate changes.	0 (password can be changed immediately) to 998 days.

Table 7.2 *continued*

Policy Type	Policy	Default Setting	Security Feature	Minimum and Maximum Values
Password	Minimum password length.	0 characters	When set to a larger number, users cannot use easy-to-guess passwords.	0 (no password required) to 14 characters.
Password	Passwords must meet complexity requirements.	Disabled	When enabled, the password is required to have a combination of other characters, numbers, and upper and lower case.	Enabled or Disabled.
Password	Store password using reversible encryption for all users in the domain.	Disabled	When enabled, passwords are encrypted.	Enabled or Disabled.
Password	User must log on to change the password.	Disabled	When the password has expired, the user can still log on; a password change will then be initiated immediately.	Enabled or Disabled.
Account Lockout	Account lockout duration.	Not defined	When defined, the Administrator sets the number of minutes that an account is locked out after the set of invalid logon attempts.	0 (account is locked out until Administrator unlocks it) to 99,999 minutes.
Account Lockout	Account lockout threshold.	0 invalid logon attempts	The user must fail at logging on for the number of attempts specified, and then will be locked out of the system.	0 (account will not lockout) to 999 logon attempts.

Table 7.2 *continued*

Policy Type	Policy	Default Setting	Security Feature	Minimum and Maximum Values
Account Lockout	Reset account lockout counter after…	Not defined	The greater the number of minutes specified here, the more likely a user may have an account locked out. This is the duration of time during which the system counts invalid logon attempts before resetting to 0. Each successful logon resets this counter to 0.	1 to 99,999 minutes.
Kerberos	Enforce user logon restrictions.	Enabled	This enables Kerberos to use the logon restrictions.	Enabled or Disabled.
Kerberos	Maximum lifetime for service ticket.	600 minutes	The duration that a Kerberos security ticket remains valid.	0 (ticket does not expire) to 99,999 minutes.
Kerberos	Maximum lifetime for user ticket.	10 hours	The duration that a user's logon remains valid without contacting a Kerberos host (KDC).	0 (ticket does not expire) to 99,999 hours.
Kerberos	Maximum lifetime for user ticket renewal.	7 days	In order to renew a previously used ticket, the user must contact a KDC in this timeframe.	0 (ticket renewal does not expire) to 99,999 days.
Kerberos	Maximum tolerance for computer clock synchronization.	5 minutes	Kerberos authentication is stamped with a start and expiration time (default of 10 hours). If the time of the KDC and the client are not synchronized, the Kerberos ticket could prematurely expire or never expire. This sets the allowable time variance.	0 to 99,999 minutes.

Administrators have tough decisions in front of them when they set up the Account policies. They must decide where to trade ease of use for security. For example, users who are forced to change passwords every day will be more likely to forget passwords and will overwhelm the help desk. However, users who are never forced to change passwords probably won't; in which case, the network is left nearly unsecured.

When deciding on the policies for your organization, you should take into account the desired level of security and likelihood of security breaches in each area. For example, if your organization is a school with one domain for teachers and another domain for students, then it would be preferred to keep high security on the teacher's domain by enforcing monthly password changes and long, encrypted passwords.

Local Policies

Three types of policies affect the local DC:

- Audit policy
- User rights assignment
- Security options

Audit policy enables the Administrator to audit the domain's activity with security events. Audited items include (but are not limited to) events such as logons, access to objects, access to system events, and policy changes. The audit can reveal whether such security events were successful or unsuccessful. An Administrator would generally prefer to know when an event has been unsuccessful, since that will provide the Administrator with the knowledge of who has tried to access something denied to him or her. Administrators may also wish to know whenever a policy change attempt has been made, whether successful or unsuccessful, since that is indicative of the use of a highly secured right.

The User Rights Assignment container provides a single place to add general rights to the local DC for users or security groups. These rights control who can shut down the server, who can change system time, who can add computers to the domain, and so forth.

Security options provide a local security system that can further lock down the DC. These security options include whether to disable using CTRL-ALT-DEL for logging on to the server, whether to automatically log off any users after a logon time expires, establishing a message text for users at the time of logon, whether to shut down the server if no more security events can be logged, and more. Although many of these items are new, others were available as Registry edits in the legacy Windows NT server.

Event Log

The Event Log settings manage the system, application, and security logs. These settings can establish the maximum size, access to the logs, and retention of the logs.

Restricted Groups

This is the same group restriction that can be set in a group policy, though it is considered more secure. When restricted groups are used in the Domain Security Policy console, the DC establishes the new security settings for groups right away. A DC must be rebooted before it accesses and uses a new group policy.

System Services

There is an associated policy for each of the default services that run. The policy is, by default, not defined. When defined, however, the Administrator is faced with the dialog shown in Figure 7.13 where the service startup mode must be selected. From this screen, the Administrator can further edit who has access to change the service. By default, the group Everyone is first offered full control of services when a policy is activated. If using Terminal Server, this should be changed to Administrators.

Registry

The Registry policy settings can secure individual Registry keys from being edited by a user. Like services, by default, the Everyone group is initially offered full control of the Registry keys, which means they can change them any way they please. You can add Registry keys to this policy and then secure those keys from being changed, or viewed, by changing the groups and users who are granted access to those keys.

File System

The file system policies can configure security for files and folders. This is a more granular control over files and folders than share-level security. It offers a single point of security administration for the local DC.

Figure 7.13 Editing a service policy.

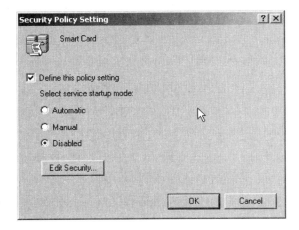

Public Key Policies

Public key policies let you add automatic certificate requests and manage the certificate authority behavior. You should install your Certificate Authority server(s) before attempting to establish these policies.

IP Security Policies on Active Directory

If you have IP Security (IPSec) established on the network, these policies will manage it. There are several ways that a DC can handle IPSec, which are discussed in greater detail in Chapter 15, "Windows 2000 Security Services."

Security Templates

Windows 2000 has several templates for security settings that you can apply to either a group policy or to the Security console. If there are changes made to a computer's security settings and the template is the organization's standard, then reapplying the template can return the computer to a working state.

To import a policy into a group policy, open the policy in the Group Policy Editor. Then, navigate to Computer Configuration | Windows Settings | Security Settings. Right-click Security Settings and select Import Policy from the pop-up menu. The security templates will appear in the window.

To import a policy into the Domain Security console, right-click the root container called Security Settings. Select Import Policy from the pop-up menu and select the desired security template.

Object Protection

With Active Directory, establishing permissions is more than just granting a user access to a file or a printer. It also involves permitting and denying access to objects for users and security groups.

Access Control Lists (ACLs)

Permissions in Windows 2000 are stored in an ACL. The ACL is accessible through the Security tab on various objects, such as the Properties of a group policy as shown in Figure 7.14.

The Security dialog screen lets an Administrator specify the groups or users who have access to the group policy. The default permission for any user to a group policy is to Read and Apply Group Policy, except for Domain Admins, Enterprise Admins, and the SYSTEM groups who are not granted the Apply Group Policy right to prevent themselves from being restricted by the policy. The Administrative groups are also granted rights that enable them to edit the policy as well. The default rights set for groups

Figure 7.14 Access Control List (ACL).

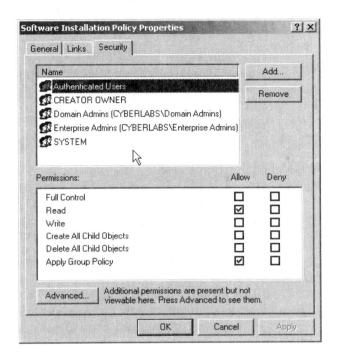

exceeds the minimum required, since Read access is not needed to use the group policy. It may mean a more secure environment to remove the Read right for Authenticated users from the ACL.

You can move any object from one OU to another within the same domain by right-clicking it and selecting Move from the pop-up menu. When you move an object from one container to another, only explicitly assigned permissions will follow the object to the new container; inherited permissions do not follow the object.

Access Control Entries (ACEs)

Each permission within the ACL is an ACE. To gain comprehensive control over the ACEs, the Administrator should click ADVANCED at the bottom of the Security dialog. This leads to the Access Control Editor shown in Figure 7.15.

When adding an ACE, there are several rights that can be granted or denied. Explicitly denying a right will take precedence over allowing the right. If a user belongs to two different groups, and one allows a right while the other denies it, then the user is denied access.

Note that many of these rights are not applicable to the Group Policy Object being edited. Instead, there is a check box at the bottom of the ACE editor that lets you establish these rights for the user or group. These

Figure 7.15 Access Control Entries.

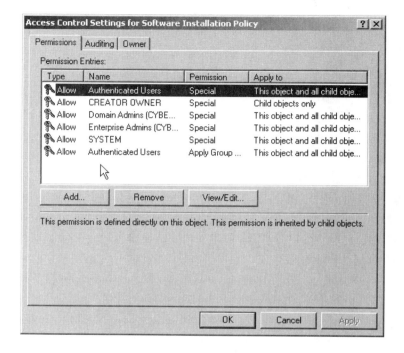

rights are then granted to any objects within the container to which the Group Policy Object belongs.

A good practice to follow when adding rights is to add them for groups only. Even if a single user is going to require a particular right, if you create a group and grant the right to the group, then other users can be added later, or the first user completely replaced. This facilitates administration that is beneficial in the long run, even though it can be a little extra work up front.

Security Descriptor

When a user authenticates to the Active Directory, the account is identified with its username and password. With a successful authentication, the system creates an access token including the Security Identifier (SID) (explained in the next section) and the SIDs of all the groups of which the user is a member. When the user generates a process after that, the access token is attached to the process.

The security descriptor is attached to network resources, rather than to users. It is the reverse of the access token in that it is the holder of the resource's ACL, which is compared to the user's access token when the user attempts to authenticate to a resource. The ACL contains the SIDs of each security principal that has been granted or explicitly denied access. It is the SID that maps the access token to the security descriptor.

Security Identifier (SID)

SIDs are created for users, groups, computers, and domains; essentially, any security principal. A SID is unique and built when the user, group, computer, or trust is generated within a domain. A SID is composed of:

- Revision number
- Authority that assigned the SID
- Domain
- Relative Identifier (RID) values

SIDs are a legacy Windows NT concept. When a user is moved from a legacy domain to an Active Directory domain, it must be issued a new SID. Because the SID is the mapping mechanism between the access token of the user and the security descriptor of the resource, it has significant implications when a SID is changed. In fact, membership would need to be reestablished for each user account. When groups are moved, new permissions would need to be granted to reestablish the ACLs.

For Managers

Secondary Logons

Run As is a secondary logon feature for Windows 2000. Using this feature enables an Administrator to execute administrative functions without logging on to a machine as the Administrator account. This adds a level of security because a PC could not be left running with an Administrator's credentials. Not only can a user walk up to that machine and execute functions with Administrative access, but a Trojan Horse attack that uses the credentials that currently exist on the PC to execute damaging functions would not have access to the credentials that enable those functions if using a standard user account rather than an Administrator's account.

Secondary logon exists as the Run As Service and can be managed on each Windows 2000 computer via the Computer Management console, or from the Component Services icon in Control Panel. To use the tool, you must be logged on as a user without rights to some application. Then, right-click the application while holding SHIFT down on the keyboard. Then select Run As from the pop-up menu.

There is a new attribute of security principals in the Active Directory called SIDHistory. SIDHistory retains a copy of a moved object's old SID. For example, a user that was upgraded from legacy NT to Windows 2000 would be able to access the same resources as before the move. Behind the scenes, the user would either authenticate as its NT4/SID or as its Windows 2000/SID—whichever has more rights. SIDHistory also works when moving a user from a domain in one forest to a domain in another forest.

However, there are also implications when the SIDHistory is retained. If a user has been moved more than one time from an NT upgrade to Windows 2000, and from forest to forest, then there will be multiple copies of the SIDHistory in the access token and it becomes overlarge. Furthermore, troubleshooting permitted access for a security principal with multiple SIDHistories is difficult.

Summary

Group Policy is an Active Directory integrated feature used to govern the user interface and computer settings. It is a newer version of the System Policies, originally introduced with Windows 95, and used in Windows 98 and Windows NT 4. Group policies allow an Administrator to control how a workstation is used. Instead of being a file-based policy (like System Policies where machines must contact a server holding a particular system policy file before the policy is applied), group policy is applied to containers within the Active Directory and applied during the computer authentication to the network and user logon to the Active Directory.

Group policies are applied in a specific order:

1. Local Group Policy Object
2. Site Group Policy Object
3. Domain Group Policy Objects
4. Organizational Unit (OU) Group Policy Objects from the parent OUs down to the user's or computer's OU location

Although there is a single Local group policy, there can be multiple policies associated with a site, domain, or OU. These policies can be changed in order to execute as the Administrator would require. The last policy to execute will override all previous policies for the same item unless a policy has been designated as "No Override." The more group policies that must be applied, the longer a user's logon sequence will take. This does not pertain to the depth of the OUs, because six policies applied to a single OU will take as long to execute a logon as six OUs deep each with a single policy. Site policies will require contact with the domain controller (DC) that manages a particular group policy, and may further increase logon time. When designing group policies, do not use site–associated policies if possible, and use as few group policies as possible.

To implement a group policy, start in the Active Directory Users and Computers console. From there, right-click the container to which the group policy will be applied, and select Properties. Click the Group Policy tab, and then add, remove, and edit group policies as needed.

When developing an OU infrastructure with Group Policies in mind, remember to:

- Group similarly configured computers in the same OU.
- Group users with similar requirements in the same OU.

Additionally, the fewer settings that a group policy contains, the less time it will take to download and apply that group policy to a computer

Security within the Windows 2000 Active Directory involves the use of Access Control Lists (ACLs) and Security Identifiers (SIDs). ACLs are lists of the groups and users who have rights to the resource, plus which rights they have been granted. SIDs are unique IDs applied to the security principal. SIDs for a user and any of the groups to which the user belongs are listed within a user's access token at the time of logon. The ACL uses SIDs to identify the users and groups. The process is simply a comparison of a user's access token to a resource's ACL. The SIDs are used when comparing an access token and security description to determine which rights are applicable to the user.

FAQs

Q: I want to deny a user access to a resource, but the user needs to belong to a group that is given full control of the same resource. Do I need to create a special group for this user?

A: That depends on how you want to manage this in the future. You do not have to create a special group with all the explicit rights for that user, and the user can remain in the group that is given full control of the resource. You can simply deny access to the resource to that user explicitly. The deny right will override all other rights to the resource. However, if you have this situation occur once, you may encounter it twice; in which case, it is recommended that you leave the user in the group with full control of the resource, then create a second group that is denied access to that resource. Adding the user to that second group will accomplish the same thing as denying access explicitly. If eventually you encounter another user who has the same requirements, you can simply add that user to the second group.

Q: Why do group policies contain many of the same features as the Domain Security Policy console?

A: Mainly because a group policy can be used to apply the same registry settings as the Domain Security Policy console, and is flexible enough to apply those registry settings to computers domainwide, or to a subset of computers within a specific OU.

Q: How can I look at the ACE for an OU?

A: The ACEs are available from the Group Policy tab. By looking at the Properties of the group policy and selecting Security, the ACL is shown. From there, click ADVANCED. At that point, you can click ADD or REMOVE to add or remove ACEs, or VIEW/EDIT to change an ACE.

Chapter 8

Managing Settings, Software, and User Data with IntelliMirror

Solutions in this chapter:

- **Introduction**
- **Deploying Software with Group Policies**
- **Managing Software with Group Policies**
- **Managing User and Computer Settings**
- **Using Scripts**
- **Folder Redirection**
- **Summary**

Introduction

IntelliMirror and group policies are a complex business requiring knowledge of Active Directory and of the supporting technologies that comprise IntelliMirror. The previous chapter provided the groundwork for IntelliMirror configuration: how to configure a policy to apply to certain predetermined groups, and how to design a group policy infrastructure. Having familiarized yourself with the way group policies interact with the Active Directory and your network infrastructure, it is time to get them to earn their keep—to help you deploy and maintain software and manage user data and settings.

Deploying Software with Group Policies

Software versions seem to change as quickly as odometer readings, with new releases of major applications a monthly occurrence. Compound this with the incredible variety of software available, and you have the potential for nightmare software management scenarios. Large organizations may require hundreds of applications to be supported on thousands of machines—an impossible task without some form of supporting infrastructure. Unfortunately, software deployment does not stop there— Administrators also have to contend with patches, revisions, and minor updates. Administrators cannot keep pace with the rate of change of software, or meet the requirement to deploy software to numerous users without offloading some of the work to an application deployment infrastructure. Allowing the deployment of software to be enforced by the infrastructure provides a scalable solution that can reduce the workload and eliminate a certain amount of human error.

We have discussed how Group Policy, a part of the IntelliMirror technology set, is used to address change and configuration management issues. Since change and configuration management encompasses software distribution, it follows that Group Policy has a well-defined software deployment component. Understanding Group Policy and its relationship to the Active Directory is integral to being able to develop a flexible and scalable software deployment strategy.

Microsoft has developed a cycle for software deployment using group policies that defines four key phases of the distribution process:

- **Preparation** To provide additional value, and to leverage the advantages of Group Policy, software has to be prepackaged into a certain format.
- **Distribution** Software that has been packaged needs to be made available at distribution points. These distribution points can later be accessed by client workstations.

- **Targeting** Not all client workstations require all packaged software, and as a result, certain clients have to be grouped together as recipients of the particular software. This is known as targeting client workstations or users.
- **Installation** Once the software has been prepared in the correct format, made available at distribution points, and the clients have been targeted, the installation of the software can take place.

Software deployment using the set of technologies that support the software installation and maintenance features of IntelliMirror provides an Administrator with centralized control over the following tasks:

- Installation, upgrade, or removal of applications
- Installation of service packs and software updates
- Assigning applications to computers or users
- Publishing applications to users
- Appearance of applications on the Start menu or in Add/Remove programs

Software is deployed using group policies by creating a Group Policy Object (GPO) that contains the details for installing the packaged software on client workstations. The targeting of clients is achieved by linking the GPO to a container and using the rules for Group Policy inheritance. Additional control can be gained by using filtering and Access Control Lists (ACLs).

There are three methods of deploying software using Group Policy:

- Assigning applications to users
- Assigning applications to computers
- Publishing applications to users

Assigning Software

Group Policy allows software to be assigned to users or computers. Assigning an application to a computer or user implies that the application is available for use at all times, even though the files and installation resources to run it may not be present. The assigned application appears as a shortcut on the desktop or an entry in the Start menu.

User Assignments

The entry point for applications that are assigned to users follows the user to every Windows 2000 computer on the network. The application is made available for the user on every machine by the advertisement of a shortcut on the desktop, or by inserting a menu item in the Start menu. If a user is assigned an application and logs on to another workstation, then an entry point on the desktop or in the Start menu will advertise that the assigned program can be run. Clicking on the shortcut for the first time seamlessly installs the application in the background, requiring no user interaction. The only difference the user will notice is a delay in the amount of time the program takes to launch. An assigned application will also install and launch if a user clicks on a file that has an association to a specific application.

Applications can be configured to be persistent; in other words, even if the user deletes them using the Add/Remove Programs applet, they will be re-advertised at next log on.

Computer Assignments

Computers that have a certain function due to their location are prime targets for applications assigned to computers. If the requirement is that anyone logging on to a specific computer should have access to a certain application, then the application should be assigned to the computer.

Computer-assigned applications are installed when the computer settings of the Group Policy are first applied at startup. This is slightly different from user-assigned applications that are installed the first time the user launches the application.

Every user who logs on to that specific computer will see the desktop shortcut or entry in the Start menu for the assigned application. Since the application is linked to the computer, the user will not be able to remove the application using Add/Remove programs. This restriction does not apply to Administrators or other accounts with similarly high privileges.

Publishing Software

Applications within the business that are not mandatory, but may be necessary to some users, can be published. Using Add/Remove Programs, users install the applications themselves. Double-clicking on a file associated with a published application can also initiate the installation process. Using Add/Remove Programs displays a list of published applications that can be optionally installed. Figure 8.1 shows a published application called Balancing Act.

Enhancements within Add/Remove Programs

The Add/Remove Programs applet is designed to help users add and remove Windows components, as well as add, remove, repair, and modify other Windows programs. The Windows 2000 Add/Remove Programs applet has seen considerably improvements over its Windows NT counterpart. As Figure 8.1 illustrates, there are three buttons in a column on the far left of the Add/Remove Programs applet. They are CHANGE OR REMOVE PROGRAMS, ADD NEW PROGRAMS, and ADD/REMOVE WINDOWS COMPONENTS.

Figure 8.1 A published application in Add/Remove Programs.

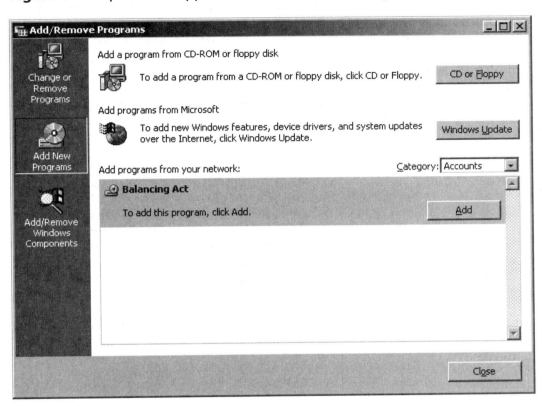

Clicking on CHANGE OR REMOVE PROGRAMS lists the set of applications currently installed on the Windows 2000 computer. Clicking on a specific application lists additional details of the installed application, such as the last time the application was used, how often the application has been used, and its size.

NOTE

The Change or Remove Programs portion of the Add/Remove Programs applet displays information about currently installed applications. The Sort by: drop-down box provides a means of ordering the list by name, size, frequency of use, and date last used. The size displayed is only an estimate, while the frequency of use is determined by measuring the number of times the application has been run in the last 30 days.

Figure 8.2 Improved functionality in Add/Remove Programs.

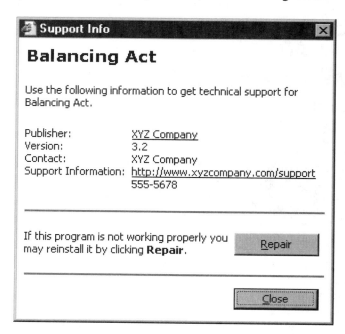

Applications that support the new method of packaging for distribution, which is discussed in the next section, can also include support information such as Web addresses and telephone numbers (Figure 8.2). The Support Info screen also provides a button to allow the application to repair itself.

The Add New Programs portion of the Add/Remove Programs applet allows users and Administrators to install a program from CD or floppy, to retrieve updates from Microsoft by clicking WINDOWS UPDATE, or to add programs that have been published on the network. Programs published on the network can be viewed by category, allowing departmental or functional delimitation of programs.

Packaging an Application

For software to be assigned or published, it needs to be packaged in a form that can be distributed using Group Policy. Windows Installer provides a packaging format that answers many of the questions posed by IT professionals regarding the setup process and application packaging.

There has been a great deal of dissatisfaction regarding the installation and setup process on the Windows platform. To address the problems faced on an almost daily basis by support staff, Microsoft developed a new installation mechanism called the Windows Installer. The native format of a Windows Installer package is the preferred format for packaging software for distribution by group policies.

Windows Installer

When Administrators imagine software being installed on client workstations, they sigh and begin to dread the imminent raft of commonly experienced problems. Will installing this software break another piece of currently functional software? Will the software uninstall properly? What DLLs will change? No standardized setup process existed previously that developers could follow, which led to each application having its own setup routine. Installing applications turns into a software version of Russian roulette—each time an application was installed, you were left wondering if another application would meet its demise.

The Windows Installer service was developed to resolve these issues, and provide a method of enforcing setup rules, managing shared resources, diagnosing and repairing problems, and easing customization. The Windows Installer is a service that resides on client workstations and is installed automatically during Windows 2000 setup. To leverage the advantages of the Windows Installer service, an application needs to be described in a standard way. The Windows Installer service is comprised of an installation service, a component management format, and a management API for applications and tools.

Installation Service

Windows 2000 includes the Windows Installer service as a standard operating system component that runs under the local system account. Using the local system account ensures that applications can be installed regardless of who is currently logged on. When presented with an application described in the standard Windows Installer format, the service installs the application, negating the need for a separate installation program for each application. The Windows Installer service is saddled with the responsibility of enforcing the installation process rules.

Component Management Format

The Windows Installer service divides applications into components, features, and products. A Windows Installer component is a set of installable resources such as files or Registry keys that are installed together. Components are visible only to the developer and not the user. The smallest entity that the Windows Installer service can manipulate is a component. Files and Registry settings are installed by installing components, and as a result, interdependent resources can be grouped together in a component to ensure that they are always installed and uninstalled together. Applications can be easily uninstalled because information is maintained at the component level, which ensures no installable resources are left behind after application removal.

> **NOTE**
>
> An installable resource can only be in one Windows Installer component. Two components cannot contain the same Registry keys or files, whether they are part of the same product or not. Components are unique and will be identical, regardless of what application they are shipped with. Each component has a Globally Unique Identifier (GUID) called the component code.

A feature is a part of the application that is available for installation. During a custom installation, the user-definable options are often comparable to features. A feature can be viewed as a way of selecting a group of components for installation. Windows Installer features provide a much more flexible set of installation types, and can be set to be:

- **Installed on Local Hard Disk**   All the relevant components are installed on to the local machine.
- **Installed to Run from Source**   The application files are fetched from a source location, such as a CD.
- **Advertised**   The application is not installed but appears to be available. The first time the user attempts to invoke the application, the relevant installable resources are installed.
- **Not Installed**   No files are copied.

A product is comprised of one or more features described by a single package file. The package file, which has the extension .MSI, describes the relationship between features, components, and resources. Packages have a database format optimized for installation performance. A Windows Installer product usually represents a full product such as the Balancing Act accounting software for the XYZ Company.

When the package file is executed, the Windows Installer interrogates it to determine what installation actions must be completed. A package file can contain the application files internally using cabinet files (.CAB files), or the application files could be placed in the same directory as the package file itself.

An example of an application that uses the MSI format is Office 2000. Word, Excel, Access, and PowerPoint are features, while Office 2000 is the product.

Management API

The management API allows applications to programmatically detail what products, features, and components are installed on a computer, to install and configure products and features, and to establish the path to Windows Installer components. The API manages file paths for the application so that the Windows Installer application can query the Windows Installer service for a path to a component. This eliminates the need for hard-coded paths. Applications that use the management API are enabled to:

- **Support roaming users**   Paths are not hard-coded and the management API allows for the installation and configuration of the application.
- **Provide on-demand install at the feature level**   If a user requested a feature not currently installed and the application has been designed to use the management API, the Windows Installer service would install the necessary feature without intervention. When a feature is available, but has not been installed, it is said to have been advertised. Since the technology required to invoke the management API is part of the application, feature-level demand installs work on Windows 9x and Windows NT.
- **Provide on-demand install at the product level**   Products can be advertised in a similar way to features, except it is the operating system, not the application, that uses the abilities of the management API. Advertising a product creates an entry point on the client to install the product. This can be in the form of a shortcut, a file extension association, or OLE registration. When these entry points are activated, it is the operating system that calls the Windows Installer service to install the product. Since the operating system must be designed to call the Windows Installer management API, product-level on-demand installs only work on Windows 2000. After installation is completed, the Windows Installer service launches the application.
- **Runtime resource resiliency**   Applications designed to use the management API can be enabled to repair themselves. The Windows Installer service performs two checks when resolving a path requested by an application. First, it determines if the feature or component has already been installed, and then it verifies that the components are installed correctly. If the Windows Installer service determines that a component is missing or corrupt, it performs an on-demand repair in a similar fashion as an on-demand install.

Additional Features

- Windows Installer provides a transacted rollback facility. During an install, the Windows Installer records an undo operation for every action it performs, and saves replaced or deleted files and Registry settings in a temporary location. If at any time the installation fails, the machine can be reverted to its original state.

- Windows Installer can interrogate multiple sources for the installation files if required for an operation such as an on-demand install.

- Windows Installer includes functionality to upgrade and patch applications. Support is included to determine if an application should be upgraded by using Upgrade Codes. Applications can also be patched using the Windows Installer.

- Transforms can modify the Windows Installer package when it is executed, and provide a way to dynamically influence the installation process.

- Windows Installer can run under the Local System Account, which has elevated privileges, or the user account. This caters to environments that do not provide the users with high privileges on their local workstations.

Creating a Package

The Windows Installer service provides a means of installing packages, but does not include a tool to package applications into the format it uses to describe the installation process. To create a package that takes full advantage of the Windows Installer service, component management format, and management API, a third-party authoring tool from vendors such as InstallShield and WinINSTALL should be purchased.

Repackaging

Though Microsoft has not bundled an authoring tool for Windows Installer packages, it has bundled a copy of the repackaging tool WinINSTALL LE on the Windows 2000 Server CD. Repackaging tools record the changes that an application makes to the computer during its installation process. A snapshot, which is a description of the computer's configuration, is taken before the application is installed (before snapshot) and after the application is installed (after snapshot). The two snapshots are compared and the differences are then packaged into a set of files and a Windows Installer description (.MSI file) of the steps to follow to install the files. Repackaged applications provide many of the same benefits as applications that have been packaged using third-party authoring tools, and can be published, assigned, and repaired. However, since applications that are repackaged were not initially designed to leverage Windows Installer, they are viewed as a single feature, and do not therefore support feature-level install on demand. WinINSTALL LE is located on the Windows 2000 Server CD in the VALUEADD\3RDPARTY\MGMT\WINSTLE directory.

ZAP Files

An alternative to using authoring or repackaging tools to package applications is to use ZAP files. These files allow an Administrator to publish the setup program that is bundled with the application itself. Since the original setup program from the application itself is being published, the application can only be installed with the options available to the original setup program. So, if the setup program has no silent option, the user will have to go through whatever setup screens are presented. Many of the benefits of using the Windows Installer are not available when using ZAP files. Applications using the ZAP file format can only be published. These applications are still available for installation and uninstallation from Add/Remove Programs, but cannot be installed using elevated privileges. Additional benefits of using Windows Installer files (.MSI) such as the rollback and repair features are not available when using ZAP files.

A ZAP file is a clear-text file similar in format to an INI file. To create a ZAP file, you should know what the commands are to install the program, what the application properties are, and what entry points the application should automatically install. An example of a possible ZAP file used to distribute Balancing Act within the XYZ Company could be:

```
; ZAP File for Balancing Act accounting software from the XYZ Company
[Application]
; The first two lines, FriendlyName and SetupCommand, are the only required entries
; FriendlyName is the name that is used by Add/Remove Programs and the software
; installation Group Policy snap-in
FriendlyName = "Balancing Act"
; SetupCommand is used to launch the application installation
SetupCommand = "setup.exe /q"
; DisplayVersion is the version that is used by Add/Remove Programs and the
; software installation Group Policy snap-in
DisplayVersion = 3.2
Publisher = XYZ Company
URL = http://www.xyzcompany.com/support
[ext]
;File extensions that cause the application to install
ACC=
```

Customizing a Package

It is often the case that different groups of users require the same application customized for their environment. Transforms allow you to modify a Windows Installer package to create custom installations. The transform file (.MST file) is applied to the package file (.MSI file), resulting in a customized version of the application.

A commonly encountered scenario occurs when departments need different features of a particular product. For example, the Accounts department requires Microsoft Word and Microsoft Excel (both features of the product Microsoft Office 2000), while the Marketing department only requires Microsoft Word. Microsoft Office 2000 is supplied with a utility (Office 2000 Customization Wizard) that allows you to generate transforms for the generic package file that is shipped with the CD. The generic package file is then transformed for each department without having to have two full installation sets.

Creating Distribution Points

Once the software has been packaged appropriately, it needs to be made available on the network. This usually implies copying all the relevant files to a suitably named directory on a network share called the distribution share, or distribution point. The files could include application files, MSI files, MST files (transforms), and ZAP files. Rights need to be set on the shared directory to allow the appropriate groups access.

Allowing Everyone Read access ensures that issues regarding access to files are negated. The obvious downside to this is that users can navigate directly to the share and install applications. Administrators, or an equivalent group, could be given Full Control or Modify rights to administer the distribution point. In large organizations, the distribution share can become a warren of files and directories. Since Windows 2000 does not supply any dedicated tools to facilitate the creation and management of distribution points, maintaining the distribution points on the corporate network can become problematic. Decide on a directory structure that provides a certain level of organization. Examples of organization schemes for the distribution share include creating departmental folders and adding applications to the appropriate departmental directory, or organizing applications along functional lines. It is imperative to maintain tight change and access controls on the distribution point. Distributed File System (DFS) can be used to increase availability of the distribution point.

Targeting Software and Using the Software MMC Snap-In

Software deployment is a feature of IntelliMirror configured using Group Policy and Active Directory. The introductory topics on Group Policy tackled in the previous chapter provided us with an understanding of how group policies work and how Group Policy Objects (GPOs) are associated with SDOUs. Software can be assigned or published to groups of computers or users by creating GPOs with the relevant packaged applications configured in the Software settings section, and linking these GPOs to Active Directory containers. The applications are then deployed to groups of users or computers according to the inheritance rules of Group Policy in the Active Directory. The Microsoft Management Console (MMC) is the common host for most administrative functions within Windows 2000, and is used when creating or modifying GPOs.

Using the Software Policy MMC Snap-In

The software settings subtree in the Computer Configuration and User Configuration nodes is actually an extension to the Group Policy snap-in. This means that an MMC console can be configured with only the software settings visible for a particular GPO, as shown in Figure 8.3.

To create a custom console with only the software settings node visible, follow these steps:

1. Launch the Microsoft Management Console by running MMC.EXE.

2. Click on the Console menu item, and select Add/Remove snap-in. CTRL-M can be used as a shortcut to this window.

3. Click ADD.

4. Select the Group Policy Snap-in, and click ADD.

Figure 8.3 Software Settings snap-in.

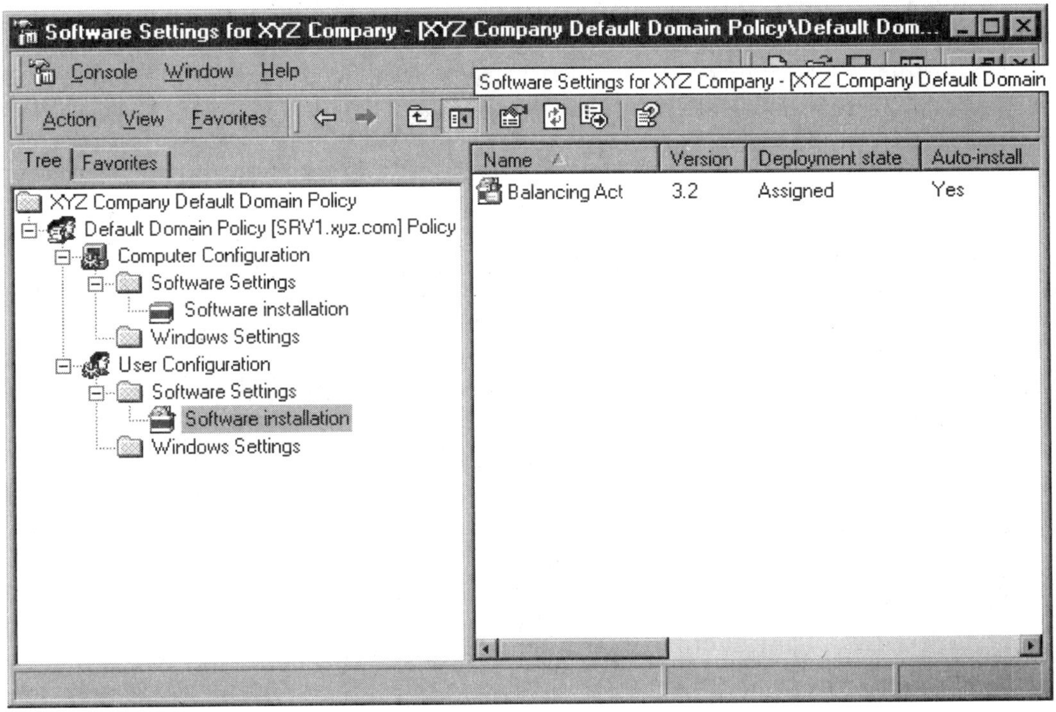

5. The snap-in then requires that you focus on a particular Group Policy Object. By clicking BROWSE, you can select the required GPO. Click FINISH and then CLOSE after the focus has been set.

6. Select the Extensions tab. This page provides a list of all the available extensions for Group Policy. Deselect the Add all extensions check box. Deselect all available extensions except Software Installation (Computers) and Software Installation (Users).

7. The Console Root can be renamed to provide a more detailed description of the GPO whose software settings you are modifying.

8. Click on Console and select Save As to save the console to the Administration tools folder.

TIP

The Microsoft Management Console provides features aimed at easing the job of the Administrator. The Favorites tab can be used to store frequently accessed or modified policy settings, or frequently modified GPOs, themselves. Fast access can be gained simply by adding frequently used GPOs to Favorites and saving the console. The next time the console is opened, the list of Favorites can be used to navigate to the relevant object you wish to modify. The console can be further modified by detailing the extensions that should be displayed in the snap-in. For example, an Administrator could create a specific console that only displays the software settings node of specific GPOs.

Using Group Policy to Assign or Publish an Application

Both the Computer Configuration and User Configuration nodes have software settings folders. This folder branches into software installation. Before deploying an application, decide whether you wish to assign or publish the application to a computer or to a user. To assign or publish an application to a user or computer, right-click on Software installation in the tree pane of the relevant computer or user configuration node. Select New, and then select Package. The common open dialog box allows you to navigate to the distribution point that contains the .MSI file for the application you wish to deploy. If you are publishing an application to a user, you can also open ZAP files. It is important that you navigate to the .MSI or .ZAP file using a network path, even if the files are local to the computer you are working on. This ensures that clients on the network have the correct path to the installation files.

Figure 8.4 Software deployment methods.

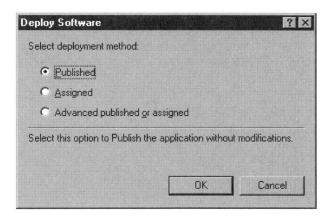

The next window, titled Deploy Software, as shown in Figure 8.4, provides three deployment options: Published, Assigned, and Advanced published or assigned.

Selecting Published or Assigned will publish or assign the application you have provided without additional configuration information. After selecting either of these two options, the Group Policy window will reappear, displaying the entry for the newly assigned or published application.

Selecting "Advanced published or assigned" allows you to configure additional properties for deployment. The application properties sheet includes six tabs. The General tab displays the name of the application, and product and support information. The Deployment tab, shown in Figure 8.5, provides the options to change:

- Deployment type from published or assigned.
- If the application automatically installs using document associations.
- If the application uninstalls when the GPO no longer applies.
- Whether to display the application in Add/Remove Programs.
- The installation interface options. Developers can choose to provide a basic interface that provides predetermined options, or a maximum interface that requires user interaction to customize the installation.

Managing Software with Group Policies

So far, we have suggested that applications be packaged in the Windows Installer format to leverage all the benefits of the new installation architecture. If applications cannot be packaged into an .MSI file, a ZAP file can be used (taking note of inherent limitations such as the inability to roll back or assign ZAP files). Once the software has been packaged, it needs to be

Figure 8.5 Advanced published or assigned deployment options.

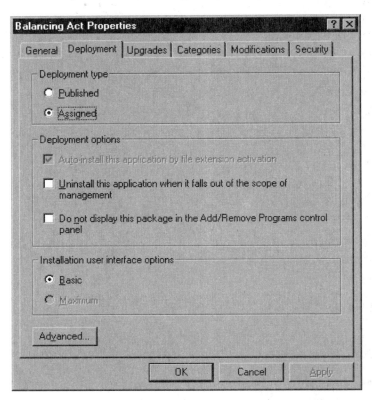

made available for distribution. The location of the package and related files is called the distribution point or distribution share. GPOs containing Group Policy settings detail what applications to install, and if they are to be assigned or published. The GPOs are then linked to sites, domains, or organizational units. Linking GPOs to SDOUs allows the Administrator to effectively target the deployment of applications by using GPO inheritance.

We now understand the framework for deploying software, but what about maintaining and managing the software once it has been deployed? What happens when an application is upgraded? How is an application removed? Who should be allowed to manage the group policy software distribution settings? Managing the software once it has been deployed is as critical as the deployment process itself.

Upgrading Software

Software applications have become business-critical, resulting in shorter cycles between new versions of products. Managing the process of upgrading to the latest release has always been problematic. The process of upgrading existing software has been integrated into the software installation and maintenance feature of Group Policy. To upgrade an existing application, an .MSI file needs to be created for the updated version of the application. Group Policy then needs to be instructed what to do during the upgrade process. Should it remove the previous version, or install directly over it? Upgrades can also be classified as:

- **Required** Upgrades are automatically installed.
- **Optional** The upgrade process allows the user to choose whether to upgrade.

To upgrade an existing application, create a new package and select the Advanced Published or Assigned deployment option (Figure 8.4). The properties for the application are displayed with six tabs. Select the Upgrades tab. The tab is divided into two sections, with the top half indicating what package this package upgrades. The bottom half of the tab indicates what packages can upgrade the current package. This tab can be used to examine existing packages to determine if they are targeted for upgrade by other packages.

The "Required upgrade for existing packages" check box determines whether the package is a required or optional upgrade. If the check box is ticked, it is a required upgrade. Click ADD to progress to the Add Upgrade Package window, as shown in Figure 8.6.

WARNING

Software upgrades should always be piloted first to provide enough time to evaluate the changes that the new version provides.

The Add Upgrade Package window provides the ability to choose a package that the current package will upgrade. The package can upgrade a package from the current GPO, or the Administrator can browse for a specific GPO. Highlight the packages that are to be upgraded in the "Package to upgrade" box and select whether the existing package should be uninstalled first, or if the package should upgrade over the existing package. Click OK and return to the Upgrades tab. The packages you selected in the "Package to upgrade" box should now appear under "Packages that this package will upgrade." Under Software Installation in Group Policy, the packages' icon should now include a small upward-pointing arrow.

Upgrading Windows 2000

The option to upgrade software using Group Policy is extremely versatile. Windows 2000 itself is nothing more than a very large and very complex piece of software. So it follows that it, too, can be upgraded to later releases

Figure 8.6 Add Upgrade Package.

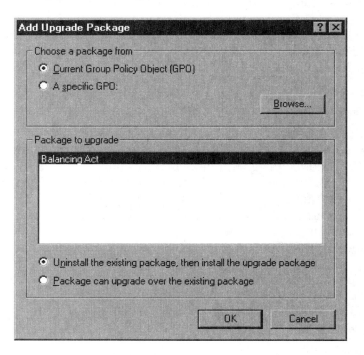

(including Service Pack releases) using Group Policy. Obviously, Group Policy cannot be used to upgrade a non-Windows 2000 computer, since Group Policy requires that the client already be a Windows 2000 computer.

Microsoft ships Windows 2000 with a Winnt32.MSI file in the \i386 directory of the Windows 2000 CD. This can be used to prepare an upgrade package that can be assigned or published. If the Windows 2000 upgrade were assigned to a user, every machine the user logs on to would receive the upgrade. A more sensible option is to assign the upgrade to computers or publish it to users.

Removing Software

Two options exist for removing software:

- **Forced removal** The next time the Group Policy is applied, the package is removed.
- **Optional removal** The software can be uninstalled when desired, but no new installations are allowed.

Right-clicking on the package that you wish to remove, selecting All Tasks and then Remove, displays the Remove Software window, shown in Figure 8.7. The option to immediately uninstall the software can be considered to be forced removal, while the second option to allow users to continue using the software is optional removal.

Figure 8.7 Removing software.

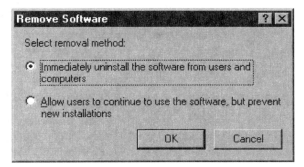

Redeploying Software

Most software will require a patch or an update to fix problems or to provide additional functionality during its lifetime. Group Policy allows for the distribution of patches and updates by providing a redeployment option.

Redeploying applications involves copying the patched or updated version of the package to the distribution point, opening the original GPO, right-clicking on the patched application, and selecting All Tasks and then Redeploy Application. A warning dialog box then informs you that the application will be reinstalled everywhere. Applications are redeployed the next time the GPO is applied. This means that applications assigned or published to a user will be redeployed at the next logon, while applications assigned to computers will be redeployed at the next reboot.

Software Installation Options

Additional software installation options are available on a per Group Policy Object basis that facilitate the management of deployed applications. Most of these settings can be unique to each GPO, allowing for a great deal of flexibility. The software installation options include:

- General deployment options.
- The default package location can be specified—whenever a new package is created for a GPO, it uses this location as the default. This location is the distribution point.
- The default deployment method when adding a new package can be specified.
- The default installation user interface level. When a Windows Installer package is added, this setting determines the default interface option.

- Whether the application should be removed when the GPO no longer applies to that user or computer.
- File extensions. Lists the file extensions, what application should be invoked, and the precedence of these applications per GPO.
- Categories. Allows you to add categories for installed applications. Categories are not local to the GPO, but are established for each domain. This provides a method to organize applications by function or department, making it easier to navigate to relevant applications in Add/Remove Programs. In Figure 8.1, the Balancing Act accounting package is displayed in the Accounts category. Applications, which can be in more than one category, will only be displayed if they have been published to a particular user.

The software installation options can be modified by right-clicking on the Software installation node and selecting Properties. Three tabs labeled General, File Extensions, and Categories provide the software installation options (Figure 8.8).

Figure 8.8 Software installation options.

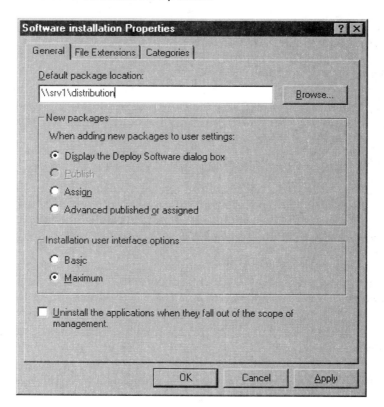

Group Policy Settings

The deployment and management of applications can be further refined and controlled using Group Policy settings. Group Policy settings of particular interest for software deployment and management are divided into those that affect Group Policy itself, and those that affect Windows Installer (Table 8.1).

Table 8.1 Group Policy Settings

Computer Configuration | Administrative Templates | System | Group Policy	User Configuration | Administrative Templates | System | Group Policy
User Group Policy loopback processing mode.	*Group Policy slow link detection.*
Forces the application of the GPO for the computer to users who log on to the computer affected by this policy.	Determines the threshold for links to be classified as slow links. Software is not deployed over slow links by default.
Software Installation policy processing.	
This allows you to specify if software installation policies should be processed even across slow links. Also allows you to process the GPO even if it has not changed.	
Group Policy slow link detection.	
Determines the threshold for links to be classified as slow links. Software is not deployed over slow links.	

The loopback processing mode is particularly useful for computers that have a special function, such as those in public places. Loopback processing has a replace mode and a merge mode. The replace mode forces the application of the user policies of the computer's GPO on any user who logs on to that particular machine. Merge mode combines the user policies of the computer's GPO and the user policies associated with the user.

Group Policy can restrict the use of snap-ins by setting the User Configuration | Administrative Templates | Windows Components | Microsoft Management Console | Restrict users to the explicitly permitted list of snap-ins. This Group Policy could be used to restrict the use of Group Policy snap-ins to just the Software Settings snap-in for either the user or computer configuration node.

Another useful Group Policy setting is Computer Configuration | Administrative Templates | System | Verbose vs. normal status messages. Using verbose messages will echo certain actions to the user when starting up or during logon (such as the installation or removal of packages).

Windows Installer also has several options that are configurable by Group Policy that help with the maintenance and management of applications (Table 8.2). Logging of Windows Installer events is particularly useful in helping to troubleshoot installation problems. An important usability feature of the Group Policy settings in the Administrative Templates folders is that a detailed explanation is included on the Explain tab of all the settings.

Table 8.2 Windows Installer Group Policy Settings

Computer Configuration | Administrative Templates | Windows Components | Windows Installer	User Configuration | Administrative Templates | Windows Components | Windows Installer
■ Always install with elevated privileges. ■ Disable rollback. ■ Disable Browse dialog box for new source. ■ Disable patching. ■ Disable IE Security prompt for Windows Installer scripts. ■ Enable user control over installs. ■ Enable user to browse for source while elevated. ■ Enable user to use media while elevated. ■ Enable user to patch elevated products. ■ Allow Administrator to install from Terminal Services session. ■ Cache transforms in secure location on workstation. ■ Logging.	■ Always install with elevated privileges. ■ Search order. ■ Disable rollback. ■ Disable media source for any install.

Application Deployment Walkthrough

In previous sections, we covered a great deal of ground on IntelliMirror, Group Policy, software deployment, software management, and the Windows Installer. The following list summarizes what we currently know about software deployment.

- Deploying software can be considered part of change and configuration management.

- Change and configuration management is addressed by IntelliMirror and Remote Operating System Installation.

- One of the features of IntelliMirror is Software Installation and Maintenance.

- To prepare applications for deployment, Windows Installer files (.MSI) and ZAP files (.ZAP) can be used. The Windows Installer format (.MSI files) is the preferred format for distributing applications. WinINSTALL LE can be used to repackage applications.

- Once applications are prepared, they need to be made available for distribution. Associated files and installation information is stored on a distribution share located on a distribution server.

- Group Policy is used by the Software Installation and Maintenance feature to deploy software.

- GPOs are linked to containers within the Active Directory to target the deployment of applications.

- Applications can be assigned or published.

- While Group Policy with Active Directory delivers the application to the right user or computer, the Windows Installer service installs the application itself.

Let us assume that the Balancing Act accounting package needs to be published to all staff in the Accounts department. An organizational unit called Accounts is a child of the XYZ.COM domain. The process to deploy and effectively manage the application using Group Policy could be as follows:

1. After investigating development costs associated with designing a version of Balancing Act for Windows Installer, the XYZ Company decided to save on the development costs and repackage the application using WinINSTALL LE. ZAP files were not considered because of their lack of functionality when compared with the Windows Installer format.

2. WinINSTALL LE generated a Balancing Act.MSI file and associated installation files. These files were placed in a directory called Balancing Act on the distribution share (\\srv1\distribution).

3. The Accounts department of the XYZ Company has only just been migrated to Windows 2000 and as a result, certain configuration options need to be set. Launch the Active Directory Users and Computers snap-in, right-click on the Accounts organizational unit, and select Properties. In the Accounts Properties window, select the Group Policy tab and click NEW. Enter the name Accounts for the Group Policy Object and then click EDIT. Expand the Software Settings folder in the Computer Configuration node and right-click on Software Installation. Select Properties, then:

   ■ The default package location needs to be set to \\srv1\distribution. This is done at the Default Package Location prompt. This should also be done for the Software Installation node in User Configuration.

   ■ Categories for published applications need to be established; though this is not mandatory, it is a recommended practice. This is done by selecting the Categories tab and adding categories suitable to the entire domain (the category need only be added at one node). A category called Accounts is added. Click OK to return to the Group Policy snap-in.

4. Select Software Installation in the Software Settings folder of the User Configuration node. Right-click Software installation, and select New and then Package. The default open dialog box is then displayed, pointing at the default package location. Navigate to the Balancing Act directory and select the Balancing Act .MSI file. The Deploy Software window then provides you with deployment methods. Select Advanced Published, or Assigned, and click OK.

5. In the Balancing Act Properties window, check that the Name, Product Information, and Support Information are all correct. Click on the Deployment tab and ensure that the deployment type is set to Published. Check the "Auto-install this application by file extension" activation box and the "Uninstall this application when it falls out of the scope of management" box. This ensures that if the user leaves the Accounts department, then the package will no longer be available to that user. Check that the Installation user interface option is set to Basic.

6. Click the Categories tab, select the Accounts category, and click SELECT.

7. Click OK to complete the configuration.

8. Users in the Accounts department can now install the application by launching Add/Remove Programs and selecting the Accounts category in the Add New Programs section.

TIP

A number of handy tools included in the Windows 2000 Support Tools distribution can provide significant help with software installation and maintenance:

- **Msicuu.exe**   Windows Installer Cleanup Utility. This tool allows you to clean up after failed Windows Installer packages.
- **Msizap.exe**   A command-line version of the Windows Installer Cleanup Utility.
- **Apcompat.exe**   The Application Compatibility Program helps during the diagnosis of application compatibility problems.
- **Depends.exe**   The Dependency Walker displays a hierarchical diagram of Windows modules such as DLLs and EXEs.

The Windows 2000 Resource Kit (a must for any Windows 2000 Administrator) also supplies a number of useful tools for application support and deployment, such as:

- **Appsec.exe**   The Application Security tool allows you to restrict file execution.
- **Inuse.exe**   This utility allows you to replace files currently in use by the operating system.
- **Appdiag.exe**   A utility that provides information on currently installed software on machines using Group Policy.
- **Instaler.exe**   Lists the changes a setup program makes to a workstation/server.

Deployment Methods

The differences between assigning and publishing packages are detailed in Table 8.3. These differences provide a means of determining if software should be assigned or published to users or computers.

Managing User and Computer Settings

Group Policy can be used to specify settings for users and their computing environment. The settings that are controlled by Group Policy include security settings, software installation and maintenance, Registry-based policy settings, folder redirection, and the scripts that are implemented for groups of users and computers. This section concentrates on controlling the user environment using Registry settings and various types of scripts.

Table 8.3 Software Deployment Methods

Application Deployment Method	Description	Examples
Assigning Applications to Computers	Applications are assigned to a computer when everyone who uses a particular computer will require a specific application. Applications are available after next reboot. Generally, all applications that are bound to the specific location of computers should be assigned to computers.	Information kiosks that require an inhouse developed guide to the company. Call centers that require the call center incident logging application.
Assigning Applications to Users	Applications are assigned to a user when a user requires the application. This often can be used with job/functional specific applications. Applications are available at next logon. Generally, all applications that are mandatory should be assigned to users.	Project managers who require project management software for time and resource planning.
Publishing Applications to Users	Applications are published to users when a user may require an application. This provides the user with the option of installing an application. Can use ZAP file format. Applications are available at next logon.	Support engineers who may need certain diagnostic tools to help facilitate troubleshooting.

Using Administrative Templates

Administrative templates (files with the extension .adm) are used in Windows 2000 to identify the Registry settings that you can modify using the Group Policy snap-in. Windows NT 4.0 also used .adm files that were modified using the System Policy Editor. The .adm files used in Windows 2000 are similar to those used in Windows NT 4.0 in that they are ASCII files that are format compatible between the two operating systems. All .adm files consist of a hierarchy of categories and subcategories that define how the options are displayed in the Group Policy snap-in of MMC. Here is an extremely small section of the system.adm file included with Windows 2000 Server.

```
CLASS MACHINE

CATEGORY !!AdministrativeServices

    POLICY !!NoSecurityMenu
       KEYNAME
"Software\Microsoft\Windows\CurrentVersion\Policies\Explorer"
        EXPLAIN !!NoSecurityMenu_Help
          VALUENAME "NoNTSecurity"
    END POLICY

    POLICY !!NoDisconnectMenu
       KEYNAME
"Software\Microsoft\Windows\CurrentVersion\Policies\Explorer"
          EXPLAIN !!NoDisconnectMenu_Help
            VALUENAME "NoDisconnect"
    END POLICY
```

Administrative Templates in Windows 2000 write predominately to two locations. The settings that apply to the Computer Configuration write to the HKEY_LOCAL_MACHINE section of the Registry, and the settings that apply to User Configuration write to the HKEY_CURRENT_USER section of the Registry. Figure 8.9 displays the items available in the Administrative Templates for Computer Configuration. The items include settings for Windows Components, System, Network, and Printers. The file used for Figure 8.10 displays the numerous items available in the Administrative Templates for User Configuration. The items include settings for Windows Components, Desktop, Control Panel, Network, and System.

For IT Professionals

Microsoft recommends that you do not use .adm files from Windows NT 4.0 on Windows 2000 clients, because the Registry keys may not match, resulting in some unexpected effects. It is also possible that if the Registry keys do match, it may lead to Registry settings that are persistent. Also note that the .adm files that ship with Windows 2000 have more options available than were present in the Windows NT 4.0 .adm files.

Figure 8.9 Administrative Templates available in the Computer Configuration section of the Default Domain Policy.

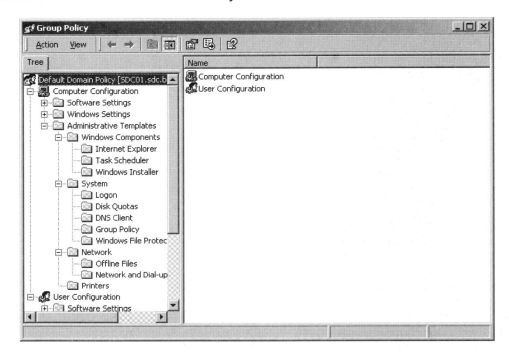

Figures 8.9 and 8.10 show the items available in the default Administrative Templates that ship with Windows 2000. The items that make up both of these Administrative Templates are contained in the files system.adm and inetres.adm. Both files contain sections that are in the User Configuration and Computer Configuration.

Assigning Registry-Based Policies

Assigning Registry-based policies means using the Group Policy MMC snap-in. For example, you have decided that you want a policy in your domain that states everyone will use a screensaver that is password protected. You could draft a memo and distribute it to your users, but how many of them would actually implement your request? You can accomplish the same goal using Group Policy to make sure that it is accomplished throughout your domain! The following steps illustrate configuring the password-protected screensaver for your Windows 2000 clients.

1. Log on to the server as Administrator and launch the Active Directory Users and Computers MMC.

2. Right-click on the relevant domain and choose Properties.

Figure 8.10 Administrative Templates available in the User Configuration section of the Default Domain Policy.

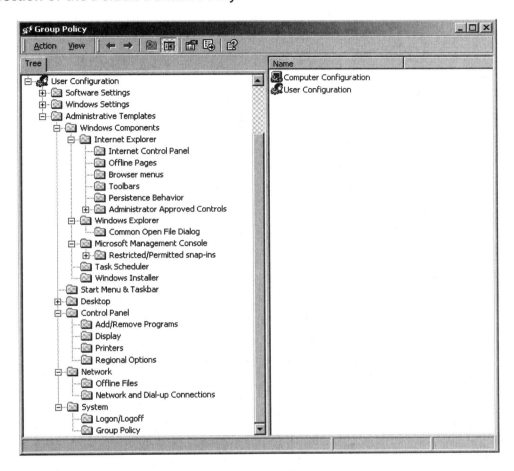

3. Select the Group Policy tab. Highlight the Default Domain Policy, and click EDIT.

4. Click the + located to the left of User Configuration. Click the + located to the left of Administrative Templates. Click the + located to the left of Control Panel.

5. Select the Display folder. In the right pane, you now see several parameters that can be set for the Default Domain Policy in regard to Display items.

6. Double-click the "Screen saver executable name" text located in the right pane. The window, as shown in Figure 8.11, is the location that you enable this policy for the domain.

Figure 8.11 Policy tab for the "Screen saver executable name" Properties window.

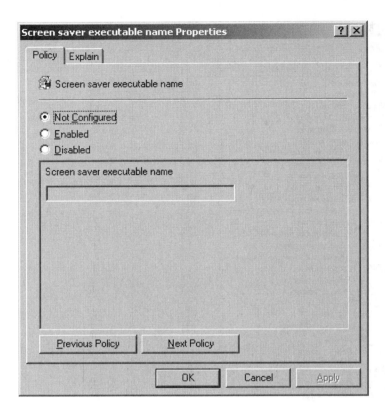

7. Select the Enabled radio button and type **logon.scr** in the "Screen saver executable name" dialog box.

8. Select the Explain tab. An explanation is given for the topic chosen. Make it a habit to check the Explain tab prior to implementing a change in domain policy for a production network to ensure you are accomplishing what you really are trying to accomplish.

9. Click OK.

10. Double-click the "Password protect the screensaver" text located in the right pane.

11. Click the Enabled radio button to enable this policy.

12. Click OK. You have now enabled these two policies in your domain as shown in Figure 8.12. It is important to note that policies take effect as soon as they are enabled.

Figure 8.12 Two Display Policies enabled for the Default Domain Policy.

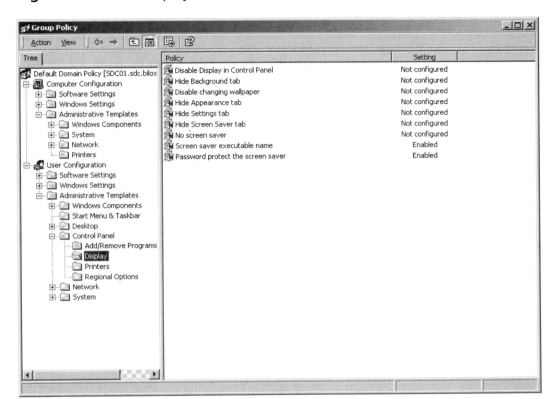

Creating Custom Administrative Templates

You may encounter situations where the choices presented in the Administrative Templates provided with Windows 2000 do not suit your needs. What do you do then? Are you stuck with the choices that Microsoft has provided? Of course not! You can create your own .adm files to fulfill your needs.

An .adm file, as we saw earlier, specifies Registry settings that take place in Group Policy. The three main attributes for an .adm file are specifying Registry locations in which changes are to be made if you make that selection, specifying any options or restrictions that are associated with the selection, and specifying a default value to use if the selection is activated.

There are several components that make up an .adm file. Recall that, at the beginning of the "Using Administrative Templates" section of the chapter, a small section of the system.adm file is presented. Each portion of that text has a purpose as shown in Table 8.4.

Table 8.4 Components Used in .adm Files

Component	Description

STRING	String variables are used in .adm files to define text strings for the user interface. String variables can be used for CATE-GORY, POLICY, PART, and DEFAULT. You assign the variable name to the component by preceding it with two exclamation points (**!!**).
	
	component **!!***variable*
	
	where *component* is CATEGORY, POLICY, PART, or DEFAULT, and *variable* is the variable you want to use for a given string.
	
	Then, in the [strings] section of the file, link the variable with the actual string to be used in the user interface. The string must be enclosed in quotation marks, and names with spaces must be enclosed in double quotation marks.
	
	For example, the following is an excerpt from the system.adm file:
	
	<pre>[strings]
	ABCDOnly="Restrict A, B, C and D drives only"
	ABConly="Restrict A, B and C drives only"
	ABOnly="Restrict A and B drives only"
	ActiveDesktop="Active Desktop"
	ActiveDirectory="Active Directory"</pre>

CLASS	The first entry you make in an .adm file must be CLASS *xxxx*, where *xxxx* can be one of the following:
	
	MACHINE: Entries found in the Computer Configuration node of Group Policy.
	
	USER: Entries found in the User Configuration node of Group Policy.
	
	Machine and User are the only two valid classes within an .adm file. The Group Policy MMC snap-in ignores nonvalid classes.
	
	The valid keywords for CLASS are:
	
	<pre>CLASS
	CATEGORY
	[strings]
	USER
	MACHINE</pre>

Table 8.4 *continued*

Component	Description
CATEGORY	The category name is displayed in the left pane of Group Policy as a node in either the Computer Configuration or the User Configuration node, depending on whether it is defined under the MACHINE class or the USER class.

The CATEGORY syntax is as follows:

```
CATEGORY !!"variable name"
[KEYNAME "key name"]
[... policy definition statements ...]
END CATEGORY
```

The *variable name* is the category name as it appears in the Group Policy list box. All names with spaces must be enclosed by double quotation marks.

The *key name* is the Registry key name to use for the category. All names with spaces must be enclosed in double quotation marks.

A policy definition statement cannot appear more than once in a single category.

End Category is used to close the category after you finish filling in the options.

The valid keywords for CATEGORY are:

```
KEYNAME
CATEGORY
POLICY
END
```

POLICY	To identify the policy that the user can modify, you use the keyword POLICY:

```
POLICY !!MyPolicy
...fill in all the policy specifics
...and then finish with:
END POLICY
```

It is possible for you to use multiple POLICY key names under one KEYNAME.

The valid keywords for POLICY are:

```
KEYNAME
VALUENAME
PART
VALUEON
VALUEOFF
ACTIONLISTON
ACTIONLISTOFF
END
HELP
CLIENTEXT
POLICY
```

Table 8.4 *continued*

Component	Description
EXPLAIN	The EXPLAIN keyword is used to provide Help text. Each policy must include one EXPLAIN keyword that has at least one space after it, followed by either the explain string in quotation marks or a reference to the explain string.
PART	You use PART to specify various options, including drop-down list boxes, text boxes, and text in the lower pane of the Group Policy snap-in.

The syntax for PART is:

```
PART [!!]name PartType
 type-dependent data
 [KEYNAME KeyName ]
 VALUENAME ValueName
END PART
```

The text that is located in *name* is the part name as you want it to appear in the Group Policy list box. If you use names with spaces, then they must be enclosed in double quotation marks.

PartType is the policy part flags. They are discussed later in this section as a separate entity.

type-dependent data is information about the part.

The use of *KeyName* is the optional. If you do not specify a key name, then the previous key name in the hierarchy is used.

The *ValueName* is used to set the data for this part.

The valid keywords for PART are:

```
CHECKBOX
TEXT
EDITTEXT
NUMERIC
COMBOBOX
DROPDOWNLIST
LISTBOX
END
CLIENTEXT
PART
```

Table 8.4 *continued*

Component	Description
PartTypes	The ADM language allows .adm files to be created that use VALUENAME of REG_DWORD type with a value of 1, or else it removes the value entirely. However, it is also possible to use the following modifiers to provide additional options:

TEXT

Displays a line of text. This is useful if you need to display a description. END is the only valid keyword for TEXT.

EDITTEXT

Displays a field that accepts alphanumeric text. There are several EDITTEXT part type values available.

DEFAULT value

Used to specify the initial string to place in the field. The field is empty if it is not specified.

MAXLEN value

The maximum length of a string.

REQUIRED

A value must be entered for this part, or else Group Policy will not allow the policy to be enabled.

OEMCONVERT

Sets the ES_OEMCONVERT style so that all text typed in the field is mapped from ANSI to OEM and back to ANSI.

The valid keywords for EDITTEXT are:

```
KEYNAME
VALUENAME
DEFAULT
REQUIRED
MAXLENGTH
OEMCONVERT
END
EXPANDABLETEXT
CLIENTEXT
```

Table 8.4 *continued*

Component	Description
NUMERIC	Displays a field that accepts a numeric value. It can have an optional spinner control if you desire. The value is set in the Registry using the REG_DWORD type.
	NUMERIC has the following options available:
	DEFAULT value
	Used to specify the initial numeric value to place in the field. The field is empty if it is not specified.
	MAX value
	Specifies the maximum value for the number. It defaults to 9999.
	MIN value
	Specifies the minimum value for the number. It defaults to 0.
	REQUIRED
	A value must be entered for this part, or else Group Policy will not allow the policy to be enabled.
	SPIN value
	Specifies the increments to use for the spinner control.
	SPIN 0
	Removes the spinner control from the item. It defaults to SPIN 1.
	TXTCONVERT
	Writes values as REG_SZ strings ("1," "2," or "128") instead of binary values.
	The valid keywords for NUMERIC are:
| | ```
KEYNAME
VALUENAME
MIN
MAX
SPIN
DEFAULT
REQUIRED
TXTCONVERT
END
CLIENTEXT
``` |
```

Adding Administrative Templates

Customized Administrative Templates files must be added to Group Policy before you can use their features. It is very easy to add custom .adm files to Group Policy. The following steps outline the process.

1. Log on your server as Administrator.

2. Open the Group Policy Object that you want to add the .adm file to.

3. Right-click on the Administrative Templates node.

4. Select Add/Remove Templates.

5. Click ADD.

6. Navigate to the .adm file that you want to add, highlight it, and click OPEN.

7. The file you selected is now displayed in the Add/Remove Templates window. Click CLOSE. The information from the .adm file is now available in the Administrative Templates node.

Group Policy in Windows 2000 is aware of Windows NT 4.0 .adm files and is alerted if there is an attempt to add them. It will accept the file, but it will show up as an Unsupported Administrative Template as shown in Figure 8.13. Unwanted .adm files can be removed from Group Policy using Add/Remove Templates.

Using Scripts

Scripts are used to manage user environments. Windows NT has always used scripts for logon, but they were somewhat limited in functionality. Scripting within Windows 2000 has undergone a much-needed overhaul, and is now able to support the following scripts:

- Computer Startup
- Computer Shutdown
- User Logon
- User Logoff

The scripts you use in Windows 2000 are not limited in functionality as they were in earlier versions of Windows NT. Windows 2000 scripts are supported by Windows Scripting Host (WSH), which includes support for both Visual Basic Scripting Edition (VBScript) and JScript scripts. Simply put, you can now use VBScript or JScript in the scripts assigned to users and computers. However, you may still use .bat and .cmd files if you wish.

Computer Startup scripts run after the computer has initialized network connections, and Computer Shutdown scripts run prior to termi-

Figure 8.13 Unsupported Administrative Templates in the Computer Configuration Policy.

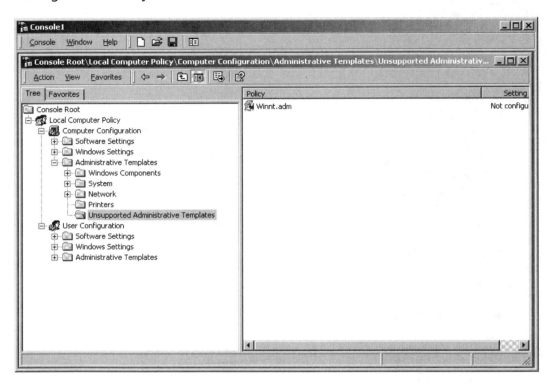

nating network connections. Since the Computer Startup/Shutdown scripts function in this manner, you can have those two scripts access network resources if necessary. User Logon scripts execute after the Computer Startup scripts and before the user logging on is handed his or her desktop. User Logoff scripts execute when the user logs off or prior to the Computer Shutdown scripts if the user is shutting down the system.

Computer Startup scripts and Computer Shutdown scripts are run in the context of the Local System account. User Logon scripts and User Logoff scripts are run in the context of the validated user. Keep this in mind when developing your scripts to ensure the proper permissions are available to perform the actions you need to perform.

Several items can be configured with regard to scripts in the Logon node of Computer Configuration as shown in Figure 8.14, and also in the Logon/Logoff node of User Configuration. These items include choices to run scripts synchronously or asynchronously, run scripts visible, and run legacy scripts hidden.

Figure 8.14 Available settings during logon for various scripts.

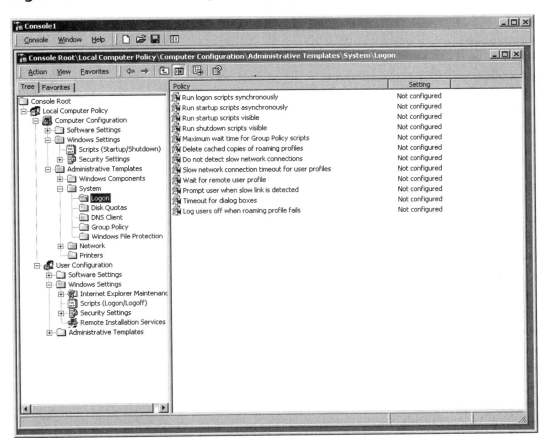

Assigning Script Policies to Users and Computers

Adding scripts to users and computers is accomplished from the Windows Settings node of the Group Policy object you choose. Refer back to Figure 8.14 to see the Startup/Shutdown Scripts selection in the Windows Settings node of Computer Configuration, and the Logon/Logoff Scripts selection in the Windows Settings node of User Configuration.

Adding scripts is the same for all script types, so we will only examine adding a script to the Startup object of the Computer Configuration portion of Group Policy.

1. Log on to the server as Administrator and open the Group Policy MMC snap-in.

2. Click the + located to the left of Computer Configuration.

3. Click the + located to the left of Windows Settings.

4. Highlight Scripts in the left pane.

5. In the right pane, click Startup, and choose Properties from the menu.

6. Click ADD.

7. In the Script Name: dialog box, type **start.vbs**.

8. Click OK.

9. Click ADD.

10. In the Script Name: dialog box, type **startup.bat**.

11. Click OK.

12. Click OK.

You have now configured two scripts to start up when the computer is first powered up as shown in Figure 8.15. Of course, the scripts do not

Figure 8.15 Adding multiple scripts to the Startup Properties.

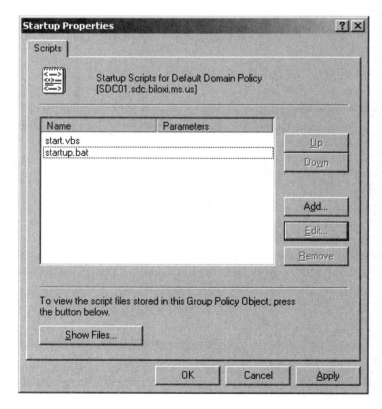

exist, so no actions will take place when the system is powered up. The purpose in adding multiple files is to illustrate that Windows 2000 can process multiple scripts. The scripts are processed in the order they are listed, from top to bottom. You may change the order by using UP and DOWN located in the Scripts Properties window. It is also possible to apply parameters to the scripts. The parameters include any item that you would type on the command line. For example, if you normally run the script from the command line using the /I (interactive) switch, then place /I in the Parameters field of your script.

Folder Redirection

Folder Redirection allows you to redirect several folders located in a user profile to another location such as a network share. The folders are Application Data, Start Menu, My Documents, My Pictures, and Desktop.

Why would you want to redirect users' folders away from their normal location? Let's look at an example and see what benefits may be gained from Folder Redirection. Imagine that you decide to redirect a user's My Documents folder to \\srv1\usersmydocs\%username%. This action ensures that the user's documents are available if he or she roams from one computer to another. It also allows the documents to be backed up, since they are located on the server instead of just being stored on the user's machine that may not be backed up regularly. A third benefit of Folder Redirection is that the user's My Documents folder is available using Offline Folders for those times when the user is disconnected from the network.

Once the My Documents folder is redirected, it is no longer part of the user's profile. Since the entire profile is processed for each log on, redirection speeds up the logon process—particularly useful if the user works with large documents.

Using Folder Redirection is accomplished from the User Configuration node. The following steps illustrate how to redirect folders for your users.

1. Log on the server as Administrator and open the Group Policy MMC snap-in.

2. Click the + located to the left of User Configuration.

3. Click the + located to the left of Folder Redirection.

4. Right-click the Desktop folder.

5. In the Target tab, select "Basic" in the Setting: dialog box. This redirects everyone's folder to the same location. Other choices available to you are "Advanced" and "No administrative policy specified" as shown in Figure 8.16.

6. Type **\\srv1\users\%username%\Desktop** in the dialog box to reflect the location where everyone's folders will be stored.

Figure 8.16 Target tab for the Desktop Properties of redirected folders.

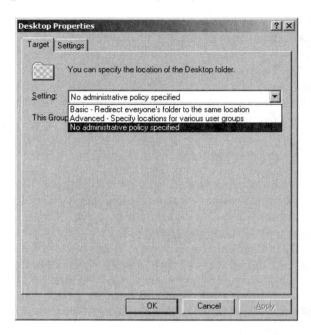

7. Select the Settings tab, and select "Grant the user exclusive rights to the Desktop." Move the contents of Desktop to the new location, and leave the folder in the new location when policy is removed, as shown in Figure 8.17.

8. Click OK. Folder Redirection is now configured for the Desktop folder.

Be very careful with the choices you select on the Settings tab of Folder Redirection. It is possible for contents of the folder to be no longer visible to the user if the Redirection Policy specifies that the folder be redirected back to the local user profile location upon policy removal, but does not specify that the contents be moved during redirection. In this instance, the user's files remain at the location that was specified when the policy was still in effect.

Figure 8.17 Settings tab for the Desktop Properties of redirected folders.

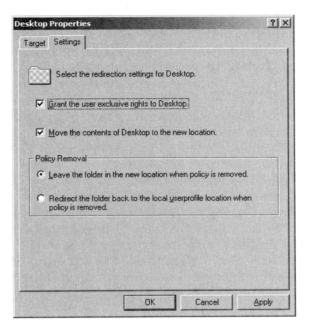

Summary

Deploying software can be broken down into preparing packages, distributing packages, targeting clients, and finally installing the package on the designated clients. Software is packaged for distribution by using a third-party authoring tool or the WinINSTALL LE repackaging tool located on the Windows 2000 Server CD. These tools create a Windows Installer package. Windows Installer is a resident installation service that is installed by default with Windows 2000. It enables applications to roll back, self-repair, and install on demand. ZAP files, which are similar in format to INI files, can also be used to describe how an application should be installed. It is important to note that ZAP files have considerably less functionality than programs described by the Windows Installer format. Once applications have been packaged, they are placed on distribution servers that are available to network clients.

Groups of computers and users are targeted for software deployment by the linking of GPOs to SDOUs and filtering. Software is then assigned or published to users and computers. Software that is assigned to a computer is installed when the computer is rebooted, and is always present on the machine, while software that is assigned to the user installs an entry point at user logon. This entry point is then used to install the application when it is first run. Published applications are visible in Add/Remove Programs and can be installed at the user's discretion. The Group Policy console used to manage software deployment can be customized to include specific GPOs, and only to display settings relevant to software deployment.

Group Policy provides for software management by allowing applications to be removed, redeployed, patched, and upgraded. Applications can be optionally upgraded, or the upgrade can be forced. Removals can also be forced or optional. Group Policy can even be used to upgrade Windows 2000 to a later version. Categories can be used to organize applications into departmental or functional groups when published to the user. These categories are visible when the Add/Remove Programs is used to install published applications. Group Policy settings can be used to configure Group Policy itself and the Windows Installer to aid in management and troubleshooting functions.

Folder redirection changes the location of a special system folder from a local disk directory to a network location. A user's My Documents folder can be pointed to a network path, making the data in the folder available to the user, no matter which computer is used to log on to the network. Other folders that can be redirected include Application Data, Desktop, My Pictures, and Start Menu.

FAQs

Q: How are policies processed during the startup of the computer and during user logon?

A: Computer Group Policy is applied prior to the Startup scripts being processed. After the user is validated by the system, the user profile is loaded. At this point, User Group Policy is applied and the logon scripts are processed.

Q: Is Group Policy only applied during the startup of the computer and user logon?

A: No, Group Policy is applied every 90 minutes for all users and computers, with the exception of domain controllers. The default is every 5 minutes for domain controllers. Setting a group policy in the Administrative Templates node can change the defaults.

Q: I'm trying to set up folder redirection for the My Documents folder in Group Policy. I set the policy to move the contents of the folder to the redirected location. When I logged on, I received a message that the contents of the My Documents folder was unavailable because they had moved or changed. What is going on?

A: Most likely, your account was already logged on another computer when you changed the policy and tried to log on. The other computer probably also received a similar error message. You need to log off both computers, and then log on one of them and check the contents of your My Documents folder. Chances are the contents are complete and now stored in the new location. (This has happened to the author more times than he cares to admit!)

Q: I set a policy to redirect the My Documents folder for a group of users to a new network server. One of my users complains that some of his files are missing and others have been changed. How did this happen?

A: If you set the policy to point the My Documents folder to a network share and did not use the %username% variable, all user objects affected by the policy are now using the same network folder as their My Documents folder. Therefore, if one user deletes a file from his My Documents folder, it will be removed from all users' My Documents folders. When using Group Policy to redirect folders to a network share, you should always use the %username% variable to create a unique folder in the share for each user, so each person has protected space for his or her data.

Q: How does software deployment with Group Policy support roaming users?

A: To support roaming users, applications can be assigned or published to the roaming users.

Chapter 9

Managing Users and Groups

Solutions in this chapter:

Introduction

Technology races ahead at a heady speed, and even the old adage "nothing is so constant as change itself" is beginning to creak under the strain of the Information Age. The modern household echoes with the pitter-patter of bits and bytes, rather than tiny feet. The computer so greatly influences the human condition that most Administrators invariably answer one simple question incorrectly: What is the most important element of the IT infrastructure?" "Servers," they reply. "No? Well then, certainly the operating system."

Actually, the answer is the users. The people behind the machines are the most important element that fuels the Information Age. Unfortunately, though, one of the most elementary (and boring) activities an Administrator undertakes is user and group administration. Though managing user and group entities can be as exciting as watching paint dry, ensuring that the correct procedures and policies are in place is critical to managing a network securely and efficiently.

A user account is a passport into the Windows 2000 network, and not surprisingly, making sure that it contains relevant and timely information is key to providing users with a rewarding and hassle-free experience. It is up to the security infrastructure to ensure that the user is authenticated and authorized appropriately, but it is up to you to issue the user with his or her electronic passport—a user account.

Additionally, if sufficient planning has been expended on understanding group roles—within the organization and within the network—administrative tasks such as permission management, rights management, and security management can be reduced dramatically.

Setting Up User Accounts

A user account is an individual's unique identifier on the Windows 2000 network. Windows 2000 uses the domain account to validate a person's identity and grant access to shared resources; in other words, to authenticate and authorize the user.

The Active Directory acts as a distributed repository for account and group information. In keeping with the initiative to pass administration through the Microsoft Management Console (MMC), the Active Directory Users and Computers snap-in is used to create and manage user accounts.

Defining an Acceptable Use Policy

Before rushing ahead and creating user accounts, it is important to develop an acceptable user-management policy. The rules included in this guide should not only cover password guidelines and account properties, but also information about network services for which the account is intended. The

For Managers

Developing an effective user-management strategy is vital to establishing and maintaining a secure network environment. Most Administrators fail to understand the importance of a good account policy, and often implement systems with major security holes. When developing a user account strategy, take into consideration:

- Standardized naming convention
- Unique account for each user
- Rules governing password settings
- Defined acceptable-use policy
- Defined audit policy and response criteria

A standardized naming convention effectively maps user logon names to an owner. When perusing log files, audit trails, and Access Control Lists (ACLs), it should be easy to identify to whom each account belongs.

It is seldom considered good practice to allow users to share accounts. No matter how extensive the security and monitoring policies, allowing users with shared accounts to access resources makes it impossible to track security violations to a single user.

Define a set of password rules that are effective without being a hindrance to the user. Administrators often get a little overzealous when they define password rules. If the rules are too strict, users may write down their passwords and leave them in obvious places, such as their day timers or under keyboards. Do not forgo password rules altogether; rather, define a set of rules that prohibit most common dictionary words and proper names. The best option is to require some combination of letters and numbers. Also, force users to change passwords on a regular basis. Despite warnings, many users will often share their passwords with others.

The options within Windows 2000 provide little value if your organization lacks a comprehensive policy statement and/or guidelines on acceptable use of network accounts and computers. The final step is to develop an audit policy that detects security breaches, and an action plan to address them. The extensive auditing capabilities of Windows 2000 include the ability to monitor network activity, file system activity, printer activity, and just about every other Active Directory object.

Continued

> Identify your most critical resources and monitor the activities relevant to that type of server (for example, attempts to crack passwords, attempts to block TCP/IP ports, attempts to access files and folders for which the user does not have permissions, and so on). The audit policy should specify not only the systems that will be monitored, but also responses to security violations.

policy should include statements regarding sharing accounts and passwords, attempts to gain access to servers without permission, and trying to acquire other users' passwords without their consent. It should be clear that the rules are enforced and violations will be dealt with in an appropriate manner. Be sure to involve the HR department when developing these policies to ensure that they comply with the necessary legal requirements. Try to ensure that the document is simple and clear, keeping in mind that the goal is not to scare or intimidate users, but to remind them of the importance of proper security.

Requirements for New User Accounts

One of the first priorities when considering user accounts is to determine an effective naming scheme. Each user has an associated display name and a logon name. The logon name is not surprisingly the name used to log on to the domain, while the display name is the name displayed to users.

Logon and display names are required to be unique throughout a domain, though a display name must be limited to 64 characters, while a logon name can be 104 characters in length. For compatibility with Windows NT 4.0 or earlier, the logon name is truncated to the first 20 characters.

Although user friendly, using first names as a logon name has a distinct limitation when scaling within organizations. It is important to adopt a consistent naming convention that is easy to use, but avoids naming conflicts as requirements grow.

A common logon naming policy in larger companies is a combination of the first and last name, such as njensen for Natalie Jensen. When a second N. Jensen requires an account, you may elect to include the middle initial or the second letter from the first name, such as najensen for Natalie Ann Jensen.

A good bet is to keep logon names somewhere between 4 and 10 characters. This allows enough length for uniqueness, but keeps the logon name short and easy to remember.

Environments that are more security conscious may require usernames to be longer and may also practice a form of obfuscation called *security by obscurity*; in other words, not providing an obvious relationship between a user and his or her logon name.

Default User Account Settings

Now that you have a naming strategy, you need to consider the default settings for each newly created account. Settings that need consideration include:

Initial password   The initial password is assigned when the account is created. The user will use it to log on the first time.

User must change password on next logon   When you set the initial password, both you and the user know what it is. If users are forced to change it at next logon, they must choose a new, private password. If this option is not enabled, you could find yourself with a community of users who all have the same password. This particular scenario highlights not only security issues, but also poor user creation practice on behalf of the Administrator.

User cannot change password   This setting could be applied to fixed-function user accounts that are used by services or by several users.

Password never expires   Another setting designed for specialized accounts and is not applicable to most user accounts. Forcing users to select a new password on a regular basis provides a safeguard against the sharing of passwords that is common in many environments despite the warnings and efforts of the Network Administrator.

Account disabled   Disabling accounts is useful for creating accounts in bulk prior to migrating users, and only reenabling them once the associated user has been migrated.

NOTE

The default Administrator account cannot be disabled. Many sites employ security by obscurity by electing to change the administrative account names to less obvious names. Changing the name does not provide a great deal of protection from determined hackers, but it does erect another barrier to unauthorized entry. Choose administrative passwords with both alphanumeric and nonalphanumeric characters.

Logon Mechanics

Earlier in the chapter, I compared a user account to a passport. In fact, when a user logs on to the Active Directory, this passport has a number of important stamps in it that provide a wealth of information that forms part of the user authentication and authorization process.

Windows 2000 identifies users and groups not by their name, but by a unique code called a security identifier (SID). Using SIDs instead of account or group names addresses issues that could arise when renaming groups or user accounts. When an account or group is renamed, the SID remains unchanged.

Active Directory, files, and Registry objects all have an associated ACL. This list contains references, called Access Control Entries (ACE), to group or user SIDs. These references detail the type of permission granted or denied to the object.

Whenever a user logs on, Windows 2000 generates an access token that contains:

Individual SID   The unique SID associated with the user.

Group SIDs   When a user is added to a group, the group's SID is attached to the user's access token.

User rights   Certain privileges, called user rights, can be granted to users or groups, and attached to their access token.

Since access tokens are generated at logon, new group membership will only take effect the next time a user logs. The logon process allows the new group SIDs to attach to the users access token.

Creating User Accounts

Domain accounts are created using the Active Directory Users and Computers snap-in. Once the snap-in has been opened, click the domain name to expand it. The domain contains four predefined groups of objects:

Builtin   The default system administration users and groups created by Windows 2000 during initial installation.

Computers   A list of all computer account objects defined by the Administrator.

Domain Controllers   The domain controllers for Active Directory.

Users   The default location for user and groups accounts created by Administrators.

Administrators can create additional organizational units to further subdivide and manage the users and computers on their network (see Chapter 4, "Implementing Domains, Trees, and Forests," for more details). Organizational units can also be used to define various security policies based on need. To create a user account:

1. Right-click the container in which you wish to create a user account. To create a user, select New→User. A window titled "Create new object – (User)" is displayed. An alternate method is to select the New User icon on the toolbar.

2. Fill in the information for the user's first and last names.

3. Select a user logon name, and click Next.

4. The penultimate step is to determine an initial password and optional settings. Most Administrators elect to check the "User must change password at next logon" option. Click Next when complete.

5. The object wizard provides a summary of the object properties, including the account name. If everything looks as expected, click Finish.

As you can see, creating a new user account is a very simple task in Windows 2000. Remember that creating an account may just be the first step in allowing a user to access resources on a Windows 2000 network.

Setting Account Policies

With Windows 2000, setting password requirements such as password length, expiration, and lockout after failed logon are known as account policies. The Security Configuration and Analysis tool provides a centralized interface to most security policies, including password, account, and Kerberos policies. A number of templates are provided as examples of different security configurations. For more information on these security templates and tools, see Chapter 15, "Windows 2000 Security Services."

The Security Configuration and Analysis tool provides a direct entry point to the same details as those stored in group policies in the Computer Configuration\Windows Settings\Security Settings\Account Policies node.

The following procedure outlines the steps necessary to set account policies using Group Policy:

1. Open the Group Policy Object for the container either through Active Directory Users and Computers or through the stand-alone Group Policy snap-in.

2. Open the Computer Configuration\Windows Settings\Security Settings\Account Policies node.

3. Double-click on any policies that require configuration, and set appropriately. A policy that is labeled as Not Defined implies that no configuration parameters have been enabled for it. Additionally, some policies can be considered to be off (disabled) or on (enabled).

Account Policy Configuration

The account policy node within Group Policy Objects consists of three nodes, each with its own set of configurable options.

Password Policy   Settings for passwords such as enforcement, and lifetimes.

Account Lockout Policy   Settings governing the activation and duration of account lockouts.

Kerberos Policy   Details Kerberos configuration parameters.

Password Policy options include:

Enforce password history   This option prevents users from cycling through two or three passwords. By default, this is set to one.

Maximum password age   The amount of time before a user must change a password. Take careful consideration when setting this value—longer password aging may make things easier for users, but it also increases the network's vulnerability profile. The default is 42 days.

Minimum password age   The amount of time that must pass before the user can change a password. Setting a minimum password age prevents users from cycling through enough passwords to overcome the Enforce password uniqueness controls. By default, this is set to 0.

Minimum password length   The shortest acceptable length for a password. A minimum length of six characters is recommended, although many Administrators insist on a minimum of eight characters. The default is to allow blank passwords—remember to change this!

Password must meet complexity requirements   Forces the user to use a mix of upper- and lower-case letters, along with a mix of alphanumeric characters. Remember that although logon names are not case sensitive, passwords are.

Store password using reversible encryption   Passwords are usually stored using a one-way cryptographic function. This option allows passwords to be recovered.

Account Lockout Policy options include:

Account lockout threshold   The number of failed logons before an account is disabled automatically. A balance needs to be established between security and allowing for those of us who have trouble finger-painting, never mind typing passwords correctly. A value between 5 and 10 is reasonable.

Account lockout duration   The amount of time an account remains locked out after the account lockout threshold has been reached. Generally, this option is not defined to prevent the account from automatically becoming reenabled.

Reset account lockout counter after   The amount of time to wait before resetting the failed logon count. The failed logon count is reset whenever a user logs on successfully, or whenever the reset time has elapsed.

Kerberos Policy options include (see Chapter 15 for more information on Kerberos):

Enforce user logon restrictions   This option enforces user account restrictions.

Maximum lifetime options   These options determine the maximum lifetimes for user tickets, service tickets, and user ticket renewal.

Chapter 7, "Configuring IntelliMirror," provides additional information on account policy configuration and the Group Policy Editor.

Modifying Properties for User Accounts

All account property management is completed through the Active Directory Users and Computers snap-in. To change the properties of an account, open the Active Directory Users and Computers snap-in and select the container that holds the required user account. To change the properties on the account, double-click on the user's name.

The User Properties window contains a number of tabs (Figure 9.1). Some of the tabs are for tracking general information, while others affect the behavior of the account. Filling in the general user information fields is considered to be good practice, since it allows the storage of information about users in a central repository that can be made available to other applications. The General, Address, Telephones, and Organization tabs should be populated with the relevant information, but on the whole, these values do not affect the account significantly except when attempting to search for the account in the directory using these fields.

The Account tab contains a number of settings related to the user logon name, how the account can be used, and when it is active. There are several attributes that can be changed, such as logon name, logon times, and account expiration date. The Profile tab is a fundamental user property tab that contains many of the most common administrative settings. The settings in the Profile tab include:

Profile Path   Allows the Administrator to specify a profile for the user's account. This is similar to the Roaming profile concept that exists in Windows NT 4.0, whereby a user has a single profile for use on every machine.

Logon Script   The script executed when the user logs on to the network. Commonly used to configure security settings, install applications, or control system configuration.

Home Directory   The home directory can be on the user's local drive, or it can be a mapped drive to a server share. If you specify a directory that does not exist, Windows 2000 will attempt to connect to the machine and

Figure 9.1 The User Properties window.

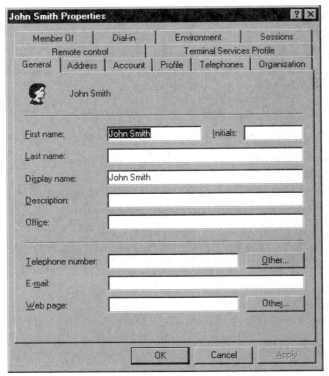

create the directory. As a shortcut, you can use the system variable %USERNAME% to reference the account name.

Network Path   This field allows an Administrator to define a network folder as a Universal Naming Convention (UNC) path that contains documents shared with other members of a group or project team. The concept is similar to a home directory for a group or project team.

The Member Of tab corresponds to the group concept of Windows NT 4.0. A list of all group memberships is in this window, with the option to add or remove groups as needed. To add additional groups, click ADD. Select the group and click ADD, then click OK to close the Add Group window. The Primary Group option is available only to Macintosh clients. The Primary Group should be set to the group with which the user most commonly shares data. It is used for permission associations when a Macintosh client creates a new folder or file.

The Dial-in tab lets an Administrator specify who can connect remotely, and how they will connect. Other options include setting static routes and defining callback options for the account.

Four tabs—Environment, Sessions, Terminal Services Profile, and Remote control—all relate to the functioning of Terminal Services. These tabs allow the Administrator to define parameters such as user session timeouts, programs to start at logon, and the location of Terminal Services profiles.

Managing User Accounts

All account administration can be completed through the Active Directory Users and Computers snap-in. The convenience of a single interface is compelling, and over time, Administrators can configure snap-ins and the MMC to host the types of administrative tasks that they most frequently perform.

Administrators can save MMC configurations as .MSC files, or create custom Taskpads. The .MSC files can be copied to other machines or carried on a disk, allowing Administrators to develop a completely customized interface that they can use from any Windows 2000 machine. Additionally, Taskpads can be used to provide a clear and unambiguous interface into particular tasks. For example, using the MMC and the Active Directory Users and Computers snap-in, a Taskpad could be created that would allow the help desk to create a new account based only on a specific template.

The Windows 2000 Server Administrative Tools (including Active Directory Users and Computers) can be installed on a workstation by running the Microsoft Installer package AdminPak.msi in the \i386 directory on the Windows 2000 Server CD-ROM.

Deleting User Accounts

The basic operations that can be performed on user accounts have been designed to be easily accessible from the Active Directory Users and Computers snap-in. For example, to delete an account:

1. Select the container of the target account.
2. Right-click the required user account, then select Delete.
3. Click YES to confirm.

Note that deleting an account will permanently delete the (unique) SID associated with the specific user. Since permissions and rights are assigned on a SID basis, this implies that all the user's individual permissions would have to be reassigned, even if a user was created in the same container with the same logon name.

Resetting Passwords

Follow these steps to reset a user password:

1. Select the container of the target account.
2. In the Results pane, right-click on the user.

3. Select Reset Password.

4. Type the new password, and confirm it.

5. If you require the user to change this password at the next logon, select the "User must change password at next logon" check box.

Disabling an Account

To disable an account:

1. Select the container of the target account.

2. In the results pane, right-click on the user.

3. Select Disable Account from the Action menu.

Enabling an Account

To enable a disabled user account:

1. Select the container of the target account.

2. In the results pane, right-click on the user.

3. Select Enable Account from the Action menu.

Other Active Directory Users and Computers Functions

To find a user account in Active Directory:

1. Open or create an MMC console with the Active Directory Users and Computers snap-in configured.

2. Right-click the domain node and select Find.

3. If you know which organizational unit the user is in, right-click the OU and select Find to narrow the search.

4. Type the name of the user you want to find in the Name box on the Users, Contacts, and Groups tab (Figure 9.2).

5. Click Find Now.

Moving User Accounts

To move a user account:

1. Select the container of the target account.

2. In the Details pane, right-click on the user and select Move.

3. In the Move pane, select the OU.

4. Select the domain and folder belonging to the place where you want to move the user account. Click Ok.

Figure 9.2 The Find Users, Contacts, and Groups window.

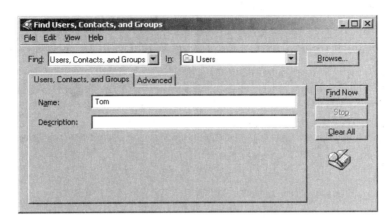

Mapping a Certificate to a User

In Windows 2000, a certificate that has been issued to a user can be mapped to the user's account. A server using public key technology can then authenticate the user via this certificate. To log on to a system, the user's certificate is authenticated. The result is the same as if the user had provided a logon name and password, yet the process is more secure.

Traditionally, computer systems have used a centralized accounts database to manage users. This technique has been widely adopted by software companies and is a familiar concept to the majority of Administrators. However, as systems become more complex, with hundreds of thousands of users, such centralized databases can become difficult to manage.

Public key certificates have the potential to help simplify these problems. Certificates can be widely distributed, issued by numerous parties, and verified by simply examining the certificate without having to refer to a centralized database. One of the key barriers to the wider acceptance of certificates is that few operating systems and administration tools understand how to deal with them. One solution that maintains the advantages of both certificates and user accounts is to create a mapping between a certificate and a user account. This allows the operating system to continue using accounts while introducing certificates for those systems that understand them.

When using certificates to log on, a user presents the certificate to the system, which determines the user account that should be logged on. In most cases, a certificate is mapped to a user account in one of two ways: a single certificate is mapped to a single user account, or multiple certificates are mapped to one user account.

UPN mapping User Principle Name (UPN) mapping is a special case of one-to-one mapping. Enterprise certification authorities place an entry into each certificate called a UPN, which looks very much like an e-mail name and is unique within a Windows 2000 domain. With UPN mapping, the UPN is used to find the user's account in Active Directory, and then the account is logged on.

One-to-one One-to-one mapping is the mapping of a user certificate to a single user account. You can either issue certificates to each of your employees from your own certification service, or you can have your employees get certificates from a certification authority approved by your organization. These certificates are then mapped to the employee's user account.

To map a certificate to a user account in Active Directory:

1. Log on as an Administrator.

2. Open Active Directory for Users and Computers.

3. Right-click on the domain name you want to administer, click View, and check Advanced Features.

4. Double-click the domain name, click on the OU, and, in the Details pane, locate the user to which you want to map a certificate.

5. Right-click the username, click Name Mappings, and select ADD.

6. Type the name and path of the .cer file. Click OPEN.

7. Do one of the following:

   ■ To map the certificate to one account, ensure that both Use Issuer for alternate security identity and Use Subject for alternate security identity are checked.

   ■ To map a certificate with many accounts, uncheck "Use Issuer for alternate security identity," and leave "Use Subject of alternate security identity" checked.

8. Click OK.

NOTE

An important note about one-to-one mapping: You cannot map the same certificate to multiple accounts using one-to-one mapping. The result will be that no account will be associated with the certificate, and any attempt to use the certificate as a user credential will fail.

Using Groups to Organize User Accounts

Groups are objects in the Active Directory that contain users, contacts, computers, and, potentially, other groups. Groups provide a method for logically organizing other objects in the Active Directory. You can then use these logical groups of objects to assign access to resources or control privileges on your network. Administrators use groups to:

- Manage access to shared resources such as Active Directory objects and their properties, network shares, files, directories, printer queues, and so on.
- Filter group policy.
- Create e-mail distribution lists.
- Grant user rights.

When assigning permissions for resources, Administrators should assign permissions to a group rather than to individual users. The permissions are assigned once to the group, instead of several times to each user. Each account added to a group receives the rights and permissions defined for that group. Working with groups instead of with individual users helps simplify network maintenance and administration.

Groups can be used to filter group policy, grant user rights, or distribute e-mail. Groups are distinct from organizational units in that some types of groups can cross domain boundaries. They can contain users, computers, or shared resources on a local server, single domain, domain tree, or forest. This is in direct contrast to organizational units that represent a collection of objects within a single domain.

Every user initially enters the network through a user account; this is the beginning point for assignment of user rights and permissions to access resources, individually or (as Microsoft recommends) through membership in security groups (Figure 9.3).

Group Types

At times you will want to group users for security purposes, while at other times you may want to group users only for distribution or high-level management purposes. Windows 2000 offers two types of groups: security groups and distribution lists. Each type of group has a specific purpose, and Administrators of large complex environments will use a combination of the two to accomplish all their administrative tasks.

Security Groups

Security groups function in a similar fashion as domain groups in a Windows NT domain. Security groups are the fundamental connection between users and security. The security group is a logical collection of

Figure 9.3 Relationship between user accounts and security groups.

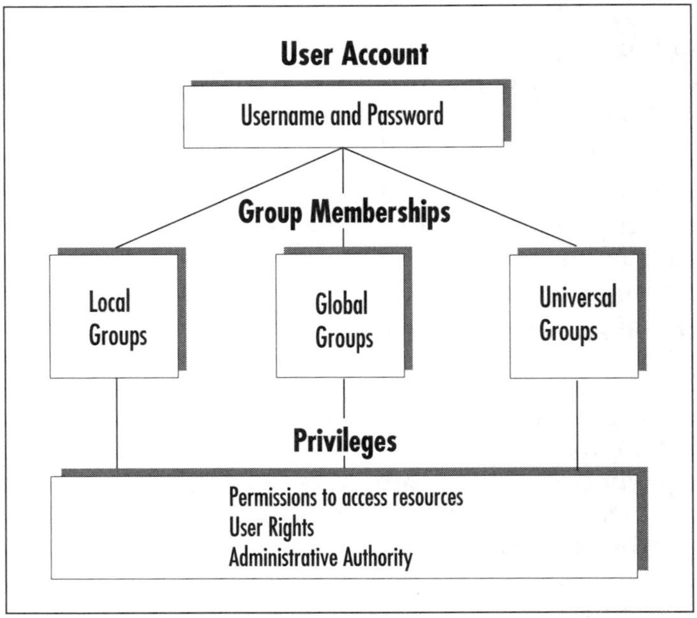

domain users that can be granted specific rights and permissions to net-work resources. Security groups can also be used to filter the application of group policy objects.

Distribution Lists

Distribution lists can be considered to be a logical collection of users stored within the Active Directory for use by applications. The most common example of an application that uses distribution lists is Microsoft Exchange. Administrators can maintain distribution lists for user notifica-tion; for example, for corporate bulletins or network problems. Note that distribution lists are used for nonsecurity purposes only.

Group Scope

When creating a group, the Administrator can control the group's scope defining whether the group can be nested or referenced in the domain or the whole forest. There are four types of scopes: Local, Domain Local, Global, and Universal.

Local

A Local group exists only on the computer on which it is created, and not on domain controllers.

- **Open membership**   You can add user accounts from anywhere in the forest.
- **Access to resources on local machine only**   You can use a Local group to control access only to a resources on the same machine as the Local group.

Domain Local

A Domain Local group is a collection of domain user accounts that can be used only to set access permission to resources in the domain. The characteristics of the Domain Local group include:

- **Open membership**   You can add user accounts from any domain, and also Global and Local groups.
- **Access to resources in local domain only**   You can use a Domain Local group to control access only to a resource in the same domain.

Global

A Global group is a collection of accounts that can be used by any server in the domain to set access permissions. The characteristics of a Global group include:

- **Limited membership**   The global group can contain user and Global group accounts only from the domain in which it was created.
- **Access to resources in any domain**   Global groups can be assigned permissions to gain access to resources in any domain in the forest.

Universal

A Universal group is accessible by any server on the network, and is most often used to assign permissions across domains. The characteristics of Universal groups include:

- **Open membership**   Any account from any domain in the forest can be added to a Universal group.
- **Access to any resource in any domain**   Administrators can use Universal groups to assign permissions to any resource in any domain in the forest.
- **Native mode only**   Before you can use Universal groups for security purposes, you must convert the domain to a native Windows 2000 domain. Universal groups are not available as an option for security groups when Windows 2000 is run in non-native mode.

Group scope also defines the membership rules for a group. The membership rules define the types of accounts that can be placed in the group. Table 9.1 provides a summary of membership rules based on the group scope.

Table 9.1 Membership Rules Based on Group Scope

Scope	Group Can Contain	Group Can Be a Member of
Domain Local	User accounts, Universal groups, and Global groups from any domain in the forest. Domain Local groups from the same domain.	Domain Local groups in the same domain.
Global	User accounts and Global groups from the same domain.	Universal and Domain Local groups in any domain in the forest. Global groups in the same domain.
Universal	User accounts, Universal groups, and Global groups from any domain in the forest.	Domain Local or Universal groups in any domain in the forest.

Implementing Groups

The process of creating groups is similar to that used for creating users. Groups are created through the Active Directory Users and Computers snap-in. By default, members of the Administrators and Account Operators groups have permission to create groups. The Windows 2000 built-in groups are discussed later in this chapter. An Administrator can delegate the ability to create groups either in the domain or in a specific organizational unit (OU). Before creating a group, a certain amount of information is required:

Group name   Every group in a domain needs a unique name. A naming convention that includes some indication of the grouping and security level is the most useful. Examples might include accounting_readonly, accounting_readwrite, or accounting_noaccess. Such names clearly indicate the group's purpose.

Group scope   The group scope defines which servers inside and outside the domain can see and use the group.

Group type   There are two types of groups: security groups and distribution lists. Security groups are used for assigning access to network resources. Distribution lists are used by applications such as Exchange to generate bulk e-mails.

For IT Professionals

Group Strategy

Before you create any user accounts or groups, it is best to develop your group strategy. The best strategy for most environments is to use a combination of Global and Domain Local groups. Follow these steps when planning your group strategy:

1. Identify the users on your network with similar job responsibilities. Add these accounts to a Global group. An example would be placing all the salespeople in a Global sales group.

2. Determine the resources or groups of resources to which users will need access. Create a Domain Local group for each of these resources. An example of a common shared resource might be a customer database, for which you would create a customers Domain Local group.

3. Identify the Global groups that will need access to a particular resource, and place these Global groups in the Domain Local group you created for the resource. For example, you would place the sales Global group in the customers Domain Local group.

4. Finally, assign access permissions to the Domain Local group. For example, you might assign read and write permissions to the customers Domain Local group for the customer database folder.

An acronym (of sorts) for this strategy is AGUGDLP: **A**ccounts are added to **G**lobal groups (that could then be nested in other **U**niversal **G**roups or **G**lobal groups) and then placed in **D**omain **L**ocal groups, which are assigned **P**ermissions. Although AGUGDLP is more reminiscent of the sound a drowning man would make, it can still prove to be useful in remembering your group strategy.

Structuring groups in this fashion gives the Administrator control over building and managing groups on the domain server, while also allowing the Administrator to combine multiple Global groups from different domains into a Local group of a stand-alone server. The amount of administrative overhead is minimized as the network grows, because user accounts are still maintained at a domain level instead of on each server.

Creating a Group

Domain groups are created in the Active Directory database using Active Directory Users and Computers. To create a group:

1. Launch the Active Directory Users and Computers snap-in.
2. Select the target container for the group.
3. Right-click the container and select New→group, or use the New Group icon in the toolbar.
4. Fill in the group name.
5. Select the group type and group scope.
6. Click OK to create the group.

Assigning Users to a Group

Users can be assigned to a group using either group settings or user settings. When a group is created for the first time and multiple users are added to the group, the group setting interface may be easier to use. When an individual account is added to a group at a later date, it may be easier to use the user settings.

Adding Users through Group Settings

To add multiple users to a group:

1. Open the group settings by double-clicking the group (Figure 9.4).
2. Select the Members tab, and click ADD.
3. Double-click on a user to add to the group list.
4. Click OK to close the Add User window and Group Settings window.

An alternate method is to add users to groups from the User Settings window by using the Member Of tab.

Configuring Group Settings

Group configuration can be completed via the Group Settings window. Group settings can be changed by double-clicking on the designated group from within the Active Directory Users and Computers snap-in. The Group Settings window offers tabs for the following parameters:

General   Most of the information in the General tab is for reference purposes and does not affect the group's behavior. It may be useful to add the e-mail address of the group Administrator on the General tab so any updates to the group can be e-mailed to him (by right-clicking on the group and selecting Send mail).

Figure 9.4 Group Settings window.

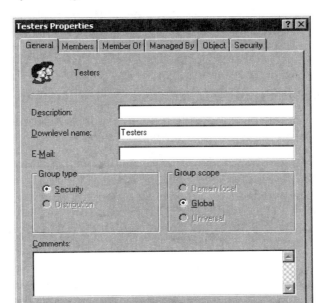

Members   The Members tab is a list of the current members of the group. You can add and remove members from the group with this tab.

Member Of   Groups can be members of other groups in certain situations.

Managed By   The Managed By tab allows you to change the users who have permission to modify the group settings. By default, the Administrator has full control over the account, but group management can be delegated to other users. This is similar to a feature within Microsoft Exchange where a user can be nominated to manage membership for a group, thereby relieving the Administrator from getting involved in the mechanics of managing membership for a particular group.

Managing Groups

Administrators are often faced with the requirement to change some aspect of a group's characteristics, such as the group's scope. Additionally, Administrators may want to search for a group within their domain, or delete a group that is no longer needed. Many of these tasks parallel their equivalent user functions.

Changing a Group's Scope

At times, it may be necessary to change the scope of a group. Administrators most commonly change the scope to one that has broader membership capabilities.

NOTE

A Global group can be changed to a Universal group only if the Global group is not a member of another Global group.

It can be a little tricky at times when converting groups, particularly in light of the fact that a Domain Local group can only be changed to a Universal group if the group being converted does not contain other Domain Local groups.

To change a group's scope:

1. Open Active Directory Users and Groups snap-in and expand the domain node.
2. Select the folder that contains the required group.
3. In the Details pane, right-click the group to display the Action menu.
4. Click PROPERTIES to display the group properties.
5. Click the General tab and change the scope.

WARNING

The scope of a Universal group cannot be changed because all other groups have more restrictive membership rules than Universal groups.

Deleting Groups

Like many other operations within Active Directory, deleting groups is a very simple task.

1. Open the Active Directory Users and Computers snap-in and expand the domain node.
2. Click the Built-in or organizational unit folder that contains the group.

3. In the Details pane, right-click the group and select Delete from the Action menu.

4. Click YES to complete the operation.

Implementing Local Groups

A Local group is a collection of user accounts created on a specific machine. Local groups can be used to assign permissions to resources on a specific machine only. These groups do not participate in the Active Directory, and reside in the local security directory. Local groups are used on individual Windows 2000 Professional workstations and stand-alone servers to control access to resources on the local machine.

Preparing to Create Local Groups

Local groups have a scope that is confined to the specific server on which they were created. This limit in scope also influences the functionality of the Local group. Before creating a Local group, you should be aware of these guidelines:

- You cannot create a Local group on a domain controller. A Domain Local group is not the same as a Local group on a member server. All account and group information for a domain controller is stored in the Active Directory, and is thus shared with all machines in the domain.

- You can use a Local group on the computer only where you created it. While you can use a Local group to assign permissions to resources, this breaks down the concept of centralized management of all accounts and resources. Local groups are not in the Active Directory, and therefore cannot be administered centrally.

The membership rules for Local groups are:

- Local groups can contain local user accounts from the computer on which they were created. They can also contain domain users, Domain Local groups, and Global groups from the domain (and other trusted domains) of which the server or workstation is a member.

- Local groups cannot be members of any other group, local or domain.

Creating a Local Group

You can use the Local Users and Groups snap-in to create and manage Local groups. To create a Local group:

1. In the Local Users and Groups snap-in, click the Groups folder.

2. Select Create Group from the Action menu.

3. Fill in the group name, description, and members.

4. Click CREATE to create the group.

Implementing Built-in Groups

Windows 2000 includes an extensive list of built-in groups with predefined security roles. The number and capabilities of the built-in groups go well beyond those included with earlier versions of Windows NT. Before creating any groups, it is important to understand the scope and role of the built-in groups.

Windows 2000 contains four types of predefined groups: Local, Domain Local, Global, and System. Windows builds these predefined groups during the install process and assigns the appropriate rights to them. You do not need to create these groups or set their user rights.

When using the Active Directory Users and Computers tool, predefined Domain Local groups appear in the Builtin folder, and Domain Global groups appear in the Users folder.

Built-in Domain Local groups   Windows 2000 creates the Domain Local groups with predefined user rights and access permissions. These accounts are designed to administer various aspects of the domain and the Active Directory. When you add an account or Global group to one of these built-in groups, it will automatically inherit the rights and permissions of the built-in groups.

Built-in Global groups   The built-in Global groups created by Windows 2000 during install have no inherent user rights or permissions. Administrators can assign rights and permissions to built-in Global groups as needed.

Built-in Local groups   Built-in Local groups are present on all stand-alone servers, member servers, and computers running Windows 2000 Professional. The built-in Local groups have user rights and permissions to perform specific tasks on individual computers. The Local groups are visible under the Groups folder in the Local Users and Groups snap-in.

Built-in System groups   Administrators cannot directly modify the Windows 2000 built-in System groups. These groups are used internally to track various states and may represent different sets of users at different times.

Built-In Group Behavior

By default, every user account created in a domain is automatically added to the Domain Users Global group. The Domain Users group represents all the user accounts created in the domain. For example, if you wanted all the users in a domain to have access to a shared resource such as a printer or shared folder, then you would assign permissions for the resource to the Domain Users group. Alternatively, you could put the Domain Users group into a Domain Local group that has permissions to access the resource. By default, the Domain Users group in a domain is also a member of the Users group in the same domain.

The Domain Admins Global group represents those users who have broad administrative rights in a domain. Windows 2000 Server does not place any accounts in this group automatically (other than the Administrator account), but if you wanted an account to have sweeping administrative rights in a domain, you would place that account into Domain Admins. Unlike Windows NT 4.0, Windows 2000 Server offers administration and delegation of authority capabilities; you will generally not have to grant such broad administrative rights. By default, the Domain Admins group in a domain is a member of the Administrators group in the same domain.

The Domain Guests Global group is a member of the Guests group in the same domain, and automatically contains the domain's default Guest user account. To secure a Windows 2000 environment, most Administrators will disable the Guest account and not use the Guests group of a domain. The better solution is to organize your domain structure so that the appropriate trusts are in place to facilitate the needed resource sharing.

The built-in Domain Local groups of a domain are primarily used to assign default sets of permissions to users who will have some administrative control in the domain. For example, the Administrators group in a domain has a broad set of administrative rights over all user accounts and resources in the domain. Table 9.2 provides a summary of some of the more common rights, along with a description of those rights, and the accounts to which the rights are granted. You can assign the same rights to other domain accounts, and add or remove rights from the existing built-in groups.

To view the current User Rights, use the Security Configuration and Analysis snap-in. To change the User Rights, use the Security templates snap-in to define the rights, then import the template into the Security Configuration and Analysis snap-in.

To view the details of a particular User Right:

1. Open the Security Configuration and Analysis snap-in.

2. Expand Local Policies and select the User Right Assignments.

3. A list of User Rights will appear on the right.

4. To view the details, double-click one of the User Rights.

Table 9.2 Common User Rights

User Right	Allows	Groups Assigned This Right by Default
Access this computer from the network	Connect to the computer over the network.	Administrators, everyone
Back up files and folders	Back up files and folders with the right to override the file and folder permissions when using a backup utility.	Administrators, backup operators
Bypass traverse checking	Move between folder to access files even if the user does not have permissions to the parent file folders.	Everyone
Change the system time	Set the time for the internal clock of the computer.	Administrators, power users
Create a pagefile	This right currently has no effect.	Administrators
Debug programs	Debug low-level OS objects such as threads.	Administrators
Force shutdown from a remote system	Shut down a computer remotely.	Administrators
Increase scheduling priority	Boost the execution priority of a process.	Administrators, power users
Load and unload device drivers	Install and remove device drivers.	Administrators
Log on locally	Log on to the computer from the local keyboard.	Administrators, power users, backup operators, everyone, guests, and users
Manage auditing and security log	Specify the types of resources to be audited, and be able to view and clear the security log.	Administrators
Modify firmware environment variables	Modify system environment variables stored in nonvolatile RAM on computers that support such configurations.	Administrators, power users
Profile single process	Perform profiling (performance monitoring) on a single process.	Administrators, power users

Table 9.2 *continued*

User Right	Allows	Groups Assigned This Right by Default
Profile system performance	Perform profiling (performance monitoring) on the entire system.	Administrators, power users
Restore files and folders	Restore backed-up files and folders. This right overrides or supersedes file and folder permissions.	Administrators, backup operators
Shut down the system	Shut down Windows 2000.	Administrators, power users
Take ownership of files and other objects	Take ownership of any resource on the system. This right supersedes any permission on the object.	Administrators

Groups—Best Practices

Here are some of the most important things to remember when using groups to organize user accounts. When you add users to a group, remember these guidelines:

- Users can be members of multiple groups.
- There is no limit to the number of groups to which a user can belong. The group object contains only a pointer to the user object, and thus multiple groups can point to the same user.
- Nesting of groups is allowed. You can place multiple domain groups inside the Local group of a server, easing the administrative tasks. One example might be your sales force. Each product sales team has a group for controlling access to its project resources. You could combine these individual sales groups into a master sales group that contains the individual groups. When you want to assign a resource to all the salespeople, you need to assign permissions only to the master group.
- Minimize the number of levels of nesting.
- While nesting is a powerful tool, it can also become a nightmare to manage if it is overused. It can be difficult to track group membership with several levels of nesting.

There are also a few points to keep in mind if you decide to use Universal groups:

- Use Universal groups only to give users access to resources spread across multiple domains. You can assign permissions to a Universal group for any resource in any domain.

- Try to keep the membership of Universal groups static. Universal groups are distributed throughout the domain tree. Changes to a Universal group may cause a significant increase in network traffic, because the change must be replicated across multiple domain controllers. Frequent changes to the Universal groups increase the overall traffic significantly.

- Use Universal groups as you would Domain Local groups, by adding Global groups to the Universal group and then assigning permissions to the Universal group. The difference between the Universal and Domain Local groups is that the Universal group can be applied to any resource in any domain. When you use a similar strategy for both types of groups, it is easier to keep track of the overall security configuration of your environment.

Windows 2000 offers two modes of operation: mixed and native. The default mode is mixed to allow backward compatibility with Windows NT 4.0. You can switch the mode to native at any time, as long as all domain controllers are running Windows 2000. Doing so makes the universal scope option for security groups available to you.

Table 9.3 provides a summary of the differences between mixed and native modes.

Table 9.3 Mixed and Native Modes under Windows 2000

Mixed Mode	Native Mode
Domain controllers can run Windows NT 3.5, 4.0, or Windows 2000.	Only Windows 2000 domain controllers are allowed. Client computers can run any version of Windows NT or Windows 2000.
Universal groups are not available.	All group scopes, including Universal groups, are available.
Only one level of nesting, adding a Global group to a Domain Local group, is allowed.	Multiple levels of nesting are available, along with more nesting options.

Administering User Accounts

Creating user accounts is only the first step in managing them. In addition to the basic account settings, Windows 2000 offers the ability to configure and manage user profiles and home directories. User profiles are an extremely powerful tool, and Microsoft has completed extensive work to improve on its Windows NT predecessors. Once you understand how user profiles fit into the overall administrative strategy, you can begin to tap their real power.

User Profiles Overview

On computers running Windows 2000, user profiles can be considered to be the settings, configuration, and files that define the users' environment when they log on. For example, the profile can contain configuration information regarding screen colors, network connections, and Start menu items. A user profile is created when each user logs on to a computer for the first time. User profiles are available for Windows 9x, but they are not enabled by default.

User profiles provide several advantages:

- Several users can use the same computer, and each receive his or her own settings at log on.
- When users log on to their workstation, they receive the desktop settings as they existed when they logged off.
- Customization of the desktop environment made by one user does not affect another user.
- User profiles can be stored on a server so that they can be downloaded to any computer at log on.

As an administrative tool, user profiles provide these options:

- A default user profile can be created that is appropriate for a specific user's tasks.
- Mandatory user profiles can be configured that will not save changes made by the user. Users can modify the desktop configuration while they are logged on, but none of these changes are saved at log off. The mandatory profile settings are downloaded to the local computer each time the user logs on.
- Default user settings can be specified that can be automatically included in all of the individual user profiles.

Types of User Profiles

The way in which you choose to administer the network will define the type of user profiles that are a best fit for your purposes. Types of user profiles include:

Local user profiles   A local user profile is created the first time a user logs on to a computer, and it is stored on the computer's local drive (the default location for user profiles is C:\Documents and Settings\<username>). Any changes made to the local user profile will be specific to the computer on which the changes were made.

Roaming user profiles   A roaming user profile is created by the Administrator and is stored on a server. This profile is available every time a user logs on. Any changes made to the roaming user profile are replicated to the server at log off.

Mandatory user profiles   A mandatory user profile is a roaming profile that can be used to specify particular settings for individuals or for an entire group of users. Only System Administrators can make changes to mandatory user profiles.

Contents of a User Profile

Every user profile begins as a copy of Default User, which is a default user profile stored on each computer running Windows 2000. The NTuser.dat file within Default User displays configuration settings from the Windows 2000 Registry. Every user profile also uses the common program groups, contained in the All Users folder.

Table 9.4 summarizes the links to various desktop items contained in profile folders.

Table 9.4 Contents of the Profile Folder

User Profile Folder	Contents
Application data	Program-specific data. Program vendors decide what data to store in the User Profile folder.
Desktop	Desktop items, including files, shortcuts, and folders.
Favorites	Shortcuts to favorite locations.
NetHood	Shortcuts in My Network Places.
My Documents	User documents.
My Pictures	User picture items.
PrintHood	Shortcuts to printer folder items.
Recent	Shortcuts to the most recently used documents and accessed folders.
Send To	Short cuts to document handling utilities.
Start Menu	Shortcuts to program items.
Templates	User template items.

The NTuser.dat file is the Registry portion of the user profile. The Registry key defined in the Ntuser.dat file overrides the current Registry settings of the local machine. Although they are not copied to user profile folders, the settings in the All Users folder are used to create individual user profiles. Windows 2000 supports two program group types:

- **Common program groups** are always available on a computer, no matter who is logged on. Common program groups are stored in the All Users folder under the Documents and Settings folder. The All Users folder also contains settings for the Desktop and Start menu.
- **Personal program groups** are private to the user who creates them.

Settings Saved in a User Profile

A user profile contains configuration preferences and options for each user—a snapshot of a user's desktop environment.

Table 9.5 describes the settings in a user profile.

Table 9.5 Options Available in User Profile Settings

Source	Parameters Saved
Windows Explorer	All user-definable settings for Windows Explorer.
My Documents	User-stored documents.
My Pictures	User-stored picture items.
Favorites	Shortcuts to favorite locations on the Internet.
Mapped network drive	Any user-created mapped network drives.
My Network Places	Links to other computers on the network.
Desktop contents	Items stored on the Desktop and Shortcut elements.
Screen colors and fonts	All user-definable computer screen colors and display text settings.
Application data and registry hive	Application data and user-defined configuration settings.
Printer settings	Network printer connections.
Control Panel	All user-defined settings made in Control Panel.
Accessories	All user-specific program settings affecting the user's Windows environment, including Calculator, Clock, Notepad, and Paint.
Windows 2000–based programs	Any program written specifically for Windows 2000 can be designed so that it tracks program settings on a per-user basis. If this information exists, it is saved in the user profile.
Online user education bookmarks	Any bookmarks placed in the Windows 2000 Help system.

Local User Profiles

The local user profile is stored on the local computer under the user's name in the Documents and Settings folder. Windows 2000 creates a user folder the first time a user logs on if no preconfigured server-based roaming user profile exists. The contents of Default User folder are copied to the user's profile folder. The user profile, along with the common program group settings in the All Users folder, combine to create the user's desktop. When the user logs off, any changes made during the session are saved to the user profile folder.

If the user has multiple accounts on the local workstation or in the domain, then a unique local user profile is created for each account. When the user logs off, changed settings are saved to only one user profile, the one used to log on.

User profiles exhibit the following behavior:

- When users log on to a computer, they always receive their personal settings, including desktop configuration and installed applications.

- Local user profiles are stored in the system partition root\Documents and Settings\<username> folder. For most systems where the C drive is the system root partition, this will be C:\Documents and Settings\<username>. The username is the account name the user used to log on.

- The user profile contains the My Documents folder, the default location for storing files and other data.

- Users have complete control over their own profiles. They can make changes to the Desktop or Network connections, and they can add files to the My Documents folder. These changes are saved each time users log off the system. The next time they log on, Windows 2000 will restore these saved settings.

Roaming User Profiles

To support a user who moves among multiple machines, roaming user profiles can be configured. With roaming user profiles, users can log on to any Windows 2000 computer within their domain and have their desktop environment follow them. The roaming user profile stored on the server is copied to the local machine, restoring all of the user's settings and documents that are stored on the server in the roaming user profile.

If you assign a user a roaming profile by entering a server-based profile path into that user's domain account, a copy of the user's local user profile is saved both locally and on the server specified in the profile path location when the user logs off. The next time the user logs on, the user profile in the user profile path location is compared to the copy in the local user profile folder. The most recent copy of the user profile is used to restore the user's settings.

If the server is not available, the local cached copy of the roaming user profile is used. If the user has not logged on the computer before, a new local user profile is created. In either case, if the centrally stored user profile is not available at logon, it is not updated when the user logs off. The next time the user logs on, he or she must specify which profile to use.

Creating Individualized Roaming User Profiles

To create a roaming profile, follow the basic steps of creating a local user profile by logging on and configuring the various settings. After creating the local user profile, copy it to a centralized location and configure the user account settings to point to this location.

An alternate way to create a new individualized roaming profile is to copy a user's local profiles from his or her primary workstation. To do this, specify the share location where the profile is to be stored in each user's account settings. The next time the user logs on and then logs off, Windows will copy his or her local profiles to the server location. This is an efficient way of converting an existing Windows network environment from local profiles to roaming profiles without having to visit each machine.

The advantages of creating an individualized roaming profile for each user include:

- Provides users with a consistent working environment. You can ensure that each profile is properly configured with the needed tools, and any extraneous applications or settings are removed.

- Provides a standardized desktop for a department or team whose members all need access to the same tools and network resources.

- Potentially simplifies troubleshooting by establishing a base configuration across all machines on the network.

- Combined with group policies, it creates an environment that is secure and easy to manage.

Mandatory Profiles

A basic roaming profile still allows users to customize settings and save those settings back to the profile on the server when they log off. A mandatory profile is a read-only version of the roaming profile. Users still get the same setting at every machine where they log on, but Windows 2000 does not save any changes they make to the settings back to the profile on the server. The profile will be the same as the original profile every time they log on.

One of the most significant advantages of a mandatory profile is that you can assign one profile to multiple users, and ensure that they always have the same configuration. When changes are required, they only need to be made to the mandatory profile. The changes are then reflected in the users' desktop environment at the next logon. This is particularly beneficial for data entry or manufacturing environments, where job responsibilities are well defined.

To change a profile from roaming to mandatory, change the name of the hidden Ntuser.dat file located in the profile folder to Ntuser.man. Windows 2000 recognizes the name change and behaves accordingly.

Setting Up a Roaming User Profile

After configuring roaming profiles on a server, Windows 2000 copies the local user profile to the roaming profile path the next time the user logs on. On subsequent logons at other machines, Windows will copy the roaming profile to the local user profile of the machine.

When configuring roaming profiles, make sure that the server has a regular backup cycle. Losing the configuration data is not critical, but losing the contents of the My Documents folder may be a disaster for some users. Ensure that the server on which profiles are located has sufficient horsepower for the task. During peak times, such as first thing in the morning, server load may be quite intensive, and an underspecified server may negatively impact logon performance.

To configure a roaming user profile:

1. On a server in your domain (member server or domain controller), create a shared folder with an intuitive name such as Profiles. You may wish to hide the share by appending a $ to the share.

2. Using the Active Directory Users and Computers application, open the Properties window of a User account.

3. Select the Profile tab, and fill in the Profile Path field using a Universal Naming Convention reference (for example, \\servername\ profiles$ \natalie).

4. Click OK to close the window and save the changes.

TIP

Windows 2000 provides a number of system variables that can be used as shortcuts when user accounts and other settings are configured. One of these is %username%, which is a system variable that corresponds to the user's logon account name.

Assigning Customized Roaming Profiles

If a group of users requires the same settings and access to common resources, a customized roaming profile can be created that they all share. The best way to do this is to create a template with all the required settings, which is then assigned to each user.

To create a template:

1. Create a user account in the domain such as marketing or manufacturing.

2. Log on to a machine in the domain using the account created.

3. Configure the machine with the required settings, including desktop settings, network configuration, shortcuts, and Start menu items, and remove anything you do not want.

4. When you log off the machine, Windows will save the profile into the standard location, which on most systems will be C:\Documents and Settings\<username>. This will become the profile you use as a template.

To assign the profile to users:

1. Log on as an Administrator to a machine in your domain.

2. Open the System Properties dialog by right-clicking the My Computer icon and selecting Properties.

3. Click the User Profile tab.

4. To copy the template profile to a server, select it from the list and click COPY TO.

5. To assign the profile to users or groups, click CHANGE to open the Choose User window.

6. Select the user or group you want to assign to the profile, and click ADD.

7. Click OK.

Creating Home Directories

In addition to the My Documents folder that is part of the user's profile, Windows 2000 also provides for home directories. Home directories are another location, generally on a server, where users can store important documents.

Home Directories and My Documents

Home directories and My Documents make it easier for an Administrator to back up user files and manage user accounts by collecting all of a user's files in a centralized location. In Windows NT 4.0, an assigned home directory became a user's default folder for the Open and Save As dialog boxes, for command prompt sessions, and for all programs without a defined working folder. An assigned home directory can be a local folder or a shared network resource. Like profiles, home directories can be assigned to an individual user or to many users.

In Windows 2000, the My Documents folder is an alternative to the home directory, but does not necessarily replace it. When a user tries to save or open a file, most programs determine whether to use the home directory or My Documents in one of two ways. Some look in the home directory for files that match the type of file being opened or saved. If a file with that extension is found, the program opens the home directory and ignores My Documents. If a file of that type is not found, the program opens My Documents. In other programs, the home directory is ignored, whether or not the home directory contains any files.

There are two advantages to home directories:

- Users can access their home directory from any computer on the network without having to share folders from each PC.
- Backup and document administration is centralized, improving reliability and reducing administrative costs.

Creating Home Directories

To specify a home directory:

1. Create a shared folder on a server in your domain. The home directories will be subfolders underneath this shared folder.

2. To secure the folder, remove the Everyone group from the Access Control List (ACL), and add either the Users group or another group that contains the users who will need access to the folder.

3. Open the Active Directory Users and Computers snap-in.

4. Right-click the user you want to configure, and select Properties.

5. Under Home Directory, select Connect To.

6. Select a Drive Letter and specify the UNC for the home directory.

TIP

If you use the %username% variable, Windows 2000 will create the home directory on the server and assign the user Full Control permissions. Windows will also remove all other users, including the Administrator, from the ACL.

When you configure home directories, remember:

- Windows 2000 includes a desktop folder called My Documents, which is an alternative to the home directory but does not replace it. To determine the location of a user's My Documents folder, log on as the user, right-click My Documents on the desktop, click Properties, and look at the location specified on the Target tab.

- A user can change the target folder location of his or her My Documents folder by right-clicking the desktop icon, clicking Properties, and then specifying a new location on the Target tab.

- You can use Group Policy Editor to change the target folder location of any user's My Documents folder, disable a user's ability to change the target folder location, remove the My Documents icon from the desktop, and choose whether programs use My Documents or a different folder as a default location.

- If no home directory is assigned, the system assigns the default local home directory to the user's account.

- To specify a network path for the home directory, you must first create the network share and set permissions that allow the user access.

Advanced Techniques

In this section, we will explore new ways to do old tasks (for example, adding a number of users simultaneously), and suggest some practices that will help reduce the amount of time spent preparing for a migration from Windows NT 4.0 to Windows 2000.

Creating Multiple User Accounts

Adding a single user is a fairly straightforward task; however, if you have many users to add, perhaps thousands, it would be extremely painful to create them one at a time. Fortunately, you don't have to. There are several methods to choose from when creating an Active Directory-based user set, whether you're migrating from Windows NT 4.0, Novell NDS, or even using an Excel spreadsheet populated with usernames.

Migrating Users from a Windows NT 4.0 Domain

When a Windows NT 4.0 domain controller or member server is upgraded to Windows 2000, any user or group accounts that were in the local SAM are automatically imported into a special Users OU beneath the root of the new domain in Active Directory. Likewise, all computer accounts are added to the Computers OU, and the built-in groups like Administrators and Account Operators are added to the Builtin OU.

If you already have a reliable method for adding Windows NT 4.0 users in bulk, such as a batch script employing the net user username /add command, this will add the user to the Users OU by default. From there, they can easily be moved into a more appropriate location within Active Directory; just select all the users you want to move and select the Move command from the Action menu.

ClonePrincipal

ClonePrincipal, included with the Windows 2000 Support Tools, is targeted at easing the migration process by supporting the incremental migration of users and groups from Windows NT 4 to Windows 2000.

The utility clones users from the Windows NT 4.0 domain, and although the SID of the cloned Windows 2000 user or group must change, the SIDHistory attribute is populated with the SID of the original account or group. This allows the cloned user to access the same resources as the original Windows NT 4.0 account (as long as the correct trusts are in place). For more information on ClonePrincipal, consult the Windows 2000 Support Tools help.

Active Directory Migration Tool

The Active Directory Migration Tool (ADMT) is a very useful snap-in that provides a number of wizards to migrate users, groups, computers, trusts, and security.

ADMT can be used to migrate user accounts and groups from a source domain to a target domain. The advantage of ADMT is that users retain access to resources. It also provides a trial-run facility that tests the process without actually migrating the accounts. ADMT can be downloaded from the Microsoft Web site.

Creating New Active Directory Users in Bulk

The Active Directory Users and Computers snap-in does not allow you to add more than one user at a time. Does this mean that you will be up all night typing in usernames? Fortunately, no. An all-night vigil can be avoided by creating an Excel spreadsheet populated with usernames. A script can then be used to read the names in from Excel and write them to the Active Directory OU of your choice. The script and a sample Excel file can be downloaded from http://msdn.microsoft.com/scripting.

The script relies on Active Directory Services Interface (ADSI). With it, you can create or modify any object in the directory, including user objects.

For IT Professionals

Group and User Guidelines

Delegate authority.   Once you have subdivided your domain into groups, define an Administrator for each major branch of the tree, and give that Administrator full ownership of all objects beneath his or her OU. You can delegate ownership easily by right-clicking an OU and selecting "Delegate control" from the menu. A wizard ensues that walks you through the delegation process, prompting you to identify the delegates and adjust what rights they should have over the OU and its contents.

Define template users.   Since so many user settings cannot be altered in bulk after the user objects have been created, think carefully about what properties you want all your users to share, and assign them to a template user. Name the template user with an underscore character, such as "_Template User," so that the template user always appears at the top of an alphabetical list. When you are not using the template user to create new accounts, keep the account disabled.

Minimize the number of Group Policy Objects.   Since processing time and network traffic per user increase with each effective GPO, try to keep the number of GPOs within your tree to a minimum. Define one Master GPO for the domain to house settings that you want to affect all users, and add additional GPOs only when you need to fine-tune settings for a particular group or override settings in the Master GPO.

ADSI can be employed from within C, C++, VBScript, PERL, and several other programming languages.

To use the script, all you need to do is populate the Excel template provided with the usernames you wish to add and the Active Directory OU where you would like to add them. Then run the script with the name of the Excel file as an argument:

```
Addusers.vbs addusers.xls
```

Importing Users from Novell Directory Services (NDS)

Windows 2000 includes two very powerful command-line utilities that can import and export information to and from any LDAP-compliant directory, including NDS. The commands are LDIFDE.EXE for importing and exporting data from other directory services, and CSVDE.EXE for importing data from comma-separated text files into Active Directory. For more information on these commands, search the online help in Windows 2000, or type the command followed by -?.

Also included in Windows 2000 is a graphical tool for migrating Novell NDS user accounts, groups, files, and their permissions directly into Active Directory. This tool, called the Directory Service Migration Tool, preserves the hierarchy of users and group memberships, but does not import NDS passwords.

Summary

The user object is one of the fundamental building blocks of a domain and the Active Directory. Administrators use user objects to control access to resources and track activity in a domain. When building a domain with shared resources, the first step is developing and implementing a user management policy. Without such a policy and process, it is impossible to create a secure server environment that supports the sharing of data and ideas.

An effective user management policy includes naming conventions, password control restrictions, and account settings. Administrators should be prepared to develop a user management policy, and have the skills needed to implement and manage it.

The next step in managing user accounts is to group users on the basis of common access requirements. Managing individual access to resources can become a burden with thousands of users. By grouping them, Administrators can make broad changes in access permissions with a single set of steps.

There are various types of groups with a variety of possible scopes. Each type of group plays an important part in an overall group structure. Windows 2000 offers a lot of flexibility in defining groups that Administrators should consider carefully before dismissing any one feature. Careful planning will significantly reduce your administrative overhead and will improve overall network security.

User profiles allow Administrators to standardize the configuration of each user's account and include desktop settings, network connections, shortcuts, and the Start menu in an effort to increase user productivity and reduce administrative overhead. Roaming profiles ensure that users always have the same configuration, no matter what machine they use to log on.

Home directories offer Administrators an option to replace the My Documents folder with a centralized network resource containing a home directory for every user. Applications can be configured to default all Open and Save dialogs to this directory. The centralization helps Administrators manage backups, and makes the information available from any machine on the network.

FAQs

Q: Can there be more than one password/account policy for a domain?

A: No, each domain has one default domain and group policy. There can only be one account/password policy for the entire domain as part of the default domain policy. If you want to set different account/password policies for different users, you will need to create additional domains.

Q: When I try to create a group, I cannot select a scope of Universal with a group type of Security. What is the problem?

A: Universal groups can be used as Security groups only if you convert your Windows 2000 environment to native mode.

Q: If I want to give an associate permission to create and manage user accounts, should I just place her in the Administrators group?

A: No. Windows 2000 offers several ways to delegate authority to administrative tasks. If you want to grant the user the right to create or modify any account in the Active Directory, you should make that user a member of the built-in Domain Local group, Account Operators. If you want the user to administer accounts for a small section of your users only, you can create an organizational unit (OU) and delegate the authority to that unit.

Q: What's the difference between a Domain Local group and a Universal group?

A: Security scope. Both kinds of groups can contain Users and Global groups from any other domain in your forest, but Domain Local groups can only be added to the Access Control List (ACL) of objects within their own domain. Universal groups can be added to the ACL of any object in the forest.

Q: Can a user with a roaming or mandatory profile log on multiple machines simultaneously?

A: Yes. The one problem for users with roaming profiles concerns making changes to the profile while they are logged on. Every time you log off, the changes are copied back to the server. If a user logs on to two machines (A and B), makes changes to the profile on A, logs off A, and then shortly thereafter logs off B, the changes will be lost.

Managing File and Print Resources

Solutions in this chapter:

- Introduction
- Windows 2000 Data Storage
- Administering NTFS Resources
- Administering Shared Resources
- Administering Printers
- Summary

Introduction

Not so long ago, information storage was dominated by the printed and written word. With alarming speed, the winds of change blew through the established methods of storage on the back of the information revolution. Suddenly, whole encyclopedias could be stored electronically on devices not much larger than the human hand. Demand grew for the safe and secure storage of huge quantities of data, and for the swift retrieval of that same data.

Operating systems and their file and print subsystems soon became overwhelmed as the information revolution spawned the information glut. Huge corporate databases and a rising level of computer literacy forced operating system vendors to develop truly scalable and reliable file and print services.

While Windows NT incorporated the first generation of reliable file and print services, Windows 2000 steps beyond those boundaries by providing a rich set of services and features that help manage all aspects of data storage, retrieval, and printing.

Windows 2000 Data Storage

With the overhaul of the Windows platform, Microsoft has not been remiss in improving on the structure and functionality of file services within Windows 2000. In fact, Windows 2000 ushers in a plethora of new functionality and features.

Windows NT 4 provided a well-structured and functional file system dubbed NTFS. At the time, NTFS boasted many improvements over its other file system counterparts, such as the File Allocation Table (FAT) and High Performance File System (HPFS). Its ability to support large disks, store large files, and recover gracefully from failure proved to be an immediate hit. To provide added value and support for the new file system, Microsoft developed a disk subsystem that supported advanced features such as Redundant Array of Inexpensive Disks (RAID).

Windows 2000 extends and surpasses the features delivered by the Windows NT disk subsystem and its associated file system, NTFS v4. By supporting new disk types, a greater breadth of file systems, and a number of eagerly anticipated storage and print features, Windows 2000 provides a true platform for mission-critical file and print serving.

Understanding Disk Types

Before we can begin to plunge into the depths of Windows 2000 file systems, we need to understand how the disks themselves are organized. Microsoft Windows 2000 supports two disk types:

- Basic disks
- Dynamic disks

Windows 2000 can provide a great deal of flexibility by supporting both basic and dynamic disks on the same physical computer.

Basic Disks

In an effort to maintain compatibility with existing disk types, Windows 2000 supports basic disks. Analogous to disk types used with Windows NT, basic disks also support a similar, but not identical, advanced feature set. The upshot of using basic disks is that they can be relocated to other non-Windows 2000 computers (providing they are using a supported file system) and can be mounted with a minimum of hassle. Similarly, disks created within a Windows NT 4 environment can also be mounted within a Windows 2000 computer. Compatibility is maintained by the reuse of the Windows NT 4 disk manager (ftdisk) for the management of basic disks.

For IT Professionals

Anatomy of a Hard Disk

The inside of a hard disk consists of metal or glass revolving discs called platters, typically organized on a common spindle. Each platter consists of concentric circles called tracks divided into sections called sectors—the smallest possible storage unit on a disk. A hard disk can contain a number of platters, with a head located on either side of the platter to read and write information to the disk.

When a Windows 2000 computer boots up, two sectors of the hard drive are processed, the Master Boot Record (MBR) and the boot sector. The MBR, which contains executable code, is located at sector 1, cylinder 0, head 0 on the first hard drive. The boot sector, which also contains executable code, is located at sector 1 of each volume.

When the data in the MBR is activated, it performs the following tasks:

1. It examines the partition table (which details the location of partitions) for the active partition.

2. After finding the active partition, it locates the start sector of that partition.

3. The executable code contained in the boot sector is then loaded into memory and executed.

The default Windows 2000 disk type is basic, though a basic disk can be upgraded to a dynamic disk at a later stage. Each basic disk consists of basic volumes that can include primary partitions, extended partitions, and logical drives. A basic disk can consist of a maximum of four primary partitions, or three primary and one extended partition.

WARNING

Basic disks do not support the management of spanned, striped, mirrored, or other RAID sets. RAID volumes created by Windows NT 4 can be migrated directly to Windows 2000 without change, but they must be upgraded to dynamic disks before they can be managed.

Dynamic Disks

Dynamic disks are a new feature of Windows 2000 and consist of a potentially unlimited number of dynamic volumes. Unlike basic disks, dynamic disks support the creation of multidisk volumes. Simple, spanned, and RAID 5 are examples of the dynamic volumes that can be created on dynamic disks. A simple or spanned volume, which is not the boot or system volume, on a dynamic disk(s) can be extended seamlessly without having to reboot or take the volume offline (users can be accessing the volume simultaneously).

Maintaining the thread of online disk management, stripes and mirrors can be created, broken, or recovered while still in use.

The changes ushered in by dynamic disks require a configuration change to the disk format in the form of a database located at the end of the physical disk containing configuration information, and the allocation of a unique signature to each disk. This change in configuration (compared to basic disks) means that dynamic disks cannot be locally mounted on Windows 9x or Windows NT computers. Note that this limitation does not apply to remote mounts such as when a Windows 9x or Windows NT computer attaches to a share located on a Windows 2000 dynamic volume. The network redirector acts as an abstraction layer, effectively hiding the physical characteristics of the disk when connecting to a network share.

The unique signature of dynamic disks means that disks can be moved to different controllers and Windows 2000 will still understand how it functions within its defined volume set.

If a basic disk is upgraded to a dynamic disk, then all partitions are converted to dynamic volumes. The upgrade process is not always a win-win situation; after being upgraded, dynamic disks cannot be extended.

NOTE

Two utilities, DiskProbe and DiskMap, are provided with the Windows 2000 Support Tools that can potentially help diagnose and resolve disk problems. These tools may not function correctly with dynamic disks. If a problem occurs that may be attributed to the MBR or the boot sector, attempt to use the fixmbr or fixboot commands in the Recovery Console. Fixmbr attempts to repair the master boot code of the boot partition, while fixboot will attempt to write a new boot sector to the system partition.

Configuring Disks

A disk can be upgraded from basic to dynamic using the Computer Management MMC snap-in. Navigate to Start | Programs | Administrative Tools, and launch Computer Management. Open the Storage node in the tree view, and select Disk Management. A tri-pane view displays the tree window, a list of the volumes, and a graphical representation of the disks and their associated volumes. Notice in the last window that each disk has a number and a type associated with it—basic or dynamic (Figure 10.1).

Figure 10.1 Disk management from the Computer Management snap-in.

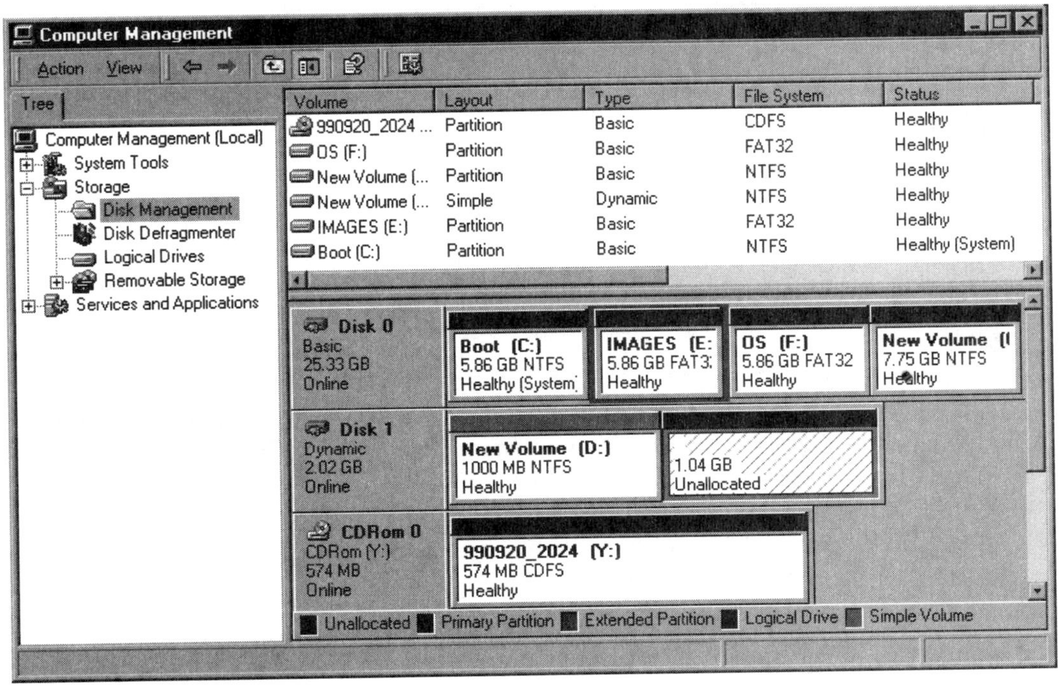

If a new disk has been added to the configuration, select the Action menu and click Rescan Disks. If the disk has been moved from another Windows 2000 computer, the disk will be marked as foreign. Right-click on the foreign disk and click Import Foreign Disk.

To upgrade a basic disk to dynamic, right-click on the disk summary in the leftmost portion of the lower window. An action menu is then displayed, offering the option to Upgrade to Dynamic Disk. Select this option and confirm the disks that you wish to upgrade in the next window. Select Upgrade in the Disks to Upgrade window.

Before proceeding with the upgrade, ensure that the disk has at least 1MB of unpartitioned space at the end of the disk to store configuration information. Another limitation of the upgrade procedure is that a disk with a sector size greater than 512 bytes cannot be upgraded.

The Disk Management snap-in provides details on the status of disks. The status information provided could be:

- **Online**   The disk is available for normal use.
- **Online (errors)**   Errors have been encountered on a dynamic disk.
- **Offline**   The dynamic disk cannot be accessed for normal use. To bring a disk back online, correct the problem related to the disk and use the Reactivate Disk command.
- **Foreign**   A dynamic disk from another Windows 2000 computer has been installed. Use the Import Foreign Disk to add the disk to the local Windows 2000 computer.
- **Unreadable**   The disk is unavailable for normal use. Take corrective action as necessary.
- **Unrecognized**   Disk type is unknown.
- **No Media**   No media is in the removable drive.

For very detailed diagnostics on disk storage, try running the dmdiag.exe command from the Resource Kit.

WARNING

Upgrading a basic disk to a dynamic disk is a one-way operation if the disk is populated with partitions. If after being upgraded, a dynamic disk needs to be reverted to a basic disk, then all information has to be copied off the drive, and all the dynamic volumes deleted. The Revert to Basic Disk command is then used to change the disk format to basic. Data can then be recopied back to the basic disk.

Manipulating Partitions and Volumes

To create a partition on a basic disk, right-click a region of space not yet allocated to a partition, and select Create Partition. The Create Partition Wizard, which is very straightforward, then walks you through the rest of the process. The partition will then be ready to be formatted with a file system of choice. To delete a partition, right-click the partition and select Delete Partition.

To create a simple volume on a dynamic disk, right-click on the unallocated space and select Create Volume. The Create Volume Wizard then walks you through the rest of the process. To delete a volume, right-click the volume and select Delete Volume.

The creation of RAID 5, spanned, striped, and mirrored volumes all follow a similar process using the Create Volume Wizard.

There are a couple of points to keep in mind when manipulating volumes. Simple volumes can be extended within the same disk, or onto other dynamic disks. Extending a volume onto another dynamic disk is called spanning. A volume can be extended if it is NTFS, if it is unformatted, and if it is not the system or boot volume. After a spanned volume has been created, none of the volumes can be reclaimed without deleting the entire spanned volume.

Windows 2000 supports spanning on up to 32 disks. While RAID 5 supports up to 32 disks, a minimum of three dynamic disks is required.

Understanding Windows 2000 File Systems

Microsoft has been particularly generous in its support of file systems in Windows 2000. Supported file systems include:

CDFS   Compact Disk File System is, just as its name suggests, a file system for use with CD-ROMs.

UDF   More generic than CDFS, the Universal Disk Format can be used as a file system for both CD-ROMs and DVDs.

FAT16   Rooted in the early days of MS-DOS, FAT16 is considered the lowest common file system denominator. Even though it is shackled by a number of limitations, FAT16 is still used in surprising quantities. Windows 2000 FAT16 volumes cannot exceed 4GB.

FAT32   Introduced with Windows 95 OSR2, FAT32 supports larger files and larger disks than FAT16. The Windows 2000 implementation of FAT32 can create volumes up to 32GB, though existing volumes larger than this can be supported.

NTFS   A new version of NTFS ships with Windows 2000 that supports a raft of powerful new features, such as reparse points and encryption. Windows 2000 supports all existing versions of NTFS.

FAT and NTFS as implemented in Windows 2000 support both long file-names (up to 255 characters) and short filenames that comply with the 8.3 naming convention.

CDFS

CDFS is an ISO 9660 compliant file system that supports long filenames. It also has a number of restrictions; for example, all file and folder names are restricted to 32 characters or less, and folders cannot go deeper than eight levels from the root directory.

UDF

UDF, the successor to CDFS, is compliant with the ISO 13346 standard and supports long filenames and sparse files. UDF is targeted at supporting a number of different media types, including DVD and CD-R. Considered the successor to CDFS, UDF is currently limited by being a read-only file system.

FAT

The grandfather of file systems, FAT has ridden the storm of change that has redefined the storage landscape. Is it limited? Oh, very. Is it slow? In certain configurations, certainly. But, is it universally accepted? Without a doubt.

Designed a computing eternity ago, FAT should be consigned to supporting small, uncomplicated data structures. The inherent speed and size limitations make FAT an unsuitable choice for the enterprise, unless compatibility with other operating systems in other physical computers is a requirement. As a troubleshooting mechanism, Administrators frequently installed Windows NT into a FAT partition rather than an NTFS partition. The driving rationale behind this is the ability of DOS to read FAT file systems and fit snugly onto a single bootable disk. Consequently, the FAT-based Windows NT installation can be accessed via floppy if the hard disk is rendered unbootable. This type of configuration is no longer necessary with Windows 2000, since the Recovery Console provides many of the same advantages of installing into a FAT partition, with none of the security drawbacks.

Windows 2000 supports the two FAT siblings: FAT16, and its bigger brother FAT32. Both implementations support long filenames. Remember that although Windows 2000 can be installed into a FAT partition, it is not recommended.

NOTE

Microsoft does not intend to extend the functionality of CDFS or FAT in the future. This implies that these file systems will be supported and maintained, but not enriched (unlike NTFS).

FAT16

Still used in surprising quantity, FAT16 still lives, even if it has lost its teeth. The size of FAT volumes is determined by the cluster size, which can range from 512 bytes to 64KB. A volume with 64KB clusters can be as large as 4GB (the maximum FAT16 volume size). Unfortunately, large cluster sizes lead to inefficient use of storage space for multiple small files. For example on a 4GB volume with 64KB clusters, one thousand 4KB files would consume 64,000KB.

FAT32 has other inherent limitations, such as the inability of the root folder to grow beyond 512 entries. Additionally, though the Windows 2000 implementation of FAT16 supports disks up to 4GB, other Microsoft operating systems such as MS-DOS and Windows 9x cannot support FAT16 volumes greater than 2GB. Of more concern is the fact there is no inherent security built into FAT16. Securing FAT16 files can only be accomplished when sharing them over the network by defining access permissions to the share itself.

A FAT volume consists of a boot sector, a File Allocation Table, a copy of the File Allocation Table, the root folder, and the files and folders.

FAT32

The Windows 2000 implementation of FAT32, the logical successor to FAT16, can be used to create volumes up to 32GB with cluster sizes ranging from 512 bytes to 16KB. FAT32 follows along similar, but not identical, structural guidelines as FAT32 in Windows 9x. FAT32 compares favorably to FAT16, in that it was designed to be more robust and efficient. These benefits were achieved by reducing cluster size, including the ability to relocate the root directory, and implementing the automatic ability to use the second backup copy of the FAT.

Initially aimed at the home market (Windows 95 OSR2 and beyond), Windows 2000 is the first Microsoft business operating system to support FAT32 natively. Due to its origins in the home market, FAT32, like FAT16, does not provide any native security.

NTFS

NTFS made its debut in Microsoft's business operating system, Windows NT, and has long been considered the enterprise file system of choice. A great deal of work was expended in an effort to allow NTFS to address many of the critical issues that surround modern enterprise storage.

Only exceptional reasons (such as computers requiring a dual boot configuration) should warrant the use of FAT in place of NTFS, and several Windows 2000 features, such as the Encrypted File System (EFS) and Active Directory, are only available on NTFS. Additionally, NTFS overcomes the shortcomings of FAT by managing disk space more efficiently, providing native security, and supporting even larger disk and file sizes.

Windows 2000 can support NTFS volumes up to a very commendable 2 terabytes. Cluster sizes can also be specified during volume creation, providing increased control over the configuration of NTFS volumes. Be aware that while the FAT siblings do not support compression, NTFS can provide compression for volumes with cluster sizes of 4KB and smaller.

The structure of an NTFS volume is described by metadata files. The Master File Table (MFT) is one such instance of NTFS metadata. Some of the metadata stored in the MFT includes a list of all files and folders on a volume, volume information, and log details.

NTFS version 5, which is bundled with Windows 2000, supports a number of important features:

- Reparse points.
- Change journal.
- Sparse file support.
- Distributed link tracking.
- Disk quotas.
- Improved chkdsk performance.
- Native property sets.

NTFS is a transaction-based file system that commits changes to log and checkpoint files. This means that manual repairs are seldom conducted on NTFS volumes, since the file system will first attempt to recover from the transaction logs.

Security is a key component of NTFS, allowing the definition of finely grained permissions. Security is further strengthened by its support for file encryption.

Many of the new features of NTFS are not accessible to Windows NT, but any Windows NT machine with Service Pack 4 or later will be able to locally access all the conventional features of an NTFS v5 volume. Remember that this restriction is only in place for volumes that are mounted on local machines; volumes mounted over the network use the network redirector to abstract the operating system from the file system structure.

WARNING

Windows 2000 automatically upgrades NTFS volumes to NTFS v5 when NTFS volumes prior to version 5 are mounted locally. The upgrade happens swiftly and does not have a significant impact on the time taken to mount a disk.

Reparse Points

Additional functionality can be incorporated into NTFS by using specialized NTFS objects called reparse points. These objects are installable file system filter drivers that can provide a wide variety of extra functionality, such as encryption and remote storage. Because reparse points are handled by the I/O subsystem, they are transparent to programs.

Microsoft has bundled a number of reparse points with Windows 2000, though software vendors can add to these by providing their own. Examples of Microsoft-provided reparse points include:

Directory junctions   Using the directory junction reparse point, a folder can be mapped to any local target directory. For example, the folder d:\data could be grafted onto the e:\accountsdata directory. Every time a user changes to the e:\accountsdata directory, he or she would in effect be traversing the d:\data directory, though the link would be transparent and nonvisible.

Volume mount points   This reparse point allows an empty directory to be resolved to a specified volume that can be any Windows 2000 supported file system. This provides the ability to cater for data growth without disrupting the directory namespace. For example, to add more space to the directory tree e:\accountsdata, an empty directory called e:\accountsdata\debtors could be created. The root of a new volume could then be mounted to that directory, providing additional disk space. To provide even further flexibility, this volume could be FAT, CDFS, UDF, or NTFS. It could even be a mirrored volume, providing the ability to mix and match storage classes in a single directory structure!

Remote storage   When a remote storage reparse point is encountered, it allows data to be retrieved from lower-cost secondary storage such as tapes.

Encrypted File System (EFS)   This reparse point allows users to securely store data using a combination of symmetric and asymmetric encryption. See Chapter 15, "Windows 2000 Security Services," for more details on EFS.

Change Journal

The change journal records all changes to the file system for a particular volume. This persistent file logs information on file deletions, additions, or modifications. It provides a central point of information for applications that need to process modifications made to the file system. Obvious examples of programs that could take advantage of the change journal would be virus protection programs and the File Replication Service. For example, an indexing program would scan a volume once to create a database of all files on the volume, and then reconcile the index according to the changes

For IT Professionals

Directory Junctions and Volume Mount Points

The method for configuring directory junctions and volume mount points is sometimes not obvious. Some utilities may be required before certain reparse points can be taken advantage of.

To create a volume mount point:

1. Open the Disk Management snap-in and right-click the volume that is to be grafted to the empty directory. Select Change Drive Letter and Path.

2. Click ADD, and choose the empty NTFS target folder, or click BROWSE, and create one appropriately.

3. Click OK twice.

Alternatively, the same effect can be achieved using the mountvol command.

To create a directory junction, a tool called linkd found in the Resource Kit is required:

1. Open a command prompt.

2. Type **linkd source destination**.

3. Source is now linked to destination via a directory junction!

Delrp.exe, found in the Resource Kit, can be used to delete all types of reparse points. Remember, never attempt to delete a junction point using Explorer, file utilities, or the del command—the directory needs unlinking first.

recorded in the change journal. In fact, the Indexing Service that is shipped with Windows 2000 uses a similar process.

Sparse File Support

Typically, databases require a significant investment in disk space, though it is not unusual for them to contain large tracks of meaningless data. Sparse files allow NTFS to allocate space only for data that is considered to be meaningful (that is, nonzero data). NTFS shields applications from knowing that the meaningless data has not been stored by submitting data as if the file were stored normally. No data is lost, it is just stored on disk more effectively.

Distributed Link Tracking

The movement of data within the corporate storage space often breaks shortcuts to files. Distributed link file tracking resolves this problem by stamping files with a particular identifier (GUID) and then storing tracking information for that file. This means that the target of a shortcut or OLE link cannot be "lost" due to files being renamed, moved within domains, or the share name or computer name it resides on being changed. Distributed Link File Tracking is implemented as a service.

Disk Quotas

The ability to track user disk space usage on a volume basis within Windows 2000 has been implemented using disk quotas. This allows Administrators to effectively manage storage assets, prevent the indiscriminate use of disk space by users, and provide a means for disk space tracking and billing.

The disk quota facility is implemented on a per-user, per-volume basis. A file is attributed to a user if he or she owns it. A user can only take ownership of a file—ownership cannot be assigned. Disk quotas are implemented in a WYSIWYG fashion—what you see is what you get. A user will only see the amount of free space left in his or her quota, even if the volume has much more free disk space.

When users exceed their assigned quota, they can be prevented from using additional disk space, and/or a warning event can be logged when a specific threshold has been exceeded. The quota limit is calculated based on uncompressed file sizes.

Though disk quotas are a much-appreciated addition to Windows 2000 NTFS, they still do not meet all requirements. Disk usage can only be computed on a per-volume basis, not on a per-folder, per-share, per-computer, or per-domain basis.

chkdsk Performance

Since NTFS is a journaling file system, the use of manual recovery features should not be a frequent occurrence. However, on those rare occasions when they are required, you typically need them to work quickly.

The performance and scalability of chkdsk has been overhauled, improving on what some refer to as the Mean Time To Recover (MTTR). Quoted performance clocks Windows 2000 chkdsk at 10 times faster than that of Windows NT 4 chkdsk.

Native Property Sets

Native property sets allow users and Administrators to attach descriptive data to a file or folder on an NTFS volume. This metadata could include

For IT Professionals

Implementing Disk Quotas

Two basic actions can be taken if a disk quota for a particular user is reached: The user can be prevented from using further disk space, or a warning event can be logged to the system log. The user can then delete files, have someone else take ownership of his files, or request a larger quota.

Default quotas can be allocated for a volume, with additional entries being required if specific users require larger or smaller quotas. To configure quotas:

1. Select the volume in Explorer that requires quotas. Right-click the volume and select properties. Select the Quota tab.

2. Click "Enable quota management."

3. Select whether to deny disk space if users exceed their quota limit.

4. Select the default quota limit for new users of the volume.

5. Select the appropriate quota logging options.

6. Click "Quota entries" if specific quota entries are required. If not, go to step 9.

7. Select Quota | New Quota Entry. Select the required user and whether to limit disk space or not. Click Oᴋ.

8. Close the Quota Entries window.

9. Click Oᴋ.

title, keywords, and comments, and is accessed by examining the properties of an NTFS object. This data can also be used by the indexing service discussed later in the chapter.

Native property sets can be accessed by right-clicking the file and selecting Properties. The Summary tab provides the native property set details.

Configuring File Systems

Most tasks can be completed through the MMC storage snap-in that is part of the Computer Management snap-in, or through the stand-alone Disk Management snap-in.

Earlier we discussed that Windows 2000 automatically upgrades NTFS volumes to NTFS v5 when they are mounted locally. This operation is transparent to the Administrator, unlike the creating, deleting, or extending volumes.

You should notice that each volume or partition has an associated status description. The descriptions include:

- **Healthy**   Volume is available for normal use.
- **Healthy (At Risk)**   Volume is available for normal use, though errors have been detected. Take corrective action.
- **Initializing**   The volume is initializing. The status should eventually change to Healthy.
- **Resynching**   Volume mirrors are resynchronizing.
- **Regenerating**   Volume is available for normal use, but RAID 5 disks are generating data from the parity information.
- **Failed Redundancy**   The volume is no longer fault tolerant, usually caused by an offline disk.
- **Failed Redundancy (At Risk)**   The volume is no longer fault tolerant, and errors have been observed. Take corrective action.
- **Failed**   The volume cannot be accessed. Take corrective action.

Formatting Volumes or Partitions

To format a volume or partition, right-click the volume and select Format. Choose the Volume Label, file system type, and sector size. Click Oĸ to proceed with the format. If a volume targeted for formatting is in use, a Disk Management dialog box is displayed, providing you with the option to abort the operation or force the format regardless.

Configuration Options for Windows 2000 Storage

Even by the standards of information technology, the rise in storage requirements has been nothing short of astonishing. The volume of data handled by the average business grows rapidly with each passing day.

Though the requirements for storage have grown quickly, the technology has struggled to keep pace. Other areas of development in memory and CPUs have yielded fantastic technological returns; unfortunately, though hard disks have gotten cheaper, there has not been a similar exponential return from storage technologies. By far, the most significant cost in data storage is not purchasing storage capacity, but managing the data once it is captured.

Recognizing that the storage and management of data would become increasingly important to the Network Administrator, Microsoft incorporated a number of features into Windows 2000 aimed at alleviating storage woes:

- Disk quotas
- Logical disk manager
- Removable storage
- Remote storage
- Distributed File System
- File Replication Service
- Indexing service
- Backup utility
- Defragmentation utility

As mentioned earlier, disk quotas provide the ability to track disk space usage on a per-user, per-volume basis. Removable storage hands off the responsibility of supporting removable storage media to the operating system, rather than to the application itself. On the other hand, remote storage provides a native facility to seamlessly store infrequently used data on cheaper, but slower, secondary storage such as tape.

Though the variety of new features is an undoubted boon to Administrators, they are a heart sore for authors! It is impossible to cover all the features in detail in one chapter; consequently, some have been given only brief coverage.

Logical Disk Manager

The Logical Disk Manager (LDM) is implemented as a driver, and acts as the disk manager for Windows 2000. The file system interfaces with LDM, which then interacts directly with the physical disks themselves.

LDM is not a homegrown Microsoft product, but was originally developed by Veritas. Earlier in the chapter, we discussed the ability to extend volumes without having to take the volume offline or reboot the Windows 2000 computer—this functionality is provided by the LDM. Additionally, the LDM allows an Administrator to create, break, and recover NTFS stripe and mirror sets without taking the volume offline. Volumes can also be forcibly dismounted, regardless of the number of open files. All this adds up to fantastic online disk management for Windows 2000!

The LDM can be accessed by launching the MMC and adding the Disk Management snap-in to the console (see Figure 10.1 earlier). Alternatively, it can be accessed by launching the Computer Management snap-in, expanding the Storage node, and selecting Disk Management.

Removable Storage Manager

Historically, backup programs used to manage the lion's share of the setup and configuration of the backup media and devices had to directly (and exclusively) access the device driver to manipulate storage media and devices. By centralizing this facility within Windows 2000, multiple applications can share and manage the same (potentially expensive) removable devices. Removable storage is implemented as a service, and can support robotic media and other changing devices such as jukeboxes.

Remote Storage Manager (RSM) exposes APIs that allow developers to accomplish a number of logical functions such as mounting and dismounting media, ejecting media, and managing storage pools. When media is mounted and ready to be accessed, RSM is removed from the loop, thereby allowing the program to access the media directly.

RSM can be accessed from the Computer Management snap-in. It is located in the storage tree under removable storage. This snap-in allows removable storage objects to be viewed, or removable storage objects to be modified, inserted, ejected, or dismounted.

Remote Storage Server

A couple of trends have hastened the development of remote storage within Windows 2000, namely:

- Least recently used files are seldom accessed again in their lifetime.
- Least recently used files take up the largest portion of disk space.
- Secondary storage is cheaper than primary storage.

The remote storage server determines, according to a set of defined policies, which files are considered to be least recently or least frequently used. These files are then moved seamlessly and transparently to secondary (slower and cheaper) storage as required. This type of storage strategy is often called Hierarchical Storage Management (HSM).

Effectively, HSM allows Administrators to migrate less frequently used files to cheaper storage while maintaining an unchanged namespace for users. The process is policy driven, allowing the Administrator to specify rules for file migration to secondary storage.

Administrators and users can visually determine if files reside on secondary storage by examining the files' icon.

Distributed File System

Due to the proliferation of servers and data stores, the corporate file namespace has become disjointed over time. Naming schemes implemented by Administrators do not necessarily provide a meaningful guide to the location of data on the network. An answer to these problems is the Distributed File System (DFS).

DFS implements a logical namespace, abstracting the physical namespace from the user. The aim of the logical namespace is to provide a simple, consistent, navigable data structure. DFS not only provides the ability to logically name shares, but to map multiple machines to the same logical name—a useful resilience feature, since if one machine is down, another machine is seamlessly used.

DFS consists of a client and server component. The server component runs on Windows 2000 Server, while the client can be Windows 9x, Windows NT, or Windows 2000.

Interestingly, the namespace used by DFS can include non-Windows entities such as NFS volumes on a UNIX server. The client and server use Common Internet File System (CIFS) for communicating details of what the logical DFS namespace resolves to in the physical world. However, when the client attempts to connect to a server, it uses the underlying protocol (if it is installed locally). For example, the NCP protocol would be used to connect to NetWare, NFS to UNIX, and CIFS to Windows.

DFS comes in two flavors: stand-alone DFS and domain DFS. Standalone DFS is only suitable for limited installations such as small businesses or workgroups. The metadata for DFS is then stored in the local Registry of the DFS server.

Domain DFS stores the metadata for the DFS topology in the Active Directory itself, benefiting from its multi-master replication topology. The root of the domain DFS namespace is accessed by using the domain name, while the root of a stand-alone DFS is accessed by using the DFS server name.

A single domain DFS link can point to multiple physical shares. If the data on the shares is synchronized (using the File Replication Service), then the user will be pointed to the share in the closest site. If this share then fails, the user would be routed to the alternate share replica.

DFS is very flexible and can be used to satisfy a variety of requirements. Common uses include user home directories and software distribution points. DFS can be managed from the MMC DFS snap-in.

File Replication Service

Ensuring that data is accurately replicated around the network has always been a difficult task, usually involving third-party products. Windows 2000 ships with the File Replication Service (FRS) targeted at providing a scalable and integrated replication service. This service replaces the Windows NT 4 LMRepl service.

FRS determines what files have changed on a particular share, and propagates the changes to a downstream partner. The FRS is an advanced feature of Windows 2000 and requires that shares be located on a Windows 2000 Server in an Active Directory network. Both the source and destination shares have to be NTFS.

The FRS replicates files from a node along an arc to the destination computer. An arc can be considered the direction in which data changes travel. The configuration of FRS follows a multi-master topology, allowing any server in an FRS set to accept changes. FRS then propagates any changes made to the master server, to the slave servers. The replication process can be scheduled by the Administrator to take advantage in lulls in server or bandwidth utilization.

A possible point of concern is the lack of a distributed locking service. A file is not locked for write access for any single user; therefore, conflicting changes could be made to the same file across multiple servers. The policy implemented in this scenario is "last writer wins"—the most recent changes are those that take effect.

DFS uses FRS to improve performance and availability. Additionally, the Sysvol directory (containing scripts and policies) on domain controllers is replicated using FRS. This provides an insight into the scalability and reliability of FRS.

Indexing Service

The Indexing Service is as important to enterprise file systems as search engines are to the Internet. Both the Internet and corporate file systems store a bewildering amount of data. The importance of the data is often negated if it cannot be found in a timely fashion.

The indexing service can be considered a search engine for Windows 2000 storage. It is a full text search that indexes files across volumes and machines so they may be searched effectively. Files can then be retrieved based on search criteria that do not necessarily have to be based on the filename, such as the information stored in the native property sets.

The indexing service can index FAT, FAT32, and NTFS volumes, but is optimized for use on NTFS because of its use of the change journal.

Backup Utility

The backup utility, originally licensed from Seagate, is a stable and functional product that is aimed at providing entry-level backup services. While it can easily meet the demands of smaller businesses, or sites, it is not the product that a corporate backup cycle should be based upon.

This said, the backup utility has undergone a number of enhancements. Wizards have been strategically placed to make it easier to use. The utility can be scheduled to back up FAT, FAT32, or NTFS volumes. It even supports the use of changers via RSM, though this does contradict the small office focus of the product somewhat.

The backup utility can dump the backup job to a single file that can be located on any media, such as a hard disk or a CD-R.

Refer to Chapter 6, "Advanced Active Directory," for a brief description of the backup process.

Defragmentation Utility

A defragmentation utility, hosted in the ever-present MMC, is distributed with Windows 2000. This GUI-based utility was developed by Executive

For IT Professionals

Disk Tuning

If the change journal is not optimally configured, it will impact disk performance. If the change journal becomes full, Windows 2000 has to flush the log—a very disk-intensive operation. To increase the size of the log, and decrease the chances of having to flush the log file, use chkdsk /L:xxxxx, where xxxxx is the new, increased size of the log file in KB.

Do not format volumes with cluster sizes greater than 4KB if you wish to be able to use the defragmentation utility on them (or compression).

Software and licensed for Windows 2000. It can be opened by launching the Computer Management or the Disk Defragmenter snap-in.

It does not take a rocket scientist to defragment a drive, requiring you only to select the relevant drive and click DEFRAGMENT.

The utility can only defragment one local volume (NTFS, FAT, or FAT32) at a time. This procedure is manual, requiring user intervention, though an inventive Administrator could write a VBScript to get around this.

The defragmentation utility decides how it should defragment the disk and where the files should be located, but it is the actual file system that shuffles the files around the disk itself. The golden defragmentation rule is "defragment early and defrag often!"

Administering NTFS Resources

The previous section discussed the underlying fundamentals of how storage and disk functionality is implemented within Windows 2000. This section discusses how files and folders are secured and manipulated on the file system itself, particularly on NTFS partitions and volumes.

NTFS permissions are used to assign access rights to files and folders. These access rights define who can access the files and folders, and what operations they can perform on them. When a permission is not explicitly allowed, then it is implicitly denied.

How NTFS Permissions Are Applied

Only an Administrator, the owner, a user with Change Permission permission, or a user with Full Control permissions can change the NTFS file and folder permissions. Before trying to adjust the permissions on a folder, ensure that you have the right access privileges.

Access Control Lists

Windows NTFS uses an Access Control List (ACL) to define who can access a file or folder, and the type of access they have. An ACL is composed of multiple Access Control Entries (ACEs). An ACE consists of a SID that identifies the user or group for whom access is allowed or denied.

As we discovered in Chapter 9, "Managing Users and Groups," when a user logs on, Windows 2000 generates an access token that contains, among other things, an individual SID and security group SIDs. When a user wishes to access a file on an NTFS partition or volume, the security subsystem compares the SIDs in the user's access token to the file or folders ACL. If an ACE matches any of the SIDs in the access token, the user is granted the permissions defined in the ACE. If the requested action matches those allowed by the assigned permission, the action will be completed.

ACEs are organized such that deny ACEs are listed before allow ACEs.

Combining NTFS Permissions

A user may have multiple ACEs that define that user's access permissions. For example, a user may have been assigned specific permissions, and one or more of the user's groups may also have been provided access permissions. In order to understand the behavior of NTFS file permissions, you need to understand the rules governing the combination of permissions and the inheritance rules of NTFS. A common cause of access problems is a lack of understanding on the Administrator's part of file permission rules. Some important points to remember include:

Permissions are cumulative   When determining a user's access to a specific resource, Windows 2000 calculates the user's effective permissions. The effective permissions are the sum of all access permissions defined in the ACL. If multiple entries match the access the user has been granted—for example, Read for the user's specific account ID, and Write for a group of which the user is a member—then the effective permissions are Read and Write.

File permissions override folder permissions   When determining access to a resource, Windows 2000 will let file permissions override folder permissions. A user may not have any access permissions to a folder, but may have full control access to a file contained in that folder.

Deny overrides all other permissions   The Deny permission completely overrides any other access permissions a user may have. This contradicts the cumulative rule, but provides a powerful means to ensure that a file/folder is properly secured.

Permission Inheritance

By default, permissions are inherited from the parent folder. This makes it easier to administer a shared folder environment by ensuring that any new files and folders created in the folder have the same ACLs as the parent. Users need not worry about adjusting the permissions on new folders and files, though it is possible to disable this behavior in Windows 2000.

NTFS Folder Permissions

NTFS folder permissions are used to assign access controls to a folder. Table 10.1 is a summary of folder permissions and the access control they provide. A user or group can have one or more folder permissions.

Table 10.1 NTFS Folder Permissions

Folder Permission	Allows
Read	Users can see the files and subfolders in the directory. They can also view the ownership, attributes, and permissions.
Write	Users can create new files and subfolders, change the folder's attributes, and view ownership and permissions.
List Folder Contents	Users can see the names of files and subfolders in the folder.
Read & Execute	Users can browse through the folder, opening folders to which they may not have explicit access. They also have Read and List Folder Contents on the files and subfolders.
Modify	Users can delete the folder in addition to the actions provided by the Write and Read & Execute permissions.
Full Control	User can perform the actions of all other permissions, and can take ownership, change permissions, and delete files and subfolders.

NTFS File Permissions

NTFS file permissions are applied to the files contained in the folders. NTFS file permissions may be more restrictive or more lenient than the permissions on the folder that contains the file, and thus may alter the user's effective access permissions. Table 10.2 is a summary of access permissions and the restrictions they enforce.

Table 10.2 NTFS File Permissions

File Permission	Allows
Read	Users can view the ownership, permissions, attributes, and contents of a file.
Write	Users can change the file's attributes or overwrite the file completely, and can view the file's ownership and permissions.
Read & Execute	Users can perform the actions provided by Read, and can execute the file if it is an application.
Modify	Users can perform the actions provided by the Write and Read & Execute permissions, and can modify or delete the file.
Full Control	Users can perform the actions provided by all other permissions, and can change permissions and take ownership.

Managing NTFS Permissions

When an NTFS file system is created, the default permission is for the Everyone group to have Full Control. Take the time to change the permission sets and inheritance on critical folders. To change the NTFS permissions of a file or folder:

1. Right-click the object and select Properties.
2. Click the Security tab (Figure 10.2).
3. From here, you can see the access permissions of each user or group by clicking on its name. Adjust the permissions as required.

To add a user to the ACL:

1. From the Security tab, click ADD.
2. Select the user or group by double-clicking on its name. You can add multiple groups simultaneously.
3. Click OK to close the Add window.
4. Select the group in the Security tab and set the desired permissions.

Figure 10.2 The Security tab of the Folder Properties window.

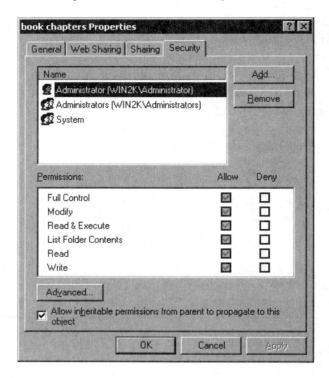

To prevent the inheritance of permissions from the parent folder:

1. Right-click the file or folder and select Properties.

2. Click the Security tab.

3. Uncheck the "Allow inheritable permissions from parent to propagate to this object."

4. You will be prompted to choose from copying the previously inherited permissions, removing the inherited permissions, or aborting the operation (Figure 10.3).

5. Select the one of the options:

   ■ **Copy** will copy over the inherited permissions from the parent folder.

   ■ **Remove** will remove all inherited permissions, retaining only those permissions you have explicitly selected.

   ■ **Abort** cancels the operation.

6. Click OK to close the Properties window.

Figure 10.3 Removing permission inheritance.

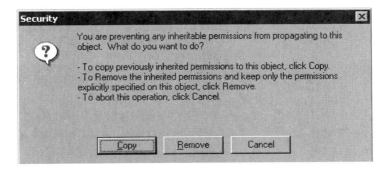

Special Access Permissions

Windows 2000 provides 12 special access permissions that give you additional capabilities beyond the normal access permissions of the ACL. Two useful special access permissions are Take Ownership and Change:

Take Ownership   The owner controls how permissions are set on an object. When an object is created, the creator automatically becomes its owner. Using the Take Ownership special access permission is one way to transfer ownership of a file or folder from one user to another. A user can be granted the right to take ownership. Administrators always have the right to take ownership of a file or folder. Note that the current owner of the file or folder, or any user with Full Control permissions on the file, can either assign Full Control or Take Ownership permissions to another user or group, allowing them to take ownership of the file or folder. Also, Administrators can always take ownership of a file or folder, regardless of the permissions on the file.

Change Permissions   The Change Permissions special access permission lets you give other users the ability to change permissions on a file without giving them full control. This gives the users some flexibility in defining the permissions on the files without completely opening access to the object.

Table 10.3 is a complete list of special access permissions, along with a short description. Special access permissions provide Administrators with flexibility in controlling access to resources on the network, and should be a part of every Administrator's tools.

Using Special Access Permissions

The special access permissions allow you to define access to folders and files in more detail, along with granting permission to Take Ownership or

Table 10.3 Special Access Permissions and Their Functions

Special Access Permission	Description
Traverse Folder/Execute File	Browse folder contents or open an application (Execute).
List Folder/Read Data	See the contents of a folder or file (List Folder Contents/Read).
Read Attributes	View the attributes of a file or folder.
Read Extended Attributes	View the extended attributes of a file or folder.
Create Files/Write Data	Create a new file (Write).
Create Folders/Append Data	Create a subfolder or append data to a file (Write).
Write Attributes	Modify the attributes of a file or folder.
Write Extended Attributes	Modify the extended attributes of the file.
Delete	Delete a file or folder from a directory. (Overridden by the Delete Subfolders and Files permission on the parent folder.)
Delete Subfolders and Files	Delete files and folders from a directory.
Read Permissions	View permissions of a file or folder.
Change Permissions	Modify the permissions of a file or folder.
Take Ownership	Take ownership of a file or folder.

Change Permissions. Windows 2000 combines multiple special access permissions to form the regular permissions set.

Setting the Special Access Permissions

The special access permissions are accessed much as are regular permissions. They can be thought of as advanced security settings. To set the special access permissions:

1. Right-click the folder or file for which you want to change the permissions, and select Properties.
2. Click the Security tab.
3. Click ADVANCED to open the Access Settings dialog box (Figure 10.4).
4. Ensure that the Permissions tab is selected.
5. Select the user for whom you want to change the permissions, and click VIEW/EDIT.

Figure 10.4 Advanced Security Setting window.

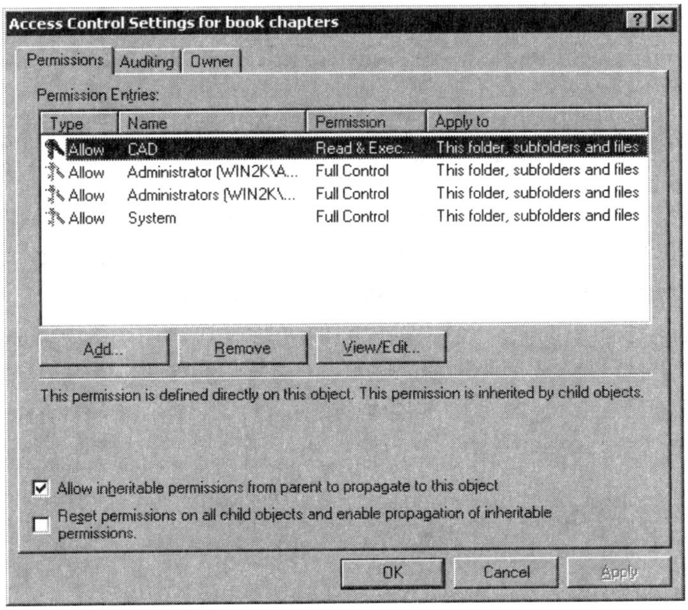

6. Adjust the permissions, and click OK.

7. Click OK to close the Advanced Settings window.

8. Click OK to close the Properties window.

Taking Ownership of Files and Folders

Once you have granted special access permission to take ownership, the user can follow a similar series of steps to take ownership of the file or folder. To take ownership of a file or folder, follow these steps:

1. Right-click the folder or file for which you want to change permissions, and select Properties.

2. Click the Security tab.

3. Click ADVANCED.

4. Select the Owner tab.

5. In the Change Owner To: field, select the user you want to designate as the new owner.

6. Check the "Replace owner on subcontainer and objects" to change the owner on all subfolders and files.

7. Click OK to close the Access Control Settings window.

Changing NTFS Permissions

When changing the permissions on an object, the new permissions apply when the object is subsequently accessed. If a user has the object open at the time when the permissions are changed, the user is allowed access according to the permissions that were in effect when the object was opened.

Explicit permissions on an object can be directly changed by user action, but inherited permissions cannot be changed directly. Thus, to change permissions on a file whose permissions are inherited, you can do either of the following:

- Change the permissions on the parent object, and specify that the changed permissions should be propagated.

- Add permissions to an object that has inherited permissions, giving the object a combination of both explicit and inherited permissions. For example, if a file inherits Read and Write permissions from its parent, and then you add Delete permission to the file, the file now has the cumulative permissions of (Read and Write) and (Delete).

Copying and Moving Files and Folders

When files are copied or moved, the permissions on the file may change. Understanding the rules that govern when the permissions will change is critical to managing access to your data. Administrators and users often set the access permissions of a file or folder, and then move or copy the object without realizing that the permissions may have changed.

Copying Files

Table 10.4 illustrates the effect of the copy operation on a file or folder. Copying files will always affect the permissions on the file, because Windows treats the copied file as a new file. In order to copy files between NTFS partitions or between folders on the same partition, you must have Write permissions to the destination. You will also become the creator-owner of all copied objects.

Table 10.4 Effects on Permissions of Copying a File or Folder

Action	Effect on Permissions
Copy a file or folder to another location on the same NTFS partition.	The file or folder will inherit the permissions of the folder to which it is being copied.
Copy a file or folder to a location on a different NTFS partition.	The file or folder will inherit the permissions of the folder to which it is being copied.
Copy a file or folder to a FAT partition.	All permissions are lost.

Moving Files

Table 10.5 shows what happens to file and folder permissions during a move. When files or folders are moved, the permissions do not always change. The specific exception is when you move a file or folder from one location on an NTFS partition to another location on the same partition.

The reason for this difference in the behavior of permissions is subtle but critical. When a file is moved within the same partition, Windows 2000 simply updates the file pointers and structures to reference the file's new location. When a file is moved to a different partition, Windows 2000 actually copies the file from the old partition to the new one, and then deletes the original file. The file on the new partition is essentially a new file, and new files always inherit the permissions from the parent folder.

When a folder is moved within an NTFS partition:

- The folder or file will retain all NTFS permissions currently defined.
- You must have Write permissions to the destination folder.
- You must have Modify permissions on the original folder, because Windows 2000 will delete the source folder once it has written the data to the new location.
- You will become the creator-owner of the file or folder.

When a file or folder is moved between NTFS partitions, these rules apply, but the files or folders inherit the permissions of the destination folder.

WARNING

When a file or folder is moved or copied to a FAT partition, all NTFS permissions are lost.

Table 10.5 Effects on Permissions of Moving a File or Folder

Action	Effect on Permissions
Move a file or folder to another location on the same NTFS partition.	The permissions will remain the same.
Move a file or folder to a location on a different NTFS partition.	The file or folder will inherit the permissions of the folder to which it is being copied.
Move a file or folder to a FAT partition.	All permissions are lost.

Administering Shared Resources

Sharing folders over the network makes the contents of the folders accessible to other users on the network. Shared folders also provide another level of security to control access to the files and folders on a computer. Shared folder access permissions apply to NTFS, FAT, and FAT32 partitions.

Securing Network Resources

Windows Explorer uses a folder with a hand underneath to represent a shared folder. To control access to shared folders, you assign the shared object access permissions. Table 10.6 lists the permissions you can assign to a shared folder.

Table 10.6 Shared Folder Permissions

Share Permissions	Actions Allowed
Read	See folder names, filename, data, and attributes; run applications.
Change	Perform all the actions of the Read permissions; create files and folders, change files, append to files, delete files and folders, and change file attributes.
Full Control	Perform all the actions allowed by Change permissions; change permission and take ownership.

While shared folders do offer an extra layer of security, there are issues to keep in mind when developing a strategy for sharing data over the network. These include:

- Shared folder permissions apply only to folders. Files cannot be shared individually. Shared folder permissions generally allow less detailed control over access than do the native Windows NTFS permissions.
- Shared folder permissions do not apply to users who have gained physical access to the machine and logged on locally.
- The Default permissions on a shared folder are Full Control for the Everyone group.

You can allow or deny any of the shared folder permissions to both users and groups. Best practice is to assign allow permissions to groups and generally avoid deny permissions, except when you specifically need to lock out a user who is a member of a group with access permissions. If you deny users access, it will override any access permissions granted to groups of which they are members.

Shared Folder Permissions

As with NTFS permissions, there are a series of rules and guidelines to follow in applying shared folder permissions. Many of the guidelines are the same, but there are a few new ones with shared folders. When applying shared folder permissions, keep in mind:

- **Shared permissions are cumulative.** If a user is a member of multiple groups, each with unique access permissions, the user's effective permissions will be the combination of all the group access permissions.
- **Deny overrides all other permissions.** As with NTFS permissions, Deny overrides any other permissions assigned to the user or any group of which the user is a member.
- **On NTFS volumes, the user must have access via the NTFS permissions in addition to the shared folder permissions.** On a FAT volume, shared folder permissions are the only security control that determines the user's access to the data in the folder. On an NTFS partition, the user must have the appropriate permissions in order to access the files and folders in the shared folder. The NTFS permissions and the shared permission will both be evaluated individually, and then the most restricted of these two results will be the effectively permissions.
- **When a shared folder is copied or moved, it is no longer shared.** This is true no matter where it is copied or moved.

Creating Shared Folders

It is easy to just jump right in to Windows 2000 and begin creating shares; however, as with most administrative tasks, planning a strategy can significantly reduce the amount of overhead involved in managing shares across your network.

Administrative Shares

Depending on the configuration of the computer, some or all of the special shares may appear when Windows 2000 presents a list of shared resources. Special shares are created by the system and should not be deleted or modified.

Windows 2000 creates several administrative shares by default. These shares are used for remote administration and are normally hidden from the nonadministrative users. All administrative shares end with a $. Table 10.7 provides a list of administrative shares and their use.

Table 10.7 Administrative Shares and Their Use

Share Name	Purpose
<drive_letter>$	A share that allows Administrators to connect to the root directory of a storage device. For example, D$ is a share name by which drive D might be accessed by an Administrator over the network.
ADMIN$	A resource used by the system during remote administration of a computer. The path of this resource is always the path to the Windows 2000 system root; for example, C:\Winnt.
IPC$	A resource sharing the named pipes used for communication between programs. It is used during remote administration of a computer and when viewing a computer's shared resources.
REPL$	This resource is created by the system when a Windows 2000 Server computer is configured as a replication export server. This resource is used only by Windows 2000 Servers that are configured as replication export servers.
NETLOGON	Used by the Net Logon service of a Windows 2000 Server computer while processing domain logon requests. This resource is used only by Windows 2000 Server.
PRINT$	This share is created the first time a printer is installed, and points to the systemroot\System32\Spool\Drivers folder. The Administrator, server operators, and print operators have Full Control permissions. The Everyone group has Read privileges. This share is used to distribute printer drivers to users when they install a printer from the server.
SYSVOL	This share is used to replicate file-based data among domain controllers in an Active Directory domain. This resource is used only by Windows 2000 Server.

NOTE

Additional hidden shares can be created by appending a $ to the end of the share name. Users can access the folder only if they know the share name and possess the relevant access permissions.

Creating a Shared Folder

To create a shared folder:

1. Right-click the folder you want to share and select Sharing.

2. Click Share this folder.

3. Configure the sharing options (Table 10.8).

4. Click OK to close the Property window.

TIP

The same folder can be shared a number of times with different names and access privileges.

Table 10.8 Options for a Shared Folder

Option	Purpose
Share Name	The name users will use to access the shared folder.
Comment	An optional description of the contents of the folder. User will see the comments when browsing the server with the View options set to Details mode.
User Limit	You can limit the number of users accessing the shared folder concurrently. Under Windows 2000 Professional, the limit is set to 10 concurrent users. With Windows 2000 Server, you can support an unlimited number of users, within the limits of the number of Client Access Licenses you own.
Permissions	Allows you to define the permissions on a shared folder. By default, the Everyone group has Full Control permissions
Caching	Settings used for offline access to the shared folder.

Assigning Permissions to a Shared Folder

Once a shared folder has been created, access permissions to the folder need to be assigned. By default, the Everyone group has Full Control. When working with shared folders on NTFS partitions, NTFS permissions must also be considered.

When folders are shared on FAT partitions, the shared folder permissions are the only permissions in effect. When folders are shared on an NTFS partition, both the NTFS and sharing permissions can be used to control access to the folders. When combining shared folder and NTFS permissions, the more restrictive permissions are always the effective permissions for the user.

NTFS permissions offer Administrators greater flexibility when defining access control to both files and folders. Share permissions offer fewer options and apply only at the folder level.

One common strategy for managing the combination of shared and NTFS permissions is to allow Authenticated Users Full Control shared permission. NTFS permissions are then used to control access to subfolders and files. The other advantage of this strategy is that NTFS permissions apply both locally and over the network. This ensures that users who gain access to the machine and log on locally have no greater access to data files than if they had connected over the network.

To assign permissions to a shared folder:

1. Open the Sharing tab of the Properties window by right-clicking on the shared folder and selecting Sharing.

2. Click PERMISSIONS.

3. Click ADD to open the Select Users, Computers, or Groups window.

4. Double-click the users and groups you want to add to the share permissions of the folder.

5. Click ADD.

6. Select each user you added, and click the share setting you want to either allow or deny them.

7. Click OK to close the Properties window.

Managing Shared Folders

Shared folders are managed completely from the Share tab of the Folder Properties window. From this window, you can start or stop sharing on a folder, limit the number of users, share the folder under another name, or modify its permissions.

To view a list of shares, sessions, or open files on a computer:

1. Open Computer Management from the Start\Programs\Administrative menu (Figure 10.5).

2. In the console tree, click Shares, Sessions, or Open Files.

NOTE

Files opened by other users are displayed, but files opened by you are not.

Figure 10.5 Viewing shares, sessions, and open files.

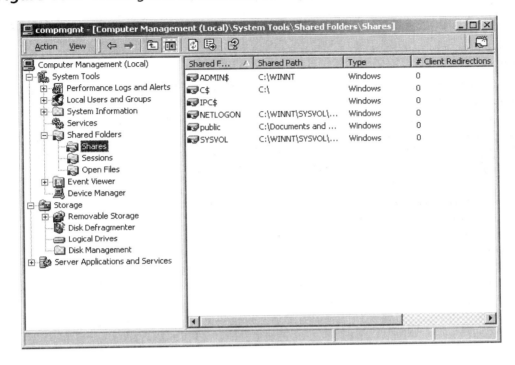

Administering Printers

There are a number of new features that enhance the printing experience in Windows 2000. Improvements include remote printer administration, Internet printing, print queue monitoring, and Active Directory integration.

The first step in discussing Windows 2000 printing issues is to clarify a few terms that are often confused:

Print device is the hardware that actually does the printing. It is connected to the print server by direct cable connection or across the network.

Print server is a computer that manages printing on the network. A print server can be a dedicated computer hosting multiple printers, or it can run as one of many processes on a nondedicated computer.

Print driver is a software program used by other computer programs to connect with printers and plotters. It translates information sent to it into commands that the print device can understand.

Printer is the software interface between the document and the print device. This is the term used for the object that is created on the server and client workstation and that provides access to the configuration and print queue.

Planning the Print Environment

A successful network printing environment is one that has been carefully planned out. While a thorough discussion of a complete printing environment plan is beyond the scope of this chapter, a few suggestions are included in this section.

Local, Remote, and Network Printers

Unfortunately, this terminology can be a bit confusing. From a workstation perspective, a printer object can be created as either a local or a remote printer. A local printer is directly connected to the workstation, while a network printer is located on a print server. The same can be done on a print server. Its printer objects can be set as local, where the print server directly controls access to the print device, or remote, where the server points to a printer on another print server.

The confusion comes in when a local printer is set up on a server. A local printer can be a local print device that is attached directly to the printer by parallel or serial cable, or it can be a network print device that is connected directly to the network. The distinction is that a local printer object on the server has direct control over the print device, whether it is connected directly to the print server or across a network link. A remote printer object on a server points to a print object on another print server.

Creating the Print Environment

Once the printing environment has been planned out, it needs to be created on the print server or servers. This process involves setting up the print queues and configurations for each print device to be set up.

Installing a Local Printer

Follow these steps to set up a printer that will be directly connected to the print server:

1. Open the Printers folder and double-click the Add Printer icon.
2. Select Local printer, and click Next.
3. Select the correct printer port, and click Next.
4. Select the printer manufacturer and the specific printer type from the menus. If an alternate driver is required, click Have Disk.
5. Specify the name for the printer. This is the name that will appear locally on the print server. If this is not the first printer installed, an option to specify this printer as the default will appear in the dialog box.
6. Specify the share name of the printer. This is the name that will be advertised on the network for the printer.

7. Fill in the location and comment fields as necessary. These can be left blank, but specifying location and other information can help identify the print device for usage or troubleshooting.

8. Review the summary information at the end of the Add Printer Wizard. If the information is correct, click FINISH to close the wizard.

Installing a Network Printer

Follow these steps to install a local printer that is not directly attached to the print server, but is not configured on another print server:

1. Open the Printers folder and double-click the Add Printer icon.

2. Click the "Create a new port:" radio button and select the appropriate port type from the Type: drop-down list. Depending on the configuration of the server, you may find options for AppleTalk Printing Devices, Local Port, LPR Port, and Standard TCP/IP Port, among others. This example will use the Standard TCP/IP Port selection (Figure 10.6).

3. Specify the IP address of the print device. The Port Name will automatically be entered as IP_, followed by the IP address entered in the Printer Name or IP Address field.

4. Select the print device manufacturer and type.

Figure 10.6 Select the port type.

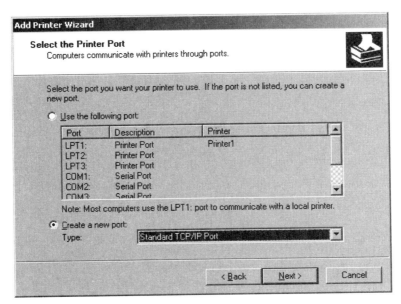

5. Specify the name of the printer and indicate whether it should be the default printer.

6. Specify the share name of the printer.

7. Fill in the Location and Comment fields as desired.

8. Review the printer information, and click FINISH if the information is correct.

Installing a Printer from Another Server

A Windows 2000 print server can also be configured to interface with a printer interface already set up on another print server. In Microsoft terminology, this is known as remote printing. The printer interface is set up on the local server, which manages print jobs as any other printer does, but print job information is sent to the remote print server instead of to a print device. Follow these steps to set up a remote printer:

1. Open the Printers folder and double-click on the Add Printer icon.

2. Click the "Remote printer" radio button.

3. Choose the method to use to locate the printer. If the printer is set up on a Windows 2000 server in the Active Directory, click the "Find a printer in the Directory" button. Otherwise, you can specify the path to the printer using the printer's UNC path or URL if it is on a Web-enabled print server.

4. Locate and load any print drivers, if necessary.

5. Review the printer information in the final wizard screen, and click FINISH if the information is correct.

Loading Printer Drivers

Creating a printer on the print server automatically installs printer drivers on the server. While Windows 2000 and Windows NT workstations will rely on the print server for the correct printer driver, Windows 95 and Windows 98 workstations must have printer drivers installed locally. When the Windows 95 or Windows 98 client installs a printer from the print server, it attempts to download the appropriate printer driver from the server. Thus, it is necessary to load the printer driver for these platforms on the print server so that the drivers are available for download.

Follow these steps to verify that the additional printer drivers are installed and to install them, if necessary:

1. Open the Printer Properties dialog box of an installed printer by right-clicking on the printer and selecting Properties from the pop-up menu, or select Properties from the File menu with the printer highlighted.

2. Click on the Sharing tab and then on Additional Drivers.

3. Scroll through the list of drivers to see whether the driver for the desired platform has been installed. If it has not, click on the check box next to each platform, and click Oκ.

4. Follow the steps for locating the printer drivers to install them.

Managing Printer Permissions

Once the printer interfaces are set up and working on the print server, the focus of printer administration changes to management and maintenance. Management of the printer objects on the server involves many different aspects of administration, from securing printer access through security permissions to managing documents in the printer queues at the client's request.

Security/Sharing Permissions

Three basic security permissions apply to Windows 2000 printing:

- **Print** allows an account to connect to a printer, print a document, and control that document in the printer queue.
- **Manage Documents** includes Print permissions, as well as the ability to control all documents in a queue and modify the job settings for those documents.
- **Manage Printers** includes the permissions for Print and Manage Documents, as well as the ability to modify printer properties and permissions, modify a printer's sharing setup, delete all documents in a print queue, and delete the printer from the server.

By default, the Everyone group is assigned the Print permission on all printers created on the server. The Creator Owner group is assigned the Manage Documents permission. The Administrators, Print Operators, and Server Operators groups are given all three permissions on each printer on the server.

Additional permissions can be set on a printer to limit access to the printer and its associated print device. For example, a Purchasing department in a company may have a print device set up that uses a special form to generate purchase orders. Having a stray print job print on the print device would waste both time and forms, so access to the printer is limited to the Purchasing department only. To do this, the Administrator would add the Purchasing group to the printer, and give that group the Print permission. In addition, the Everyone group would be removed from the security list so that accounts not belonging to the Purchasing group would not have access to the printer.

As another example, the Purchasing department has determined that its internal billing group has been sending invoices to the purchase order printer by accident, and has asked the Administrator to block that group from the printer. To achieve this, the Administrator will add the Billing group to the security list, but will check the Deny box for the Print permission. This will prevent any member of the Purchasing group that is also a member of the Billing group from submitting any jobs to the printer. This example also illustrates why the Everyone group was not denied access to the printer in the first example. The Deny permission always overrides the Allow permission, so if the Everyone group had been set to Deny, no one on the server would have been able to print to the printer.

Printer Ownership

The account that creates the printer on the server becomes the owner of the printer. Ownership of the printer gives all printing permissions to the associated account. Usually, this is an Administrator account, but accounts that have been given permissions to create printers on a server will be given full control over the printer or printers created by the account.

If the owner of a printer is no longer able to perform that role, resulting from a job role change or an individual's leaving the company, ownership of the printer can be reassigned to another account. Ownership of a printer can be changed in the Access Control Settings dialog box, which is found by clicking ADVANCED on the Security tab of the printer properties. The ownership information is in the Owner tab and indicates which account is the current owner of the printer, as well as which accounts can become the owner of the printer.

Managing Printers

Information about more advanced printer management topics can be used to help fully customize the printing environment and perform advanced maintenance tasks.

Creating a Printer Pool

Occasionally, network printing will increase to such a level that a single print device is unable to keep up with the printing demands. The solution is, of course, to add another print device, but printing clients may become confused if they are instructed to use a new printer on the server for their print jobs. Through printer pooling, Administrators can add print devices to the network and lessen the demands on existing printers without adding more confusion.

In order for printer pooling to work, all print devices in the pool must be of the same type, as they will be driven by the same printer driver. A printer port must be set up for each print device on the server, and then the printer must be configured to print to multiple ports. This configuration is done in the Ports tab of the Printer Properties dialog.

When a printer is set up for a single print device, the Ports tab can only have one port checked at a time. To specify additional ports for the printer, the "Enable printer pooling" check box must be checked, and then multiple ports can be checked in the window. If a print server has two LaserJet 5Si printers connected to LPT1: and LPT2:, checking both these ports in the Ports tab will share that printer between the two print devices. When a print job comes into the queue, it begins spooling to the first available print device. This decreases the time a print job must wait before spooling to the print device. Network clients will be much happier when their one- or two-page memo doesn't have to wait for a 600-page presentation to finish on a print device before going through.

Specifying Printer Priorities

The printing environment can also be configured in the reverse way, in which two printers are set up to print to a single print device. One reason for setting this up is to create a fast track for critical documents to be printed quickly, even if other jobs had been printed earlier. This can be accomplished by setting up two printers for a print device and giving them different print priorities. One printer might be called Printer1 and assigned a priority of 1, and another called Printer1 Critical and assigned a priority of 99. Network clients would use Printer1 by default, with their print jobs being serviced on a first-come, first-served basis. If someone had a critical job to print out, he or she would then use the Printer1 Critical printer, and that job would be the next one printed out, since that printer has a higher priority than the Printer1 printer. Printer priority is set in the Advanced tab. The desired value is set in the Priority selector, with 99 being the highest priority, and 1 being the lowest.

Redirecting a Printer

Sometimes, printer maintenance cannot take place after business hours. There are times when the print device dies during the day, and it must be diagnosed or repaired right away. To keep printing chaos to a minimum, the printer can be redirected to another print device, and the clients can be told to pick up their printouts from the alternate print device without having to change their printing configuration. This only works, however, when the alternate printer is the same kind as the one that has been made unavailable.

Redirecting a printer is as simple as selecting a different printer port in the printer configuration, provided that an identical print device or one that can emulate the same print device exists on that port. This is done in the Ports tab of the Printer Properties. No configurations have to be changed on the client workstation after the change is made on the server—the server simply begins routing the print jobs to the new port.

Removing Printer Drivers

In a highly dynamic printing environment where printers are added, removed, and changed on a regular basis, the print server can end up with a large number of unused printer drivers installed. In addition, the Administrator might find a problem in a printer driver and would like to install a newer driver. In either case, removing the printer drivers is a good practice.

Information about installed printer drivers is located in the Server Properties window, not in the Printer Properties dialog. To access Server Properties, select Server Properties item from the File menu in the Printers folder. Click on the Drivers tab to manage the printer drivers. From this window, drivers can be added, removed, updated, and modified manually, ensuring that the Administrator has full control over how the drivers are installed.

Managing Documents in a Print Queue

The server Administrator or printer owner will periodically have to perform basic maintenance over the printer queue and the documents in it. This does not happen very often, and usually only at a client's request. Clients might ask that a job be canceled on the printer because they printed to the wrong printer, or perhaps there was something wrong with the job or the print device. These are the document management actions:

- **Pause** puts a print job on hold, either to allow another job to print or to fix a problem with the print device.
- **Resume** continues processing of a print job that had been put on hold.
- **Restart** halts current processing of a print job, and starts over from the beginning of the document.
- **Cancel** deletes the print job from the queue entirely.

Sometimes a print job will hang in the queue, and will continue to show in the queue even after being canceled. If other print jobs can continue to print around the stuck job, this is only a cosmetic problem. However, if other jobs are being blocked from printing as a result, then action must be taken. In both cases, the stuck job will be removed by stopping and restarting the spool services on the server. To do this, open a command prompt, and type:

net stop spooler

followed by

net start spooler

to restart the print spooler. This will remove the stuck job, but may also jumble the order of other jobs that are in the queues on the server. Only members of the Administrator group will be able to recycle the spooler service.

Setting Priority, Notification, and Printing Time

In addition to setting a priority on a printer object, individual print jobs within a queue can be prioritized. Each print job has its own properties, including priority, notification, and print time settings. The properties of a print job can be viewed by selecting the Properties item under the Document menu in the print queue window. The owner of the document, the owner of the print queue, and any server or printer Administrator can modify the properties of a document.

By default, the name of the account that created the print job is specified in the Notify box as the account to receive notification when the print job has completed. If an account other than the creator of the jobs needs to be notified when the job is complete, enter the name of the account. To change the priority of the print job relative to the other jobs in the queue, move the Priority slider to the desired priority level—1 being the lowest, and 99 being the highest. Or, to specify a specific time for a job to print, make the necessary changes in the Schedule fields in the Document Properties window.

Administering Printers by Using a Web Browser

Not all administration of a printer must be done on the print server or an authorized workstation, or on a PC for that matter. Windows 2000 allows the server Administrator to enable Web administration of the printers on the server. Internet Information Services (IIS) must be installed and running on the print server to make Web-based administration possible. An authorized individual can access the printer properties from a computer with a Web browser that can connect to the printer server computer. The URL to use to access the printer information is http://servername/Printers, where servername is the domain name or IP address of the print server. The Web server will authenticate the client by asking for a username and password combination, and when access is authorized, the client will see the printer configuration as illustrated in Figure 10.7.

In the main window, the client sees all the printers that are configured on the print server, the status of each printer, the number of jobs in the printer's queue, and the location, model, and comment configured for the printer. The page will update and show any changes in status and number of jobs. Each printer name is a hyperlink that will load a page showing all the current documents in the printer queue.

In this page, the client sees all the jobs that are waiting to be printed in the queue, including the status, the owner, the number of pages in the printout, the file size, and the time the job was submitted. The client can then click a specific document in the list and manage the document with the actions in the left of the screen. The client can also perform actions on the printer itself from this screen, including pausing the printer, resuming the printer, and canceling all jobs in the printer. Authorization prompts may be given if the initially authorized connection does not have permissions to perform the selected actions. The client can also select to view the properties of the current printer by clicking the Properties link on the left of the page.

In this page, the browser displays configuration information about the printer, but only in display mode. The actual configuration of the printer cannot be changed through the Web interface. However, by giving configuration information about the printer, a client would be able to more easily

Figure 10.7 This is the Web browser interface for printers on Server1.

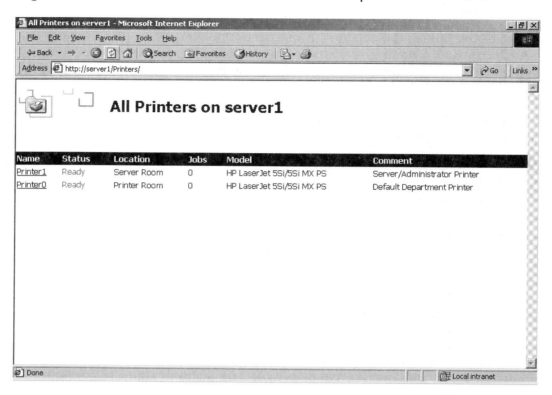

locate a specific printer that would suit his or her printing needs without having to contact the print server Administrator or other designated contact. In addition, the Web interface is easier to navigate than the printer folder interface.

Summary

Windows 2000 supports two types of disks: basic and dynamic. Basic disks are very similar in structure to disks formatted under Windows NT 4. Dynamic disks provide additional functionality, but are not compatible when installed on local machines with other operating systems. A basic disk can easily be upgraded to a dynamic disk.

RAID, mirroring, and striping are all supported by dynamic disks. Additionally, dynamic disks can be extended while still in use. A basic disk consists of partitions, while a dynamic disk consists of volumes.

Windows 2000 supports a wide variety of file systems, including FAT16, FAT32, NTFS, CDFS, and UDF. NTFS version 5, which is bundled with Windows 2000, supports a number of important features:

- Reparse points
- Change journal
- Sparse file support
- Distributed link tracking
- Disk quotas
- Improved chkdsk performance
- Native property sets

Microsoft incorporated a number of features into Windows 2000 aimed at alleviating storage woes:

- Disk quotas
- Logical disk manager
- Removable storage
- Remote storage
- Distributed File System
- File Replication Service
- Indexing service
- Backup utility
- Defragmentation utility

With a thorough understanding of both NTFS and shared permissions, you will be ready to start building a network server environment that is secure and encourages the collaboration of users.

Windows NTFS uses an Access Control List (ACL) to define who can access a file or folder, and the type of access they have. An ACL is composed of multiple Access Control Entries (ACEs). An ACE consists of a SID that identifies the user or group for whom access is allowed or denied. If an ACE matches any of the SIDs in the user's access token, then the user is granted the permissions defined in the ACE. If the requested action matches those allowed by the assigned permission, then the action will be completed.

Some important points to remember when implementing NTFS permissions are that permissions are cumulative, file permissions override folder permissions, and deny overrides all other permissions.

When creating shares, note that permissions are cumulative, that deny overrides all other permissions, and that when a shared folder is moved or copied, it is no longer shared.

There a number of new features that enhance the printing experience in Windows 2000. Improvements include remote printer administration, Internet printing, print queue monitoring, and Active Directory integration. Windows 2000 printing terms can be confusing, but can be defined as follows:

- **Print device** is the hardware that actually does the printing.
- **Print server** is a computer that manages printing on the network.

- **Print driver** is a software program used by other computer programs to connect with printers and plotters.
- **Printer** is the software interface between the document and the print device.

FAQs

Q: When I try to upgrade to a dynamic disk, I receive an error message that there is not enough disk space.

A: Dynamic disks install a database at the end of the disk and require free space to create the database. You can back up the disk, delete the partitions, upgrade the disk to dynamic, create the desired volumes, and then restore all the data. Or, if there are multiple partitions, back up and delete the last partition, and then upgrade to dynamic, followed by the creation of the last volume and the restore of its data.

Q: When users create a file or folder in a shared public directory, they do not have enough privileges to delete the folder. How can I assign permissions so that they can delete the folders they create?

A: Use the built-in System group Creator Owner with access permissions of Full Control. Any new files that users create will have an ACE that lists their user account with Full Control permissions. With Full Control permissions, users can delete the files they create.

Q: I have a shared folder in which I assigned the Users group Change permissions. I have also verified that the group has Change permissions for the folder on the NTFS partition. Users are still not able to access all the files in the folder. What is the problem?

A: There are two problems here. First, file permissions always override folder permissions. Check to see if your file permissions are more restrictive than the folder permissions. Second, the file permissions are probably different because you have managed to turn off inheritance. If you want all the files and subfolders to have the same permissions as the parent directory, ensure that inheritance is turned on.

Q: I've set up the printer queue and the printer is on, but when I print a test page, nothing prints on the print device.

A: The printer might have the wrong port selected, and the test page is going to another printer. Also, the wrong print driver might be loaded, and the printer is unable to process the job (such as sending PCL code to a PostScript printer).

Inside Windows 2000 TCP/IP

Solutions in this chapter:

- Introduction
- A TCP/IP Primer
- The OSI Model
- The TCP/IP Protocol Suite
- Windows TCP/IP
- Using TCP/IP Utilities
- Using Windows 2000 Monitoring Tools
- Summary

Introduction

In times gone by (on a planet far, far, away...), TCP/IP was accepted unreservedly only in UNIX environments. The adoption of TCP/IP and DNS as the foundation for the Internet caused many vendors to hurriedly reexamine their network and Internet strategies. With Windows 2000, Microsoft has embraced TCP/IP and its associated applications as the protocol of choice. In fact, Windows 2000 is touted as an operating system that embraces (some) open standards. Considering Microsoft's previous history, the irony of this turn of events is not lost on many industry observers.

A number of the networking changes in Windows 2000 revolve around TCP/IP and its suite of protocols, including DNS, DHCP, and IPSec. This chapter provides an outline of the basic features in Windows 2000 TCP/IP and some background on TCP/IP, while later chapters cover DHCP, DNS, WINS, and TCP/IP security and routing in more detail. Windows 2000 has added and enhanced a number of protocols and services related to TCP/IP; it is critical to understand these enhancements to derive the maximum benefit from Windows 2000 Server.

A TCP/IP Primer

TCP/IP is a network protocol based on a 32-bit addressing scheme that enables networks to be interconnected with routers. The bits in each address are separated into four sets of 8 bits, called octets, which are separated by periods. With the binary number system, 8 bits can be used to signify any number from 0 to 255, so the lowest theoretical IP address is 0.0.0.0, while the highest is 255.255.255.255.

Each device, or host, on the network must have a unique IP address to communicate on the network. In order to communicate on the Internet, IP addresses must be registered with the organizations that manage the Internet so that routing can be configured correctly. Two specific network addresses and a range of network addresses are reserved for private use and are not routed on the Internet. These two network addresses— 10.0.0.0, 192.168.0.0, 172.16.0.0–172.32.255.255—are used on networks that are not connected to the Internet or connected by using network address translation (NAT) or proxy hosts. NAT and proxy hosts have two IP addresses, one on the private network and one registered on the Internet, and handle all communications between the private network and the Internet.

IP Address Classes and Subnets

As you can see in Table 11.1, IP addresses are divided into classes, or blocks of addresses, for administrative purposes. Each class is also assigned a default subnet mask. The class structure is simply a way to manage address space. For example, the United States government might have one or two Class A address spaces instead of thousands of Class C addresses.

Table 11.1 IP Addresses Are Divided into Three Usable Classes

Class	Range	Default Mask	Addresses per Network
A	0.0.0.0–126.255.255.255	255.0.0.0	16 million +
B	128.0.0.0–191.255.255.255	255.255.0.0	64,000 +
C	192.0.0.0–223.255.255.255	255.255.255.0	254
D	224.0.0.0–239.255.255.255	Reserved for multicast addressing	
E	240.0.0.0–254.255.255.255	Reserved for experimental use	

The subnet mask determines which bits in the IP address are the network address, and which bits are the host address. If we assumed that the default subnet mask was 255.0.0.0 for a Class A address, then from Table 11.1 it would imply that the first 8 bits (which equals 255) are the network portion of the address, and the three remaining octets are available for host addresses. It is not realistically possible to have 16 million hosts on a single network, or even 64,000, without segmenting the network with routers. Accordingly, networks with Class A and B addresses do not typically use the default mask; often, their subnet masks end up similar to those of Class C networks.

When a mask other than the default is used, subnets are created that enable the address space to be split up into several smaller networks and route traffic between them. A Class B network address could be split into 255 networks by using a 255.255.255.0 subnet mask. The actual number of usable networks, however, is a bit less than 255, due to network and broadcast addresses.

Subnets and Routing

Routers are devices that connect networks together and relay traffic between networks according to routing tables that are configured in their memory. IP networks that are not on the same logical network must have a router to connect them in order for their hosts to communicate. TCP/IP neophytes are often baffled when two machines cannot "see" each other, even though they are on the same physical wire. The point they should remember is that the combination of IP address and subnet mask can segregate the physical network into logically separate networks.

In the example illustrated in Figure 11.1, Network A has a network address of 192.168.10.0, since its subnet mask is 255.255.255.0. This is a

Figure 11.1 IP subnets are connected by routers.

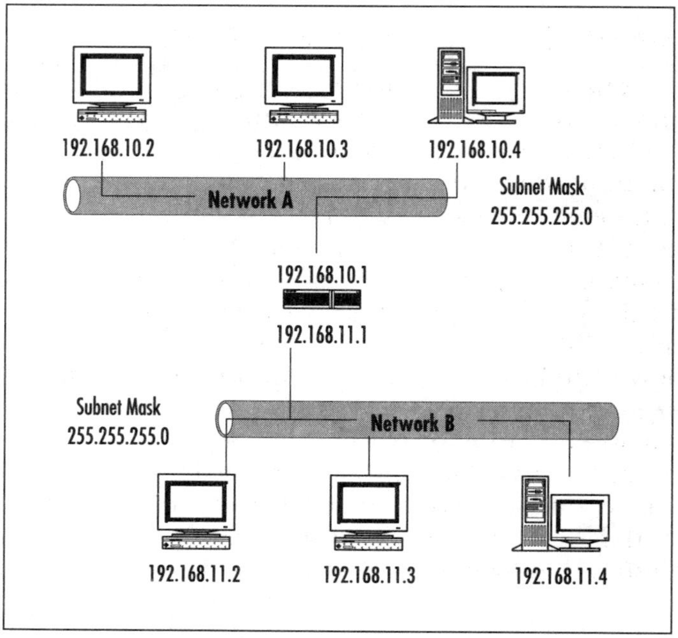

simple case, since the first three octets of the subnet mask are 255, meaning that all bits in the first three octets of each IP address are the network address, and the last octet is the host address. The network address of Network B is 192.168.11.0, and since it is on a different subnet (logical network), it must be connected to Network A by a router. In this specific example, the physical networks are parallel with the subnets. However, if both subnets were on the same physical network, either a router would be necessary for hosts on the 192.168.10.0 network to communicate with the hosts on the 192.168.11.0 network, or the routing tables on each computer could be individually configured.

Multiple routes can be configured between networks, providing TCP/IP with a measure of fault tolerance. Computers can act as routers if they are running software to perform that function. Routers are, in fact, computers designed for the specific purpose of routing network traffic. Windows NT and Windows 2000 Server can also perform the functions of routers with the Routing and Remote Access Service.

The OSI Model

The OSI model is used as a broad guideline for describing the network communications process. Not all protocol implementations map directly to the OSI model, but it serves as a good starting point for gaining a general understanding of how data is transferred across a network.

Seven Layers of the Networking World

The OSI model consists of seven layers. The number *seven* carries many historical connotations; it is thought by some to signify perfect balance, or even divinity. Whether this was a factor when the designers of the model decided how to break down the functional layers, the Seven Layers of the OSI Model are at least as legendary as the Seven Deadly Sins and the Seven Wonders of the World (within the technical community).

Data is passed in a top-down fashion through the layers on the sending computer until the Physical layer finally transmits it onto the network cable. At the receiving end, it travels back up in reverse order. Although the data travels down the layers on one side and up the layers on the other, the logical communication link is between each layer and its matching counterpart, as shown in Figure 11.2.

Here's how that works: As the data goes down through the layers, it is encapsulated, or enclosed, within a larger unit as each layer adds its own header information. When it reaches the receiving computer, the process occurs in reverse; the information is passed upward through each layer,

Figure 11.2 Communication between corresponding OSI layers.

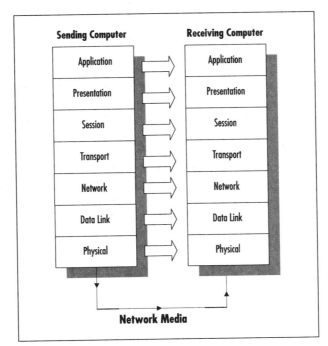

Figure 11.3 Each OSI layer except the Physical layer adds header information to the data.

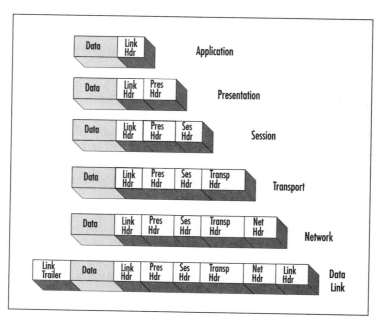

and as it does so, the encapsulation information is evaluated and then stripped off one layer at a time. The information added by the Network layer, for example, will be read and processed by the Network layer on the receiving side. After processing, each layer removes the header information that was added by its corresponding layer on the sending side.

It is finally presented to the Application layer, and then to the user's application at the receiving computer. At this point, the data is in the same form as when sent by the user application at the originating machine. Figure 11.3 illustrates how the header information is added to the data as it progresses down through the layers.

Note that in Figure 11.3, the header information that is added by the Application layer is called a link header, as is that added by the Data Link layer. These headers mark the first and last headers to be added. The Data Link layer also adds a Link Trailer. Many books teach the OSI layers upside down; that is, starting with the bottom layer. In fact, the Physical layer is often referred to as Layer 1, the Data Link layer as Layer 2, and so on. Other descriptions start (seemingly logically) at the topmost layer. Which way you look at it depends not on which hemisphere you live in, but on whether you're addressing the communication process from the viewpoint of the sending or the receiving computer.

The TCP/IP Protocol Suite

Though the OSI model provides a well-understood and modular architecture to describe network communications, not all communication methods map directly to it—including TCP/IP (Figure 11.4).

As TCP/IP has matured, it has grown to include a number of protocols and applications. Actually, TCP/IP is somewhat of a misnomer, because TCP isn't used by every application that communicates on an IP network. As you can see in Figure 11.4, applications use either TCP or UDP to communicate with IP on the Internet layer. The other Internet layer protocols listed, ARP, ICMP, and IGMP, are used by IP to resolve IP addresses to hardware addresses and route packets. In the Transport layer, UDP is a connectionless protocol and does not guarantee delivery of network packets; so most applications do not use it. Therefore, since most applications use TCP, the name TCP/IP has become common usage for referring to IP networks and components. The other common applications and protocols that are usually present in a TCP/IP implementation are included with TCP and IP to comprise what is known as the TCP/IP protocol suite.

The TCP/IP protocol suite grows as new application protocols are introduced to provide functionality for IP networks. Hypertext Transfer Protocol

Figure 11.4 The TCP/IP model and protocols compared to the OSI model.

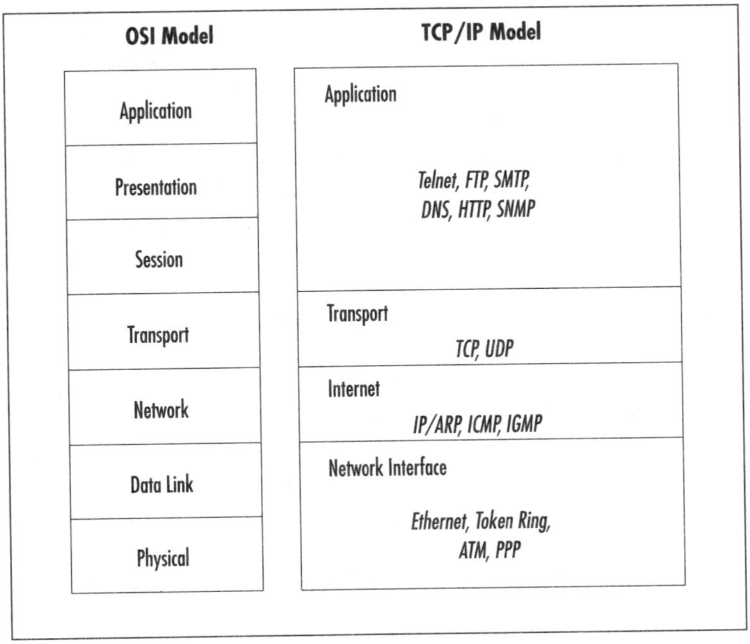

(HTTP) was created to transmit Hypertext Markup Language (HTML) documents over TCP/IP, and was introduced in 1991. It was swiftly absorbed into the TCP/IP protocol suite, in no small part due to its rapid proliferation throughout the Internet community. It is amazing to think that prior to 1991, the World Wide Web did not even exist, and in the space of a decade, it has become one of the primary vehicles ushering in the global village.

Using some of the other TCP/IP applications has been made easier by HTTP technology. Web browsers have incorporated the ability to use File Transfer Protocol (FTP), which is much simpler than using a command-line FTP interface. They can also be used to access e-mail, providing a much simplified and ubiquitous e-mail client. Although you are probably not intimidated by command-line interfaces and SMTP configurations, many users would not even use these applications if it weren't for the World Wide Web.

When viewed from a different perspective, the TCP/IP protocol suite becomes something far greater than just a conglomeration of protocols. This technology combined with others has changed the lives of a multitude of people in a startling number of ways. Discussing the details of the technology may be less appealing than considering the way it changes the world, but this is a technical book, so we must.

TCP/IP Core Protocols

There are a handful of protocols that are the mainstay of the TCP/IP suite, the real bread-and-butter protocols. These protocols handle all of the network connections and routing so that applications are simply concerned with handing data to the protocols at the Transport layer.

TCP

Transmission Control Protocol (TCP) works on the Transport layer of the TCP/IP model, providing connection-based communication with other IP hosts. When an application passes data to the Transport layer, it is often too much data to transmit in one packet, so TCP segments the data on the sending side and reassembles it at the receiving end according to sequence information that is packaged with the packet. TCP sends acknowledgments to confirm successful delivery, and analyzes each packet according to checksum information to ensure data integrity.

TCP uses a system of ports to manage communication. Applications bind to a specific TCP port, and any inbound traffic delivered to that port will be picked up by the application. This enables multiple applications on one host to use TCP at the same time, and also standardizes the way a client can connect to a given service on a server. For instance, Telnet's standard TCP port is 23, so Telnet clients try to establish connections on port 23 by default. Port assignments are flexible; that is, you can change the port a client or server uses for a specific application if needed. Although Web servers typically use port 80 for HTTP communication, the Web server application can be bound to a different port, but clients will need to know which port to use in order to establish a connection since it differs from the default (Table 11.2).

Table 11.2 TCP Ports Used by Common Applications

TCP Port	Application
20	FTP (data)
21	FTP (control)
23	Telnet
53	DNS zone transfers
80	HTTP
139	NetBIOS session

UDP

UDP also provides Transport layer services, and is a connectionless protocol that does not guarantee delivery or sequencing of data. UDP can be used when data transfer is not critical, or when the application is designed to ensure correct delivery of data. Since it does not acknowledge successful transfer, it is faster and uses less network bandwidth than TCP (Table 11.3).

Table 11.3 UDP Ports Used by Common Applications

UDP Port	Application
53	DNS name queries
69	Trivial File Transfer Protocol
137	NetBIOS name service
138	NetBIOS datagram service
161	SNMP
520	Routing Information Protocol

IP

When TCP and UDP are ready to send data, they pass it to IP for delivery to the destination. IP is connectionless and unreliable, which is why TCP is designed to establish connections and guarantee delivery. IP does not try to detect or recover from lost, out-of-sequence, delayed, or duplicated packets. IP is the foundation of the TCP/IP protocol suite.

For IT Professionals

The Three-Way Handshake

Computers using TCP to communicate have both a send window and a receive window. At the beginning of a TCP communication, the protocol uses a three-way handshake to establish the session between the two computers (Figure 11.5). Because TCP (unlike its Transport layer sibling, UDP) is connection oriented, a session, or direct one-to-one communication link, must be created prior to sending and receiving of data. The client computer initiates the communication with the server (the computer whose resources it wants to access). The handshake includes the following steps:

1. **Sending of a SYN (synchronization request) segment by the client machine.** An initial sequence number, sometimes just referred to as the ISN, is generated by the client and

Figure 11.5 The TCP three-way handshake that establishes a communication session.

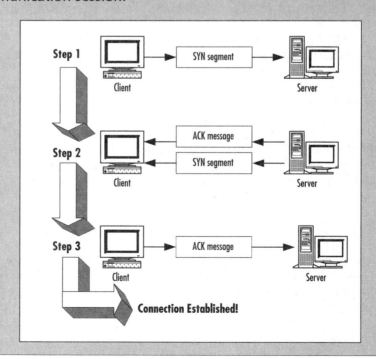

Step 1 — Client → SYN segment → Server

Step 2 — ACK message ← Server; SYN segment ← Server → Client

Step 3 — Client → ACK message → Server

Connection Established!

Continued

sent to the server, along with the port number the client is requesting to connect to on the server

2. **Sending of an ACK message and a SYN message back to the client from the server.** The ACK segment is the client's original ISN plus 1, and the server's SYN is an unrelated number generated by the server itself. The ACK acknowledges the client's SYN request, and the server's SYN indicates the intent to establish a session with the client. The client and server machines must synchronize one another's sequence numbers.

3. **Sending of an ACK from the client back to the server, acknowledging the server's request for synchronization.** This ACK from the client is, as you might have guessed, the server's ISN plus 1. When both machines have acknowledged each other's requests by returning ACK messages, the handshake has been successfully completed and a connection is established between the two.

NOTE

Packets are often referred to as datagrams at this level. These datagrams contain the source and destination IP addresses, which will be translated to MAC (physical) addresses at a lower layer.

IP receives TCP segments (or UDP for connectionless communications such as broadcasts) and then passes it down to the Network layer. Before handing it down, however, IP performs an important function: It looks at the destination IP address on the packet and then consults its local routing table to determine what to do with the packet. It can pass the data to the network card (or if it is a multihomed system, determine which of the attached network cards to pass it to), or it can discard it.

When a Windows 2000 computer starts, the routing table is constructed. Certain entries, such as the addresses for the loopback, the local network, and the default gateway (if configured in TCP/IP properties) are added automatically. Other routes can be added by ICMP messages from the gateway, by dynamic routing protocols (RIP or OSPF), or you can manually add routes using the route command at the command prompt.

ARP

The Address Resolution Protocol resolves IP addresses to Media Access Control (MAC) addresses. MAC addresses are unique IDs that are assigned to network interface devices. ARP uses a broadcast, after checking the ARP cache, to send out a query that contains the IP address of the destination host, which replies with its MAC address. When the request is answered, both the sender and the receiver record the IP and MAC addresses of the other host in their ARP table cache to eliminate the need for an ARP broadcast for every communication.

ICMP

Internet Control Message Protocol is used by network devices to report control, error, and status information. ICMP messages are delivered by IP, which means that they are not guaranteed to reach their destinations. ICMP is used by routers to indicate that they cannot process datagrams at the current rate of transmission, or to redirect the sending host to use a more appropriate route. Most of you are probably familiar with the ping utility, which sends ICMP echo requests and displays the replies it receives.

IGMP

Internet Group Management Protocol is used to exchange and update information regarding multicast group membership. Multicasting is a system of sending data to one address that is received and processed by multiple hosts. Multicast addresses are in the Class D IP address range, and addresses are assigned to specific applications. For instance, the 224.0.0.9 address is used by RIP (Routing Information Protocol) version 2 to send routing information to all RIP routers on a network (Table 11.4).

Table 11.4 TCP/IP Core Protocols and Their Related RFCs

Protocol	RFCs
ARP	826
IP	791
ICMP	792
IGMP	1112, 2236
UDP	768
TCP	793

TCP/IP Applications

TCP/IP would be rather useless without applications to run on top of it. In addition to the applications that are considered part of the TCP/IP protocol suite, there are numerous proprietary applications that work on IP networks as well. For instance, NetBIOS over TCP/IP (NetBT) is Microsoft's implementation of NetBIOS for IP. Since NetBT is typically only found on Windows computers, it is not considered part of the TCP/IP protocol suite. We will discuss the most popular TCP/IP applications and protocols, but an entire book could be filled if each application and protocol were covered in detail.

SMTP   Simple Mail Transport Protocol is a protocol designed for applications to deliver mail messages. SMTP defines the specific commands and language that mail servers use to communicate, and the format of the messages to be delivered. For instance, if an SMTP server receives a mail message that is addressed to a user that is not defined, according to SMTP standards it will reply to the sender and include information regarding the failed delivery.

HTTP   The child prodigy of Internet protocols, Hypertext Transport Protocol is used by Web browsers and Web servers to conduct their business with each other. HTTP defines how browsers request files and how servers respond. HTTP works in conjunction with Hypertext Markup Language (HTML), graphics, audio, video, and other files to deliver the killer application of the 1990s, the World Wide Web.

FTP   File Transfer Protocol is a client/server application designed to enable files to be copied between hosts regardless of the operating systems. FTP can also be used to perform other file operations, such as deletion, and it can be used from a command-line interface or a GUI application. The latest versions of popular Web browsers include complete FTP functionality, although many shareware FTP clients offer interfaces that are faster and more powerful.

Telnet   Telnet is an application that enables a remote command-line session to be run on a server. Telnet is available for most operating systems, including Windows 2000. By using Telnet to log on to a server, you can run programs and perform other operations on the server. It's the next best thing to being there!

DNS   Domain Name System is used by most of the other applications in the TCP/IP protocol suite to resolve host names to IP addresses. A Web browser, for example, cannot establish a connection to a Web server unless it knows the IP address of the server. DNS is used to resolve host names, such as www.microsoft.com, to IP addresses. DNS is a distributed database that is essential for TCP/IP to be used on a massive Internet-size scale. It provides a function that hides the complexity of IP addresses from users, and makes things such as e-mail and the World Wide Web much easier to use.

SNMP   Simple Network Management Protocol was designed to provide an open systems management infrastructure for hardware and software vendors to implement on their systems. This enables management software to be developed that can query a host for information defined in its Management Information Base (MIB). Devices running SNMP software can also send traps, which are simply messages formatted according to SNMP specifications, to a management server when a certain event occurs. Since SNMP is an open platform protocol, SNMP management console software can interoperate with systems of various types as long as they comply with SNMP standards.

Windows TCP/IP

Most of you have worked with TCP/IP on Windows NT and other Windows operating systems, so you are familiar with how to use it and TCP/IP related services such as WINS and DHCP. Microsoft has implemented support for most cross-platform TCP/IP applications such as DNS, SMTP, and FTP, as well as adding one additional service, Windows Internet Naming Service (WINS), which is unique to Windows networks. This section discusses some of the more important Windows TCP/IP services, while the enhancements and new protocols related to TCP/IP are covered in the next.

Windows 2000 TCP/IP Stack Enhancements

The most important enhancements that Microsoft has made to the TCP/IP protocol stack in Windows 2000 are related to performance increases. These include:

- RFC 1323 TCP extensions: scalable TCP window size and timestamping.
- Selective Acknowledgments (also called SACK) in accordance with RFC 2018.
- Support for IP over ATM (Asynchronous Transfer Mode) as detailed in RFC 1577.
- TCP Fast Retransmit.
- Quality of Service (QoS).
- Resource Reservation Protocol (often referred to as RSVP).
- IP Security (IPSec).
- The Network Driver Interface Specification version 5.0.

NetBT and WINS

If you have worked with Windows in a network environment, you know that Windows computers have a computer name that is used to identify each system on the network. This computer name is the NetBIOS (Network Basic Input/Output System) name. NetBIOS, which has a history extending back to 1983, is a networking API that was used by Windows computers to register and locate resources. NetBIOS names have a maximum length of 15 characters and a flat namespace, two factors that are severely limiting on a large network.

NetBT is simply the application of NetBIOS working on a TCP/IP network, and WINS was introduced to help manage the NetBIOS names on a TCP/IP network. WINS is a service that registers IP addresses with the associated computer names and services in a database, and responds to queries from clients who need to resolve a NetBIOS name to an IP address. Without WINS, Windows clients had to rely on broadcasts or static files located on each PC to resolve names to IP addresses. WINS was introduced to reduce the amount of broadcast traffic on a Windows network and provide the ability to resolve addresses for computers throughout a WAN.

Windows 2000 has taken a big step away from NetBIOS, NetBT, and WINS, but they are still there to support existing Windows networks. NetBT uses the following TCP and UDP ports:

- UDP port 137 (name services)
- UDP port 138 (datagram services)
- TCP port 139 (session services)

Windows 2000 requires NetBIOS over TCP/IP to communicate with prior versions of Windows NT and other clients. In accordance with the move away from NetBIOS, Windows 2000 supports direct hosting to communicate with other Windows 2000 machines. Direct hosting uses the DNS (on port 445) for name resolution, instead of the NetBT.

NOTE

Windows 2000 by default enables both NetBIOS and direct hosting. When establishing a new connection, both protocols are used simultaneously, and the one that connects first is the winner. In many configurations, NetBIOS should be disabled for performance and security reasons. To force Windows 2000 to use direct hosting:

1. Click Start | Settings | Network and Dial-up Connection. Right-click on the Local Area Connection and click Properties.
2. Select Internet Protocol (TCP/IP), and click Properties.
3. Click ADVANCED.
4. Click the WINS tab, and select Disable NetBIOS over TCP/IP.

Windows 2000 introduces several new features for WINS that improve its manageability. Chapter 12, "Managing Windows 2000 DHCP Server," discusses WINS and the enhancements you will find in Windows 2000.

DHCP

Windows has long included support for Dynamic Host Configuration Protocol on both the server and client sides, and Windows 2000 is no exception. DHCP enables clients to request the lease of an IP address from a server. The server will also automatically configure other TCP/IP items such as gateways, DNS servers, and WINS servers. Windows 2000 includes several new DHCP features, including performance monitor counters, integration with DNS, disabling NBT on clients, and detection and shutdown of unauthorized DHCP servers on Windows 2000 servers by integration with Active Directory. Chapter 12 contains detailed information regarding DHCP, and configuring and managing the DHCP service on Windows 2000 computers.

DNS

Windows NT 4.0 ships with a DNS server service, and organizations that have deployed it will benefit when they upgrade to Windows 2000. As mentioned previously, Active Directory relies on DNS in order to function, and some older versions of DNS servers will not be suitable. In order for Active Directory to work, it must register SRV records with the DNS service, which are not supported on some DNS servers. A detailed discussion of Windows 2000 DNS is presented in Chapter 12.

SNMP

An SNMP service ships with Windows NT and Windows 2000, enabling them to participate as SNMP managed hosts. Third-party software is also available so that a Windows NT or 2000 computer can be an SNMP network management station. DHCP, IIS, and other Windows services install custom MIBs so that they can be managed via SNMP. Microsoft Systems Management Server includes a client service, Event to Trap Translator, which converts Windows NT and 2000 events into SNMP traps. This feature is a very useful tool to integrate Windows NT and Windows 2000 into large organizations that depend on an SNMP management infrastructure.

Using TCP/IP Utilities

The Windows 2000 distribution ships with a number of command-line utilities to assist in troubleshooting TCP/IP network problems. If you have been supporting Windows NT TCP/IP (or even UNIX), you are probably familiar with most of these utilities. Some of the utilities have been enhanced, and one new utility, pathping, has been added to the tool set.

ARP

The ARP utility is not one that you will use often, but is very useful in certain situations. ARP can be used to display, delete, and add entries in the computer's ARP table. The ARP table contains IP address to MAC address assignments, and you shouldn't need to modify it except under extreme circumstances. The ARP utility is helpful when troubleshooting problems that are related to duplicate IP addresses or duplicate MAC addresses on a segment.

The ARP utility allows you to add and delete entries in the ARP cache. When you add an entry into the ARP cache, you create a static entry. A static entry will appear as static in the type field in the ARP cache. You might want to create static ARP entries for frequently accessed servers on the segment, or perhaps for the default gateway. When you create static entries, the source machine does not need to issue ARP broadcasts to resolve IP addresses to MAC addresses.

Hostname

The hostname utility simply returns the host name of the computer. There are no command-line switches.

Ipconfig

Ipconfig is a utility that can be used to display IP configuration, manage the DHCP client, and manage and display the DNS cache. New switches for the ipconfig command include /flushdns, /registerdns, and /displaydns.

Running ipconfig with no switches displays the IP address, subnet mask, and default gateway for each network adapter on the computer. This is especially useful when troubleshooting to see whether a client has received a DHCP address. Let's discuss of the command-line options, since ipconfig is a utility you will probably use more than most of the other TCP/IP utilities.

Important switches for ipconfig include:

/?   Displays command-line options, syntax, and examples.

/all   Displays a multitude of configuration items for all network adapters, including node type, MAC address, IP address, subnet mask, default gateway, DHCP server, and primary and secondary WINS servers.

/renew   You can force the DHCP client to refresh its configuration from the DHCP server by using the /renew switch.

/release   This switch will remove the IP configuration from all adapters with DHCP configuration. This operation can also be performed on a specific adapter by appending its name after the release switch.

/flushdns   The DNS cache is flushed by using the /flushdns switch with ipconfig.

/registerdns   This switch renews DHCP leases on adapters, and performs dynamic registration for DNS names and IP addresses. Useful in environments that use dynamic DNS.

/displaydns   The DNS resolver cache can be displayed by using the /displaydns switch. To be useful, you may need to pipe this command to a text file so that you can see all of it (ipconfig /displaydns > c:\temp\displaydns.txt).

/showclassid   Returns information on the DHCP Class ID that is configured on the client.

/setclassid   Class IDs on network adapters can be set by using the /setclassid switch with the network adapter name trailing it. The function of Class IDs is to control DHCP configuration for specific groups if the same configuration is not appropriate for all users.

TIP

TCP/IP parameters for Windows 2000 are stored as Registry values and can be located at HKEY_LOCAL_MACHINE\SYSTEM\CurrentControlSet\ Services\Tcpip\Parameters. Remember to back up any keys before changing them!

Nbtstat

Nbtstat is a utility used to view protocol statistics and current TCP/IP connections using NBT. There are a number of command-line switches available to allow you to view adapter status and name tables of remote computers, local NetBIOS names, the cache of NetBIOS names, names resolved by WINS or broadcast, and session information. The following example illustrates that, if interpreted correctly, nbtstat can provide a wealth of information in a Windows network. Examining the results of issuing the command nbtstat –a 192.1.1.1 allows us to determine that the node 192.1.1.1 is a domain master browser [1B], and that the Administrator is logged on.

```
Node IpAddress: [192.1.1.1] Scope Id: []

              NetBIOS Remote Machine Name Table

         Name               Type         Status
         ----               ----         ------
         YODA        <00>   UNIQUE       Registered
         YODA        <20>   UNIQUE       Registered
         JEDI        <00>   GROUP        Registered
         JEDI        <1C>   GROUP        Registered
         JEDI        <1B>   UNIQUE       Registered
         YODA        <03>   UNIQUE       Registered
         JEDI        <1E>   GROUP        Registered
         JEDI        <1D>   UNIQUE       Registered
```

```
INet~Services   <1C>   GROUP     Registered
.._MSBROWSE__.<01>    GROUP     Registered
IS~YODA........<00>   UNIQUE    Registered
ADMINISTRATOR   <03>   UNIQUE    Registered

MAC Address = 02-00-4C-4F-4F-50
```

Netstat

Netstat also displays protocol statistics and current TCP/IP connections. Several command-line switches are available to display information such as all connections and listening ports, Ethernet statistics, addresses and port numbers, connections by protocol type, the routing table, and statistics by protocol.

The netstat –s switch provides detailed statistics regarding protocol performance. You can limit which protocols are reported on by using the –p switch, or if you want performance statistics on all TCP/IP protocols, use only the –s switch.

By using a combination of the –a and –n switches, a list of open ports on the machines and their current status is displayed. The –n switch speeds up the screen print process by preventing netstat from translating port numbers to services. Try it with and without the –n switch and you'll see what I mean. *Listening* means that the port is open, but no active connections have been made to it. *Established* indicates that the connection is active. *Time-Wait* and *Close-Wait* represent connections that have been established, but are in the process of timing out and closing.

The netstat command can provide you with a wealth of information. Every Systems Administrator should run this command on a periodic basis to assess the state of the ports on his servers for security reasons, and to obtain quick TCP/IP statistics. Using the /? switch will display information you need to use the utility.

TIP

A couple of things to watch out for when netstat –s statistics are displayed are the discards entries. These should be hanging around zero. If you find a large number of discards, you likely have problems with the network card itself, or the segment is very busy, and messages are lost or corrupted in the NIC buffer.

Nslookup

Nslookup is a utility used to troubleshoot DNS issues. This is one command where you cannot use the /? switch to get help on how to use the utility. Nslookup can be used as an interactive utility by running the executable with no command-line options. When nslookup is started, you will be greeted with a greater-than prompt. More information on the options available can be displayed after launching nslookup and typing **?** or **help**. The Windows 2000 Help file also has information regarding nslookup.

Ping

The ping utility (Packet Internet Groper) sends an ICMP ECHO request to the specified host, and displays statistics on the replies that are received. Ping is one of the first IP troubleshooting tools to use when you are trying to resolve a network problem. See Table 11.5 for command-line switch options for this "oldie, but goodie."

Table 11.5 Command-Line Switches for the Ping Utility

Switch	Description
-?	Displays syntax and command-line options.
-t	The –t switch is useful when you want to continuously monitor a connection. For example, you want to restart a machine remotely, and then want to know when the machine is up again so that you can reestablish your remote connection. Use the ping –t command and watch when the destination computer begins to respond, and then reestablish the connection.
-n count	If you don't want to continuously ping a remote host, you can specify the number of ICMP echo request messages sent to the destination by using the –n switch.
-l size	Size of send buffer.
-f	Set Don't Fragment flag in packet.
-i TTL	The default Time-To-Live (TTL) set on the ICMP echo messages is 252, but you can change that value by setting the –i switch.
-v TOS	Type of Service.
-r count	The –r command shows you the routes taken with each ping attempt. Think of this as a quick-and-dirty way to investigate your routing configuration.
-s count	Timestamp for count hops.
-j host-list	Loose source route along host-list.
-k host-list	Strict source route along host-list.
-w timeout	Use the –w switch to configure a custom timeout period on your requests. The default timeout is 1000 milliseconds. If you don't want to wait that long for a timeout, change the value using the –w switch.

Route

The route command enables you to view, add, remove, or modify the IP routing table on a computer. The route table maintains four different types of routes:

- **Host**   The route to a specific destination IP address.
- **Subnet**   A route to a subnet.
- **Network**   A route to a network.
- **Default**   Used when no other route applies.

Routes, which are available even after rebooting, are called persistent routes and are contained in the Registry key HKEY_LOCAL_MACHINE\ SYSTEM\CurrentControlSet\Services\Tcpip\Parameters\PersistentRoutes. Use the –p switch to add a persistent route, and –f to clear the routing table. The -? switch will display usage options, and the Windows 2000 Help file can be consulted for supplementary information.

TIP

If you have partitioned one physical network into logical subnets, you can eliminate the requirement to install a router to reach a different logical subnet. This can be achieved by using the route command and then letting ARP do all the work for you. For example, on host 10.1.1.1, the command would be:
route add 0.0.0.0 MASK 0.0.0.0 10.1.1.1

Tracert

The tracert utility allows you to trace the path of routers to a destination host. You can use the tracert utility to assess whether a router on the path to the destination host may be congested.

The tracert utility sends a series of ICMP echo requests, with each request having a incrementally higher TTL value. The first echo request has a TTL of 1. When the first router receives the message, it will decrease the TTL by 1. Since the TTL on the request was 1, it now is 0, and the router will return a Time Exceeded message to the requesting computer.

The tracert utility then increases the TTL to 2 on the ICMP echo request message. When the message hits the first router, the TTL is decreased by 1, and when it hits the second router, it is decreased by 1 again. The second router then sends a time-exceeded message to the source host. The process continues until all the routers have been traversed to the destination host.

See Table 11.6 for command-line options, or just run the executable without indicating a target system, and the command usage will be displayed.

Table 11.6 Tracert Command-Line Options

-d	Don't resolve addresses to host names.
-h max_hops	Maximum number of hops to target.
-j host-list	Loose source route along host-list.
-w timeout	Milliseconds to wait for replies.

Pathping

Pathping, a utility that is new to the Windows operating system, discovers the route to the destination host, pings each hop for a period of time, and then reports the statistics. The PATHPING utility sends ICMP echo request messages to each router along the path to the destination host, and calculates how long it takes the roundtrip from request to reply. The default number of hops is 30, period 250 milliseconds, and queries to each router 100.

NOTE

The Pathping tool combines the capabilities of both tracert and ping, and gives you additional information that you can't get easily from using either tool individually. Pathping will calculate roundtrip times, percent of requests that were lost at each router, and percent of requests lost between the routers.

Pathping provides some interesting statistics because it gives you information regarding where the packet loss is taking place, and the level of stress a particular router may be experiencing.

Note that PATHPING first does a tracert and identifies all the routers in the path to the destination, and provides a list of those routers in the first section. Then, PATHPING provides statistics about each router and each link between routers. From this information, you can assess whether a router is being overloaded, or whether there is congestion in the link between the routers (Table 11.7).

The last two columns provide the most useful information when troubleshooting routers and links. Notice in the last column the name of the router, the IP address, and the percentage to the left of the router. If there is a high number of lost pings to a router, that is an indication that the router itself may be overloaded.

Table 11.7 Pathping Command-Line Switches

Switches	Description
/?	Displays pathping options.
/n	Do not resolve address to host names.
/h maximum_hops	Maximum number of hops to destination.
/g host-list	Loose source route along host-list.
-p period	Number of milliseconds between pings.
-q num_queries	Number of pings per hop.
-w timeout	Milliseconds to wait for each reply.
-T	Test each hop with Layer-2 priority tags.
-R	Test each hop for RSVP awareness.

Just under the name of the router, you see a | character. This represents the link between the router and the next-hop router. When there is a large percentage of lost pings for the link, it indicates congestion on the network between hops. In this case, you would want to investigate problems with network congestion rather than with the router itself.

NOTE

The pathping algorithm takes advantage of the fact that there are two paths the ping request can take: the fast path and the slow path. The fast path is that taken when a router just passes the packet to the next hop, without actually doing any work on that packet. This is in contrast to the slow path, where the router is the recipient of the ICMP echo request and must use processing resources to respond to the request by issuing an ICMP echo reply.

Netdiag

The netdiag command is new with Windows 2000. It is the Swiss Army Knife of network diagnostics for your Windows 2000 installation. When you run this command, it sets forth to test 24 different aspects of the networking subsystem for the machine.

When netdiag is run without any switches, it prints the results to the screen. But, you will likely want to save the results of the analysis, and netdiag allows you to save everything it has discovered to a log file, which you can read at your leisure (or send to somebody else so he or she can figure out what's wrong!).

Perhaps the greatest value of the netdiag command is you can easily tell a user or a junior Administrator to run this command and not have to worry about walking him or her through 24 different command-line tests and switches, which would in all probability lead to a minor disaster.

A list of the tests run when the netdiag command is issued without switches appears in Table 11.8.

Table 11.8 Tests Run by Netdiag

Test	What the Test Does
Ndis	Tests the NIC.
IpConfig	Runs ipconfig.
Member	Tests the machine's Domain Membership.
NetBTTransports	Tests NetBIOS over TCP/IP Transports.
Autonet	Autonet address test.
IpLoopBk	Pings the loopback address.
DefGw	Pings the default gateway.
NbtNm	NetBT name test.
WINS	Tests the WINS servers.
Winsock	Tests Winsock integrity.
DNS	Tests that correct names are entered in DNS.
Browser	Tests the Workstation Services and Browser Service.
DsGetDc	Discovers Domain Controller availability.
DcList	DC list test.
Trust	Tests Trust Relationships.
Kerberos	Kerberos test.
Ldap	Tests Lightweight Directory Access Protocol.
Route	Tests the routing table.
Netstat	Runs netstat and records the results.
Bindings	Bindings test.
WAN	Tests the WAN configuration.
Modem	Performs Modem Diagnostics.
Netware	Tests NetWare connectivity.
IPX	Tests IPX components.

The netdiag command includes several switches, which you can find by typing **netdiag /?** at the command prompt. The /q switch will only show you the errors that netdiag finds, so that your screen (hopefully) does not get too busy with the results from all the tests. If you want the real nitty-gritty details, use the /v switch to get the verbose output printed to the screen. If verbosity is your middle name, use the /debug switch to wring out every possible bit of information and print that to the screen. The most useful switch is the /l switch, which allows saving all the output to a log file.

When you have users at a remote site reporting problems with connectivity, have them run netdiag with the /debug and the /l switches. Then have them e-mail the NetDiag.log file to you as an attachment. This is an excellent way to start troubleshooting without having to ask a lot of questions of someone who might have marginal understanding of the networking subsystems of the machine.

Make the netdiag utility your first line of offense when troubleshooting connectivity programs. An entire report takes less than a minute to complete, and the information gathered is invaluable.

SNMP

The Simple Network Management Protocol is not a utility in and of itself. Rather, it is a protocol used to communicate status messages from devices distributed throughout the network to machines configured to receive these status messages. Machines that report their status run SNMP Agent software, and machines that receive the status messages run SNMP Management software.

How Does SNMP Work?

SNMP allows you to audit the activities of servers, workstations, routers, bridges, intelligent hubs, and just about any network-connected device that supports the installation of agent software. The agent software available with the Windows 2000 implementation allows to you monitor Windows 2000 Server and Professional operating system parameters, the DHCP service, the WINS service, the Internet Information Services, QoS Admission Control Services, the Routing and Remote Access Service (RRAS), and the Internet Authentication Service (IAS). All these Windows 2000 services can be monitored remotely by SNMP Management software.

In order for agent software to collect information regarding a particular service, a Management Information Base (MIB) must be created.

NOTE

The MIB is a database and a collection of instructions about how and what information should be gathered from a system. The MIBs included with Windows 2000 allow the agent software to communicate a wide range of information.

The agent is responsible for reporting the information gathered by the MIB. However, agents rarely volunteer information spontaneously. Rather, the agent must be queried by an SNMP management system before it gives up its knowledge.

There is an exception to this: a trap message. A trap message is sent spontaneously by an agent to SNMP Management System for which is has been configured to send. For example, we could set a trap message to indicate that the World Wide Web service is hung. We would then configure the agent to send a trap message to the IP address of our computer running the SNMP Management software so that we can quickly handle this catastrophic event. SNMP messages themselves are sent to UDP Port 161 for typical GET and SET type messages, and UDP Port 162 for trap messages.

NOTE

A GET message is a request that is sent from an SNMP Management System requesting information from an agent. A SET message allows the SNMP Management System to write changes to MIB, and therefore extend its information-gathering abilities.

Installing the Agent

In order for a system to report to the SNMP Management System, you have to install the agent software first. To install the agent on Windows 2000 machines, go to the Control Panel, open the Add/Remove Programs applet, select Add/Remove Windows Components, scroll down to find Management and Monitoring Tools and select it, then click DETAILS. Place a check mark in the Simple Network Management Protocol check box, and click OK.

Once the agent software is installed, its behavior can be configured. The way to configure the SNMP agent behavior in Windows 2000 is by launching the Services applet from Administrator Tools | Services. Then scroll down to the SNMP Service. After you install the service, it should start automatically. Right-click on the SNMP Service entry, click Properties, and click the Agent tab. This tab is for descriptive purposes only. SNMP Management Systems can obtain information about a contact person and location from information provided here. Also, information about what type of system the agent is running on is indicated by the selections made in the Service frame area. Click the Traps tab.

If you want the agent to initiate a trap message, you need to make the agent part of a community that the agent and the SNMP Management software have in common. The community name can be anything you like, and it is not related to domain names, usernames, or any other security principle you might think of in Windows 2000.

WARNING

The community name does represent a somewhat primitive degree of security, because only machines from the same community can communicate with the agent. Microsoft documentation states that you should make your community name hard to guess. However, since the community name is transmitted in clear text, it really doesn't make much of a difference how difficult to guess the name of the community might be!

One way around this problem is to use IPSec encryption between the SNMP Management station and the SNMP agent. In this way, the clear-text messages are encapsulated in encrypted IPSec packets and are not vulnerable to network sniffers.

After configuring at least one community membership, you then need to enter the IP addresses or host names of the machines that will receive the trap message. You do so by clicking ADD under the Trap destinations text box.

On the Security tab, you can configure some basic security parameters for the SNMP agent. In the "Accepted community names" frame, you can add new communities that the agent can report to, and define the level of permissions for Management Station access to the agent and MIBs.

After clicking ADD, the SNMP Service Configuration dialog box is displayed. Several security rights can be configured for the community:

- **None** means no permissions.
- **Notify** means only traps will be sent to the Management Station, and that the Management Station cannot make SNMP requests.
- **Read Only** allows the Management Station to read the values of the information provided by the MIBs.
- **Read Write** and **Read Create** do the same thing, which is to allow a SET command to be sent to the agent.

Figure 11.6 Customizing trap events using the Event to Trap Translator.

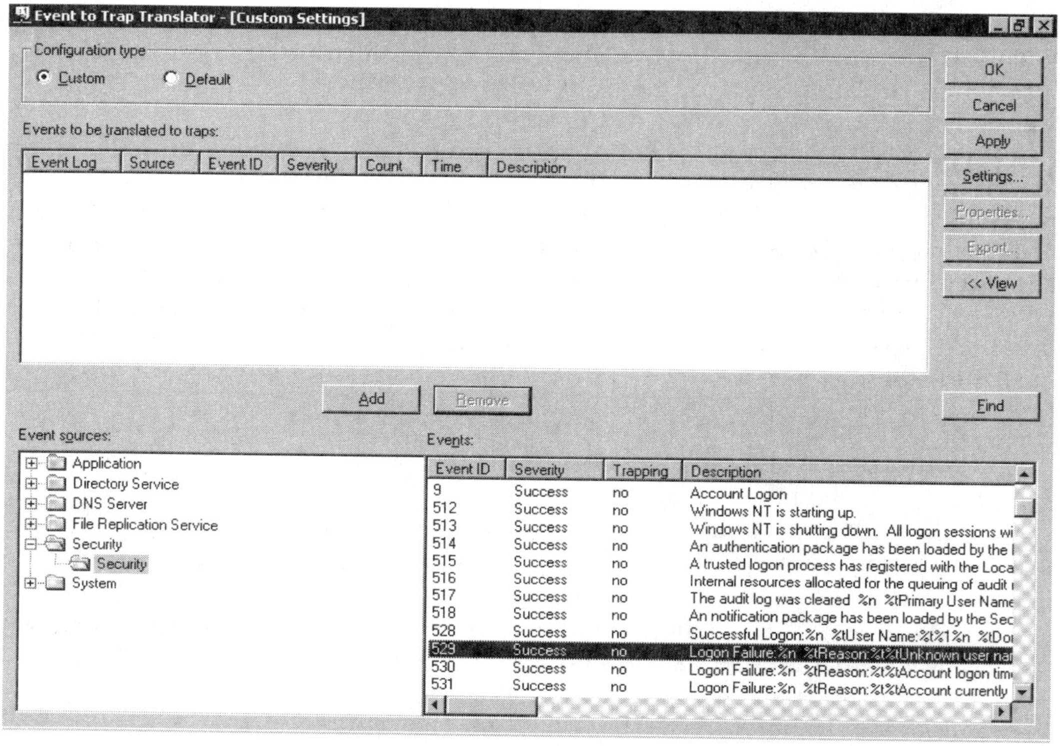

One really nice addition to the Windows 2000 SNMP agent is a GUI utility that allows you to configure which events will elicit a trap message. By default, no events will send a trap, which isn't very useful. However, there is a GUI utility that you can access from the Run command. Type **evntwin.exe** at the Run command and click Oκ.

This launches the Event to Trap Translator, which allows you to configure which events will elicit trap messages. Notice the DEFAULT option button is selected, and list of events that are configured to send trap messages by default. That's right, none! In order to configure trap events, click CUSTOM, and then click EDIT. In the lower-left pane titled Event sources, double-click on the Security folder. You should see another security folder under that one. Click on that security folder, scroll down to Event ID 529, and click on that. A similar window to Figure 11.6 should be displayed.

Note that in the lower-right pane, you are able to select from a number of different security events for which you can elicit trap messages to be sent to a management station. After selecting Event ID 529, click ADD. You can decide if the trap will be sent after a certain number of instances take place over a specified time interval. Click Oĸ, and this event will be listed in the top pane of the Translator window.

If you prefer a command-line version of this program, type **evntcmd.exe** at the command prompt and you will receive some help on how to use the command-line version of the program.

Using Windows 2000 Monitoring Tools

At times it is necessary to collect information about the state of the network (and TCP/IP) by drilling down deeper into its technical core. This can take the form of network analysis where TCP/IP traffic is captured and analyzed, or system monitoring where an individual host is monitored for particular system activity. The tools described in this section are extremely useful for analyzing not only TCP/IP activity, but also a plethora of other protocols, system objects, and activities.

Microsoft has included two powerful network-monitoring tools with Windows 2000: the Performance Console and the Network Monitor. With these tools, you can monitor the health of your network from a single location, and you can listen in on network activity in real time. Both of these utilities allow you as the Administrator to have more control over the health and efficiency of your network.

Before diving into the tools, let's talk first about some basic monitoring guidelines that will help optimize your use of the tools discussed in this chapter.

Basic Monitoring Guidelines

When monitoring aspects of your network, you need to have a good idea of what it is that you're looking for. Are you looking for clues for logon validation errors? Are you looking for reasons for complaints of network sluggishness from users? Are you looking for possible security leaks? Are you just obtaining baseline measurements so that you have something to compare to when the network is acting abnormally? When monitoring, a few basic steps should be followed:

1. **Baseline** This is the process of collecting information on a network when everything is working the way you want it to work. It would make no sense to collect baseline information when the network is acting up, or is the subject of complaint and ridicule.

2. **Document** A system must be in place that allows you to quickly and efficiently return to previous measurements, and to measure trends that may exist in the measurements you have taken.

3. **Back up** It is important that you back up this information to multiple locations for fault-tolerance reasons.

4. **Analyze** After you have decided on a location to keep your precious data, you need a system to collate it and bring it together so that you can spot trends. Most of the tools that we will work with in the chapter allow you to save data in some kind of delimited text file.

Performance Logs and Alerts

The application formerly known as Performance Monitor has undergone a name change and a minor overhaul in its appearance in Windows 2000. In fact, it appears to have a couple of different names, depending on the Microsoft documentation you read. It is called either Performance or System Monitor.

You can use the Performance Console to obtain real-time data on network performance parameters such as TCP, Web, FTP, and Proxy server statistics. This information can be saved in a log file for later analysis, and it can even be replayed. To open the Performance Console, go to the Administrative Tools and click Performance.

Note that there are two panes in the Performance Console. On the left, you see entries for the System Monitor, and then several options for Performance Logs and Alerts. The System Monitor is the counterpart of the Windows NT 4.0 Performance Monitor.

There are three views available in the System Monitor:

- Chart view
- Histogram view
- Report view

When working with the Chart view, note that it will display up to 100 units of time. You select the unit of time for which measurements are taken by right-clicking anywhere on the chart area itself, and selecting Properties.

Notice the area next to the "Update automatically" field to enter the update period. You can enter the number of seconds you want the chart updated, and the entire chart will contain data for up to 100 update intervals.

TIP

If you would like to see an entire day's worth of activity on one chart screen, you could divide the number of seconds in one day by 100, or 86400/100 = 864 seconds. By setting the chart interval to 864 seconds, you'll be able to see an entire day's worth of data on a single chart screen.

Counters

There are a great variety of network-related counters that can be added to the System Monitor. A noncomprehensive list of these counters includes IP, IIS Global, ICMP Browser, FTP Server, UDP, TCP Redirector, SMTP Server, and Network Interface.

One of the nice things about the System Monitor application in Windows 2000 is that you can populate the Chart view with a number of counters without having to repopulate the Report view. To select all counters from a performance object, select the "All counters" option button and click ADD.

After the counters are added to the Chart view, statistics gathered from those counters are displayed in both the Report and the Histogram views. If you would like to create a log file to view the information at a later date, click on the Counter Logs object, then right-click in the right pane and select New Log Settings. Input the name of the log into the New Log Settings dialog box. Make it something meaningful and descriptive so you can find the information later. The first tab displayed is the General tab, and this is where you begin to add new counters to the log file. Click ADD and add counters as you did in the Chart view. After adding the counters, they will populate the area labeled Counters.

Log File Format

In the Log file type drop-down list box, you can choose what format you want the log file to be saved in. The main choices are binary format and delimited text formats. If you save the logs in delimited text formats, you can import the data into an Excel or Access database. Regardless of the format you choose, you can still bring the information back to the System Monitor Console for later analysis in the same way you were able to open log files for later viewing using the Windows NT 4.0 Performance Monitor.

Alerts

To create an alert, click the Alerts object in the left pane, and then right-click in the right pane and select New Alert Settings from the context menu. Enter the name of the alert and click OK. Counters are added for alerting by clicking ADD. The Actions tab allows the setting of what actions should be taken if the alert is triggered. This action can take the form an entry in the application event log, a network message, starting up of a performance log, or the running of a program. Remember that if alerts are to be sent to a NetBIOS name, then it must be enabled on both the machine generating the alert and the machine receiving an alert. With the Schedule tab, the system can be instructed to look for alert conditions at certain specified times.

Network Monitor

The Microsoft Network Monitor is a software protocol analyzer that captures and analyzes traffic on the network. The version of Network Monitor that ships with the Windows 2000 server family has unfortunately been limited in scope by not allowing the network adapter to be placed in promiscuous mode.

When an adapter is placed in promiscuous mode, it is able to listen to all the traffic on the segment (also referred to as a collision domain), even if that traffic is not destined for the machine running the Network Monitor software. However, one of the advantages of this state of affairs is that because promiscuous mode capturing can potentially overtax your computer's processor, it won't happen.

NOTE

A more full-featured version of Network Monitor that allows for promiscuous mode is included with Microsoft System Management Server (SMS).

Even with these limitations, Network Monitor is an extremely useful tool for assessing network activity. It can be used to collect network data and analyze it on the spot, or to save recorded activities for a later time. Network Monitor allows network activity to be monitored and triggers to be set when certain events or data cross the wire. This could be useful, for instance, when looking for certain key words in e-mail communications moving through the network.

Filtering

The Network Monitor program captures only those frames that you are interested in, based on protocol or source or destination computer. More detailed and exacting filters can be applied to data that has already been collecting, which allows you to pinpoint the precise elements you might be looking for in the captured data. We'll discuss how to filter what data you want to capture, and how to fine-tune the captured data after you've collected it.

Security Issues

The Network Monitor program is a network sniffer. Any person with Administrative privileges can install it on a Windows 2000 server family computer and start listening to activity on the wire. If you feel this is a cause for concern, you are correct. This easy availability of such a powerful tool should lead to even further consideration during the assignment of administrative privileges. Fortunately, the Network Monitor is able to detect when someone else on the segment is using Network Monitor, and provide

Figure 11.7 The Network Monitor Capture window.

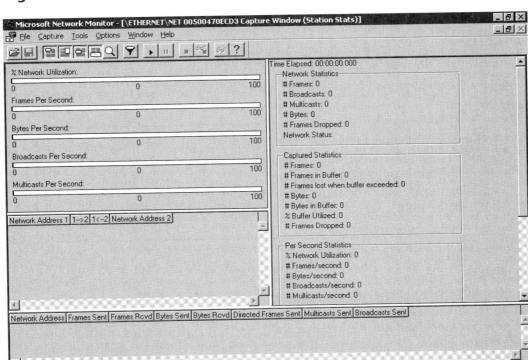

you with his or her location. However, the usefulness of this feature is in doubt due to a lack of consistent results during testing.

Using Network Monitor

Network Monitor is not part of the default installation and can be installed via the Add/Remove Programs applet in Control Panel. After you have installed the program, go to the Administrative Tools menu and click Network Monitor. If multiple adapters are installed on the machine, you may be asked to pick a default adapter. The Network Monitor capture window will then be displayed consisting of four panes (Figure 11.7).

Capture Window Panes

The top-left pane is depicted with a gas-gauge type format, providing real-time information on percent network utilization, broadcasts per second, and other parameters.

Just below that is a pane that provides information about individual sessions as they are established, showing who established a session with whom, and how much data was transferred between the two. The right pane is the local machine's session statistics pane, and provides detailed summary (is that an oxymoron?) information about the current capturing session.

The bottom pane provides information about each detected host on the segment, and statistics gathered on the host's behavior.

TIP

To determine other instances of Network Monitor currently on the network, select the Tools menu, and then click Identify Network Monitor Users. Nbtstat can also be used to track down Network Monitor users, since Network Monitor registers NetBIOS names with a service identifier of [BFh] or [BEh].

Buffers

By clicking the Capture menu item and selecting Buffer settings, you can configure Network Monitor's buffer size and frame size. The buffer size, in megabytes, determines the amount of data that can be captured in a single recording session. Since the buffer is eventually written to disk, remember to ensure that there is more available hard disk space than the amount specified in the buffer size. The second setting in the Capture Buffer Settings window is frame size, which determines how many bytes of the frame should be captured.

Collecting Data

Now that we're finished with the preliminaries, let's get to the job of collecting some data. The first thing to try out is a capture without filters, just to get a feel for how the capture process works. There are a couple of ways to get the capture started: by either selecting the Capture menu and then clicking Start, or clicking the little right-pointing arrow in the toolbar. Either one will begin the capture. When it is running, you'll see the gas gauges moving, and the statistics being collected on the recording session.

After letting the capture run for a little bit, or after the % Buffer Used value is 100, click the button that has the eyeglasses next to a square (the stop and view button). This stops the capturing process and provides a view of the frames that have been captured. You'll see the Capture Summary window as seen in Figure 11.8.

This window provides a list of all the frames that were captured during the session. If you scroll to the bottom of the list, you'll note that there is a

Figure 11.8 Capture Summary window.

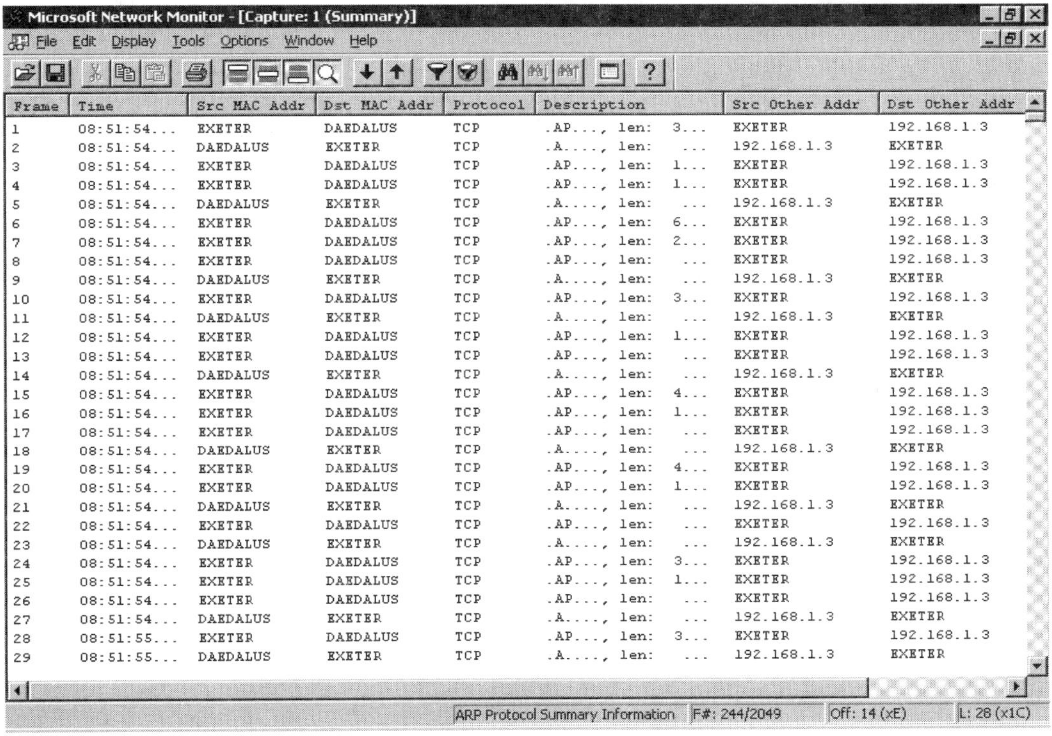

Frame	Time	Src MAC Addr	Dst MAC Addr	Protocol	Description	Src Other Addr	Dst Other Addr
1	08:51:54...	EXETER	DAEDALUS	TCP	.AP..., len: 3...	EXETER	192.168.1.3
2	08:51:54...	DAEDALUS	EXETER	TCP	.A...., len: ...	192.168.1.3	EXETER
3	08:51:54...	EXETER	DAEDALUS	TCP	.AP..., len: 1...	EXETER	192.168.1.3
4	08:51:54...	EXETER	DAEDALUS	TCP	.AP..., len: 1...	EXETER	192.168.1.3
5	08:51:54...	DAEDALUS	EXETER	TCP	.A...., len: ...	192.168.1.3	EXETER
6	08:51:54...	EXETER	DAEDALUS	TCP	.AP..., len: 6...	EXETER	192.168.1.3
7	08:51:54...	EXETER	DAEDALUS	TCP	.AP..., len: 2...	EXETER	192.168.1.3
8	08:51:54...	EXETER	DAEDALUS	TCP	.AP..., len: ...	EXETER	192.168.1.3
9	08:51:54...	DAEDALUS	EXETER	TCP	.A...., len: ...	192.168.1.3	EXETER
10	08:51:54...	EXETER	DAEDALUS	TCP	.AP..., len: 3...	EXETER	192.168.1.3
11	08:51:54...	DAEDALUS	EXETER	TCP	.A...., len: ...	192.168.1.3	EXETER
12	08:51:54...	EXETER	DAEDALUS	TCP	.AP..., len: 1...	EXETER	192.168.1.3
13	08:51:54...	EXETER	DAEDALUS	TCP	.AP..., len: ...	EXETER	192.168.1.3
14	08:51:54...	DAEDALUS	EXETER	TCP	.A...., len: ...	192.168.1.3	EXETER
15	08:51:54...	EXETER	DAEDALUS	TCP	.AP..., len: 4...	EXETER	192.168.1.3
16	08:51:54...	EXETER	DAEDALUS	TCP	.AP..., len: 1...	EXETER	192.168.1.3
17	08:51:54...	EXETER	DAEDALUS	TCP	.AP..., len: ...	EXETER	192.168.1.3
18	08:51:54...	DAEDALUS	EXETER	TCP	.A...., len: ...	192.168.1.3	EXETER
19	08:51:54...	EXETER	DAEDALUS	TCP	.AP..., len: 4...	EXETER	192.168.1.3
20	08:51:54...	EXETER	DAEDALUS	TCP	.AP..., len: 1...	EXETER	192.168.1.3
21	08:51:54...	DAEDALUS	EXETER	TCP	.A...., len: ...	192.168.1.3	EXETER
22	08:51:54...	EXETER	DAEDALUS	TCP	.AP..., len: ...	EXETER	192.168.1.3
23	08:51:54...	DAEDALUS	EXETER	TCP	.A...., len: ...	192.168.1.3	EXETER
24	08:51:54...	EXETER	DAEDALUS	TCP	.AP..., len: 3...	EXETER	192.168.1.3
25	08:51:54...	EXETER	DAEDALUS	TCP	.AP..., len: 1...	EXETER	192.168.1.3
26	08:51:54...	EXETER	DAEDALUS	TCP	.AP..., len: ...	EXETER	192.168.1.3
27	08:51:54...	DAEDALUS	EXETER	TCP	.A...., len: ...	192.168.1.3	EXETER
28	08:51:55...	EXETER	DAEDALUS	TCP	.AP..., len: 3...	EXETER	192.168.1.3
29	08:51:55...	DAEDALUS	EXETER	TCP	.A...., len: ...	192.168.1.3	EXETER

summary frame that contains statistics about the current capture. Take note of the column headers, which are pretty self-explanatory.

Notice something unusual about the data in Figure 11.8? The data in the Src MAC Addr and Dst MAC Addr fields have been translated into machine names. This feature takes a small portion of the mystique away from packet capturing by substituting sensible names for MAC addresses. To activate this feature, select the Display menu, and then click the Find All Names.

After double-clicking one of the frames, the display transforms into a tri-pane view (Figure 11.9). The top pane is similar to the one displayed in Figure 11.8, while the middle pane contains translated information from the captured frame detailing frame headers and protocol information. The bottom pane presents the raw Hex and translations of the collected frame data. At the very bottom of the window, in the status bar area, there is a description of the frame selected in the top pane (which in this case is Ethernet/802.3 MAC Layer), the frame number out of the total number of frames, and an offset value for the selected character in the bottom pane.

Figure 11.9 Tri-pane view in the Capture Summary window.

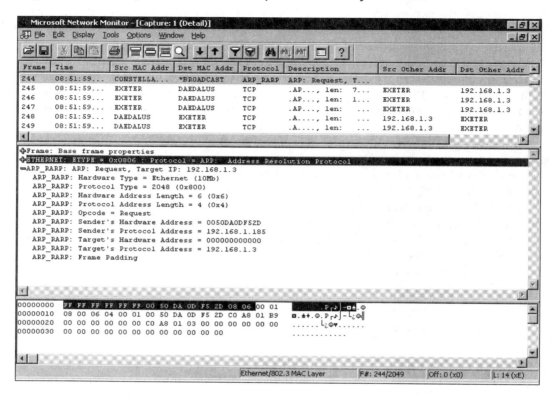

In the preceding example, frame number 244 was selected, which is an ARP broadcast frame. Notice the detail in the middle pane. It indicates the hardware type and speed, and the source and destination IP and hardware address. The destination hardware address is the Ethernet broadcast address [FFFFFFFFFFFF], because the whole purpose of the ARP broadcast is to resolve the IP address to a hardware address (Figure 11.9).

The capture was taken from EXETER. The ARP broadcast was issued by CONSTELLATION for DAEDALUS, which is the machine with the IP address of 192.168.1.3. Would the ARP reply be found later in the capture? The answer is no, because the reply will not be sent to the hardware broadcast address, but to CONSTELLATION's hardware address; therefore, the Network Monitor on EXETER would be able to capture that conversation. The only reason the ARP request was captured initially was because it was directed to the hardware broadcast address, which means that every machine on the segment had to evaluate the request to see if it was for them.

The bottom pane in this instance isn't very exciting. It shows the Hex data on the left and an ASCII translation on the right.

Filtered Captures

The capture displayed in Figure 11.8 was an unfiltered capture. The advantage of doing an unfiltered capture is that data can be gathered on every communication in to and out of the computer doing the capture. However, this method may result in an inordinate amount of information, some of which is unnecessary and could serve to obscure the data that is actually being looked for. If, for example, it is only necessary to capture conversations to one specific host, the captured frames could be limited by using a capture filter.

The purpose of the capture filter is to limit the frames that are actually saved in the capture buffer. This also makes better use of buffer space, since the buffer can be devoted to the precise targets of interest. It also reduces the amount of extraneous information (sometimes called noise) that could obscure important information.

In order to create a capture filter, select the Capture menu, and click Filter. Click OK to pass through the warning dialog. A Capture Filter dialog box will then be displayed.

There are two ways to filter capture information:

- By machine address pairs
- By a specified pattern in the frames that are examined during the capture sequence

Filtering by Address Pairs

Up to four address pairs can be defined for filtering. For example, suppose there are 30 computers on a segment that is running Network Monitor, and only capture information from four specific computers is required. To start adding address pairs, double-click on the [AND] (Address Pairs) statement. A window similar to Figure 11.10 would then be displayed.

A close look at the elements of the dialog box reveals two option buttons, Include and Exclude. Any address pair selected for Include will be included in the capture. Any address pair selected for Exclude will be excluded from the capture. For example, if *Any was selected (which indicates all frames coming to and leaving this computer), then a pair of computers could be excluded so that messages being sent to and arriving from that machine are ignored.

Under the Include and Exclude options are three panes: Station 1, Direction, and Station 2. Station 1 and Station 2 will define the computers named in the address pairs that will be included or excluded from the filter, with Station 1 always being the machine running the Network Monitor application. The Direction arrows allow you to filter based on the direction of the traffic. The ←→ symbol represents traffic leaving Station 1 to Station 2 and arriving from Station 2 to Station 1, the → represents traffic leaving

Figure 11.10 The Address Expression dialog box.

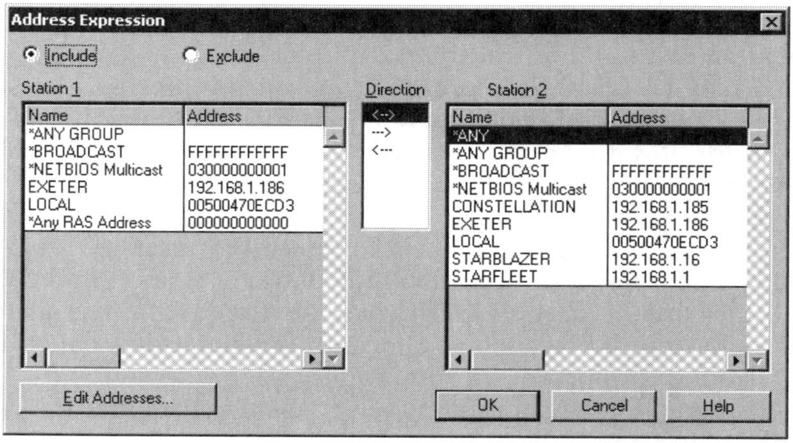

Station 1 to Station 2, and the ← represents traffic arriving from Station 2 to Station 1.

The chances that the machine that you wish to designate as Station 2 is not included in the list are relatively high. To add the machine of interest to the list, click EDIT ADDRESSES. This shows the Addresses Database in its current state on the machine running Network Monitor. The first column gives the machine's NetBIOS name, the second column the machine's addresses, the third column denotes the type of address included in the second column, and the fourth column includes a comment about the entry in the database.

To add a new entry, click ADD. A window similar to Figure 11.11 will then be displayed.

In the Add Address Information dialog box, enter the name of the machine, whether this is a permanent name for the machine, the address, the type of address, and an optional comment. Click OK, and the address is then entered into the database.

These addresses will only stay in the database for the time that Network Monitor is open. If several addresses have been added, it is a good idea to save these addresses. To do so, click SAVE, and choose a location and a name for the file. The addresses can then be loaded during subsequent monitoring sessions.

After clicking CLOSE, the Address Expression dialog box is displayed again. In Figure 11.12, EXETER has been selected for Station 1, CONSTELLATION for Station 2, and the double arrow for traffic direction.

With this capture filter in place, only traffic between EXETER and CONSTELLATION will be retained in the capture filter, and all other packets will

Figure 11.12 A completed capture filter.

be rejected. This implies that all packets continue to be examined by the application, and that is true.

> **TIP**
>
> The filtering process can be processor intensive, especially in the case of complex filters. Keep this in mind before running an extended capture session on a machine that is already heavily taxed.

Now the capture session can commence. Click OK in the Capture Filter dialog box to remove it from sight. To start the capture, click the right-pointing arrow in the toolbar.

After letting the capture run for a very short period of time, click the stop and view button on the toolbar.

Display Filters

Now that some data has been captured, the second filter type can be applied, known as a display filter. The display filter allows the captured data to be mined for very specific elements, allowing for a much more refined filtering than can be accomplished with the capture filter.

> **NOTE**
>
> A display filter can be used as a database search tool, where the capture frames are the data in our database.

Figure 11.13 The Expression dialog box.

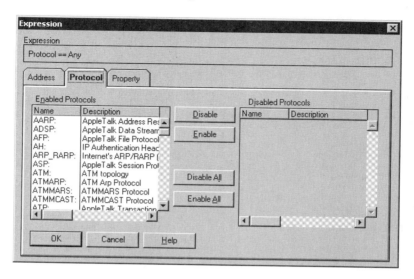

Assume that the purpose of capturing the data is to determine what types of messages are being passed around the network regarding Windows 2000. The first decision is to determine what kind of messages need to be searched for. In this case, assume the requirement is to determine if users have been using the net send command to exchange ideas or opinions regarding Windows 2000.

To get started, select the Display menu (from the Capture Summary screen), and click Filter. Everything other than the protocol of interest needs to be filtered out, and then a key phrase contained within the protocol of interest needs to be identified. It is common knowledge that Net Send uses the SMB protocol, so the search will begin there.

Double-click on the line that says Protocol==Any to display the Expression dialog box (Figure 11.13).

Notice that the Protocol tab is the default. By default, all protocols are enabled, which means that the filter is letting frames from all protocols appear. The objective is to allow only frames from the SMB protocol to appear. The first step is to click DISABLE ALL. This causes all the protocols to be moved to the right pane, into the Disabled Protocols section. The SMB protocol can then be found by scrolling through the disabled protocols. Click on the SMB protocol, and then click ENABLE.

When the display filter is enabled, only the SMB frames will be visible. However, only the SMB frames that contain the term *Windows 2000* need to be displayed. In order to drill down to just those frames, click the Property tab.

After clicking the Property tab, scroll down the list of protocols until the SMB protocol is found. Double-click on the protocol to see all the SMB

Figure 11.14 The SMB protocol Properties dialog box.

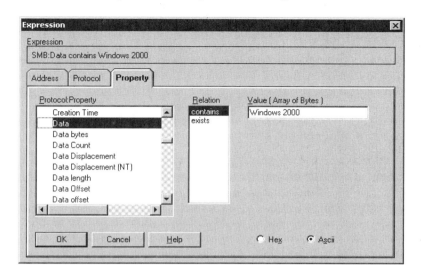

frame properties. Then scroll down the list of SMB frame properties until the Data property is found. A window similar to Figure 11.14 should then be displayed.

In Figure 11.14, the contains option has been selected in the Relation text box with an associated value of Windows 2000. This will filter out any SMB frames that do not contain the text string Windows 2000. Note toward the bottom of this dialog box there are two option buttons, Hex and ASCII, and that ASCII is selected.

After clicking Oκ, and then Oκ again, a single frame containing a reference to Windows 2000 is displayed (Figure 11.15).

Apparently, the rollout of Windows 2000 on the network is being well received!

Summary

In the computer industry, time moves at a pace that is different from the rest of the world. By those standards, the TCP/IP protocol suite has a (relatively) long and venerable history. TCP/IP is the protocol stack of the global Internet and for Windows 2000.

TCP/IP as we know it today consists of an entire suite of protocols. To understand how various protocols in the suite work together, one of the popular networking models can be used as a reference point. Models provide a way to graphically represent and better understand the process of communication between computers that share their resources with one another.

Figure 11.15 The result of the display filter.

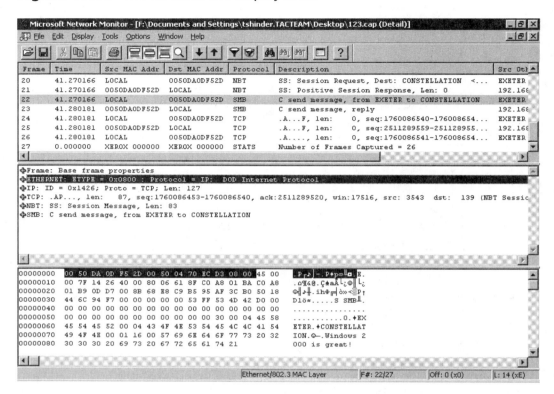

The Open Systems Interconnection (OSI) model is the current recognized standard. It provides a set of common specifications to which networking components can be designed. Compliance with the standard ensures that products made by different manufacturers will still be able to interoperate.

The Windows 2000 operating system includes a suite of TCP/IP command-line utilities that allow Administrators to monitor and assess the current status of network performance and communications. Some of these tools include:

- netstat
- nbtstat
- netdiag
- ipconfig
- ping
- tracert
- pathping

Devices running an SNMP agent to communicate with machines running SNMP Management Software use the Simple Network Management Protocol.

The System Monitor tool (also known as Performance) has new and improved capabilities. One of the most powerful tools for investigating the network and TCP/IP is the Network Monitor. The version of Network Monitor that comes with Windows 2000 Server family products is limited to some extent, because it can only capture information arriving to and leaving the machine running the Network Monitor software. However, it still provides a great deal of functionality.

FAQs

Q: When can I disable NetBIOS over TCP/IP (NetBT)?

A: Microsoft states that you can remove NetBT once you have a pure Windows 2000 environment. Since WINS relies on NetBT, you cannot disable NetBT until you are no longer relying on WINS for name resolution. Additionally, legacy applications and logon scripts often use NetBIOS names, and these must be modified to use DNS name resolution before you can remove NetBT. You can disable NetBT via DHCP on Windows 2000 clients when you are ready to make the change.

Q: I am having problems with logon validation with one of my downlevel (NT) clients. It seems as if it isn't able to contact any of the backup domain controllers. These downlevel clients are only able to log on when a primary domain controller is online. Can I use any of these tools to investigate the problem?

A: Yes. In order to do this, you'll need the version of Network Monitor that comes with Systems Management Server, or you'll need to run a monitoring session from every computer that is a domain controller on your network. What you want to do is monitor all traffic coming in to and out of the machine that is having problems logging on. After the capture is complete, filter the data so that you see only the netlogon protocol activity. This should give you an indication of what the problem might be.

Q: Can I obtain information about other machines on my network using the System Monitor?

A: Yes. In order to do this, you have to have the Network Monitor Agent installed on the target machines. You can install the agent from the Add/Remove Programs applet in the Control Panel, and then click Add/Remove Windows Components. After you add the Network Monitor

Agent, you will be able to collect performance data from other machines on the network. If you wish to collect information from downlevel clients (NT machines), you must be sure that the Network Monitor Agent from Systems Management Server 2.0 is installed on these clients.

Q: What is the difference between TCP ports and UDP ports? What are some of the well-known ports?

A: TCP ports are more complex and they operate differently from UDP ports, although both are used for the purpose of identifying a packet's destination more specifically within a frame. A UDP port operates as a single message queue. The UDP port is the endpoint for UDP communications. Each TCP port, on the other hand, is identified by dual endpoints (one address/port pairing for each connected host). Well-known ports include TCP ports 20 and 21 (FTP), 23 (Telnet), 53 (DNS zone transfer), 80 (Web server), and 139 (NetBIOS session). Well-known UDP ports include 69 (TFTP), 137 (NetBIOS name service), 138 (NetBIOS datagram service), 161 (SNMP), and 520 (RIP).

Chapter 12

Managing Windows 2000 DHCP Server

Solutions in this chapter:

441

Introduction

Most common network protocols assign each computer a unique identifier. NetBEUI uses a 16-character NetBIOS name, while the TCP/IP protocol uses an IP address. In a TCP/IP environment, the Dynamic Host Configuration Protocol (DHCP) can be a Network Administrator's best friend—unless he or she fails to configure it properly, in which case, it can be the source of his or her worst nightmare.

DHCP is designed to assign IP addresses dynamically as computers attach to the network. Computers require minimal configuration to retrieve an IP address (and other TCP/IP configuration information) from a DHCP server. Automatic DHCP configuration saves time, provides greater accuracy, and uses IP address spaces more efficiently than manual methods.

A significant advantage of using the DHCP service bundled with Windows 2000 is that it is integrated with Microsoft DNS Server. This new feature allows a Windows 2000 DHCP server to communicate IP addressing and host name information to a Windows 2000 Dynamic DNS (DDNS) server. This provides dynamic IP addresses to host name registration and resolution. As application standards move toward using the Winsock interface, it is critical in large corporate networks to locate clients by host name and IP address.

DHCP is a mission-critical feature of enterprise networks. Most corporate networks have moved to TCP/IP and rely on DHCP for IP address administration. It is up to the Network Administrator to ensure that the DHCP service is configured optimally for his or her environment.

DHCP Overview

As mentioned earlier, DHCP provides IP addressing information for DHCP clients. To obtain IP addressing information, the client must obtain a lease from a DHCP server. In this section, we examine the process of lease assignment and integration of DHCP with DDNS. Some lease configuration strategies to optimize the allocation of IP addresses will also be examined.

The Process of Obtaining a Lease

The DHCP client and server participate in a dialog that consists of four primary interchanges:

- DHCPDISCOVER
- DHCPOFFER
- DHCPREQUEST
- DHCPACKNOWLEDGMENT

The result of this dialog is the assignment of an IP address and additional TCP/IP parameters. Let's look at each of these messages in more detail.

DHCPDISCOVER

When the DHCP client initializes, it broadcasts a DHCPDISCOVER message to the local segment. The destination address is the limited broadcast address, 255.255.255.255. All DHCP servers on the segment will respond to the DHCPDISCOVER message (including non-Microsoft DHCP servers). The DCHP client has not yet received an IP address, so it includes with the DHCPDISCOVER message its Media Access Control (MAC) address (identified as the ciaddr field in a packet analysis). Other information in the DHCPDISCOVER message includes:

- The client's host name
- A parameter request list that includes the DHCP option codes the client supports
- The hardware type of the client's network interface card (NIC), such as 10Mb Ethernet

DHCPOFFER

All DHCP servers on the segment respond to the client's DISCOVER message by offering an IP address from their pool of available IP addresses. This offer is made in the form of a DHCPOFFER message. The DHCP client works on a first-come first-serve basis, and will accept the IP address from the first DHCPOFFER message it receives.

The DHCPOFFER message is a broadcast message. In order for the correct client to receive the information, the destination MAC address is included in the ciaddr field. Other information in the DHCPOFFER message includes:

- DHCP server IP address
- The offered IP address
- The offered subnet mask
- DHCP option information—WINS and DNS servers, default gateway
- Lease interval
- First and second lease renewal intervals (Renewal [T1] and Rebinding [T2] Time Values)

The DHCPOFFER message contains the basic IP addressing information the client computer will use when the TCP/IP stack is initialized.

DHCPREQUEST

The client responds to the offer by issuing a DHCPREQUEST broadcast message. The question might come to mind at this point, "Why use a broadcast message? Doesn't the client now have an IP address?" Recall that all DHCP servers respond to the initial DCHPDISCOVER message. The purpose of the DHCPREQUEST broadcast is just a polite way of informing other DHCP servers that their offers have been rejected. The rejected DHCP servers (now, don't feel sorry for them) then return the IP addresses they offered to their pools of available IP addresses.

The DCHPREQUEST message is a confirmation of the information sent to the client in the DHCPOFFER message. The DHCPREQUEST message includes:

- The client's hardware address
- The DHCP server's IP address
- The client's requested IP address
- The client's host name

DHCPACKNOWLEDGMENT (DHCPACK)

Finally, the DHCP server responds to the DHCPREQUEST message with a DHCPACK broadcast message. The reason this message is broadcast is that the client does not officially obtain its IP address until it is acknowledged. Again, the client's MAC address is included in order to identify the proper destination of this message.

The DHCPACK message contains information similar to that included with the DHCPOFFER message, and acts as a confirmation of the DHCPREQUEST message. At this point, the client has leased the IP address and can use it for network communication. The address is marked as leased by the DHCP server and will not be leased to any other client during the active lease period.

DHCP Negative Acknowledgment (DHCPNACK)

After a reboot, the client will attempt to renew its lease. The client will broadcast a DHCPREQUEST message in an attempt to retain its current IP address. If the server determines the client can keep this address, it will return to the client a DHCPACK message.

However, if the server decides the client cannot keep its current IP addressing information (perhaps the address has been given to another computer), then the DHCP server will issue a DHCP Negative Acknowledgment (DHCPNACK). The DHCPNACK message is similar to the DHCPACK message in that it contains the client's MAC address and is a broadcast message. Also included is the IP address of the DHCP server that issued the Negative Acknowledgment.

When the client receives the DHCPNACK, it will broadcast a DHCPDISCOVER message. The message is similar but not exactly the same in content and form as the original DHCPDISCOVER message. The difference lies in the fact that the client will attempt to obtain its previous IP address. This DCHPDISCOVER message contains the field, DHCP: Requested Address, that was not part of the DHCPDISCOVER message when the client did not yet have an IP address. If the IP address is available again for some reason, the client will receive the same IP address. If the original IP address continues to be unavailable, the client will be assigned another IP address from any responding DHCP server's pool of available IP addresses. If the client is unable to obtain a lease from a DHCP server, TCP/IP will be shut down, and the computer will no longer be able to participate in network activity.

Integration of DHCP with DNS

An extremely useful extension of the DHCP service is its integration with the Windows 2000 DNS. The most significant extension is the Windows 2000 DHCP server's ability to deliver host name and IP addressing information to a Windows 2000 DDNS server.

After assigning a DHCP client an IP address, the Windows 2000 DHCP server can interact with a Windows 2000 Dynamic DNS server in one of three ways:

- It will update the DNS server by providing information to create an A (Address) record and PTR (Pointer) record on the DNS at the client's request.
- The DHCP server will update both the A record and the PTR record regardless of client request.
- The DHCP server will never register information about the DHCP client. However, the client itself may contact the Dynamic DNS server directly with this information.

The DCHP/DDNS interaction varies with the type of client receiving the IP addressing information from the DHCP server. The Windows 2000 DHCP server supports the Client Fully Qualified Domain Name (FQDN) Option (Option Code 81), which allows the DHCP client to communicate its FQDN to the DHCP server. Only Windows 2000 clients support Option Code 81. The interplay between the Windows 2000 client and Windows 2000 DHCP encompasses the following:

1. The Windows 2000 client broadcasts a DHCPREQUEST message and receives an IP address via a DHCPACK. After officially obtaining a lease, the Windows 2000 client will register its own A Record with the Dynamic DNS server.

2. The DHCP server will register the client's PTR record with the DDNS server. This is the default behavior for a Windows 2000 client and Windows 2000 DHCP server.

3. Client and server configuration can be manipulated to allow the DHCP server to update both A and PTR records. If desired, the DHCP server and DCHP client can be configured so that no dynamic update of client information reaches the DDNS server.

Figure 12.1 Advanced TCP/IP Settings dialog box.

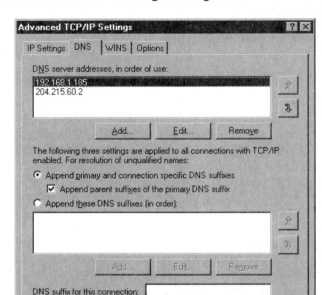

To prevent the client from registering directly with the DDNS server, you must alter the default settings. Figure 12.1 shows the Advanced TCP/IP Settings dialog box.

You can remove the checkmark for "Register this connection's addresses in DNS." This will prevent the computer's FQDN as defined in the Network Identification tab in the System Properties dialog box from registering directly with DDNS. The second option, "Use this connection's DNS suffix in DNS registration," refers to entries made in the "Append these DNS suffixes (in order)" text box, or those assigned to the specific network connection via DHCP. Each network connection can be customized to provide its own DNS name information. Removing the checkmark from both of these prevents the client from registering directly with the Dynamic DNS server.

We now know what happens when dealing with pure Windows 2000 clients and servers. However, downlevel clients are not able to communicate A record information to a DDNS server. In this case, the DHCP server acts as a proxy and forwards both Address and PTR information to the DDNS server.

Windows 2000 computers configured with static IP addresses will update their own A and PTR records with the DDNS server. If you change the name or IP address of a Windows 2000 client that has a static IP address, you can manually update that client's entry in the DDNS server by issuing the command:

ipconfig /registerdns

Downlevel clients with static IP addresses are not able to communicate directly with the DDNS server. DDNS entries for these clients must be manually reconfigured at the DDNS server.

What Are Leases?

A lease is an agreement to let someone use something for a specified period. The DHCP client leases IP addressing information from the DHCP server, and in accordance with the definition of a lease, it does not keep this information forever. This allows the DHCP server to maintain a dynamic pool of IP addresses. The lease process prevents computers no longer on the network from retaining IP addresses that could otherwise be returned to the pool and assigned to other computers.

The length of the lease is defined at the DHCP server. The default lease period on a Windows 2000 DHCP server is eight days. This can be changed, depending on the needs of the Network Administrator.

A DHCP client must renew its lease. The DHCPOFFER and DHCPACK messages include the amount of time a client is allowed to keep its IP address. Also included are times when the client will be required to renew its lease. The DHCPOFFER message includes the lease period, a Renewal Time Value (T1), and the Rebinding Time Value (T2).

The Renewal Time Value represents 50% of the lease period. At this time, the DHCP client will attempt to renew its IP address by broadcasting a DHCPREQUEST message containing its current IP address. If the DHCP server that granted the IP address is available, it will renew the IP address for the period specified in the renewed lease. If the DHCP server is not available, the client will continue to use its lease, since it still has 50% of the lease period remaining.

The Rebinding Time Value represents 87.5% of the lease period. The client will attempt to renew its IP address at this time only if it was not able to renew its lease at the Renewal Time. The client broadcasts a DHCPREQUEST message. If the server that granted the IP address does not respond, the client will enter the Rebinding State and begin the DHCPDISCOVER process, attempting to renew its IP address with any DHCP server. If it cannot renew its IP address, it will try to receive a new one from any responding DHCP server. If unsuccessful, TCP/IP services are shut down on that computer.

Leasing Strategy

How you time your leases depends upon the level of dynamism of your network or network segments. The default lease period is eight days for Windows 2000 DHCP servers, though this can be reconfigured as required. Lease periods are configured on a per-scope basis. Increase the lease duration for segments that do not add or remove clients frequently. Segments that have an excess of IP addresses benefit from extended lease periods. The amount of network traffic due to DHCP broadcasts can be reduced by lengthening the lease period. Extended lease periods also allow the Network Administrator more time to fix a downed DHCP server before client leases begin to expire.

Shorten the default lease duration from the default if you have segments that see many computers joining and leaving on a frequent basis. The typical example is that of a Sales division with many laptop users joining and leaving the network. It would not take much time to exhaust all of the available IP addresses for that scope if their segment had a long lease period. The truncated lease period allows the DHCP server to rapidly reclaim IP addresses from computers that have left the network. Segments that have a narrow required/available IP address ratio benefit from shortened IP lease durations. This maximizes the chance of a computer gaining a lease when the number of available IP addresses is tight.

The definition of long and short lease periods is debatable. However, consensus dictates that lease periods of 30–60 days are adequate for stable networks, while highly volatile networks might require lease periods of 24 hours or less. Be aware that more broadcast traffic is generated when lease intervals are shortened.

Operating without a DHCP Server

A TCP/IP network does not require a DHCP server. The DHCP server provides the convenience of IP address allocation and management. In small or very stable networks (such as home or SOHO locations), DHCP server functionality does not enhance ease of use.

Problems commonly associated with decentralized management of IP addressing information include assigning multiple machines the same IP address or misconfiguring TCP/IP parameters such as WINS, DNS, or default gateway.

If you choose not to use a DHCP server, Windows 2000 clients can avoid the problem of duplicate IP addressing by using Automatic Private IP Addressing (APIPA).

Automatic Client Configuration

Automatic Client Configuration, or APIPA, allows Windows 2000 computers configured as DHCP clients to assign their own IP addresses. This technology is available on Windows 98SE clients and is now part of Windows 2000. A Windows 2000 DHCP client unable to contact a DHCP server may assign itself an IP address.

There are two scenarios where APIPA is useful. The first scenario occurs when the machine has not previously bound an IP address. In this case:

1. The Windows 2000 computer configured as a DHCP client starts up. A DHCPDISCOVER message is broadcast to the segment. If the machine does not receive a reply, it will attempt to autoconfigure its IP address.

2. The machine will select, at random, an IP address from the Microsoft reserved Class B network ID 169.254.0.0 with the default Class B subnet mask of 255.255.0.0.

3. A gratuitous ARP message will be broadcast for this randomly selected IP address. If no machine responds to the ARP request, the machine will bind the new IP address to the network adapter configured as a DHCP client.

4. If a machine responds to the ARP request, the self-configuring computer will choose another IP address and issue another ARP request. It will continue this process for up to 10 addresses. If the machine cannot configure an IP address after 10 attempts, it will stop and disable TCP/IP.

If a DHCP client that has an active lease starts up and cannot contact a DHCP server, the process is a little different.

1. When the DHCP client with a valid lease starts up, it will issue a DHCPREQUEST broadcast to renew the lease.

2. If the client does not receive a DHCPACK from the DHCP server, it will start to ping the IP address of the default gateway configured in its lease.

3. If the default gateway responds, the machine "assumes" there must be a problem with the DHCP server itself. The DHCP client attempts to renew its lease at 50% and 87.5% of the lease period.

4. If the default gateway fails to respond to the ping, the machine assumes it has been moved. In this case, the machine will abandon its lease and autoconfigure itself as described previously.

In both cases, the DHCP client will issue a DHCPDISCOVER message every five minutes in an attempt to contact a DHCP server. If the client receives a DHCPOFFER message at any time, it will bind a valid IP address from the DHCP server sending the offer.

Windows 2000 DHCP computers communicate with NDIS 5.0 compliant NIC drivers to obtain information about network connection status. This media sense capability allows the operating system to detect whether the computer has been removed from the network. If the operating system senses the computer has been removed from a network and plugged into another, it will begin the lease renewal and autoconfiguration process.

A DHCP client can be configured to not autoconfigure. To suppress autoconfiguration, find the following Registry key:

HKEY_LOCAL_MAHCINE\SYSTEM\CurrentControlSet\Services\Tcpip\Interfaces\adapter_name

Once there, add the following value:

IPAutoconfigurationEnabled: REG_DWORD
Set the value to 0

Keep in mind that APIPA is only useful on single segment networks where all machines are using APIPA. Otherwise, the self-configuring machines will assign themselves to a different network ID than the other clients on the segment.

Manual IP Addresses

The Administrator can completely forgo DHCP and Automatic Client Configuration and manually set IP addressing information on all the computers on the network. Elements that require configuration include IP address, subnet mask, default gateway, WINS address, DNS address, alternate DNS address, NetBIOS node type, and many others.

In a large installation with thousands of computers, the manual IP addressing method is a prescription for error. IP addressing information must then be tracked by manual methods. This can be done with the help of tools such as Microsoft Access or Excel. If the network team coordinates their efforts and is assiduous in recording TCP/IP information in a spreadsheet or database, this solution may be viable.

The vast majority of enterprise networks use DHCP for systemwide IP address assignment and configuration. This avoids the overhead of manual record keeping and attendant human error.

Design of a DHCP Configuration

Optimal placement of DHCP servers across the organization is pivotal to successful DHCP deployment. When planning the locations for DHCP servers, it is vital to consider the following:

- DHCP messages are broadcasts.
- Broadcasts do not traverse routers without special configuration.
- DHCP servers do not share information with each other, unlike WINS.
- DHCP server location must be done with these issues firmly in mind.

Placement of Servers

The simplest setup is the nonrouted, single-segment network. A single segment will likely represent a single network ID. A single scope on a solitary DHCP server is all that is required. Unless otherwise noted in this text, segment and subnet will be used synonymously.

The complexity of the DHCP server placement problem increases with the number of segments on the network. Allowance must be made for the fact that DHCP messages are broadcast-based. One solution is to put a DHCP server on each segment. This obviates the need for broadcast messages to traverse routers. This solution can be costly and manpower intensive if there are a large number of subnets to be managed. This distributed approach will complicate issues for the Administrator who seeks a more centralized management solution.

However, for a small network consisting of only two or three segments, you might consider placing a server on each segment. In this case, enabling the DHCP service and creating a scope would be a simple task that requires nominal administration.

Another option is to use fewer DHCP servers and place these machines in central locations. To solve the problem of broadcast management, routers can be configured to pass DHCP/BOOTP messages selectively. If one cannot or will not change router configurations, then placing a DHCP Relay Agent on each segment allows DHCP clients and server to communicate. The Relay Agent will communicate with a DHCP server and act as a proxy for DHCP messages sent to remote segments.

Link speed is an important issue in DHCP server placement. If you choose to locate the DHCP server remotely from the DHCP clients, you need a fast, reliable path between them. Segments separated by WAN links are typically slower than intranet connections. At least one DHCP server should be placed on each WAN link for performance and fault-tolerance reasons.

Using DHCP Routers or DHCP Relay Agents

Routers that conform to RFC 2132 (which supercedes 1542) can be configured to pass DHCP/BOOTP broadcast messages. These broadcast packets pass through UDP Port 67. This is known as BOOTP/DHCP relay. Most modern routers support BOOTP/DHCP relay. If your router does not, contact the router manufacturer for a software or firmware upgrade.

If you cannot upgrade routers to support BOOTP/DHCP messages, you can engage a Windows NT or Windows 2000 server to become a DCHP Relay Agent. The DHCP Relay Agent will listen for DHCP broadcast messages and forward these to a DHCP server on a remote subnet. When the remote DHCP server receives the messages from the DHCP Relay Agent, it forwards replies to the source subnet and requesting client.

The details of this exchange when an RFC-compliant router acts as a Relay Agent are:

1. The DHCP client broadcasts a DHCPDISCOVER message.

2. The DHCP Relay Agent intercepts the message. In the message header, there is a field for the gateway IP address. If the field is 0.0.0.0, the Relay Agent will insert its own IP address.

3. The DHCP Relay Agent forwards the DHCPDISCOVER message to the remote DHCP server.

4. When the DHCPDISCOVER message arrives at the DHCP server, the service examines the gateway IP address (giaddr). The server determines whether it has a scope for the network ID specified in the giaddr.

5. The DHCP server prepares a lease for the client, and issues a DHCPOFFER message directly to the address included in the giaddr.

6. Since the client does not yet have an IP address, the local router interface broadcasts the DHCPOFFER to the subnet.

7. The same processes take place for the DHCPREQUEST and DHCPACK messages.

RRAS Integration

The Routing and Remote Access Service (RRAS) is able to call upon a DHCP server to assign IP addresses to RRAS clients. The RRAS server acts as a proxy between the RRAS client and the DHCP server. The way the RRAS server uses the DHCP server to distribute IP addresses is different from the way LAN clients receive their IP address information.

If the RRAS server is configured to use DHCP to assign IP addresses, it will obtain a group of IP addresses from the DHCP server in a block. This block of IP addresses is obtained when RRAS services initialize. RRAS clients do not directly receive information from the DHCP server. The number of IP addresses retrieved is equal to the number of RAS ports configured on the RRAS server plus one. The RRAS server itself uses the additional IP address.

The IP addressing information available to RRAS clients is limited compared to LAN DHCP clients. When the RRAS server obtains its group of IP addresses, any option information sent from the DHCP server to the RRAS server is ignored. Typical DHCP option parameters such as WINS and DNS server IP addresses are obtained from the specific RRAS connection itself. Each RRAS connection can be independently configured.

The RRAS client lease is different from the LAN client lease. There is no effective lease period for the RRAS client. The lease immediately expires after the connection is terminated. You can perform an ipconfig on the client machine to see DHCP configuration parameters the RRAS server has assigned.

Configuring a DHCP Server

A DHCP server becomes functional after a pool of IP addresses is made available to DHCP clients. The DHCP server is able to deliver, when so configured, additional information to DHCP clients. DHCP messages are broadcasts, which do not cross routers by default.

We will examine these issues in this section on configuring a DHCP server. Other topics include how a DHCP server provides information to BOOTP clients, the new Vendor and User Class options, and superscopes.

DHCP Scopes

A scope defines a range or pool of IP addresses. A single scope includes all the IP addresses that may be made available to DHCP clients on a single subnet. Only one scope can be created for each subnet. A single DHCP server can manage several scopes. The server itself does not need to be local to all scopes it services. Remote hosts can access the DHCP server via RFC-compliant routers or DHCP Relay Agents.

Each scope must consist of at least the following elements:

- Scope name
- Start and end IP address
- Lease duration
- Subnet mask

The scope typically includes all available IP addresses for the network ID or subnetwork ID. An exception to this is when the available addresses are split among DHCP servers to provide fault tolerance for the scope. If you have clients with static IP addresses, such as WINS, DNS, or other DHCP servers, you can configure a range of excluded IP addresses. These excluded IP addresses are removed from the scope and are not available for distribution.

Creating a new scope in Windows 2000 is a much easier task because it is wizard-driven. Most configuration options are included in the wizard, which helps the Administrator define and configure the scope.

At the end of this chapter, we will perform a walkthrough on the steps involved in creating a new scope.

Configuring Leases

A lease contains all information provided to the client by the DHCP server. The lease is not permanent, unless you wish to create a permanent lease assignment. The default lease period is eight days for a Windows 2000 DHCP server.

Leases periods should remain short for volatile networks. Longer lease periods are appropriate for stable networks where new clients are not added frequently.

DHCP Options

The DHCP server can deliver to the DHCP client more information than just an IP address and subnet mask. Configuration details such as the IP address of the WINS server, DNS server, and default gateway can be included in a client lease. These additional configuration details are referred to as DHCP options.

There are several levels of DHCP options. These include:

- Server Options
- Scope Options
- Client Options
- Vendor Class or User Class Options

Each level shares a similar set of DHCP Options. There are a large number of options available in the Windows 2000 DHCP server. Microsoft client operating systems support a small number of these options. Of the standard set of DHCP options, Microsoft clients support:

003 Router   The IP address of the default gateway.

006 DNS   The IP address of the DNS server.

015 Domain Name   The DNS domain name the client should use.

044 WINS/NBNS Servers   The IP address of the WINS server.

046 WINS/NBT Node Type   The NetBIOS node type.

047 NetBIOS Scope ID   The NetBIOS scope ID.

Each of these options is configured at the DHCP server. Let's now look at the different option levels and see how to configure options for each level.

Server Options

Server Options apply to all scopes on a single DHCP server. For example, you have three scopes on your DHCP server for the following network IDs:

192.168.1.0

192.168.2.0

192.168.3.0

Assume that the WINS server address is configured to 192.168.1.16. Clients receiving their lease from any of these scopes will be given the same WINS server address.

To configure Server Options:

1. Open the DHCP management console.

2. In the left pane, expand the server name, and then click on the Server Options folder. If there are any existing Server Options, they will appear in the right pane.

Figure 12.2 Setting Server Options.

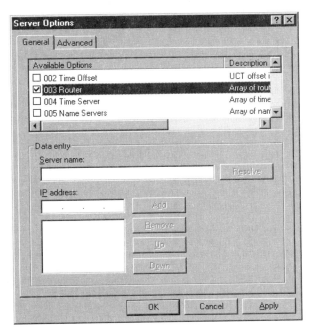

3. Right-click on the Server Options folder, and select Configure Options. A dialog box similar to Figure 12.2 should be displayed.

4. Select the desired option and put a checkmark in the box. The Data entry pane will change to allow configuration of the option. When completed, click APPLY and then OK to close the dialog box.

Scope Options

Scope Options allow the specification of DHCP Options that apply to a single scope. For example, you want the default gateway to be on the same subnet as the clients. Therefore, a different default gateway is configured for each scope. It wouldn't make much sense to assign the same default gateway to all the scopes.

To configure Scope Options:

1. Open the DHCP management console.

2. In the left pane, expand the server name, and then expand the Scope folder. You will need to already have a scope in place to do this. Right-click on the Scope Options folder, and then click Configure Options.

3. Select and configure options as described previously.

Client Options

Client Options are assigned to computers configured to receive the same IP address from the DHCP server each time the client starts. This client is also known as a reserved client. Creating reserved clients allows you to assign functionally "static" IP addresses to computers that require these, such as WINS and DNS servers. DHCP servers also require a static IP address. However, the DHCP server itself cannot be a DHCP client. Client Reservations allow you to centrally manage IP addressing information on machines that might otherwise require manual configuration.

To create a Client Reservation, perform the following steps:

1. Open the DHCP management console.

2. In the left pane, expand the server name, and then expand the Scope folder. You will need to already have a scope in place to do this. Click on the Reservations folder.

3. Right-click on the Reservations folder, and select New Reservation.

4. In the New Reservation dialog box, enter the following information:

   Reservation name   The host name of the computer.

   IP address   The IP address of the computer.

   MAC address   The Media Access Control address (do not include dashes).

   Description   An optional field to describe the reserved client.

   Support types   Indicate whether this reservation is for a DHCP client, a BOOTP client, or both.

5. Click Add to complete the operation, then click Close.

A reserved client's IP address must be included in an existing scope. Some Administrators conclude that since the reserved client's IP address is not available to any other client, they should exclude its IP address. That is not correct. Client Options can be now be configured. To create Client Options:

1. Open the DHCP management console.

2. In the left pane, expand the server name, expand the Scope folder, and then expand the Reservations folder. You need to have a scope in place to do this. Right-click on the name of the Client Reservation you want to configure options, and then click Configure Options.

3. Continue adding options as described previously.

DHCP Options Order of Precedence

There is an order of precedence that applies when conflicts arise among DHCP options. This order is:

1. Client Options
2. Scope Options
3. Server Options

Should a conflict arise among the options delivered to the client, Client Options will override Scope Options, and Scope Options will override Server Options.

BOOTP/DCHP Relay Agent

The Routing and Remote Access Service must be installed prior to configuring the DHCP Relay Agent. After installing RRAS, open the Routing and Remote Access console, expand the server name, expand the IP routing node, then click on the DHCP Relay Agent node. In the right pane, you will see a list of interfaces listening for DHCP broadcasts. Double-click on the interface of choice. The Internal Properties dialog box should then be displayed.

Put a checkmark in the Relay DHCP Packets box to enable DHCP Relay. The Hop Count Threshold allows you to configure the number of DHCP Relay Agents that determines the number of hops a DHCP message can take before being discarded. This prevents DHCP messages from looping endlessly throughout the network. The maximum setting is 16.

The Boot Threshold defines the number of seconds the Relay Agent waits before forwarding DHCP messages. This option is useful if you are using a combination of local and remote DHCP servers, as in the case of fault-tolerant setups. The Relay Agent should forward DHCP messages only if the local server becomes unavailable. This setting helps prevent a flood of routed DHCP packets. Do not implement both a DHCP Relay Agent and RFC-compliant router pass-through. If you choose the DHCP Relay option, reconnoiter your network and disable BOOTP/DHCP forwarding on your routers to minimize pass-through broadcast traffic.

Vendor-Specific Options

RFCs 2131 and 2132 define vendor classes, which allow hardware and software vendors to add their own options to the DHCP server. If a manufacturer wants custom DHCP options sent to the DHCP client, this custom option information can be made available when the DHCP client initializes and requests IP a lease from the DHCP server. A DHCP client can be configured to send vendor class identification to the DHCP server. The DHCP server will recognize the vendor's class identifiers and forward the vendor-configured options to the client.

The Vendor Options must be installed and configured on the DHCP server. Microsoft has included Vendor Class Options for Windows 2000 and Windows 98 clients, as well as a generic Microsoft Operating System Vendor Class. The latter is used to deliver DHCP options to any Microsoft operating system that includes "SFT" as a client identifier during the client initialization.

Microsoft vendor-specific options include:

Disable NetBIOS over TCP/IP (NetBT)   Allows an option to be sent to the client to disable NetBT.

Release DHCP lease on shutdown   Informs the client to release its lease on shutdown. This could be used with laptop computers that move on and off the network frequently. This will free up IP addresses in the scope.

Default router metric base   Sets the default base metric for the DHCP client. This value is used to calculate the fastest and least expensive routes.

Proxy autodiscovery   Used only by clients that have Internet Explorer 5.0. This option informs the client of the location of the Internet Explorer 5.0 automatic configuration file.

The Administrator cannot create the Vendor Class Options provided by the hardware or software vendor. The Administrator can implement these options when available.

User Class Options

User Classes are part of a proposed Internet Standard under consideration by the Internet Engineer Task Force (IETF). User Classes allow DHCP clients to identify their class membership to a DHCP server. The server can then return to the client a specific set of options relevant to the class.

Prior to implementing User Classes, you must define the Class at the DHCP server. For example, you could classify a group of computers, which should use a specific IP address, subnet mask, and default gateway, as portable by first creating the portable class at the DHCP server. Then define DHCP Options at the server, which will be returned to any client that identifies itself as a member of the portable class. Next, configure the client to use the class, by issuing the ipconfig /setclassid command at the client.

Microsoft has included some built-in classes that are available out of the box, including Users Classes with special options for BOOTP and Remote Access Clients.

TIP

Scope Options override Server Options, Client Options override Scope Options, and User Class Options override all other options. For example, if we have a machine with a Client Reservation, this machine's reserved Client Options will override any other options that might be set for the server or for the scope. However, if the reserved client identifies itself as a member of a certain User Class, the User Class Options will override any reserved Client Options that are in conflict.

To create a new User Class:

1. In the DHCP management console, right-click on the server name, and then click on Define User Classes.
2. The DHCP User Classes dialog box appears. Click ADD. The New Class dialog box should then be displayed.
3. Enter the display name of the class, and a description. To enter the User Class ID in ASCII, click on the right side of the lowest text box under ASCII and type in the Class ID. This is the Class ID you will use with the ipconfig command on the clients to configure them to send their class membership to the DHCP server.
4. Click OK, and then click CLOSE to close the DHCP User Classes dialog box.

At the client machine, type in the following command to have the client identify itself as a member of the class:

ipconfig /setclassid adapter [classidtoset]

User Options allow a greater level of granularity in the assignment of DHCP Options. This improved granularity gives the Administrator greater control over the TCP/IP parameters configured on the DHCP clients in his or her network.

BOOTP Tables

BOOTP (Bootstrap Protocol) is the predecessor to DHCP. It was originally designed to provide IP address configuration of diskless workstations that booted from the server. DHCP was developed to improve on the host configuration services offered by BOOTP, and address some of the problems encountered in using it.

Similarities between DHCP and BOOTP

Because DHCP is based on BOOTP, they are alike in many ways. For instance, the request and reply messages they use are basically the same, using one 576-byte UDP datagram for each message. The headers are almost the same as well, although there is a slight difference in the final message header field that carries optional data: it is called the vendor-specific area in BOOTP, whereas DHCP calls it the options field. The size of the field differs, too; the vendor-specific area is only 64 octets, while the DHCP options field can hold as much as 312 bytes of information.

Another aspect that the two protocols have in common is the use of the same UDP ports for communication between server and client. UDP 67 is used for receiving client messages, and UDP 68 is used to accept replies from a server.

Because of these similarities, Relay Agents generally don't distinguish between BOOTP and DHCP packets, and treat them both the same.

Differences between DHCP and BOOTP

Despite the similarities noted in the preceding section, there are some important differences between the two host configuration protocols. The IP address allocation methods are not alike—BOOTP normally allocates one IP address per client, which it permanently reserves in its database on the BOOTP server. DHCP, as its name implies, leases addresses dynamically, assigning an address to the client from a pool of available addresses and only temporarily reserving it in the server's database.

Many of the differences between BOOTP and DHCP stem from the difference in intended purpose. Unlike BOOTP, DHCP was originally designed to configure addressing information for computers with hard drives from which they could boot, especially laptops and other computers that are moved frequently.

Due to this, BOOTP uses a two-phase configuration process, in which client computers first contact a BOOTP server for address assignment, and then contact a TFTP (Trivial File Transfer Protocol) server to transfer their boot image files to boot the operating system. DHCP clients, which are capable of booting from their own hard drives, use a one-phase configuration process; the client negotiates a leased IP address from the DHCP server, which contains any other needed TCP/IP configuration details (such as subnet mask, default gateway, DNS and WINS server addresses).

Another difference is that BOOTP clients must restart in order to renew the configuration with the server. DHCP clients, however, can automatically renew their leases with the DHCP servers at preset intervals. It is valuable for a Windows 2000 Administrator to be aware of the characteristics of BOOTP, since it is the foundation upon which automatic host configuration was founded.

Superscopes

Microsoft recommends the use of superscopes when more than one DHCP server is present on a subnet. A superscope is a Windows 2000 DHCP feature that lets you use more than one scope for a subnet. The superscope contains multiple child scopes, grouped together under one name and manageable as one entity. The situations in which superscopes should be used include:

- When many DHCP clients are added to a network.
- When the IP addresses on a network must be renumbered.
- When two (or more) DHCP servers are located on the same subnet for fault-tolerance purposes.

Using superscopes gives the Administrator the flexibility to support DHCP clients in multinet configurations. A multinet is a network configuration in which multiple logical networks reside on the same physical segment. The Administrator is able to activate the individual scope ranges of IP addresses used on the network, and provide leases from multiple scopes to the DHCP clients on the same physical network.

Superscopes are valuable in situations where the available DHCP addresses have almost been used up, and there are additional computers that need to join the network. Using a superscope will allow you to extend the address space for the network segment. In this situation, you can create a superscope with two child scopes: the original scope of addresses that is almost depleted, and a new scope for the additional computers that need to join the network.

Windows 2000 includes a New Superscope Wizard that guides you through the process. To start the wizard, access the DHCP management console (Start | Programs | Administrative Tools | DHCP), right-click on the server name, and select New superscope from the context menu.

Managing DHCP Servers

Managing DHCP servers is easier and more efficient than ever. Windows 2000 DHCP servers include Enhanced Monitoring and Statistical Reporting, as well as Rogue DHCP Server Detection.

Enhanced Monitoring and Statistical Reporting for DHCP Servers

The Windows 2000 DHCP server supports enhanced ease of use and more statistical counters compared to its Windows NT counterpart. You can view DHCP statistics such as the number of Discovers, Offers, Requests, Acks, and Declines by viewing them through a window in the DHCP management console.

The Performance console contains DHCP objects counters, including Informs/sec, Nacks/sec, Offers/sec, Releases/sec, and Requests/sec as shown in Figure 12.3.

Authorizing DHCP Servers

DHCPDISCOVER is a broadcast message, which means it is indiscriminate. If an unofficial DHCP server is introduced to the network, an error in IP address assignment can occur. A rogue DHCP server (a DHCP server that has not been approved by the IT department) is likely to contain invalid scopes and DHCP options. Rogue DHCP servers can assign inaccurate IP addressing information to DHCP clients, which may disrupt network communications for these hapless clients.

Windows 2000 networks running only Windows 2000 DHCP servers can recognize and stop the DHCP Server service on rogue DHCP servers, by keeping a list of authorized DHCP servers in the Active Directory. Any DHCP server that starts up and is not included in the authorized list will be shut down automatically.

Figure 12.3 The Add Counters dialog box.

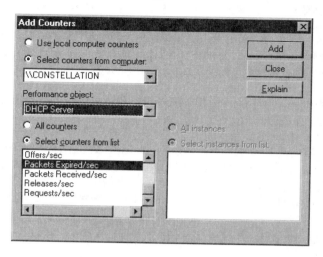

Only Windows 2000 DHCP servers can detect rouge DHCP servers, and the rogue DHCP server must be a Windows 2000 computer. Rogue DHCP server detection will fail to detect an unauthorized Windows NT DHCP server.

How Rogue DHCP Servers Are Detected

When a Windows 2000 DHCP server initializes, it broadcasts a DHCPINFORM message to the local segment. The DHCPINFORM message contains vendor-specific option codes that can be interpreted by Microsoft Windows 2000 DHCP servers. These option types allow the Windows 2000 DHCP server to obtain information about the network from other Windows 2000 DHCP servers on the segment.

The DHCPINFORM message submits queries to other Windows 2000 DHCP servers, and when a Windows 2000 DHCP server on the segment receives this message, it responds to a DHCPINFORM query. This query asks for information about the Enterprise root name and location. The queried Windows 2000 DHCP server responds by sending back a DHCPACK that includes Directory Services Enterprise Root information.

NOTE

The new DHCP server will receive DHCPACK messages from all the DHCP servers on its segment. This allows the new DHCP server to collect domain membership information about all Windows 2000 DHCP servers on its segment.

If the new DHCP server receives information about an existing Directory Services Enterprise Root, it will query the Active Directory, which maintains a list of DHCP servers that are authorized to participate in the domain. If the machine's IP address is on the list, it will successfully initialize DHCP server services. If not, DHCP server services will not initialize. The new DHCP server will start DHCP server services if:

- There are other DHCP servers on the segment that are authorized DHCP servers, and the new DHCP server is listed in the Active Directory's list of authorized DHCP servers, or
- The new DHCP server is the only DHCP server on the segment (if the new DHCP server does not receive a response to the DHCPINFORM message query, the new DHCP server cannot be made aware of existing Directory Services Enterprise Roots), or
- The new DHCP server is on a segment with other Windows 2000 DHCP servers that are workgroup members, or all other DHCP servers on the segments are downlevel systems (such as Windows NT DHCP servers).

In the second and third instances, the new DHCP server is unable to contact another DHCP server that has information about a Directory Services Enterprise Root. The lone DHCP server will send a DHCPINFORM message every five minutes. If the new DHCP server later receives a DHCPACK from a DHCP server that contains information about the Enterprise Root, the new DHCP server will look to see if it is authorized in the Active Directory, and if not, will disable its DHCP server services.

Authorizing a DHCP Server

A new DHCP server must be authorized to issue addresses in the Active Directory. This exercise runs through the procedure for authorizing a DHCP server.

1. Open the DHCP management console.
2. Right-click on the computer name, and click on Authorize (Figure 12.4).

The DHCP server is now authorized. To confirm that the DHCP server was successfully authorized in the Active Directory, perform the following steps:

1. Log on as Administrator at a DC in the domain that the DHCP server was authorized in.
2. Open the Active Directory Sites and Services management console. Right-click on the top level and select the View menu. Click on Show services node. A Services node should now be displayed in the left pane.

Figure 12.4 Using the DHCP MMC to authorize your new DHCP server.

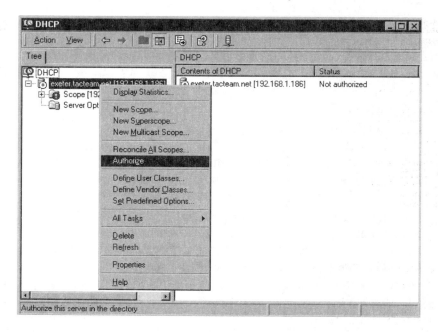

3. Expand the Services node, and click on the folder NetServices. In the right pane, the Fully Qualified Domain Name (FQDN) of the newly authorized DHCP server with the type DHCPClass should be visible. In Figure 12.5, exeter.tacteam.net has been authorized.

Deploying DHCP

Several factors to consider when deploying a DHCP solution in an enterprise network are related to its physical configuration. Important considerations include:

- The number of physical segments on the network
- Options you want to deliver to the DHCP clients
- Where WAN links connect network segments

Within a LAN environment, a single DHCP server can service multiple physical segments. You can place a DHCP Relay Agent on segments that do not house a DHCP server; however, segments without a DHCP server can be negatively impacted if intersegment traffic is interrupted.

If segments are joined by WAN links, it is a good idea to place a DHCP server on each side of the link. WAN links tend to be frail and less reliable than LAN connections. Placing a DHCP server on both sides of the WAN will insure more reliable lease assignment.

Figure 12.5 Finding the FQDN of your newly authorized DHCP server.

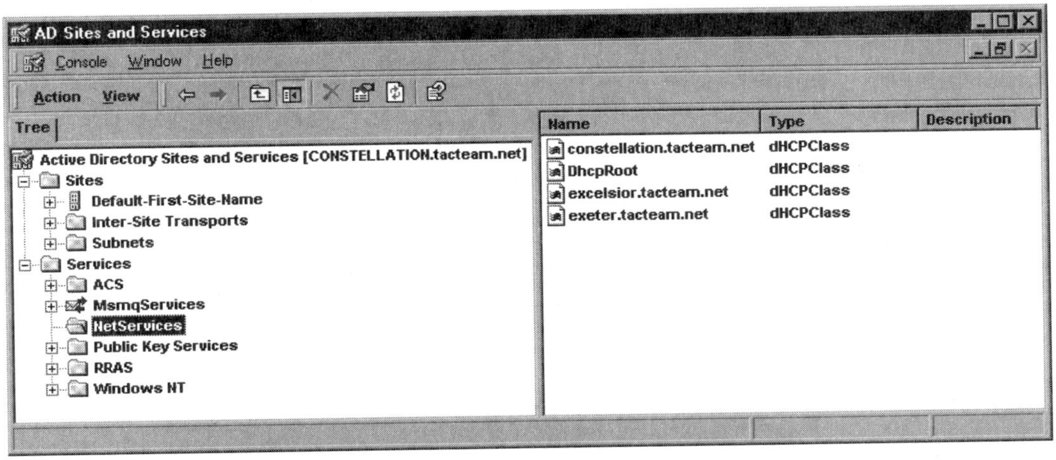

The success of a DHCP deployment depends, to a large degree, on planning. You should determine beforehand what DHCP Options need to be assigned to each DHCP scope, as well as any Global Options that should be assigned. You should also decide in advance what computers will require Client Reservations and what blocks of IP addresses should be configured from the scope.

DHCP, when properly deployed, can reduce administrative headaches, decrease the time spent on TCP/IP configuration, prevent configuration errors that occur when addresses are entered manually on each client, and help you avoid the problem of IP address conflict. Windows 2000 makes it easier than ever to administer DHCP services with the management console, which integrates the DHCP administration tools into one centralized location. Windows 2000 also includes command-line DHCP tools.

TIP

Remember that the DHCP server itself cannot be a DHCP client; it must be manually configured with a static IP address and other TCP/IP configuration information.

Best Practices

Windows 2000 DHCP server allows DHCP to be customized on a per-network basis. Optimum DHCP lease assignment depends on the size of the network, its physical characteristics (routed or nonrouted), and the nature of its client connections (for example, whether there are remote access clients using DHCP).

Microsoft provides some guidelines and recommendations for the most effective and efficient implementation of DHCP in typical network configurations.

Optimizing Lease Management Practices

The default lease duration of eight days strikes a good medium for most networks. You can customize this value to optimize performance based on the unique characteristics of each network. The Administrator can change the lease duration on a per-scope basis. In this section, we will examine when it is advantageous to lengthen or shorten the lease period.

Lengthening Lease Duration

Windows 2000's DHCP server configuration allows you to change the duration of the leases. If the network is extremely stable, and especially if it consists of multiple physical LANs connected by routers, it may be beneficial to increase the duration of the leases beyond the default (eight days). The overall amount of DHCP-related broadcast traffic on the network could be reduced by providing longer lease periods. Extended lease periods can range from 9 to 60 days, depending on the nature of change on your network.

This solution should be used only if there are plenty of extra scope addresses available, to ensure that the longer lease duration doesn't result in a shortage of addresses when the clients "hold on to" their leases for an increased period.

NOTE

It is possible to set the lease duration for an infinite time, but this is not generally recommended.

Shortening Lease Duration

Conversely, when your supply of available IP addresses in the DHCP scope is limited, or if your client configurations are not fixed (such as when computers often change location), it may be best to decrease the lease duration so that addresses are returned to the pool more quickly.

There are also special situations in which you can optimize performance by reducing the duration of the lease for certain clients; for example, when you have a segment that sees a lot of laptop computers entering and exiting the segment. In this way, their leases will be released more quickly to be available for assignment to other DHCP clients. Another situation in which you would benefit from temporarily shortening the lease period is if you plan to reconfigure the IP infrastructure of the network (such as changing WINS, DNS, or domain controller IP addresses).

You can create a User Class for laptop computers, as discussed previously.

> **NOTE**
>
> Remember that RRAS clients obtain their address lease through the RRAS server, which receives a group of addresses from the DHCP server to distribute to its clients, and the RRAS server can specify options to the clients that use these proxied leases. RRAS clients do not obtain Option information from a DHCP server.

Determining the Number of DHCP Servers to Use

The number of clients, segments, and WAN links in the organization determines the optimum number of DHCP servers. There is no hard-and-fast rule regarding the exact number of servers required, and there is no theoretical limit on the number of clients a single DHCP server can service. However, DHCP is very disk and CPU intensive. It is recommended that you use the performance console to assess how your machines are impacted by DHCP services, and add DHCP servers as required.

A DHCP server should definitely be in place on each side of a WAN or dial-up link, since these links can be slow or unreliable.

If DHCP servers service remote segments, do not put all of the servers on the same segment. Placing them in different segments will prevent failure of DHCP services if the single segment is isolated from the rest of the network.

Fault-Tolerant Planning

DHCP fault tolerance can be achieved by providing for more than one DHCP server on each subnet. This gives the DHCP clients a backup, so that if one server becomes unavailable, the other will still be able to grant new leases or renew existing ones.

A good rule of thumb for balancing the load between the servers is the 80/20 Rule. This DHCP design standard recommends that, when spreading a single scope of addresses between two DHCP servers, you should have one server distribute 80% of the addresses, and have the second server distribute the other 20%.

Router Support Required

If you chose to enable pass-through of DHCP messages, you will require a router that is RFC 2132 compliant. Most modern routers support DCHP Relay and can be configured to do so based on the individual router's manufacturer's instructions.

However, older routers may not include software or firmware that support DHCP Relay. If this is the case, first try contacting the router manufacturer to obtain a software upgrade. You may need to purchase new routers if no upgrade is available. The alternative is to use a Windows NT or Window 2000 computer as a DHCP Relay Agent.

DHCP Walkthroughs

This section contains a number of walkthroughs for common DHCP activities such as installation and configuration.

Installing a DHCP Server

Follow this procedure to install the DHCP Service:

1. Log on as Administrator and open the Control Panel.
2. Open the Add/Remove Programs applet, and select the Add/Remove Windows Components icon.
3. The Windows Components Wizard is then launched. Scroll down to the Networking Services option. Highlight it, but do not remove the checkmark from the check box.
4. Click DETAILS in the Windows Components Wizard dialog box. Place a check in the box next to Dynamic Host Configuration Protocol. Then click OK.
5. After clicking OK, you are returned to the Windows Components Wizard dialog box. Click NEXT.
6. When the installation of the DHCP server software is complete, you will be notified of a successful installation. Click FINISH.
7. Close the Add/Remove Programs dialog box.

Creating Leases

To create leases, a scope must be created and configured. Windows 2000 includes a Create New Scope Wizard, that greatly simplifies the process. In this walkthrough, we will create a new scope using the wizard.

1. Click Start | Programs | Administrative Tools | DHCP.
2. Expand all levels in the left pane displaying the server name and a folder for Server Options.

3. Authorize the server if you have not already done so. Follow the procedure detailed earlier to authorize your server. After authorization, the server status will be labeled running.

4. Click on the computer's name, taking notice of the toolbar changes.

5. To create a new scope for network ID 192.168.2.0 with a subnet mask of 255.255.255.0 (the default Class C subnet mask, which uses 24 bits), either right-click on the computer's name and select New Scope, or click on the rightmost icon in the toolbar (it looks like a video screen).

6. This opens the New Scope Wizard and the Welcome screen. Click NEXT.

7. Enter the name of the scope and a description that may serve as a reminder of some of the characteristics of the machines using the scope. Click NEXT.

8. Enter the first and last IP addresses in the range of addresses this scope will hand out. Include the appropriate subnet mask. Enter 192.168.2.1 as the Start IP address and 192.168.2.254 as the End IP address as seen in Figure 12.6. Click NEXT.

9. The wizard provides the facility to exclude some IP addresses from the range defined earlier. To exclude the bottom 5 and top 10 IP addresses, enter the Start IP address 192.168.2.1 and the End IP address 192.168.2.5, and then click ADD. Enter the Start IP address

Figure 12.6 Defining the scope address range.

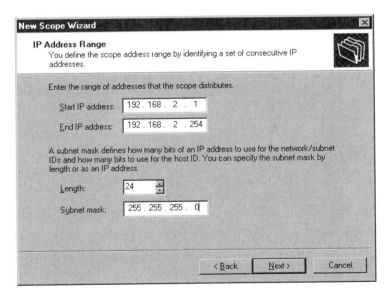

Figure 12.7 Excluding addresses from the scope's range.

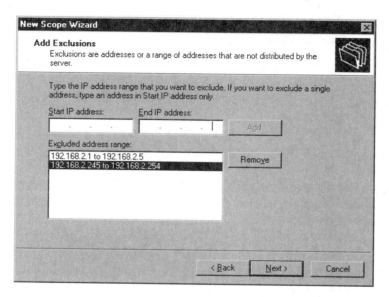

192.168.2.245 and the End IP address 192.168.2.254, and click
ADD. This screen should look similar to Figure 12.7. Click NEXT.

10. Set the lease duration for IP addresses delivered by this scope.
Change the lease duration to 14 days. Then click NEXT.

11. This dialog box offers you the opportunity to configure DHCP
Options. Select the "Yes, I want to configure these options now"
option button. Then click NEXT.

12. The first option is for the Router (default gateway). Enter
192.168.1.16 in the IP address space, and then click ADD. Click
NEXT.

13. Choose the parent domain your DNS clients will use for DNS name
resolution. You can also configure your DNS server name or
address. Enter 192.168.1.185 in the IP address box as seen in
Figure 12.8. Then click NEXT.

14. Enter the IP addresses or names of the WINS servers. In the IP
address box, enter 192.168.1.185, and click ADD. Click NEXT.

15. The wizard asks if the scope should be activated. Select the option
button for "Yes, I want to activate the Scope now." Click NEXT.

16. Click FINISH.

On returning to the DHCP management console, it should appear similar to Figure 12.9.

Figure 12.8 Choosing the DNS server.

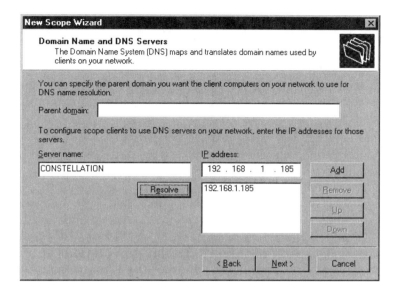

Figure 12.9 Viewing the newly created scope in the DHCP MMC.

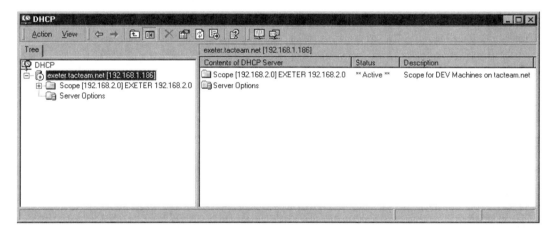

Troubleshooting DHCP

Many problems with TCP/IP connectivity turn out to be IP addressing problems. Although manually assigning IP addresses to each computer increases the likelihood of human error (mistyping or transposing numbers), using DHCP or allowing APIPA to assign addresses on the network will not absolutely guarantee trouble-free address assignment.

As might be expected, the majority of DHCP problems stem from incorrect initial configuration or failure to update the configuration on the DHCP server. Configuration problems can cause address conflicts to occur with the automatic addressing services.

The DHCP Database

The DHCP database can become corrupt, or data may be accidentally deleted or destroyed due to hardware problems, power problems, viruses, or other reasons.

The database files are stored in <systemroot>\System32\DHCP and include the following files:

- Dhcp.mdb
- Dhcp.tmp
- J50.log and J50#####.log
- J50.chk

Windows 2000 backs up the DHCP database by default at one-hour intervals. You can edit the Registry to change the backup interval. To do so, use a Registry editor to open the key:

HKEY_LOCAL_MACHINE\SYSTEM\CurrentControlSet\Services\DHCP\Parameters

NOTE

The DHCP database backup files are stored on the DHCP server in the <systemroot>\System32\DHCP\Backup\Jet directory. A copy of the DCHP\Parameters subkey of the Registry is stored in the Backup directory with the filename DHCPCFG.

If the operating system detects that the DHCP database has become corrupt, it will automatically restore from backup when the service restarts. To manually restore the database from the backup files, you must edit the Registry. Navigate to HKEY_LOCAL_MACHINE\SYSTEM\CurrentControlSet\Services\DHCPServer\Parameters and set the RestoreFlag value to 1.

Multiple Clients Fail to Obtain IP Addresses

If multiple clients are unable to obtain leases for IP addresses, check the following:

- The DHCP server is up, and that its IP address has not been changed.

- The DHCP server's IP address is in the same network range as the scope it is servicing.
- Multiple DHCP servers have not been configured on the same subnet with overlapping scopes.
- Within an Active Directory environment, the DHCP server has been authorized.

Duplicate Addresses

Duplicate addresses can be a problem in a network where some of the IP addresses are manually assigned, especially if there is more than one Administrator responsible for configuring TCP/IP properties on computers.

There are several ways to locate the guilty parties when address duplication occurs. If it is a Windows 2000 or Windows NT computer, there will be an event entered in the System Log reporting the conflict, although the computer that "got there first" will be able to continue using the address.

You can also use the tracert command on the address to find out the name of the computer using it, or you can use arp –a to find out the physical address of the computer using the IP address, as long as the other computer is on your local subnet.

Summary

The Dynamic Host Configuration Protocol was designed to fill the need for automatic and centralized assignment and administration of IP addresses in a large TCP/IP-based network. DHCP is implemented as a client/server protocol. Upon initialization, the DHCP client requests an IP address from a DHCP server, which is configured with a pool of addresses to assign to DHCP clients. The DHCP server can be configured to also send additional information to the DHCP client.

DHCP clients do not usually keep IP addresses indefinitely; instead, IP addressing information is leased to DHCP clients. There are four steps to the lease process: DHCPDISCOVER, DHCPOFFER, DHCPREQUEST, and DHCPACK. All DHCP messages are broadcasts.

A client must have a valid lease to retain an IP address, and will not be able to continue network activity if is does not retain a valid lease.

The pool of available IP addresses is called a scope. Scopes typically include all the available IP addresses for a specific network ID. Clients that require static IP addresses can be excluded from the scope. Excluded addresses will not be allocated to DHCP clients.

The DHCP server can deliver additional IP addressing information in the form of DHCP Options. A large number of DHCP Options are available, but Microsoft network clients support only a small number of DHCP Options. An example of DHCP Options information that can be delivered to DHCP clients would be the IP addresses of the WINS server and DNS server.

DHCP options can be configured at several levels. These include Server Options, Scope Options, Client Options, and Vendor Class/User Class Options. Server Options apply to all scopes configured on a single server. Scope Options apply only to a single scope. Scope Options override Server Options.

A DHCP server can deliver the same IP address to a machine each time it renews a lease, if a client is designated as Reserved. A Reserved Client is a computer whose MAC address and IP address have been configured at the DHCP server.

Vendor Class Options are introduced for the first time in the Windows 2000 DHCP server. They allow for a hardware or software manufacturer to add to the available set of DHCP Options. The DHCP client can identify itself as a member of the Vendor's Class, and the DHCP server will send class members a custom set of options.

The DHCP Administrator configures User Class Options, which are delivered to machines identifying themselves as a member of a particular User Class.

DHCP clients unable to contact a DHCP server can autoconfigure their IP address. APIPA (Automatic Private IP Addressing) allows DHCP clients to self-assign an IP address from the 169.254.0.0 Class B network ID.

The Windows 2000 DHCP server also supports dynamic assignment of IP addresses to BOOTP clients, and Client Reservations can be configured for BOOTP clients as well. The name of a TFTP server and the location of the Boot Image are configured in the DHCP server Boot Table.

A single physical network containing multiple logical subnetworks is called a multinet. A superscope must be configured to support multinet configurations. To create a superscope, first create the individual scopes. Then use the Superscope Wizard to join the individual scopes into a single administrative unit.

FAQs

Q: What protocol and ports does DHCP use?

A: DHCP uses UDP ports 67 and 68.

Q: How does the DHCP server know what subnet the DHCP request came from?

A: The "giaddr" (Gateway Internet Address) field in the DHCP message includes the source network ID. The DHCP server will use this information to search for a scope to service the client's request.

Q: Do any routers have DHCP server functionality?

A: DHCP servers are very disk intensive; consequently, major router manufacturers have not included any DHCP functionality in their products.

Q: Can I use DHCP for assigning IP addressing information to my routers?

A: You can do this, but it is not recommended. Gateway IP addresses need to be reliable and accessible to all clients. If the gateway address changes, some clients will not be able to connect to remote subnets.

Q: The DHCP server log shows NACKs being returned to DHCP clients requesting leases. I have tried to renew the client's lease manually, but am unable to do so. What is the problem, and how do I solve it?

A: This situation will occur if the IP address range configured for the DHCP server is conflicting with (overlapping) the range that some other DHCP server on the network is offering. Change the address pool for the scopes on one or both servers so that they do not overlap. Add exclusions if needed. You can also enable address conflict detection on the server by right-clicking on it in the management console, selecting Properties | Advanced, and setting the value for Conflict Detection Attempts to a number greater than 0.

Managing Windows 2000 DNS Server

Solutions in this chapter:

- Introduction
- Understanding DNS
- Understanding Name Resolution
- Active Directory and DNS Integration
- Installing DNS Server Service
- Configuring DNS Services
- Configuring the DNS Client
- DNS Walkthroughs
- Summary

Introduction

The Domain Name System (DNS) is yet another classic illustration of the fact that it is people who drive the Internet and computing in general, not computers themselves. Computers exist in a finite world of black and white, zeros and ones. Humans embrace an entire universe of sounds, smells, tastes, and emotions.

So, what is the difference between 196.168.12.244 and www.bluen-imbus.com? Nothing—except in the interpretation. And this is the service that DNS provides: It interprets the bland combination of digits that make up an IP address and translates it into a human-friendly format, painting names with color, dimensions, and emotion.

The DNS is a distributed database whose function is to resolve host names to IP addresses. DNS solves a basic problem when connecting to servers on an intranet and on the Internet: Names are easier to remember than numbers, and they add a human dimension.

With the integration of Active Directory and Dynamic DNS (DDNS), Microsoft has started along the path toward eliminating NetBIOS. DDNS allows computers to update their host names dynamically, allowing Administrators to wean their networks from the NetBIOS standard.

It is important to remember that DNS is not a Windows-based protocol, such as NetBIOS. Rather it is a naming system and protocol used not only by companies worldwide, but also by the burgeoning namespace occupied by the global Internet. If you elect to replace your existing DNS infrastructure with Windows 2000 DNS, you will be responsible for host name resolution not only for the Windows 2000 infrastructure, but also UNIX servers, mainframe computers, and the Internet.

Understanding DNS

As mentioned earlier, DNS maps friendly names to IP addresses. It is similar to a phonebook, pairing host names and IP addresses much in the same way as people's names are paired with their telephone numbers.

Quite obviously, no one person or entity can track the millions of host computers on the Internet. Consequently, a method was developed to cater for the distribution of responsibility for tracking and organizing local groups of computers. These groups have their own database of host name to IP addresses. The isolated databases are then unified to create a single large distributed database.

The distributed database approach solves an additional problem. Large, flat databases take a very long time to search, causing name resolution queries aimed at flat files to take an unreasonable amount of time to complete. Significant performance gains can be realized by partitioning the database in much the way the DNS does.

Domain Namespace

The domain namespace is a hierarchical construct. Examples of familiar hierarchical constructs include the file namespace you see in the Windows Explorer, and the organizational namespace in a corporate organizational chart. In comparing the DNS to the file system namespace, you could consider each domain analogous to a folder. Just as a folder can contain files and/or other folders, a domain can contain hosts and/or other domains.

Perversely, the highest level of the DNS hierarchy is Root. A single period ("."") represents the Root domain. Underneath the Root domain are the top-level domains. Frequently encountered top-level domains include .com, .net, .org, .edu, .mil, and .gov. Other top-level domain names include a country code such as .ca or .au, representing Canada and Australia, respectively. Top-level domain names are assigned by the Internet Society (ISOC).

The domain names directly beneath the top-level domains are the second-level domains. Familiar second-level domains include microsoft.com, syngress.com, and osborne.com. Assigning second-level domain names was the sole responsibility of Network Solutions, Inc. (NSI, previously known as InterNIC) until 1999. Other organizations can now register second-level domain names, and are collectively known as the Domain Registrars.

The only centralized aspect of the Internet is the management of top- and second-level domains. Thereafter, each organization is responsible for managing its portion of the domain namespace once it is assigned a second-level domain name.

Domains under the second-level domains are called subdomains. A DNS Administrator's primary duty is managing his second-level domain and the subdomains it contains. It is the responsibility of the IT services of each company to design, implement, and maintain subdomains.

Like any database, the DNS database contains records. Each domain contains Resource Records containing information about the DNS infrastructure. There are many types of DNS database records, with the most common database record being the A Address record. The Address record contains a single host name and IP address mapping.

Several domains and subdomains can be managed from a single DNS server, and a group of contiguous domains can be managed from a single DNS database file. All domains managed in a single DNS database file are members of the same zone.

NOTE

A single DNS server can contain information about many domains. A zone may contain multiple contiguous domains. Multiple zone files may be placed on a single DNS server.

Domain Naming Conventions

Each domain name is separated by a "." (referred to as "dot"). Each domain or host name is a label, which can be no greater than 63 octets (or bytes). A single ASCII character consists of 8 bits or 1 byte, with 8 bits defining an octet. The entire Fully Qualified Domain Name (FQDN) cannot exceed 255 octets.

NOTE

A single domain or host label is limited to 63 octets (or bytes). The UTF-8 standard allows a single character to span more than a single octet. This is why it is more accurate to enumerate octets rather than characters.

Windows 2000 DNS servers support the UTF-8 standard. UTF-8 allows for extended character set entries as DNS labels. Not all DNS servers support the UTF-8 standard. Only use extended characters in DNS labels when your DNS environment contains only Windows 2000 DNS servers. Standard characters for DNS label characters are a–z, A–Z, 0–9, and the hyphen. Note that the underscore is not supported. Standard DNS servers are not case sensitive; www.bluenimbus.com is the same as www.BlueNimbus.com and resolve to the same IP address. Filenames included in a URL may be case sensitive depending on the Web server implemented.

WARNING

DNS servers using the standard label character convention do not support the underscore. If your NetBIOS naming scheme includes machines with underscores in their names, now is a good time to rename them. Any new machines introduced into the network should conform to standard naming conventions. This will save you many headaches when upgrading your domains to Windows 2000.

Host and Domain Names

Most Microsoft network operating systems are based on the NetBIOS naming standard. NetBIOS names represent endpoints of communication between two computers using NetBIOS applications.

NetBIOS programs must know the NetBIOS name of the target computer to establish a session. NetBIOS protocols use the NetBIOS name to identify computers on the network. Conversely, the TCP/IP protocol uses IP addresses and port numbers as endpoints of communication. TCP/IP is oblivious to NetBIOS names.

How do we make TCP/IP care about NetBIOS names? This is the function of NetBIOS over TCP/IP, or NetBT. On TCP/IP networks, the NetBIOS name must be resolved to an IP address. Resolution of NetBIOS names to IP addresses can lead to additional broadcast traffic on the network.

Host Names

Applications written specifically for TCP/IP networks use the Winsock session layer interface. Winsock applications do not require the name of the destination computer to establish a session, but do require the IP address and port number. A Winsock computer name is a host name. Host names are not required to establish sessions between computers using the Winsock interface; only the destination IP address and port number are required. The host name is injected into the foray for convenience and the human element. In comparison, NetBIOS names are integral and required in NetBIOS networking. So, in fact, a TCP/IP network could exist without host names.

NetBIOS names are required to be unique. If a second computer tries to join the network with a duplicate NetBIOS name, it receives a negative name registration response and will consequently not initialize its network subsystem.

The hierarchical nature of the DNS allows two computers on the same network to share the same host name. This is a function of the hierarchical structure of the Domain Name System. Duplicate host names are not a problem as long as they are not on the same level and branch of the DNS tree.

Fully Qualified Domain Names

Host names are qualified by identifying their position in the DNS tree. When a host name is combined with its parent DNS domain name path, it is called a Fully Qualified Domain Name (FQDN). Consider the addresses www.bluenimbus.com and www.microsoft.com. These two computers share the same host name: www. However, the DNS path to these hosts is different.

This is comparable to mailing addresses. Two homes can have the same house number, such as 21. However, the complete path to the home includes the street and city name. 21 Berry Close, London, and 21 Berry Close, Dallas are obviously very different since the path to 21 is different.

As it is read from left to right, note that the FQDN moves from specific to general. Now it should be clear why so many Internet servers can share www as their host name. This also explains the occasional URL containing an unusual host name, such as www2, which may signify that the corporation maintains more than one Web server on the Internet. It should also be evident that the www does not represent a protocol or service.

WARNING

It is an Internet convention to name hosts by the services they provide. You give a Web server the host name www. An FTP server is ftp, while a mail server is smtp. These host names are not service identifiers. A server named mail.bluenimbus.com may not have any e-mail function at all. Mail is the host name and nothing more.

Zones

To recap, domain names can be top level, second level, or subdomains. Each domain has its own resources described in Resource Records. Management of resources within domains is achieved through DNS zone files.

A DNS zone file is a database. Each domain or group of domains included in a zone file is a member of the same DNS zone. There are two standard zone types: forward lookup zones and reverse lookup zones. A forward lookup zone allows for resource name to IP address resolution (for example, determining the IP address of www.bluenimbus.com). The resource type can vary. Examples of resources include Mail Exchangers, Host Addresses, and Aliases. The different types of resources are discussed later in the chapter. A reverse lookup zone allows for IP address to resource name resolution (for example, determining the host name of 192.168.12.244).

Using Zones

Let's look at an example. Assume that .com is the top-level domain, and that the second-level domain is bluenimbus.com. Bluenimbus has facilities in Dallas, Seattle, and Boston. We want to partition bluenimbus.com's resources into three domains: bluenimbus.com, west.bluenimbus.com, and east.bluenimbus.com. The west.bluenimbus.com domain contains resource records for machines in Seattle. The east.bluenimbus.com domain contains resource records for machines in Boston, and the bluenimbus.com domain contains resource records for machines at the headquarters in Dallas.

NOTE

Be aware that DNS domain names are not Windows NT 4.0 domains. A Windows NT 4.0 domain represents a security context in which all domain members participate. DNS domains that are used to organize resources so they can be found use DNS queries.

The main operation is in Dallas, and the majority of employees and computer personnel are located there. The Seattle facility has programmers and a small Systems Administration division. The Boston office has Sales and Marketing personnel, but has no IT support presence onsite.

We would manage the three domains using two zones to assure accurate and timely management of the DNS database. One zone includes both the bluenimbus.com and the east.bluenimbus.com domains. The other zone includes only the west.bluenimbus.com domain.

The zone containing both the east.bluenimbus.com and the bluenimbus.com domains is named the bluenimbus.com zone. Bluenimbus.com represents the highest-level domain represented in the zone, and therefore makes it the root domain in the zone. Moreover, the name of the zone is derived from the zone's root domain. The west.bluenimbus.com domain is contained in the west.bluenimbus.com zone. West.bluenimbus.com is the only domain in the zone and therefore is the root.

Why Partition Three Domains into Two Zones?

Partitioning allows us to distribute responsibility for maintaining domain resource records to personnel capable of administrating them. Zones and domains are not the same. Domain information is saved in zone files. Multiple contiguous domains can be included in a single zone file. A single DNS server can house multiple zone files. Zone information is stored in files on a physical disk. Each domain can be considered a different table in the zone database.

Reverse Lookup Zones

Reverse lookup zones allow, unsurprisingly enough, for reverse lookups. Many diagnostic tools such as nslookup and domain security assessment programs make extensive use of reverse lookup queries.

Forward lookup queries resolve an IP address from a host name. A reverse lookup query does the opposite: it resolves a host name from an IP address. Forward lookup zone files are not structured to perform reverse lookups, so a specialized zone—the reverse lookup zone—must perform reverse lookups.

The reverse lookup zone is contained in a domain known as in-addr.arpa. Subdomains of the in-addr.arpa domain are based on the dotted quad representation of each network ID, but the order of the octets is reversed. Don't worry, it will all become clearer!

For example, consider a network ID of 131.107.0.0. The name of the reverse lookup zone would be 107.131.in-addr.arpa. If you had a network ID of 192.168.2, the reverse lookup zone would be 2.168.192.in-addr.arpa. A network ID of 10.1.0.0 would have a reverse lookup zone of 1.10.in-addr.arpa.

Reverse lookup zones are created independently of forward lookup zones. Reverse lookup zones are not mandatory and use Pointer (PTR) records to provide IP address-to-host-name resolution. Pointer records can be entered manually, or created automatically each time you enter an A Address record to a forward lookup zone.

Zone Transfer

When a zone is created, it becomes the master copy of that zone. The DNS server containing this copy is called a Primary DNS server, and holds the only read/write copy of the zone database file.

Domain name servers share information via zone transfer, where the master copy of the zone file can be copied to another DNS server, with the receiving DNS server called the Secondary DNS server. Additionally, a Master DNS server is one that sends a copy of its zone information to a Secondary DNS server.

Note that DNS servers can take on multiple roles. A DNS server can be a Primary for one zone, and a Secondary for another zone. A Secondary DNS server can be a Master to another Secondary DNS server when it copies a zone file to another DNS server.

NOTE

A Master DNS server does not need to be a Primary DNS server. Secondary servers can transfer zone files to other Secondary servers. A Secondary Master server copies the zone database to another Secondary.

Primary and Secondary DNS servers allow for fault tolerance. If the Primary DNS server is disabled, DNS clients can access zone information from a Secondary DNS server. Secondary DNS can also optimize DNS query performance.

For example, a DNS client is located in a satellite office that is separated from the Primary DNS server via a 56k Frame Relay. The Frame Relay link is often saturated during normal business hours. DNS queries are slow during times of network congestion. A Secondary DNS server can be placed at the satellite location. This avoids reaching across the WAN to query the DNS server. The satellite DNS server receives zone information from the Primary DNS on the other side of the WAN through zone transfer.

Methods of Zone Transfer

Previous versions of Microsoft DNS servers transferred the entire zone database during a zone transfer. The Secondary DNS server initiates zone transfers by sending a pull request to the Primary DNS server. The first record the Primary DNS server sends is the Start of Authority (SOA) record.

The SOA record contains the refresh interval. The Secondary DNS server waits the length of the refresh interval before requesting another update to its zone file. The refresh interval determines how often the zone database on the Secondary updates.

When a new zone is created, it has a serial number of 1. Each time a change is made to the zone database, the serial number is incremented by 1. Each time the Primary updates the Secondary's zone file, the Secondary's zone serial number updates. The serial number is included in the SOA record sent by the Primary DNS server. The Secondary examines the serial number in the SOA record and compares it to the serial number of its own zone file. If the SOA number is larger, the Secondary sends an AXFR request. An AXFR request instructs the Primary DNS server to send the entire zone database.

The Retry Interval

The Primary DNS server may at times be unavailable; consequently, the Secondary server waits a specified period of time before attempting another pull operation. This time period—the retry interval—is detailed in the SOA record on the Secondary server.

Compatibility of DNS Server Versions

The zone transfer sends a compressed version of the zone database in an effort to speed file copy over the network. Care must be taken when running a mixed DNS server environment. DNS servers running versions of BIND earlier than 4.9.4 do not support this method of transfer.

Incremental Zone Transfers

Windows 2000 DNS servers support a more efficient mode of zone transfer than the method (AFXR) implemented with Windows NT DNS Server. AFXR zone transfers require the entire zone database to be copied during each update. Zone transfers can consume a significant amount of bandwidth, even when the zone database is compressed. This is especially true in large DNS installations and voluminous zone databases.

Windows 2000 DNS servers support incremental zone transfers. An incremental zone transfer sends only new or changed records. RFC 1995 delineates incremental zone transfer standards.

The Windows 2000 Secondary DNS server pull request sends an IXFR query rather than an AXFR query. The Master server responds to an IXFR query by sending new and changed records.

The Master server keeps a zone database change history. Serial numbers are associated with changes to the zone file. When the Secondary sends an IXFR query, the Master and Secondary's serial numbers are compared, and records added or changed since the Secondary's serial numbers are transferred. The Secondary updates its zone database with the new and changed records and the zone serial number increments to reflect that of the Master DNS server at the time of zone transfer.

Your existing DNS servers may not support IXFR query requests. Downlevel DNS servers do not support incremental zone transfer. Downlevel DNS servers only issue AFXR queries. In this scenario, the Windows 2000 Master DNS server responds to the AXFR query by sending the entire zone database.

DDNS Dynamic Updates

Resource records on downlevel DNS servers must be manually updated. There are significant limitations to manual updates:

- They can be very time consuming during large-scale DNS rollouts or upgrades.
- It is unrealistic to include DHCP clients in the DNS. DHCP clients could potentially change IP addresses on a regular basis.

Windows 2000 premieres the first Microsoft Dynamic DNS server (DDNS). A DDNS updates resource records dynamically in a fashion similar to a WINS server. Clients can update their own Address and PTR records when configured to do so. Dynamic DNS update standards are described in RFC 2136.

A Windows 2000 DHCP server supports dynamic updates for downlevel clients. When a downlevel client uses both Windows 2000 DNS Server and Windows 2000 DHCP Server, the Windows 2000 DHCP server sends both Address and Pointer record information on the behalf of the downlevel client to the DDNS server.

Only the Primary DNS server can receive dynamic updates in a standard DNS zone. When the DNS zone database is integrated with the Active Directory, any domain controller in the domain can accept dynamic updates. Windows 2000 DNS client computers send an UPDATE message to the DDNS computer to update their records. Downlevel clients cannot update their own Address records, but the DHCP server can handle this task.

Understanding Name Resolution

Winsock applications require the IP address of the destination host to establish a session, while users work with host names rather than IP addresses. The process of finding the IP address for a particular host is referred to as host name resolution. Resolver software formulates and issues query statements sent to the DNS server. Resolver software can be included in the Winsock application, or in the case of Windows 2000, it can be a component of the operating system. Winsock programs with resolver software include:

- Web browsers (such as Microsoft Internet Explorer)
- FTP clients (such as the command-line FTP program found in Windows 2000)
- Telnet clients
- DNS servers themselves

NOTE

Any program or service that issues DNS queries uses resolver software.

Recursive Queries

When you type an FQDN in the address bar of a Web browser, the resolver sends a query to the client's Preferred DNS server. The DNS server must respond to the query either positively or negatively. A positive response returns the IP address. A negative response returns a "host not found" error. A recursive query is one that requires a definitive response, either affirmative or negative. Referral is not an option.

Iterative Queries

Iterative queries allow the DNS server to make a best-effort attempt at resolving the DNS query. If the DNS server receiving an iterative query is not authoritative for the domain in the query, it can return a referral response. The referral contains the IP address of another DNS server that may be able to service the query.

The DNS client sends a recursive query to its Preferred DNS server. If the Preferred DNS server is not authoritative for the host domain in the query, it will issue iterative queries to other DNS servers. Each DNS server can respond with a referral to another DNS server that brings the query closer to resolution.

Looking Up an Address from a Name

The following list represents the sequence of events during the host name resolution process using both recursive and iterative queries. In this example, we want to connect to a Web server at bluenimbus.com.

1. Type **andromeda.bluenimbus.com** in the address bar of the Web browser, and press ENTER. The resolver formulates a recursive query to send to the Preferred DNS server.

2. The Preferred DNS server checks to see if it is authoritative for the domain in the query. The Server first checks its cache to see if it has recently resolved the same host name. If the IP address is not in its cache, and if the DNS server is not authoritative (does not contain a zone for the target domain) for the queried domain, it sends an iterative query to an Internet root name server. At this point, the Preferred DNS server becomes a DNS client itself. The Preferred DNS server starts the iterative query process in order to complete recursion. Once recursion is complete, a definitive answer can be returned to the client.

3. The root name server is not authoritative for bluenimbus.com. However, the Internet root DNS server is authoritative for all top-level domains. This includes the com domain. The root server sends the IP address of the DNS server authoritative for the domain to the Preferred DNS server.

4. The Preferred DNS server connects to a DNS server authoritative for the com domain. The com domain DNS server is not authoritative for the bluenimbus.com domain. In a best-effort attempt, the com domain DNS server returns to the Preferred DNS server the IP address for the DNS server authoritative for the bluenimbus.com domain.

5. At this point, the Preferred DNS server queries the DNS server authoritative for the bluenimbus.com domain. The bluenimbus.com DNS server checks its zone files for an Address record containing andromeda.bluenimbus.com. Andromeda is located in the bluenimbus.com domain, and there is an Address record for it in the zone database. The bluenimbus.com DNS server responds to the Preferred DNS server with the IP address of host computer, Andromeda.

6. The Preferred DNS server has completed recursion. It responds to the client with a recursive response, and sends the IP address of andromeda.bluenimbus.com. You can establish a connection to the destination host because the IP address is known. If the bluenimbus.com DNS server did not have an Address record for Andromeda, the Preferred server would have issued a recursive response in the negative.

Note that both the requesting host and the Preferred server acted as resolvers in the preceding process.

NOTE

The DNS server caches the results of successful queries. This reduces Internet traffic to Internet root servers. Extended periods of uptime allow the DNS cache to build. DNS requests speed up significantly after the DNS server has built up a large cache of successful queries.

Looking Up a Name from an Address

Occasionally, it is required to resolve a known IP address to a host name. IP address to host name resolution can aid in investigating suspicious activity. Many security analysis programs use IP address to host name resolution.

A HOSTS file can be used to map host names to IP addresses. It is simple task to search the HOSTS file to find an IP address to host name mapping. However, this situation becomes much more complex when dealing with a worldwide distributed database.

The primary index for the DNS is the domain name. The forward lookup is based on this indexing scheme. Finding a domain name using the IP address as the index value would require an exhaustive search of the entire DNS. You can perform reverse lookups in this fashion, but don't make plans for dinner.

The answer lies in creating another domain that uses IP addresses as the index value. Then we can search this domain in the same way as we did the forward lookup domain. This domain is called the in-addr.arpa domain.

Each node in the in-addr.arpa domain is named after numbers found in the w, x, y, and z octets of the network ID. Each level in the in-addr.arpa domain can contain 256 domains corresponding to the possible values for each octet. At the bottom are the actual resource records (PTR records) that contain the IP address to host name mapping.

As we saw earlier, the in-addr.arpa domain notation is the reverse of the forward lookup domain convention. For example, if bluenimbus.com has a network ID of 21.18.189.0, the in-addr.arpa subdomain is 189.18.21.in-addr.arpa. This maps to the domain name bluenimbus.com.

IP addresses, like domain names, are hierarchical. Network IDs are assigned in a fashion similar to domain names. Like subdomains within the second-level domain, you can subdivide or subnet your network ID any way you like.

Authority can be delegated in the same way as is done for the forward lookup domain when the leftmost octet is made the top of the hierarchy. For example, the 126.in-addr.arpa domain contains reverse mappings for all hosts whose IP addresses start with 126. The Administrator of network 126 can delegate authority for the 255 subdomains of the 126 domain.

The iterative and recursive query process works the same when performing reverse lookups as it does when performing forward lookups.

WARNING

As the Administrator of your own subdomains, you are not required to create or maintain reverse lookup zones, but some network security analysis software will not work correctly if reverse lookup zones are not created.

Active Directory and DNS Integration

In the first pass through the intricacies of DNS, the focus has been on traditional DNS zone management. Windows 2000 allows DNS integration with the Active Directory, a marriage of convenience that provides a number of advantages.

DNS is a requirement when using Active Directory, since Windows 2000 DCs are located via DNS queries. The Netlogon service searches for a logon server via DNS. Prior to Windows 2000, WINS servers provided this function. However, Windows 2000 is no longer dependent on NetBIOS. Core network functionality is mediated through the Winsock interface.

The more efficient and fault-tolerant Active Directory replication model provides the primary advantage of integrating DNS with the Active Directory. In addition, Dynamic DNS updates can be secured by using Active Directory Integrated zones.

When Active Directory is installed on a DC, it seeks out a DNS server authoritative for the domain. If it cannot find an authoritative DNS server, or if the authoritative DNS server does not support dynamic updates and SRV records, the installer is required to create a DNS server on that machine. Active Directory domain names are also DNS domain names.

It is not required that DNS zones be integrated with the AD. The option is available to use either standard or AD Integrated zones. As indicated earlier, standard zones are stored in text-based files with the .dns extension.

Zones stored in the Active Directory are located in the Active Directory tree. Each Directory Integrated zone is stored in a Microsoft DNS container object.

Microsoft recommends that in an Active Directory environment, DNS zones should be integrated with the AD to take advantage of multi-master replication and enhanced zone fault tolerance. Also, since workstations are dynamically entered into DDNS via DHCP, there will be many DNS changes (more than when only the servers are entered). Thus, the more efficient replication scheme finds its best application when DHCP is in widespread use.

Using Active Directory to Replicate and Synchronize DNS

In a standard zone environment, the DNS Primary contains the only read/write copy of the zone database. Zone transfers take place when the refresh interval has expired and the Secondary DNS server sends a pull request to Master DNS servers to receive the zone database. The Secondary DNS server contains a read-only copy of the zone database. This standard zone schema has a single point of failure. If the Primary server for the zone is disabled, accurate zone updates and zone transfers are halted.

The Active Directory Integrated zone does not have a single point of failure. DNS zone information is stored in the AD, and each authoritative server contains a read/write copy of the zone database. A single downed DC will not prevent zone transfers and zone updates. Updates and transfers continue to take place among all other AD domain controllers for the domain.

RFC 2137 Secure DNS Updates

Security measures in AD Integrated zones can be implemented that are not available in standard zones. RFC 2137 defines the standards for secure updates to AD Integrated zones. You can control which computers or groups can update resource records by setting access controls in the Active Directory. This prevents unauthorized and potentially malicious attempts to alter information in the zone database. Secure updates are the default for AD Integrated DNS zones.

Zone transfer takes place in a secure fashion immediately upon adding a new AD domain controller. You do not need to configure DNS server properties to set up and tune the zone transfer process.

Changing Zone Types

The zone type can easily be changed from AD Integrated to standard via the DNS management console. A standard zone can be changed into an AD Integrated zone, and vice versa, simply by clicking on an option button in the DNS management console.

AD Integrated zone management is easier from the planning and design perspective. If the Active Directory and Standard DNS zones are used, a plan will be required to configure two separate replication strategies: one for AD database replication and the other for DNS zone database replication. AD Integrated zones provide a unified entity for replication and management of domain and zone information. This also decreases the amount of bandwidth required for zone transfer. Rather than sending the entire record, AD Integrated zone transfers only replicate property information that has changed.

Integration with DHCP

Windows 2000 DHCP is a significant improvement over the DHCP server bundled with Windows NT, delivering host name and IP addressing information to a Windows 2000 DDNS server.

The Windows 2000 DHCP server interacts with a Windows 2000 Dynamic DNS server in one of three ways after assigning a DHCP client an IP address:

- It will update the DNS server by providing information to create an A Address and PTR (pointer) record at the request of the DNS client.

- The DHCP server will update both the Address and the Pointer records regardless of client request.

- The DHCP server will never register information about the DHCP client. However, the client itself may contact the Dynamic DNS server directly with this information.

The DCHP/DDNS interaction varies with the client receiving the IP addressing information from a DHCP server. The interplay between the Windows 2000 client and Windows 2000 DHCP encompasses the following:

1. The Windows 2000 client broadcasts a DHCPREQUEST message and receives an IP address. The Windows 2000 client will register its own Address record with the Dynamic DNS server after official obtaining a lease.

2. The DHCP server registers the client's PTR record with the DDNS server. This is the default behavior for a Windows 2000 client and Windows 2000 DHCP server.

3. Client and server parameters can be manipulated to allow the DHCP server to update both Address and PTR records. If desired, the DHCP server and DCHP client can be configured so that no dynamic updates are made to the DDNS server.

This only occurs in a pure Windows 2000 environment. Downlevel clients are not able to send A Address record information to a DDNS server, so the DHCP server acts as a proxy and forwards both Address and PTR information to the DDNS server.

Windows 2000 computers configured with static IP addresses update their own Address and Pointer records with the DDNS server. If the name or IP address of a Windows 2000 client with a static IP address is changed, the client's entry in the DDNS server can be manually updated by issuing the command:

ipconfig /registerdns

This command should be completed from the command prompt. Downlevel clients with static IP addresses are not able to communicate directly with the DDNS server, and DDNS entries must be manually configured for these clients.

WARNING

You should use only Windows 2000 DHCP servers on your network to guarantee that dynamic updates are successful on downlevel clients.

Registration of Server in DNS Using the SRV Record

Active Directory domain controllers must be registered in the DNS, since DC entries in the DNS include special SRV records that contain information regarding their DC status. The Netlogon service on domain controllers automatically registers these SRV resource records via a DDNS update.

Windows 2000 DCs are able to dynamically update SRV records on a DDNS server and provide information about available services. Examples of such services include LDAP, FTP, and WWW. Domain clients must find a SRV record for a DC in the DNS database in order to find a DC to authenticate logon. There is a SRV record for Kerberos information allowing Kerberos clients to locate the Key Distribution Service in their domain.

Every DC dynamically registers a host resource record containing the name of the domain where the DC is located. The A Address record makes it possible for clients that do not recognize SRV records to locate a domain controller by means of a generic host lookup. This process is similar to the domain name registration process on WINS servers.

Situations do arise when a SRV record for a DC will have to be added manually. An unfortunate example is the Administrator who inadvertently deletes these records. It is important to restore these records on a timely basis, since domain clients are dependent on these records for domain activity.

To view the SRV resource records that were created by a domain controller, open and view the Netlogon.dns file. The Active Directory Installation wizard created this file during setup, and it can be found in %systemroot%\System32\Config\Netlogon.dns.

Be sure when creating a new SRV record for a domain controller that the record is placed in the appropriate container object in the AD as indicated by the path defined in the Netlogon.dns file.

Installing DNS Server Service

Installing the DNS server service is a relatively simple affair that is outlined at the end of the chapter. Prior to installing the DNS service, you will need to plan the location and roles of the DNS servers on your network. Once the DNS server is installed, it requires configuration. This section explores some of the options available for DNS server roles in an enterprise network, and configuration options for the DNS service.

DNS Server Roles and Security Topology

Careful consideration is required not only in determining the placement of DNS servers, but also what roles these servers will play in the overall DNS infrastructure. The focus for this section will be on standard DNS setup.

When the zone database is integrated with the Active Directory, many of the concepts discussed in this section will not apply. Further discussion of Active Directory Integrated zone databases is included later in this chapter.

A Domain Name Server can take one of several different roles. A single DNS server can assume multiple roles depending on zone topology. A DNS server's principal roles include:

- Primary DNS server
- Secondary DNS server
- DNS forwarder
- Caching-only server
- DNS slave server

Each role determines how the zone database is maintained on the server, and/or how DNS client queries are evaluated.

The IP infrastructure of the internal network is uncovered when an intruder gains access to a DNS zone database. With this information, an intruder can easily compromise internal host systems. It is imperative that the internal DNS servers remain secure. Different ways to position DNS servers that optimize internal infrastructure security are discussed later in the chapter.

Primary DNS Server

A Primary DNS server contains the only write copy of the zone database, and is considered authoritative for the domain or domains contained in its zone files. Primary DNS servers are authoritative because they can respond directly to client DNS queries.

Primary DNS servers share characteristics with all DNS servers, including:

- Storing zone database information in the <systemroot>\system32\dns directory
- The ability to boot from either the Registry or a boot file
- Caching of resolved queries
- A cache.dns file

All zone files are stored in the %systemroot%\system32\dns directory. Zone file names are based on the name of the zone and are appended with the .dns file extension. For example, the bluenimbus.com zone file is bluenimbus.com.dns.

A Windows 2000 DNS server's configuration information is stored in the Registry. Server configuration is completed via the DNS administrative console. This is the default setting.

However, you can administer the DNS server via a file called BOOT. UNIX Administrators are accustomed to administrating DNS servers by manipulating the BOOT file. The Registry will need editing to administer the DNS server via the BOOT file. The Registry key is:

HKEY_Local_machine\System\CurrentControlSet\Services\DNS\Parameters\ BootMethod

Set this value to 0 to boot from the BOOT file.

All DNS servers cache resolved queries. A DNS server can receive and issue query requests. When a DNS server issues an iterative query to another DNS server, the result is placed in the DNS server's cache. Cached information is stored in system memory and is not written to disk. The cached information is lost after a server reboot. DNS servers are most effective when frequent reboots are avoided.

The cache.dns file (also known as the Root Hints file) contains host name and IP address mappings for the root Internet DNS servers. If a DNS server receives a recursive query for a domain for which it is not authoritative, it must complete recursion by issuing iterative queries. The iterative query process begins with the root DNS servers. The cache.dns file is located in the same directory as the zone files.

The Internet root server mappings change periodically. The current Internet root server mappings can be downloaded from ftp://ftp.rs.internic.net/domain/root.zone.gz.

A DNS server can be authoritative for multiple domains. For example, the bluenimbus.com.dns zone file can contain entries authoritative for bluenimbus.com and dev.bluenimbus.com. It is authoritative because the server does not need to issue an iterative query in order to resolve recursive queries for bluenimbus.com and dev.bluenimbus.com.

A Primary DNS server can act in the role of Secondary DNS server. A Primary DNS server that receives zone transfers from another Primary server acts in the role of Secondary. Any DNS server can contain either or both Primary and Secondary zone files. The only difference between the two is that the Primary zone file is read/write, while the Secondary zone file is read only.

This leads us to the next subject. How do we provide fault tolerance for zone database files? A corporation is highly dependent on reliable host name resolution in order to access both intranet and Internet servers. In order to provide for fault tolerance we configure a Secondary DNS server.

Secondary DNS Server

The DNS should include at least two DNS servers authoritative for each zone. Secondary DNS servers are authoritative for their zones and provide the following functions:

- Fault tolerance
- Load balancing
- Bandwidth conservation

Like Primary servers, Secondary DNS servers contain a zone database file. The copy is received via a zone transfer. A Primary DNS server for the zone acts as a Master server and transfers the zone file to the Secondary during a zone transfer. Secondary DNS servers can answer DNS client queries. DNS clients are configured with the IP addresses of both the Primary and Secondary DNS servers for their domain. This provides fault tolerance should the Primary DNS server become disabled. Name resolution services continue without interruption by querying the Secondary server.

Load balancing allows for distributing the DNS query load among multiple DNS servers. A DNS server could be overwhelmed by name query traffic if all client computers were to access a single Primary DNS server simultaneously. Clients on different segments can be configured to query local Secondary DNS servers. This disperses the query load among Primary and Secondary DNS servers for a zone.

Fault tolerance, load balancing, and bandwidth conservation provide cogent reasons to implement Secondary DNS servers. Secondary DNS server placement must be included in every DNS deployment plan you create. If you plan to maintain your own DNS servers on the Internet, the Domain Registrar will require you to have at least one Primary and one Secondary DNS server for your second-level domain.

Caching-Only Servers

All DNS servers cache results of queries they have resolved. The caching-only DNS server does not contain zone information or a zone file. The

Figure 13.1 The Root Hints tab in the DNS server Properties dialog box.

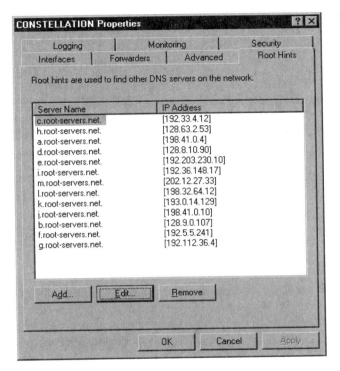

caching-only server builds its database of host names over time from successful DNS queries.

All DNS servers have a cache.dns file containing the IP addresses of all Internet root servers. The Windows 2000 cache.dns file is referred to as the root hints file. The contents of the root hints file can be viewed via the DNS server properties dialog box, as seen in Figure 13.1. The caching-only server uses this list to begin building its cache. It adds to the cache as it issues iterative queries when responding to client requests.

Caching-only servers are valuable because:

- They do not generate zone transfer traffic.
- They are extremely efficient when placed on the far side of a slow WAN link.
- They can be configured as forwarders.

Caching-only servers do not contain zone information, and are therefore not authoritative for any zone. There is no need for zone transfers to caching-only servers.

Satellite locations are often connected to the main office via slow WAN links. These locations benefit from caching-only servers for a couple of reasons:

- There is no zone transfer traffic.
- DNS queries do not have to traverse the WAN after the cache is built from resolved queries.

These caching-only servers do not require expert administration. A satellite office is unlikely to have trained DNS administrative staff onsite. This saves the cost of having an experienced DNS Administrator visit the site on a periodic basis.

There is no risk of an intruder obtaining zone information from a caching-only server. Therefore, caching-only servers make excellent candidates for forwarders. We'll cover forwarders in the next section.

DNS Forwarders and Slave Servers

A DNS forwarder is a DNS server that accepts DNS queries from another DNS server. Caching-only servers make good forwarders, and can be used to protect an internal DNS server from the Internet.

A DNS client sends a recursive query to its Preferred DNS server. The request is for a host in a domain for which the DNS is not authoritative.

The DNS server must resolve the host name for the client or return a "host not found" error. The DNS client's Preferred DNS server can be configured to forward all queries for which it is not authoritative. This DNS server issues a recursive query to another DNS server called the forwarder.

Some of the terms used in the forwarding process require clarification. In our example, the client's Preferred server is forwarding the request to the forwarder. The client's Preferred server is the forwarding DNS server. The DNS server receiving the forwarding server's query is the forwarder. Therefore, the process of forwarding a DNS query involves both a forwarding DNS server and the forwarder DNS server.

The forwarder begins to resolve the host name in the query. It can do this by retrieving the record from its cache, from a zone file, or by issuing a series of iterative queries. If successful, it will answer the recursive query affirmatively and return the IP address to the forwarding server. The forwarding server completes its recursion by returning this IP address to the DNS client that initiated the query.

If the forwarder cannot resolve the host name to an IP address, it will return to the forwarding DNS server a "host not found" error. If this happens, the Preferred DNS server (the forwarding server) will attempt to resolve the host name itself. The forwarding server will check its cache, zone files, and perform iterative queries to resolve the host name. If unsuccessful, a "host not found" error is finally returned to the client.

It may not be appropriate to have the forwarding DNS server issuing iterative queries to servers located on the Internet. This may be true when the forwarding server is an internal DNS server. Internal DNS servers that issue iterative queries for Internet host name resolution are easy targets for hackers.

The forwarding server can be configured to not resolve the host names when the forward fails to return a valid IP address. When the forwarding computer is configured in this fashion, it is referred to as a slave server. The slave server accepts responses from the forwarder and relays them to the client without attempting host name resolution itself.

Security Considerations and DNS Server Location

A slave server/caching-only forwarder combination can be implemented to protect zone data information on internal DNS servers. A secure intranet is isolated from the Internet by a firewall. The forwarding server is on the intranet side of the firewall, while the forwarder is located on the Internet side of the firewall. The forwarder is configured as a caching-only server because of its high Internet visibility.

The firewall must be configured to allow DNS query traffic between the forwarding server and the forwarder. DNS traffic passes through UDP Port 53, and the firewall needs to be configured to limit pass-through of DNS queries to only the two server's IP addresses on the necessary port.

For example, at bluenimbus.com we have an internal DNS server we use to resolve internal DNS requests. DNS queries for intranet resources do not represent a security risk. However, what happens when we need to resolve Internet host names?

When the recursive request for Internet host name resolution hits our internal DNS server (which is authoritative for only bluenimbus.com and dev.bluenimbus.com), it begins the iterative query process. The Internet DNS servers send their responses to our internal DNS server through the firewall. This exposes our internal DNS server, and its zone data, to the Internet. How can we avoid this potentially disastrous scenario?

We can place a caching-only forwarder on the outside of the firewall and configure the internal DNS server to be a slave server. Now when a client issues a name resolution request for an Internet host, the internal DNS server will forward the request to the forwarder on the outside of the firewall. The forwarder resolves the FQDN to an IP address. If successful, the forwarder will return the IP address to the internal DNS server. The internal DNS server will return the IP address to the client. If the forwarder is unsuccessful, it will send a "host not found" error to the internal server, which returns this information to the client. Our internal slave server will not issue iterative queries to resolve the host name itself.

At no time does an Internet DNS server send a response to the internal DNS server. In this way, internal zone records are safe.

Configuring DNS Server Options

Installing the DNS server service is a simple procedure that is covered in a walkthrough at the end of the chapter. Configuration parameters are made after installation. Open the DNS management console, right-click on the server name, and click Properties to access the DNS server configuration property sheets.

The DNS server Properties dialog box first presents you with the Interfaces tab, with which you configure which interfaces the DNS server should listen for queries. This is an issue only for multihomed machines. On multihomed machines, the servicing of DNS queries can be limited to selected adapters by entering the IP addresses of the adapters that should accept queries.

Click on the Forwarders tab and put a checkmark in the "Enable forwarders" check box to make the server a forwarding DNS server. Enter the IP address(s) of the forwarder in the "P address" text box. The "Forward time-out (seconds)" text box allows you to define how long the server will continue attempting to contact and use a listed forwarder. The server will try the next server on the list if the server is unable to contact the forwarder by the end of the time-out period.

This server will be a slave server if the "Do not use recursion" check box is selected. Combining slave servers with caching-only servers is an excellent method to ensure DNS zone database security (Figure 13.2).

The Advanced tab includes some extended features of the Windows 2000 DNS server, as seen in Figure 13.3.

Six advanced server options can be configured as seen in Figure 13.3. The details of each of these options are included in Table 13.1.

The Name checking option allows for the definition of valid DNS name conventions when the DNS server accesses the validity of zone records. Non-RFC (ANSI), UTF-8, and All Names are options for this setting. The "Load zone data on startup" list box configures the boot method for the DNS server.

Figure 13.2 DNS slave and forwarder protecting the internal DNS zone information.

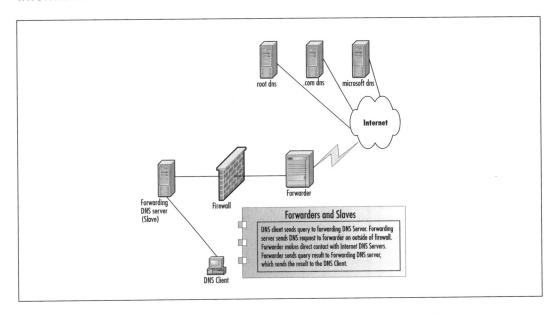

Figure 13.3 The Advanced tab in the DNS server Properties dialog box.

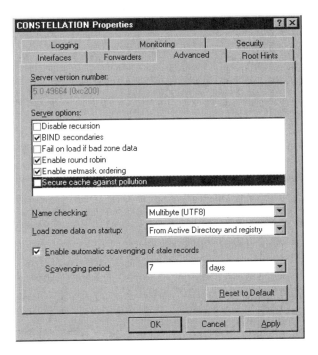

Table 13.1 Advanced DNS Server Options

Option	Properties
Disable recursion	Allows recursion to be disabled. Recursion is enabled by default.
BIND secondaries	Allows the Windows 2000 DNS server to use compression and include multiple records in a single TCP message when transferring zone data to BIND secondary servers. This is the default zone transfer method for Windows 2000 DNS servers. BIND-based DNS servers that run versions 4.9.4 and later support this zone transfer method.
Fail on load if bad zone data	Selecting this option will prevent the DNS server from loading zone data if errors are detected in zone records. This is disabled by default.
Enable round robin	Selecting this option enables DNS round robin. DNS round robin is used to rotate and reorder a list of multiple A Address resource records when the queried host is configured with multiple IP addresses. DNS round robin is an ideal vehicle for load balancing all types of Winsock-related services. DNS round robin is enabled by default.
Enable netmask ordering	The DNS server can reorder a list of multiple A Address records based on local subnet priority if the queried host name is for a multihomed computer. This is enabled by default.
Secure cache against pollution	Windows 2000 DNS servers use a secure response option that prevents adding unrelated resource records included in a referral answer to the cache. Typically, any names added in referral answers are cached. This expedites resolving subsequent DNS queries. When this feature is enabled, the server will determine if referred names are potentially polluting or are unsecured and discard them. The server determines whether to cache the name offered in a referral by determining whether it is part of the DNS domain name tree for which the original queried was made. For example, if the original query was for dev.bluenimbus.com, and a referral answer provided a record for a name outside of the bluenimbus.com domain name tree, such as syngress.net, the syngress.net referral would not be included in the cache.

A DNS server can retain old or stale DDNS registrations over time, in a manner similar to that seen with WINS servers. Put a checkmark in the check box for "Enable automatic scavenging of stale records" to allow the DDNS server to clean out these records. When this option is enabled, it sets the default for all zones defined on this server. Each zone can be configured independently of this default setting.

The Root Hints property sheet displays the server name and IP addresses for the Internet root DNS servers. Entries can be added, edited, or removed as required.

The Logging property sheet allows for the configuration of advanced debug logging options. All debugging options are disabled by default. You can selectively enable debugging options. The DNS Server service will perform trace-level logging that aids in debugging the server when error conditions are extant. These specialized debugging options are disk and processor intensive. Enable them only when actively troubleshooting a problem with the DNS server.

Configuring DNS Services

After installing the DNS service it must be configured. There is a wealth of configuration options available, but your primary responsibilities will be to manage and configure forward and reverse lookup zones. Let's examine some of the configuration options available for both.

Creating Forward Lookup Zones

A forward lookup zone contains resource records for hosts in domains included in the zone. Each zone can contain one or more domains. The zone database is stored in a file with the zone name and a .dns extension at the end of the name.

New zones are easy to configure in Windows 2000. The New Zone Wizard provides a walkthrough of process of creating a new zone. A walkthrough on how to create a new zone is included at the end of the chapter.

After the new zone is created, it must be configured to meet the required specifications. The forward lookup zone configuration options are available after right-clicking on the name of the zone and then selecting Properties. The Zone Properties General Tab reports on the server status. If you need to pause the DNS service without shutting it down, you can do it from here.

When creating a new zone, you are asked whether the zone is to be a Standard Primary, Standard Secondary, or Directory Integrated zone. The zone type can be changed at a later stage by clicking CHANGE.

Dynamic updates are not enabled by default. To enable dynamic updating of the DNS, click the down arrow in the "Allow dynamic updates?" drop-down box and select YES.

If a DDNS client registers its own Address records and does not shut down properly before being removed from the network, the host's Address record will not be removed from the DDNS server. Laptop users who plug in to the network and leave frequently can also leave behind outdated and invalid Address records.

This creates problems similar to those seen with WINS servers. Unlike WINS, there is no method for tombstoning a record. Problems arise when too many outdated or stale records remain in the database:

- They take up disk space and increase the size of the zone database. This increases the amount of bandwidth required during zone transfer.
- It takes longer to search large zone databases. This impairs the performance of the DDNS server.
- The existence of stale records can lead to incorrect host name resolution.

To solve these problems, aging/scavenging of stale resource records can be initiated. Click AGING and you will be presented by the Zone Aging/Scavenging Properties dialog box.

Scavenging is not enabled by default—and for good reason. If the Administrator is not fully aware of the implications of scavenging, valid resource records could be removed from the DDNS zone database.

Selecting the Start of Authority (SOA) tab presents a window similar to Figure 13.4.

The Serial number field is used to track changes to the zone database. Each time there is a change to the zone database, the serial number will be incremented. You can manually increment the serial number by 1 if INCREMENT is depressed.

The Primary server text box contains the name of the server housing the master copy of the zone. Click BROWSE and select another server to change this value.

The Responsible person text box contains the e-mail address of the DDNS server Administrator. Include the e-mail address of the DDNS Administrator here in FQDN format. For example, if the DDNS Administrator's e-mail address is soniabarrett@bluenimbus.com, you would enter soniabarrett.bluenimbus.com (notice the substitution of the @ for a .).

The Secondary DDNS server will check for updates to the zone database on a periodic basis. The amount of time the secondary DDNS will wait between update checks is defined by the refresh interval. The default is 15 minutes. You can change this by manipulating the time periods in the appropriate drop-down boxes. If you do not have clients that dynamically update their records, you might want to increase the refresh interval.

Figure 13.4 The Start of Authority (SOA) tab in the zone Properties dialog

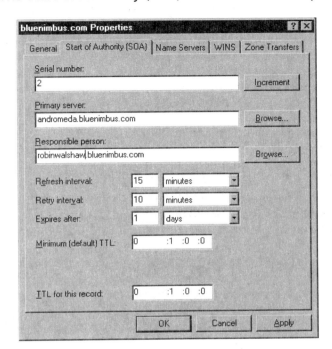

If a secondary DDNS server is not able to contact the Master server, it will repeat the zone transfer request. How often this request is repeated is determined by the retry interval. The default retry interval is 10 minutes and should be set to a value smaller than the refresh interval.

When a DDNS server queries another DNS server, the responding DNS server will send information about how long the record should be considered valid. This is known as the Time to Live (TTL). The Time to Live can be set in the Minimum (default) TTL text box. This is the default value for records emanating from this server. Individual records can be configured with their own TTL values, which will override the server TTL. The default period is 60 minutes. The SOA record has its own TTL, which you can modify in the TTL for this record text box.

Click on the Name Servers tab to see a list of name servers that are authoritative for the zone. Lists of name servers are configured for either the server or zone. This displays a list of DNS servers configured to be authoritative for the zone. In most cases, this includes all other servers that are configured as zone secondaries. In order to make a server authoritative for a zone, it must have a Name Server (NS) record configured in the zone.

DDNS servers that cannot locate a resource record for a requested host name can be configured to look up the host name in a WINS database. To configure the DDNS server to use WINS forward lookup (resolving NetBIOS name to IP address), click on the WINS tab.

Place a checkmark in the "Use WINS forward lookup" to enable WINS forwarding. The "Do not replicate this record" check box is enabled if you have non-Microsoft DNS servers acting as secondaries. A zone update failure might occur if you include WINS resource record information in the zone transfer to non-Microsoft DNS servers. If all the secondaries are Microsoft DNS servers, leave the check box clear so that WINS resource records are included in the zone transfer.

If the WINS forward lookup is enabled, enter the IP addresses of the WINS servers to be queried. An ordered list of WINS servers to be queried can be configured. If the first WINS server fails to respond, the next one on the list is tried.

Consider adding a new WINS-enabled DDNS lookup zone dedicated to WINS lookup requests. When naming the zone, use a subdomain added to an existing DNS domain that is used just for WINS-specific referrals added to your DNS domain namespace.

For example, consider a domain named dev.bluenimbus.com with a new zone, wins.dev.bluenimbus.com. The new WINS referral zone is then used as the root zone for any WINS-aware computers with names not found in other DNS zones.

To make the WINS referral zone work, its domain name in a DNS suffix search order for the clients is needed. This can be configured manually at the client, or the DNS suffix search order can be configured as an option delivered by a DHCP server. When the name of the WINS referral zone is included in the DNS suffix search order list, any DNS names not resolved in other zones will be resolved using the WINS referral subdomain.

DDNS servers acting as Master servers are able to transfer their zone databases to configured Secondary servers or to other domain controllers. Click on the Zone Transfers tab to configure zone transfer options, as seen in Figure 13.5.

Not strangely, to allow zone transfers, you check the "Allow zone transfers" box. You then decide who is allowed to transfer the zone. The three options are:

- To any server
- Only to servers listed on the Name Servers tab
- Only to the following servers

If you allow transfer to any server, anyone configuring a DNS server can transfer a zone, whether you desire that transfer or not. The second option allows you to restrict zone transfers to computers that are known authoritative secondaries for the zone. If for some reason you want more granular control of zone transfer, you can enter the IP addresses of

Figure 13.5 The Zone Transfers tab in the zone Properties dialog box.

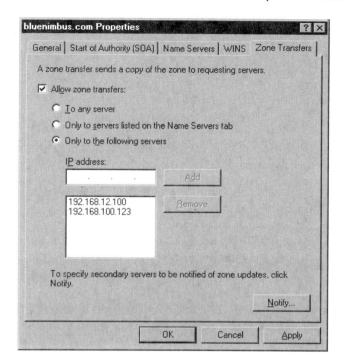

selected DNS servers in the IP address box under the "Only to the following servers" option.

Without further configuration, DNS servers will only update their zone
files according to the amount of time configured in the refresh interval. The
Master server can be configured to immediately notify secondaries when
there is a change to the zone database. Click NOTIFY to enable this feature.

To enable notification, put a checkmark in the "Automatically notify"
check box. Then select whether you want servers listed on the Name Server
tab or a custom set of DNS servers to be notified. If you choose the latter,
then enter the IP addresses of those servers.

Creating Reverse Lookup Zones

A reverse lookup zone allows you to find host names via IP addresses. This
is the opposite of the forward lookup where you wish to resolve host names
to IP addresses. In order to accomplish this, you must configure a reverse
lookup zone.

The reverse lookup zone takes on the format of <network_ID_in_reverse>.
in-addr.arpa. For example, to create a reverse lookup zone for network ID
192.168.2.0, you would create a reverse lookup zone 2.168.192.in-addr.arpa.

Queries directed to hosts located in network ID 192.168.2.0 would be directed to this reverse lookup zone for IP address to host name resolution. Reverse lookup zones are populated with Pointer resource records.

Reverse lookup zones are easy to configure in Windows 2000. A New Zone Wizard dedicated to creating a new reverse lookup zone can be launched, and all you need do is right-click on the Reverse Lookup Zones node in the left pane of the DNS administrative console and select New Zone. The wizard will ask for the network ID, and will automatically create a zone database file with the .dns extension based on the reverse lookup zone's name.

Configuration options for the reverse lookup zone are almost exactly the same as those found for forward lookup zones. The only tab that is different in the reverse lookup zone is the WIN-R tab.

A reverse WINS lookup allows a client to perform IP address to NetBIOS name resolution. The WINS database is not indexed by IP address; therefore, the DNS service cannot send a reverse name lookup to a WINS server.

The DNS service solves this problem by sending a node adapter status request directly to the IP address implied in the DNS reverse query. A node adapter status request causes the target computer to respond with a list of NetBIOS names registered for the adapter.

The DNS server will append the DNS domain name listed in the domain to append to returned name text box onto the NetBIOS name provided in the node status response. The result is forwarded to the requesting client.

Record Types

The DNS forward lookup zones are populated with a variety of resource records. The most common resource records include:

- Host or A Address
- Pointer (PTR)
- Service location (SRV)
- Mail Exchanger (MX)
- Alias or Canonical Name (CNAME)

Table 13.2 lists the types of records and their functions in the DNS database.

The SRV record has been recently introduced to the Microsoft DNS server. The primary purpose at this time is to record the information about domain controllers in the DNS. The SRV record is similar in function to the Service Identifier used in the NetBIOS name, which is saved in the WINS database. Examples of such services include LDAP, Telnet, and SMTP. A DNS client can then locate a server with the desired service based on the SRV record entry.

Table 13.2 Resource Record Types

Resource Record Type	Name	Description
SOA	Start of Authority	The SOA identifies the DNS server as authoritative for the data within the domain. The first record in any zone file is the SOA. Several configuration parameters are included in the SOA RR.
NS	Name Server	The NS record defines a DNS server that will return an authoritative answer for the domain. This includes the Primary DNS server for the zone, and Secondary DNS servers to which you delegate authority for the zone.
A	Address	The Address record contains the host name to IP address mapping for the particular host. The majority of the records in the zone will be host A Address records.
SRV	Service	The SRV denotes a service running on a particular host. This is similar to the service identifier in NetBIOS environments. If a host is looking for a domain controller for authentication, it will check for a SRV record to find an authenticating server.
CNAME	Canonical Name	This is an alias record. There must be a computer with an existing A Address record. For example, an alias could be created for a computer named proxima if that computer is also a Web server. The most common CNAME record for Web servers is www.
MX	Mail Exchanger	Identifies the domain's preferred mail servers. Several servers in the same domain can have MX records. An order of precedence determines which MX records will be delivered to the client.
HINFO	Host Information	HINFO records provide information about the DNS hardware and software. Entries include CPU, operating system, interface type, and other server characteristics. This is a primitive resource tracking method.
PTR	Pointer	The Pointer record is created for reverse lookups. Reverse lookups are valuable when doing security analysis and checking authenticity of source domains for e-mail.

A service record conforms to the following syntax:

```
service.protocol.name  ttl  class  SRV  preference  weight  port  targe
t
```

An example:

```
_ldap._tcp.ms-dcs   SRV  0 0    389 andromeda.bluenimbus.com
                    SRV 10 0    389 crabnebula.bluenimbus.com
```

Two fields of interest are the priority and weight fields. The priority field determines which target hosts are contacted first, in order of priority, for a specific service. The weight field is used to provide for load balancing when multiple servers are listed in the target field, and all have the same priority number. When all target servers have the same priority value, this value is used to set an added level of preference that can determine the exact order or balancing of selection for the target hosts used in an answered SRV query. If you use any value but 0, servers of equal priority are tried in proportion to the weight of this value. The range of values is 1 to 65535 for both priority and weight values. Use a value of 0 in the weight field if load balancing is not desired.

Manually Adding Records

At this time, the only resource records that are dynamically updated are the A Address, Pointer (PTR), and SRV records. The DDNS Administrator must manually create all other records.

Adding resource records is time consuming but easy to do. To manually add a new RR:

1. Open the DNS console.

2. Expand all Nodes and right-click on the node you wish to add the new RR. A context menu similar to Figure 13.6 should be displayed.

3. Select the type of RR you wish to create. For example, selecting New Host will cause the New Host dialog box to appear.

4. Enter the host name of the machine in the Name text box. Enter the IP address of the host in the IP address text box. To have the server automatically enter the Pointer record for reverse lookups, place a checkmark in the "Create associated pointer (PTR) record" check box. The option is available to change the Time to Live for the record.

5. Click ADD HOST. The new record should appear in the DNS console.

Configuring the DNS Client

The DNS client can be configured manually or via a DHCP server. The preferred method is to have the DHCP server automatically configure DNS set-

Figure 13.6 Context menu for the selected domain.

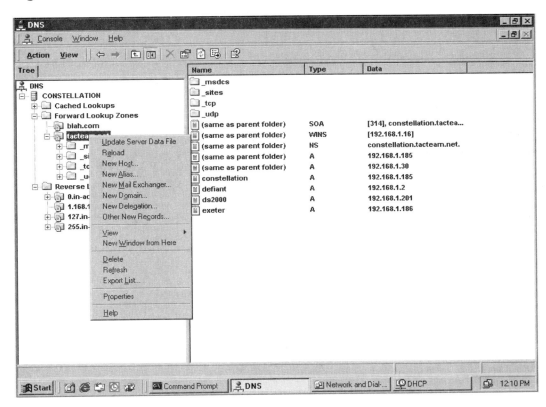

tings for DHCP clients. This avoids error inherent in going from machine to machine manually configuring DNS settings. We will look at both approaches in this section.

Manually

This has to be performed at the machine in question and cannot be completed remotely. Manually configuring the client's Preferred DNS involves the following:

1. Log on with an account that has administrative privileges.

2. Right-click on My Network Places, and click Properties.

3. This opens the Network and Dial-up Connections window. You should see at least two icons: one for Make New Connection and a second for Local Area Connection. Right-click on Local Area Connection, and then click Properties.

4. Scroll through the list and find Internet Protocol (TCP/IP). Click once on the text (not on the checkmark, or you may remove it inadvertently), and then click PROPERTIES just underneath it. The Internet Protocol (TCP/IP) Properties page is then displayed.

5. Select the option "Use the following DNS server addresses" and type in the IP for the Preferred DNS server. For fault tolerance, type in the IP address of an Alternate DNS server.

6. Click OK, and then click OK again.

The foregoing procedure allows for basic client configuration. Other client configuration options are available by clicking ADVANCED.

From here, you can add additional servers to the DNS servers address list. The search order can be changed by using the up and down arrow buttons on the right side of the DNS servers list.

One area of confusion regarding DNS client setup relates to the three options displayed beneath the DNS servers list. The option "Append primary and connection specific DNS suffixes" refers to what DNS suffixes should be included in a request to a DNS server if an unqualified DNS request is sent to a DNS server.

For example, if http://andromeda is typed in the address bar of a Web browser, it would be considered an unqualified request since there is only a host name, and no domain name, included in the request. A DNS server must use an FQDN in order to process a request. The Primary suffix is the computer's domain membership included in the Network Identification tab of the System Properties dialog box.

The computer's Primary membership can be changed by clicking PROPERTIES. The machine's domain membership can then be changed via the Identification Changes dialog box.

Using DHCP

A significant amount of unnecessary administrative tasks can be avoided by using DHCP to assign DNS Preferred server addresses. To assign the DNS options at the DNS server:

1. Install a DHCP server. See Chapter 12, "Managing Windows 2000 DHCP Server," on how to install and configure a DHCP server.

2. Create a scope on the DHCP server. It is best to configure DNS server addresses on a per-scope basis. You want clients to use local DNS servers prior to querying remote DNS servers. Instructions on how to create a scope are found in Chapter 12.

3. Expand all nodes in the left pane. Right-click on the Scope Options node and select Configure Options. The Scope Options dialog box is then displayed (Figure 13.7).

Figure 13.7 Configuring DNS Scope Options.

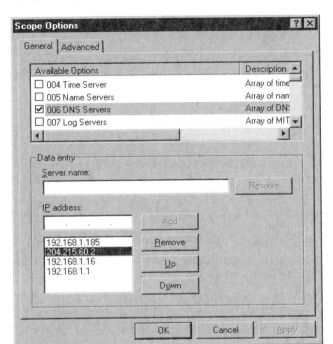

4. Check the "006 DNS Servers" option and type in the IP address of the DNS servers to be used for the scope. The DNS servers are listed in priority order. Enter the server IP addresses in the IP address text box, and then click ADD. Move the Preferred DNS server to the top by clicking UP or DOWN.

5. Click OK. The DHCP console will then display the new DNS options in the right pane.

DNS Walkthroughs

Installation of a DNS Server

DNS can be installed during the Windows 2000 installation process, or can be deferred until later. To install the DNS service when it has not been included in the Windows 2000 setup:

1. Click Start | Settings | Control Panel | Add/Remove Programs.

2. Click ADD/REMOVE WINDOWS COMPONENTS. This displays the Windows Components Wizard. Scroll down and select Networking Services.

3. Click DETAILS. This opens the Networking Services dialog box. Click the check box to the left of Domain Name System (DNS) to place a checkmark there. Click OK, and then click NEXT. The service will then commence installation.

4. Click FINISH to complete the installation

Creating a Forward Lookup Zone

1. Select Start | Programs | Administrative Tools | Computer Management.

2. Expand Services and Applications. Scroll down to the DNS entry and expand the computer name. Note if any zones appear in the left pane.

3. Right-click on the computer name, and then click New Zone.

4. The Welcome to the New Zone Wizard starts. Click NEXT.

5. Assuming that a Standard Primary Zone is required, select this option. Click NEXT.

6. The Wizard requests whether a forward lookup zone or a reverse lookup zone is required. Always create the forward lookup zone before creating the reverse lookup zone. The reverse lookup zone will contain the Pointer records for resources in the forward lookup zone. Click NEXT.

7. Type in the name of the new zone. Click NEXT.

8. By default, the wizard creates the new zone file based on the domain name, and then appends the .dns extension. This file will is stored in the %systemroot%\system32\dns folder, and can easily be transferred to another DNS server if required. Click NEXT.

9. The wizard presents a datasheet listing the responses to the wizard. If everything looks good, click FINISH.

10. Return to the Computer Management window. Expand all zones to see the new forward lookup zone.

Creating a Reverse Lookup Zone

Now let's configure our reverse lookup zone. The computers in the blue-nimbus.com domain are located on network ID 192.168.1.0 and use the default Class C subnet mask 255.255.255.0.

1. Log on with an account that is a member of the local Administrators group if not already logged on as such.

Figure 13.8 Configuring the reverse lookup zone.

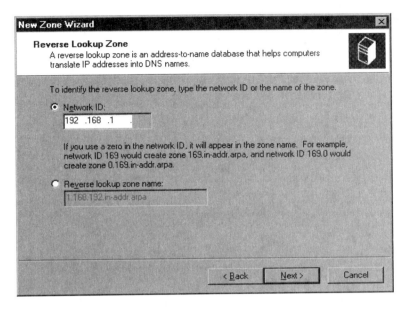

2. Click Start | Programs | Administrative Tools | Computer Management.

3. Expand all levels in the DNS node.

4. Right-click on your computer name, and click New Zone.

5. The New Zone Wizard starts. Click NEXT.

6. The wizard then asks whether to create a Standard Primary, Standard Secondary, or an Active Directory Integrated zone. Select Standard Primary. If Active Directory is already installed, you should select Active Directory Integrated to take advantage of the benefits of Active Directory. Click NEXT.

7. Select Reverse Lookup Zone. Click NEXT.

8. The wizard requires the network ID that is serviced by this reverse lookup zone, as seen in Figure 13.8. The network ID and subnet mask can be entered; alternatively, directly enter the name of the zone file yourself. If you wish to enter the lookup zone name manually, begin with the network ID in reverse, then a period, then type **in-addr.arpa**. For example, if the network ID were 131.107.0.0, the reverse lookup file would be 107.131.in-addr.arpa. Click NEXT.

9. The wizard then requests confirmation of the name of the file. Unless you have an old reverse lookup file to import, select the default. Click NEXT.

10. The last screen confirms the data entered data. Click FINISH.

11. Return to the Computer Management screen to confirm the creation of your new reverse lookup zone.

Testing the DNS Server

The zone should now be populated with resource records. A Address records are the most common type of record, and can be configured by:

1. Log on with an Administrative account.

2. Click Start | Programs | Administrative Tools | Computer Management.

3. Expand the Services and Applications node and the DNS node.

4. Right-click on the bluenimbus.com forward lookup zone. Click New Host. A New Host Properties dialog box similar to Figure 13.9 is then displayed.

5. Enter the host name, bluto, of the new computer. Enter the IP address of the host. Be sure to select "Create associated pointer (PTR) record" so that DNS will automatically create this record for you and place it in the inverse lookup zone.

Figure 13.9 Entering resource records for host computers.

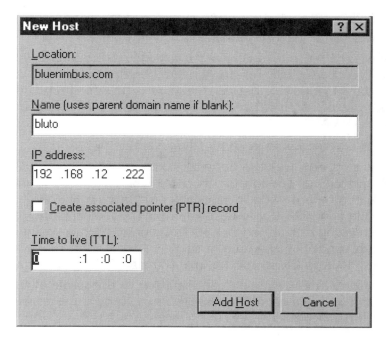

6. Now a resource record for host bluto at bluenimbus.com has been configured. Open a command prompt. At the command prompt, type:

nslookup bluto.bluenimbus.com

The host should successfully resolve.

Summary

The Domain Name System is a distributed database that allows for host name to IP address resolution. Domain names are arranged in a hierarchical structure, with the Root domain occupying the uppermost position in the hierarchy.

Top-level domains lie just beneath Root. Common top-level domains are .com, .net, and .edu. Second-level domains lie under the top-level domains and frequently take on the name of the organization they represent. Microsoft.com is an example of a second-level domain. Root, top-level, and secondary-level namespaces are centrally managed. Administrators of second-level domains are responsible for their portion of the DNS database. This distributes the responsibility for managing what would otherwise be an unmanageable database.

Each computer in the DNS namespace has a host name. A Fully Qualified Domain Name (FQDN) is the computer host name combined with the full domain path to that computer. Unqualified names do not include a full domain path to the host.

When a DNS client needs to resolve a host name to an IP address, it issues a recursive query to its Preferred DNS server. If the Preferred DNS server is not authoritative for the destination domain, it will issue a series of iterative queries to other DNS servers to find one authoritative for the zone. The response from the authoritative DNS server is sent to the client's preferred DNS server, which forwards the answer to the DNS client.

Each domain's resources are contained in a zone file. Multiple contiguous domains can be included in a single zone. Zone files are stored on DNS servers. DNS clients can query DNS servers containing a zone of interest to look up a resource. A single DNS server can be responsible for multiple zones.

Resource records track domain resources. You use an A address record to add resources to the domain. You use other resource records types to identify zone resources such as Mail Servers. The NS resource record defines servers that are authoritative for domains.

The Primary DNS is the one on which the first zone was created. The Primary contains the only read/write copy of the zone database. Read-only copies of the zone database are kept on Secondary DNS servers. Secondary DNS servers allow for fault tolerance in the event the Primary DNS server becomes unavailable. Secondaries are also useful in providing load balancing.

The Primary DNS server copies the zone database to the Secondary. Traditional zone transfer copied the entire zone database file from Primary to Secondary. Windows 2000 DNS servers support incremental zone transfer. Incremental zone transfer copies only new or changed records to the Secondary DNS server.

Windows 2000 DNS servers support dynamic update of Address records. A Windows 2000 DNS client can update its own Address and Pointer records. Downlevel clients are unable to update their own records in the DNS. Using DHCP as a mediator can provide support for dynamic DNS update for downlevel clients. DHCP will update both Address and Pointer records for downlevel DHCP clients.

Zones can be either "Standard" or Active Directory Integrated. Active Directory Integrated zones provide for multi-master replication, more efficient zone transfer, and secure updating of the zone database.

AD Integrated DNS servers are all Primary DNS servers. Zone transfer is from an AD domain controller to another. The Primary DNS server replicates only change properties, rather than entire records. You provide security on a granular level, and access controls can be placed on objects in the zone database. This prevents updating of resource records without requisite permissions.

FAQs

Q: How do I make DNS rotate through the available addresses for a service—say, www.bluenimbus.com—to obtain a load-balancing effect, or similar?

A: Create several A Address records for www.bluenimbus.com, and give each entry a different IP address. The DNS server will rotate through the entries so that the same server isn't hit twice in a row.

Q: I want to set up DNS on an intranet. Are there any special considerations?

A: You do not need to use the cache hints file included with the Windows 2000 DDNS server. Replace that file with the host names and IP addresses of your internal root servers. This has the advantage of not having to obtain a new cache.dns file on a regular basis.

Q: Where does the caching name server store its cache?

A: The cache is completely stored in memory, it is never written to disk at any time. The cache can become very large in a short period of time in a large organization. DDNS servers dedicated as caching servers must have generous amounts of RAM to respond to DNS client queries on a timely basis.

Q: What happens after I restart my caching DDNS server?

A: The cached entries disappear. It is recommended that a caching DDNS server be very stable and rarely rebooted for this reason.

Q: How many times does a DNS client query a DNS server, and for how long?

A: The DNS client will query each DNS server on the list in order of succession. The client will wait three seconds and then issue another query. Total time spent on each server is 15 seconds, or a total of five queries. The client will then move to the next server on the list and repeat the process.

Q: Is DNS necessary in Windows 2000?

A: No. DNS is only required if you implement Active Directory domain controllers. Windows 2000 client computers can participate in Windows NT 4.0 domains. Windows NT domains are NetBIOS based and do not require host name resolution services. DNS is required if you do implement a Windows 2000 domain model.

Q: Can I use "illegal" characters with Windows 2000 DDNS servers?

A: Yes, but they are no longer illegal. New DNS specifications allow for the use of an extended character set for label names. Microsoft Windows 2000 DDNS servers support UTF-8, which is based on the Unicode character set. The Unicode character set allows for characters from virtually all known languages. Great care must be taken if you use non-standard characters, because not all DNS servers support the extended character set.

Q: Why should I use Directory Integrated DNS zones?

A: There are many reasons to implement Active Directory Integrated DNS zones. The two foremost reasons are secure updates and streamlined directory replication. Non-Directory Integrated servers cannot prevent unauthorized dynamic updates. Directory-enabled zones allow the Administrator to control access to the zone database on a granular basis. Zone database replication is faster for Directory-enabled zones. Non-Directory Integrated zones can transfer records using either AXFR or IXFR. While IXRF is more efficient than AXFR, the entire record must be sent for those records that have changed. Directory Integrated zones send only changed property information and not the entire record.

Managing Windows 2000 WINS Server

Solutions in this chapter:

- Introduction
- WINS Functional Description
- WINS Configuration
- New Features in Windows 2000 WINS
- WINS Walkthrough
- Summary

Introduction

The success of the Windows platform belongs in no small part to Microsoft's strict observance of two basic principles: compatibility and ease of use. Each iteration of Windows became easier to use, while simultaneously maintaining backward compatibility with previous releases. Though admirable and sometimes necessary, these principles also mean that a certain amount of baggage from the past still exists in the bright new computing world of the future.

Classic examples of modern-day Windows coelacanths include DOS, ISA support, and WINS. Though the Windows Internet Name Service (WINS) may be regarded as a necessary evil in some environments, it can still provide a great deal of functionality. Legacy platforms and even Windows 2000 can use WINS as a robust, if not universally adopted, name resolution solution. Its purpose is to provide a method of resolving names to IP addresses.

Thanks to the improvements in Windows 2000, WINS Administrators are able to maintain their investment in WINS with a minimal amount of effort.

WINS Functional Description

WINS provides NetBIOS name resolution on the network via a dynamic database that matches friendly NetBIOS names to IP addresses. Users prefer names to numbers; it's easier for human beings to think of a particular computer on the network as MyServer than as 192.168.0.9.

IBM introduced the NetBIOS interface in the early 1980s. Microsoft then developed NetBIOS as an Application Programming Interface (API) for MS-DOS programs to use for network communication, and it became a standard for PC LANs. NetBIOS uses a flat namespace (in contrast to the hierarchical namespace of DNS), with each name limited to 16 characters in length. However, when a NetBIOS name is created (for instance, when a name is designated for a computer during installation of Windows 2000), only 15 characters can be used. The 16th character is hexadecimal and is used to identify the resource type.

NetBIOS names are registered dynamically when the computer starts up on the network or the user logs on. They cannot be duplicated on the network; for instance, if two computers are given the same NetBIOS name, the second one that attempts to log on to the network will not be allowed to register its name.

All Windows operating systems prior to Windows 2000 required NetBIOS in order to function in a networked environment. The NetBIOS interface is not a requirement for networking Windows 2000 computers; DDNS can handle all name resolution. However, Windows 2000 supports WINS and includes an improved version of the service, as many Windows

2000 networks will still include downlevel computers on the network that require NetBIOS for network communication.

The Windows 2000 core networking functions use the Winsock interface, thus disassociating it from the NetBIOS. Computer names are now host names, which can be dynamically registered, and queried for, using the new Windows 2000 Dynamic DNS server.

However, NetBIOS is still required for interoperability with legacy or downlevel operating systems and applications. To provide support for these clients, Microsoft provides a new and improved implementation of its NetBIOS Name Server (NBNS): the Windows Internet Name Server (WINS).

There are many benefits to using WINS; it provides the Administrator with a centralized database of NetBIOS names that is updated dynamically, and reduces broadcast traffic on the network. A Windows 2000 server can be a WINS server, implementing the TCP/IP over NetBIOS (NetBT) standards to register and resolve names for NetBIOS-enabled computers.

NetBIOS Name Resolution

Programs written to the NetBIOS API are required to know the name of the destination host in order to establish a session. However, the TCP/IP protocol only requires the destination IP address and port number in order to establish a session. It is important to remember that TCP/IP is unaware of the presence of NetBIOS names. The challenge then faced by NetBIOS applications on TCP/IP networks is to match up a NetBIOS name with an IP address, in a process known as NetBIOS name resolution.

NetBIOS over TCP/IP, or NetBT to its friends, is a component of the NetBIOS interface. When NetBIOS applications send a request to the network, NetBT intercepts this request and resolves the NetBIOS name to an IP address before the request is sent further down the TCP/IP protocol stack.

Microsoft provides several mechanisms for resolving NetBIOS names, including:

- NetBIOS name cache
- NetBIOS name server
- Broadcasts
- LMHosts file
- HOSTS file
- DNS

The order in which these methods are employed depends on the NetBIOS node type of the host computer. The NetBIOS node types are:

- B-node
- P-node
- M-node
- H-node

B-Node

B-node clients depend primarily on broadcasts to resolve NetBIOS names. Broadcasts are limited because they do not normally cross router boundaries. Additionally, they do not use NetBIOS name servers to resolve NetBIOS names. Microsoft's implementation of B-node is known as enhanced B-node. The enhanced B-node client preloads entries marked with the #PRE tag in the LMHosts file into the NetBIOS name cache.

The NetBIOS name cache is a reserved area in memory that stores recently resolved NetBIOS names. Entries stay in the NetBIOS name cache for two minutes, unless a destination client is contacted again before the end of the two minutes. If a client is contacted, then the name remains in the NetBIOS name cache for 10 minutes. The maximum time an entry can stay in the NetBIOS name cache is 10 minutes, regardless of how many times the client is contacted.

Microsoft enhanced B-node is the default NetBIOS name resolution method when the client is not configured as a WINS client. The order of resolution for the enhanced B-node client is as follows:

1. NetBIOS name cache
2. Broadcast
3. LMHosts file
4. HOSTS files
5. DNS

P-Node

A P-node client does not use broadcasts to resolve NetBIOS names; instead, it depends primarily on a NetBIOS name server to resolve NetBIOS name query requests. The following is the order of NetBIOS name resolution methods for P-node clients:

1. NetBIOS name cache
2. NetBIOS name server
3. LMHosts
4. HOSTS
5. DNS

M-Node

The M-node client uses both a NetBIOS name server and broadcasts in order to resolve a NetBIOS name. The M-node client will broadcast before issuing a NetBIOS name query request to a NetBIOS name server. M-node implementations might be helpful when there is a small group of computers at a branch office that communicate primarily with each other, and the only NetBIOS name server is on the far side of a slow WAN link. Since the branch office only contains a few computers, broadcast traffic is not significant. In this scenario, broadcasts are faster and more efficient than querying a NetBIOS name server on the far side of a slow WAN link.

NetBIOS name resolution methods for M-node clients proceed as follows:

1. NetBIOS name cache
2. Broadcast
3. LMHosts
4. NetBIOS name server
5. HOSTS
6. DNS

H-Node

H-node clients use NetBIOS name servers before they issue a NetBIOS name query request broadcast. When a computer is configured as a NetBIOS name server client, H-node becomes the default NetBIOS node type for Microsoft operating systems. In fact, one might think of H-node as enhanced H-node. An H-node client parses the LMHosts file at startup and preloads any entries in the LMHosts file that have the #PRE tag into the NetBIOS name cache. The order followed for NetBIOS name resolution for an H-node client is:

1. NetBIOS name cache
2. NetBIOS name server
3. Broadcast
4. LMHosts
5. HOSTS
6. DNS

Note that all node types will attempt to resolve NetBIOS names using a HOSTS file and a DNS server. HOSTS files contain Fully Qualified Domain Name (FQDN) to IP address mappings. DNS servers resolve FQDNs to IP addresses.

When a NetBIOS name is sent to the HOSTS file for resolution, only the host name component of the FQDN is queried. Similarly, when a NetBIOS name resolution request is sent to a DNS server, only the host name is portion is queried. When a DNS server receives a NetBIOS name to resolve, it only checks its own zone and does not refer the request to other DNS server for name resolution.

What Does WINS Do?

The Windows Internet Name Server (WINS) is Microsoft's implementation of a NetBIOS name server. WINS provides a centralized mechanism to resolve NetBIOS names to IP addresses. When computers are configured as WINS clients, they automatically register their names and IP addresses with a WINS server. When a NetBIOS client application requires resolution of a NetBIOS name to an IP address, it can query the WINS server to obtain this information.

To configure a computer to be a WINS client, the address(es) of one or more WINS servers can be added in the Advanced TCP/IP Settings Properties sheet of the client computer, as shown in Figure 14.1. If the computer is configured to obtain its IP address from a DHCP server, the DHCP server can provide the WINS server address information.

Prior to the development of WINS, NetBIOS names could be resolved by broadcast on the local subnet, or by use of an LMHosts file for IP addresses on other subnets.

Figure 14.1 WINS and the Advanced TCP/IP Settings properties.

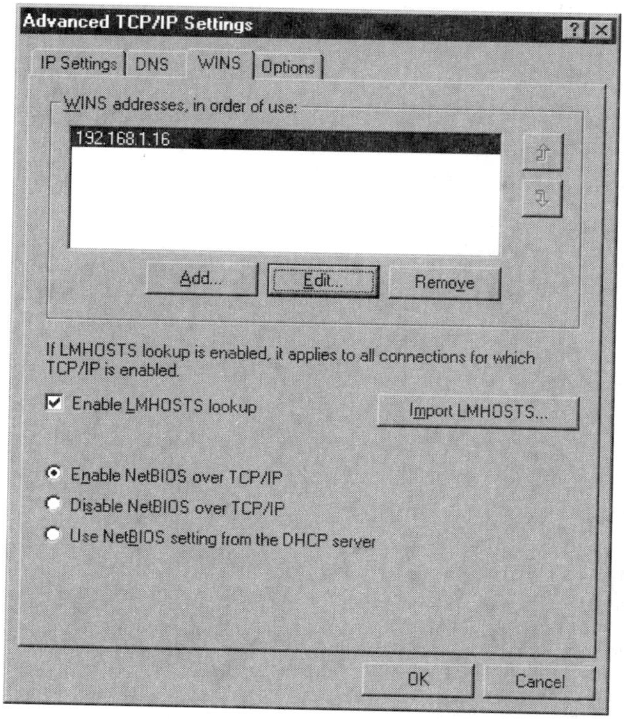

Name resolution using broadcasts is limited, because most routers stop NetBIOS broadcast traffic. Broadcast-based name resolution is only useful if the NetBIOS names to be resolved are on the local subnet. If a computer uses only broadcasts for NetBIOS name resolution, it will not be able to resolve NetBIOS names to IP addresses for computers on subnets other than its own.

One solution to the broadcast limitation is the LMHosts files. The LMHosts file contains NetBIOS names and IP address mappings. A computer can examine an LMHosts file for the IP address of remote computers that would otherwise be inaccessible via NetBIOS Name Query broadcast messages.

LMHosts files are limited by their static nature. In dynamic networks, such as those using DHCP, IP addresses change on a frequent basis for computers throughout the network. Each time a computer changes its IP address, the LMHosts file will need to be updated. On large internetworks, this can become an overwhelming task. In addition, LMHosts files need to be placed on every machine on the network (unless a central LMHosts file is configured). Furthermore, a flat text file is not the most efficient database structure. This becomes even more problematic when the number of NetBIOS hosts on the internetworks runs into the thousands.

WINS was developed specifically to address the limitations inherent with broadcasts and LMHosts.

Broadcasting vs. WINS

One way to resolve a NetBIOS name to an IP address is by using broadcasts. When a computer wants to send a message to a computer named Yoda, the originating computer sends a broadcast message to the network. A broadcast is a message that does not have a specific destination address; instead, it is transmitted to all computers on the subnet. This broadcast message is a name query. It is as if the computer is shouting to a crowd, "Yoda, are you out there?" If the target computer is on the subnet, it returns a response informing the first computer of its address, and then the message intended for Yoda can be sent.

There are two major drawbacks to the broadcast method of name resolution:

- Broadcasts create extra traffic on the networks, since they are sent to all computers on the subnet.
- Broadcasts do not normally cross routers, so if the destination computer is on a different subnet on the network, it will not "hear" the broadcast.

This is where the LMHosts file, discussed earlier, comes in. LMHosts files can be configured with the names and IP addresses of remote hosts, thereby circumventing the limitation of local NetBIOS name query requests.

> **NOTE**
>
> In an effort to alleviate some of the traffic congestion caused by broadcasts, a computer in a broadcast-based network (called B-node) will first check its name cache before broadcasting. The cache contains those names that were used recently, or an LMHosts file can be configured to preload certain names into the cache by adding the #PRE designation.

LMHosts vs. WINS

The biggest problem with using the LMHosts file for NetBIOS name resolution is the fact that it is a static file. If names and/or IP addresses change, or are added or removed, an Administrator must manually edit the file. Manual updating is tedious, time consuming, and prone to error. Thus, LMHosts is a viable method of resolving NetBIOS names only on a small and relatively stable network.

LMHosts is static, but WINS is a dynamic solution to the name resolution dilemma. A WINS server maintains a database with information similar to that in the LMHosts text file, but its name-to-IP mappings are updated automatically. When a WINS-enabled computer attaches to the network, it registers its name and IP address with the WINS server.

The WINS database contains an entry for each name, which is replicated to other WINS servers called replication partners.

The following sections explain the interactions a NetBIOS client has with a WINS server.

NetBIOS Name Registration Request

The name registration process is initiated when a WINS client requests to register its name, which is required to be unique, on the network. If the name requested does not already exist in the WINS database, the request is accepted and it is entered, timestamped, given a version ID, and a positive name registration response is sent back to the requesting computer.

If the requested name already exists in the database, one of several things occurs, depending on whether the IP address or the name registered in the WINS database is the same as that of the requesting computer, and further depending on the state of the entry.

If the IP address in the database is the same as that of the requesting computer then:

- If the name already exists and the IP address associated with the entry is the same as the one on the request, WINS will check the state of the entry to determine whether it is marked active, tombstoned, or released. If it is marked active and is owned by this WINS server, the timestamp will be updated and the requesting computer will receive a positive response, and is then able to use the name on the network.

- If it is marked tombstoned (discussed later) or released, or is owned by another WINS server, it is treated as a new registration. Again, a positive response is returned to the requesting client.

If the IP address in the database is different from that of the existing computer then:

- If the name already exists but the database entry shows a different IP address, and the entry is marked tombstoned or released, WINS can assign the name to the new IP address.

- If the name already exists with a different IP address and the entry is marked active, the WINS server will challenge the name. First, it sends a Wait for Acknowledge (WACK) message to the requesting computer, specifying an amount of time it should wait for an answer to its request. Then the server sends a name query to the IP address that is registered to the name in the database. If it receives a positive response, indicating that a computer is still on the network and using the name, it will reject the requesting computer's request to register the name. If the server does not receive a positive response to the name query after three tries, it will send the requesting computer a message accepting its request, and will enter the name and new IP address in the database.

Name Renewal

As part of the registration process, the WINS server gives the client computer a Time To Live (TTL) indicating that the registration must be renewed after a certain amount of time or it will expire and eventually be removed from the WINS database.

By default, the TTL is six days. However, WINS clients begin the attempt to renew their registrations when 50% of the designated time has elapsed, so renewals will usually be done every three days.

Figure 14.2 WINS server settings are made using the WINS console.

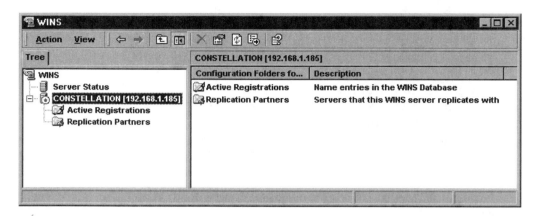

NOTE

Static WINS entries, which are manually entered in the database, do not have to be renewed and do not expire.

The renewal process is similar to the initial name registration process. The WINS client sends a refresh request to the WINS server at the 50% mark. If there is no response, the client will continue to send requests until it receives a positive response.

The renewal interval is set on the WINS server through the WINS properties sheet, which can be accessed as follows:

1. Start | Programs | Administrative Tools | WINS. This will open the WINS console, as shown in Figure 14.2.

2. To change the interval settings, right-click on the WINS server name and select Properties, then select the Intervals tab, as shown in Figure 14.3.

WARNING

If you have multiple WINS servers that are replication partners, they should all use the same renew interval. If you change the interval from the default, be sure to change it on all partners, or network operation may be disrupted.

Figure 14.3 The renew, extinction, and verification intervals.

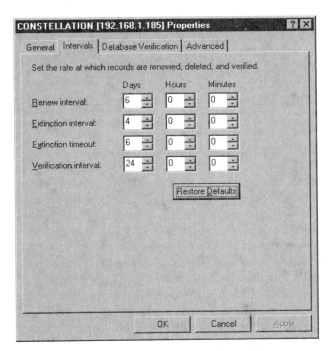

The WINS Properties sheet also allows you to set the intervals for extinction and verification, and the extinction timeout. The extinction interval is the amount of time between when an entry is marked as released and when it is marked as extinct in the WINS database. The extinction timeout is the amount of time between when the entry is marked extinct and when it is scavenged (removed) from the database. The verification interval determines the time after which the WINS server will verify that old names (that are owned by other servers) are still active.

NetBIOS Name Release

When a WINS client shuts down properly, it sends a message to the WINS server releasing its name. The computer user can also cause the name to be released without shutting down the system by issuing the command nbtstat -RR at the command line. When either of these occurs, a message called a name release request is sent to the WINS server. The server then marks the registration entry as released and sends a release confirmation message to the client.

If the entry has been marked released, and a computer attempts to register that name with a different IP address, the WINS server will allow the new registration because it knows the name is no longer being used with the former IP address.

If a computer shuts down abnormally, without releasing the name, when it attempts to connect again and register its name, the WINS server will challenge the earlier registration. However, in this case there would be no response to the challenge, so the new registration would be allowed.

The client can also release the name by broadcasting if it sends a release request and does not receive a release confirmation from a WINS server.

NetBIOS Name Query Request

A WINS client first checks its NetBIOS name cache to see if it has recently resolved the NetBIOS name of the computer it is seeking to contact. If the address mapping is not in the NetBIOS name cache, the WINS client will send a NetBIOS name query request to its Primary WINS server. If the Primary WINS server does not respond after three attempts (500ms apart), the Secondary WINS server is tried.

The WINS server searches its records for an IP address mapping for the requested NetBIOS name. If the NetBIOS name-IP address mapping is contained in the WINS database, a positive NetBIOS name query response is sent to the WINS client. If the WINS server does not contain a mapping, a negative NetBIOS name query response is sent to the WINS client.

If the WINS client receives a negative NetBIOS name query response, it will query a Secondary WINS server. The WINS client continues to query Secondary WINS servers until it receives a positive NetBIOS name query response.

WINS Configuration

In the previous section, we covered the fundamentals of WINS and its processes. Now that the foundations have been laid, it is time to discuss how to optimally configure WINS.

Configuring Static Entries

A WINS client can look up the IP address of another WINS client by querying the WINS database. But how are IP addresses of non-WINS clients resolved?

The WINS-enabled client would normally continue through the normal NetBIOS name resolution process, causing a potential delay in name resolution. An effective method of resolving this problem is to add a static mapping for the non-WINS client into the WINS database.

A static mapping is a nondynamic entry in the WINS database. The static mapping information must be entered manually into the WINS database in a similar fashion to entries made in standard DNS databases. Static mappings are not typically overwritten by dynamic name registrations unless the "migrate on" option is enabled.

A classic example of static entries involves a Windows-based WINS client that needs to contact a UNIX server running a NetBIOS application. In order for the Windows-based client to establish a session with the UNIX server, its NetBIOS name must be resolved. The Windows client is located on a remote subnet and does not have a mapping for the UNIX host in its LMHosts file. The solution to this problem is to create a static mapping for the UNIX machine in the WINS database. The WINS client is then able to locate a mapping for the UNIX host and resolve its NetBIOS name to an IP address.

Obviously, a number of Microsoft operating systems can act as WINS clients, including:

- Windows 2000
- Windows NT versions 3.5*x* and 4.0
- Windows 9*x*
- Windows 3.*x* with Microsoft TCP/IP-32 add-on
- Microsoft Network client 3.0 for MS-DOS
- LAN Manager 2.2c for MS-DOS

To add a static mapping to the WINS database, right-click on the Active Registrations node in the left pane of the WINS management console and click New Static Mapping.

The only information required is the NetBIOS name, an optional scope ID, the type of mapping, and the IP address of the statically mapped host. Table 14.1 defines the types of static mapping entries that can be created. Table 14.2 lists the different NetBIOS names registered in the WINS database.

Table 14.1 Types of WINS Static Mappings

Type	Explanation
Unique	Configure a Unique mapping when a single IP address defines the host computer. Three NetBIOS names are associated with Unique static mappings. A NetBIOS name associating the host name for the workstation service (redirector), messenger service, and server service are created. For example, NOSTROMO will have three entries in the WINS database: NOSTROMO[00h], NOSTROMO[03h], and NOSTROMO [20h].
Group	If the computer is a member of a workgroup, a Group entry can be configured for the machine. The IP address of the host is not included, and Group name resolution is performed via local subnet broadcasts only. This known as a Normal Group.

Table 14.1 *continued*

Type	Explanation
Domain Name	A Domain Name entry creates a [1Ch] mapping in the WINS database. This mapping points to domain controllers in Windows NT environments. A WINS client queries the WINS database for [1Ch] entries for a machine to authenticate a logon.
Internet Group	Configure an Internet Group when you want to create Administrative Groups of shared resources that appear as members of the group when browsing for resources. Examples include grouping file servers and print servers into such Administrative Groups. The Group identifies itself by the shared group name with the [20h] service identifier.
Multihomed	Use the Multihomed mapping to configure multiple IP address for a single NetBIOS host computer. A computer may have multiple adapters or multiple IP addresses bound to a single adapter.

Table 14.2 Some Unique NetBIOS Name Types

NetBIOS Name with Service Identifier	Explanation
computer_name [00h]	NetBIOS clients running the Workstation Service (redirector) register their NetBIOS name with the [00h] service identifier.
computer_name [03h]	NetBIOS clients running the messenger service register their NetBIOS name with the [03h] service identifier.
computer_name [20h]	NetBIOS clients running the server service register their NetBIOS names with the [20h] service identifier.
computer_name [21h]	NetBIOS clients running the RAS client service register their NetBIOS names with the [21h] service identifier.
domain_name [1Bh]	The Domain Master Browser (Is the Primary Domain Controller) registers its domain name with the [1Bh] service identifier.
username[03h]	Usernames are registered with the WINS server when the user logs on to a NetBIOS client. The username is appended with the [03h] service identifier. The messenger service will search for a user when a net send command is issued by searching for the [03h] service identifier attached to the username.

An s attribute denotes a static mapping in the WINS database. When static mappings replicate, replication partners respect their status as static entries and do not overwrite them with dynamic name registrations.

Connecting WINS Servers through Replication

Multiple WINS servers allow for fault tolerance and a more efficient NetBIOS name resolution process. In order to maintain consistency among all WINS servers on a network, there must be a method for sharing information in the WINS databases among the WINS servers. This method of sharing information among WINS servers is known as WINS replication.

WINS clients typically register their NetBIOS names with their Primary WINS server, and if the Primary WINS server is not reachable, the WINS client registers with one of its Secondary WINS servers. In large networks, multiple WINS servers service the name registration requests of WINS clients near them. Those same WINS servers also answer NetBIOS name queries.

A problem arises when clients register their names with different WINS servers. Imagine that on subnets 192.168.1.0 and 192.168.2.0, all the WINS clients are configured to use a single WINS server at IP address 192.168.1.2. On subnets 192.168.3.0 and 192.168.4.0, all the WINS clients are configured to use a Primary WINS server at IP address 192.168.3.2.

When clients on the 192.168.1.0 need to resolve a NetBIOS name for a client on subnet 192.168.2.0, they can query the WINS server, and a mapping for that client is located in the WINS database. If a client on the 192.168.3.0 subnet needs to resolve a NetBIOS name for a client on the 192.168.4.0 subnet, it can do so successfully because a mapping for clients on both the 192.168.3.0 and 192.168.4.0 subnets are in its WINS database. But what happens when a client on the 192.168.1.0 subnet needs to resolve a NetBIOS name of a client on the 192.168.4.0 subnet?

The client on the 192.168.1.0 subnet issues a NetBIOS name query request to its Primary WINS server at 192.168.1.2. However, no mappings exist for clients on the 192.168.4.0 subnet in its database. To solve this problem, WINS servers need to be configured as replication partners.

Replication partners share their information with each other. In this way, any WINS client will be able to query any WINS server and successfully resolve a NetBIOS name, regardless of what WINS server originally received the NetBIOS name registration.

WINS servers are configured as replication partners in two ways: pull partners and push partners. The pull partner receives WINS database information based on a configured replication interval. A push partner sends database information based on how many changes have taken place in the WINS database.

A WINS server is notified by its pull partner when it's time to request the changes that have taken place in the WINS database since the last time that server received replicated information. This determination is made based on

WINS database version IDs. If the pull partner's WINS database has a version ID higher than the one last pulled by the WINS server, it will request the changes. If the database version is the same or lower (an unlikely event, but possible), then records are not replicated from the pull partner.

Push replication causes the push partner to send a change notification based on how many changes were made in its WINS database. Then, after the minimum number of changes have been made, the push partner sends a change message to its partner, and the partner will then request the changes. Windows 2000 WINS servers are able to maintain persistent connections, which allow push partners to announce changes as soon as they take place.

Microsoft recommends that replication partners be configured as both push and pull partners. This reduces the chance of inconsistencies occurring in the WINS database. A notable exception to this policy is when WINS servers are separated by slow WAN connections. In this type of configuration, it may be more efficient to configure the WINS servers on either side to be pull partners. These pull partners can be configured to exchange WINS database information during times of reduced network utilization, and therefore not impact normal networking communications to such a large extent.

To configure replication partners:

1. Open the WINS management console and expand all nodes. Right-click on the Replication Partners node, and click New Replication Partner.

2. Type in the NetBIOS name of the WINS server you want to make a replication partner, or click BROWSE and select the WINS server from the Browse list.

3. You can see the list of replication partners in the right pane of the WINS management console, as seen in Figure 14.4.

4. Right-click on one of the replication partners, and click Properties. Select the Advanced tab to display a window similar to Figure 14.5.

5. In the Replication partner type: drop-down list, Push/Pull, Push, or Pull can be selected. Select the Push/Pull option. This defines CONSTELLATION as the push and pull partner of Exeter.

6. After selecting the Push/Pull option, the text boxes for configuring both push and pull partnerships are made available. In the Pull replication frame, you can configure the Start time and Replication interval. The start time represents the time of day on a 24-hour clock. The start time by default is set to midnight, with a replication interval of 30 minutes. So, EXETER will send a pull notification to CONSTELLATION every 30 minutes to inform it to get any existing WINS database changes.

Figure 14.4 The WINS management console displaying Replication Partners for Exeter.

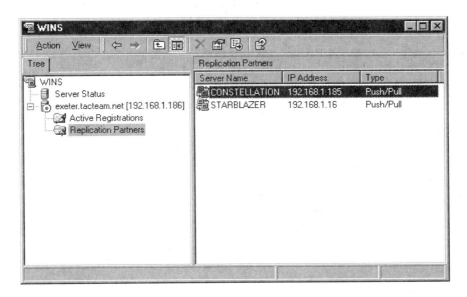

Figure 14.5 Configuring push and pull partner properties.

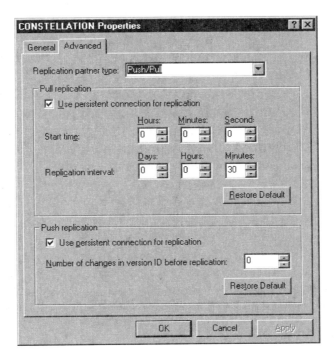

7. The Push replication frame contains the "Number of changes in version ID before replication" text box. You can configure the number of changes in the WINS database before EXETER sends a push message to CONSTELLATION so that it will request any existing WINS database changes.

8. For both push and pull replication, a persistent connection can be maintained between the partners. By placing a checkmark in the "Use persistent connection for replication" check box, you avoid the overhead of opening and closing connections between the replication partners. Replication, therefore, will have less impact on the server as a whole when this option is selected.

Designing a Network of Multiple WINS Servers

Small networks with two or three WINS servers can be configured to have all WINS servers as push and pull partners. However, larger networks will require configurations that are more sophisticated.

Imagine an organization with 50,000 clients and 10 WINS servers. Configuring all 10 WINS servers to be push and pull partners would lead to needless and potentially adverse levels of network traffic during replication. A more efficient method of configuring replication partners in a large network is the hub-and-spoke model of WINS database replication.

The hub-and-spoke model allows multiple WINS servers to partner with a single hub WINS server. The hub collects information from all its partners, and then distributes the information from all the partners back to each one. This is reminiscent of how the Browser services works, with the Domain Master Browser acting as a central point of collection of information from multiple subnets (Figure 14.6).

In our example, there are three main sites as pictured in Figure 14.6. Each site has a single hub WINS server. Each hub WINS server is partnered with three spoke WINS servers. Each hub server is configured to be a push and pull partner to its related spoke servers. Each spoke server is configured to be a push and pull partners to its related hub server.

The hub servers are also configured to be replication partners. There are several different ways you can configure the Hub servers. One approach is to configure one of the hub servers as a hub for the hub servers themselves. In Figure 14.6, Dallas could be configured as the hub server, with Seattle and Austin as spokes. Each spoke would be a pull partner of the hub in Dallas, and Dallas would be a pull partner for the spokes in Austin and Seattle.

Another way to configure the replication relationships among the hub servers is to configure a chain. The chain arrangement is displayed in Figure 14.7.

Figure 14.6 Hub-and-spoke WINS server deployment.

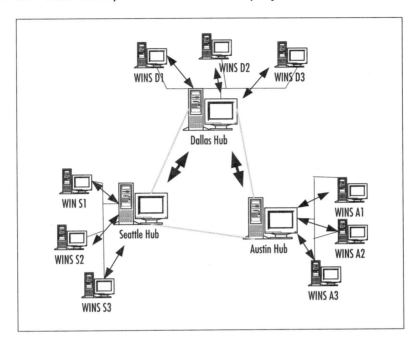

Figure 14.7 Chain replication in a WINS hub network.

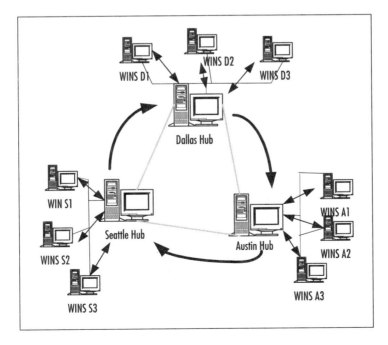

In the chain design, the Austin server is configured as a pull partner of the Dallas server, the Seattle server is configured as a pull partner of the Austin server, and the Dallas server is a pull partner of the Seattle server. While the chain arrangement consumes less overall bandwidth, convergence time is longer.

When configuring multiple WINS servers in such a distributed fashion, we have to consider the amount of time it takes for database changes to distribute themselves to all WINS servers in our WINS network. This time period is referred to as convergence time, which is the amount of time it takes for changes to the WINS database of a single WINS server to converge or be distributed to all other WINS servers in the network.

Let's look at the example in Figure 14.6 again. We will configure the pull interval between the peripheral spoke servers with their hub servers to be 15 minutes. Let's configure the Dallas server to be the hub of the hub servers, and the pull interval among the hub servers is 30 minutes. Remember that Dallas is a pull partner of Seattle and Austin, and Seattle and Austin are pull partners of Dallas.

How long will it take a change made one of the spoke WINS servers in Austin to be replicated to one of the spoke WINS servers in Seattle? In a worst-case scenario, the change on the spoke server in Austin will take 15 minutes. That change is replicated from Austin to Dallas in 30 minutes. The change is then replicated to Seattle from Dallas 30 minutes later, and the Seattle hub sends the change to the Seattle spoke 15 minutes after that. When we add all the intervals together, the worst-case scenario has the convergence time set to 90 minutes.

You need to plan how much time you can allow for full convergence to take place. WINS clients will not be able to resolve NetBIOS names of hosts whose IP addresses have changed during this interim period. Your decision on how much convergence time is acceptable is dependent upon how dynamic your network infrastructure is. The majority of the problems are related to DHCP. Clients configured with static IP addresses will not send changes to the WINS database, and their records are stable.

Backing Up WINS Databases

Backing up the WINS database can protect against numerous problems, should the database file be corrupted by power fluctuations or disk errors. A large WINS database can take a long time to rebuild, and all WINS clients on the network would have to reregister their names with their WINS server. Immediately thereafter, all the WINS servers would need to complete the replication process. As you can imagine, this could take a LONG time to complete.

A good backup policy is to make the WINS database folder part of the regular tape backup routine. The WINS database and its supporting files are stored in %systemroot%\system32\wins.

It is good practice to keep a local backup copy of the WINS database so that you can rapidly recover in the event the original WINS database file becomes corrupt. Restoring the local copy is faster than searching and restoring a copy from tape.

To back up the WINS database, first create a folder on another physical drive that will contain the WINS database files. Do not use a mapped network drive, or the procedure will fail. You can name this folder anything you like. Open the WINS management console, right-click on the WINS server's name in the left pane, and click Backup Database.

Select the folder that you created for the WINS database backup files, and click Oĸ. A dialog box confirming that the database backed up successfully will then be displayed.

To restore the WINS database from the local backup, first stop the WINS service. The WINS server service can be stopped by launching a command prompt and typing **net stop WINS**, or by right-clicking on the WINS server name in the left pane of the WINS management console, selecting All Tasks, and then Stop.

After stopping the WINS server service, the Restore Database command is available. Click RESTORE DATABASE. The Browse for Folder dialog box appears. Select the directory housing the WINS database backup files, and click Oĸ. The database is restored, and the WINS server service is restarted automatically.

New Features in Windows 2000 WINS

The Windows 2000 WINS server includes all the functionality of previous versions of Microsoft WINS servers, as well as additional and enhanced functionality and an enhanced user interface. Windows 2000 WINS servers can maintain persistent connections with replication partners, block replication from selected WINS servers.

Persistent Connections

Earlier versions of the Microsoft WINS server had to establish a new connection to replication partners each time a replication event took place. The connection was then closed after completion. This opening and closing of connections between WINS servers required processor cycles on both machines. Establishing and breaking down connections on a frequent basis diminished the overall performance of the WINS servers.

The Windows 2000 WINS server allows replication partners to maintain persistent connections. Persistent connections circumvent the need to repeatedly open and close sessions; consequently, the server does not need to expend additional processor cycles servicing connection requests. This improves the overall performance of the WINS server.

Another benefit of persistent connections between replication partners is the ability to immediately update partners of WINS database updates. In the past, push updates were configured according to a target number dubbed the update count. This counter had to be reached or exceeded before the push update message was sent to replication partners. This was sometimes set to a high number to avoid frequent opening and closing sessions between partners. An update count of 0 allows persistent connections to obviate this limitation.

A nominal amount of bandwidth is used to maintain a persistent connection because the channel is idle most of the time. When immediate updates are sent, only a small amount of data is sent over the wire, minimizing potential bandwidth implications.

There is a walkthrough at the end of the chapter where persistent connections for replication partners are configured.

Manual Tombstoning

Tombstoning is the process of marking records in the WINS database as invalid. If a WINS client fails to renew its NetBIOS name within the renewal interval, its WINS database record is marked as released. The record stays in the released state for a duration defined by the extinction interval. After the extinction interval has passed, the record is marked as tombstoned. The record remains in the tombstoned state for the entirety of the extinction timeout interval. At the end of the extinction timeout interval, the record is removed from the WINS database. Figure 14.8 depicts the lifecycle of a WINS database record.

You may wonder, why tombstone a record? Why doesn't the WINS server just delete the record? Tombstoning a record prevents that record from being replicated back to the WINS server that owns it. The owner is the WINS server that received the original NetBIOS name registration from the WINS client.

Imagine a computer with the NetBIOS name of W2K1. W2K1 registered with its primary WINS server when it started up. Later, when W2K1 is removed from the network, releasing its NetBIOS name, the WINS server waits the period defined in the extinction interval before marking W2K1's record as tombstoned. When the WINS server that is the owner of W2K1's record replicates, W2K1's tombstoned status replicates as well. After the extinction timeout period has passed, the tombstoned records remove themselves from the owner's WINS database, and from the databases of all its replication partners.

After the extinction timeout, the tombstoned record removes itself from both the server that is the owner of the record and all replication partners receiving the tombstoned record. The record cannot be rereplicated because it removes itself from all WINS databases.

Figure 14.8 The lifecycle of a WINS database record.

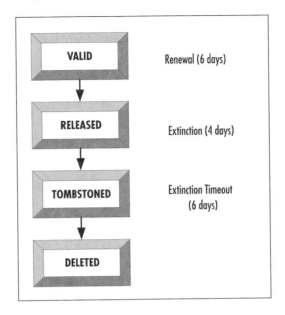

What would happen if we just deleted the record, rather than tomb-stoning it? Let's just delete W2K1's record from the WINS server that owns his record. Consider what has happened before W2K1 went offline. Most likely, W2K1 renewed its NetBIOS name a time or two. In addition, W2K1's Primary WINS server replicated its database during this time. A valid record now exists in the WINS databases of the owner's replication partners.

After deleting W2K1's record from its owner's database, the WINS server continues to replicate with its partners. Since W2K1's record is now absent from the database, no information regarding W2K1 is included in the repli-cated records.

However, what happens when W2K1's Primary WINS server receives replication from its partners? These WINS servers still have W2K1 in their WINS databases. The record is marked as active in their databases. After replication, W2K1's Primary WINS server receives W2K1's record again. Its status is marked as active! You can see how deleting records, rather than tombstoning them, can cause them to loop back and forth among WINS replication partners.

To manually tombstone a record, open the WINS management console. Expand all nodes, and click on the Active Registrations node. Right-click on one of the records in the right pane of the WINS management console, and click DELETE.

You can manually tombstone or mark a record as extinct by selecting the option "Replicate deletion of the record to other servers (tombstone)."

It is much better to tombstone records rather than delete them. Take advantage of this new capability to manually tombstone in the Windows 2000 WINS server.

Improved Management Tools

Windows 2000 uses the WINS management console for WINS server management. The WINS management console features can be accessed by opening the dedicated WINS management console, opening the Computer Management console, or creating a new console and adding the WINS plug-in.

Several new features have been added to the WINS management console that provide control of how WINS records are replicated in the WINS network. These include the ability to overwrite or update static WINS entries, and the ability to prevent records from specific WINS servers from replicating.

Static mappings allow WINS records to be added for machines that are not WINS clients, or for those machines that have client reservations on a DHCP server. When a machine has a static mapping, it does not dynamically update its WINS records and is not required to renew its name. By default, if a machine tries to overwrite a static mapping, it will fail.

When a WINS server receives a name registration request, it searches its database for another computer claiming the same NetBIOS name. If another record is found with the same name, the WINS server will send a challenge message to the IP address of the owner. If the owner of the NetBIOS name doesn't respond, the name registration request is honored, and the new computer is allowed to register its NetBIOS name and IP address. When the entry in the WINS database is a static mapping, the results of the challenge have no bearing on the result; the new computer will not be allowed to register its name.

When static mappings replicate, they are marked as static mappings. All WINS servers that receive the static record honor the no-overwrite status of a static mapping. No WINS server tombstones the static mapping; therefore, static mappings replicate indefinitely unless manually tombstoned. You must tombstone the record, because static mappings are not subject to extinction or extinction timeouts. Normally this is not a problem. When you want to remove a static mapping, you just right-click on its entry in the WINS database and select the tombstoning options.

But, what if the WINS server goes offline and you do not plan to bring that machine back online? All the static mappings on that machine have replicated to its WINS replication partners. Those partners will continue to copy the static mappings indefinitely until you manually delete all of them. Also, any machine that needs to claim the NetBIOS name will be denied registration because of the statically mapped computer's entry in the WINS database.

To solve this problem, you could go to every WINS machine in your WINS infrastructure and delete the record manually, or you could tombstone the record and wait for the convergence interval to complete. However, there is a less labor-intensive way to accomplish your goal of removing these static entries and allowing dynamic updates of the NetBIOS names to which they lay claim.

The problem can be solved by choosing to make the records owned by the absent WINS server persona non grata. This blocks the replication of records owned by the WINS server marked as such. In Windows NT 4.0, the persona non grata value had to be entered manually into the Registry. In Windows 2000, you can enter the IP address of the removed WINS server to block replication of the records it owns. Figure 14.9 shows where to configure persona non grata servers, and Figure 14.10 shows a WINS record and owner information. After adding IP addresses of the computers for which you want to block entries, restart the WINS service to ensure the settings take effect.

While this solves the problem involving replication of static mappings owned by absent or disabled WINS servers, it does not allow computers to update or overwrite the information contained in the static mappings. In

Figure 14.9 Configuring the persona non grata server.

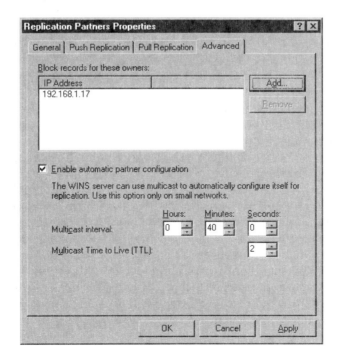

Figure 14.10 WINS record with IP address of owner.

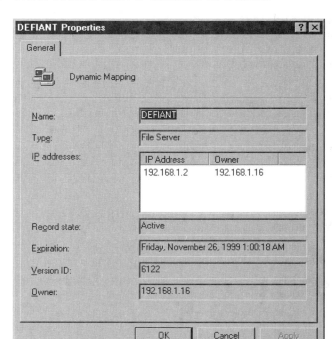

order to accomplish this goal, you must enable what was known as Migrate On in Windows NT 4.0.

The Migrate On feature is called the "Overwrite unique static mappings at this server (migrate on)" option in Windows 2000. When enabled, WINS clients can register the NetBIOS name and IP address when a client with a static mapping fails to respond to the WINS server challenge. Some types of static mappings will not be overwritten, such as those WINS entries designating a computer as a domain controller [1Ch].

Higher Performance

The WINS service now uses the jet blue database engine. This is the same database technology used by the Active Directory and Exchange server. The more efficient database design improves the speed and efficiency of the Windows 2000 WINS server compared to its predecessors.

The WINS management console itself is more flexible than its ancestors were. The WINS console is a multithreaded application that allows multiple tasks to engage simultaneously. While you are waiting for a task on one WINS database to complete, you can start work on another WINS server listed in the WINS management console.

Enhanced Filtering and Record Searching

Large WINS installations can gather tens of thousands of WINS records in the WINS database. In the past, if you wanted to find a record or a group of records in the WINS databases, you had to sift through the list manually. Windows 2000 WINS servers have enhanced record finding and filtering.

If you want to find all servers that begin with LAX, all you need to do is type LAX in the "Find names beginning with" text box and click FIND NOW. The right pane in the WINS manager will display the results of the query. If you want to see all the records in the database, you can type an asterisk (*) in the text box instead of a computer name string. Note that this is the only wildcard type of search you can do. The only searches done by the "Find by name" dialog box are for the entries beginning with the letters typed in the text box.

Figure 14.11 shows the Find by Owner dialog box.

Using this search tool, you can find all records owned by selected servers, or view records owned by all servers. The IP address of the server and the highest version ID number is also included on this list.

Figure 14.12 shows the contents of the Record Types tab in the Find by Owner dialog box. You can filter and view records that have specific service identifiers. So, if you wanted to find all domain controllers registered in the WINS database, you could limit your search for only entries with the [1Ch] service identifier.

Figure 14.11 The Find by Owner dialog box.

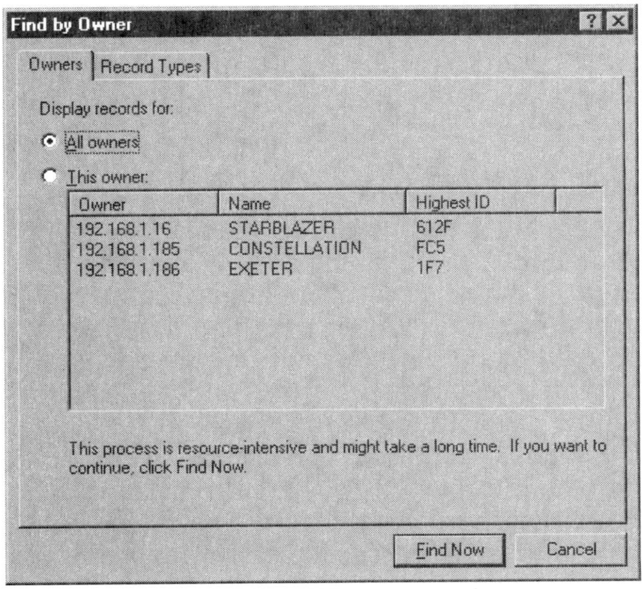

Figure 14.12 Selecting records by service identifier.

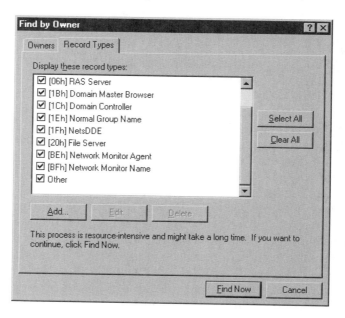

The find and filter feature makes life a lot easier for the Administrator in a large enterprise environment.

Dynamic Record Deletion and Multiselect

Deleting records is a lot easier using the Windows 2000 WINS management console. In the WINS management console, multiple records can be selected by holding down either SHIFT or CTRL on the keyboard and then right-clicking on the selected records to either delete or tombstone them.

Increased Fault Tolerance

Windows 2000 WINS clients can be configured with up to 12 Secondary WINS servers. Downlevel clients support only Primary and Secondary WINS server configuration. Windows 2000 clients benefit from a higher level of fault tolerance for NetBIOS name resolution by supporting more WINS servers.

A WINS client contacts its Primary WINS server when registering its NetBIOS name or when resolving a NetBIOS. If the Primary WINS server fails to respond after three attempts to contact it, the client will contact a Secondary WINS server. In addition, the client will contact Secondary WINS servers when the Primary WINS server returns a negative NetBIOS name query response. If there are multiple Secondary WINS servers, the client will try each of these three times before the client moves to the next one on the list.

Assigning multiple Secondary WINS servers appears to be a no-lose situation. You must strike a balance between fault tolerance and speed of name resolution. The normal NetBIOS name resolution process for H-node machines includes:

1. Checking its own NetBIOS name.
2. Searching the NetBIOS name cache.
3. Querying configured WINS server(s).
4. Issuing a broadcast.
5. Searching the LMHosts file.
6. Searching the HOSTS file.
7. Querying the Preferred DNS server.

The efficiency of name resolution depends on services available on the network. It may be more efficient for a WINS client to move through the entire NetBIOS name resolution algorithm than to query up to 12 WINS servers. Consider this when configuring clients with multiple Secondary WINS server addresses.

Burst Handling

WINS servers can be overwhelmed with NetBIOS name registration requests. The typical example is when a systemwide power outage takes place and all machine come online simultaneously and attempt to register their NetBIOS names with their WINS server. The WINS server can cache a certain number of requests, after which it will begin to drop subsequent requests.

Windows NT 4.0 WINS servers with Service Pack 3 and above support high-volume WINS registration requests via a process called burst handling. Windows 2000 WINS servers also support WINS server burst mode responses.

When a large number of NetBIOS name registration requests arrive at a WINS server in rapid succession, the WINS server will not be able to complete processing of each request in a timely fashion. The WINS server holds these requests in a queue for processing until the resources on the server become available. Then the requests are fully processed and written to disk in the WINS database.

The number of virtually simultaneous requests may be so great that the efficiency and accuracy of name registration may suffer. In this scenario, the WINS server will switch into burst mode. When the WINS server is in burst mode, any name registration requests received over a predefined number receive immediate acknowledgment. However, the WINS server does not check the NetBIOS against the WINS database; it does not issue a challenge against duplicate names, and it does not write an entry to the WINS database.

The default queue size is 500. When the number of pending registration requests exceeds 500, the WINS server switches into burst mode and immediately acknowledges the WINS client's request for NetBIOS name registration. For the first 100 registrations over 500, the clients are given a name renewal period of five minutes. For the next 100 pending name registrations, the WINS clients receive a name renewal interval of 10 minutes. This pattern of incrementing the name renewal period by five minutes per 100 pending requests continues until the TTL reaches 50 minutes (1000 pending registrations). Then the process starts all over with the WINS server sending the next 100 pending registration requests a TTL of five minutes.

The maximum number of queued responses is 25,000. After that point, the WINS server starts dropping the requests.

Note that when the WINS clients receive an immediate acknowledgment, there is a risk of registering duplicate NetBIOS names on the network. This is because the WINS server does not challenge duplicate names in the WINS database prior to acknowledging the client while in burst mode. The assumption is that the WINS server will be less impacted when the client attempts to renew its name, and then the WINS server will be able to complete the normal process of the NetBIOS name registration request.

Figure 14.13 shows the configuration options for WINS server burst handling.

Figure 14.13 Configuration options for WINS server burst handling.

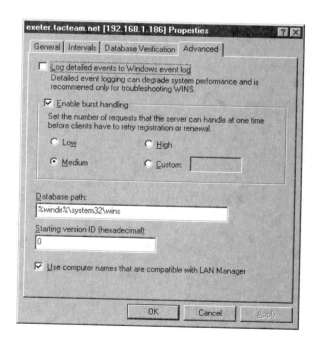

The configuration options are Low, Medium, High, and Custom. Each configuration option determines how many name registration requests can be in the queue before burst mode is enabled. Low allows 300, Medium 500, and High 1000. A custom value can be selected by entering it in the text box next to the Custom option.

Dynamic Reregistration

Windows NT 4.0 clients had to be restarted in order to reregister or update their WINS records after NetBIOS names or IP addresses change. Windows NT clients with Service Pack 4 and above, as well as Windows 2000 WINS clients, support reregistration without restarting the client machines.

To reregister a WINS client's entry in the WINS database, open a command prompt and type:

Nbtstat –RR

If the name conflicts with another active registration in the WINS database, TCP/IP is disabled on that adapter. In this case, selectively disconnect that adapter from the network and change the NetBIOS name of the computers. Reconnect to the network and reregister the client again.

WINS Walkthrough

Installing and Configuring a WINS Server

In this walkthrough, we'll install and configure a WINS server, and then configure a Windows 2000 client to use the new WINS server.

In order to complete these exercises, you'll need two computers: one Windows 2000 server family computer to install the WINS server, and a second computer to use as a WINS client. The WINS server computer should have a static IP address. If you don't have a second computer, you can configure the WINS server machine as a WINS client pointing to itself.

1. Log on as Administrator at the computer that will be the WINS server.
2. Click Start | Settings | Control Panel.
3. In the Control Panel, open the Add/Remove Programs applet.
4. Click ADD/REMOVE WINDOWS COMPONENTS on the left side of the Add/Remove Programs applet.
5. In the Add Components Wizard window, scroll down the list of components and find the Networking Services entry.

6. Click once on Networking Services to select it. Do not click on the check box or you may inadvertently remove some networking components. Click DETAILS.

7. Scroll down the list and locate the entry for Windows Internet Name Service (WINS). Click in the check box to place a checkmark for Windows Internet Name Service (WINS). Then click OK. Then click NEXT in the Windows Components Wizard.

8. The wizard installs the software and then presents a dialog box indicating the installation is complete. Click FINISH.

This completes the installation of the WINS server. Next, we configure the WINS server to meet the specifications of our network environment. We focus primarily on configuration settings for the WINS console, WINS server status checking, WINS server properties, and replication partner properties.

1. Click Start | Programs | Administrative Tools | WINS.

2. The WINS administrative console is now open. First, add a server to the WINS console. You can manage all WINS servers from a single location. Right-click the WINS node at the top of the left pane, and click ADD SERVER.

3. You see the Add Server dialog box. Click BROWSE. In the Look in: list box, be sure to select your domain. Scroll through the list of computers and select your WINS server computer. Click OK, and then click OK again to close the Add Server dialog box.

4. Expand all nodes. If you see an error message saying that you cannot connect to the server, click on the Action menu and click Refresh. If that does not correct the problem, then right-click on your computer name in the left pane, trace down to All Tasks, and then trace over and click Restart. Click Refresh one more time if you still see the error.

5. Right-click the WINS node on top of the left pane, and click Properties.

6. Choose to display servers by name, and put a check in the "Show DNS names of WINS servers." Put a checkmark in the "Validate cache of WINS servers at startup" to have the system check for the status of WINS servers added to the console at system startup. Click APPLY, and then OK.

7. Right-click on your WINS server name and then click on Properties. You will see the Properties sheet of your WINS server as shown in Figure 14.14.

Figure 14.14 The WINS server Properties sheet.

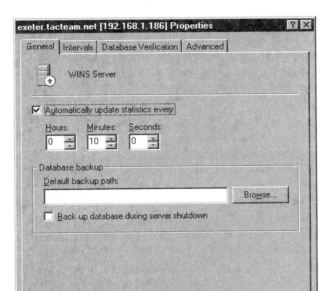

8. Ensure that the "Automatically update statistics every:" check box is selected, and change the update interval to 15 minutes. In the "Default backup path:" text box, type **c:\WINSbak** and place a checkmark in the "Back up database during server shutdown" box. You must create the WINSbak directory manually before the WINS database will back up to that location.

9. Click on the Intervals tab and examine the Renew, Extinction, Extinction timeout, and Verification intervals. The defaults are adequate for most situations and do not need to be reconfigured.

10. Click on the Database Verification tab to display a window similar to Figure 14.15.

11. Put a checkmark in the "Verify database consistency every:" check box and set the number of hours to 24. Start verifying at 2 A.M. by changing the value in the Hours text box to 2. Change the "Maximum number of records verified each period:" value to 30,000. Select "Owner servers" to whom you will verify against.

12. Click the Advanced tab to see what appears in Figure 14.16. Put a check in the "Log detailed events to Windows event log." This takes

extra disk and processor time, so do not leave this setting on for an extended period. Set burst handling to Medium. This will allow up to 500 name registration requests to stay in the queue before activating burst mode handling. Leave the checkmark in the "Use computer names that are compatible with LAN Manager." LAN Manager compatible computer names include 15 user-configurable characters, plus a 16th hexadecimal character to use as a service identifier.

Figure 14.15 The Database Verification tab.

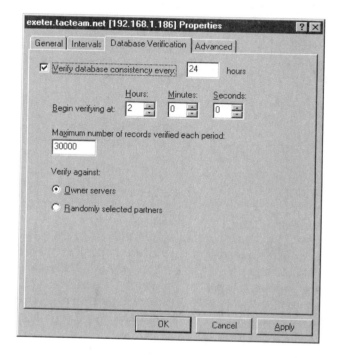

12. Click APPLY, and then OK to close the WINS server Properties dialog box.

Configuring Replication Partners

In the next exercise, we will examine and configure the Replication Partners node in the WINS management console.

1. Right-click on the Replication Partners node in the left pane, and click Properties. You should see the Replication Partners Properties dialog box.

2. Put a checkmark in the "Replicate only with partners" check box to ensure that replication of the WINS database takes place only

among configured WINS replication partners. Put a checkmark in the check box for "Overwrite unique static mapping at this server (migrate on)." The Migrate On configuration allows dynamic mappings to overwrite static mappings. This is useful for a network transitioning from an LMHosts name resolution configuration to a dynamic WINS name resolution scheme.

Figure 14.16 The Advanced tab.

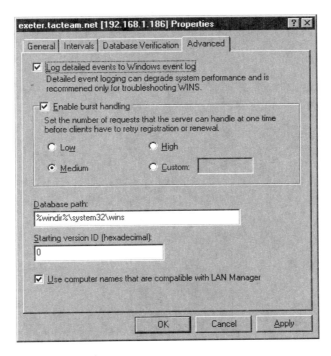

3. Click on the Push Replication tab to display a window similar to Figure 14.17.

4. Put a checkmark in the check box for "At service startup" to start push replication with replication partners at startup. To immediately update replication partners every time a record is updated, put a checkmark in the check box for "When address changes." If you choose not to update immediately, put a number in the "Number of changes in version ID before replication" text box. Put a checkmark in "Use persistent connections to push replication partners."

5. Click the Pull Replication tab.

6. Enter the time of day when you want a pull replication to take place in the "Start time:" text boxes. Enter the amount of time you

want to pass between pull requests to replication partners in the "Replication interval:" text boxes. The "Number of retries:" text box determines how many times the WINS server will try to establish failed connections. Put a checkmark in the "Use persistent connections for pull replication partners" check box to enable persistent connections between configured replication partners.

Figure 14.17 The Push Replication tab.

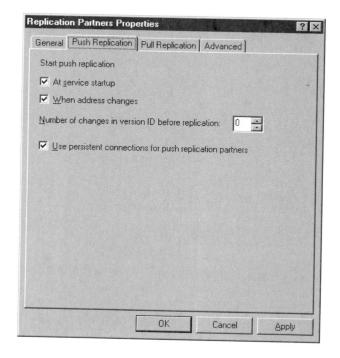

7. Click the Advanced tab to display a window similar to Figure 14.18.

8. If there are WINS servers that you want to block or prevent replication from, click ADD to add their IP addresses. (This was known as persona non grata in Windows NT 4.0, and had to be set in the Registry.) Automatic partner configuration uses multicast addresses to allow WINS servers to automatically use themselves as replication partners. All WINS servers will identify themselves as part of the same multicast group. Configure how often you want WINS servers to announce themselves as members of the multicast group in the "Multicast interval:" text boxes. Autoconfigured partners will pull records from each other every two hours.

9. Click OK to close the Advanced tab.

Figure 14.18 The Advanced tab.

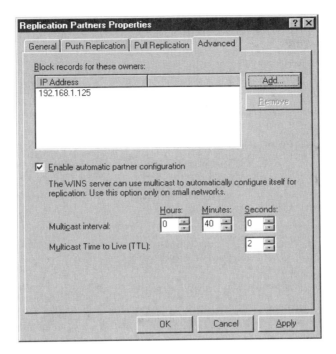

Summary

Windows 2000 provides a number of methods to resolve NetBIOS names to IP addresses, including the NetBIOS name cache, WINS, broadcast, LMHosts, HOSTS, and DNS. Of these choices, WINS is the superior solution. A WINS server maintains a database of NetBIOS names and their corresponding IP addresses.

When a computer is configured as a WINS client, it can register its name and IP address automatically on startup with a WINS server. The host accomplishes this via a NetBIOS name registration request. A NetBIOS name registration refreshes in order for its record to remain valid in the WINS database. If the NetBIOS host computer does not refresh its NetBIOS name within the period known as the refresh interval, its name is marked as released in the WINS database. A released name then becomes available to any other computer that wishes to register the same name in the WINS database.

The NetBIOS name continues to be marked as released until the extinction interval is completed. At that point, the record is marked as tombstoned. The tombstoned record remains in the WINS database for the period defined in the extinction timeout interval. When the extinction timeout interval passes, the record is removed from the WINS database.

WINS clients issue a name query request to resolve a target computer's NetBIOS name to an IP address. The first WINS server the client contacts is the Primary WINS server. If the Primary WINS server fails to respond after three tries, the client contacts a Secondary WINS server. Windows 2000 WINS clients support up to 12 Secondary WINS servers. Use caution when configuring multiple Secondary WINS servers. Too liberal assignments of Secondary WINS servers can extend the time required to resolve a NetBIOS name to an IP address.

A WINS client will send a NetBIOS name release message to its WINS server. This marks the NetBIOS name release and makes it available to other WINS clients for registration.

Networks large enough to require multiple WINS servers need a method to ensure that all WINS servers maintain the same entries in their databases. WINS servers are able to share information by replicating database records to configured replication partners. WINS replication takes two forms: push and pull. You configure WINS servers as push partners, pull partners, or both.

A push partner sends a trigger to its replication partner to pull records from its WINS database after certain numbers of changes have taken place in the WINS database. The WINS Administrator configures this number. Windows 2000 WINS servers allow for persistent connections. You can take advantage of persistent connections between replication partners and send immediate updates of each change. Persistent connections avoid the overhead inherent in establishing and breaking down connections among replication partners.

A pull partner is configured to send a trigger to its partner at a certain time, and then at regular intervals after the start time. In general, it is wise to configure replication partners as both push and pull partners. However, a pull partner relationship only may be advantageous when defining replication parameters for WINS servers separated by a slow WAN connection.

Enterprise environments may require more than two or three WINS servers. These environments are likely geographically distributed and connected by a variety of slow- and high-speed links. To optimize WINS replication in such a distributed environment, a WINS network based on the hub-and-spoke model works best. You configure spoke WINS servers as push/pull partners of their respective hubs; hub servers are configured in a chain, ring, or star arrangement of pull partners.

The amount of time required to synchronize all WINS servers in a WINS network is the convergence time. NetBIOS name query requests can be in error for some WINS clients until the convergence time is over. Configuring the push and pull parameters for the participants in the WINS network alters convergence time. Stable networks do not demand quick convergence, while highly dynamic networks that make widespread use of DHCP may require quicker convergence.

The Windows 2000 WINS server includes several new features unavailable or improved upon from the Windows NT 4.0 version of the WINS server: persistent connections, manual tombstoning of records, easier-to-configure burst handling, and an improved interface in the form of the WINS management console. Many of the functions that required Registry edits (such as persona non grata records and burst handling) can now be configured via the WINS management console's GUI interface.

FAQs

Q: I thought Dynamic DNS replaced WINS in Windows 2000. Why is it still included?

A: While Microsoft's stated goal is to eliminate NetBIOS from Windows-based networks, it is not realistic to do so at the present time. The majority of network-enabled applications created for Microsoft networks are NetBIOS based. To run a mixed network environment that includes Windows 2000 and downlevel network clients, you must enable NetBIOS support on your Windows 2000 network. DNS only resolves host names, not NetBIOS names. To allow optimal NetBIOS name resolution on your Windows 2000 network, you should run WINS.

It will be several years before NetBIOS is completely eliminated from Microsoft networks.

Q: I have a number of multihomed servers on my network. Is there any way to have my clients rotate through the adapters they connect to on each multihomed server?

A: Yes. The Windows 2000 WINS server supports rotation through IP addresses assigned to a single multihomed server in a manner similar to that seen with DNS round robin. When WINS clients query a WINS server for multihomed clients, they will receive the list of IP addresses in a different order each time, and try to connect to the first IP in the list. This balances the load on each network adapter connected to the multihomed server.

Q: What is a WINS Proxy Agent?

A: A WINS Proxy Agent intercepts NetBIOS name query requests. This is of particular help when you have non-WINS-enabled client that needs to resolve NetBIOS names. The WINS Proxy Agent will intercept the name query request and forward it to a WINS server. The WINS server will respond to the WINS Proxy Agent, which in turn will return the answer to the client issuing the original request.

The WINS Proxy Agent caches the results of WINS queries. This reduces the amount of query-related traffic. The WINS Proxy Agent also checks the name of the requesting non-WINS client for duplication in the WINS database; it does not register the name in the WINS database.

To make your machine a WINS Proxy Agent, use a Registry Editor (for example, regedt32.exe) to open HKEY_LOCAL_MACHINE\SYSTEM\ CurrentControlSet\Services\NetBT\Parameters, and set the EnableProxy parameter to 1.

Q: Am I required to have a WINS server on my network?

A: No. A WINS server is not required. If you must enable NetBIOS name resolution on your network, you can open UDP Ports 137 and 138 and TCP Port 139 on your routers, or you can implement LMHosts files. A WINS server is a superior solution to LMHosts and NetBIOS broadcast passthrough.

If your network does not require NetBIOS name resolution, you can completely disable NetBT by making a configuration change in the TCP/IP properties on all computers on the network. If you use DHCP for IP addressing, Microsoft provides vendor-specific options that allow you to disable NetBT on DHCP clients.

Keep in mind that although the Windows 2000 core networking compo-nents do not require the NetBIOS interface to be enabled, all non-Winsock applications require NetBIOS name resolution. Therefore, NetBT must be enabled to support these applications.

Windows 2000 Security Services

Introduction

Computers and networks have undoubtedly revolutionized the way we work. Why rifle frustratingly through mountains of paper when you can retrieve the information from a database in another continent in seconds? Unfortunately, the radical way in which the workplace has changed has not only empowered the worker, but also the unsavory characters who would maliciously damage computer systems and those who seek to gain corporate information for personal gain.

Securing your network has the advantage of preventing unwanted intrusions, and helps avoid the inevitable accidents that can arise from allowing users (and Administrators) too much flexibility. Some pundits would have you believe that there are legions of bespectacled hackers toiling away in darkened rooms in an attempt to pull off the ultimate coup—to break into your system. The reality is that you are more likely to be compromised by someone from inside your network than from outside!

Make no mistake; there are a large number of people dedicating time to infiltrating computer networks. The proliferation of easy-to-use hacker toolkits has seen the rise of the script kiddie – a nontechnical user who runs hacking tools to do all the technical hacking work for them. But locking all the doors to your house does not help if the thief is already inside. Security is not just about preventing intrusions from external sources, but from internal sources too.

An oft forgotten, but crucial aspect of security strategy is that security should not be a barrier to business, but a means of enabling the business to do more *because* it is secure.

Windows 2000 Security Infrastructure

A greater emphasis has been placed on security in Windows 2000 than in any previous iteration of the Windows product family. Existing services been strengthened, and new services and functionality have been incorporated into the operating system, making Windows 2000 an excellent platform for secure computing.

The three primary responsibilities of a complete security infrastructure is to ensure:

- **Confidentiality**   Has information that has been branded confidential remained private during transit and during storage?
- **Integrity**   Has the content of the information remained unchanged?
- **Authenticity**   Have the identities of the security principals involved been confirmed?

In this chapter, we exam the issue of authenticity by discussing Kerberos. We also consider confidentiality of data storage with the use of the Encrypted File System (EFS). Windows 2000 also provides an easy-to-use security configuration tool set that allows Administrators to easily manage security configuration in a distributed network.

In Chapter 16, "Securing TCP/IP Connections," the basic three elements—confidentiality, integrity, and authenticity (ominously dubbed CIA)—are covered with specific reference to security within TCP/IP networks.

Authentication Protocols

One of the cornerstones of network security is authentication. How does a server or directory service determine that a person/application/device requesting access is not an imposter? By going through the process of authentication, that's how. Windows 2000 supports five methods of authenticating the identity of users:

- Windows NT LAN Manager (NTLM)
- Kerberos v5
- Distributed Password Authentication (DPA)
- Extensible Authentication Protocol (EAP)
- Secure Channel (Schannel)

Windows 2000 uses NTLM and Kerberos for network authentication, while the other three protocols are used for authentication over dial-up connections or the Internet.

Windows NT 4.0 uses Windows NT LAN Manager (NTLM) as the default network authentication protocol. For that reason, NTLM is still available in Windows 2000 to maintain backward compatibility with previous versions of Microsoft operating systems. It is also used to authenticate logons to Windows 2000 stand-alone computers (or to establish trusts with Windows NT 4 domains).

Kerberos is the default network authentication for Windows 2000. Kerberos is a widely used authentication protocol based on an open standard. Windows 2000 uses Kerberos v5 for authentication under all circumstances, except when connecting to a downstream service such as a Windows NT Server or a Windows NT domain. In both cases, Windows 2000 will use NTLM instead of Kerberos.

DPA is an authentication protocol used on the Internet to allow users to use the same password to connect to any Internet site that belongs to the same membership organization. Though Windows 2000 supports DPA, it is a separately purchased add-on product.

EAP is an extension to the Point-to-Point Protocol used for dial-up connections. The purpose of EAP is to allow the dynamic addition of authentication plug-in modules at both the server and client ends of a connection. Secure channel includes four related protocols:

- Secure Sockets Layer (SSL) v2.0
- Secure Sockets Layer (SSL) v3.0
- Private Communication Technology (PCT) v1.0
- Transport Layer Security (TLS) v1.0

The primary purpose of using Schannel is to provide authentication, data integrity, and secure communication over the Internet. Most people who have purchased goods over the Internet will have used SSL (which is covered in Chapter 16) in some form or another. All four protocols in Schannel provide authentication by using digital certificates.

NTLM and LM

NTLM, or NT LAN Manager security, is the mainstay of Windows NT and was considered a relatively powerful protocol in its heyday. However, NTLM suffers in comparison to Kerberos for several reasons:

- Authentication with NTLM is slower than with Kerberos.
- NTLM performs one-way authentication only, which allows server spoofing.
- NTLM trusts are one-way and nontransitive, and thus harder to manage.
- NTLM is proprietary, and not compatible with non-Microsoft networks.

Weaknesses aside, NTLM is alive and kicking in many Microsoft networks. To maintain compatibility with its older siblings, Windows 2000 supports three challenge/response mechanisms:

LAN Manager (LM)   Windows 2000 can use this protocol to connect to Windows 9*x* computers using share-level security. LM is also used to authenticate Windows 95 and Windows 98 systems to a Windows 2000 infrastructure.

NTLM v1   Windows 2000 can use this protocol to connect to a Windows NT 4 domain. Windows NT 4 clients can also use this protocol to authenticate to Windows 2000 infrastructure.

NTLM v2   Only available for Windows NT in Service Pack 4 and beyond, this protocol allows Windows 2000 to connect to Windows NT domains more securely than when using NTLM v1.

Windows 2000 can use all of these protocols by default. NTLM is also necessary for establishing trusts with NT domains, as well as for authenticating downlevel clients. By default, Windows 2000 Active Directory is installed in

Figure 15.1 Windows 2000 Server responding to a Windows 98 logon request.

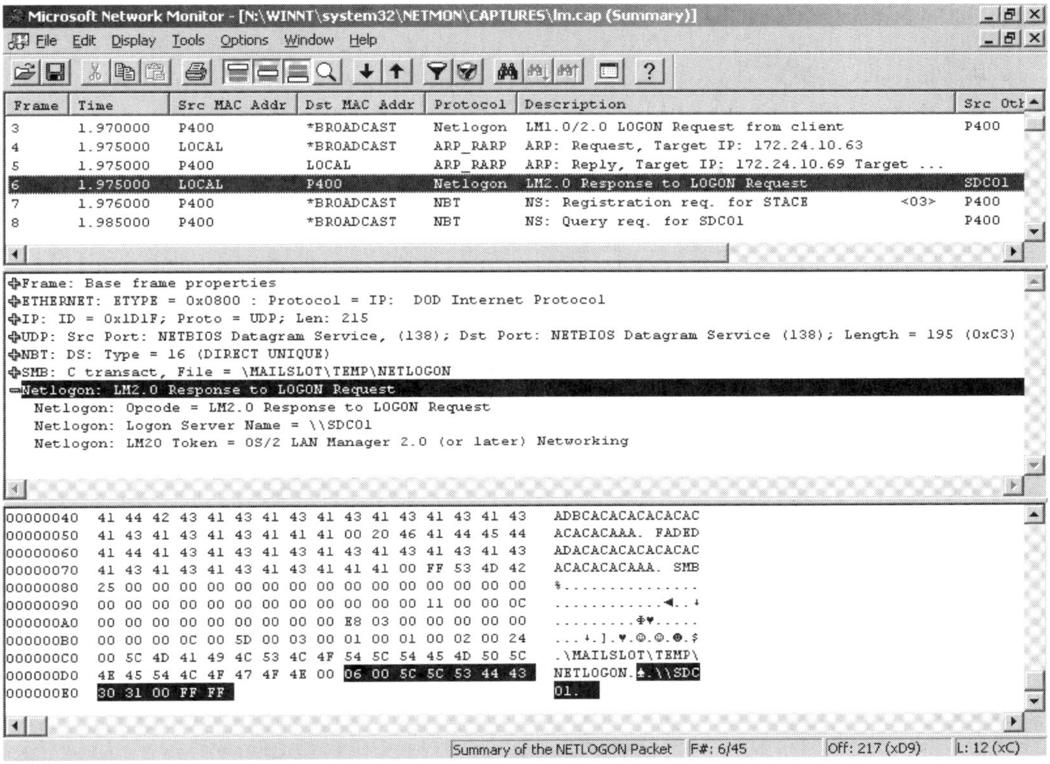

mixed mode, meaning that the directory can contain any combination of Windows NT 4.0 domains (or DCs) and Windows 2000 domains. If you do not have a mixed-mode network (that is, if you have upgraded the network to a pure Windows 2000 domain controller environment), you can disable NTLM authentication by switching to native mode at a domain controller.

Figure 15.1 shows a packet capture of the response sent to a Windows 98 client requesting to log on to a Windows 2000 Server domain. The Windows 98 machine sends out a broadcast LM1.0/2.0 LOGON Request. The Windows 2000 Server then responds with a LM2.0 response to the logon request.

Kerberos

Kerberos is widely used in UNIX and other networking environments, and is the default authentication protocol for Windows 2000. Kerberos is a private key (also called secret key) encryption protocol. In private key cryptography, the same key, called a shared secret, is used for both encryption and decryption of data.

Benefits of Kerberos Authentication

Several benefits provided by Kerberos make it a considerably better choice than NTLM for enterprise authentication. Unlike NTLM, Kerberos is based on existing standards, allowing Windows 2000 to interoperate with other networks that use Kerberos v5 as their authentication mechanism. Connections to application and file servers are faster when Kerberos authentication is used. This is because the Kerberos server needs to examine only the credentials supplied by the client to determine whether access is allowed. The same credentials supplied by the client can be used for the entire network logon session. When NTLM is used, the application and file servers must contact a domain controller to determine whether access is allowed for that client.

Kerberos authentication provides authentication for both ends of the communication path. Both the client and the server are authenticated, while NTLM provides authentication only of the client. NTLM clients do not know for sure that the server they are communicating with is not a rogue server. Kerberos is the basis for transitive domain trusts, with each domain sharing a key.

Extensions to the Kerberos Protocol

Microsoft has enhanced the version of Kerberos in Windows 2000 so that the initial authentication of users can be accomplished using public key certificates instead of the standard shared secret keys normally used by Kerberos v5. Extending Kerberos in this manner allows interactive logons to Windows 2000 using smart cards. The extensions Microsoft implemented in Kerberos for Windows 2000 are based on the draft specification *Public Key Cryptography for Initial Authentication in Kerberos*, proposed to the Internet Engineering Task Force (IETF) by numerous third parties such as Digital Equipment Corporation (DEC), Novell, CyberSafe Corporation, and others.

Private/Public Key Pairs and Certificates

Public key cryptography differs from Kerberos in that it uses a pair of keys; one is public and available to everyone, and the other is private. In general, one of these keys is used to encrypt the message, and the other is used to decrypt it.

Windows 2000 uses a certificate authority to store the public and private keys. Digital certificates are used to verify that the public key really belongs to the user to whom it is supposed to belong. The certificate is issued by a trusted third party—in this case, Microsoft Certificate Services running on the Windows 2000 server—and guarantees that the public key you are using is valid.

Windows 2000's Public Key Infrastructure (PLI) support is based on the X.509 standard, first established in 1995 to specify the syntax and format of digital certificates, and the certificates are called X.509 v3 digital certificates. PKI and shared key pairs are discussed in Chapter 16.

Encryption Technologies

Window 2000 uses encryption in a variety of ways to help secure communication and data storage. The confidentiality of data stored on an NTFS volume can be maintained by using the Encrypted File System (EFS). Encryption is also used to maintain the confidentiality of network communication when using virtual private network (VPN) technologies and IPSec (both discussed in Chapter 16).

Encryption technologies are often divided into symmetric and asymmetric encryption. Security principals involved in symmetric encryption possess the same key to unlock (and lock) the encrypted data. In asymmetric encryption, the security principals may possess different keys.

Security Configuration Tool Set

Windows 2000 provides a number of configurable options for security, providing a great deal of flexibility in security configuration. In many network environments, this flexibility is offset by the inability to manage the security configurations effectively.

The security configuration tool set is Windows 2000's answer to the problem of security configuration and management.

Secure Authentication Using Kerberos

In Greek mythology, Kerberos (Greek spelling) or Cerberus (Latin spelling) is the three-headed dog that guards the entrance to Hades. In Windows 2000, Kerberos has undergone intensive house training, and now instead guards the entrance to a much nicer place: your network.

Kerberos provides mutual authentication for both servers and clients, and server to server, unlike other protocols that authenticate only the client. Kerberos operates on the assumption that the initial transactions between clients and servers are completed over an insecure network.

Basic Concepts

A shared secret is shared only with those required to know the secret, allowing those who know the shared secret to verify the identity of others who also know the shared secret. Kerberos depends on shared secrets to perform its authentication. Kerberos uses symmetric encryption as the mechanism for implementing shared secrets. One entity encrypts information, and another entity successfully decrypts the information; this is proof of the knowledge of the shared secret between the two entities.

Windows 2000 domain controllers run the Kerberos server service (and Windows 2000 client computers run the Kerberos client service). Kerberos passwords (called keys) and identities are stored in Active Directory, reinforcing security/directory services integration. Kerberos includes these elements:

KDC The Key Distribution Center stores and distributes Kerberos tickets. The KDC runs on Windows 2000 domain controllers and uses Active Directory for secure storage.

Tickets Just as you do at the movies, you need a ticket to get in (in this case, to get into the domain itself, or access a network resource). The process is a little more complex than at the theater, though, since with Kerberos you have to have a ticket to get a ticket. After authenticating a client, the KDC issues a ticket-granting ticket (TGT) for this purpose.

Hash Having absolutely nothing to do with corned beef, this is a fixed-size numerical result that is generated when a one-way mathematical formula is applied to a string of text (the formula is called the hash algorithm).

Kerberos logon authentication follows a well-defined procedure: A user at a Windows 2000 client machine types in a username and password to log on to the network. The user's password is hashed and bundled, and this little package, called an Authentication Service (AS) request, goes to the KDC.

The KDC has its own copy of the user key, which it uses to hash the user's password, and compares the result to the hash received in the AS request. If they match, the KDC issues a TGT to the client, which can be used to get service tickets to access network services within the domain.

Now when the client attempts to access a network resource, the TGT is sent back to the KDC, along with a ticket-granting service request (TGS). The TGT is checked, as are the user's access permissions, and if all is in order, the KDC issues a session ticket, which is used to access the requested service.

Cross-domain authentication is dependent on yet another ticket type, the referral ticket, which is the basis for the transitive trust model.

Kerberos provides tight security for network resources with relatively low overhead, which helps explain why Microsoft made it Windows 2000's primary security protocol.

Key Distribution Center

Just as the Kerberos in Greek mythology had three heads, in computing, Kerberos also has three parts. The Kerberos authentication protocol has a client, a server, and a trusted authority. The Key Distribution Center (KDC), the trusted authority used in Kerberos, maintains a database with all account information for principals in the Kerberos realm. A principal is a uniquely named entity that participates in network communication, and a realm is an organization that has a Kerberos server. Since the system running the KDC service contains the database with security account information, it needs to be physically secure. A portion of this security information is the secret key that is shared between a principal and the KDC. Each principal has its own secret key, and it has a long lifetime, which is why this key is also known as the long-term key. When the long-term key is based on a human user's principal, it is derived from the user's password. This long-term key is symmetric in nature.

Another key used with the KDC is the session key, which is issued by the KDC when one principal wants to communicate with another principal. For example, if a client wants to communicate with a server, the client sends the request to the KDC, and the KDC in turn issues a session key so that the client and server can authenticate with each other. Each portion of the session key is encrypted in the respective portion of the long-term key for both the client and server. In other words, the client's long-term key encrypts the client's copy of the session key, and the server's long-term key encrypts the server's copy of the session key. The session key has a limited lifetime that is good for a single logon session. After the logon session is terminated, the session key is no longer valid. The next time the same client needs to contact the same server, it will have to go to the KDC for a new session key.

Session Tickets

The client receives an encrypted message from the KDC that contains the client's copy of the session key. On the server, a session key is contained in a session ticket, which also contains information about the client and is encrypted with the shared secret of the server and KDC. The client cannot access the session ticket because it does not know the shared secret key the server and KDC share.

Now that the client has received the client session key and the servers' session ticket from the KDC, it can successfully contact the server. The client sends a message to the server that contains the session ticket and an authenticator that has been encrypted with the session key. After the server receives the credentials from the client, it decrypts the session ticket using its shared secret key (shared between the server and the KDC) and extracts the session key sent by the KDC. It then uses the session key to decrypt the authenticator sent by the client. The server believes in the stated identity of the client because the KDC, the trusted authority, told the server the identity of the client. At this point, mutual authentication can take place if the client has requested it, if the correct flag is set in the message it sends.

This is one of the differences between Kerberos and other authentication mechanisms that only validate clients. If the client has requested mutual authentication, then the server encrypts the timestamp, including the milliseconds from the client's authenticator using its copy of the session key, and then sends it back to the client.

Session tickets can be reused for a set period of time that is determined by the Kerberos policy in the realm. The KDC places the time period in the structure of the ticket. This alleviates the principal's need to go to the KDC each time it wants to communicate with another principal. The client principal maintains the session tickets it needs to communicate to other principals in its credentials cache. On the other hand, a server principal does not keep session keys in its credentials cache. It simply waits until a client principal sends it a session ticket and decrypts it, using its shared secret key.

Ticket-Granting Tickets

Session tickets are not the only tickets used in Kerberos. The KDC communicates and verifies that principals are really who they say they are by using a ticket-granting ticket (TGT). A user who logs on to a Kerberos realm uses a password that is run through a one-way hashing algorithm that results in a long-term key. The results of the hashing are then sent to the KDC, which in turn retrieves a copy of the hash from its account database. When the client sends the long-term key, it also requests a session ticket and session key that it can use to communicate with the KDC during the entire length of the logon session. The ticket returned by the KDC to the client is the TGT. The TGT is encrypted in the KDC's long-term key, and the client's copy of the session key is encrypted in the client's long-term key. After the client receives the reply message from the KDC, it uses its long-term key (which is cached on the client system) to decrypt the session key. After the session key is decrypted, the long-term key is flushed from the client's cache, because it is no longer needed to communicate with the KDC for the remainder of the logon session or until the TGT expires. This session key is also known as the logon session key.

The client principal contacts the KDC to retrieve a session ticket to communicate with another principal such as a server. The client uses the logon session key to set up an authenticator, and then it sends off the authenticator, TGT, and a request for a session ticket for the server it wants to access to the KDC. When the KDC receives the message from the client, it decrypts the TGT, using its long-term key to extract the logon session key, and uses that to verify the authenticator sent by the client. Each time the client sends the TGT to the KDC, it must send a new authenticator.

Services Provided by the Key Distribution Center

The KDC separates its duties between two services. The authentication service (AS) is used to issue TGTs, and the ticket-granting service (TGS) is used to issue session tickets. This means that when a client first contacts the KDC, it is communicating with the AS, and when it needs to contact a server, it passes the ticket-granting ticket issued by the AS side of the KDC to the TGS side of the KDC so that it can issue a session ticket for communication to the server.

Cross-Realm Authentication

The KDC is broken down into two different services, even though one service of the KDC could perform both functions, so that Kerberos can support authentication over multiple realms. One reason multiple realms may be used in an organization is to lessen the load on a single KDC. No matter what the reason is, multiple realms can exist only if an interrealm key is shared between the KDCs. After the interrealm key is shared, the TGS of each realm becomes a security principal in the other's KDC.

When a client in realm 1 wants to access a server that is in realm 2, it does not go straight to the KDC of realm 2. First, it must log on the AS in realm 1. The AS in realm 1 sends a TGT back to the client. The client determines that it needs to contact the server in realm 2, so it requests a session ticket for the server from the TGS in realm 1. The TGS determines that the server is not in its realm, so it issues a referral ticket to the client. The referral ticket is a TGT encrypted with the interrealm key shared between realm 1 and realm 2. The client uses the referral ticket and sends a message to the TGS in realm 2. The TGS in realm 2 uses its copy of the interrealm key to decrypt the referral ticket, and if it is successful, it sends a session ticket for the realm 2 server to the realm 1 client. Figure 15.2 shows the series of steps taken in cross-realm authentication.

Figure 15.2 The steps taken in cross-realm authentication.

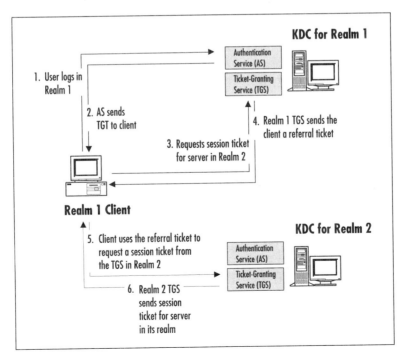

Tickets

Tickets are at the heart of the Kerberos authentication system. A variety of messages are used to request and send tickets between principals. Tickets contain a flag field that is 32 bits wide. Tickets can be used by the principal holding the ticket as many times as necessary, as long as it is within the inclusive period shown between the start time and the end time. The time for a ticket is set by the KDC and is based upon the current time unless the client has requested a different start time. Clients do not have to request a start time, but they do include the time they want the ticket to expire. The KDC consults the Kerberos realm policy and adds the time indicated in the policy to the start time. If the client has requested a specific end time, the KDC adds the requested end time to the start time. Whichever time is shorter, the time calculated using the Kerberos policy or the time calculated using the client requested time, is the time used for the end time.

If a client sends an expired session ticket to a server, then the server rejects it. It is then up to the client to go back to the KDC and request a new session ticket. However, if the client is already communicating with the server and the session ticket expires, communication continues to take place. Session tickets are used to authenticate the connection to the server. After the authentication has taken place and the connection is established, the session ticket can expire, but the connection will not be dropped.

Ticket-granting tickets also expire based on the time set in the Kerberos realm policy. If a client attempts to use an expired TGT with the KDC, then the KDC rejects it. At that point, the client must request a new TGT from the KDC, using the user's long-term key.

It is possible to renew tickets as well as flag settings. The Kerberos realm policy dictates whether tickets are renewable. If the policy allows tickets to be renewed, then the renewable flag is set in every ticket issued by the KDC. In this situation, the KDC places a time in the end time field and another time in the renew till time field of tickets. The time set in the renew till time field is equivalent to the time set in the start time field added to the maximum cumulative ticket life set in the Kerberos realm policy. The client must submit the ticket to the KDC before the original expiration time shown in the end time field. Every time the client sends a ticket back to the KDC, it must send a new authenticator also. When the KDC receives the ticket from the client, it checks the time set in the renew till time field. If the time has not already passed, then the KDC creates a new copy of the ticket that has a new time set in the end time field as well as a new session key. By issuing a new session key, the KDC helps to alleviate the possibility of compromised keys.

Proxy Tickets and Forwarded Tickets

Within tickets, the proxy and forwarded flags are used in situations in which a client connects to one server, and that server connects to another server to complete the transaction for the client. This is known as delegation of authentication. Kerberos operates using tickets, so the first server must have a ticket to connect to the second server. Proxy and forwarded flags operate on different principles, and they must be specifically allowed in the Kerberos realm policy.

Proxy tickets operate on the principle that the client knows the name of the second server that will be contacted. If the policy for the Kerberos realm allows proxy tickets, then the KDC sets the proxiable flag in the TGT it sends to the client. When the client requests a ticket for server 2, it sets the flag stating that it wants a proxy ticket and includes the name of server 1, which is the server that will act on behalf of the client. The KDC generates the ticket for server 2, sets the proxy flag, and sends it to the client. The client then sends the ticket to server 1, which uses the ticket to access server 2 on behalf of the client.

If the client does not know the name of server 2, it cannot request a proxy ticket. This is where forwarded tickets are used. Forwarded tickets operate on the principle that the client gives server 1 a TGT that it can use to request tickets for other servers when necessary. The client requests a forwardable TGT from the KDC notifying the KDC the name of the server, in this case server 1, that is authorized to act on behalf of the client. The KDC generates the forwardable TGT for server 1 and sends it back to the client. The client then sends the forwardable TGT to server 1. When server 1 needs to contact another server such as server 2, it sends the client's TGT to the KDC. The KDC detects that the TGT is forwardable, so it creates a forwarded ticket for server 2 and sends the ticket to server 1. Server 1 can then use that ticket to access server 2 on behalf of the client.

Kerberos and Windows 2000

As discussed earlier, Microsoft has added its own extensions to Kerberos; consequently, the implementation in Windows 2000 is called Microsoft Kerberos. After Microsoft Kerberos has verified the identity of the user, then the Local Security Authority (LSA) authorizes or denies access to the resource.

Key Distribution Center

The KDC is integral to the operation of Kerberos, and Windows 2000 implements the KDC as a domain service. The KDC uses Active Directory as the source of its account database.

The KDC service, along with the Active Directory, is located on every Windows 2000 domain controller. This allows each domain controller to accept authentication and ticket requests instead of depending on a single KDC.

Every Kerberos KDC has its own principal name. The name used in Windows 2000 is krbtgt, which follows the guidelines given in RFC 1510. When a Windows 2000 domain is created, a user account named krbtgt is

Figure 15.3 The krbtgt account is used by the Key Distribution Center.

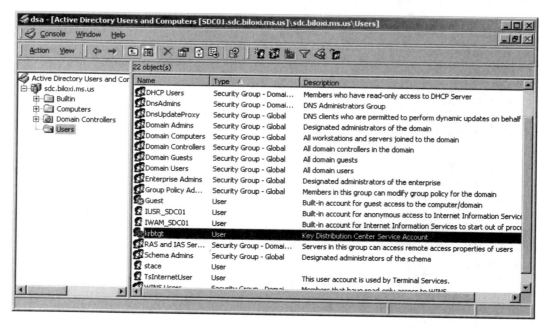

created for the KDC principal, as shown in Figure 15.3. This account is a built-in account, so it cannot be deleted, renamed, or enabled for normal user use. Even though it appears that the account is disabled, in reality it is being used by the KDC.

The password for the account is generated automatically by Windows 2000, and is changed automatically by the system on a regular basis. The key used by the krbtgt account is based on its password, just like a normal user's long-term key. The long-term key of krbtgt is used to encrypt and decrypt the TGTs it gives out. The krbtgt account is used by all KDCs in a domain. For example, a Windows 2000 domain may have five domain controllers; each of which, has its own functioning KDC, but each of the KDCs, uses the krbtgt account. This allows each KDC to encrypt and decrypt TGTs using the same long-term key. A client knows which KDC to communicate with because the client computer queries the Domain Name System (DNS) for a domain controller. After the client locates a domain controller, it sends a Kerberos Authentication Service Request message to the KDC service on that domain controller.

Kerberos Policy

Policy for Kerberos in Windows 2000 is set at the domain level. As a matter of fact, Microsoft uses the word *domain* instead of *realm* when referring to Kerberos policy. Kerberos policy is stored within Active Directory, and only

Figure 15.4 The default Kerberos domain policy.

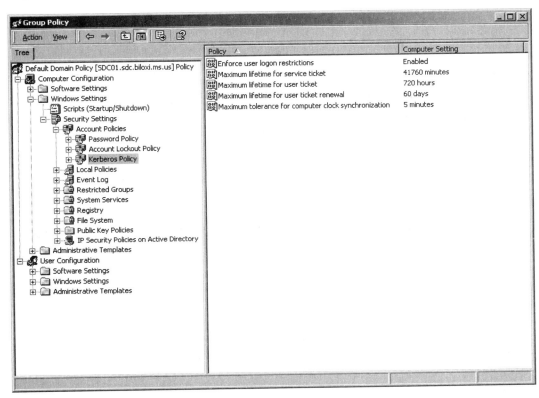

members of the Domain Admins group are allowed to change the policy. Figure 15.4 shows the options available in the Kerberos policy for the domain.

The settings included in the Kerberos domain policy are:

- Enforce user logon restrictions
- Maximum lifetime that a user ticket can be renewed
- Maximum service ticket lifetime
- Maximum tolerance for synchronization of computer clocks
- Maximum user ticket lifetime

"Enforce user logon restrictions" is enabled by default and is used to validate every request for session tickets by making sure that the client has the correct user rights for logging on to the destination server. This setting can be disabled; it takes extra time to perform, and may slow network performance.

The maximum lifetime that a ticket can be renewed setting is set in days. A reasonable setting is seven days for this attribute.

The maximum service ticket lifetime is set in minutes. Do not let the term *service ticket* confuse you; it is just the name Microsoft decided to use for session tickets. The setting for the lifetime of the service ticket cannot be more than the time specified in the maximum user ticket lifetime or less than 10 minutes. A reasonable setting for this option is to make it the same as the maximum user ticket lifetime.

The maximum tolerance for synchronization of computer clocks setting determines how much difference in the clocks is tolerated. This setting is in minutes, and 5 minutes is a reasonable setting.

The maximum user ticket lifetime is set in hours. Microsoft has decided to use the term *user ticket*, but in Kerberos terms, it is a TGT. A reasonable setting is 10 hours for this attribute.

It is easy to change an attribute by double-clicking the attribute and changing the setting.

Contents of a Microsoft Kerberos Ticket

There are additional items contained in Microsoft Kerberos tickets that are not in other Kerberos implementation tickets. Windows 2000 uses Security Identifiers (SIDs) just as in previous versions of Windows NT. SIDs are used to represent user accounts and groups. The SID for a user, along with any SIDs for the groups to which the user belongs, is included in tickets used by the client and is known as the Privilege Attribute Certificate (PAC). The PAC is not the same thing as a public key certificate. The user's name, also known as User Principal Name, is added to the ticket as UPN:name@domain. For example, UPN:natalie@Walshaw.com is placed in a ticket to identify the user Natalie.

Delegation of Authentication

Kerberos supports two methods of delegation: proxiable tickets and forwardable tickets. Microsoft Kerberos provides support for forwardable tickets only, and the default Kerberos policy for Windows 2000 domains assigns this permission only to members of the Domain Admins group. It can be provided to individual users by modifying the user's account in Active Directory Users and Computers. To access user accounts in Active Directory, click Start | Programs | Administrative Tools | Active Directory Users and Computers. The account option for enabling delegation is available on the Account tab of a user's properties. An account option is also available to not allow the acceptance of delegated credentials.

Preauthentication

In Kerberos authentication, some of the messages have a preauthentication field. Microsoft Kerberos uses preauthentication in domains by default. The data contained in this field is the encrypted timestamp of the client. If it is necessary, preauthentication can be turned off for user accounts on an individual basis. It may be necessary to turn off preauthentication if you are integrating Microsoft Kerberos with other variations of the Kerberos protocol.

Security Support Providers

When the system is booted, Windows 2000 Server automatically starts two Security Support Providers (SSPs): the Kerberos SSP and the NTLM SSP. Both SSPs are started by the Local Security Authority (LSA), and both are available to authenticate network logons and connections between clients and servers. Windows 2000 Server defaults to using the Kerberos SSP unless the client is not capable of using Kerberos, as is the case with Windows 9x and Windows NT Workstation clients. In that case, the NTLM SSP is used. The NTLM SSP is also used for Windows 2000 servers that are configured as member servers or stand-alone servers, and when a Windows 2000 computer is authenticating to a Windows NT 4.0 domain controller. (Figure 15.5 outlines the process used when you log on locally.) The Kerberos SSP is used first for authentication because it is the default for Windows 2000. However, if the user is logging on locally, an error is sent to the Security Support Provider Interface (SSPI), and then the SSPI sends the logon request to the NTLM SSP.

Figure 15.5 The logon process for local logons.

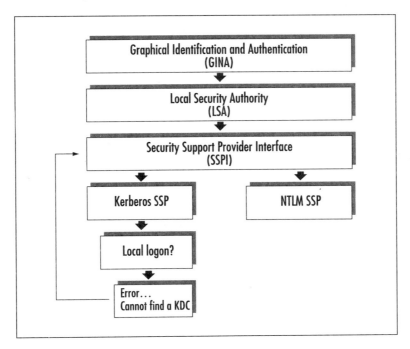

Credentials Cache

The client uses an area of volatile memory called the credentials cache. This area of memory is protected by the LSA, and it can never be put in the pagefile on the hard disk drive. When the user logs off the system, everything in the area of memory used for the credentials cache is flushed.

The Kerberos SSP controls the credentials cache and is used to attain and renew tickets and keys. The LSA is responsible for notifying the Kerberos SSP when these functions need to be performed.

The LSA also keeps a copy of the user's hashed password in a secure portion of the Registry while the user is logged on. Once the user logs off, the hashed password is discarded. The LSA keeps a copy of the hashed password in case the TGT expires; it then gives the Kerberos SSP a method of obtaining another TGT without prompting the user to input a password. This allows this task to be smoothly accomplished in the background.

DNS Name Resolution

Microsoft Kerberos depends on the Domain Name System (DNS) to find an available KDC to send the initial authentication request. All Windows 2000 domain controllers are KDCs, and the KDC is registered as _kerberos._udp. nameofDNSdomain in the DNS service location record (SRV record). Clients can query for this SRV record to locate the IP address for computers running the KDC service. A client that cannot find the SRV record can query for a host record (A record), using the domain name.

If a Windows 2000 computer is a member of a different Kerberos realm (not a Windows 2000 domain), it cannot look for the SRV record. In this case, the name of the KDC server is stored in the Registry of the Windows 2000 computer. When the computer needs to locate the KDC, the Microsoft Kerberos SSP locates the domain name for the KDC server from the Registry and then uses DNS to find out the IP address for the system.

UDP and TCP Ports

When a client sends Kerberos messages to the KDC, it defaults to using User Datagram Protocol (UDP) port 88 as long as certain criteria are met. On an Ethernet network, the Maximum Transmission Unit (MTU) that can be carried is 1500 bytes. If the Kerberos message is smaller than 1472 bytes, Microsoft Kerberos uses UDP as the transport mechanism. If the message is between 1473 bytes and 2000 bytes, IP fragments the frame over UDP on port 88. If the Kerberos message is over 2000 bytes, it is sent by the Transmission Control Protocol (TCP) on port 88. RFC 1510 states that UDP port 88 should be used for all Kerberos messages, but since Microsoft Kerberos messages may very well be more than 2000 bytes, because user and group SIDs are included, Microsoft also uses TCP port 88. A draft revision to RFC 1510 has been submitted to the Internet Engineering Task Force (IETF) proposing the use of TCP port 88, but it has not been included in the formal RFC yet. Interoperability should not be affected with other Kerberos realms; the communications are between Windows 2000 computers only.

Using the Security Configuration Tool Set

This section introduces the functions and uses of the Windows 2000 Security Configuration Tool Set. The tool set is a response to Systems Administrators' need for a central, easy-to-use program that will allow configuration of domains, organizational units (OUs), and local security. In addition to conveniently bringing together formerly widely disparate programs into a single interface, the Security Configuration and Analysis snap-in allows the Administrator to analyze a local machine's current configuration. This analysis can be performed against security templates so that the Network Manager can compare the present configuration to a proposed ideal configuration, which can then be applied with a couple of simple clicks of the mouse.

Security Configuration Tool Set Overview

The four main components of the Security Configuration Tool Set are:

- Security Configuration and Analysis snap-in
- Security Settings Extension to Group Policy
- The command-line tool, secedit.exe
- Security Templates snap-in

Security Configuration and Analysis Snap-In

The Security Configuration and Analysis snap-in is a security tool that allows you to create, test, and apply a variety of security scenarios. From within the Security Configuration and Analysis snap-in, you can create text-based files that contain security settings than can be transported and applied to any Windows 2000 computer. The text files are saved with the .inf extension, and can be easily edited with basic text editors such as Notepad. When you manipulate security configuration, you should use the graphical interface to minimize mishaps.

Information about different security configurations are saved to a personal database that the Administrator creates for personal use. Use the Security Configuration and Analysis snap-in to import other security configurations that have been saved as security templates. You can create multiple security templates and merge them into a single security database. Each personal database contains a scenario based on the security templates that have been imported into the database.

After creating a security configuration, the Administrator can test the scenario against the current security configuration on that machine. After the analysis, the Security Configuration and Analysis snap-in will report what current settings deviate from the scenario stored in the database.

An Administrator who is pleased with the scenario results can then use a simple point-and-click procedure to update the local machine's own security configuration to match that of the scenario stored in the database.

Security Setting Extensions to Group Policy

A security configuration can be saved using the Security Configuration and Analysis snap-in and then applied to the local computer. An Administrator can export security scenarios as text-based template files that can be imported into the group policy of a domain or OU. This provides a tremendous degree of flexibility for the Administrator who wishes to obtain granular control over the security infrastructure of an enterprise.

The ability to save security settings in a template file, which can be saved and backed up, provides a high degree of fault tolerance for the organization's security plan. If an administrative misadventure causes complex alterations to the domain security policy, the Administrator can restore the original security policy by importing and applying a template.

Security Templates

Microsoft provides a full set of templates that conform to a number of common security scenarios. These security templates can be broken down into two general categories: Default and Incremental. The Default or Basic templates are applied by the operating system when a clean install has been performed; they are not applied if an upgrade installation has been done. The incremental templates should be applied after the Basic security templates have been applied. The four types of incremental templates are Compatible, Secure, Highly Secure, and Dedicated Domain Controller.

The Administrator can save time and effort during an initial rollout by applying these templates to workstations, domain controllers, and member and stand-alone servers. Then, as time allows, the Administrator can customize and fine-tune security settings for local computers, OUs, or an entire domain.

The secedit.exe Command-Line Tool

The secedit.exe command-line tool offers much of the functionality of the Security Configuration and Analysis snap-in from the command line. This allows the Administrator to script security analyses for many machines across the enterprise, and save the results for later analysis.

The reporting capabilities of the secedit.exe tool are limited. Although you can perform a security analysis from the command line, you cannot view the results of the analysis with secedit.exe. You must view the results of the analysis from the graphical Security Configuration and Analysis snap-in interface.

Security Configuration and Analysis Database

The Security Configuration and Analysis snap-in database contains all the existing security properties available for Windows 2000 computers. It does not add any additional settings or extend the security capabilities of the operating system. The Security Configuration and Analysis snap-in database contains the Administrator's security preferences. The database is populated with entries derived from security templates. You have the choice to import multiple templates and merge the contents of those templates, or you can import templates in their entirety after the previous database entries have been cleared.

The database is central in the security analysis process. The Administrator can initiate a security analysis after configuring the entries in the database to meet the organization's perceived needs. The security analysis will compare the settings in the database with the actual settings implemented on the local computer. Individual security settings will be flagged by an icon that will change, depending on whether the actual security settings are the same or different from those included in the database. You will also be informed if there are settings that have not been configured at all, and thus may require the Administrator's attention.

The formulation of a well thought-out security policy is a time-consuming process. To add a measure of fault tolerance, the database entries can be exported to a text file template, which can be saved for later use on the same machine, or can be applied to another machine, domain, or OU.

The procedure used to export the template to be saved is simple: just right-click on the Security Configuration and Analysis snap-in node and choose Export Template.

The exported template is saved as an .inf file, and can be imported to other computers, domains, and OUs. In this way, the security parameters can be reproduced exactly from one machine to another.

Security Configuration and Analysis Areas

The Security Configuration and Analysis snap-in brings together in a single workspace security configuration components that were formerly spread throughout many different programs in NT 4.0. The different nodes that can be configured are illustrated in Figure 15.6.

The nodes in the snap-in include:

Account Policies   The Account Policies node includes those configuration variables that were formerly manipulated in the User Manager for Domains applet in NT 4.0, such as maximum password age.

Local Policies   This node provides policies for the local machine only. The Security Options subnode offers the Administrator many options that formerly were available only by the manipulation of the Windows NT 4.0 Registry; that is, message text for users attempting to log on.

Figure 15.6 Security Configuration and Analysis nodes.

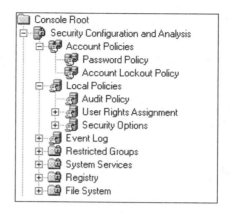

Event Log   This node allows you to configure security settings for the security log file. These settings include maximum log sizes, configuring guest access to the security log, and whether the computer should shut down when the security log is full.

Restricted Groups   You can configure a group membership list in the Restricted Groups node, and then configure an approved list of members by reapplying the security template you have created.

System Services   The Security parameters of all system services can be defined in the database via the System Services node. You can define whether a service startup should be automatic, manual, or disabled.

Registry   The Registry node allows you to set access restrictions on individual Registry keys.

File System   The File System node allows you to set folder and file permissions.

Security Configuration Tool Set User Interfaces

There are two user interfaces available to configure system security settings: the graphical interfaces and the secedit.exe command-line interface.

You should do most of your work from the graphical interface. From the graphical interface, you will design your security scenarios, test them against extant security settings, and then apply scenarios stored in the security database after testing. After security scenarios are customized to the Administrator's needs, the scenario can be exported in a plan text file, which can be saved for later use.

The exported text file can be edited by hand using any available text editor. However, Microsoft recommends that users confine themselves to the graphical interface, so as to not introduce random elements into the structure of the file and inadvertently corrupt its contents.

Your interfaces with the Security Tools set will be via these interfaces:

- Security Configuration and Analysis snap-in
- The secedit.exe command-line tool
- Security Extensions to the Group Policy Editor

Security Configuration and Analysis Snap-In

You use the Security Configuration and Analysis snap-in to control local machine security policies. You cannot directly affect domain or OU security policies from the Security Configuration and Analysis snap-in. This limits the use of the snap-in somewhat, since you cannot use it to test different scenarios against the prevailing domain or OU's security configuration.

Nonetheless, the Security Configuration and Analysis snap-in remains a powerful tool. To get started, you must first create an MMC that will allow you to work with the Tool Set. To create a Security Configuration Tool Set Console:

1. From the Run command, type **mmc** in the text box, and click OK.

2. From the MMC menu, click Add/remove snap-in, and then click ADD.

3. Select and add:
   - Security Configuration and Analysis
   - Security Templates
   - Group Policy

After adding these, save your MMC as Security Tool Set or any other name you wish. You now need to open an existing database, or create a new one. It is against these entries in the database that you will test your present security configuration. You can also apply the settings saved in the database to the computer itself, thus updating the local machine's security configuration.

1. Right-click Security Configuration and Analysis, and select OPEN Database.

2. If there is already an existing database, you can open that one. If there are no databases currently defined, you can create a new one by entering the name of the database in the filename box. Click Open.

3. After you click OPEN, the Import Template dialog box appears. You need to populate the database with security configuration entries. The templates contain this information. Select the template that contains the information that most closely represents the level of security you are interested in, and then click OPEN.

4. In the right pane, you will see instructions on how to Analyze or Configure your computer. Right-click the Security Configuration and Analysis node, and select either Configure or Analyze. Be careful; if you select Configure, it will apply the settings that you have imported into the database to the active security configuration of the computer.

After the database has been created, you can test your configuration. You have two options: You can merge settings from another template file into your working database, or you can clear the working database so that it will contain only entries from the new template being imported. Merging templates allows the Administrator a great deal of flexibility in analysis and in the application of different security scenarios.

In order to merge or replace the entries in the database:

1. Right-click Security Configuration and Analysis, and select Import Template. You will see the Import Template dialog box.

2. You have two choices at this point. You may select a template and then click OPEN. By doing this, you will merge the entries from the template with those already in the database. However, if you would prefer to start with a "clean" database by clearing the entries in the database before you import the new entries, you can select "Clear this database before importing" by putting a check in the box. Then click OPEN.

The Security Settings Extension to the Group Policy Editor

The Security Configuration and Analysis snap-in allows you to configure local machine policies easily. However, for the configuration of security structure of an entire domain or OU, you need to use the Security Settings Extension to the Group Policy editor.

You cannot use the Security Configuration and Analysis snap-in to configure the security settings of a domain or OU. To apply a security configuration to an OU:

1. Open the Active Directory Users and Computers console from the Administrative Tools menu. Right-click an organizational unit, and select Properties.

2. The Organizational Unit's Properties box appears. Click the Group Policy tab.

3. Click NEW. Type a name for the Group Policy Object. Make sure the new object is selected, and then click EDIT.

4. Expand Computer Configuration, then expand Windows Settings. There are two subnodes of Windows Settings: Scripts and Security Templates. Select the Security Templates node.

5. Right-click the Security Settings node, and select Import Policy. Notice that the policies are template files with the .inf extension. You have the option of merging the template's entries into the present organizational unit's security setup, or you can clear the present OU's security settings and have them replaced by the settings in the imported template. Click OPEN to enact the new policy.

You are not given the option to test the template settings against the present OU's security configuration. The settings are enabled after you import the policy via the .inf file.

The secedit.exe Command-Line Tool

The secedit.exe command-line interface allows the Administrator to:

- Analyze system security
- Configure system security
- Refresh security settings
- Export security settings
- Validate the syntax of a security template

Common switches include:

```
secedit /analyze
```

The analyze switch is used to initiate a security analysis.

```
secedit /configure
```

Secedit applies a template by using the configure switch.

```
secedit /refreshpolicy
```

This command updates the system security policy after changes have been made.

```
secedit /export
```

Use the export switch to export the template stored in the database to an .inf file.

Configuring Security

The Administrator can configure the entries in the security database via each of the nodes in the Security Configuration and Analysis and Security Templates snap-ins. New security attributes cannot be defined; only modification of existing Windows 2000 security elements are configurable. Microsoft or third parties may include extensions to the security attributes in the future.

Account Policies

Account Policies define aspects of security relating primarily to passwords and account lockout. The password Policy contains entries related to password aging and password length. Account Lockout Policy determines how many bad tries a person gets before the account is locked out. Kerberos Policy applies only to domain controllers, since local logons do not use Kerberos. Entries include maximum lifetimes for various tickets, such as user tickets and user renewal.

Local Policies and Event Log

Local Policies include the Audit Policy, User Rights Assignment, and Security Options. Some Audit Policy selections include auditing logon events, use of user privileges, systems events, and object access. The User Rights Assignment node includes granting or denying user rights such as the right to add workstations to the domain, change the system time, log on locally, and access the computer from the network.

The most profound improvements are represented in the Security Options node, where you can make changes that could be made only via direct Registry edits in Windows NT 4.0. Example of such Security Options include clearing the pagefile when the system shuts down, message text during logon, number of previous logons kept in cache, and shut down system immediately if unable to log security audits.

The improvements in local policy management are numerous with the addition of the configurable objects available in the Security Options node.

Event Log

Event Log Configuration settings allow you to configure the length of time logs are retained, and the size of the event logs. You can also configure that the system should shut down if the security log becomes full.

Restricted Groups

The Restricted Groups node lends a new dimension to the security configuration options available in Windows 2000. You can define, as part of security policy, the members of a group. There are times when the Administrator needs to temporarily add users to groups with a higher classification than the users' typical group membership. This might be the case when an Administrator goes on vacation and another member of the team is assigned full administrative rights. However, often the temporary promotion ends up being an inadvertently permanent one, and the user remains in the Administrators group. Groups may also become members of other groups, when this is not part of the company security plan. By defining Restricted Group membership rules, you can return group membership to that defined by security policy.

You can add users to restricted groups by double-clicking on the group in the Results pane and adding new members from there. You can also restrict what groups the group itself can be a member of (a type of recursive checking), using the nested group capabilities now available in Windows 2000.

Registry Security

Registry keys can be protected by policy. You can define a security policy for a Registry key or value in the database, and then customize the propagation of the setting using the Key properties dialog box. This approach is much easier and less error prone than controlling the security of Registry entries via the Registry editor.

File System Security

The File System Security node allows you to configure NTFS permission for all local drives. It is common for a number of different Administrators to get into Explorer and customize the NTFS permissions on file and folders through the file system. File and folder security should be part of a well thought-out and implemented security plan. This security plan can be realized by setting File System Policy in the templates (seen in Figure 15.7). You can then periodically audit the status of the file system to look for inconsistencies between the plan and the actual state of NTFS permissions in the local environment.

In the template, the volume letters are not assigned. You can do this by right-clicking on the File System node, and then picking the volumes that you would like to include in the template.

Figure 15.7 File System security settings.

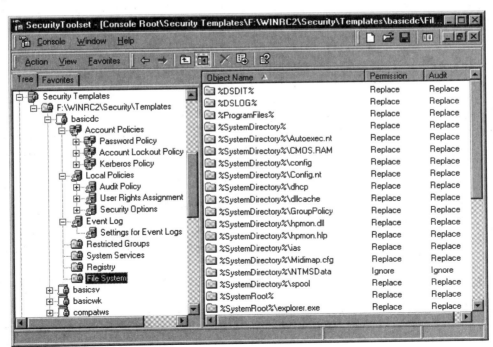

System Services Security

The System Services node allows you to control security and startup policy on all the services defined in the template. Controlling the startup behavior of system services can save the Administrator many headaches over time. Consider the situation of users starting up their own RAS services or DHCP services haphazardly. This type of situation creates a large security risk for any network. You can set restrictive networking services startup properties, and assign all computers that require certain services to an OU that does have the right to start up particular networking services.

Analyzing Security

One of the most useful features of the Security Configuration and Analysis snap-in is the ability to compare the desired security policies as they are set up in the template with the actual state of the local machine. The Administrator is able to glean a tremendous amount of insight regarding the currently security configuration of the machine by using the Analyze feature of the Security Configuration and Analysis snap-in.

Running the analysis is easy. After you import the security settings from the appropriate templates, all you need to do is right-click on the Security Configuration and Analysis node and select the Analyze Computer Now command. The machine will run an analysis and show you its progress. Security analyses can be run against various selected templates. Figure 15.8 shows the results of an analysis on the local audit policy.

Group Policy Integration

You can use the features of the Security Configuration Tool Set to configure group policies. This is important to the Administrator who is interested in configuring the security of an entire domain or OU. By extending the group policy capabilities of the Security Configuration Tool Set to the group policy objects of choice, the Network Manager is able to speed deployment of uniform policy through many computers in the domain.

Security Configuration in Group Policy Objects

The Security Configuration Tool Set allows for the configuration of security policy, which is one aspect of group policy. Security policies designed and tested using the Security Configuration and Analysis snap-in can be exported and applied to domains and OUs.

A significant limitation at this time is the inability to export security configuration parameters from a domain or OU. This limits the full functionality of the Security Configuration and Analysis snap-in to analyzing security parameters of the local machine only. You cannot, at this time,

Figure 15.8 Results of an Audit Policy analysis.

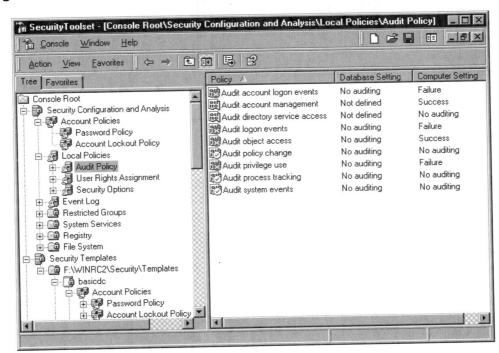

export the domain or OU's security policy for analysis. However, you can import a security policy that has been saved as an .inf file.

Security policy can be edited in the Group Policy Object. These include all Windows 2000 security configuration objects.

Additional Security Policies

IPSec policy   IPSec security policies can be configured and analyzed in the Security Configuration and Analysis snap-in. For more information on IPSec, see Chapter 16, "Securing TCP/IP Connections."

Public Key policies   Included in the public key policies are the encrypted data recovery agents, Root certificates, and certificate trust lists.

Using the Tools

Let's put what we have covered into practice. In this section, we will walk through using both the Security Configuration and Analysis snap-in and the Security Settings Extension to the Group Policy Editor.

Using the Security Configuration and Analysis Snap-In

It is possible to configure a Security console that includes both the Security Configuration and Analysis snap-in and the Security Templates. That console can be used to configure a new security template, and then import that template into a database that would restrict membership to the Administrator's Local group as demonstrated in the following steps.

1. From the Run command, type **mmc** in the text box, and click OK.

2. From the MMC menu, click Add/remove snap-in, and then click ADD.

3. Select and add:
   - Security Configuration and Analysis
   - Security Templates

4. Expand the Security Templates node. Right-click on the basicsv node and select Save As. In the Save As dialog box, type **practicebasicsv** and press ENTER.

5. Expand the practicebasicsv node and select the Restricted Groups node. Right-click that node and select the Add Group command. Click BROWSE.

6. In the Select Groups dialog box, click the down arrow in the Look in box, and select the name of your computer. Then select Administrators, click ADD, and then click OK. Click OK again to close the Add Group dialog box.

7. In the results pane, you should see the Administrators Group listed. Right-click on the Administrators Group, and select the Security command.

8. Click the "Add for the Members of this group:" text box. Next, click BROWSE in the Add Member dialog box. This brings up the Select Users or Groups dialog box. In the Look in box, make sure the local machine is selected. Then select the Administrator account, and click ADD. Click OK, and then click OK again. Click OK one more time to close the Configure Membership for Administrators dialog box. Right-click the practicebasicsv node and click Save to save the changes you have made to the template.

9. Now the template is properly configured. The next step is to open or create a new database to import the security entries from the template. Right-click the Security Configuration and Analysis node, and select the Open database command.

10. In the Open Database dialog box, type **practice**, and then click OPEN. You are now asked what template you want to use to populate the database. Select the practicebasicsv template, and click OPEN. The entries in the template are imported into the practice.sdb database.

Using Security Settings Extension to Group Policy Editor

To use the Security Settings Extension to the Group Policy Editor:

1. At the Run command, type **mmc** to start an empty console.
2. Click the Console menu, and then select the Add/Remove Snap-in command.
3. Click ADD, and then select Group Policy from the list of Standalone snap-ins. Click ADD.
4. In the Select Group Policy dialog box, click BROWSE and select the Default Domain Policy, then click OK. Click FINISH, click CLOSE, and then click OK.
5. Expand the Default Domain Policy node, expand the Computer Configuration node, expand the Windows Settings node, and then expand the Security Settings node.
6. Double-click the Account Policies node, and select the Password Policy node.
7. Double-click the Minimum Password Age entry, and change the value to 14.

You have successfully changed the domain password age policy.

Encrypted File System

Windows 2000 provides a much-needed addition to the administrative security toolkit: file encryption. As the use of computers continues to surge, and laptop use is at an all-time high, the concern over data security increases for everyone, not just the System Administrator. The fact that data is hidden behind a firewall, and that Windows NT includes mandatory logon and access control for files, does not guarantee that data is protected from unauthorized eyes. To keep data from being viewed or modified by an unauthorized user, technology has now turned to the process of file encryption.

Windows 2000 provides native file encryption incorporated in the NTFS file system called the Encrypted File System (EFS). In an effort to provide a security infrastructure that does not restrict functionality, Microsoft has ensured that EFS is transparent, while at the same time providing industrial-strength security.

How EFS Works

EFS is implemented with a combination of secret key encryption (a fast and less secure process) and public key encryption (a slow but more secure process). When a request is received to encrypt a file, EFS gener-

Figure 15.9 The encryption process.

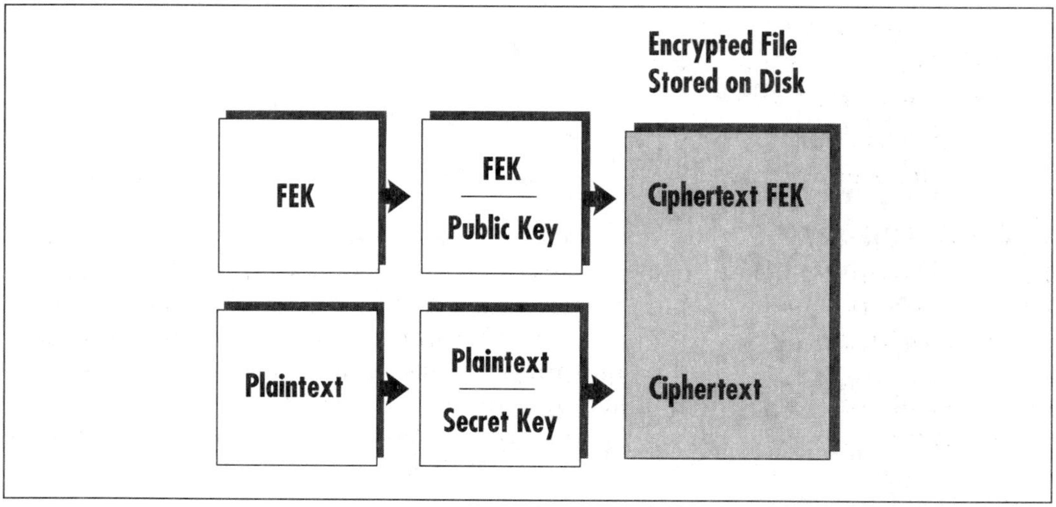

ates a random number for the file, and this random number is known as the file's File Encryption Key. With this File Encryption Key, a modified DES algorithm, called DESX, is used to generate the encrypted file and store it on disk.

When a file needs to be decrypted, the File Encryption Key (FEK) is used again. Storing the FEK on disk with the file ensures that the file can be decrypted at any time. Anyone who needs to decrypt the file and has access to it, also has access to the file's File Encryption Key.

To tighten the security of the File Encryption Key, EFS uses the user's public key to encrypt the FEK. This prevents users from sharing the same decryption key. Public key encryption is used only on the relatively small FEK, minimizing the impact on the host machine. What is stored with the encrypted file is the ciphered FEK. Only the user, with that user's private key, can decrypt the ciphered FEK, which in turn is needed to decrypt the actual file. Figure 15.9 demonstrates the encryption process.

User Operations

EFS is native to all versions of Windows 2000 and requires only that the files be located on a Windows 2000 NTFS volumes. No administrative tasks involving installation and configuration of the Encrypting File System need to be completed in order for it to work.

A user can manipulate an encrypted file much like a normal file. The following operations can be conducted on a file:

- Encrypt a file
- Access an encrypted file
- Copy an encrypted file
- Move and rename an encrypted file
- Decrypt a file
- Encrypt a directory
- Recovery operations

File Encryption

EFS uses a public key pair and a secret key in the encryption/decryption process. When a user tries to encrypt a file, EFS determines whether a user key pair is in existence for the user, or whether it must be created. If a key pair needs to be created, the generation occurs on a domain controller or on the local computer. Other tasks completed by EFS include creating the actual ciphered file, ciphering the File Encryption Key, creating a log, creating a backup file, and deleting the log and backup file used in the encryption process.

In order to manage encrypted file resources, the user must first identify what data needs to be protected, and then use either Explorer or the Cipher command utility to encrypt the file.

Any folder or file, as long as it is stored on a NTFS volume, can be encrypted by the owner. The easiest way to maintain encrypted files is to first create an encrypted folder where you plan to store all sensitive data. After creating the folder, right-click on the directory and select Properties. Click ADVANCED on the General tab, which then displays the Advanced Attributes window. Check the "Encrypt contents to secure data" box, as in Figure 15.10.

Figure 15.10 Marking a directory for encryption.

The process for encrypting an individual file is identical, except that the file should be selected first before right-clicking to navigate to Properties.

Any newly created file or subdirectory stored in the marked encrypted directory from this point on will be automatically encrypted. If the directory is marked for encryption and it already contains existing files and subdirectories, the user receives a message asking whether to encrypt files and subdirectories in the directory.

A tradeoff exists between compressed and encrypted files: a file can only be encrypted or compressed, not both. The encryption process will fail if a file that has the system bit set is targeted for encryption.

Decrypting a File

The decryption process occurs when a user accesses an encrypted file during normal operations. The file is unencrypted on-the-fly, though the file remains encrypted on the disk. Windows 2000 will also go through the decryption process when the owner of the file decides that the added security method is no longer needed.

When the user wants to read and/or modify the contents of the encrypted file, the Windows 2000 operating system decrypts the file as it is moved from the hard drive into physical memory. The decryption of the file for use is transparent to the user, and the ciphered file is still stored on the hard drive. The user does not have to decrypt the file manually before each use. EFS must have the user's private key in order to decrypt the file.

To permanently decrypt a file, the user can use the Explorer interface and clear the encryption attribute, or use the Cipher Utility and execute the appropriate command. When an individual file is selected for decryption, only that file is affected. When the user at the directory level requests decryption, a message is displayed, asking whether the user wishes to decrypt all files and subdirectories found within this directory.

This decryption process at the directory level is exactly like the process for changing permissions at the directory level. Use these steps to decrypt a file:

1. Using Explorer, select the file you want to decrypt, and right-click to bring up the Context menu.

2. Select Properties, and click ADVANCED on the General tab.

3. In the Advanced Attributes dialog box, clear the check box to "Encrypt contents to secure data."

4. Click OK. On the General tab, click OK or APPLY to mark the file as unencrypted.

Cipher Utility

Windows 2000 provides users with a command-line interface for file encryption. The general format of the Cipher Utility is:

```
>cipher  [ /e ]   [ /d ]  [ /s [dir]]  [ /a ]  [ /i ]  [ /f ]  [ /q ]  [filename]
```

When the cipher command is executed without any switches or file-name, the result will be a display of the encryption status of the current directory and any files in that directory. Typing **cipher /?** at the command prompt will display the switches that can be used with the command.

Directory Encryption

As discussed earlier, we noted that EFS allows encryption to be set at the directory level. When the directory is selected for encryption, any new object placed in this directory, including files and subdirectories, are encrypted.

When a directory's attributes are modified to include encryption, the directory itself is not technically encrypted; rather, the directory is marked for encryption. This encryption mark controls all the new objects becoming encrypted.

Recovery Operations

Windows 2000 contains an Encrypted Data Recovery Policy (EDRP), which is part of the local security policy in a workgroup environment or part of the domain security policy for domains. The Security Subsystem in user mode is responsible for the enforcement of this policy. This subsystem is responsible for caching the EFS policy so that the policy can be applied offline.

A first step is to ensure that the System Administrator sets up a Recovery Policy. Windows 2000 contains a Recovery Agent Wizard, in which Recovery Agents are assigned along with their corresponding key pairs. The Microsoft Base Cryptographic Provider is used to create a Data Recovery File for each Recovery Agent.

To recover an encrypted file that the owner cannot manipulate:

1. The person responsible for the recovery operation—the Recovery Agent—should use a Backup utility and restore a copy of the user's ciphertext file on the computer that has the recovery certificates.

2. Using Explorer, the encrypted file's Properties should be displayed.

3. On the General tab click ADVANCED.

4. The clearing of the Encrypt contents to secure data check box will use the Recovery Agent's private key and decrypt the file.

5. The decrypted file should now be backed up and restored to the user.

Note that recovery keys can be exported as a file and stored on different physical media, such as floppy disk.

A command-line utility can also be used to recover an encrypted file. If you decide to use the EfsRecvr utility, the same steps should be applied in order to back up the file and restore it on the computer that contains the recovery keys.

The EfsRecvr command-line utility uses this general format:

```
EFSRECVR  [ /S [:dir] ]  [ /I ]  [ /Q ]  [ filename […] ]
```

Summary

Windows 2000 supports several authentication protocols, including NTLM, Kerberos v5, Distributed Password Authentication, Extensible Authentication Protocol, and Secure Channel. The two protocols used for network authentication, for logging on locally or as an interactive user, are NTLM and Kerberos v5. Kerberos is the default authentication protocol used in Windows 2000; NTLM is provided for backward compatibility and is also used to authenticate Windows 2000 member and stand-alone servers.

Kerberos provides several advantages over NTLM, which was the authentication protocol of choice in previous versions of Windows NT. One of the advantages is that Kerberos provides mutual authentication wherein the client can also verify the identity of the server, which cannot be accomplished using NTLM. Another advantage is that Windows 2000 Kerberos domains can communicate with Kerberos realms of other implementations of Kerberos. This cannot be accomplished with NTLM, which is proprietary to Microsoft operating systems.

Kerberos is made up of several components, including the Key Distribution Center, session tickets, and ticket-granting tickets. The Key Distribution Center is comprised of two services, the Authentication Service and the Ticket-Granting Service.

The Security Configuration Tool Set introduces a new and more efficient way to manage security parameters in Windows 2000. Using this new set of configuration and management tools, the Administrator can configure and manage the security policies for a single machine, or an entire domain or OU.

The tool set includes the Security Configuration and Analysis snap-in, Security Templates, the secedit.exe command-line tool, and the Security Settings Extensions to the Group Policy Editor. Together, you can use these tools to create and configure security policies for local machines, domains, or OUs.

The Security Configuration and Analysis snap-in allows the Administrator to create a database with security configuration entries. These security configuration entries can be used to test against the existing security configuration of a local machine.

Security configuration can be saved as templates, which are text files that contain security configuration information. These templates are imported into the Security Configuration and Analysis snap-in database for analysis and application.

Windows 2000 now supplies the user with the ability to encrypt files that contain sensitive information. The Encrypting File System can be set both at the directory and file level. Basic file encryption is accomplished using two methods. Secret key encryption uses the same key for encrypting and decrypting data. The Secret key algorithm is relatively fast, and therefore is appropriate for encrypting a large amount of data.

Public Key Cryptography uses a key pair: the public key is used for encryption, and the private key is used to decrypt the file. This method of encryption provides more security, because only a private key can unscramble the ciphertext back into plaintext. The price you must pay for better security is that the process is slow; it should be used only on a small amount of data.

Windows 2000 uses both methods of encryption. The file is encrypted using a Secret Key called a File Encryption Key, along with the DESX algorithm. To protect the File Encryption Key from dishonest people, the File Encryption Key is then encrypted by the owner's public key.

FAQs

Q: How does a Windows 2000 client find a Microsoft KDC?

A: It uses DNS to locate KDCs in the domain.

Q: Why are ticket-granting tickets necessary?

A: To prove to the KDC that the clients requesting a session ticket are really who they say they are. The KDC issues the TGT to the client when the user first logs on to the domain.

Q: I would like to analyze a number of computers in my domain using scripts. What tool would I use to accomplish this?

A: The secedit.exe command-line tool allows the Administrator to analyze a number of machines by creating scripts that can be automated. You can then view the results of the analysis by opening up the database file that the analysis was run against.

Q: What happens to the data if the system crashes during the encryption process?

A: The Encrypting File System is designed to be fault tolerant. Throughout the entire encryption process, a log file keeps track of certain operations as they are completed. If the system crashes before the file is completely encrypted, the Local Security Authority Server looks for log files at boot time. If the LSASRV locates any Encryption log file, the contents are read. Usually, the LSASRV copies the backup file over the original semi-encrypted file, and then deletes the backup and log files. If the LSASRV finds that the original file has not been modified, it deletes the backup and log files.

Securing TCP/IP Connections

Solutions in this chapter:

- Introduction

- Secure Sockets Layer

- Secure Communications over Virtual Private Networks

- IPSec for Windows 2000

- Deploying IPSec

- Summary

Introduction

To the uninitiated, TCP/IP is a jumble of meaningless letters as indecipherable as quantum physics. To the network professional, however, it is the life force of the Internet that drives its organic growth.

A few years ago, ubiquitous connectivity would have been considered a computing nirvana. Businesses now share data with partners, allow customers to access account information, and provide dial-up access to the corporate network for employees. Broadband technologies are delivering high-speed access into homes across the world.

Nowadays, we take the connectivity for granted and seek out extra value from the networks that span the globe. For businesses today, it is insufficient to be highly connected. Connectivity on its own is meaningless if a business is to thrive in a competitive world, but secure connectivity—that's the ticket.

In this chapter, we examine several technologies that provide the extra value; that make communication secure across TCP/IP networks. These technologies include Secure Sockets Layer (SSL), Point-to-Point Tunneling Protocol (PPTP), and Layer 2 Tunneling Protocol/Internet Protocol Security (L2TP/IPSec). Each of these provides secure data communication between computers on either a public or a private network. We cover the theory of each technology and its implementation in Windows 2000.

Secure Sockets Layer

The Secure Sockets Layer (SSL) describes an encryption technology widely used on the Internet to secure Web pages and Web sites. In this section, we take a mile-high view of SSL and discuss the methods used by SSL to encrypt information to keep it secure.

Overview of SSL

SSL is classified as a Transport layer security protocol, since it secures not only the information generated at the Application layer, but at the Transport layer as well. It is considered a secure protocol by providing the mechanisms for supporting the basic elements of secure communications, namely:

- Confidentiality
- Integrity
- Authentication

Authentication ensures that the information received is indeed from the individual believed to be the sender. Integrity guarantees that the message received is the same message that was sent, while confidentiality protects data from inspection by unintended recipients.

SSL lies between the Application and the Transport layers (review Chapter 11, "Inside Windows 2000 TCP/IP," for more details on the TCP/IP and OSI models). It protects information passed by application protocols such as FTP, HTTP, and NNTP. An application must be explicitly designed to support SSL's security features. Unlike Layer 3 protocols (such as IPSec covered later in this chapter), it is not transparent to Application layer processes.

SSL uses several protocols to provide security and reliable communications between client and server SSL-enabled applications. Specifically, the handshake protocol negotiates levels and types of encryption, and sets up the secure session. These include SSL protocol version (2.0 or 3.0), authentication algorithms, encryption algorithms, and the method used to generate a shared secret or session key.

SSL uses a record protocol to exchange the actual data. A shared session key encrypts data passing between SSL applications. The data is decrypted on the receiving end by the same shared session key. Data integrity and authentication mechanisms are employed to ensure that accurate data is sent to, and received by, legitimate parties to the conversation.

SSL uses an alert protocol to convey information about error conditions during the conversation. It is also used by SSL hosts to terminate a session.

How a Secure SSL Channel Is Established

To understand how a secure channel is formed, let's examine how an SSL client establishes a session with an SSL Web server:

1. A URL is entered into a Web browser using https rather than http as the protocol. SSL uses TCP Port 443 rather than Port 80. The https entry requests the client to access the correct port on the target SSL Web server.

2. The SSL client sends a client Hello message. This message contains information about the encryption protocols it supports, what version of SSL it is using, what key lengths it supports, what hashing algorithms to use, and what key exchange mechanisms it supports. The SSL client also sends to the SSL server a challenge message. The challenge message will later confirm the identity of the SSL-enabled server.

3. The server then sends the client a Hello message. After examining methods supported by the client, the server returns to the client a list of mutually supported encryption methods, hash algorithms, key lengths, and key exchange mechanisms. The client will use the values returned by the server. The server also sends its public key, which has been signed by a mutually trusted authority (a digital certificate of authenticity).

4. The client then verifies the certificate sent by the server. After verifying the server certificate, the client sends a master key message. The message includes a list of security methodologies employed by the client and the session key. The session key is encrypted with the server's public key (which the server sent earlier in the server Hello message).

5. The client sends a client finished message indicating that all communications from this point forward are secure.

Almost all messages to this point have been sent in clear text, implying that anyone listening in on the conversation would be able to read all parts of the exchange. This is not a problem, since no information other than the session key is secret. Moreover, the session key is safe because it is encrypted with the server's public key. Only the server is able to decrypt the session key by using its private key. The next series of events takes place in a secure context.

1. The server sends a server verify message to the SSL client. This message verifies that the server is indeed the server with which the client wishes to communicate. The server verify message contains the challenge message the client sent earlier in the conversation. The server encrypts the challenge message with the session key. Only the legitimate server has access to the session key. When the client decrypts the challenge message encrypted with the session key, and it matches that sent in the challenge, then the server has verified itself as the legitimate partner in the communication.

2. The last message used to set up the secure SSL channel is the server finish message. The SSL server sends this message to the SSL client informing of its readiness to participate in data transmission using the shared session key. The SSL session setup is complete, and data passes through a secure SSL channel.

The setup procedure is dependent on several security technologies, including public key encryption, symmetric encryption, asymmetric encryption, message hashing, and certificates. In the following sections, we define these terms and see how SSL uses them to create a secure channel.

Symmetric and Asymmetric Encryption

The two major types of encryption algorithms in use today make use of either symmetric or asymmetric encryption keys. Symmetric techniques use the same key to encrypt and decrypt information, and asymmetric methods use different keys to encrypt and decrypt data. Both types of encryption are examined in the coming sections.

Symmetric Encryption

Symmetric encryption uses the same key to lock and unlock data. There are two elements involved in the data encryption process: an encryption algorithm and a key. The most commonly used symmetric encryption algorithm is the Data Encryption Standard (DES). There are actually several flavors of DES, each using a different encryption methodology and key length. Single DES uses a 56-bit encryption key, while a stronger form of DES, known as Triple DES or 3DES, uses a 168-bit encryption key. The advantage of triple DES with its longer key length is that it provides a higher degree of security. However, this advantage is not achieved without cost: 3DES is slower than DES. In general, symmetric encryption algorithms are faster than asymmetric ones.

An obvious question when considering symmetric encryption is, how is the value of the encryption key known? It could be sent with the message, but if someone intercepted the message, he or she would have access to the key. This is analogous to writing your PIN on the back of your automated teller machine card. The key could be sent via courier; however, that would take time, prove to be expensive, and make it difficult to change keys frequently. A method is required to allow keys to be changed frequently to guard against an intruder discovering the identity of the key.

Asymmetric Encryption

We know that data can be swiftly and securely encrypted using symmetric encryption, but a method is still required to exchange the shared session keys used to encrypt data passing between secure partners. To exchange the shared session key, a secure mechanism that is fast and inexpensive is required. To provide secure passage for shared session key exchange, asymmetric or public key encryption is used.

A Public Key Infrastructure (PKI) uses key pairs: a public key and a private key. The public key is available to anyone and everyone, and is not considered confidential. The private key, on the other hand, is secret, and is available only to the rightful owner of the private key. If the private key is stolen, it is no longer valid, and any messages from the owner of that private key are suspect.

Messages can be encrypted using either the public key or the private key. When a message is encrypted using a public key, a secret message is being sent that cannot be read (decrypted) by anyone other than the holder of the corresponding private key. By encrypting a message with someone's public key, you are assured that no one but the owner of the corresponding private key can read (decrypt) it. Encrypting a message using the recipient's public key provides a digital envelope for the message.

If the sender of a message wants the recipients to be sure of the message's origin, it is encrypted with the sender's private key. Consequently, anyone with the sender's public key can open the message. When you encrypt a message with your private key, it is termed *signing the message.* No one else can sign a message with your private key, since you are the only one who has access to it. Encrypting a message with a private key provides a type of digital signature.

> **NOTE**
>
> The basic concepts of public and private keys can be boiled down to: Messages encrypted with a public key are secret, and can only be read by the holder of the corresponding private key. Messages encrypted with a private key can be read by anybody, since it can be decrypted using the freely available public key. Private key encryption provides a way of signing a message.

Consider the following example: A lawyer needs to send a confidential message to a client. To ensure that only the client can read the message, the lawyer encrypts it with the client's public key. Remember that the client's public key is freely available. When the client receives the message, he decrypts it with his private key, since only the client's private key can decrypt a message encrypted with the same client's public key. Additionally, since no one else has access to the client's private key, the message has consequently remained private between the lawyer and the client.

Though the lawyer is sure that message has remained confidential, how does the client know that the message actually came from the claimed source, his lawyer? Perhaps a third party impersonated the lawyer and set up the secure communication channel. To assure the client that the message was from the lawyer, the lawyer encrypts the message with his private key. The only way the client can then read the message is by decrypting it with the lawyer's public key. Only messages encrypted with the lawyer's private key can be decrypted with the lawyer's public key. If the message cannot be opened with the lawyer's public key, then the client knows the message did not come from him. When a message is encrypted using a private key, the source of the message can then be authenticated.

Hash Algorithms

Using public and private key pairs, we can confirm the authenticity of a message and maintain its confidentiality. But how do we validate the integrity of a message? In other words, how do we know that the message sent by the lawyer to the client was not changed in transit?

Hash algorithms are used to accomplish this task. The two most commonly used hash algorithms are Message Digest 5 (MD5) and Secure Hash Algorithm 1 (SHA-1). These hash algorithms take the content of a message and convert it to a constant-length string. These hashes are safe to transmit because the hashed output cannot be reverse engineered to reproduce the original message; in other words, they are a one-way mathematical function. The hashed output can be used to create a digital signature for the document. To create a digital signature, the hashed output (also known as the message digest) is encrypted with the lawyer's private key.

When the document is received, the message is run through the same hash algorithm. After running the hash algorithm on the message, a message digest based on the document received is created. Then the digital signature is decrypted using the lawyer's public key. Finally, the digest attached to the message and the one generated by the client are compared. If they are the same, the document received is indeed the one that was sent. If the digests differ, then the message has been altered in transit.

As you can see in this example, the digital signature provides two functions: authentication and message integrity. The sender is authenticated because the recipient was able to decrypt the message digest using the sender's public key. Message integrity was also ensured, since the digest calculated proved the same as the one sent with the message.

Unfortunately, there is still one more conundrum to resolve. Recall how the client receives the lawyer's public key—it was sent to the client directly. How does the client know it was really the lawyer who sent him the public key?

This problem can be solved by using digital certificates of authority.

Digital Certificates

A digital certificate is a public key signed by a mutually trusted third party. The trusted third party signs your public key by first hashing your public key, and then encrypting the message digest with its private key. If I can open the message digest using the mutually trusted third-party's public key, and successfully decrypt messages with your public key, then I know for sure that you are the one who sent the message. I am able to authenticate you by virtue of your digital certificate.

Continuing with the lawyer/client analogy, suppose the client wants to verify the lawyer's identity. The client asks the lawyer for his public key. The lawyer responds by providing a public key that has been signed by a party trusted by both the lawyer and the client. The trusted third party has confirmed the lawyer's identity. The client already possesses the public key of the trusted third party, and uses it to decrypt the message digest of the lawyer's public key. If they match, then the lawyer's identity has been confirmed. The lawyer has then been authenticated.

Certificate Authorities

A certificate authority (CA) is responsible for verifying the identities of those who hold certificates signed by them. A certificate authority is a trusted third party. You can create your own key pair, and submit it to the CA for signing, or you can request the CA to create a signed key pair for you. The CA will verify your identify via telephone, personal interview, e-mail, or a combination thereof.

The public key of the CA must be signed too. How do you know that the public key from the certificate authority is valid? Because its certificate is signed too! Certificate authorities can consist of a chain of certificate authorities. On top of this chain or hierarchy is the root certificate authority. Subauthorities are child authorities. Each child authority has its digital certificate signed by a certificate authority above it in the hierarchy. These higher-level certificate authorities are parent authorities.

The single point of failure for security in this scheme is the certificate root authority. If the private key of the root authority is compromised, all signed certificates from the root, and all its child authorities, are suspect and should be considered invalid. Similarly, whenever a private key from any child authority is breached, all signed certificates from that child authority and all of its children, are also compromised, and must be considered invalid.

One method to protect against fraud when private keys of certificate authorities are compromised is to publish a Certificate Revocation List (CRL). The certificate authority makes public the serial numbers of invalid certificates. The CRL contains a list of serial numbers from certificates that are no longer valid for reasons other than that they have expired.

Grasping the mechanics of PKI and certificates is not necessarily an easy process, and you may want to read through this section a few times to cement your understanding.

SSL Implementation

Windows 2000 Server family includes a Certificate Server that can be used to grant certificates to Web site operators. After the Web site operator has a digital certificate, he can implement SSL and protect the contents of communications between the Web server and Web client.

The Windows 2000 root certificate authority must be installed on a domain controller (DC) running Active Directory. Child certificate authorities can be created on member servers. In this exercise, we will install the certificate server on a member server.

1. Log on as Administrator at a member server in your domain.

2. Open the Control Panel, and then open the Add/Remove Programs applet.

Figure 16.1 Selecting the Certificate Authority type.

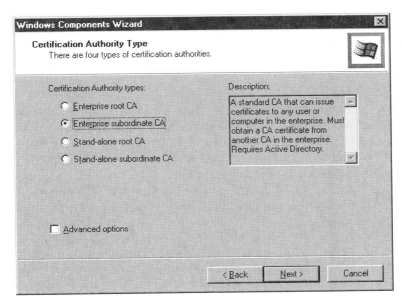

3. In the Add/Remove Programs applet, click on ADD/REMOVE WINDOWS COMPONENTS on the left side of the window.

4. In the Windows Components Wizard window, place a checkmark in the Certificate Services check box. A warning dialog detailing that domain membership cannot be changed after installing certificate server will appear. Click YES.

5. Choose a Certificate Authority type. Since the certificate server is being installed on member server, it cannot be the Enterprise Root CA. Select Enterprise subordinate CA as seen in Figure 16.1. Click NEXT.

6. Enter identifying information (such as CA name, organization, organizational unit (OU), and e-mail address) in all the fields. Click NEXT.

7. Specify the local paths for the Certificate Database and the Certificate database log. Then click NEXT. The following screens determine how the certificate request is processed. Configuration options include sending the request directly to a parent certificate authority, or saving the request to a file that can be sent later to a parent certificate authority. In this example, select the "Send the request directly to a CA already on the network" option button. Click BROWSE to select a CA to send the request to.

Figure 16.2 The Certificate Server management console.

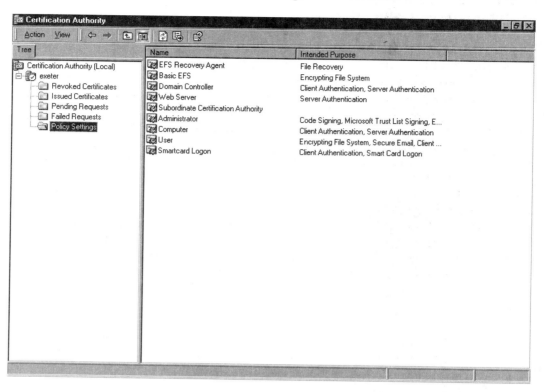

8. After choosing the CA, the name of the computer and the name of the parent CA appear in the request text boxes. Click NEXT. A dialog box appears, warning that Internet Information Services will be shut down if it is running on this computer. Click OK. Insert the Windows 2000 CD-ROM, or point to the location of the Windows 2000 installation files and following the onscreen instructions.

9. The wizard completes the installation of the Certificate Server and presents a dialog box informing you of this. Click FINISH to complete the installation.

10. To confirm successful installation of the certificate server, open the Certificate Server management console (Figure 16.2), which is located in Administrative Tools, and there should be a green checkmark on the certificate server's name indicating that it is functioning correctly.

The installed certificate server can now issue certificates that will enable Web sites to use SSL for secure communications.

Secure Communications over Virtual Private Networks

Remote connectivity is becoming a popular solution to a variety of problems: the need for sales personnel to access company databases while on the road, the need for traveling executives to stay in touch with the office, and the need for telecommuting employees to view and manipulate files on corporate servers. The ability to extend the reach of the corporate network to remote locations is no longer a luxury, but a necessity.

There are several ways to establish a remote connection to a private network. One option is to dial in directly over the public telephone lines, using a modem on the remote computer to connect to a modem on the company server. With security concerns on the increase, this type of basic remote access infrastructure is not always cost effective and does not stand up to close cost scrutiny when taking into consideration the three pillars of secure communication: confidentiality, integrity, and authentication. Another possibility is to have dedicated leased lines installed from one point to another.

A third, increasingly attractive solution, is to take advantage of the widespread availability of Internet connectivity to establish a Virtual Private Network (VPN), which circumvents long-distance charges, doesn't require expensive capital outlays, and can be done from virtually anywhere.

In the past, a VPN was considered to be a somewhat exotic, high-tech option that required a great deal of technical expertise. With Windows 2000, setting up a VPN connection is a simple process—there is even a wizard to guide you.

Tunneling Basics

A VPN can use the public network (Internet) infrastructure, yet maintain privacy and security by encrypting and encapsulating the data being transmitted. This is often referred to as tunneling through the public network.

VPN Definitions and Terminology

To understand how a VPN works, it's important to first define the terms used in conjunction with this technology.

Tunneling protocols are used to create a private pathway or tunnel through an internetwork (typically the Internet) in which data packets are encapsulated and encrypted prior to transmission to ensure privacy of the communication. Windows 2000 supports two tunneling protocols: PPTP and L2TP.

Data encryption provides a method of transmitting private data over public networks in a secure form. Modern VPN technologies use both encryption and encapsulation to provide an easier-to-implement and more flexible way to transmit private data over the public network. In a

Windows 2000 VPN using the Point to Point Tunneling Protocol (PPTP), encryption keys are generated by the MS-CHAP or EAP-TLS authentication process, and Microsoft Point to Point Encryption (MPPE) is used to encrypt a PPP frame.

Encapsulation inserts one data structure into another. VPN technology encapsulates private data with a header that provides routing information that allows the data to travel over the Internet to the private network.

How Tunneling Works

Tunneling emulates a point-to-point connection by wrapping the datagram with a header that contains addressing information to get it across the public network to the destination private network. The data is also encrypted to further protect the privacy of the communication. The tunnel is the part of the connection in which the data is encapsulated and encrypted; this becomes the virtual private network.

Data encryption is performed between the VPN client and the VPN server; thus, the connection from the client to the Internet Service Provider (ISP) does not need to be encrypted.

IP Addressing

The VPN connection will use a valid public IP address, usually supplied by the ISP's DHCP server, to route the data. This data packet, containing internal IP addresses of the sending and destination computers, is inside the envelope of the VPN, so even if you are using private (nonregistered) IP addresses on the private network, they will never be seen on the Internet. Encryption and encapsulation protect the addresses of the computers on the private network.

Security Issues Pertaining to VPNs

The concept of using an open, public network like the vast global Internet to transfer sensitive data presents obvious security concerns. For virtual networking to be feasible for security-conscious organizations, the privacy component must be ensured. Security over a VPN connection involves encapsulation, authentication of the user, and security of the data.

Encapsulation

The encapsulation of the original data packet inside a tunneling protocol hides its headers as it travels over the internetwork, and is the first line of defense in securing the communication.

User Authentication

Windows 2000 VPN solutions use the same authentication protocols used when connecting to the network locally; authentication is performed at the destination, so the security accounts database information is not transmitted onto the public network.

Windows 2000 can use the following authentication methods for VPN connections:

- **CHAP** Challenge Handshake Authentication Protocol, which uses challenge-response with one-way hashing on the response, allows the user to prove to the server that he knows the password without actually sending the password itself over the network.
- **MS-CHAP** Microsoft CHAP, which also uses a challenge-response authentication method with one-way encryption on the response.
- **MS-CHAP v2** An enhanced version of Microsoft-CHAP, which is a mutual authentication protocol requiring both the client and the server to prove their identities.
- **EAP/TLS** Extensible Authentication Protocol/Transport Level Security, which provides support for adding authentication schemes such as token cards, one-time passwords, the Kerberos V5 protocol, public key authentication using smart cards, certificates, and others.

Data Security

Data security is provided through encapsulation and encryption, but the greater the security, the more overhead and the lower the performance. IPSec was designed to work with different encryption levels and provide different levels of data security based on the organization's needs.

NOTE

PPTP uses Microsoft Point to Point Encryption (MPPE) to encrypt data. When using L2TP for VPN connections, data is encrypted using IPSec.

L2TP over IPSec uses certificate-based authentication, which is the strongest authentication type used in Windows 2000. A machine-level certificate is issued by a certificate authority, and installed on the VPN client and the VPN server. This can be done through the Windows 2000 Certificate Manager or by configuring the CA to automatically issue certificates to the computers in the Windows 2000 domain.

Windows 2000 Security Options

Windows 2000 provides the Network Administrator with a great deal of flexibility in setting authentication and data encryption requirements for VPN communications. Table 16.1 shows possible security settings combinations for both PPTP and L2TP.

Table 16.1 Authentication and Encryption Requirement Settings

Validate My Identity Using	Require Data Encryption	Authentication Methods Negotiated	Encryption Enforcement
PPTP			
Require secured password	No	CHAP, MS-CHAP, MS-CHAP v2	Optional encryption (connect even if no encryption)
Require secured password	Yes	MS-CHAP, MS-CHAP v2	Require encryption (disconnect if server declines)
Smart card	No	EAP/TLS	Optional encryption (connect even if no encryption)
Smart card	Yes	EAP/TLS	Require encryption (disconnect if server declines)
L2TP			
Require secured password	No	CHAP, MS-CHAP, MS-CHAP v2	Optional encryption (connect even if no encryption)
Require secured password	Yes	CHAP, MS-CHAP, MS-CHAP v2	Require encryption (disconnect if server declines)
Smart card	No	EAP/TLS	Optional encryption (connect even if no encryption)
Smart card	Yes	EAP/TLS	Require encryption (disconnect if server declines)

These settings are configured on the Security tab of the Properties sheet for the VPN connection. To access this dialog box, from the Start menu, select Settings | Network and Dialup Connections | [name of your VPN connection]. Then click PROPERTIES and select the Security tab.

Selecting the Advanced radio button and clicking SETTINGS displays the Advanced Security Settings dialog box shown in Figure 16.3, where the

Figure 16.3 Custom security settings in the Advanced Security Settings dialog box.

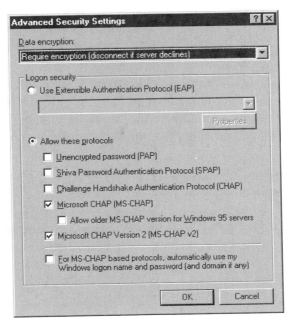

authentication and encryption setting combinations can be adjusted (see Chapter 17, "Connecting Windows 2000 Server," for more information).

This dialog box allows you to select whether encryption is optional, required, or not allowed; whether to use EAP or allow other designated protocols; and whether to automatically enter the logged-on account's Windows username and password for MS-CHAP authentication.

If you choose to use EAP (for instance, to enable authentication via smart card), you will need to configure the properties for the smart card or other certificate authentication. You can choose from a list of recognized root certificate authorities (CAs).

NOTE

A CA is an entity entrusted to issue certificates to individuals, computers, or organizations that affirm the identity and other attributes of the certificate. VeriSign is an example of a remote third-party CA recognized as trustworthy throughout the industry.

Common VPN Implementations

VPNs are commonly used by companies to provide a more cost-effective way for employees, customers, and other authorized users to connect to their private networks. The VPN is a viable alternative to direct dial-in, which incurs long-distance charges, or the hefty initial and monthly expense of a dedicated leased line.

VPNs are typically used to allow a remote user to connect a stand-alone computer, such as a home desktop system or a laptop/notebook computer when on the road, to the corporate network. However, VPNs can also be used to connect two distant LANs to one another using their local Internet connections, or to securely connect two computers over an intranet within the company.

Remote User Access Over the Internet

A typical scenario is the traveling employee who needs to connect to the company's network from a remote location. The traditional way to do so was to dial in to the company RAS server's modem. While a workable solution, it can prove costly if the remote user is not in the company's local calling area. If the remote user has an ISP local to his location, however, he can avoid long-distance charges by dialing the ISP instead of the company's modem, and setting up a VPN through the Internet.

Figure 16.4 Accessing the corporate network through a VPN.

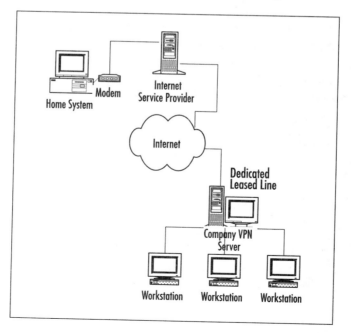

Figure 16.4 details a common example of this type of scenario.

See Chapter 17, "Connecting Windows 2000 Server," for instructions on setting up a client computer to use a VPN connection.

> **NOTE**
>
> An active Winsock Proxy client will interfere with the creation of a VPN by redirecting data to the proxy server before the data can be processed by the VPN. You must first disable the Winsock Proxy client before attempting to create a VPN connection.

Connecting Networks Over the Internet

Another use of the VPN is to connect two networks through the Internet. If you have offices in two cities with a LAN at each office location, it may be advantageous to connect the two LANs so that users at both locations can share one another's resources. One way to do so is to purchase a leased line such as a T1 line to connect the two networks, but this could prove to be expensive. An alternate option is to create a VPN between the two sites.

Sharing a Remote Access VPN Connection

If both offices already have Internet connections, perhaps through dedicated ISDN lines or DSL service, the existing connection to the Internet can be used to set up a VPN between the two offices. Figure 16.5 illustrates a situation where a VPN could be used to connect two distant networks.

In this case, setup will be slightly more complicated than connecting a single remote computer to a company network. In order to give all the computers on both LANs access to the resources they need, a VPN server on each side of the connection would have to be configured, as well as VPN client connections. The VPN client connection could then be shared with the rest of the LAN via Internet Connection Sharing (which is discussed in Chapter 17).

Another level of security can be employed by restricting the VPN client to access resources only on the VPN server and not on the rest of the network.

Using a Router-to-Router Connection

Another way to connect two networks via a VPN is to use a router-to-router VPN connection with a demand-dial interface. The VPN server then provides a routed connection to the network of which it is a part. Routing and Remote Access Service (RRAS) is used to create router-to-router VPN connections, so the VPN servers acting as routers must be Windows 2000 servers or NT 4.0 servers with RRAS.

Figure 16.5 A VPN connecting two LANs in disparate locations.

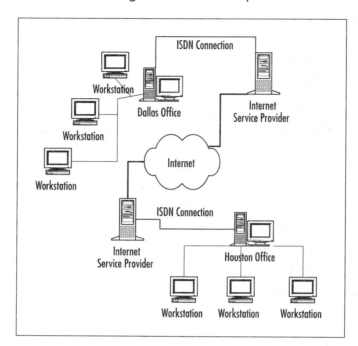

Mutual authentication is supported, so that the calling router (VPN client) and answering router (VPN server) authenticate themselves to one another. Figure.16.6 illustrates a typical example of a router-to-router connection.

In a router-to-router connection, the VPN works as a Data Link layer connection between the two networks. In Figure 16.6, the Windows 2000 computer acting as a router to the Austin office is the VPN client that initiates the connection to the VPN server, which is the computer acting as a router to the Dallas office. Note that the VPN server will need to have a dedicated connection to the Internet, unless the ISP supports demand-dial routing to customers, which is not common.

The endpoints of a router-to-router connection are the routers, and the tunnel extends from one router to the other. This is the part of the connection in which the data is encapsulated.

Tunneling Protocols and the Basic Tunneling Requirements

Establishing a secure tunnel through a public or other internetwork requires that computers on both ends of the connection are configured to use Virtual Private Networking, and they must both be running a common tunneling protocol. Windows 2000 Server can be a VPN client, or it can be

Figure 16.6 The VPN server can provide a routed connection to the network to which it belongs.

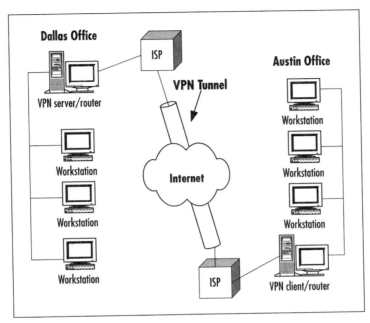

a VPN server accepting PPTP connections from both Microsoft and non-Microsoft PPTP clients.

Windows 2000 Tunneling Protocols

As mentioned earlier, Windows 2000 supports two tunneling protocols for establishing VPNs: PPTP and L2TP. A primary difference between the two is the encryption method: PPTP uses MPPE to encrypt data, while L2TP uses certificates with IPSec.

Point to Point Tunneling Protocol (PPTP)

The Point to Point Tunneling Protocol (PPTP) was developed as an extension to the popular Point to Point Protocol (PPP) used by most ISPs to establish a remote access connection to the Internet through the provider's network. PPTP allows IP, IPX, and NetBIOS/NetBEUI datagrams or frames to be transferred through the tunnel. From the user's perspective, the tunneling is transparent.

PPTP allows for Windows NT 4 authentication, using the insecure Password Authentication Protocol (PAP), Challenge Handshake Authentication Protocol (CHAP), and Microsoft's version of CHAP, MS-CHAP. PPTP is an open standard.

Layer 2 Tunneling Protocol (L2TP)

The Layer 2 Tunneling Protocol (L2TP) provides the same functionality as PPTP, but overcomes some of the limitations of PPTP. Unlike PPTP, it does not require IP connectivity between the client workstation and the server. L2TP can be used as long as the tunnel medium provides packet-oriented point-to-point connectivity, which means it works with such media as ATM, Frame Relay, and X.25.

L2TP is an Internet Engineering Task Force (IETF) standard, which was developed in a cooperative effort by Microsoft, Cisco Systems, Ascend, 3Com, and other networking industry leaders. It combines features of Cisco's Layer 2 Forwarding (L2F) protocol with Microsoft's PPTP implementation. L2TP can use IPSec to provide end-to-end security (see the section on IPSec later for more information).

Using PPTP with Windows 2000

PPTP is installed with RRAS. It is configured by default for five PPTP ports. PPTP ports can be enabled with the Routing and Remote Access wizard. The PPTP ports are displayed as WAN miniports in the RRAS console.

The status of each VPN port can be displayed, refreshed, or reset by double-clicking on the port name to display the status sheet and clicking the appropriate button.

How to Configure a PPTP Device

To configure a port device, right-click on Ports in the left panel of the console and select Properties. Highlight the RRAS device you wish to configure, and then click CONFIGURE.

In the device configuration dialog box, you can set up the port to be used for inbound RAS connections and/or inbound and outbound demand-dial routing connections.

NOTE

A device can be physical, representing hardware (such as a modem), or virtual, representing software (such as the PPTP protocol). A device can create physical or logical point-to-point connections, and the device provides a port, or communication channel, that supports a point-to-point connection.

A standard modem is a single-port device. PPTP and L2TP are virtual multiport devices. You can set up to 1000 ports for PPTP and L2TP devices. Five is the default number of ports.

Using L2TP with Windows 2000

Layer 2 Tunneling Protocol (L2TP) over IPSec provides Administrators the facility to provide end-to-end security for a VPN connection. L2TP does not rely on vendor-specific encryption methods to create a completely secured virtual networking connection.

How to Configure L2TP

To enable the server to be a VPN server for L2TP clients, RRAS must be installed if it has not already. Open the RRAS console: Start | Programs | Administrative Tools | Routing and Remote Access. In the left pane of the console tree, right-click the server to be enabled, and click Configure and Enable Routing and Remote Access. This starts the wizard, which guides you through the process. After the service is installed and started, con-figure the properties of the server by right-clicking on the server name and selecting Properties.

On the General tab, be sure that the "Remote access server" check box is selected. On the Security tab, under Authentication Provider, you can confirm the credentials of RRAS clients by using either Windows 2000 security (Windows Authentication) or a RADIUS server. If RADIUS is selected, RADIUS server settings need to be configured for the RADIUS server or RADIUS proxy.

In the Accounting Provider drop-down box, choose Windows or RADIUS accounting. Accordingly, remote access client activity can be logged for analysis or accounting purposes.

Next, click AUTHENTICATION METHODS, and choose the authentication methods that are supported by the RRAS server to authenticate the creden-tials of remote access clients, as shown in Figure 16.7.

> **TIP**
>
> Microsoft remote access clients generally will use MS-CHAP authentica-tion. To enable smart card support, use EAP authentication.

On the IP tab, verify that the "Enable IP routing" and "Allow IP-based remote access and demand-dial connections" check boxes are both checked. Next, configure the L2TP ports for remote access. In the RRAS console, right-click on Ports and select Properties. Select the L2TP ports.

How L2TP Security Differs from PPTP

L2TP is similar to PPTP in many ways. They both support multiprotocol VPN links and can be used to create secure tunnels through the Internet or

Figure 16.7 Authentication method used by RRAS clients.

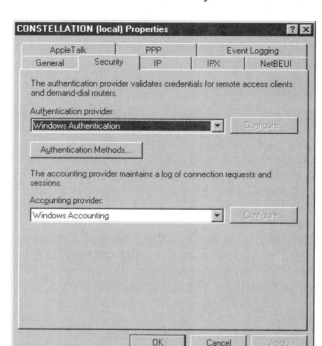

another public network to connect to a private network that also has a connection to the internetwork. L2TP can be used over IPSec to provide for greater security, including end-to-end encryption, whereas Microsoft's PPTP connections are dependent upon MPPE for encryption. L2TP is derived from L2F, a Cisco Systems tunneling protocol.

With L2TP over IPSec, encapsulation involves two layers: L2TP encapsulation and IPSec encapsulation. First, L2TP wraps its header and a UDP header around a PPP frame. Then IPSec wraps an ESP (Encapsulating Security Payload) header and trailer around the package, and adds an IPSec authentication trailer. Finally, an IP header is added, which contains the addresses of the source (VPN client) and destination (VPN server) computers. The data inside the IPSec ESP header and authentication trailer, including the PPP, UDP, and L2TP headers, is all encrypted by IPSec.

Data authentication is available for L2TP over IPSec connections, unlike for PPTP connections. This is accomplished by the use of a cryptographic checksum based on an encryption key known only to the sender and the receiver.

Interoperability with Non-Microsoft VPN Clients

A Windows 2000 VPN server can accept client connections from non-Microsoft clients, if the clients meet the following requirements:

- The clients must use PPTP or L2TP tunneling protocol.
- For PPTP connections, the client must support MPPE.
- For L2TP connections, the client must support IPSec.

If these requirements are met, the non-Microsoft clients should be able to make a secure VPN connection. No special configuration changes on the VPN server are required to allow non-Microsoft clients to connect.

IPSec for Windows 2000

IPSec defines a network security architecture that allows secure networking for the enterprise while introducing a minimum of overhead. By performing its services at the Network layer, IPSec secures information in a manner that is transparent to the user and to the protocols that lie above the Transport layer. IPSec provides Layer 3 protection.

The IPSec security architecture exercises an end-to-end security model. Only the endpoints of a communication need to be IPSec aware. Computers and devices that serve as intermediaries of message transfer do not need to be IPSec enabled. This allows the Administrator of a Windows 2000 network to implement IPSec for end-to-end security over diverse network infrastructures, including the Internet. Transit network devices such as bridges, switches, and routers can be oblivious to IPSec without compromising its efficacy.

NOTE

IPSec provides protection of the data transmission from end to end. This is different from the PPTP model that only protects the link.

This end-to-end capability can be extended to different communication scenarios, including:

- Client to client
- Gateway to gateway

When IPSec is used to protect communications between two clients—for example, on the same LAN—the machines can use IPSec in what is known as transport mode. In transport mode, both clients must use TCP/IP as their network protocol. In this example, the endpoints of the secure communication are the source machine and the destination host.

In contrast, with a gateway-to-gateway solution, information traversing a transit network (such as the Internet) is protected by IPSec. Packets are protected as they leave the exit gateway and then decrypted or authenticated at the destination network's gateway. In this scenario, the host and destination computers do not employ IPSec, and can use any LAN protocol supported by IPSec (IPX/SPX, AppleTalk, NetBEUI, TCP/IP).

When gateways represent the endpoints of secure communication, IPSec works in tunnel mode. A tunnel is created between the gateways, and client-to-client communications are encapsulated in the tunnel protocol headers. Tunnels can be created using IPSec as the tunneling protocol, or you can combine IPSec with L2TP, which stands for Layer 2 Tunneling Protocol and allows for data encryption via IPSec. In this case, L2TP rather than IPSec creates the tunnel.

Overview of IPSec Cryptographic Services

IPSec ensures secure communications by providing robust solutions that support confidentiality, integrity, and authenticity (CIA). It is a worthwhile exercise to revisit the aspects of CIA and understand how they apply to IPSec.

Message Integrity

Message integrity implies that the contents of a message have not changed during transit. Creating a digital signature can protect message integrity, acting almost as a digital fingerprint. This fingerprint represents the contents of the message. If someone were to capture and change the contents of the message, the fingerprint would change. The destination host could detect the fraudulent fingerprint and would be aware that "other hands" had touched the document. The assumption is that if other hands have touched the document, then the message is invalid. It has lost its integrity. Hash algorithms create these fingerprints.

Hashing Messages

The result of a hash is a fixed-length string known as a message digest. The message digest represents the hashed output of a message. Microsoft's implementation of IPSec uses one of two algorithms for hashing:

- **Message Digest 5 (MD5)** processes each message in blocks of 512 bits. The message digest ends up being 128 bits.

- **Secure Hash Algorithm (SHA-1)** processes messages in blocks of 512 bits. However, the resulting message digest is 160 bits long. This makes the message more secure. It is more processor intensive, and therefore slower than MD5.

Each partner in the communication must use the same key in order to come up with the same hashed result. Though we have already discussed the use of public key infrastructure and key exchange, we will touch on these topics again.

Message Authentication

When a host is authenticated, its identity is confirmed. While integrity is concerned with the validity of the contents of a message, authentication is aimed at confirming the validity of the sender. IPSec can use any of the following methods to authenticate the sender:

- Preshared key authentication
- Kerberos authentication
- Public key certificate-based digital signatures

Preshared Key Authentication

Preshared key authentication schemes depend on both members of the communication having preselected a secret key that will be used to identify them to each other. Data leaving the sending computer is encrypted with this agreed-to key, and is decrypted on the other end with the same key.

You can use the preshared key to authenticate a computer using the following procedure:

1. The sending computer hashes a piece of data (a challenge) using the shared key and forwards this to the destination computer.
2. The destination computer receives the challenge, performs a hash using the same secret key, and sends it back.
3. If the hashed results are identical, both computers share the same secret and are thus authenticated.

Preshared keys are effective and simple to implement. They circumvent potential complications introduced when other authentication schemes are used. However, the shared-key approach is not very scaleable or mutable. The shared key must be manually entered into every extant IPSec policy. An organization with a large number of organizational units, all using different IPSec policies, would find it difficult to track all the keys. In addition, the keys should change frequently. Manually changing the keys can be an arduous process within large organizations.

Kerberos Authentication

The Kerberos authentication method is also based on the shared secret principle. In this case, the shared secret is a hash of the user's password.

Public Key Certificate-Based Digital Signatures

When a private key encrypts a hash, the message digest forms a digital signature. A message is authenticated after it is decrypted with the source's public key and then run through the hash algorithm.

In a public key infrastructure, each computer has a public and a private key. The public key is open and available to the public at large; it is not secret. The private key is a secret key that is only available to the owner of the private key. The private key must remain private. If the private key is ever compromised, all messages from the owner of that private key should be considered suspect.

A viable public key infrastructure includes elements:

- Secret private keys
- Freely available public keys
- A trusted third party to confirm the authenticity of the public key

The trusted third party will digitally sign each party's public key. This prevents people from providing a public key that they claim is theirs, but is in fact not the public key of the person they are impersonating.

Public key authentication is used when non-Kerberos-enabled clients need to be authenticated and no preshared key has been established. You must also use public key authentication when using L2TP tunneling and IPSec.

Confidentiality

Neither integrity nor authentication is concerned with protecting the privacy of information. In order to ensure confidentiality, data is encrypted using algorithms such as the Data Encryption Standard (DES) or the Cipher Block Chaining (CBC).

DES is a symmetric encryption algorithm. DES works on 64-bit blocks of data. The DES algorithm converts 64 input bits from the original data into 64 encrypted output bits. While DES starts with 64-bit keys, only 56 bits are used in the encryption process. The remaining 8 bits are for parity. CBC prevents each DES block from being identical. This DES-CBC algorithm makes each ciphertext message appear different.

IPSec Security Services

IPSec engages two protocols to implement security on an IP network:

- Authentication header (AH)
- Encapsulating security protocol (ESP)

Authentication Header (AH)

The authentication header ensures data integrity and authentication. The AH does not encrypt data, and therefore provides no confidentiality. When

Figure 16.8 Datagram as it appears after the authentication header is applied in transport mode.

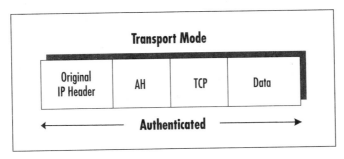

the AH protocol is applied in transport mode, the authentication header is inserted between the original IP header and the TCP header, as shown in Figure 16.8. The entire datagram is authenticated using AH.

Encapsulating Security Payload (ESP)

The encapsulating security payload protocol can provide authentication, integrity, and confidentiality to an IP datagram. Authentication services are available with ESP, but the original IP header prior to application of the ESP header is not authenticated. The ESP header, in transport mode, is placed between the original header and the TCP header, as shown in Figure 16.9. Only the TCP header, data, and ESP trailer are encrypted. If authentication of the original IP header is required, you can combine and use AH and ESP together.

Figures 16.8 and 16.9 demonstrate packet configurations when AH or ESP is used in transport mode. Transport mode is used when point-to-

Figure 16.9 Datagram after the encapsulating security payload header is applied in transport mode.

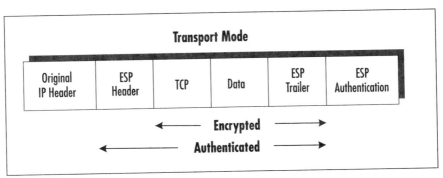

Figure 16.10 This is a datagram with ESP header in tunnel mode.

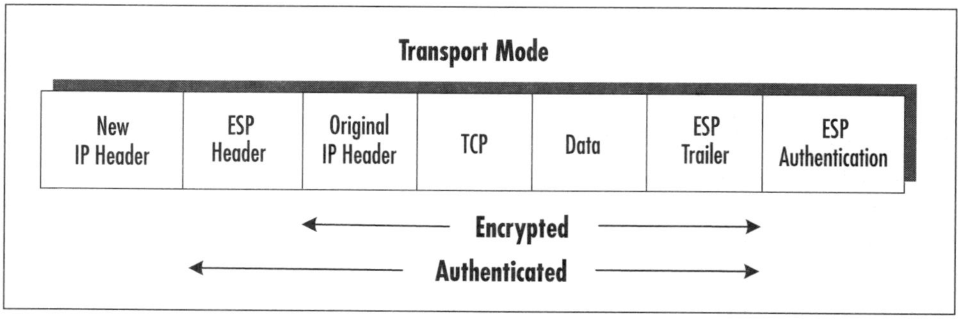

point communications are taking place between source and destination computers. AH and ESP can be applied at a gateway machine connecting the LAN to a remote network. In this case, tunnel mode would be used.

In tunnel mode, an additional IP header is added that denotes the destination tunnel endpoint. This tunnel header encapsulates the original IP header, which contains the IP address of the destination computer. Figure 16.10 shows a packet constructed for tunnel mode.

Security Associations and IPSec Key Management Procedures

When two computers establish a connection using IPSec, they must come to an agreement regarding which algorithms and protocols they will use. A single security association (SA) is established for each link a computer maintains with another computer via IPSec. If a file server has several simultaneous sessions with multiple clients, a number of different SAs will be defined, one for each connection via IPSec.

Each security association has associated with it these parameters:

- An encryption algorithm (DES or 3DES)
- A session key (via Internet Key Exchange, or IKE)
- An authentication algorithm (SHA1 or MD5)

A security parameters index (SPI) tracks each SA. The SPI uniquely identifies each SA as separate and distinct from any other IPSec connections current on a particular machine. The index itself is derived from the destination host's IP address and a randomly assigned number. When a computer communicates with another computer via IPSec, it checks its database for an applicable SA. It then applies the appropriate algorithms, protocols, and keys, and inserts the SPI into the IPSec header.

An SA is established for outgoing and incoming messages, necessitating at least two security associations for each IPSec connection. In addition, a single SA can be applied to either AH or ESP, but not both. If both are used, then two more security associations are created. One SA for inbound and one SA for outbound communications will be created.

IPSec Key Management

Keys must be exchanged between computers in order to ensure authenticity, integrity, and confidentiality. Key management defines the procedure of how the keys are formed, the strength of the keys, how often they are changed, and when they expire. The establishment of a shared secret key is critical to secure communications. The shared secret can be manually established using the prearranged key method, but this technique does not scale very well because of its inherent lack of flexibility.

Automated key management is the preferred method of key exchange. Automated key management uses a combination of the Internet Security Association Key Management Protocol and the Oakley Protocol (ISAKMP/Oakley). This combination of protocols is often referred to collectively as the Internet Key Exchange (IKE). The IKE is responsible for exchange of key material (groups of numbers that will form the basis of new key) session keys, SA negotiation, and authentication of peers participating in an IPSec interaction.

The IKE takes place across two phases: Phase 1, in which the two computers agree upon mechanisms to establish a secure, authenticated channel, and Phase 2, where Security Associations are negotiated for security protocols; either AH, ESP, or both.

The first phase establishes what is called the ISAKMP security association (ISAKMP SA), and the second phase establishes the IPSec SA.

Phase 1: Establishing the ISAKMP SA

The following points detail the sequence of events during the ISAKMP SA:

1. The computers establish a common encryption algorithm, either DES or 3DES.

2. A common hash algorithm is agreed upon, either MD5 or SHA1.

3. An authentication method is established. Depending on policy, this can be Kerberos, public key encryption, or prearranged shared secret.

4. A Diffie-Hellman group is agreed upon in order to allow the Oakley protocol to manage the key exchange process. Diffie-Hellman provides a mechanism for two parties to agree on a shared master key, which is used immediately or can provide keying material for subsequent session key generation. Oakley will determine key refresh and regeneration parameters.

Phase 2: Establishing the IPSec SA

After a secure channel has been established by the creation of the ISAKMP SA, the IPSec SAs will be established. The process is similar, except that a separate IPSec SA is created for each protocol (AH or ESP) and for each direction (inbound and outbound). Each IPSec SA must establish its own encryption algorithm, hash algorithm, and authentication method.

One important difference is that each IPSec SA uses a different shared key than that negotiated during the ISAKMP SA. Depending on how policy is configured, the IPSec SA repeats the Diffie-Hellman exchange, or reuses key material derived from the original ISAKMP SA. All data transferred between the two computers will take place in the context of the IPSec SA.

Deploying IPSec

In the implementation of IPSec in an organization, planning takes on special importance in the design of a security infrastructure.

The planning phase is followed by the implementation phase. Windows 2000's graphical interface makes it easy to develop an IPSec policy for any organization. IPSec policy, filters, filter actions, and interoperability with downlevel clients and other operating systems are a vital part of implementation.

Building Security Policies with Customized IPSec Consoles

IPSec configuration and deployment is intimately intertwined with Active Directory and group policy. You must create a policy in order to deploy IPSec in the organization. A policy can be applied to a site, a domain, an organizational unit, or a single computer.

It is within the group policy that we can choose from built-in policies or create custom policies to meet our specialized needs. These policies can be configured by creating an MMC and then using the appropriate MMC plug-in.

It is possible to configure a custom IPSec console that is used to configure IPSec policy and monitor significant IPSec-related events.

Building an IPSec MMC Console

1. Create a new console by starting the Run command and typing **mmc**. Click OK to open an empty console.

2. Click the Console menu, and then click Add/Remove Snap-in. Click ADD, select Computer Management, and click ADD. A dialog box will appear that will want to know which computer the snap-in will manage. Select Local Computer (the computer this console is running on). Then click FINISH.

3. Scroll through the list of available snap-ins, select Group Policy, and click ADD. At this point, a wizard will appear that will query you on what Group Policy Object you want to manage. In this case, confirm that it says Local Computer in the text box, and click FINISH. If you want to define a policy for another group policy object, click BROWSE and select from the list.

4. Scroll through the list of Group Policy Objects again, this time looking for Certificates. Select Certificates, and click ADD. A dialog box will appear asking you what you want the snap-in to always manage certificates for. Select Computer Account, click NEXT, and then select Local Computer for the computer that you want the snap-in to manage. Then click FINISH.

5. Click CLOSE on the Add Standalone Snap-in dialog box, and then click OK in the Add/Remove Snap-in dialog box. Expand the first level of each of the snap-ins.

   IPSec policies can be configured and managed from this custom console. In this example, IPSec policy is managed for a single machine. This might be appropriate when configuring IPSec policy for a file or application server. If you wanted to manage policy for an entire domain or organizational unit, you would select the appropriate policy when selecting the Group Policy snap-in configuration.

Flexible Security Policies

Now that we have our console, we can get to the business of building IPSec security policy. Three built-in IPSec policies can be used, and custom policies can be created.

To begin, you need to find where the IP security policies are located. Expand the Local Computer policy, expand the Computer Configuration object, expand the Windows Settings object, then click IP Security Policies on Local Machine. In the right pane, you will see listed the three built-in IPSec policies: Client (Respond Only), Secure Server (Require Security), and Server (Request Security). You screen should look similar to Figure 16.11.

The Client (Respond Only) policy is used when secure IPSec connections are required once another computer requests them. For example, a workstation requires connectivity to a file server that requires IPSec security. The workstation with the built-in Client policy enabled negotiates an IPSec security association. However, this client never requires IPSec security; it will only use IPSec to secure communications when requested to do so by another computer.

The Server (Request Security) policy is used when IPSec security is requested for all connections. This could be used for a file server that must serve both IPSec-aware (Windows 2000) clients and non-IPSec-aware

Figure 16.11 IPSec Security console with three built-in IPSec policies.

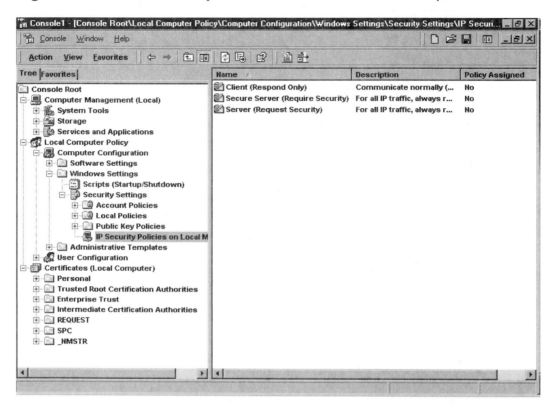

clients (such as Windows 9*x* and Windows NT). If a connection is established with an IPSec-aware computer, the session will be secure.
Unsecured sessions will be established with non-IPSec-aware computers.
This allows greater flexibility during the transition from mixed Windows
networks to native Windows 2000 networks.

The Secure Server (Require Security) policy is used when all communications with a particular server need to be secured. Examples include file
servers storing sensitive data and security gateways at either end of an
L2TP/IPSec tunnel. The server with the Secure Server policy will always
request a secure channel. Connections will be denied to computers not able
to respond to the request.

Security policies are bidirectional. If a Secure Server attempts to connect to non-IPSec-aware network servers such as DNS, WINS, or DHCP
servers, the connection will fail. It is imperative that all scenarios are tested
in a lab that simulates a live network before implementing IPSec policies.
During the testing phase, it is important to assiduously check the event
logs to ascertain what services fail because of IPSec policies.

Rules

An IPSec policy has three main components: IP security rules, IP filter lists, and IP filter actions. Double-click the Server Policy to see the Server (Request Security) Properties sheet, as shown in Figure 16.12.

Rules are applied to computers that match criteria specified in a filter list. An IP filter list contains source and destination IP addresses. These can be individual host IP addresses or network IDs. When a communication is identified as a participant included in an IP filter list, a particular filter action will be applied that is specific for that connection.

The All IP Traffic filter list includes all computers that communicate with the server via TCP/IP. Any instructions in the filter action associated with All IP Traffic will be applied to all computers.

First, double-click All IP Traffic filter list. This opens the Edit Rule Properties dialog box for the All IP Traffic filter. You should see a tabbed dialog box consisting of five tabs.

The option button for the IP filter list is selected, and a description is included which explains the purpose of the list. Double-click All IP Traffic filter list to see the details of the All IP traffic filter. The Name, Description, and the details of the filter are displayed in the details (Figure 16.13).

Figure 16.12 Server (Request Security) Properties sheet.

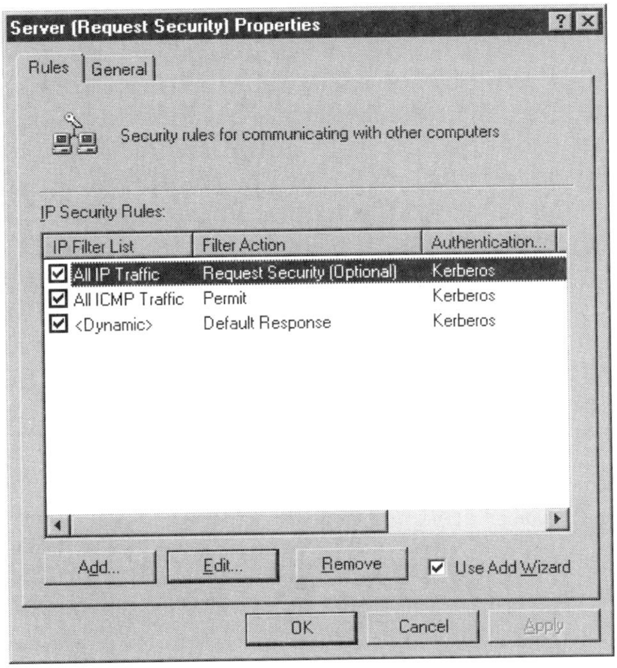

Figure 16.13 IP Filter List details dialog box.

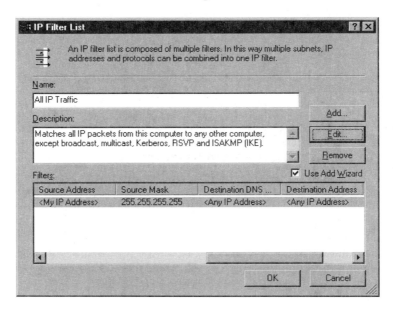

If you want to see more details regarding the Addressing, Protocol, and Description of the filter, you can click EDIT. Click CANCEL twice to return to the Edit Rules Properties dialog box.

Filter Actions

Filter Actions define the type of security and the methods by which security is established. The primary methods are Permit, Block, and Negotiate security. The Permit option blocks negotiation for IP security. This is appropriate if you never want to secure traffic to which this rule applies. The Block action blocks all traffic from computers specified in the IP filter list. The Negotiate security action allows the computer to use a list of security methods to determine security levels for the communication. The list is in descending order of preference. If the Negotiate security action is selected, both computers must be able to come to an agreement regarding the security parameters included in the list. The entries are processed sequentially in order of preference. The first common security method is enacted.

Click the Filter Action tab, and click Request Security (Optional) to view these options. Of the check boxes at the bottom of the dialog box, "Accept unsecured communication, but always respond using IPSec," allows unsecured communication initiated by another computer, but requires the computers to which this policy applies to always use secure communication

Figure 16.14 Authentication Methods configuration tab.

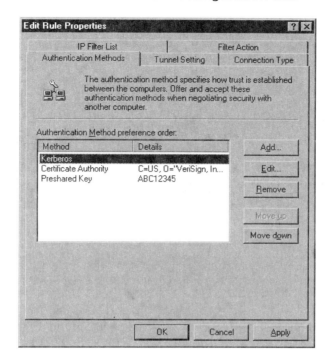

when replying or initiating. This is essentially the definition of the Secure policy. The "Allow unsecured communication with non-IPSec-aware computer" option allows unsecured communications to or from another computer. This is appropriate if the computers listed in the IP filter lists are not IPSec-enabled. However, if negotiations for security fail, this will disable IPSec for all communications to which this rule applies.

Perhaps the most important of these options is the session key Perfect Forward Secrecy. When you select this option, you ensure that session keys (or keying material) are not reused, and new Diffie-Hellman exchanges will take place after the session key lifetimes have expired.

Click CANCEL to return to the Edit Rule Properties dialog box. Click the Authentication Methods tab. Here you can select your preferred authentication method. Kerberos is the default authentication method. You can include other methods in the list, and each will be processed in descending order. You can click ADD to include additional authentication methods, as shown in Figure 16.14.

Click the Tunnel Setting tab if the endpoint for the filter is a tunnel endpoint. Click the Connection Type tab to apply the rule to All network connections, Local area network (LAN), or Remote access.

Figure 16.15 Custom Security Method Settings dialog box.

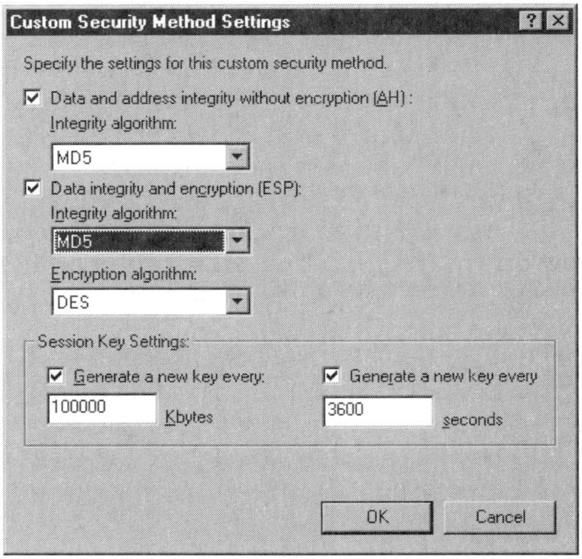

You cannot delete the built-in policies, but you can edit them. However, it is recommended that you leave the built-in policies as they are, and create new policies for custom requirements.

Flexible Negotiation Policies

Security method negotiation is required to establish an IPSec connection. The default policies can be used, or custom policies can be created. To add a new filter action, which will be used to create a new security policy, click ADD after selecting the Filter Action tab. When the wizard has completed, you can edit the security negotiation method.

When you double-click on the Request Security (Optional) filter action, you will see the Request Security (Optional) Properties dialog box. If you select the Negotiate security option, and then click ADD, you can add a new security method.

You may fine-tune your security negotiation method by selecting the Custom option, and then clicking SETTINGS. After doing so, you will see the Custom Security Method Settings dialog box, as shown in Figure 16.15.

Here you can configure whether you want to use AH, ESP, or both. For each option, you can select the integrity algorithm, encryption algorithm, or both. All algorithms supported in Windows 2000 are included. Session key lifetimes can be customized by entering new key generation intervals by amount of data transferred or time span.

Filters

Rules are applied to source and destination computers or networks, based on their IP addresses. To create a new filter, you can avail yourself of the New Filter Wizard. To do this, return to the Edit Rule Properties dialog box, click on the IP Filter List tab, and then click ADD. This brings up the IP Filter List dialog box, where you enter in the name of the new filter and a description of the filter. Click ADD to start the wizard.

When the wizard starts, you see the Welcome dialog box. Click NEXT. Choose the source address of the wizard. Your options appear after you click the down arrow on the list box. Note that you can identify the source by individual IP address, all IP addresses, DNS name, or subnet. Click NEXT to continue.

The next dialog box asks for the destination IP address. You are afforded the same options as when you designated the source. Click NEXT to continue through the wizard. At this point, you can select which protocols will be included in the filter. All protocols are included by default, but you can select from a list of protocols or define your own by selecting Other and entering a protocol number.

Click NEXT, and then click FINISH. Your new filter will appear in the IP filter list included in the IP Filter List tab of the Edit Rule Properties dialog box.

Creating a Security Policy

Consider the following scenario: You are the Administrator of the network for a large hospital. The network is subdivided into multiple subnets. The Medical Records department contains a large amount of data that must be kept secure. The hospital would suffer a large amount of liability if security were breached. Computers within the Medical Records department are closely monitored, and therefore the overhead of confidentiality is not required, but authentication and integrity should be applied to intradepartmental communications.

The Medical Records department must regularly send information to the hospital floor. The network infrastructure is more open to attack between the well-guarded Medical Records department and the less secure, open hospital environment. All computers within the Medical Records department are located in network ID 192.168.1.0, and all floor computers that access medical records database information are located on network ID 192.168.2.0. The default Class C subnet mask is used.

In order to implement your new security policy, you need to:

1. Create a security policy for the hospital's domain. In this way, all computers in the domain will inherit the IPSec policy.

2. Computers in the Medical Records department need to communicate with two sets of computers: machines within their own depart-

ment, and the machines on the hospital floor. Characterizing these machines by subnet, you could say that machines on subnet 192.168.2.0 need to communicate with machines on 192.168.1.0, and machines on 192.168.1.0 need to communicate with machines on 192.168.2.0. When selecting the protocols, you would select All so that all IP traffic is filtered. Therefore, you need to create two filters, so that you can assign different filter actions to each filter.

3. Now you need to create two filter actions (Negotiation policy); the first filter action will be applied to intradepartmental communications, in which just authentication and integrity are important, and the second filter action will be applied to extradepartmental communication, where authenticity, integrity, and confidentiality are required. The first filter action might use AH, which provides for authenticity and integrity. The second filter action might use a combination of AH and ESP, to provide the highest level of authentication and integrity, while also providing confidentiality.

By implementing these combinations of filters and filter rules, you can effectively secure traffic in a customized fashion. You can easily implement this solution by invoking the Security Rule Wizard after you create the new security policy.

Making the Rule

The rule will create a filter for all communications emanating from 192.168.1.0 that are directed to 192.168.2.0. After the filter is created, you will create a filter action. In this case, you need to ensure secure communications, because you are communicating with the unsecured hospital floor. You need to insure integrity, authentication, and confidentiality.

1. Click Start | Programs | Administrative Tools | Active Directory Users and Computers. When the console opens, right-click on a domain name, then click Properties. In the Domain properties dialog box, click on the Group Policy tab.

2. Select Default Domain Policy, and click EDIT.

3. This opens the Group Policy Editor. Expand Computer Configuration, expand Windows Settings, expand Security Settings, and then right-click on IP Security Policies on Active Directory. Click Create IP Security Policy.

4. A wizard starts up, welcoming you. Click NEXT.

5. You now need to enter the name of the Policy. Name it **MedRecToFloor**, and then click NEXT. Remove the checkmark in the "Activate the default response rule" check box. Click NEXT.

6. Now you are at the end of the Wizard. Leave the check in the Edit Properties box, and click FINISH.

7. At this point, you have no IP filter lists. Use the Add wizard to create a new filter list and filter action. Together they create a filter rule. Make sure there is a check in the "Use Add Wizard" check box, and click ADD.

8. This takes you to the Security Rule Wizard. The first dialog box is a Welcome box. Click NEXT.

9. The next dialog box asks whether the rule applies to a tunnel end-point. In this case, it does not, so select "This rule does not specify a tunnel." Click NEXT.

10. The wizard now asks what network connections this rule should apply to. Select "All network connections," then click NEXT.

11. Now decide what the default authentication protocol should be used. Select Windows 2000 default (Kerberos V5 protocol), as shown in Figure 16.16. Then click NEXT.

12. Create the IP filter list by adding a filter for all traffic sent from 192.168.1.0 with the destination of 192.168.2.0. Click ADD as shown in Figure 16.17.

Figure 16.16 Selecting the Authentication protocol.

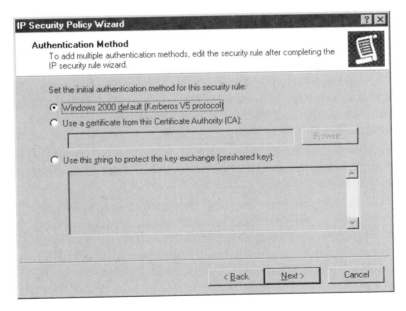

Figure 16.17 Adding a new filter list.

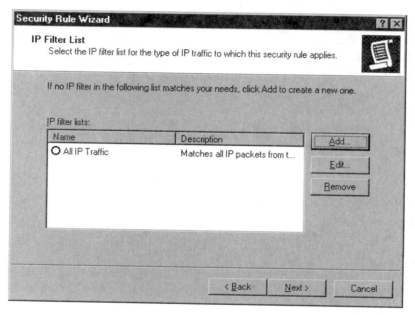

13. You now see the IP Filter List dialog box. Type **Secure from MedRec to Floor**, and make sure the Use Add Wizard check box is filled. Now click ADD.

14. The IP Filter Wizard (yes, another wizard!) appears. Click NEXT to move past the Welcome dialog box. Now you are at the IP Traffic Source dialog box. Click the down arrow under Source address and select A specific IP Subnet. Type **192.168.1.0** and a subnet mask of **255.255.255.0**. Then click NEXT.

15. Now enter the IP traffic destination. Under the Destination address, click the down arrow and select A specific IP Subnet. Then type the destination subnet **192.168.2.0** with a subnet mask of **255.255.255.0**. Click NEXT.

16. You want all the protocols to be included in the filter, so select Any for the protocol type and click NEXT, and then click FINISH to complete the wizard.

17. This takes you back to the IP Filter List dialog box. Click EDIT (Figure 16.18). Mirrored should checked. Match packets with the exact opposite source and destination addresses, to ensure that machines from the destination subnet are also included in the incoming filter. Click OK to close the dialog box, and then click CLOSE. You are now back to the IP Filter List dialog box in the

Figure 16.18 Filter Properties dialog box.

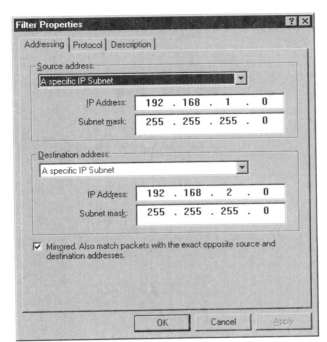

Security Rule Wizard. Select the Secure from MedRec to Floor filter list, and then click NEXT.

18. At this point, configure a filter action. Select the Require Security option. Make sure there is a check mark in the Use Add Wizard check box, and then click ADD.

19. The IP Security Filter Action Wizard starts. Click NEXT to move past the Welcome dialog box. Here you are asked for a name; enter **SecureMedRec**, and click NEXT.

20. The Filter Action General Options dialog box asks for a filter action behavior. Select Negotiate security, and click NEXT.

21. This dialog box asks whether you want to support communications with computers that do not support IPSec. Select the "Do not communicate with computers that do not support IPSec" option. Click NEXT.

22. Now select the security method for IP traffic. To ensure confidentiality, authentication, and integrity, select Custom, and then click SETTINGS (Figure 16.19). Select the "Data and address integrity with encryption" check box, and then click the down

Figure 16.19 Custom Security Method Settings.

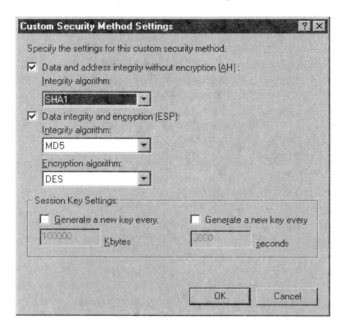

arrow and select SHA1. Make sure there is a checkmark in the
"Data integrity and encryption (ESP)" check box, and select MD5
and 3DES. Do not set the session key settings; you will select
Perfect Forward Secrecy later. Click OK, then click NEXT. The final
dialog box appears. Ensure that a check is in the Edit box, and
then click FINISH.

23. You are brought to the New Filter Action Properties dialog box.
Check "Session key Perfect Forward Secrecy." Click OK to return to
the Security Rule Wizard, then click NEXT.

24. This is the last dialog box for the Security Rule Wizard. Click
FINISH. Click OK to close the New Rule Properties dialog box. You
are returned to the MedRecToFloor Properties box. Click the
General tab. You can configure how often the Policy Agent checks
for policy changes here. Click ADVANCED to control the Internet Key
Exchange Process.

25. Here you control the security of the Internet Key Exchange process,
as shown in Figure 16.20. Click METHODS to configure the security
methods that are used to protect identities during the Key
Exchange process as shown in Figure 16.21.

26. Click OK, click OK, and then click CLOSE. Your new security policy
appears in the console.

Figure 16.20 Key Exchange Settings dialog box.

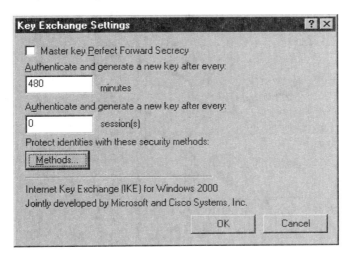

Figure 16.21 Key Exchange Security Methods dialog box.

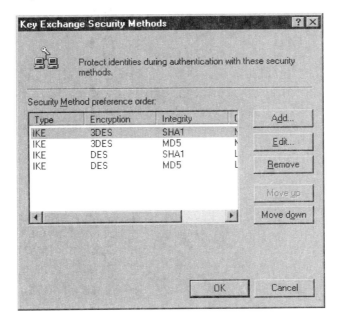

As you can see, what looks easy on paper can be somewhat daunting when you actually apply the principles! With the rule you created, all traffic leaving 192.168.1.0 to 192.168.2.0 will be secured according to the filter rule you set up. Because it is mirrored, the same rule applies in the other direction.

Summary

The Secure Sockets Layer (SSL) describes an encryption technology widely used on the Internet to secure Web pages and Web sites. In this section, we took a high-level look at SSL and the methods used by SSL to encrypt information to keep it secure.

Windows 2000 provides the Administrator with a new tool in defense against security violations. IPSec allows the Administrator to secure information as it crosses the network. IPSec secures data at the Network layer and carries out its activity transparently in the background. Users and applications do not need to be aware of IPSec. IPSec's implementation at the Network layer gives it an advantage over security protocols, such as SSL, that applications must be specifically written for to support.

Hallmarks of secure communications ensure authentication, integrity, and confidentiality. Authentication assures the receiver that a message was indeed sent by the individual who claimed to have sent it. Data integrity ensures that the contents of messages have not been altered during transit. Confidentiality ensures that others cannot read data during transit. Combining all three provides solid end-to-end security between any two communicating hosts.

IPSec uses two protocols that add their own headers to IP datagrams. The authentication header (AH) provides for authentication and integrity, but not confidentiality. The encapsulating security payload (ESP) provides for authentication, integrity, and confidentiality. The two protocols can be combined to provide a higher degree of security.

Each IPSec connection a computer establishes has its own security association (SA). There are two types of SAs: the ISAKMP SA and the IPSec SA. The ISAKMP SA provides a secure channel for the exchange of keying information to provide for a master key, and the IPSec SA defines parameters for each secure IPSec channel between computers. A separate IPSec SA is created for both inbound and outbound connections. Each IPSec SA is individualized by assigning it a security parameters index (SPI).

Network security enabled by IPSec is policy-driven. Policies are integrated into Active Directory on domain machines, or they can be implemented as local machine policies. Each IPSec-aware computer uses a policy agent, which checks for IPSec policy during startup, and periodically afterward.

IPSec policies are implemented as a series of rules. These rules include IPSec filter lists and IPSec filter actions. If a computer seeks to establish a session with a computer whose IP addressing information matches a number in one of the filter lists, then a filter action affiliated with that list will be triggered. The creations of IPSec policies, filter lists, and filter rules can be easily accomplished via wizard-driven interfaces. You can create your own policies, or use one of the three built-in policies. The built-in policies are the Client, Server, and Secure Server IPSec policies.

FAQs

Q: Does SSL have any drawbacks?

A: Yes. The Secure Sockets Layer provides strong security for Web pages and Web sites. However, SSL is enabled on a per-page basis, which can be time consuming to configure, and difficult to audit for large and comprehensive Web installations. Another limitation of SSL is that it is processor intensive. You might have noticed reduced responsiveness when connecting to SSL-enabled Web pages. Processor cycles used by a single SSL process affect all services running on the machine. If you are planning to use SSL, be sure to benchmark all processes on that machine while SSL are active. This will provide you with an accurate assessment of how your server's overall performance will play out in a production environment.

Q: In what environment would I use the Microsoft Certificate Server?

A: You can use Microsoft Certificate server to create your own digital certificates of authenticity. However, these certificates are of limited use when running an Internet Web site. The Microsoft certificate server finds its best use in a corporate intranet. You can create certificates for both servers and users. A server certificate authenticates a server for the users connecting to it. A client certificate authenticates the users connecting to an SSL-enabled server. You can "map" user certificates to Windows 2000 user accounts. This provides granular control over intranet server resources. Another scenario where certificate server is helpful is the corporate "extranet." You can create a user certificate to a corporate partner, and then require that certificate when the partner accesses an "order entry" system on your SSL-enabled IIS server. If that partner were to fall in arrears in payments, you could revoke that partner's certificate.

Q: Can I use IPSec to secure communications with my Win 9x machines?

A: No. At this time, only Windows 2000 clients and servers can participate in IPSec-secured communications. Microsoft source material suggests that Windows CE may support IPSec in the future, but there are no plans to support downlevel clients.

Q: Does my VPN server require a dedicated connection to the Internet?

A: Your VPN server requires a dedicated IP address. In most instances, this means your VPN server needs to be connected to the Internet at all times. A small number of ISPs support "on demand" routing, which will cause the ISP to dial up your VPN server when incoming requests are received for its IP address. However, to ensure highest availability, it is best to have a dedicated connection. Remember that the VPN clients will "dial in" to your server using its IP address, and therefore that IP address must be constant.

Q: Is there a way for me to monitor the IPSec connections to my server?

A: Yes. Microsoft provides a tool called ipsecmon.exe. You can start this tool from the Run command. The IP Security Monitor allows you to assess when failures take place in negotiating security associations, when bad Security Parameters Index packets are passed, and many other statistics. The Oakley Main Mode indicates the number of master keys exchanged, and the Quick Mode number indicates the number of session keys. The Options button allows you to configure the update interval of the displayed statistics.

Connecting Windows 2000 Server

Introduction

In the space of a handful of years, the Internet has become as essential to many modern businesses as the telephone. The wholehearted adoption of the Internet was a surprise to many, and even such industry luminaries as Bill Gates did not predict the runaway success of the Internet.

Businesses are either clamoring to set up their virtual storefronts on the Internet, or seeking a way to economically tap its vast information reservoir. With the adoption of several open standards that have taken root in the Internet, such as DNS and HTTP, Windows 2000 Server is geared toward providing Internet productivity through a number of mechanisms.

Windows 2000 offers a number of ways for companies to connect to the Internet, and provides services that permit users to connect to the corporate network over the Internet and over normal telephone lines. This chapter provides details on how to configure Internet Connection Sharing (ICS), Network Address Translation (NAT), Virtual Private Networks (VPNs), and remote access services.

Connecting to the Internet with Windows 2000 Server

There is no need to begin listing the benefits of connecting your business to the Internet—mainly because most are well known, but also because more ingenious uses for the Internet seemingly spring up with every passing day.

With Windows 2000 and Internet Connection Sharing (ICS), connecting your network to the Internet through a modem or ISDN/DSL adapter is simple and requires no extra hardware or software. In fact, access sharing is a new, compelling reason to network a small company's computers that were previously operating in a stand-alone capacity.

Internet Connection Sharing (ICS)

With ICS, all the computers in a workgroup will be able to access the Internet simultaneously. ICS works with e-mail clients, Web browsers, and most other Internet client software. Different users can access different Web sites (or FTP sites, mail servers, etc.) at the same time, without interfering with one another's activities.

What Do You Need to Use ICS?

In order to use ICS to connect a network to the Internet, at least one computer running Windows 2000 must have an Internet connection. This can be either a dial-up or dedicated connection. Many small businesses and home networks will use ICS with regular analog telephone lines and a standard modem, but it will also work with an ISDN terminal adapter or other high-speed access methods.

The Internet-capable computer must also have a connection through a network interface card (NIC) to the LAN. Internet sharing must be enabled on this NIC. Later in this chapter, we will walk through the steps necessary to enable ICS and configure the other computers to go through the ICS gateway from your LAN to the Internet. First, though, we will discuss some of the concepts involved in sharing an Internet connection. We will look at characteristics of ICS as it applies to Windows 2000, and then examine NAT (Network Address Translation), which is available as part of the Windows 2000 Server operating systems. ICS and NAT can be considered variations on the same theme.

ICS uses the TCP/IP protocol and IP autoconfiguration in conjunction with private network addressing to make it possible for workgroup computers to simultaneously use the same dial-up or always-on connection. Let's take a look at each of those components, and how they are used in Windows ICS.

TIP

Before attempting to set up connection sharing, ensure that that the Internet is accessible from the ICS host computer. Much time and effort can be wasted troubleshooting the ICS connection when the problem is actually that the primary computer has lost its connection to the Internet.

ICS and TCP/IP

In order to use ICS, TCP/IP must be installed on the computer that connects to the Internet, and bound to both the Internet connection device (modem or ISDN/DSL adapter) and to the NIC that connects the computer to the LAN. Additionally, TCP/IP is required on all computers on the local network that want to take advantage of ICS.

How APIPA Works

Automatic Private IP Addressing (APIPA) is used in conjunction with DHCP to automate the IP configuration of computers on a TCP/IP network. If a computer's TCP/IP properties are set up to obtain an IP address automatically, when that computer is booted up and comes online it will first attempt to contact a DHCP server. If a DHCP server is

found on the network, the computer will go through the process of negotiating to lease an IP address from the range of addresses that has been
specified by the Administrator on the DHCP server. See Chapter 12,
"Managing Windows 2000 DHCP Server," for more information about
DHCP and the lease process.

In legacy versions of Windows if no DHCP server was located, the
TCP/IP connection failed. The computer was not able to participate in
the network using the TCP/IP protocol, because it had no way of
obtaining an IP address. That's where APIPA comes in—with a Windows
2000 client, the inability to reach a DHCP server is not fatal. The computer goes to Plan B, assigning itself an address in the range
169.254.0.1–169.254.255.254 and the subnet mask of 255.255.0.0 after
checking to determine that the address is not being used by another
APIPA computer on the network.

This self-assigned address can be used until a DHCP server is located,
allowing the computer to communicate on the network, although with some
limitations. The computer will only be able to communicate with other computers that are also using APIPA, or that are manually configured with IP
addresses on the 169.254.0.0 subnet.

Together, DHCP and APIPA make the configuration and maintenance of
a small TCP/IP LAN easier, and provide for more reliable connectivity.

ICS Address Autoconfiguration and the DHCP Allocator

When ICS is enabled on a computer so that it can connect to the Internet
and other computers on its local network can share its connection, that
computer becomes a DHCP allocator. It has a preset range of IP addresses
that it can hand out to the other computers as they come online.

A DHCP allocator differs from a DHCP server because its IP address
range is predefined, and Windows 2000 Professional with ICS enabled can
be a DHCP allocator, even though it is not running a server operating
system.

The use of the DHCP allocator for ICS connections also differs from
APIPA, where the DHCP-enabled computer assigns itself an address after
failing to find a DHCP server. These three concepts all relate to automatically assigning IP addresses, but it is important that you understand the
differences between them, and when and where each is used.

Private Network Addresses vs. Public Addresses

One of the advantages of using Internet connection sharing instead of a
routed connection (aside from the cost of the router itself) is the ability to
use private IP addresses on the internal network. Instead of having to purchase a block of addresses from an ISP, only one valid public address is
required, which is used by the computer that acts as the gateway from the
LAN to the Internet (the Windows 2000 computer on which ICS is

installed). This can result in substantial savings in time as well as cost, considering the administrative effort involved in changing the internal IP addresses in order to access the Internet.

Using Internet Connection Sharing

ICS was designed to be easy to set up and use. On a Windows 2000 Professional or Server computer, you just select a dial-up connection or virtual private network (VPN) connection that has already been configured (for example, the modem connection to the ISP). Then, enable ICS on the Internet Connection Sharing tab (in Windows 2000 Professional) or Sharing tab (in Windows 2000 Server).

Using ICS with a VPN Connection

Typically, ICS is used to share a dial-up connection to the Internet. However, you can also share a VPN connection using ICS, if you want the ICS client computers to be able to connect to a private network, such as your company network, through a secure tunnel over the Internet.

You can set up the VPN connection on the Windows 2000 ICS gateway, using either Point-to-Point Tunneling Protocol (PPTP) or L2TP (Layer 2 Tunneling Protocol), both of which are supported by Windows 2000. The tunneling protocol encapsulates the packets, which can then be using any protocol used on the private LAN (TCP/IP, IPX/SPX, or even NetBEUI).

For more details on setting up a VPN, see Chapter 16, "Securing TCP/IP Connections."

On-Demand Dialing

A few options are available when configuring ICS. The on-demand dialing feature can be enabled, which will cause the ICS computer to automatically dial up the Internet connection whenever an ICS client computer tries to start an Internet dependent program.

For example, consider a Windows 2000 Server computer with a modem that is configured to dial up to an ISP. ICS could be installed on the server, and other network clients could be configured to use it as their Internet gateway. Then, when someone opens a Web browser on one of the other computers, or clicks on Send and Receive in an e-mail program, that will signal the ICS computer, if it is offline, to dial up and connect to the ISP. To the user, all this means is a slight delay while the connection is established; if you have a high-speed digital connection type such as an ISDN dial-up account, the delay is not even noticeable.

Configuring Applications and Services

Another option when configuring ICS is to configure certain applications and services to work properly across the Internet. Those applications, and certain services such as the Web server service, must be configured on the ICS computer before the connecting computers will be able to use them. This is achieved by clicking SETTINGS on the Internet Connection Sharing tab of the connection's property sheet.

ISP Static IP Addressing

Many ISPs use DHCP on their servers to assign a new IP address to your connection each time you dial up. By default, Windows 2000 will attempt to get an IP address and other TCP/IP information from a DHCP server when making a dial-up connection.

However, some ISPs issue static addresses, which never change. In this case, you must configure TCP/IP on the dial-up connection to use the static address. To do this, open the Properties sheet for the dial-up connection, double-click on TCP/IP (or select it and click PROPERTIES), and then enter the static IP address, subnet mask, and default gateway addresses issues by the ISP. When using static addresses, you will also need to check the "Use the following DNS server addresses" check box and enter the address(es) for the ISP's DNS server(s).

NOTE

ICS acts as a DNS proxy, passing on the internal computers' requests for name resolution to an Internet DNS server and returning the results. It does not act as a WINS proxy; however, Network Address Translation (NAT) can perform the WINS proxy function.

What Happens When You Enable ICS?

There are several things to be aware of when using ICS. By default, when enabling ICS, the NIC that you are using to connect to the local network is given a new static IP address, 192.168.0.1, with a subnet mask of 255.255.255.0. Unless this happens to be the address that was already assigned to this system on the internal network, this will cause any already existing TCP/IP connections between the ICS computer and the other computers on the LAN to be lost.

The second thing that occurs when enabling ICS is that it becomes a DHCP allocator for the other computers connecting to the Internet through it. It will assign those computers IP addresses from its preset range. Using ICS, you cannot disable the DHCP allocator or modify the address range. You also cannot configure inbound mappings. To do any of those things, you will need to use NAT to share your Internet connection.

NOTE

ICS is intended for smaller networks only, and it is not recommended for use on networks running Windows 2000 domain controllers, DNS servers, DHCP servers, or other computers that are assigned static IP addresses. In these situations, NAT should be deployed instead.

Network Address Translation (NAT)

The terminology used in Windows 2000 can be confusing, since both ICS and NAT are translated connections that provide addressing and name resolution for a small LAN to connect to the Internet. Although their function is similar, they differ primarily in terms of simplicity and flexibility. ICS lets you get a small network's Internet connection up and running quickly, with a minimum amount of configuration involved. However, it is not very configurable and is not designed to work on a more sophisticated small network.

How NAT Differs from ICS

NAT can be thought of as ICS's big brother. It accomplishes the same end result, but provides Administrators with the ability to customize the configuration to a much greater degree. It allows Administrators to change the range of allocated addresses assigned to internal computers, to map the internal addresses to multiple external, public addresses on the Internet. While ICS supports only one interface to the local network, NAT can support multiple interfaces.

TIP

A Windows 2000 Professional computer or a Windows 2000 (non-domain controller) server can be set up to be an ICS computer. However, NAT is part of the Routing and Remote Access (RRAS) component that is found only on Windows 2000 server.

What Is NAT?

While ICS is perfect for the typical home or simple small business network, Microsoft designed its Windows 2000 Network Address Translation protocol with the more sophisticated small business network in mind. NAT is designed to provide an Administrator with the flexibility that ICS lacks, so that you can fine-tune the address translation process depending on your organization's needs.

NAT performs three basic activities, and thus can be divided into three elements:

Address allocation   The computer on which NAT is enabled acts as a DHCP allocator for the other computers on the local network that are configured to use DHCP. The NAT computer can assign an IP address and subnet masking information, and can designate the DNS and WINS server addresses.

Address translation   The main function of a NAT-enabled computer is to translate private IP addresses with corresponding TCP or UDP port numbers to public addresses, and back again.

Name resolution   The NAT-enabled computer acts as a DNS and WINS proxy for the rest of the computers on the network.

Note that you cannot run DNS, WINS, or DHCP services when NAT is enabled. Typically, NAT is used to translate multiple private addresses to a single public IP address provided by the ISP. If your ISP has provided you with a block of addresses, NAT can be configured to translate to multiple public addresses.

Setting Up the NAT Computer

Setting up NAT is a bit more complicated than enabling ICS. First, the IP address of the NAT computer's LAN network adapter should be manually configured to 192.168.0.1, with a subnet mask of 255.255.255.0 (these are recommended addresses, though other addresses can be used). This is done in the TCP/IP Properties for the NIC.

The next step is to enable Routing and Remote Access Server (RRAS). This is achieved through the RRAS configuration MMC snap-in, accessed by navigating to Start | Programs | Administrative Tools | Routing and Remote Access.

Right-click the name of the server to be NAT enabled, and click CONFIGURE and Enable Routing and Remote Access in the context menu. This will open the RRAS Wizard, which will guide you through the steps.

Next, enable routing on the dial-up port. To do this, in the RRAS snap-in, click Ports in the console tree, right-click and select Properties, choose the Devices tab, and select the device you want to configure (Figure 17.1).

Click CONFIGURE and select Demand-dial routing, then click OK. Now you have to add a demand-dial interface to your ISP. Again, go to the RRAS console, and click Routing Interfaces. Right-click, and choose New Demand Dial Interface, as shown in Figure 17.2. This will invoke the Demand-dial Wizard, which will guide you in setting up the interface.

Figure 17.1 Configuring the dial-up port for routing.

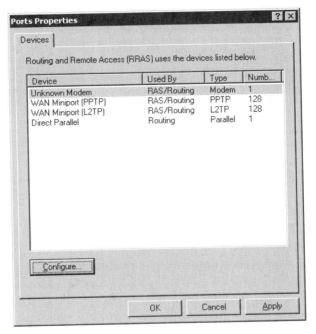

Figure 17.2 Creating a new demand-dial interface.

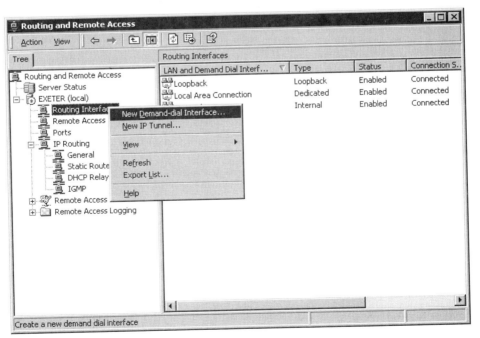

Figure 17.3 Adding the Network Address Translation routing protocol.

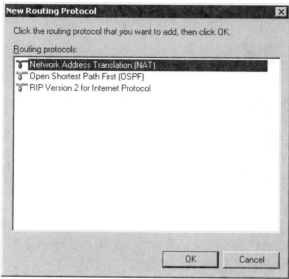

Next, create a default static route for the interface that connects to the Internet. To do this, in the RRAS console tree, click Static Routes and choose New Static Route. Click on the interface you want to use as the default static route. Enter 0.0.0.0 in the Destination box, and the same in the Network mask box. (These settings are used to indicate this is the default route. You may also have other static routes, which will have the IP and subnet information entered. The Gateway parameter will be grayed out because this is a demand-dial route.) Check the "Use this route to initiate demand-dial connections" check box. Enter 1 for Metric.

Finally, we can add the NAT protocol. In the RRAS console tree, select General, located under the IP Routing node, right-click, and select New Routing Protocol. Choose Network Address Translation, as shown in Figure 17.3, and click OK.

Now it's time to add the Internet connection interface to NAT. In the RRAS console tree, right-click NAT and select New Interface. Click the interface for your Internet connection, and click OK. On the General tab, click Public Interface connected to the Internet, and check the Translate TCP/UDP headers check box.

Go through the same process to add the private network interface to NAT, this time selecting "Private interface connected to private network" on the General tab in NAT properties.

In order for the NAT computer to act as a DNS and WINS proxy, you must enable NAT name resolution. To do so, right-click on NAT in the

Figure 17.4 Configuring NAT name resolution.

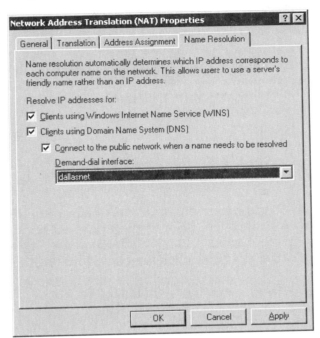

RRAS console tree, and check both the WINS and DNS check boxes on the Name Resolution tab, shown in Figure 17.4. For on-demand dialing to occur when one of the internal computers sends a DNS name resolution request, check the "Connect to the public network when a name needs to be resolved" check box, and then select the name of the interface to be used in Demand-dial Interfaces.

NOTE

In most cases, you would not want to enable WINS name resolution if the NAT computer is providing address translation for clients to connect to the public Internet. This would be enabled when NAT is used to share a VPN connection to a private network.

The last step is to enable addressing and name resolution. Back in the RRAS console tree, right-click NAT, and click Properties. Select the Address Assignment tab, and check the "Automatically assign IP addresses by using DHCP" check box.

If you will be using multiple public IP addresses, configure the range (see the following section, *Multiple Public Addresses*).

Multiple Public Addresses

Configuring NAT to translate to multiple public addresses requires some knowledge of subnet masking. You must determine whether the range of IP addresses assigned by your ISP can be expressed by an IP address and a mask. For instance: The four public IP addresses 200.100.100.212, 200.100.100.213, 200.100.100.214, and 200.100.100.215 can be expressed as 200.100.100.212 with 255.255.255.252 as the mask. This works when the number of addresses is a power of 2.

The alternative method is to enter the starting and ending addresses of the range. This is done in the RRAS configuration MMC snap-in, accessed as noted earlier.

Double-click NAT in the console tree, right-click the interface in the right pane, and click Properties. Choose the Address Pool tab, click ADD, and enter the range of addresses in the dialog box shown below. When you have added the address range(s), click OK twice to close the dialog boxes.

Setting Up the NAT Client Computers

The other computers on the local network, which will connect to the Internet through the NAT computer, need to have TCP/IP installed and configured to obtain an IP address automatically (as in the earlier section on ICS). The NAT computer will also supply them with the subnet mask, default gateway, and DNS and WINS server addresses.

A NAT Example

Let's say your small local area network uses the 192.168.0.0 network ID for internal computers, and you purchase a dial-up access account from an ISP, which will assign you one public address when you establish a connection, using DHCP.

The computer on which NAT is enabled has a modem, and connects to the ISP. After being authenticated on the network, it is assigned an IP address of 204.215.60.72. This legitimate public address will be used for the duration of the session by the NAT computer to communicate over the modem with computers on the Internet.

So far, this is the same thing that happens when a stand-alone computer uses a modem to connect to the Internet through an ISP. Here's where NAT comes in, as shown in Figure 17.5.

The NAT computer is also connected to the LAN with a network adapter card, which has been assigned the IP address 192.168.0.1. The other computers on the LAN are using addresses with the same network ID and unique host IDs (192.168.0.x).

Figure 17.5 A small network using NAT to connect to the Internet.

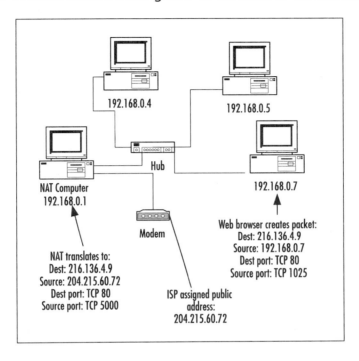

A user at the computer whose network card is using the IP 192.168.0.7 wants to connect to a Web site on the Internet that has the IP address 216.136.4.9. He opens his browser and types in the URL for that Web site. Here's what happens:

The user's computer creates a packet with the following header information:

- Destination IP address: 216.136.4.9
- Source IP address: 192.168.0.7 (the originating computer's private address)
- Destination port: TCP port 80
- Source port: TCP port 1025

The packet is sent to NAT, which will translate the addresses of the outgoing packet to:

- Destination IP address: 216.136.4.9
- Source IP address: 204.215.60.72 (the NAT computer's public address)
- Destination port: TCP port 80
- Source port: TCP port 5000

Note that a port is the endpoint in a TCP/IP communication. Because several different applications could be communicating over TCP/IP simultaneously from the same computer (using the same IP address), each application uses a different port number to identify packets sent to and from it. TCP port 80 is the common port used by Web servers, and port 1025 is the port normally used by Web clients to send a request for a Web page to the Web server. NAT maps the internal client's port to port 5000 on the NAT host machine to identify that particular client's request. The NAT protocol maintains a mapping table, which in this case will map {192.168.0.7 TCP 1025} to {204.215.60.72 TCP 5000}. Now the translated packet can be sent over the Internet, using the public address, which is legal on the global network. When the response is returned with a destination address of 204.215.60.72 TCP 5000, NAT will consult the mapping table and route the response to the computer at 192.168.0.7 on TCP port 1025.

WARNING

NAT works properly only with protocols in which the IP address and port numbers are contained in the headers. Some protocols, such as FTP, store these addresses in the payload instead of the header. Others, such as PPTP, don't use TCP or UDP headers. In these cases, address translation requires additional software, called a NAT editor. Windows 2000 includes NAT editors for the FTP, PPTP, and ICMP protocols. Editors for SNMP, LDAP, COM, and RPC are not included. (Address translation will not work with IPSec traffic, even with an editor.)

Accessing Other Computers' Printers and Network Drives

The computers on a small TCP/IP network, once configured to share an Internet connection, can also share other resources with one another. The type of access control used will depend on whether the network is set up as a workgroup (peer-to-peer network) or uses a domain controller running server software to authenticate logons. For the Windows 2000 computers on the local network to access one another's files and folders, printers, and other resources, several conditions must be met:

- The server service must be installed and started on each computer that wants to share its resources with other computers.
- The resource must be specifically shared.
- The user accessing the resource must have permission to do so.

To share a resource, such as a printer, folder, or an entire logical drive, right-click on the resource in My Computer or Windows Explorer, and select Sharing. Here you can elect to share the resource, give the share a name to identify it on the network, and set access permissions.

If the Windows 98 or Windows 95 computer is a member of a workgroup, share-level access control could be used; this means a password must be set on each shared resource. When another user attempts to access the resource across the network, the user will be prompted to enter the password. If the computer is part of a Windows 2000 or Windows NT domain, user-level access permissions are assigned. Users will be able to access the resource based on the individual permissions granted to their accounts or the security groups to which they belong. If the resource resides on a partition formatted in NTFS, the NTFS permissions also are applied, with the effective permissions being the most restrictive. In a Windows 2000 domain, Active Directory security will also control access to all directory objects.

Accessing Other Computers' Resources over the Internet

When a computer is connected to the Internet, it becomes part of that huge global network of networks. Others can access your resources over the Internet if they know the account name and password of a user who is a member of the Administrators, Backup Operators, or Server Operators group. A user who does gain access to your computer's hard drive, whether over the network or the Internet, may be able to view all folders and files on that drive. This includes those that are protected by NTFS permissions, if those NTFS permissions allow access to members of the Administrators, Backup Operators, or Server Operators groups.

Protecting Your Computer from Unauthorized Access

You should always use very strong passwords for the accounts that belong to these groups, and it is a good idea to change the passwords on a regular basis. If you want to ensure that no one will be able to access your computer across the network or the Internet, you may want to consider disabling the server service. When you do this, your computer ceases to share its resources; you can think of the server service as the sharing service. You will still be able to access other computers' resources from this computer, however.

If you wish to be able to share your computer's resources with others on the local network, but do not want anyone from the outside to be able to access them when you are connected to your ISP through a dial-up or dedicated connection, you can uninstall File and Print Sharing for Microsoft Networks on the Internet connection only. This is done by right-clicking on the connection icon in Network and Dialup Connections, on the General tab selecting File and Print Sharing for Microsoft Networks, and then clicking UNINSTALL.

Comparison of ICS, NAT, and Windows Routing

We have seen how both ICS and NAT translate all of your network's private IP addresses to one or more public addresses. However, there is another way to connect your LAN to the Internet if your ISP has provided you with multiple public addresses: IP routing.

You may wonder why Microsoft has given you three different means of accomplishing the same result; ICS, NAT, and Windows routing are all used to connect the computers on an internal network to the Internet through one dial-up or dedicated link. Which one is best for your small office depends on your particular situation, as well as performance and security considerations.

A Windows 2000 Routed Connection

If you have a legal address for each computer that you want to connect, you can use a Windows 2000 computer with RRAS acting as a software router to connect to the global network, without any address translation required. A routed connection requires manual configuration of IP addresses on all the LAN computers or the use of a full-fledged DHCP server with the proper scope configured. Thus it is more complex to configure than either of the translated connection methods, but it also provides maximum flexibility and allows all IP traffic between Internet and local hosts. The Windows 2000 software router supports both IP and IPX packet filtering, in addition to PPTP and L2TP over IPSec.

Windows 2000 routing requires that the computer is running any version of the Windows 2000 Server operating systems.

Performance Considerations

One common complaint about NAT is the performance hit caused by large address tables in a high-traffic situation. Certainly, the translation process requires resources and time; consequently, NAT will perform best in a smaller, lower-traffic network. In general, NAT will work well with a network in which 10 or fewer users simultaneously access the Internet through the NAT computer. However, the number of users NAT can accommodate without unacceptably lowered performance will vary depending on the nature of access, the Internet connection itself (analog modem vs. ISDN, DSL, or cable), and the speed of the internal network (for instance, 10Mbps vs. 100Mbps Ethernet). You will recall that ICS is designed to work in a peer-to-peer situation, where there are only workstation computers and perhaps member servers (non-domain controllers) set up to belong to a workgroup. NAT must be run on a server, but you cannot run the DNS, WINS, and DHCP services in conjunction with it.

Windows routing can be used in a Windows 2000 domain, and is the method of choice for the larger network when sufficient public IP addresses are available.

Which connection method will perform best for you thus depends on what type of network environment you have.

Security

Remember that any time you establish a link from your local network to the Internet, you open your LAN up to possible risks. This is true regardless of which method you use to connect. However, Windows 2000 provides security features that will let you enjoy the benefits of officewide Internet connectivity with less chance of security-related problems.

How Do NAT and ICS Protect My Network?

Connecting to the Internet through a NAT computer hides the internal IP addresses from "outsiders" on the Internet. External computers communicate only with the NAT computer's public IP address, and none of your internal addresses are exposed.

Additionally, in its typical configuration, NAT allows only outbound connections, traveling from your local network to the Internet. The only inbound packets that are allowed are those sent over a connection that was initiated by an internal computer. For example, when a computer on your local network uses a Web browser to send a request to a Web server on the Internet, the response to that request can come back into the internal network. Otherwise, traffic from the Internet cannot cross the NAT boundary.

NOTE

If you do want to allow access to resources on your local network from the Internet, you can do so by assigning a static IP address to the computer on which the resources are located. Exclude that address from the DHCP allocator's range, and configure a special port to map the inbound Internet connection to the resource server's address on your local network.

Since ICS and NAT are configured to allow only traffic that originated as an outbound connection, this offers some protection, as does the cloaking of internal addresses from the rest of the world through the address translation component. On the other hand, NAT prevents the encryption of anything that carries an IP address or information derived from an IP address (such as the TCP-header checksum). Application-level encryption can still be used in most cases, but the TCP header cannot be encrypted.

Security Issues with Routed Connections

A routed connection to the Internet means that communication can occur with any host on the Internet; it also means that the computers on your LAN will be exposed to hackers or others with malicious intent on the Internet. You counteract this is by using packet filtering, which must be configured on the Windows 2000 router to keep undesirable Internet traffic off your internal network.

Comparison of Features

Table 17.1 shows some of the similarities and differences between Internet Connection Sharing, Network Address Translation, and Windows software routing.

Table 17.1 Feature Comparison at a Glance

Feature	ICS	NAT	Routing
NAT	Yes	Yes	Yes
IPX/NetBIOS	No	No	Yes
Configuration	Check box	Manual	Manual
Address range	Fixed	Configurable	Configurable
Proxy	DNS	DNS and WINS	–
LAN interface(s)	Single	Multiple	Multiple

Microsoft cautions that ICS and NAT are not designed for connecting two LANs, but only for establishing a link from an internal network to the Internet. Windows routing, on the other hand, serves a much broader purpose, and can be used to connect local networks and to connect local networks to the outside network.

Establishing VPNs over the Internet

As you learned in Chapter 16, "Securing TCP/IP Connections," VPNs provide the capability to securely join separate physical LANs into one logical network across the Internet. In this chapter, we will look at exactly how this can be accomplished, and also look at the simpler task of connecting one client to a LAN via a VPN over the Internet.

PPTP and L2TP

Before you begin implementing a VPN solution, it is important to first gather the requirements and decide what type of VPN you are going to deploy. Windows 2000 supports VPNs based on PPTP and L2TP, and while one is easier to implement for most Windows platforms, the other is of a less proprietary nature.

PPTP VPNs are supported in Windows 2000, Windows NT 4.0, Windows 95, and Windows 98. However, Windows 2000 is the only Microsoft operating system that is capable of establishing an L2TP VPN. Consequently, you will need to provide PPTP services for legacy Windows systems in your organization.

PPTP relies on proprietary encryption, and Windows systems that support PPTP use Microsoft Point-to-Point Encryption (MPPE). Since MPPE is built in to the networking components of the operating system, it requires fewer steps to implement. A VPN that uses L2TP relies on IPSec for encryption, and accordingly must have security certificates installed on VPN servers and clients.

A Windows 2000 server providing VPN connections can support both PPTP and L2TP connections at the same time, so it won't be difficult to provide for both. You may want to plan to install certificates on all computers that are upgraded to or are delivered with Windows 2000. This will enable you to use L2TP for these machines, and when your network no longer has any legacy Windows systems, you can remove the PPTP ports on the VPN server, effectively forcing all VPN connections to be L2TP-based.

An L2TP VPN is established as described in the following steps:

1. An IPSec security association is generated.

2. An L2TP tunnel is created between the client and server.

3. A challenge is sent by the server.

4. An encrypted response is sent by the client.

5. The response is compared to the user accounts database.

6. The server accepts the connection if the remote access policies and user account properties are appropriate.

PPTP connection attempts are processed in the following order:

1. A PPTP tunnel is created by the client with the VPN server.

2. A challenge is sent to the client from the server.

3. An encrypted response is sent to the server from the client.

4. The response is compared to the user accounts database.

The server accepts the connection if the remote access policies and user account properties are appropriate.

As you can see, the only major procedural difference between PPTP and L2TP is that L2TP establishes an IPSec association before creating the tunnel. This is not to say that the two protocols are identical otherwise—they certainly aren't. This extra step provides another layer of authentication, since IPSec is based on computer certificates.

VPN Solutions

Windows 2000 VPNs can be implemented in two ways: client to server, and server to server. The type that you select will depend on the needs of your network and the hardware available for use.

Client/Server VPN

To provide remote clients with access to a LAN, a client-to-server VPN can be implemented, which enables a client PC to access all resources on the VPN server's LAN. This connection can be made through the Internet, so any client connected to the Internet via any method can establish a VPN connection. This type of VPN is used primarily to provide mobile users or a single computer on a separate LAN access to LAN resources. Windows 2000 components for a client-to-server VPN include RRAS on the server with VPN ports configured, and a VPN network connection configured on the client. If a VPN utilizing L2TP and IPSec is used, each computer must also have a security certificate installed.

A server-to-server (or router-to-router) VPN is used to create one logical network out of two or more physical networks across the Internet, an intranet, or another public network. With this method, you can create a WAN without buying expensive dedicated connections between physical locations. Each office participating in the VPN simply needs to have an Internet connection and a Windows 2000 Server computer running RRAS with the VPN connections and appropriate routes configured.

Creating a VPN connection between servers requires that a demand-dial interface is configured to establish the VPN connection when the server starts. Demand-dial interfaces can be configured to dial when network traffic needs to be routed to the other network, or to remain connected continuously. The demand-dial interface configuration includes the IP address or host name of the remote VPN server, the dial-up connection association if it is a dial-up link, a username and password to authenticate, and protocol information. The terminology may be a bit misleading here, since a demand-dial interface may not actually be dialing anything if it doesn't require a modem-based connection. A demand-dial interface for a VPN may use either a permanent network connection or a dial-up connection.

It is important to remember that the appropriate routes must be configured in RRAS for the VPN servers to properly forward traffic to other networks. This requires a fundamental understanding of IP routing concepts and a familiarity with RRAS configuration (Figure 17.6).

Figure 17.6 Demand-dial interfaces that establish server-to-server VPN connections.

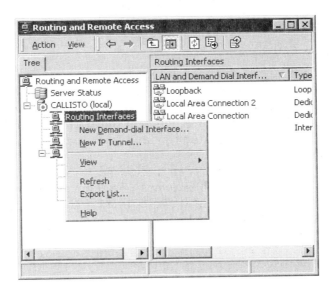

Creating a VPN Router

In order to create a VPN, a VPN router is required. Creating a VPN router with Windows 2000 is a rather simple task, as detailed next. VPN connections are available through configuring Routing and Remote Access and will allow clients and other routers to establish VPNs across the Internet, an intranet, or by dial-up. Most VPN implementations will be over the Internet, so that will be our focus in this chapter.

1. Run the Routing and Remote Access management console by clicking Start | Programs | Administrative Tools | Routing and Remote Access.

2. Expand the tree below the server. If it does not expand and displays a red dot on the server, then you must enable RRAS. Do this by right-clicking on the server and selecting Configure and Enable Routing and Remote Access.

3. Click NEXT, select Virtual private network (VPN) server, and then click NEXT.

4. The available protocols to be tunneled are displayed, and you are given the opportunity to add more protocols. Click NEXT when all of the protocols are displayed.

5. The next dialog contains a list of available network connections (Figure 17.7). Select the interface that is connected to the Internet. If you do not have a specific interface that is connected to the

Figure 17.7 Selecting the Internet connection during RRAS VPN configuration.

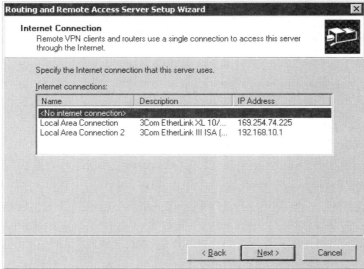

Internet, then select <No internet connection>. Click NEXT after you have made your selection.

6. If you selected <No internet connection>, or if there are more than two network adapters, you will be asked to select the network to which clients must be assigned for addressing purposes. This is the network with which the VPN will be established. Select the appropriate network connection, and click NEXT to continue.

7. Now select the method for assigning IP addresses to VPN clients. Choose either automatic assignment or specify a range of addresses. Select the appropriate method, and click NEXT.

8. If DHCP was selected and the network connection selected earlier has a static IP address, you will see a warning urging you to make sure the DHCP addresses will be compatible with the static address of the network connection.

9. If a specified range of addresses was selected, you will now need to create the address ranges to assign to clients.

10. Click NEXT to proceed. A dialog box asking if you want the server to use an existing RADIUS server is then displayed. For this exercise, select NO, and click NEXT to move ahead.

11. Click FINISH, and click OK at the message notifying you of the need to configure the DHCP Relay Agent to support relaying DHCP messages from remote access clients.

12. The RRAS service starts, and you now have a VPN server! Expand the tree under your server in the management console and you will see the various RRAS components. Click on Ports to see the VPN devices. When a VPN connection is active, the status column for that port will change to Active, and you will be able to see details by double-clicking the port.

Connecting a VPN Client

Creating a single client connect is quite easy, and only requires that you know the name or IP address of the VPN router. The following sequence provides an insight on how to do this.

1. Right-click on the My Network Places icon on the desktop, and select Properties.

2. Double-click the Make New Connection icon, and click NEXT at the Welcome screen.

3. Select "Connect to a virtual private network through the Internet" (Figure 17.8), and then click NEXT.

4. Enter the IP address or host name of the VPN server or router to which you are connecting, and click NEXT.

5. Select whether the VPN connection is to be available for all users or only to the currently logged on user, and click NEXT.

Figure 17.8 Specifying the network connection type.

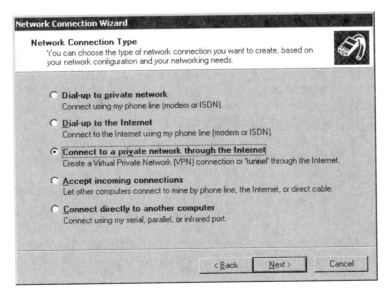

Figure 17.9 VPN connections are signified by the cloud in the connection icon.

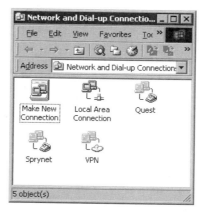

6. Give the connection a descriptive name, and uncheck the box at the bottom if a shortcut is not required on the desktop. Click NEXT to continue.

7. A Connect dialog will now appear. Enter a username and password for an account on the remote server that has dial-in permission enabled. Click CONNECT to establish the VPN connection.

8. An icon in the Network and Dial-up Connections window is now available for the VPN connection (Figure 17.9). Right-click the new icon, and select Properties.

9. The General tab can be used to change the IP address of the VPN server, or to configure the connection to connect using another network connection (dial-up to the Internet, for example).

10. Click on the Options tab to configure whether the connection displays connection progress, prompts for username and password before connecting, and redial options.

11. Select the Security tab if you need to set specific encryption and authentication protocol settings. To see the advanced settings, select ADVANCED and click SETTINGS.

12. Click the Networking tab to select the type of VPN and to see the transport protocols, network clients, and services enabled for the connection (Figure 17.10).

13. Select the Sharing tab if you wish to share this connection with other clients. This may be used in very small branch offices to enable other clients to use the VPN connection. For everything other than very small offices, a server running RRAS would be the appropriate solution.

14. Click OK when you are finished configuring the VPN connection.

Figure 17.10 VPN Connection Properties

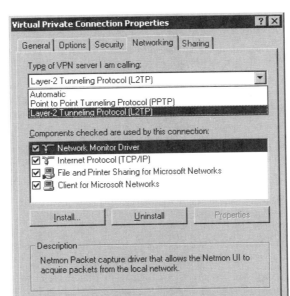

Tunneling Non-TCP/IP Protocols

Despite the popularity of TCP/IP, some networks still use IPX and NetBEUI on some workstations and servers. These computers can still be accessed via a VPN, since these protocols can be tunneled across the Internet. A computer can transmit an IPX or NetBEUI datagram, which will be encapsulated in an IP datagram, transmitted to the remote network, unencapsulated, and delivered to the destination. As can be seen in Figure 17.10, each protocol can be enabled or disabled for use over the VPN connection.

Dial-Up Access

The Windows Remote Access Service (RAS) enables computers to establish modem connections with servers or workstations on a LAN, and can make all network resources on the LAN available to the dial-up client. RAS became very popular with Windows NT 4.0, and those of you who have experience with Windows NT 4.0 RAS will find the Windows 2000 implementation of dial-up network services a little different. However, you are still dealing with essentially the same devices and services, so it won't take you long to learn how to configure and manage RAS services in Windows 2000.

RRAS first became available as a downloadable add-on for Windows NT 4.0, and enabled Windows NT 4.0 Server to become a full-fledged router and provide VPN services. If you have used RRAS in Windows NT 4.0, then you'll find the transition to Windows 2000 RAS a bit easier, since RAS is integrated into Routing and Remote Access Service (RRAS).

The simplest RAS implementations of RAS will have only one or two modems, and the only hardware configuration required is for the system to recognize and install the modems. An enterprise RAS server, however, may have dozens of modems connected to interface cards that provide a COM port for each modem. In this case, the COM port adapter must be correctly installed before the modems will be recognized by the system. The hardware manufacturer will provide you with drivers and information regarding the configuration of the COM port adapter.

Configuring RAS

When RRAS is enabled on the server, it creates an icon in the Network and Dial-up Connections window (Figure 17.11), which enables you to select modems and ports for inbound access, to change users' connection permissions, and to configure network protocols, clients, and services.

To change the ports available for incoming connections, right-click on the Incoming Connections icon and select Properties. The Properties dialog will list all of the available modems and ports, and the check box beside each item will indicate whether it is enabled for incoming connections. The layouts of the Users and Networking tabs are similar, with check boxes designating which users have dial-in permissions, and which network protocols, clients, and services are bound to incoming connections.

Within the RRAS management console, you can view the status of RAS modems in the list of ports (Figure 17.12) and see the details of a port by double-clicking on it. The detailed status provides information on the connection speed, bytes in and out statistics, error statistics, and protocols in use.

Figure 17.11 An Incoming Connections icon is created when RRAS is enabled.

Figure 17.12 RAS port status.

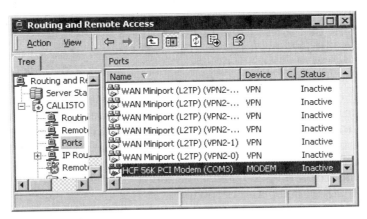

There are several options you can configure from the RRAS console by right-clicking on the server in the left pane and selecting Properties. From this dialog, you can enable/disable remote access, enable/disable IP routing, specify authentication methods, authentication providers, accounting providers, and whether to assign IP address from a static pool or use DHCP.

Security Concerns

Since RAS provides an entry point into your network, you need to make certain that an acceptable level of security is established so that unauthorized users are not able to gain access. There are several things you can do to reduce your risks without imposing additional administration or impairing usability.

Secure the Telephone Number

Telephone numbers used for dial-in access should not be published. Since this is the first thing an intruder needs in order to attempt a RAS break-in, the number should not be readily available to anyone who searches for it. This is one example of why it is advantageous to have Windows NT or Windows 2000 on laptop computers that have dial-up connections configured. In order to see the dial-up configuration to get the number, an intruder must first be able to log on to the system. A stolen laptop running Windows 95/98 will not provide much of a challenge for a savvy user to get the dial-up information.

User Accounts

Users must be given dial-in permission, which is not granted by default when a user account is created. It is beneficial to grant dial-in permission only to those who actually need it instead of giving it to everyone, since intruders need to compromise a username and password to gain access. The risk of having an account compromised is greater if a hacker can select any user account for RAS access. If only one of every 10 users has dial-in permission, any attempts at brute force will be less likely to succeed since, there is only a 1-in-10 chance the account they are trying to compromise can even use RAS.

Password security is also very important. Please see section in this chapter on Internet security for more information regarding passwords.

Account lockout is another feature that you will want to have enabled to secure a VPN server. This is not related to the account lockout feature that is associated with the user account on the Windows domain. With account lockout enabled, attempts by unauthorized users to establish a VPN connection will be thwarted after a specified number of bad password attempts. Unfortunately, this feature can only be configured by editing the Registry on the RAS server. Set the MaxDenials entry to the number of failed attempts to allow before account lockout in the following Registry key:

HKEY_LOCAL_MACHINE\SYSTEM\CurrentControlSet\Services\RemoteAccess
\Parameters\AccountLockout

The ResetTime (mins.) value is set to 48 hours by default, and specifies the length of time before the failed attempts counter is reset. To reset a user account that has been locked out, delete the following Registry key:

HKEY_LOCAL_MACHINE\SYSTEM\CurrentControlSet\Services\RemoteAccess
\Parameters\AccountLockout*domain name:username*

A malicious individual can use the account lockout feature to deny VPN services to authentic users. If someone obtains valid usernames, he or she can simply make multiple bad logon attempts and cause the account to be locked out. Although the individual has not gained access to your network, he or she has denied service to an authorized user and has created some work for you. If this becomes a problem, you would have to pursue a time-consuming investigation to determine who is causing the problem.

Authentication and Encryption

There are a number of encryption and authentication methods that can be configured on a Windows 2000 server providing RAS services. Windows 2000 includes some new protocols, such as MS-CHAP version 2 (Microsoft Challenge Handshake Authentication Protocol) and EAP (Extensible Authentication Protocol), that are not compatible with legacy Windows systems, so you will have to enable other protocols to support them.

Caller ID and Callback

If you have a known set of numbers from which users will be calling, you can enable caller ID security in Windows 2000. Caller ID security is dependent upon the proper hardware and drivers to support it, so you will need to do a little homework before enabling it. If caller ID security is enabled, the user must be calling from a specified telephone number for the connection to be accepted. For VPN access, caller ID can be enabled to accept connections only from specific IP addresses. Caller ID security will be applicable for home users who dial in to the corporate network, but will not be a good option for mobile users, since the phone numbers from which they dial are always changing.

Outsourcing Dial-Up Access

Since using VPN connections provides secure access to your network over the Internet, you have the option of using an ISP to provide mobile users access to your LAN. Many organizations maintain their own remote access servers, which requires a significant hardware investment and ongoing maintenance. Additionally, remote users out of the local calling area must connect using long distance or a toll-free number. The cost of these items in addition to the monthly cost of the phone lines, floor space for equipment, and other costs, can easily be greater than a flat monthly fee per user charged by a national ISP.

Outsourcing dial-up services can provide you with some significant savings, but there are a few issues that can create more support work if outsourcing is not carefully planned and deployed. First, the provider you select must have an easy method for users to select a local telephone number. When a user travels from one city to another, it is not reasonable to expect him or her to look up the dial-up number for that city and manually change the configuration. Several of the national ISPs provide software that keeps a database of dial-up numbers so users can easily find and dial a local number. This is definitely an option to look for when selecting a dial-up provider.

You will also need to create VPN connections on every client that will be using this method to access your network. This will require the time of support personnel, detailed instructions for users to follow, or development of an automated process. It is important to know how this will be accomplished before you plan a timeline for the project to outsource dial-up access. Additionally, support personnel must be trained in order to assist users with problems they may experience. The ISP will handle any issues regarding dial-up access to their network, but any problems with establishing a VPN connection must be resolved internally.

RADIUS

RADIUS (Remote Authentication Dial-in User Service) is a standards-based protocol defined in RFCs 2138 and 2139 that provides accounting, authentication, and authorization services in a distributed dial-up networking environment. RADIUS is most commonly used by Internet service providers, and enables a dial-up server acting as a RADIUS client to receive user authentication and authorization from a RADIUS server.

Windows 2000 RAS includes RADIUS client capabilities, enabling deployment in RADIUS environments. RADIUS authentication and accounting can be configured separately, so you can utilize either component or both depending on your needs. These items are configured on the Security tab of the server Properties dialog in the RRAS management console.

Windows 2000 Internet Authentication Service (IAS) provides the RADIUS server component. IAS will enable you to contract with an ISP that will provide Network Access Servers (NAS) to which your users can connect when they are mobile. Using RADIUS, the NAS will contact your Windows 2000 server to authenticate your users and report accounting information. The advantages are that you are able to control which users are authorized to use the ISP's network, and data regarding usage of the service is up to date on your system.

Summary

In this chapter, we examined three different ways to connect a small office network to the Internet without the need for multiple modems, telephone lines, or ISP accounts. All of these methods are built in to the Windows 2000 server operating systems, and ICS is included in Windows 2000 Professional. We saw that Internet Connection Sharing (ICS) and Network Address Translation (NAT), although configured differently and intended for different types of networks, both use the same basic technology: translation of private addresses used for communication on the internal network to one or more public addresses used to communicate on the Internet. We also defined private and public addressing, and discussed how the translating computer keeps track of where packets originated and to which computers packets should be returned on the internal network. We then looked at how the address translation methods differ from Windows routing, and some of the advantages and disadvantages of each connection type. Finally, we walked through the process, in a step-by-step manner, of connecting a two-computer network to the Internet using the easy-to-configure Internet Connection Sharing component of Windows 2000's dial-up networking. The goal of many small businesses is to get everyone in the office online, but most of them are limited in financial resources and technical expertise; they need a simple and inexpensive way to do it. Windows 2000 provides those organizations with not just one, but three ways of doing so, one of which is sure to meet the specific needs of your organization.

There are many choices to be made when considering Internet access for your network. You must determine which type of access will best suit your needs and budget, whether it is dial-up, ISDN, leased line, or one of the newer technologies such as cable and ADSL modems. Each method has advantages and disadvantages, which can vary depending on your needs and your location. Some of the access methods, such as cable and ADSL modems, are not currently available in all areas, but will be available in most metropolitan areas soon.

Windows 2000 has several Internet connection technology improvements, including NAT functionality in RRAS, a new VPN based on RFC-standard technologies, IPSec, Internet Connection Sharing, and more. Establishing a secure and functional connection to the Internet is easier than ever, and many organizations will be using Windows 2000 to provide secure services to remote users.

FAQs

Q: If I have a small peer-to-peer network with no servers, which type of Internet connection sharing is the best choice for my office?

A: Both NAT and Windows routing require a Windows 2000 server with RRAS installed. For a peer-to-peer (workgroup) network, you must use ICS.

Q: If I have DHCP, DNS, and WINS servers on my Windows 2000 domain network, and my ISP has assigned me IP addresses for each computer on the local network, which connection solution is best for my office?

A: In this situation, Windows software routing will allow you to use your public IP addresses without the need for translation, and utilize your DHCP, DNS, and WINS servers.

Q: I'm confused! I don't understand the difference between ICS and NAT. Are they the same thing?

A: Yes and no. Both ICS and NAT use address translation—ICS is actually a simplified implementation of NAT that is available on both Windows 2000 Professional and Server. ICS can be set up with just a few clicks of the mouse, through the Network and Dialup Connections Properties sheet. To use Windows 2000 NAT, you must first install and configure RRAS on a Windows 2000 server, and then proceed through several steps of manual configuration. NAT is more sophisticated and allows for more flexibility.

Q: Why doesn't SNMP work with NAT?

A: Some protocols do not put IP addressing information in the packet headers. These will not work with NAT unless you use a NAT editor, which is a software component that modifies the IP packet so it will work with NAT. Windows 2000 includes built-in NAT editors for the FTP, ICMP, and PPTP protocols, but does not include an SNMP editor.

Q: If I run a Web server on one of the ICS client computers my local network, what must I do so that Internet users will be able to access it?

A: You will have to configure the Web server service on the Services tab in the Internet Connection Sharing Settings property box for that connection on the ICS computer. To do this, you will need to enter the service port number (in this case, TCP port 80), and the name or IP address of the computer where the service resides.

Q: Does NAT work with the new Windows 2000 IP Security protocol?

A: No. IPSec cannot be translated by NAT, even with a NAT editor.

Index

E

Q

R

The Global Knowledge Advantage

Global Knowledge has a global delivery system for its products and ser-vices. The company has 28 subsidiaries, and offers its programs through a total of 60+ locations. No other vendor can provide consistent services across a geographic area this large. Global Knowledge is the largest inde-pendent information technology education provider, offering programs on a variety of platforms. This enables our multi-platform and multi-national customers to obtain all of their programs from a single vendor. The com-pany has developed the unique CompetusTM Framework software tool and methodology which can quickly reconfigure courseware to the proficiency level of a student on an interactive basis. Combined with self-paced and on-line programs, this technology can reduce the time required for training by prescribing content in only the deficient skills areas. The company has fully automated every aspect of the education process, from registration and follow-up, to "just-in-time" production of courseware. Global Knowledge through its Enterprise Services Consultancy, can customize programs and products to suit the needs of an individual customer.

Global Knowledge Classroom Education Programs

The backbone of our delivery options is classroom-based education. Our modern, well-equipped facilities staffed with the finest instructors offer programs in a wide variety of information technology topics, many of which lead to professional certifications.

Custom Learning Solutions

This delivery option has been created for companies and governments that value customized learning solutions. For them, our consultancy-based approach of developing targeted education solutions is most effective at helping them meet specific objectives.

Self-Paced and Multimedia Products

This delivery option offers self-paced program titles in interactive CD-ROM, videotape and audio tape programs. In addition, we offer custom develop-ment of interactive multimedia courseware to customers and partners. Call us at 1-888-427-4228.

Electronic Delivery of Training

Our network-based training service delivers efficient competency-based, interactive training via the World Wide Web and organizational intranets. This leading-edge delivery option provides a custom learning path and "just-in-time" training for maximum convenience to students.

Global Knowledge Courses Available

Microsoft
- Windows 2000 Deployment Strategies
- Introduction to Directory Services
- Windows 2000 Client Administration
- Windows 2000 Server
- Windows 2000 Update
- MCSE Bootcamp
- Microsoft Networking Essentials
- Windows NT 4.0 Workstation
- Windows NT 4.0 Server
- Windows NT Troubleshooting
- Windows NT 4.0 Security
- Windows 2000 Security
- Introduction to Microsoft Web Tools

Management Skills
- Project Management for IT Professionals
- Microsoft Project Workshop
- Management Skills for IT Professionals

Network Fundamentals
- Understanding Computer Networks
- Telecommunications Fundamentals I
- Telecommunications Fundamentals II
- Understanding Networking Fundamentals
- Upgrading and Repairing PCs
- DOS/Windows A+ Preparation
- Network Cabling Systems

WAN Networking and Telephony
- Building Broadband Networks
- Frame Relay Internetworking
- Converging Voice and Data Networks
- Introduction to Voice Over IP
- Understanding Digital Subscriber Line (xDSL)

Internetworking
- ATM Essentials
- ATM Internetworking
- ATM Troubleshooting
- Understanding Networking Protocols
- Internetworking Routers and Switches
- Network Troubleshooting
- Internetworking with TCP/IP
- Troubleshooting TCP/IP Networks
- Network Management
- Network Security Administration
- Virtual Private Networks
- Storage Area Networks
- Cisco OSPF Design and Configuration
- Cisco Border Gateway Protocol (BGP) Configuration

Web Site Management and Development
- Advanced Web Site Design
- Introduction to XML
- Building a Web Site
- Introduction to JavaScript
- Web Development Fundamentals
- Introduction to Web Databases

PERL, UNIX, and Linux
- PERL Scripting
- PERL with CGI for the Web
- UNIX Level I
- UNIX Level II
- Introduction to Linux for New Users
- Linux Installation, Configuration, and Maintenance

Authorized Vendor Training
Red Hat
- Introduction to Red Hat Linux
- Red Hat Linux Systems Administration
- Red Hat Linux Network and Security Administration
- RHCE Rapid Track Certification

Cisco Systems
- Interconnecting Cisco Network Devices
- Advanced Cisco Router Configuration
- Installation and Maintenance of Cisco Routers
- Cisco Internetwork Troubleshooting
- Designing Cisco Networks
- Cisco Internetwork Design
- Configuring Cisco Catalyst Switches
- Cisco Campus ATM Solutions
- Cisco Voice Over Frame Relay, ATM, and IP
- Configuring for Selsius IP Phones
- Building Cisco Remote Access Networks
- Managing Cisco Network Security
- Cisco Enterprise Management Solutions

Nortel Networks
- Nortel Networks Accelerated Router Configuration
- Nortel Networks Advanced IP Routing
- Nortel Networks WAN Protocols
- Nortel Networks Frame Switching
- Nortel Networks Accelar 1000
- Comprehensive Configuration
- Nortel Networks Centillion Switching
- Network Management with Optivity for Windows

Oracle Training
- Introduction to Oracle8 and PL/SQL
- Oracle8 Database Administration

Custom Corporate Network Training

Train on Cutting Edge Technology

We can bring the best in skill-based training to your facility to create a real-world hands-on training experience. Global Knowledge has invested millions of dollars in network hardware and software to train our students on the same equipment they will work with on the job. Our relationships with vendors allow us to incorporate the latest equipment and platforms into your on-site labs.

Maximize Your Training Budget

Global Knowledge provides experienced instructors, comprehensive course materials, and all the networking equipment needed to deliver high quality training. You provide the students; we provide the knowledge.

Avoid Travel Expenses

On-site courses allow you to schedule technical training at your convenience, saving time, expense, and the opportunity cost of travel away from the workplace.

Discuss Confidential Topics

Private on-site training permits the open discussion of sensitive issues such as security, access, and network design. We can work with your existing network's proprietary files while demonstrating the latest technologies.

Customize Course Content

Global Knowledge can tailor your courses to include the technologies and the topics which have the greatest impact on your business. We can complement your internal training efforts or provide a total solution to your training needs.

Corporate Pass

The Corporate Pass Discount Program rewards our best network training customers with preferred pricing on public courses, discounts on multimedia training packages, and an array of career planning services.

Global Knowledge Training Lifecycle

Supporting the Dynamic and Specialized Training Requirements of Information Technology Professionals

- Define Profile
- Assess Skills
- Design Training
- Deliver Training
- Test Knowledge
- Update Profile
- Use New Skills

Global Knowledge

Global Knowledge programs are developed and presented by industry professionals with "real-world" experience. Designed to help professionals meet today's
interconnectivity and interoperability challenges, most of our programs feature
hands-on labs that incorporate state-of-the-art communication components and
equipment.

ON-SITE TEAM TRAINING

Bring Global Knowledge's powerful training programs to your company. At Global
Knowledge, we will custom design courses to meet your specific network requirements. Call (919)-461-8686 for more information.

YOUR GUARANTEE

Global Knowledge believes its courses offer the best possible training in this field.
If during the first day you are not satisfied and wish to withdraw from the course,
simply notify the instructor, return all course materials and receive a 100%
refund.

REGISTRATION INFORMATION

In the US:
call: (888) 762–4442
fax: (919) 469–7070
visit our website:
www.globalknowledge.com